For Reference

Not to be taken from this room

MASTERPLOTS II

British and Commonwealth Fiction Series

MASTERPLOTS II

BRITISH AND COMMONWEALTH FICTION SERIES

2

Fin-Liv

Edited by
FRANK N. MAGILL

SALEM PRESS

Pasadena, California   Englewood Cliffs, New Jersey

Library of Congress Cataloging-in-Publication Data
Masterplots II: British and Commonwealth fiction
series.
   Bibliography: v. 1, p.
   Includes index.
   Summary: Includes more than 350 interpretative
essays on the themes, plots, and techniques of
works of twentieth-century fiction published in England, Ireland, Canada, India, Nigeria, and other
areas of the British Commonwealth of Nations.
   1. English fiction—20th century—Stories, plots,
etc. 2. English fiction—Commonwealth of Nations
authors—Stories, plots, etc. 3. Commonwealth of
Nations in literature. [1. English fiction—20th century—Stories, plots, etc. 2. English fiction—20th
century—History and criticism. 3. English fiction—Commonwealth of Nations authors—Stories, plots, etc. 4. English fiction—Commonwealth
of Nations authors—History and criticism] I.
Magill, Frank Northen, 1907-   . II. Title: Masterplots 2. III. Title: Masterplots two.
PR881.M39 1987   823'.009'24   87-4639
ISBN 0-89356-468-0 (set)
ISBN 0-89356-470-2 (volume 2)

LIST OF TITLES IN VOLUME 2

LIST OF TITLES IN VOLUME 2

MASTERPLOTS II

British and Commonwealth Fiction Series

THE FINANCIAL EXPERT

Author: R. K. Narayan (1906-   )
Type of plot: Regional comedy
Time of plot: The late 1940's
Locale: Malgudi (based on Mysore), in southern India
First published: 1952

Principal characters:

MARGAYYA, the protagonist, a manipulator of loans to needy, bad-risk villagers and peasants

DR. PAL, self-described as an academician, sociologist, journalist, and author

MADAN LAL, the principal printer in Malgudi

BALU, Margayya's son, an academic failure and runaway

ARUL DOSS, an old Christian, the head servant of the Co-operative Bank

The Novel

Margayya (who adopted his name, which means "one who shows the way"), a financial expert, is one of the minor businessmen who are to be found in most Indian towns and cities. Neither a moneylender nor really a banker, he is a manipulator of others' affairs who accumulates a modest income by giving financial advice, selling forms, and showing illiterate farmers and peasants how to obtain loans from the Central Co-operative Land Mortgage Bank in Malgudi. His role as middleman is lucrative, for he has almost no overhead: His pen, ink, blotter, and account book are contained in an old, gray tin box that he carries with him and that constitutes his office when he sits under a banyan tree across the lawn from the bank. When he is rebuked by Arul Doss, the chief peon of the bank, for being a nuisance on the premises (normally trying to obtain loan application forms or even new clients), Margayya decides that large sums of money—necessary for the type of life and position in society of which he judges himself deserving—are not to be made from villagers' small transactions; rather, they are to be made by devotions to Lakshmi, the Hindu goddess of wealth, whose favors to the elect are almost boundless.

A priest from a run-down local temple prescribes special rituals for obtaining the favor of Lakshmi: mixing the ashes of a red lotus with the milk of a smoke-colored cow, exorcising rodents and cockroaches from his house, decorating the doorways with mango-leaf garlands, and repeating a special mantra a thousand times daily for forty days. The result is that Margayya becomes a devotee not of Lakshmi but of money itself.

During his search for the red lotus, Margayya meets Dr. Pal, author of a 150-page manuscript, "Bed-Life, or the Science of Marital Happiness," and he decides to become the publisher of his manuscript rather than a seller of snuff or tooth powder—two possibilities that attract him now that he is almost penniless after his forty-day absence from his banyan-tree "office," during which his son, Balu, has thrown his account book into a sewer canal.

Madan Lal, the proprietor of the Gordon Printery on Market Road, reads Pal's manuscript and offers to publish it in partnership with Margayya under the title *Domestic Harmony*—though it is really an amalgam of the *Kama Sutra* and the writings of Havelock Ellis. Sold at one rupee a copy, *Domestic Harmony* (promoted as sociology but in reality a work of prurience) becomes Margayya's means to unexpected riches and position (as secretary of the town elementary school—through a manipulated election).

Yet in spite of his newfound social status resulting from his increased wealth, Margayya is distressed by the lack of academic progress by his son Balu. Even after teachers are pressured, Balu fails to gain admission to a university and so runs away to Madras, confessing that he hates studies and examinations.

Word is received that Balu has died—but the cause is unknown. Margayya (to economize) takes a third-class train to Madras, where, with the help of an inspector of police, he learns that Balu is alive and that the postcard announcing his death was written by a madman, who is a cinema owner; Balu is the supervisor of street urchins who wear sandwich-board advertisements for films. After reconciliation, Margayya and Balu return to Malgudi.

After preliminary inquiries about a bride for Balu, Margayya is aided by Dr. Pal, who persuades an astrologer to manipulate horoscopes. Balu and his bride, Brinda, move into a fashionable new house, and Dr. Pal becomes a tout for Margayya, who decides to become a deposit-taker rather than a lender. He quickly achieves celebrity status, and he is virtually a currency-hoarder.

Balu has fallen under the influence of Dr. Pal, however, who is part owner of a "house of debauchery," and Margayya assaults Dr. Pal, who then spreads rumors about Margayya's bank being insolvent. There is a ruinous run on the bank, and even Balu's house and property are attached. In about four months, Margayya, crushed, suggests that Balu take up the old, gray tin box and set up office under the banyan tree while he plays at home with his grandson.

The Characters

If, as has been suggested by some distinguished critics, *The Financial Expert* is the quintessential Narayan novel, then its characters are fully representative of the entire range of the writer's invention and thus of India itself, for Malgudi is as representative of urban life on the subcontinent as is any other town or city in modern literature, and it is drawn in greater detail and with greater fidelity and sympathy. That is to say, the characters are both individuals and representatives of the types to be found in their multifarious modifications throughout South India.

Margayya, aware that his grandfather and his grand-uncles were corpse-bearers (and hence of one of the lowest castes), has nevertheless managed to rise above his origins through providing a service of sorts to illiterate and intimidated villagers; he is hardworking, frugal to the point of penuriousness, and—aware that knowledge is power—ever careful to become acquainted with others' finances while remaining secretive about his own. His relationships reveal his character in all of its complexity. First, in typical fashion, he treats his wife, Meenakshi, as unworthy of being apprised of his business dealings and unworthy of love, or even of respect. (There is no word for love, as it is defined in English, in Indian languages.) Second, he regards Balu as a projection of himself and tries to force him into a mold quite unsuited to him; he shows him neither paternal affection nor true understanding but wants him to achieve academic success so that he might become a government official or a business success. By indulging him after his return from Madras, he merely ensures Balu's future failure—though his last act is to recommend that Balu follow in his father's footsteps. It seems certain that the son, like the father, will never "pass on to the grade of people who [are] wealthy and not merely rich."

It is Margayya's consuming desire for wealth and position that blinds him to the machinations of Dr. Pal and Mr. Lal, author and publisher, respectively, of *Domestic Harmony*. All three men illustrate one side of Indian society: the puritanical public attitude toward sex (and even to normal heterosexual behavior) that coexists with the erotic, in the form of temple statuary and the *Kama Sutra*, which are almost compulsively exhibited to Western visitors. Dr. Pal, in particular, represents the seamy side of Indian academic life: He is, by his own account, a sociologist, psychologist, journalist, author, and tourist director, but in fact, he ekes out a living through illicit enterprises and by performing lowly tasks. He is, in essence, a social parasite. Mr. Lal, on the other hand, is merely a furtive businessman: He loves to read a titillating manuscript and sees in it ready profit from surreptitious sales.

Arul Doss, however, although he plays a seemingly minor role as chief servant of the Co-operative Land Mortgage Bank, is an important foil to Margayya, whose cupidity and self-interest (if not also his deviousness) are contrasted to the values that have been represented for years by the Bank: cooperation, frugality, regularity, punctuality, moderation, and caution. That is, the Bank represents the Puritan ethic of Western culture. Doss is ready to address Margayya on terms of equality and with politeness, but it is not a reciprocal attitude. Doss has an inherent dignity as a functionary that suggests a basis in Christian theology and in a philosophy of service and equality—service to employer and customers alike.

Even the minor characters—such as Balu's wife, Brinda; the inspector of police; and the mystic owner of the Madras theater—add materially to R. K. Narayan's panorama of Indian characters. Brinda is the arranged bride, sought out by negotiation and consultation with astrologers yet dutiful, retiring, complaisant, and devoted to her domestic duties; the inspector is diligent, resourceful, modest, and professional in the execution of his work; the theater owner is one of those mystics who pervade the Indian scene—partly religious, partly profane, they seem to belong to neither world entirely, yet they influence both. When impoverished villagers, prostitutes, filmmakers, and small-time vendors are included, one has a picture of Indian urban life of remarkable detail and comprehensiveness.

Themes and Meanings

At the conclusion of the novel, Margayya calmly alludes to Balu's earlier request for his inheritance upon attaining the age of eighteen and directs him to the old tin box that served as office under the banyan tree opposite the Bank: Seemingly unremarkable, this gesture and counsel can be seen as the essence of Indian life—and of the novel. Though many and great events have taken place, and though riches have come and gone, life will continue as determined by forces beyond the comprehension of mere mortals. One proceeds at the whims of the deities in one's progress toward Nirvana. Performing *puja* is necessary in order to placate the gods, but their goodwill and favors cannot be taken for granted or assumed to be permanent. Lakshmi, the goddess of riches, is capricious, and she must perpetually be courted. In like manner, Brahma, Vishnu, and Shiva must be appeased if one is to lead a life of reasonable comfort and satisfaction. Life is, after all, a mere stage between creation and destruction and the inevitable re-creation. The whole atmosphere of the novel suggests this truth, and all the characters and events have a timeless quality that approaches the ineffable. By these means, Narayan conveys this fundamental tenet of Hindu belief: The past determines the present as the present determines the future, and all things are determined by the will of the gods, whose favors must be sought.

Within this general framework, Narayan develops the theme of family relationships and responsibilities as protection against the outside world, though the frictions that arise in interpersonal relationships (even when duties are strictly observed) are not excluded. Human weaknesses—vanity, cupidity, indolence—are shown as crucial elements in the destruction of individual dreams and fortunes, in the unfolding of lives of sadness and defeat.

In the development of character, there are frequent epiphanies: As Margayya meets Arul Doss, Dr. Pal, Mr. Lal, the inspector of police, and the priest of Lakshmi, he has new insights into life that change his actions and his attitudes—all, unfortunately, temporarily only, it seems. Once again, however, Narayan develops his central thesis: that despite the vicissitudes of life, everyone is fundamentally of one essence.

Critical Context

Narayan was first championed by Graham Greene, who saw in the Indian writer's work the continuation of the best elements of comedy, which had (he thought) been superseded in European writing by farce and satire. In large measure, Narayan's work depends for its comic tone upon his basic identification with the society in which he places his characters and yet upon his ability to perceive its inconsequentialities, its irrelevancies, and its irreverences as much as its departure from the ideal. He is never the satirist intent upon demolition or poking fun at the foibles of men, nor is irony his pervading mode, for he does not dwell upon the dissonance between proclaimed principle and performance. He smiles rather than laughs at his neighbors' idiosyncrasies and shortcomings, remembering that even the observer has his faults. It is this gentleness that pervades his writing and makes his novels so appealing to sensitive readers; it is the gentleness one finds also in the works of Anton Chekhov.

The comic in Narayan is balanced by the genuinely pathetic, which indicates the point of view of the philosopher-novelist. Yet there is never any truly tragic circumstance any more than there is a melodramatic one: The Hindu philosophy almost excludes the possibility of tragedy, and there is never a clear good/bad dichotomy that would produce melodrama. It is this deft and rare handling of character and circumstance that gives Narayan's work such an inimitable quality, whether his protagonist is a vendor of sweets, a schoolteacher, a filmmaker, a painter of signs, a guide, or a financial expert.

Sources for Further Study

Garabian, Keith. "Narayan's Compromise in Comedy," in *The Literary Half-Yearly*. XVII, no. 1 (1976), pp. 77-92.

Gowda, H. H. A. "R. K. Narayan: The Early Stories," in *The Literary Half-Yearly*. VI, no. 2 (1965), pp. 25-39.

Iyengar, K. R. Srinivasa. *Indian Writing in English*, 1962.

Naik, M. K. *The Ironic Vision: A Study of the Fiction of R. K. Narayan*, 1984.

Walsh, William. *R. K. Narayan*, 1971.

───────────. *R. K. Narayan: A Critical Appreciation*, 1982.

A. L. McLeod

FIRE FROM HEAVEN

Author: Mary Renault (Mary Challans, 1905-1983)
Type of plot: Historical novel
Time of plot: 351-336 B.C.
Locale: Macedon, the Greek peninsula, Athens
First published: 1969

> *Principal characters:*
> ALEXANDER, the prince of Macedon, later known as
>   Alexander the Great
> PHILIP, the king of Macedon, his father
> OLYMPIAS, his mother
> HEPHAISTION, his closest friend and lover
> PTOLEMY, his half brother
> ANTIPATROS, a statesman and adviser to Alexander in his
>   regency
> ARISTOTLE, the philosopher and the tutor of Alexander
> LYSIMACHOS, a friend of Alexander and a pedagogue, known
>   to Alexander as Phoinix

The Novel

Fire from Heaven is a historical *Bildungsroman* depicting the career of the boy who was to go down in history as Alexander the Great from the ages of five to twenty, when he succeeded his father, Philip, as king of Macedon. As the novel opens, the child Alexander wakes to find a snake in his bed. Thinking that it is Glaucos, his mother Olympias' sacred snake, he slips out of bed to return it. It is not, however, Glaucos but a larger snake; they recall the legend of the young Hercules, the patron god of Achilles, one of Olympias' ancestors. Olympias tells Alexander that the snake has come from the god, and Alexander names him Tyche, "fortune." Alexander's father, Philip, appears, drunk, and, flinging off his clothes, approaches the bed. Olympias cannot shield Alexander from his father's wrath. Philip throws him out bodily, and he is comforted by the guard.

Thus, in the opening pages, Mary Renault establishes the major themes and characters: Alexander's fearlessness and his attraction to both logic and legend; Olympias' superstition and sorcery; Philip's drunkenness, lust, and anger; the parents' hostility toward each other and rivalry for Alexander; Alexander's need for love and his ability to inspire the love and loyalty of the soldiers. In the Macedonian court, Alexander grows up quickly. When he is eight, he has two meetings significant for his future. Envoys arrive from Persia; Philip is not there, and the boy receives them. He is somewhat naïve and boyish, but he goes through the proper forms and asks some very pertinent questions. Philip, talking with him afterward, is impressed, the episode showing a hint of the mature relationship which is to develop between them.

Alexander also meets Hephaistion, who will act as a Patroclus to his Achilles, though their mature and intense friendship does not begin until some years later. Leonidas, devoted to Spartan methods of education, is engaged as his tutor, as are masters to teach Alexander music, mathematics, philosophy, and, above all, the Greek language. Macedonian is regarded as a barbarous language. To provide the constant supervision an active and intensely inquisitive young boy needs, Lysimachos, a wellborn, longtime family friend, becomes his pedagogue. Alexander is very fond of him and sensitive enough to know that Lysimachos' discipline is necessary; he calls him Phoinix, after the friend who stands in the relation of father to Achilles. The *Iliad* (ninth century B.C.) was to remain a major influence throughout Alexander's life.

The Spartan training enables Alexander to endure hardship and to reconfirm his very un-Macedonian moderation and sobriety. Gradually, he begins to understand his father better, but first he must establish his own identity and manhood. At twelve, young even by Macedonian standards, he sets out to earn his swordbelt by killing a man in battle. Following one of Philip's soldiers, who is going on leave to avenge a family feud, he not only kills his first man but he also leads and wins a battle. Then, at a horse fair, he asks for a horse which Philip himself cannot ride. At first angry, Philip laughs and says that the horse is Alexander's, if he can ride him. This, of course, is the legendary Bucephalus, Oxhead in Renault's literal rendering of the Greek.

Alexander's education is entrusted to Aristotle, who is then about forty. Under his guidance, Alexander, with a group of wellborn young men, known as the Prince's Companions and traditionally attached to the Macedonian heir, are sent to their own residence outside Pella. Philip wants to get Alexander away from Olympias and her palace intrigues; Alexander equally wants to be away from Olympias and with Hephaistion, one of the first companions. His education ends when, at sixteen, Alexander is summoned to fight by his father's side. Philip soon accepts Alexander as an equal, testing him by making him regent of Macedon, with the guidance of Antipatros, and then assigning him, at eighteen, his own cavalry troop. Father and son quarrel over one of Philip's many state marriages. Macedonian kings traditionally took wives after conquests, but Alexander is outraged when Philip marries the fifteen-year-old daughter of a leading Macedonian, and, at the wedding, the father-in-law toasts the "true heir" to the throne that will come of the match. After the ensuing brawl, Alexander is sent into exile, some of the Companions joining him. Philip and Alexander are reconciled, but, soon after, Philip is assassinated, and Alexander inherits the throne of Macedon and turns his thoughts to the conquest of Asia, which Philip had been planning at his death.

The Characters

Alexander is the most completely and complexly drawn of *Fire from Heaven*'s characters. Not only is he the central figure but also he is seen from boyhood on; the others, except for brief glimpses of Hephaistion, are adults whose characters have been formed. With Alexander, Renault carefully builds detail upon detail, foreshadowing in the episodes of childhood the leader to come. Each of the other characters is shown in relation to Alexander; from each, a facet of his character is reflected and developed.

Established at the outset are Alexander's fearlessness, resourcefulness, intellectual acuity, kinship with Achilles, and worship of Hercules. Most important, Alexander, while reverencing the gods and aware of his descent from heroes, possibly even from a god (Achilles was half god), nevertheless always has a practical interpretation of events and portents as well. His inquiring mind and his moderation save him from the excesses of his parents. As he grows older, he becomes more sympathetic to Philip, but the latter's excesses stand in the way of their ever developing a genuinely close relationship. Olympias is uncontrolled in her religious passions; as a priestess of the cult of Dionysius, her excesses are physical as well. Alexander grows to distrust her, particularly her practice of black magic. Philip, while hostile to her barbarous superstitions, has his own barbarisms: his lust and his ill temper. Alexander's moderation is in some ways a reaction to his parents' extremes.

Alexander's relationship with Hephaistion is another paradox of his nature. Although Renault makes it clear that they are lovers, physical love is the least of Alexander's concerns, though not of those of Hephaistion. The latter learns moderation from Alexander. In the *Iliad* and from Leonidas and Lysimachos, Alexander finds values and guides to life other than those of his parents. Identifying strongly with Achilles, he sees Hephaistion as Patroclus. Alexander, though, is not uncritical of Achilles' conduct as a warrior, and he soon adds Xenophon to his mentors. Xenophon's writings, ranging from how to evaluate horses to a study of Cyrus of Persia as a philosopher-king, influence the Alexander who is to conquer and administer the then-known world.

Renault creates an impressive gallery of portraits, all in relation to Alexander and his growth. Some are minor, but telling. The guard, Agis, who rescues the five-year-old Alexander from his father's wrath, is drawn to Alexander in a combination of affection, loyalty, and physical attraction; his example, in turn, shows Alexander that even these must not stand in the way of doing one's duty. Aristotle, though dominantly a rational, empirical philosopher, always teaching Alexander to ask why and seek out evidence, reveals strong personal loyalty both to his home city, devastated by war, and to a friend who has been tortured and killed by the Persians. His example, as much as his precepts, teaches Alexander friendship. When Aristotle is ready to leave the court, Philip and Alexander keep the promise to rebuild Stagira for the philosopher so that he can spend his declining years there.

Themes and Meanings

Fire from Heaven is a study in contrasts between a philosophical and rational outlook and that of the ancient religions, between barbarian Macedon and civilized Athens, between reason and superstition. Alexander's development is a major focus of these themes, of which the other characters embody facets. Aristotle and Hephaistion, after Alexander, most clearly approach the balanced ideal. Renault here seems to endorse the great man theory of history—"events are made by men"—and the value of unification by conquest. Though choosing to mirror as accurately as possible the time in which she writes, she is not uncritical. It is in keeping with Alexander's character that he at once seeks glory and honor and is horrified or saddened by the aftermath of war. As commander and victor, he pardons enemies, though not traitors, and founds, rather than sacks, cities.

Ancient religions, traditions, and superstitions are also presented as the characters experience them, creating an atmosphere of comprehension and acceptance of the role these play in the characters' lives. Alexander questions his own paternity, especially before he reaches some understanding of Philip. Some of the other characters do the same—notably those who stand to gain by Alexander's not being Philip's heir. Philip's relationship with Alexander silences most of these. Alexander finally questions Olympias, insisting on the truth about his birth. Her answer is not recorded; one knows only that it satisfies Alexander, who does not tell even Hephaistion. It is possible that Alexander may realize that Olympias' superstition and her habit of intrigue may prevent her from ever telling the full truth about anything. Quite early, a teacher of Alexander sums up the situation. Asked if he believes the "whispers" about Alexander's birth, he replies, "Not with my reason. He has Philip's capacity, if not his face or his soul." Alexander himself, while one aspect of him may believe the "whispers," does cause his own exile by challenging a public questioning of his birth.

The relationship of Macedon to Athens, intellectually and culturally, foreshadows the relationship of Greece to Persia. In Athens, Alexander finds not only that his dress, manners, and moderation, unusual or even unique in Macedon, are commonplace but also that he must be on his guard lest he seem rude there. The final impression left in *Fire from Heaven* is not of a choice between the various opposite alternatives but of a fusion to produce a new outlook and era. From Olympias, Alexander learns reverence and a time when one must trust one's own intuitions or the promptings of one's god; from Leonidas, he learns Spartan discipline without espousing Spartan rudeness; from Phoinix, he learns unswerving loyalty; from Aristotle, he learns to temper friendship with moderation; and from Philip, he learns how to lead an army and a nation. This capacity to unite diverse philosophies and cultures under a single just rule will become Alexander's goal as he sets out for Persia and the conquest of the then-known world.

Critical Context

Mary Renault is in general acknowledged as a fine novelist and, indisputably, a master of the historical novel. Unfortunately, her general critical reputation has been diminished by the reputation of the historical novel as a genre. Genre fiction—historical, detective, Western, science fiction, romance—is not usually accorded a high critical standing. The historical novel as a genre presents special difficulties to the critic. With a range of examples to consider which includes Leo Tolstoy's *War and Peace* (1865-1869), Nathaniel Hawthorne's *The Scarlet Letter* (1850), William Faulkner's *Absalom, Absalom!* (1936), Pär Lagerkvist's *Barabbas* (1950; English translation, 1951), and Willa Cather's *Death Comes for the Archbishop* (1927), conventions and forms are not easily defined. Conversely, a genre whose practitioners include several Nobel Prize winners and which numbers established classics cannot be dismissed as mere escapist entertainment. One difficulty is that few critics are qualified in both history and literature; fewer still have these qualifications and a mastery of the language, if the work and its sources are not in a language with which the critic is familiar. Most authors of major historical novels, however, have also written novels dealing with their own time and place. Renault's contemporary novels are all early works and, with the exception of *The Charioteer* (1953), are apprentice work.

Renault's skill not only as a historical novelist but also simply as a novelist is evidenced in her treatments of Alexander. He appears as a character in four novels: *The Mask of Apollo* (1966), *Fire from Heaven*, *The Persian Boy* (1972), and *Funeral Games* (1981), and in her biographical study, *The Nature of Alexander* (1975). In each of these works, Alexander is seen from a different perspective, and each has a different style. Nikeratos, an actor, the narrator of *The Mask of Apollo*, perceives Alexander's beauty, but also, even at the early age he meets him, his air of command, his awareness of being a man among men, and his inquiring mind. Bagoas, the narrator of *The Persian Boy*, sees Alexander from a lover's and intimate's perspective, holding the man and the legend in balance. *Fire from Heaven*, *Funeral Games*, and *The Nature of Alexander*, though all in the third person, are again different from one another and the other works. In *Funeral Games*, Alexander is glimpsed briefly at the end of his life and in death; the style is heavy and elegiac, the legend uppermost. In *The Nature of Alexander*, Renault judiciously weighs evidence and cites sources, giving her reasons when she chooses among conflicting interpretations. Her style is objective but flowing and readable. *Fire from Heaven* is told in a compellingly dramatic narrative style. In contrast to the variety of styles, each of the novels is linked by the themes clustered around the character of Alexander: his heroic identification with the *Iliad* (Nikeratos sees him after a performance of Aeschylus' *The Myrmidons*), his mastery of himself and of other men, the blending of cultures, and his ability to be simultaneously awed by and questioning of a situation.

Taken as a whole, Renault's novels present a broad portrait of the Greek world, ranging from the Mycenaean period to the post-Alexandrian. In each, style and theme give the reader a sense of the past, each subtly differing from the others yet linked by the common theme of the development of Greek culture and values. In the treasure of fine novels written in English, Renault's works are small gems but ones of outstanding quality and brilliance.

Sources for Further Study

Brunsdale, Mitzi M. "Mary Renault," in *Critical Survey of Long Fiction, English Language Series*, 1983. Edited by Frank N. Magill.

Dick, Bernard F. *The Hellenism of Mary Renault*, 1972.

The New Yorker. Review. XLV (December 27, 1969), p. 57.

Renault, Mary. "History in Fiction," in *The Times Literary Supplement*. March 23, 1973, pp. 315-316.

Time. Review. XCIV (December 19, 1969), p. 82.

Warner, Rex. Review in *The New York Times Book Review*. December 14, 1969, p. 42.

Wolfe, Peter. *Mary Renault*, 1969.

Katharine M. Morsberger

504

FIRE ON THE MOUNTAIN

Author: Anita Desai (1937-   )
Type of plot: Domestic realism
Time of plot: The 1970's
Locale: Kasauli, India
First published: 1977

> *Principal characters:*
> NANDA KAUL, the protagonist, an academic vice chancellor's
> wife who has retired to her "country" home, Carignano
> RAKA, her great-granddaughter, who is spending the summer
> at Carignano
> ILA DAS, Nanda Kaul's friend since childhood, currently a
> social worker near Kasauli
> RAM LAL, Nanda Kaul's cook and Raka's friend

The Novel

The plot of *Fire on the Mountain* is relatively brief and uncomplicated, the significant action occurring within the psyches of Nanda and, to a lesser extent, Raka, her great-granddaughter. When Ila Das is raped and killed, that violent action happens "offstage" at the end of the novel, almost simultaneously with Raka's announcement that she has set the forest on fire. While there are few important "events" in the rest of the novel, Anita Desai prepares the reader for the horrific ending by carefully embedding violence in her imagery and in her symbolism. In effect, the "fire" metaphorically smolders within her characters before it literally ignites at the end of the novel.

Part 1 of *Fire on the Mountain* provides the geographical and psychological setting prior to the arrival of Raka, Nanda's great-granddaughter. After the death of her husband, Nanda has apparently chosen to live an isolated life in her retirement. Except for an occasional telephone call and a visit from the postman, which she regards as unwelcome intrusions, only the presence of Ram Lal, her cook, disturbs her solitude. Carignano, her literal and metaphorical "retreat," is perched on the side of a cliff, and its setting suggests the precarious nature of the life she has established there. That life, free from obligations to others, is threatened by the visit of the postman, who brings her a letter informing her of the impending visit by Raka. When Ila Das, a friend since childhood, telephones Nanda and also asks about visiting her, Nanda realizes that her "pared, reduced, and radiantly single life" is in jeopardy.

The second part of the novel concerns the interaction—and lack of it—between Nanda and Raka, who, despite the generational gap, are quite similar in behavior. At first, Nanda considers Raka an "intruder, an outsider," and resists being drawn into the child's world. Nanda soon discovers, however, that she and her great-granddaughter have much in common, primarily their aloofness and determination to pursue their own secret lives. Raka is distant not only emotionally but also spatially, and her Kasauli is not Nanda's: Raka frequents, despite Ram Lal's warning, the forbidden ravine behind and below Carignano. In spite of their initial mutual rejection, Nanda comes to miss Raka during the child's forays into the ravine; Nanda finds "the child's long absences as perturbing as her presence was irksome." Consequently, Nanda insists on accompanying Raka on some walks, notably the one to a peak called Monkey Point, but Raka spurns Nanda's overtures and prefers her own secret world.

When her ploys prove unsuccessful, Nanda whets Raka's curiosity by telling the child about her own childhood in Kashmir, where her idealized father had a zoo, including a pangolin, a "hard, scaly creature in its armour." (Nanda's father, in direct contrast to Raka's brutish one, obviously interests Raka, who resembles the pangolin, also the object of the father's loving care.) Nanda's stories, however, succeed only temporarily, and she is reduced to thinking of giving Carignano to Raka. Meanwhile, Raka continues her exploration of the ravine and also visits an abandoned burned house near Carignano. When Raka leaves her ravine, which is associated with nature and death, to visit the clubhouse, which is associated with civilization, she is, ironically, threatened for the first time in Kasauli. At the club the masked revelers appear as "caged, clawed, tailed, headless male and female monsters" who remind her of her father returning from a party and beating her mother senseless. At this point, reality impinges upon her secret world and transforms it into a nightmare.

The final part of the novel also concerns a visit: Ila Das arrives at Carignano after being taunted and physically abused by a group of boys. Although she is aware of Ila Das's desperate financial plight, Nanda adroitly steers the conversation away from any discussion of Ila Das moving into Carignano. When the two old women persist in the "game of old age," Raka slips away and steals some matches. Finally, Ila Das leaves Carignano, and on her way home in the dark is raped and killed by the father of a young girl whose marriage to an old landowner she had opposed. When the police call Nanda with the news of the murder, Nanda realizes that "it was all a lie," that her stories about her father, her loving husband, and the circumstances leading to her stay at Carignano were all fabrications. While she holds the phone, Raka announces, "I have set the forest on fire."

The Characters

As is the case in Desai's other novels, *Fire on the Mountain* is more memorable for its characters than for its plot or "action." In fact, plot is important only in terms of what it reveals about the characters, Desai's primary concern. Desai focuses not so much on physical appearance—unless it reflects an inner reality or serves a symbolic purpose—as on her characters' inner lives. Nanda, the protagonist, is a case in point, for Desai tells her readers little about Nanda's appearance but does tell the readers, through the use of a stream of consciousness narrative technique, much about her thoughts, values, fears, suppressed hostility, and unconscious need for love.

Carignano, Nanda's "retreat," suggests Nanda's determination to withdraw from her former active life, replete with its duties, obligations, and roles. Among the roles she rejects is the role as sacrificing nurturer of others: "The care of others . . . had been a religious calling she had believed in till she found it fake." At the end of part 1, she pleads, "Discharge me. I've discharged all my duties." In her desire to simplify her life, Nanda "jettisons" her past, strips it to its necessities, and attempts to reject other people. Like Carignano, she is "barren," and like the garden, through age and "withering away" she has arrived at a "state of elegant perfection." The setting is both "perfected and natural" in that she has imposed her will on stubborn nature. Like the apricot trees that flourish in stony soil, however, she cannot resist her natural impulse to reach out to her great-granddaughter, Raka.

Although she resembles Nanda in her aloofness, Raka is not "exactly like" her great-grandmother: While Nanda's rejection of Raka is "planned and wilful," Raka's rejection of Nanda is "natural, instinctive, and effortless," at least as Nanda sees it. Since Desai presents most of the story through Nanda's perspective, readers know more about Nanda than they do about Raka, who remains, with the exception of the clubhouse revelations, an enigma throughout the novel. As seen by Nanda, Raka is a part of nature, a child whose natural habitat is the ravine and whose behavior is described in animal imagery. When she first meets Raka, Nanda compares her to a "dark cricket" and a "mosquito," comparisons that continue until Nanda discovers a rapport between the two. In addition to the negative insect imagery, there are references to Raka as one of the "newly caged," which suggests that Nanda will not be able to domesticate her "natural" great-granddaughter. Raka seeks her freedom, which is epitomized by the eagles with which she identifies at Monkey Point. (Ironically, Nanda also identifies with eagles, but it is the "low, domestic call" of the cuckoo that she hears just before Raka's visit.) Raka cannot really escape from the civilized world, regardless of how much she attempts to repress her memories of her parents' behavior. Like Nanda, Raka fears human contact because it has brought her pain.

Like Raka, Ila Das tests Nanda's commitment to physical and emotional isolation. A pathetic creature whose most notable feature is her "cackle," Ila Das appeals indirectly to Nanda's charity and compassion. Despite her desperate financial status and ridiculous appearance, however, Ila Das has much in common with Nanda: Both are "old, beaten, and silent" as they reenact the past. Ila Das, in fact, is superior to Nanda, in that she has not withdrawn from life but has instead reached out to help the people she serves as a social worker.

Themes and Meanings

One of the themes of *Fire on the Mountain* is certainly withdrawal, with its associated theme of loneliness, especially as embodied in Nanda and Raka. In Nanda's case the withdrawal results from a failed, if enduring, marriage, while in Raka's case the withdrawal is from domestic violence; for both, a man causes the alienation. The violence of a predatory world cannot, however, be escaped, as Ila Das's fate so forcefully indicates. Nor is the "retreat" without its symbolic violence, which is played out in nature. As Nanda anticipates Raka's visit, she sees a white hen drag out a worm until it snaps in two: "She felt like the worm herself, she winced at its mutilation." Nanda also sees herself as a predatory cat in pursuit of the lapwing, and later she sees the hoopoe bird feeding its young with insects. While Desai tends to depict the ravine as a symbol of nature and as a refuge for Raka, who cannot abide the civilization of Carignano and the clubhouse, even the ravine is "blighted" by civilization's waste and polluted by the smoke from the chimneys of the Pasteur Institute.

The Institute serves as an appropriate symbol for the contradictory nature of civilization or progress, since it serves people through its production of serum, but at a cost: the smell of "dogs' brains boiled in vats, of guinea pigs' guts, of rabbits secreting fear in cages packed with coiled snakes, watched by doctors in white." Desai does not, however, seem to be nostalgically yearning for the past, even though colonialism offered a surface grandeur (the decline of Kasauli seems attributable to the town going "native"). The colonial past is also marked by violence, which the postman traces with black humor in his account of Carignano's various owners: Colonel Macdougall's corrugated roof blows off, decapitating a coolie; the pastor's wife attempts to poison him and then to stab him; Miss Jane Shrewsbury pokes a fork into her cook's neck, and he dies. In Desai's fictional world, one simply cannot escape violence by retreating from one's obligations to others. Nanda's failure to "connect" with Ila Das and with Raka indirectly causes the former's death, and Raka's refusal to "connect" with her great-grandmother leads to her decision to destroy a world she can neither accept nor tolerate.

Critical Context

Fire on the Mountain, Desai's fifth novel, has much in common with her earlier short story "Grandmother," in which the grandmother, like Nanda, is a product of her experiences and has become an isolated soul. Like the novel, "Grandmother" concerns the confrontation between an older woman and a child, except in the short story the child has not, like Raka, withdrawn from the world. The novel also is linked with *Cry, the Peacock* (1963), which uses stream-of-consciousness narrative and imagery to depict the diseased psyche of a woman who is slowly disintegrating and who, like Nanda, is very much a prisoner of her past. Maya, the protagonist, becomes alienated from her husband, just as Nanda has become alienated from her husband in *Fire on the Mountain*. The themes of alienation and lack of communication in married life also appear in *Where Shall We Go This Summer?* (1975), a novel that stresses the impact of the past on the future.

Desai also tends to concentrate on the inner world of her characters and often uses setting to mirror or to effect a character's development. Setting and character interact most prominently in *Voices in the City* (1965), which concerns a young man in Calcutta who is unable to "connect" with other people, while in *Bye-Bye, Blackbird* (1971) an Indian immigrant in England (who resembles the protagonist of *Voices in the City*) struggles with an alien culture. Desai's themes and characters lend themselves to the short, poetic novel or the *novella*, and she also seems to prefer the three-part structure she uses in *Fire on the Mountain* and in two other novels. In a real sense, the structure appears dialectic, with thesis, antithesis, and synthesis corresponding, in the case of *Fire on the Mountain*, to Nanda's tenuous withdrawal, Raka's threat to her aloofness, and the concluding death and fire which act as a kind of purification, bringing self-awareness.

Sources for Further Study

Asnani, Shyam M. "The Themes of Withdrawal and Loneliness in Anita Desai's *Fire on the Mountain*," in *Journal of Indian Writing in English*. IX (January, 1981), pp. 81-92.

Ganguli, Chandra. "*Fire on the Mountain*: An Analysis," in *Commonwealth Quarterly*. VI (December, 1981), pp. 40-44.

Krishna, Francine E. "Anita Desai: *Fire on the Mountain*," in *Indian Literature*. XXV (September/October, 1982), pp. 158-169.

Maini, Darshan Singh. "The Achievement of Anita Desai," in *Indo-English Literature: A Collection of Critical Essays*, 1977. Edited by K. K. Sharma.

Prasad, Madhusudan. "Imagery in the Novels of Anita Desai: A Critical Study," in *World Literature Today*. LVIII (Summer, 1984), pp. 363-369.

Singh, R. S. *Indian Novel in English*, 1977.

Thomas L. Erskine

THE FIRE-DWELLERS

Author: Margaret Laurence (1926-1987)
Type of plot: Domestic realism
Time of plot: The 1960's
Locale: Vancouver and the fictional prairie town of Manawaka
First published: 1969

Principal characters:

STACEY CAMERON MACAINDRA, the protagonist, a middle-aged wife and mother

CLIFFORD (MAC) MACAINDRA, her husband, a salesman

KATIE MACAINDRA, her fourteen-year-old daughter

BUCKLE FENNICK, Mac's best friend, who dies in a traffic accident

LUKE VENTURI, a young science-fiction writer who has an affair with Stacey

MATTHEW MACAINDRA, Stacey's father-in-law, a clergyman

The Novel

The "doom everywhere" message that Stacey Cameron MacAindra, the protagonist of *The Fire-Dwellers*, allows to permeate her outlook on life is a projection of the inner turmoil she is experiencing. The real inferno of the novel burns in Stacey's agitated consciousness. Stacey struggles to get a grip on herself, to accept her inadequacies, to accept that her family is never going to be like a Norman Rockwell painting, and to accept that she must aspire to represent sanity in what she sees as an insane world. The omniscient narrator gives credence to Stacey's assessment of life yet maintains a distance needed for the reader to be objective about Stacey's character, as the primary mode of narration is Stacey's interior monologues, used for acute self-evaluation and expressing her indomitable wrath. Without Stacey's sardonic burbles, this would be simply another novel about an oppressed woman ready to have a nervous breakdown. Stacey is too much of a survivor to crack up, but she is caught in a self-defeating groove in which she is communicating her own awfulness to herself without communicating anything constructive to anyone else.

The events of the novel transpire over several months before Stacey's fortieth birthday. Reaching forty is enough of a crisis, but Stacey, housewife and mother of four, is not certain about anything anymore. She goes through the motions of being alive; she looks after her husband and children and tries to cope with world events, but it all seems a bit much for one person to shoulder. Stacey wants to communicate with her family, but she cannot make the right connections. Her family takes her for granted; her husband, Mac, is only interested in his job; her teenage daughter, Katie, seems to hate her mother; her two sons, Duncan and Ian, fight like Cain and Abel; and her two-year-old, Jen, will not speak a word. God, with whom she carries on one-sided conversations, even though she is not sure He exists, provides no illumination from on high.

One day, Stacey gets a strange feeling that God may have forgiven her, because Mac arrives home and proclaims that he has a new car, a new haircut, and a new job. She is elated until he describes this new job: He is not simply selling Richalife vitamins; he is selling a way of life. To Stacey, the promises of Richalife are absurdly phony; she is not the kind of wife who says that the sun is the moon if her husband says it is, and she is disappointed that he is so tainted by modern society that he would even consider selling such a product.

Mac locks himself away in his study and becomes even more of a stranger at a time when Stacey needs him the most. To comfort herself, she drinks gin and tonic and fancies having an affair with Mac's best friend, Buckle Fennick, whom she dislikes. The gods, however, turn on Stacey. Buckle can have sex only with himself in front of a witness, and as if being that witness is not punishment enough, Stacey suffers further humiliation when Buckle tells Mac that she forced him to have sex with her. Mac believes Buckle, and Stacey's marriage becomes a fire burning out of control.

Stacey goes to the Sound, where she finds some relief in a young science-fiction writer, Luke Venturi, who treats her as a human being and as a desirable woman. Stacey knows that having sex with a man other than her husband, though healthy for the ego, does not solve her problems. Buckle's pointless death—he is killed while playing chicken—does not bring Mac and Stacey permanently closer together; even Mac's getting a promotion, her father-in-law's moving into her house, and her mother and sister's moving into her city do not change Stacey. Finally, she accepts that she is not going to undergo the transformation for which she has yearned; as she says to herself,

> I used to think there would be a blinding flash of light someday, and then I would be wise and calm and would know how to cope with everything and my kids would rise up and call me blessed. Now I see that whatever I'm like, I'm pretty well stuck with it for life. Hell of a revelation that turned out to be.

The Characters

Stacey MacAindra thoroughly dominates the novel. Margaret Laurence uses her to examine the role of wife/mother in a modern family in which the mother feels both nourished and devoured by her children. Although Stacey performs all the routine duties associated with being a mother and knows that bringing up four children is a worthwhile occupation, she fears that she is spending her life in one unbroken series of trivialities. She wants something of her own. She wants to stand as herself and communicate with her husband, her children, and the world. It is not simply the crisis of turning forty that causes her to exclaim to God,

> I stand in relation to my life both as child and as parent, never quite finished with old battles, never able to arbitrate properly the new, able to look both ways, but whichever way I look, God, it looks pretty confusing to me.

This woman facing forty is a frightened little girl who senses that her inability to communicate with others cannot be all her fault. She is a prairie girl from Manawaka who left home at nineteen for the big city of Vancouver, certain that life there would be better than it was in the tomblike silence in which she dwelled with her parents. Her life is indeed better than her parents' lives, but better is not good enough. Stacey wants to express her true self to the people she loves. She is a responsible person and has no real intention of walking away from her obligations. She will survive if all survival means is to cope from day to day.

It is difficult for Stacey to accept that a man and a woman can live together for almost twenty years and not communicate. Her marriage to Mac, however, is a perfect example of such a marriage. Mac is seen through his actions, conversations with other characters, and Stacey's interior monologues. The reader never knows what hides behind his icy exterior. He is a provider who does not want to admit that any problems exist. He deals with Jen's inability to talk or Duncan's insufficient masculinity by refusing to discuss these concerns. Stacey tries to reach out to Mac, but he is not reachable. He is able to handle his problems without discussing them; he, therefore, sees no reason for anyone else to discuss theirs. Stacey comes to accept that Mac will never communicate the way she wishes he would in "full technicolor and intense detail."

Katie's relationship with her mother is complicated by Stacey's seeing herself in her daughter: Katie is attractive and rebellious, just as Stacey was when she was Katie's age. Stacey seems to say and do everything deliberately to annoy Katie, who sees Stacey as very "square" and unable to get along with Mac. She wants Stacey to be a mother and is incapable of relating to Stacey as a person. Yet Stacey sees the future in her. Katie is on her own because Stacey does not have all the answers and can only hope that life turns out better for her.

Themes and Meanings

The central theme of *The Fire-Dwellers* is the difficulty of achieving genuine communication among individuals. The novel opens with Stacey viewing her life through a full-length mirror. She sees images there that are "less real than real and yet more sharply focused because isolated and limited by a frame." Everything in the frame is shabby and filtered as if displayed on a television screen. Stacey is caught up in a wasteland existence in which an internal fire keeps her from communicating with her family and with herself. A nursery rhyme—"Ladybird, ladybird,/ Fly away home;/ Your house is on fire,/ Your children are gone"—haunts Stacey throughout the novel. Stacey's most sincere fear is that God, to punish her for her constant complaining or sinning, will take her children away from her or allow them to be harmed in some way.

Stacey develops from an exasperated woman into one who thinks that maybe trivialities are not so bad after all because they are something on which to focus. She wonders, "Will the fires go on, inside and out?" She is stronger than she thinks and will plod on out of conviction that she loves her children and is willing to accept even silence as a form of positive communication. She has learned that all communication does not have to be in the color and detail she would like it to be.

Laurence's style is related to what she is attempting to do thematically. The novel shifts abruptly between third person and first and includes fantasies, dreams, flashbacks, and media headlines. The style reinforces the fragmented, out-of-control nature of the characters' frantic lives; the multi-layered narrative technique is appropriate for a novel in which it is imperative for the reader to see the contrast between Stacey's thoughts and her actions and words.

Critical Context

The Fire-Dwellers is the third in a loosely connected sequence of five books (four novels and a collection of stories) involving the fictional prairie town of Manawaka. *A Jest of God* (1966) is the novel in this series most closely related to *The Fire-Dwellers*. Stacey's story can be seen as a sequel to *A Jest of God*, which is narrated by her younger sister, Rachel Cameron. Stacey is first introduced to readers in Rachel's narrative. *A Jest of God* ends with Rachel and her mother planning to move from Manawaka to Vancouver, where Rachel believes that Stacey lives an idyllic life. Rachel, a withdrawn spinster, has always been envious of Stacey, who always seemed so sure of herself. Rachel seems to believe that, by leaving Manawaka, Stacey has set herself free of the place. Manawaka is a state of mind, however, and the root of Stacey's turmoil lies in her inability to break away from the conditioning that she received in Manawaka.

The Fire-Dwellers is well regarded by feminist critics. Stacey exists in a male-oriented, chauvinistic society, but she is not aware that she is oppressed because she is a female. Stacey never considers getting a job and letting someone else care for her children or her house. She is conditioned to believe that every woman wants to be married and to have a family and that all it takes for a woman to be happy is to be a member of a family that loves and communicates with one another. Mac shares Stacey's conditioning about

what a woman needs to be fulfilled. Mac remarks while viewing a very nervous girl speaking at a rally that all the girl needs is the love of a good man,
and Stacey agrees. Laurence in no way, however, presents Stacey's narrative
in the shrill manner of some feminist writing of the time.

Sources for Further Study
Morley, Patricia. *Margaret Laurence*, 1981.
New, William H., ed. *Margaret Laurence: The Writer and Her Critics*, 1977.
Thomas, Clara. *The Manawaka World of Margaret Laurence*, 1975.
Woodcock, George, ed. *A Place to Stand On: Essays by and About Margaret
    Laurence*, 1983.

Brenda Adams

FIREFLIES

Author: Shiva Naipaul (1945-1985)
Type of plot: Social satire
Time of plot: The 1960's
Locale: Port of Spain, Trinidad
First published: 1970

> *Principal characters:*
> VIMLA LUTCHMAN (BABY), the heroine, a cousin to the Khojas
> RAM LUTCHMAN, first a bus driver, then an employee in the
> ministry of education
> BHASKAR, the Lutchmans' firstborn, who is driven to cynicism
> by repeated failures
> ROMESH, the second-born son, who becomes a criminal
> GOVIND KHOJA, the head of one of Trinidad's most important
> families, a disciple of Jean-Jacques Rousseau
> SUMINTRA KHOJA, his paranoid wife, who is neurotically
> attached to dolls, which are her substitute children

The Novel

Set in Trinidad, Shiva Naipaul's birthplace, *Fireflies* is a massive chronicle, in two parts, of the fortunes (good and bad) of Vimla Lutchman (nicknamed Baby). At first she is the rather passive wife of an undistinguished bus driver, but being the great-niece of the elder Mrs. Khoja, she is circumscribed by the impressive social and material background of the Khojas, one of the wealthiest, most powerful, and most important families in the region. Baby is powerless in that family, in which all veneration is paid to Govind Khoja and in which all domestic affairs are influenced by his six sisters. After her marriage to Ram Lutchman, Baby discovers another side to her life: a submission to Ram's sordid bouts of violence, drunkenness, and unapproachable taciturnity. She grows fat, and her lust for commerce waxes. She remains devoted to her husband even when he has an affair with Doreen James, a purported anthropologist. Baby worries about her two sons, Romesh and Bhaskar, and occasionally seeks refuge with Gowra, a distant cousin.

Ram Lutchman develops fitful obsessions—with Doreen, gardening, swimming, photography—but these come and go. His life becomes a sequence of ridiculous failures. His wife stays with him, however, through all of his quirks of fortune, sometimes defending him with a ferocity as comically useless as it is poignantly loving. When Ram dies suddenly after a heart attack, her grief prompts her to collect some of his charred bones from the cremation site, but when she begins to suffer nightmares, she throws the bones into a river, and her nightmares stop.

The second part of the novel opens with the gradual disintegration of the Khoja clan, as a rebellious faction of sisters develops (headed by Urmila, Shantee, and Badwatee) against Govind. This conflict is part of the important subplot that fuels Baby's struggle for independence. As a widow, she is drawn more strongly into the Khoja sisters' circle, and deciding to follow Urmila's commercial example, she takes in lodgers to finance her dream of success for her sons—particularly for Bhaskar, who wants, very unrealistically, to be a doctor. She comes to depend naïvely and foolishly on the fraudulent prophecies of her neighbor, Mrs. MacKintosh, a rather desolate, impoverished Scottish woman, deserted by her husband and left with a polio-stricken son and a daughter. Seeing her opportunity to trade her crackpot predictions for free food, Mrs. MacKintosh delivers whatever prophecies she knows will appeal to Baby's hunger for good news.

To inspire the mediocre Bhaskar, Govind spins a parable of a boy who overcomes economic deprivation by his resourcefulness. Lacking the convenience of electric light, the boy captures fireflies in a bottle and studies by their light. It is an absurdly exaggerated tale, perfectly in keeping with Govind's propensity for moralizing but comically irrelevant to Bhaskar's essence as a youth. When Bhaskar goes abroad to an Indian university, his brother Romesh develops quickly into a dangerous failure. His passion for cinema so warps his personality that his life is overrun by violent fantasy. Festering with contempt for the memory of his dead father and filled with hate for the Khojas, he brutally attacks Govind and his wife, Sumintra.

The whole edifice of Khoja respectability cracks. Trouble brews in the home of Saraswatee, another of the Khoja sisters, when her daughter Renouka, influenced by her Catholic education, turns against Khoja values. Rudranath, Saraswatee's husband, turns against this modernity and goes berserk. He never recovers from the blow to his puritanical mania. Renouka takes up with her cousin Romesh, while also pursuing an affair with a "commercial traveler." Govind, who has been deprived of his authority as the head of the family, decides to play the guru to the people at large and forms the People's Socialist Movement, which he leads disastrously in an election. Assassination threats are made against him, and the Khoja rebels campaign against him.

Baby survives all the shame brought on her by her criminal son, just as she survives Bhaskar's sequence of career failures. Bhaskar's newly developed cynicism—he eventually dismisses Govind's tale of the fireflies as pure rubbish—counterpoints his mother's optimism. Yet the heroine's life is cast in a downward spiral. She loses the friendship of Mrs. MacKintosh and the sympathy of her lodgers. She therefore sells the house and moves with Bhaskar into cousin Gowra's home. She assists Govind with his "naturalist" school, but the venture fails. Bhaskar embarks for England with a bride, and Baby is left alone and empty.

The Characters

Baby is Shiva Naipaul's detailed portrait of a dreamer out of touch with reality. She is not a powerful or particularly colorful figure, but she is intensely and touchingly human in her natural foibles, suffering, and yearnings. At first, she is little more than a conventional Hindu wife, who is subject to her husband's will and whim. She bears his cycles of violence and calm, drunkenness and abstinence, brutality and concern. She even abides his adulterous relationship with Doreen James. Her resignation, patience, and unquestioning loyalty to Ram mark her as an acquiescent victim of domestic exploitation, but because her worldview is marked by an indifference to the formal arrangement of laws, duties, and social forces, her world does not fall apart easily.

She derives substantial emotional solace from the Khoja sisters, who, as a group, are a corporate entity. Although foils to her patience and soulless devotion, the sisters provide her with the emotional coherence and consistency she lacks from her husband. While each of the sisters has her own speciality—Urmila, her voice; Shantee, her shared confidences with Govind's wife; Badwatee, her obsession with Catholicism; Indrani, her defiant solitariness; Darling and Saraswatee, their compliancy—together they constitute a formidable feminine force and represent the grasping and conspiratorial power of a family that is a pillar of the Trinidadian community.

Baby shares with her cousins a confusion of religion with magic. She so wishes her life to be blessed with good luck that she turns desperately to Mrs. MacKintosh for tea-leaf fortunes. Absurd but pitiable, she is not selfish: Her dreams are more for her family rather than for herself. It is only when, little by little, almost all of her emotional supports are taken away from her that she deteriorates into a figure of desolate emptiness. She becomes, in effect, a lost one.

Shiva Naipaul, like his famous elder brother, V. S. Naipaul, has a genius for telling satiric details—so much so that subsidiary or supporting characters have a palpable, colorful existence in the novel. Doreen James is sketched in all of her snobbish affectation and incapacity to love. Sumintra Khoja is poignantly limned as a woman of arrested emotional development, whose dolls are a substitute for children. Mrs. MacKintosh is delightfully weird and shrewdly exploitative of Baby's gullibility. The priest Ramnarace, with his concessions to modernity, is an exotic anomaly.

Ultimately, however, the most lasting impression is created by the Khojas, Baby, and her family. Naipaul's world is one of illusions and delusions. Mocked by failure, his characters often try to abstract themselves from the world that hurts them, but they are not simply victims. They all have their own foibles and failings—sometimes disturbingly violent (as in Ram and Romesh), sometimes absurdly self-victimizing (as in Govind and Baby). In a society in which no soul is pure and no vision uncorrupted, the more the inhabitants attempt to escape their enclosed world of hierarchical functions and powers, the more victimized they become. Their failures, though sharp and sometimes destructive, are glossed by their eccentricities or absurdities, so that they are almost tragicomic.

Themes and Meanings

Shiva Naipaul chronicles the erosion of human idealism and power. The world of the Khojas and Lutchmans is one in which reality is distorted into false fable, before asserting itself with unrelenting pitilessness. In this world, expectation exceeds fulfillment, and passion dwindles into wastefulness. Although they differ from one another in scale and status, the characters share a common fate: They are compelled to acknowledge the futility of their efforts to transform their world and shape their destinies.

The smaller characters—Ram, Romesh, Bhaskar, Doreen, Mrs. Mac-Kintosh—are plagued by bad luck or disillusionment. With no real economic or social power of his own, Ram is simply a tyrant at home, and a failure at his obsessions. Romesh is an absurd victim of his own cinematic fantasies. He thinks and acts like a Hollywood gangster until reality catches up with him. Doreen's love life is a maze of confusion and misunderstanding, but fundamentally she is punished by life for her selfishness. Mrs. MacKintosh, deserted by an unreliable husband, seeks to exploit others before they can exploit her, but she, too, is nothing more than a lonely, rather desperate woman who can barely eke out a meager existence in a world that wastes little sympathy on its victims. The world turns some characters into cynics: Bhaskar's sullen solitariness in the later stages of the book is a natural result of his disappointment in life.

Even the larger characters are circumscribed by this pattern of failure. Govind Khoja, the superficially sophisticated disciple of Jean-Jacques Rousseau, is full of sententious precepts and advice, yet none of his ideals ever materializes the way he envisages: His book is never completed, his political campaign is sabotaged, and his naturalist school fails. Even his power in the Khoja clan diminishes. As for Baby, the massive exposure to the workings of human nature and circumstance render her a powerless victim. Like the Khojas, she learns the hard way that a passion for controlling life leads to a diminution of control.

The acute description of rituals in the novel is not simply a sociological curiosity but also a subtle suggestion of how life becomes a sequence of empty rites and ceremonies. The religious customs are meant to evoke Hindu spiritual forces, yet they are mocked by events. Ram Lutchman's gardening is a fruitless attempt to set down roots and to transform his small, seedy world into a Garden of Eden. Unable to succeed in life, he is mocked even in death, for his cremation is spoiled by Romesh's refusal to participate in the rites. The *puja* that Baby organizes for Bhaskar is slyly mocked by the Khoja sisters and undercut by the fact of Bhaskar's mediocre prospects.

There are special images that convey Naipaul's themes—the landscape, the houses occupied by various characters, and, most of all, the fireflies of the title. Although the specific tale of the fireflies is but a brief one, Naipaul subtly builds up to the fable. The first significant instance of insect imagery is when Ram Lutchman watches an insect struggling desperately to escape from a lampshade. The whirring wings, gradually decreasing in effect and conviction, prefigure his own futile actions and eventual decline. Insects are, by nature, instinctive and most ephemeral, and are accordingly good analogues for the characters (particularly Ram, Romesh, and Bhaskar), whose passions are short-lived and whose impact on their world is negligible.

The major importance of the fireflies is that they are at the heart of an absurd fable concocted by a pretentious dreamer. Govind Khoja is a man who lives for effect, but his effects are often miscalculated or frustrated. When he exaggerates the reality of fireflies into a sentimental fable, he seems to signal his own false conceptions of existence. There is nothing beneath the tissue of his fable—only an empty posture of heroic persistence and unyielding willfulness. He is eventually reduced by life, and the only true (but ultimately unhappy) example of resolve is Baby, whose instinct is for survival, although her experiences eventually cripple her will.

Critical Context

Fireflies is, perhaps, underrated. It lies in the shadow of *A House for Mr. Biswas* (1961)—that masterpiece by Shiva Naipaul's older brother—and certainly lacks the driving force, unrelenting central focus, and architectural coherence of its predecessor. Yet it is a massive success in its own right. It won the Jock Campbell Award, the John Llewelyn Rhys Memorial Prize, and the Winifred Holtby Memorial Prize of the Royal Society of Literature.

Like his brother, Shiva Naipaul was Hindu by instinct, if not by doctrine. His story conveys a strong sense of detachment and resignation, for in it the heroine, unable to alter the grim course of life, gives up the struggle in the end.

In a sense, Naipaul could be accused of exercising the fashionable pessimism of existentialism, but there is a sweet flavor amid the bitterness and sourness of his story. His gritty satire saves the writing from wearying pessimism, and his perceptive renderings of human nature offer a cool irony. Yet it is not a cold, heartless book, for the satirist's penetrating and scalding wit is balanced by sympathy for suffering. Like the fireflies of the title, the heroine's struggle sheds light before being extinguished. Its light is an illumination of human nature. Naipaul's comedy thus distances readers from facile pity without alienating them from the vulnerabilities that make us helplessly human.

Sources for Further Study

Blackburn, Sara. Review in *The Washington Post Book World*. April 18, 1971, p. 2.

Grant, Annette. Review in *The New York Times Book Review*. LXIV (February 7, 1971), p. 6.

Hess, Linda. Review in *Saturday Review*. LIV (March 20, 1971), p. 37.

The Times Literary Supplement. December 11, 1970, p. 1437.

Keith Garebian

THE FISHER KING

Author: Anthony Powell (1905-   )
Type of plot: Psychological realism
Time of plot: The early 1980's
Locale: On board the *Alecto*, cruising around the British Isles
First published: 1986

Principal characters:

SAUL HENCHMAN, a famous photographer maimed in World
    War II, the "Fisher King" of the title
BARBERINA ROOKWOOD, Henchman's young assistant, once a
    very promising dancer
VALENTINE BEALS, a writer of historical thrillers and the
    primary narrator of the events of the novel
LOUISE BEALS, his wife
PIERS MIDDLECOTE, an adman and a narrator
FAY MIDDLECOTE, his wife
GARY LAMONT, a newspaper tycoon, an admirer of Barberina
    Rookwood
ROBIN JILSON, a young invalid and an aspiring photographer

The Novel

Anthony Powell employs a variety of narrative forms to recount the drama
of the *Alecto*'s cruise; each fresh perspective adds to the irony of the novel.
The structure is reminiscent of the English "whodunit": A small, enclosed
society—in this case isolated aboard a ship—attempts to solve a mystery in
its midst. There is no murder at the core of *The Fisher King*, but rather a
puzzle involving the vagaries of the human heart. Saul Henchman is the ultimate enigma: Famous for his photographs, controversial for his manner of
living, pitied for his disabilities, he is immediately recognized as a celebrity.
Nevertheless, Henchman is shrouded in mystery; a shadowy past, apocryphal
tales from his war service, gossip about his relationships might illustrate the
outer man, but the novel makes it painfully clear that attempts to fathom the
inner man are inept, at best. Barberina Rookwood is his partner in mystery.
Their fellow passengers long to know the precise nature of her relationship
to Henchman. Her celebrity derives not only from her companionship to
Henchman, who is said to be impotent, but also from her immense sacrifice
in giving up a career in ballet that promised fame and fortune. Was this supreme renunciation her idea or Henchman's?

As the novel unfolds, the reader slowly gains at least a partial understanding of the characters. The reader's limited knowledge has at its base the mis-
apprehensions and lack of perception in the narrators. Valentine Beals, the

primary narrator, first observes Saul Henchman and Barberina Rookwood as they board the *Alecto* to begin the cruise. While Beals has never seen either in the flesh, he immediately recognizes their names on the passenger list and spots the couple—Henchman by his crutches and camera, Barberina by her effortless grace and delicate beauty. Beals, an author of swashbuckling historical romances, is always on the lookout for a story, adventure, or prototype hero, and he is immediately fascinated by the complexities of the Henchman-Rookwood partnership. Aided and abetted by his interested wife and the Bealses' friends and traveling companions, the Middlecotes, he engages himself in a minute scrutiny of the pair's actions. The four stockpile rumors, facts, gossip, and opinions to attempt an understanding of the famous couple; all keep an eagle eye on them during the cruise and witness the breakup of the partnership.

Beals's most fascinating addition to the narrative stockpile is his assertion that Henchman is the archetypal Fisher King of Arthurian legend. Beals's "innate taste for pin-pointing archetypes" seems to spread to others during the cruise; Elaines, Don Juans, and Loathly Damsels find their way among the passengers. When Beals tries his theory out on his wife and friends, they are unimpressed at first. Beals mentions the parallels: kingship with celebrity and power; the thigh wounds and impotence, the same in both cases; fishing as a hobby, the same; a young apprentice knight, Perceval, who fails to restore the Fisher King, later equated with Robin Jilson, the apprentice photographer. The myth of the Fisher King involves the reader in two realms: the shadowy, ancient world of the Arthurian court and T. S. Eliot's brooding, modern epic, *The Waste Land* (1922).

From his post as observer, Beals is able to spot an early complication in the Henchman-Rookwood enjoyment of their holiday. Gary Lamont, a recently bereaved widower and newspaper tycoon, is on board hoping to further his infatuation with Barberina. Beals, always ready with a parallel, sees Lamont as a "latterday Gatsby, a Gatsby retired from a life of open illegality, while retaining the Midas touch in commercial dealings; buccaneering ventures tempered in his own eyes with a few high ideals, one of them probably the image of the Perfect Woman." Once on board, Lamont gives every indication that Barberina is his Perfect Woman and that he believes she should be restored to the stage, freed from her Sleeping Beauty bondage to dance again. Some of Lamont's zeal may be based on a heart condition that does not indicate a long future.

Another invalid on board besides Henchman and Lamont is young Robin Jilson, who is afflicted with a rare muscular condition of the cranial motor nerves as well as with an anxious, garrulous mother. Jilson, although dismissed by most of the narrators as a very ordinary young man, attracts the attention of Henchman and, more important, of Barberina. Henchman offers Jilson help in launching himself as a photographer; Barberina falls in love with him, only to be outmaneuvered by the bossy, antiseptic Dr. Lorna Tiptoft. Barberina's decision to leave Henchman is revealed in a silent gesture—one only Henchman and the observant Beals can comprehend. An incident as simple as Barberina dancing to the ship's orchestra's selection from *Swan Lake* tells Henchman that Barberina's companionship is lost to him forever. Henchman leaves the *Alecto* early to fish a Scottish loch; Barberina must continue alone, knowing that the balance of Jilson's affections are tipped in the Loathly Lady Doctor's favor.

The novel ends at The Ring, a circle of standing stones, where past, present, and future merge. There Henchman leaves his fellow travelers: "Come. Let us leave these pilgrims seeking forgetfulness of the Present in a Promised Land of the Past." Yet forgetfulness is not the aim of these particular pilgrims; the story of Saul Henchman and Barberina Rookwood has made a profound and memorable impact upon each human heart.

The Characters

The characters so meticulously created, Henchman and Barberina, partially exist in the minds of their creators, the Bealses and the Middlecotes. The reader is well aware that material given is selected primarily by Valentine Beals. A writer of fiction, Beals might manipulate the narrative to create certain artistic effects. When the narrative involves direct reporting and quotation from Henchman or Barberina, however, the reader pays close attention. Henchman is everything gossip reports him to be—disfigured, difficult, peremptory, ironic. At times, he is silent, nearly spectral; then he may suddenly wax loquacious about his experiences. Both Louise Beals and Fay Middlecote find Henchman extraordinarily attractive for all of his disabilities; his impotence somehow renders him more appealing rather than the reverse. Fay Middlecote attempts fairly direct flirtation, while Louise Beals, once enamored of her homosexual doctor—another man who could not return her affections—contents herself with admiration from afar. Henchman wears the gloss of celebrity with an ill will that distinguishes him from others; perhaps this impatience with image makes his character so ironic as it is his profession to create images for others. Professionally, nearly all the male characters work with the manipulation of images—Lamont in his newspaper, Middlecote in his advertising campaigns, and Beals in his novels.

Barberina is nearly as complex as Henchman. Marked as a dancer from childhood, protected and cosseted by her grandmother, given a taste of early success, Barberina's desertion at seventeen to share Henchman's life can only be termed a *coup de foudre*. She tends him lovingly; she is as much nurse as assistant. The Bealses and Fay Middlecote believe that Barberina is still a virgin; Beals especially likes the idea, as it backs up his notion of the Fisher King and the importance of virgins and courtly love in the Arthurian legends. It is evident that Barberina is a strong woman of great inner repose;

"I've never seen waters so still," remarks Fay Middlecote. Barberina makes her decision to leave Henchman as quickly as she made her earlier move to live with him; the Middlecotes and Bealses can only guess at her feelings.

Anthony Powell's use of flawed narrators is done with gentle irony. The reader must understand and sympathize with the curious quest of Valentine Beals. Celebrity has a built-in drawing power; it is a rare individual who admits no curiosity about or desire to observe the famous or notorious. Neither Beals nor Middlecote is a mere power worshiper; both are rich, successful, and quite well-known in their own spheres. Nevertheless, Henchman and Barberina mesmerize these characters; for the length of the holiday cruise, Beals and Middlecote define all relationships and emotions by the terms they observe in the mysterious partnership.

Louise Beals and Fay Middlecote maintain an interest on a different level; they are bound in admiration of Barberina as well as in fascination with Henchman. Fay Middlecote, more direct in her approach to the mystery, also has the most moral qualms. When Henchman allows her to interrogate him near the end of the novel, "she was afraid she was going to cry, which would have been a dreadful humiliation to her. . . . She herself was ashamed of just feeling trite curiosity about it all. She wanted to tell him that." While the Bealses and Middlecotes comment on their observations, they reveal bit by bit their personal philosophies on life and love.

Powell includes a variety of minor characters on board ship. Some he quickly sketches, such as the inseparable pair of American men identified only by the slogans on their T-shirts (Basically Bach and Marginally Mahler); others he draws more carefully. The reader scarcely notes a lesser luminary, Mr. Jack, with Barberina and Henchman ablaze in the sky of Beals's regard. Mr. Jack is an aged barfly with long-winded tales; "The Ancient Mariner was a terse reporter compared to him," groans Beals after one encounter. Yet Mr. Jack has a link with Henchman's past and is destined to be Henchman's final companion, a drunken Fool to a crippled Lear. Powell meticulously handles characterization and conversation in *The Fisher King*; both contribute to the depth of psychological insight and elegant wit of the novel.

Themes and Meanings

Despite Beals's comparison of Mr. Jack to the Ancient Mariner, it is actually Beals's fate to tell the drama of the *Alecto*'s cruise over and over to "listeners not over-curious as to the workings of human nature and the emotion of love." Certainly *The Fisher King* exists as a tale of lovers both real and mythic; some are tragic, others comic. Love can be two opposites at once—a sacrifice and a demand.

Sacrifice and demand also exist as the elements of celebrity, an important thread in the novel. The demands of fame force Henchman and Barberina to play out the end of their relationship under the scrutiny of the public eye.

The nature of celebrity makes Beals believe that he "owns" a part of Henchman and Barberina simply because he recognizes them as public property. Powell also employs power as an underlying theme; in an unusually talkative mood, Henchman bandies definitions of power with Sir Dixon Tiptoft. Henchman identifies power as an imposition of the will, then goes on to explain his photography as such. Photography, according to Henchman, gives the practitioner power over the Living and the Dead:

> Photography is one of the aspects of Death and Regeneration. Those who live more photographic lives than one, have more photographic resurrections than one, as well as more deaths. Nowadays a dead person depends almost entirely on photographs for the manner in which he or she is physically remembered. . . . If that is not power, I don't know what is."

Even as Henchman ironically claims power over the Living and the Dead, he recognizes Death's nearness on board. All three of the men whom Barberina has been drawn to are marked by severe illness. Even Mr. Jack seems too decrepit, too debilitated by drink to live long. How each character chooses to live identifies him more clearly than the shadow of death.

Last, Powell works with the interplay of myth, legend, and literature with the more mundane elements of life. Powell's allusions are legion. The Arthurian element is most prominent, as is evidenced by the novel's title. Besides the Fisher King, Elaine, Perceval, and the Loathly Damsel, the legends of Tristan and Isolde and the search for the Grail find their way into the novel. The novel's locale, particularly the stops to visit Hadrian's Wall and the Stone Circle, regenerate other English and Celtic myths. A proposition that Mr. Jack is Don Juan promotes lively debate on yet another archetype and his literary treatment. Erudition, wit, and psychological insight combine to give meaning to the social alignments in *The Fisher King*.

Critical Context

Powell's literary reputation rests largely on his twelve-volume novel series *A Dance to the Music of Time*. The first novel of the series, *A Question of Upbringing*, appeared in 1951; the last, *Hearing Secret Harmonies*, in 1975. Together the twelve novels are considered one of the outstanding achievements in twentieth century British fiction. Covering British social and political values from the end of World War I until the early 1970's, the series captures people and events through the eyes of its narrator, Nicholas Jenkins. After completing *A Dance to the Music of Time*, Powell turned to his memoirs until he published a novella, *O, How the Wheel Becomes It!*, in 1983. *The Fisher King* marks his return to the full-length novel.

While *The Fisher King* does not attempt the scope of *A Dance to the Music of Time*, its aim is to distill and concentrate the essences of modern

British life. A few days' holiday, dotted with conversation and encounter, are all the materials Powell needs to craft his story and render its deeper, darker significance.

Sources for Further Study
Brennan, Neil. *Anthony Powell*, 1974.
Library Journal. Review. CXI (September 15, 1986), p. 101.
The New York Times. Review. CXXXVI (September 23, 1986), p. C17.
Powell, Anthony. *The Strangers All Are Gone*, 1982.
Publishers Weekly. Review. CCXXX (August 1, 1986), p. 66.
Tucker, James. *The Novels of Anthony Powell*, 1976.

Kathryn V. Graham

FLAUBERT'S PARROT

Author: Julian Barnes (1946-   )
Type of plot: Critical novel
Time of plot: The early 1980's
Locale: France and England
First published: 1984

Principal characters:
GUSTAVE FLAUBERT, the great nineteenth century French
  novelist and letter writer
LOUISE COLET, his mistress during the composition of
  Madame Bovary (1857)
MAXIME DU CAMP,
LOUIS BOUILHET, and
ALFRED LE POITTEVIN, Flaubert's close friends
GEOFFREY BRAITHWAITE, a retired contemporary British
  physician, who is obsessed with Flaubert's life
ELLEN BRAITHWAITE, his adulterous dead wife

The Novel

This is a tantalizingly elusive work of fiction, exhibiting elements of biography, autobiography, literary monograph, parody, novel, and anthology of maxims and epigrams. It is narrated by Dr. Geoffrey Braithwaite, a retired British general practitioner in his sixties, widowed from a wife whom he never understood, who becomes obsessed with seeking to understand the essential nature of Gustave Flaubert.

Braithwaite begins—and finally ends—his quest by attempting to identify the particular green stuffed Amazonian parrot which Flaubert borrowed for a model while writing "Un Cœur simple." In that tale, a simple, sacrificial Norman domestic, Félicité, devotes her life to serving a largely ungrateful family. The last object of her love is a parrot, Loulou, whom she comes to regard as the incarnation of the Holy Ghost. Braithwaite discovers a green stuffed parrot in Rouen, perched above an inscription certifying that Flaubert had been lent the bird by the city's museum and had kept it on his desk for three weeks while writing "Un Cœur simple." A few weeks later, in Croisset, the village where Flaubert lived most of his life, Braithwaite discovers another parrot, also stuffed, also green. Which is the authentic model for Félicité's Loulou?

Braithwaite ascertains that Flaubert described an ugly English matron he met aboard a boat from Alexandria to Cairo as looking "like a sick old parrot." In *Salammbô* (1862), Carthaginian translators sport parrot tattoos on their chests. In *L'Éducation sentimentale* (1869), the protagonist Frédéric Moreau peers into a shop window and sees a parrot's perch. Flaubert's niece, Caroline, insists in her memoirs that Loulou had a real-life model, as did Félicité. The second and incomplete section of *Bouvard et Pécuchet* (1881) includes a passage wherein the copying clerks are to transcribe a newspaper account of a lonely misanthrope who comes to love a magnificent parrot and teaches it to pronounce, one hundred times daily, the name of the woman who rejected him. After the parrot dies, the owner takes to perching in a tree, squawking, extending his arms like wings. He is committed to a *maison de santé*. Finally, the small house in Croisset where Flaubert wrote was called *un baton de perroquet*, "a parrot's perch."

Braithwaite is strongly tempted to regard the parrot as emblematic of the author, as the magic madeleine whose dissolution in the waters of Flaubert's complex life will provide the key to his tormented temperament. Could the parrot be the Life which repeats and mocks itself, just as Braithwaite remarks on episodes in Flaubert's life that parrot his work? Or could the parrot, as the only creature capable of making human sounds, symbolize the supremacy of Language to which Flaubert offered all other opportunities for happiness? Braithwaite muses,

> Félicité + Loulou = Flaubert? Not exactly; but you could claim that he is present in both of them. Félicité encloses his character; Loulou encloses his voice. You could say that the parrot, representing clever vocalisation without much brain power, was Pure Word. . . . I imagined Loulou sitting on the other side of Flaubert's desk and staring back at him like some taunting reflection from a funfair mirror. No wonder three weeks of its parodic presence caused irritation. Is the writer much more than a sophisticated parrot?

Braithwaite looks at Flaubert from many perspectives, collecting the views of the writer's friends, critics, relatives, particularly his mistress for five stormy years, Louise Colet. He presents the traditional portrait of the artist consumed by the demands of his art to the peril of his relations with women, of the man who insists that love remain in the back room of his life while he cultivates the religion of Writing. What remains in the foreground of Flaubert's life, in addition to literature, is his lifelong devotion to his dour mother, to three male friends who became intimate confidants, and to the romantic symbol of Sacred Love represented by Elisa Schlésinger, regarding whom he maintained for forty years an unconsummated admiration. Then Braithwaite dramatizes the agonized liaison involving the Parisian actress Louise Colet, with whom Flaubert was "ill-matched in temperament and incompatible in aesthetics." Flaubert met Louise in 1846 but interrupted their affair from 1849 to 1851 to travel in the Middle East with Maxime Du Camp and there enjoy the favors of lice-ridden prostitutes, such as the locally celebrated courtesan Kuchuk Hanem.

Braithwaite apes Flaubert's *Dictionnaire des idées reçues* (1910) with his own *Dictionary of Accepted Ideas* in which he weighs, in Flaubert's cynical eyes, the comparative merits of Kuchuk's bedbugs, sandalwood oil, and syphilis opposed to Louise's lyric poetry and cleanliness. The outcome: "He found the issue finely balanced." After all, prostitutes were the necessary means by which the nineteenth century's distinguished writers could contract syphilis, "without which no one could claim genius"—whereupon the narrator lists, as "wearers of the red badge of courage," not only Flaubert but also Alphonse Daudet, Guy de Maupassant, Jules de Goncourt, and Charles Baudelaire. (He omits Leo Tolstoy, probably because his lens is wholly focused on French authors.)

Braithwaite loves to compile a miscellany of little-known facts about Flaubert: that he was born so delicate that his father, a surgeon, had a small grave dug in anticipation of the infant's death; that his present statue in Trouville replaces the original the Germans removed in 1941; that *Salammbô* furnished the name for a newly marketed *petit four* in 1862; that George Sand wrote him, "You produce desolation, and I produce consolation"; that Flaubert derived immense amusement from a five-legged sheep he found at a fair; that in *Madame Bovary* the author loses track of an Italian greyhound bitch beloved by Emma; that Flaubert received only eight hundred francs for the publication rights to *Madame Bovary* but spent five hundred francs on gloves; that the scene in *Madame Bovary* which has Léon use a closed cab to seduce Emma became so quickly notorious that in Hamburg, the year after the novel's publication, cabs hired for sexual use were called "Bovarys"; and that Flaubert, after having savaged the bourgeois Homais in *Madame Bovary* by awarding him the Légion d'honneur, permitted himself in 1866 to become a Chevalier de la Légion d'honneur: "Consequently, the last line of his life parroted the last line of his masterpiece."

In the thirteenth of the book's fifteen chapters, Braithwaite at last reveals the tale he has hesitated to tell: that of his own tortured marriage to a wife, Ellen, who died in 1975 at the age of fifty-five. Being a discreet, inhibited man, he finds it difficult to confess his deepest wounds, yet being also melancholy, clearheaded, and candid, he finds it purgative to expose them. His leitmotif becomes a regularly repeated refrain: "I loved her; we were happy; I miss her. She didn't love me; we were unhappy; I miss her." His wife, he assures the reader, was kind, caring, prudent with money, and always good to him. Yet she had a secret life which became manifest to him over and over again: Like Emma Bovary, she was an adulteress. Unlike Emma, she never ran up large bills, and never embarrassed him publicly. She simply never loved him, while he never stopped loving her. They kept an unspoken compact never to discuss her promiscuity. In an impulsive manner he refuses to describe, she committed what amounts to suicide. Yet, he insists, "hers is a pure story."

The Characters

By stressing the pains and losses Flaubert had to endure, Julian Barnes presents him in a more compassionate light than is usually shed by the chilling legend of a literary genius who repels most people as cold, cruel, narcissistic, depressed, dogmatic, sexually vulgar, and sardonic. Barnes/ Braithwaite takes an inventory of such inflictions as Flaubert's subjection to shattering attacks of epilepsy; his hopeless infatuation with Elisa Schlésinger; the deaths of both his father and his beloved sister Caroline when Gustave was twenty-five; the possessive hysterics of Louise Colet; the death of his dearest friend, Alfred le Poittevin, aged thirty-two; the ravages of syphilis, contracted when he was twenty-nine; his victimization in financial affairs by his niece's husband, Ernest Commanville, to the point at which Flaubert had to plead with him and his niece not to eject him from Croisset; and his lonely death at fifty-nine, after years of illness, poverty, and increasing social isolation.

In one chapter, the narrator compiles a summary brief of "the case against" Flaubert, only to refute it, point by point. The most eloquent response is offered to the charge that Flaubert teaches no affirmative values. Not so, insists Braithwaite: He teaches one "to sleep on the pillow of doubt," to value language, to venerate truth and beauty, feeling and style, to hate hypocrisy, to conduct one's life courageously and stoically, to cherish one's friends, to distrust the doctrinaire and the moralistic.

In a bravura chapter, Barnes has Louise Colet slip her arm into the reader's and defend her side of the romance with Flaubert while walking with her captive auditor. When she and Gustave met, he was twenty-four to her thirty-five: "I was the candle; he was the moth." She describes him as erotically ardent, softly playful, yet military about women: "I fired five shots into her." He humiliated her incessantly, even refusing her entry to his Rouen residence after severely rationing his trips to join her in Paris. She was not even allowed to correspond with him directly, having to mail her letters via Maxime Du Camp. He lied to her, ridiculed her writing, disparaged her opinions of his, and burned her letters. Her conclusion is fatalistically resigned: "you are elected into love by a secret ballot against which there is no appeal." In thirty pages, Barnes has etched a poignantly intense, double-edged profile of a relationship in equal measure impassioned and impossible.

The characterization of Braithwaite is another triumph. As a Flaubertian, he is plausibly eccentric, antic, tenacious, and driven. Yet he avoids the traps of stuffiness, pettiness, or preciosity. Instead, he shows a persuasive capacity for reflection and self-examination. His quest for the essential Flaubert becomes a quest for the essential Braithwaite; Emma and Charles Bovary, Flaubert and Colet are both paralleled and contrasted to Geoffrey and Ellen Braithwaite. To what meaning? Braithwaite murmurs the melancholy maxim: "*Les unions complètes sont rares.*"

Themes and Meanings

Flaubert's Parrot is a Proustian exercise in searching for, recovering, and analyzing the past—Flaubert's, Braithwaite's, everyone's. In the final chapter, the narrator meets the oldest surviving member of Croisset's Societé des Amis de Flaubert. This man recalls that the curator of Flaubert's Croisset museum applied in 1905 at Rouen's Museum of Natural History for the parrot which had served Flaubert as the model for Loulou. He was taken to the museum's bird section and there given his choice of fifty Amazonian parrots. When another Flaubert Museum was established in Rouen after World War II, the same procedure was followed. In each case, the parrot which most closely resembled the bird described in "Un Cœur simple" was selected. Braithwaite draws the only logical conclusion: "So you mean either of them could be the real one? Or, quite possibly, neither?"

Having a neatly nuanced sense of irony, Braithwaite gracefully accepts the failure of his chase after the authentic Flaubertian parrot: "Well, perhaps that's as it should be." Being both intelligent and sensible, he recognizes that the joke is on him and on the reader. Behind every parrot is another parrot; behind every truth is another truth. The Past with a capital P remains elusive; Truth with a capital T is a chimera. All man can do is delight in the search for the sake of the search; in a fundamentally romantic way, the journey is itself the goal. Thus, the essential Gustave Flaubert remains undiscovered and undiscoverable—as does the essential Louise Colet, Geoffrey Braithwaite, Ellen Braithwaite, you, I, everyone. Julian Barnes has written this novel as a reminder that the most probing questions have only mysteries for answers.

Critical Context

Julian Barnes read French at Oxford University and has held such establishment literary posts as lexicographer for the *Oxford English Dictionary Supplement* (1969-1972) and deputy literary editor of the *London Sunday Times* (since 1979). His two previous novels, *Metroland* (1980) and *Before She Met Me* (1982), share with *Flaubert's Parrot* the overriding theme of obsession. In *Metroland*, a bookish schoolboy is too caught up in the French classics of passion to participate in the Parisian student riots of 1968 or seize the amatory opportunities offered him. In the second novel a man is crazed by suspicions of his wife's adulteries.

In all three works, Barnes's tone is urbane, wry, and winningly worldly. Like John Fowles, Barnes combines erudition with emotion, elegance with warmth. The obvious counterpart to *Flaubert's Parrot* is Vladimir Nabokov's *Pale Fire* (1962), both literary parodies, both tales of passion told with complex resonances by pedants who construct dense, many-layered rinds of lists and commentaries. Yet one difference is crucial: Nabokov's protagonist, Charles Kinbote, is an insufferable and insane ass, while Braithwaite is a sensitive, soundly balanced, dignified gentleman who acts as Barnes's alter ego.

If Barnes's novel has a major flaw, it is probably the involuted brilliance of its many cross-fertilizing literary echoes, the occasional archness of its many witticisms. On balance, however, this is a distinguished and original novel by a highly gifted writer who bridges the gap between the nineteenth century's sentimentality and the twentieth century's self-mockery.

Sources for Further Study

Brooks, Peter. *The New York Times Book Review*. XC (March 10, 1985), p. 7.

Kermode, Frank. *The New York Review of Books*. XXXII (April 25, 1985), p. 15.

Rafferty, Terrence. Review in *The Nation*. CCXLI (July 6-13, 1985), p. 21.

Updike, John. Review in *The New Yorker*. LXI (July 22, 1985), p. 86.

Time. Review. CXXV (April 8, 1985), p. 78.

Gerhard Brand

THE FOUNTAIN OVERFLOWS

Author: Rebecca West (Cicily Isabel Fairfield, 1892-1983)
Type of plot: Psychological realism
Time of plot: The end of the nineteenth century
Locale: The Scottish countryside and London
First published: 1956

> *Principal characters:*
> ROSE AUBREY, the narrator, a young girl
> MARY,
> CORDELIA, and
> RICHARD QUIN, her siblings
> CLARE, her mother, a talented concert pianist who
> relinquished her career to rear her family
> PIERS, her father, a newspaper editor and writer of political
> pamphlets
> CONSTANCE, a childhood friend of Clare and the wife of
> Clare's cousin Jock
> ROSAMUND, her daughter, a friend of the Aubrey children

The Novel

The Fountain Overflows concerns the Aubrey family and their adventures and misfortunes as the four Aubrey children grow up. One of these children, Rose, is the narrator, and through her eyes the reader sees the events that affect the family, events as varied as a visitation by a poltergeist, murder, and poverty. Her childhood is not a typical one, and the difference can be attributed to her parents, the fountain that overflows, providing the children with a source of energy and an abundance of experiences.

Her handsome and eccentric father, Piers, is a newspaper editor and occasionally writes persuasive political tracts. Unfortunately, he can become so involved with his concern for justice that he antagonizes his friends and benefactors and ignores his family. At other times, however, he devotes many hours to carving intricate wooden toys for the children. Yet his compulsive gambling on the stock exchange has driven his family into poverty. Rose's mother, Clare, gave up a promising career as a concert pianist when she married and began rearing a family. She notices keenly her husband's lack of attention to the details of living. Being constantly in debt, dealing with bill collectors, and tolerating her husband's infidelity, she has worried herself into a scarecrow of her former appearance, now "thin and wild-looking and badly dressed." Because of her interest in music, however, she is able to provide her children, except for Rose's older sister Cordelia, with a strong base on which to develop.

At the beginning of the novel, the family, previously subjected to sudden shifts in locale brought on by Piers's inability to get along with his superiors and his colleagues, is in Scotland contemplating yet another move, this time to London. Since it is summer, though, the children and Clare stay on a Scottish farm while Piers begins his job as an editor for a small paper in London and prepares for their arrival. Farm life is wholesome and delightful for the children, but Clare is worried, as well she might be. Piers neglects to write, she discovers that he has sold her prized antique furniture, and as the summer draws to a close, she does not know the address of the London house to which she and the children must move.

London proves to be their home for several years as the children approach adolescence. Rose and her twin sister, Mary, planning to be concert pianists, are taught music by their mother. It is understood that they have inherited their mother's talent. Unfortunately, Cordelia has not, but she persists in playing the violin. Unlike Rose and Mary, Cordelia suffers under her family's poverty. She practices the violin desperately because she sees it as a means to a more comfortable future. Her desire to be a famous musician is encouraged by Miss Beevor, her music teacher at school, who idolizes her and is unaware of Cordelia's lack of musicality. Miss Beevor suggests that Cordelia give paid performances, an idea which horrifies Clare, but she is helpless to prevent it. Should Clare refuse to allow it, Cordelia would believe that she had been cruelly used.

There are two additional families which figure in the novel. One of these families consists of Constance, Clare's childhood friend; her husband, Clare's cousin Jock; and their daughter Rosamund, about the age of Rose and Mary. Since Constance also lives in London, Clare wants to reestablish their previously close relationship, but Constance hesitates. Clare, taking the initiative, visits, discovering Constance's house to be inhabited by a poltergeist. Perhaps the happenings are real, perhaps they are tricks perpetrated by Jock, a lout despite his being Clare's relative, or perhaps Rose (being a young girl) perceives ordinary occurrences as extraordinary. As Rose reports, however, the strange happenings cease with Clare and Rose's visit. Constance and Clare renew their friendship, and the Aubrey children have found an understanding companion in Rosamund.

There is also the Phillips family, whose daughter Nancy is Cordelia's classmate. Wealthy though the Phillipses are, their money does not prevent tragedy. The mother, Queenie Phillips, is accused of poisoning her husband. To provide Nancy and her Aunt Lily a haven away from the gossip of their neighbors, the Aubreys take them in. Nancy soon goes to live with her father's brother, but Aunt Lily remains throughout the trial of Queenie. Since the judge assumes Queenie's guilt, the trial is a farce. Because of the obvious prejudice, Piers rightly thinks that he can win Queenie a reprieve. Risking going to jail himself, he argues the point in an as-yet-undistributed pamphlet. The government, fearing the public reaction should the pamphlet be released, commutes the death sentence.

After the trial, a period of calm ensues for the Aubrey family, but eventually it is disrupted by Piers's new project, writing a book. Either the subject of the book or the act of writing it throws him into despair. His situation deteriorates, until one day he does not recognize his wife when he passes her on the street, Soon after, he abruptly abandons his family, leaving only a note. Even though he was eccentric and often estranged from the family, his absence is deeply felt. Rose comments, "He had apparently given us more than we knew, for now we felt bitterly cold." Clare's prime concern, however, is with her husband's well-being. Discovering that a hidden wall cabinet has been opened, she is somewhat relieved, hoping that whatever Piers took is valuable.

Her children's comfort is assured, for unknown to anyone, Clare has all along provided for them in case of a disaster: The family portraits, long thought to be fakes, are real, including the one by Thomas Gainsborough. The sale of the portraits will provide for the needs of the children until they are established in their careers. It is already decided that Rose and Mary are to be musicians, and Richard Quin, the youngest, will also go in that direction, but Cordelia is more difficult, since she insists that she is a musician when she is not. A crisis is precipitated when the unfortunate Miss Beevor takes her to a cruel but famous teacher who reveals the truth. Cordelia, devastated, tries to poison herself. Through the careful ministrations of Rosamund, who plans to become a nurse, Cordelia gradually puts music aside, takes an interest in sewing, and seems to be headed for marriage. The conclusion mirrors the hope that Rose has had throughout. As she earlier remarked, "we . . . believed that whatever happened we would be all right. Certainly we would be all right. But it might take some time before we could get things settled."

The Characters

The character of Rose Aubrey is largely autobiographical. Rebecca West's mother gave up a promising musical career to rear a family. Similarly, her father had interests in writing and politics, repeatedly lost money on the stock exchange, and abandoned his family. Afterward, West's mother sold a valuable painting to provide for her children. Much of the rich texture in the novel can be attributed to West's vivid memories of her childhood in such a household.

Rose, as the narrator, unifies the text; her consciousness colors all the elements in the novel. There are, however, two different Roses. The first is the young girl, who, luckily for the reader, is uncommonly perceptive for a child. The second is the mature Rose, who, after a span of fifty years, is reflecting on her childhood. Some of the novel's quiet optimism comes from this double vision.

The characters in the novel can be categorized according to their stabilizing influence or lack of it. Generally, the women in the novel provide order in a chaotic world. Clare is the center of her family. Her warmth, understanding, and accessibility provide the children with security in spite of the ragged clothes and decrepit furniture. In addition, she teaches the children the value of music, enabling them to see beyond their poverty. Like Clare, Constance has the fortitude to overcome difficult situations. Their children—Rose, Mary, and Rosamund—have the same ability to meet disasters and to survive, an important trait in the world of the novel where men are in control and are, nevertheless, a destabilizing force.

The most important male figure in the novel is Piers, whose gambling throws his family into poverty and whose wholehearted devotion to his ideas threatens to fragment the family. Rose, understanding her father's commitment to justice, is proud of him, and she pities those who do not have her father as their father. Yet she also realizes that his strong commitment often means that his family is secondary. Realizing that he is willing to go to jail for his beliefs and knowing that he gives little thought to the fact that the family would be destitute, Rose comments, "I had a glorious father, I had no father at all."

While Clare is able to negate the detrimental influence of Piers on Rose, Mary, and Richard Quin, she cannot alleviate Cordelia's pain. To their acquaintances, Cordelia seems to be more normal than the other Aubrey children; even the teachers like her, a situation that worries Rose. Concerned with surface appearances, Cordelia imitates the mannerisms of famous performers, and she affects "to be mindless and will-less as grown-ups like pretty little girls to be." As such, her life is concerned with the outward show, and so, the lack of nice clothes, a stylish house, and a typical father causes her great consternation.

The major characters are carefully drawn, with the exception of Rosamund and Richard Quin, who never fully materialize. They are presented only through the soothing effects that they have on others. Rosamund plays chess with Rose's father so that he can relax, and she cares for Cordelia after her suicide attempt. As for Richard Quin, he has the capacity to calm the most anxious and is often chosen by his sisters to comfort the mother. Their own likes and dislikes, however, are never described.

Yet the minor characters are often invested with life. There is Queenie Phillips, who is consumed with her thoughts that apparently lead to the murder of her husband. There is the boorish cousin Jock, who acts the fool because of his depressing worldview. There is talkative Aunt Lily, whose outlandish costumes must be moderated so that she does not harm Queenie's case, and Miss Beevor, who sees in Cordelia all that is beautiful but who harms her through her desire to help. These characters are unforgettable in their fullness.

Themes and Meanings

The novel depicts a constant struggle between the powerful and the disenfranchised. The wealthy manipulate and dominate the poor. Aunt Theodora, in giving money to the Aubreys, expects subservience from Clare; the other children at school look down on the Aubrey girls not because of their different values, as Rose believes, but because their clothes are shabby; the wealthy Mrs. Phillips is amazed that the poverty-stricken Clare and Constance can block her desires to have Rose read her fortune. The children are twice oppressed: As Rose points out, "Most adults are rude to children, and many rich people are rude to the poor. We were children, we were poor, so we were victims of a double assault." Clare and Piers treat their children as understanding and feeling people, but others do not. Cousin Jock is shocked that Rose, a child, would dare to touch his piano even though he knows that she has long been studying music; Mrs. Phillips, underestimating Rose's intelligence, tries to bribe her with chocolate. The more strongly placed in society, the rich and the adults, impose on the weaker.

The most obvious example of oppression, however, is found in the relationship of the men and women. In the novel, Piers controls the family finances, often gambling away their meager resources, leaving Clare to scramble to pay the debts. She must accept Piers's conduct even though she is obviously better suited to the management of the household budget. Constance is also placed in a position of trying to make ends meet, but for different reasons. Cousin Jock has an ample income as a chief accountant of a firm and as a director of one of its subsidiaries, but he is stingy, preferring to keep his family in a dismal neighborhood while he squanders money on his interest in spiritualism. As a result, Constance and Rosamund take in piecework from London shops in order to have sufficient money: "They had to prepare [clothes] for women who were probably not richer than themselves but were not persecuted by their natural protectors." Rosamund, mild and seemingly oblivious, has learned to anticipate her father's tantrums and to outmaneuver him. Preparing his dinner, she makes several different sandwiches so that if he complains about the ham being too thick in one, she can offer a second, or if he objects to black pepper, she has one prepared with white.

The novel is also a discussion about the value of art. West, in an essay included in *The Strange Necessity: Essays and Reviews* (1928), asks why art matters. *The Fountain Overflows* supplies the answer. Art (and in a broader sense, the imagination) shapes experiences and orders reality, allowing the individual to transcend the trivial and petty concerns of daily existence. In the novel, imagination as a creative force surfaces in the games the children play; their invisible horses and dogs come to life; even flowers possess sensation. Imagination also surfaces in their music; they instinctively understand the intentions of the composers. Music saves Rose and Mary from being concerned with appearances and the opinions of their school friends. Cordelia, without music to save her, loathes her situation, desperately wanting to escape. Music gives to Rose and Mary a sense that there is something beyond the here and now and that everything will be all right. The novel is a strong affirmation of the dignity of life.

Critical Context

In her seventy-year career as a writer of fiction, criticism, history, biography, and journalism, Rebecca West wrote a half dozen novels, each radically different from the others. The most critically acclaimed and the most popular, however, is *The Fountain Overflows*, published in 1956, twenty years after her previous novel. Among its strengths are the strong voice of the narrator; the sharply detailed London setting; the richly described minor characters, prompting one reviewer to call it "a real Dickensian Christmas pudding of a book"; and the discussions of feminism and art, long-standing concerns of West. She wrote on the role of art in society in earlier works, in *The Strange Necessity* and in her novel *Harriet Hume: A London Fantasy* (1929). Her interest in feminist issues extended for an even longer period. Her first publications appeared in 1911 in the feminist journal *The Freewoman*. In order to save her family the embarrassment of having a daughter who wrote for a journal that advocated free love, she changed her given name, Cicily Isabel Fairfield, to Rebecca West after a character in Henrik Ibsen's play *Rosmersholm* (1886).

The Fountain Overflows was intended as the first book of a trilogy. The second volume, *This Real Night* (1984), was published a year and a half after West's death and received mixed reviews. West did not finish the third and concluding volume, which was published in 1985 as *Cousin Rosamund*. While West's reputation will rest securely on her journalism and her nonfiction works, in particular *Black Lamb and Grey Falcon: The Record of a Journey Through Yugoslavia in 1937* (1941)—a commentary not only on Yugoslavia but also on the political situation in Europe in the period preceding World War II—her novels, especially *The Fountain Overflows*, should not be slighted.

Sources for Further Study

Deakin, Motley F. *Rebecca West*, 1980.

Kobler, Turner S. "The Eclecticism of Rebecca West," in *Critique: Studies in Modern Fiction*. XIII, no. 1 (1971), pp. 30-49.

Ray, Gordon N. *H. G. Wells and Rebecca West*, 1974.

Redd, Tony. *Rebecca West: Master of Reality*, 1972.

Wolfe, Peter. *Rebecca West: Artist and Thinker*, 1971.

Barbara Wiedemann

THE FOX

Author: D. H. Lawrence (1885-1930)
Type of plot: Psychological realism
Time of plot: During World War I
Locale: The Midlands of England, probably near Berkshire
First published: 1922

> *Principal characters:*
> ELLEN (NELLIE) MARCH, a robust joint owner of the Bailey
>   Farm, about thirty
> JILL BANFORD, about the same age, the delicate co-owner of
>   the farm
> HENRY GRENFEL, about twenty, the grandson of William
>   Grenfel, former owner of the farm
> THE FOX, a devastating predator, symbolically related to
>   Henry as a similar force of masculine vitality

The Novel

Set in the Berkshire district of England during World War I, *The Fox*, like many of D. H. Lawrence's other major works, treats the psychological relationships of three protagonists in a triangle mating-complex of love and hatred. Without the help of any male laborers, Nellie March and Jill Banford struggle to maintain a marginal livelihood at the Bailey Farm. A fox has raged through the poultry, and although the women—particularly the more nearly masculine Nellie—have tried to shoot the intruder, he seems always to elude traps or gunshot. Once Nellie confronts the fox, but his "demon" eyes hold her spellbound; she cannot fire her rifle. A symbol of masculine energy, the fox appears in Nellie's nightmares as a dominating (and sexually threatening) force that both attracts and repels her. At this point of deadlock, Henry Grenfel, a soldier on leave who enlisted in the military forces in Canada, returns to the farm, which was once owned by his grandfather. Although he has no legal claim to this property, the women feel an obligation to take him in. Both are charmed by his boyish vigor, but Nellie, in particular, identifies him with the fox. In a troubled and symbolic dream, she psychologically submits to the mesmerizing willpower of the beast, to his sadistic sexual domination over her repressed instincts.

Henry's sly presence on the farm upsets the affectionate harmony that previously existed between the two women. Motivated to court Nellie (in order both to take control of the property and to subdue her will to his desire), he breaks down her resistance to his proposal. She accepts—then, more coolly, in a letter rejects—his offer of marriage. Her reason is that she has deeper obligations to Jill. Henry, however, obtains another furlough, obstinate in his quest. Observing the women attempting, with little success, to cut down a tree, he offers to fell it with an ax, insolently taunting Jill to get out of the way. She is stubborn, as Henry calculated she would be; the tree—a symbol of the male phallus—falls upon and kills Jill. Witnesses to the act, including the horrified Nellie and Jill's father, cannot hold the youth responsible. Having disposed of his rival, Henry continues his courtship of Nellie, successfully this time. She agrees to go with him to Canada, to start a new life together. Yet Nellie's heart is not in the venture. The youth has captured her and subdued her will, but she has not given her heartfelt consent to his scheme. His victory is bleak.

The Characters

Lawrence makes quite clear to the reader that Nellie March and Jill Banford share an affectionate and committed friendship. The relationship between them is homoerotic, although perhaps not physically homosexual. In her letter to Henry, Nellie writes: "I know her and I'm awfully fond of her, and I hate myself for a beast if I ever hurt her little finger. We have a life together." In other works, Lawrence is less sympathetic toward the homoerotic attachments of women. Winifred Inger in *The Rainbow* (1915), for example, is an intellectual lesbian whose influence Ursula Brangwen finally rejects as oppressive. In the 1929 poem "Ego-Bound Women," Lawrence's hostility to lesbianism is unmistakable. Yet in *The Fox*, Lawrence treats with dignity and matter-of-factness the erotic friendship of Nellie and Jill. Although they are, from a stereotypical erotic-fantasy point of view, "butch" and "femme," Nellie and Jill reverse their roles in their relationship toward Henry. He is attracted to the more nearly "masculine" Nellie rather than the "feminine" Jill. Also, counter to the stereotypical erotic-fantasy, Nellie surrenders none of her homoeroticism by submitting to Henry; he fails to dominate or "change" her sexually.

Henry, similarly, departs from the conventional erotic-fantasy stereotype of the virile male in playing his part in the triangular relationship. He falls into neither of the two major types of Lawrence's male lovers (or would-be lovers): neither the sexually unassertive, fastidious, charming heroes such as Paul Morel (*Sons and Lovers*, 1913), Cyril Mersham ("A Modern Lover"), Bernard Coutts ("The Witch a la Mode"), or Edward Severn ("The Old Adam"), nor the virile, direct, unself-conscious models of Oliver Mellors (*Lady Chatterley's Lover*, 1928), Maurice Pervin ("The Blind Man"), or Tom Vickers ("A Modern Lover"). Instead, Henry is always described as a "boy." Assertive, magnetic, and uncomplicated like Lawrence's virile heterosexual males, he is also—unlike the finer types—insensitive, manipulative, cunning. His sexuality has turned predatory, like the aggressiveness of the fox. He represents the male heterosexual as destroyer of women.

Themes and Meanings

In *The Fox*, Lawrence treats the theme of erotic willpower used to dangerous ends, demonstrating the limitations of mere animal magnetism in love that coerces rather than persuades the object of its love. In *The Ladybird* (1923), Count Dionys exerts a powerful attraction over Lady Daphne—the attraction of willpower supported by animal vitality. Yet he controls this power with restraint, refusing to violate Lady Daphne sexually. He will be her lover "in spirit." Similarly, in *The Captain's Doll* (1923), Captain Alexander Hepburn dominates Hannele by asserting his strong will, but he allows her the option of accepting or rejecting his rigorous terms of marriage. She is free to consent to a marriage without "love" but with the promise of respect and honor in place of sentimental manipulation. Yet this choice is denied Nellie. She must submit, having no other practical option, to Henry's demand for marriage. Such an assertion of brutal willpower, Lawrence maintains, is terrible—for the tyrannized and the tyrant alike. Lawrence mercifully draws a veil over the final section of the story; one does not know for certain what fate in marriage Henry and Nellie may enjoy as they embark for Canada, but one fears for them.

Critical Context

Lawrence's most powerful fiction often runs against the reader's expectations or prejudices. Often the author treats a subject that appears to arouse erotic fantasies—usually male fantasies—then alters the expected climax by means of a psychologically realistic twist. In *Lady Chatterley's Lover*, *The Virgin and the Gipsy* (1930), "The Princess," and other tales depicting male sexual domination over a submissive female, Lawrence tampers with the pattern in significant ways. *The Fox*, also, seems to follow a pattern in which a sexually capable male is supposed to interfere with a lesbian couple's relationship and to dominate one (or, in pornographic models, both) of the partners. Lawrence, however, alters the rules of the game. Henry is by no means the anticipated male teacher—nor is Nellie the anticipated student—in an erotic game that ought, in fantasy, to end in the sexual education (or grateful fulfillment) of the woman. By forcing Nellie to submit to his will, he has deprived her of free choice—of her consent—so he has neither fairly won nor satisfied his mate.

For Lawrence, the symbol of male domination and aggressiveness is the fox. In popular myths cunning, deceptive, and rapacious, the fox is treated as compulsive as well. In other stories ("The Witch a la Mode," "The Lovely Lady") Lawrence examines the mythos of the femme fatale, the fatal or dangerous woman. Like a witch or vampire, such a woman absorbs the vital energy of her lover, depleting him of virility. In *The Fox*, however, Lawrence treats as counterpart the dangerous male, the predator who, like a fox, overpowers his lover through sheer strength of will. Instead of offering readers a comfortable ending in which the domineering male captures his swooning bride as a prize, this novella shows with great psychological acumen the error of manipulating people to change their erotic natures. For their destiny, a reader cannot help but pity Henry and Nellie alike.

Sources for Further Study
Daleski, H. M. *The Forked Flame: A Study of D. H. Lawrence*, 1965.
Hough, Graham. *The Dark Sun: A Study of D. H. Lawrence*, 1957.
Moore, Harry T. *The Life and Works of D. H. Lawrence*, 1951.
Spilka, Mark. *The Love Ethic of D. H. Lawrence*, 1955.

Leslie B. Mittleman

FRANKENSTEIN UNBOUND

Author: Brian W. Aldiss (1925-   )
Type of plot: Science fiction
Time of plot: The years 2020 and 1816
Locale: Texas and Switzerland
First published: 1973

Principal characters:

> JOSEPH "JOE" BODENLAND, a deposed presidential adviser,
> who is transported by a timeslip from the twenty-first to
> the early nineteenth century
> VICTOR FRANKENSTEIN, a Swiss scientist
> MARY WOLLSTONECRAFT GODWIN, the author of *Frankenstein*
> and the mistress and future wife of Percy Bysshe Shelley
> GEORGE GORDON, LORD BYRON, the English Romantic poet
> PERCY BYSSHE SHELLEY, the poet and the lover and future
> husband of Mary Godwin
> THE FRANKENSTEIN MONSTER
> THE MONSTER'S MATE
> ELIZABETH LAVENZA, Frankenstein's betrothed
> JUSTINE MORITZ, a maidservant who has been accused of
> killing a child

The Novel

Frankenstein (1818), which can be considered the first real science-fiction novel, is subtitled "The Modern Prometheus." Its author, Mary Wollstone- craft Godwin, was the mistress and later the wife of Percy Bysshe Shelley, the Romantic poet who wrote *Prometheus Unbound* (1820) and who was in part the model for Victor Frankenstein. In *Frankenstein Unbound*, Brian W. Aldiss combines the titles of Mary and Percy Bysshe Shelley's books and sends a time traveler from the twenty-first century back to Geneva in 1816, when Mary was engaged in writing her as yet uncompleted novel.

Frankenstein Unbound begins in the summer of 2020, in a series of letters from Joseph Bodenland—a liberal presidential adviser ousted by right-wing extremists and now staying at his ranch in New Houston, Texas—to his wife in Indonesia. The world is at war, but Joe hopes that the news of a space- time rupture will stop further conflict. Meanwhile, he is enjoying the com- pany of his grandchildren, who still believe in myths. Their mythic make- believe games cause him to think of the major myth of his own time: "that ever-increasing production and industrialization bring the greatest happiness for the greatest number all round the globe. . . ."

The infrastructure of space has become unstable because of nuclear warfare above the stratosphere. Joe thinks that "the Intellect has made our planet unsafe for intellect. We are suffering from the curse that was Baron Frankenstein's in Mary Shelley's novel: by seeking to control too much, we have lost control of ourselves." In New Houston, Joe experiences a thirty-five-hour timeslip back to the Middle Ages. Then, Mrs. Bodenland receives a cable stating that during a second timeslip, her husband rode out alone into an altered countryside, and when the ranch snapped back into the present, he and his car disappeared into the vanished land.

From that point onward, the novel is the taped journal of Joe Bodenland, relating his experience. He discovers that he has slipped in time and place back to Switzerland in 1816, when people are discussing the just-ended Napoleonic Wars. His years as a diplomat had made him knowledgeable about the country and fluent in its languages. He also finds that he has become young again and full of vigor. At an inn, he overhears gossip about a local murder, in which a maidservant named Justine Moritz was to stand trial for killing a small boy, William. Joe is surprised when a gentleman whose table he is sharing insists that Justine is innocent and that guilt lies on his own shoulders. Following his distraught acquaintance to Geneva, Joe learns that the man is Victor Frankenstein. "I felt myself in the presence of myth and, by association, *accepted myself as mythical!*" Joe follows Victor into the mountains, where they both see the monster.

As a child, Joe had read *Frankenstein*, but the original was confused for him by "the deplorable pastiches and plagiarizations put out by the mass media." He remembered that Mary Shelley was the author but thought that Victor was purely fictitious. Falling in love with the unspoiled world of 1816, Joe hates the "conquest of Nature" by which the Age of Science has destroyed it and caused "the loss of man's inner self." Blaming Victor for this, Joe tries to undo the damage caused by his experiments. He attends Justine's trial and hears her sentenced to be hanged. In vain, he tries to make Victor help her; Victor is too obsessed with himself, and Joe finds that a three-month timeslip has occurred and transported him overnight from May to August, when Justine is already dead.

Failing with Victor, Joe goes to the Villa Diodati, where he encounters Lord Byron. When Byron introduces Joe to Percy Bysshe Shelley and then to Mary, Joe finds that his "severance with the old modes of reality [is] complete." They all engage in a debate about the role of science and the future. Shelley predicts the coming liberation of mankind through machinery, but Mary thinks that humanity first "will have to change its basic nature." Byron suspects that machines may strengthen the evil in man's nature and that "new knowledge may lead to new oppression." Joe tells them that there will continue to be inequality, that "culture will become enslaved by the machines," that goodness will become irrelevant because machines "become symbols of class and prosperity," and that as systems become more complex, they become impersonal, have more danger of going wrong, and make it more difficult for the individual to operate them for good.

Alone with Mary, Joe tells her that her characters are alive, only a few miles away, while she insists that they are invented. Accepting "the equal reality of Mary Shelley and her creation," Joe wants to borrow a copy of the novel to use it to ambush and kill the monster. He finds, however, that Mary has not yet completed the book. She tells him the story to the point at which Frankenstein agrees to make the monster a mate; beyond that, she has not written. Joe, in turn, assures her that she will finish the novel, marry Shelley, and become famous. For an idyllic day, Joe and Mary become lovers. Then he returns to Geneva, determined to persuade Victor not to create a female and to help him destroy the existing monster. When Joe goes to the Frankenstein house, Victor's fiancée, Elizabeth Lavenza, and friend Clerval have him arrested, charged with murdering Victor. From prison, he writes a long letter to Mary, comparing his era to hers.

When a flood hits the prison, Joe is freed. Two other escaped convicts beat him and steal his fire. During a dreadful, freezing night in the mountains, the monster visits Joe, rebuilds his fire, and leaves him food. After recuperating, Joe returns to Geneva and discovers that a slip in both time and space has occurred; the lake has vanished, and a new ice age has come. Joe finds Victor again and goes with him to his secret laboratory, where they debate the role of science and the responsibility of the scientist. Victor is creating a mate for the monster and refuses to be dissuaded by Joe, who is shocked to find that Victor has given the mate the face of Justine Moritz. Joe then decides to kill both Frankenstein and his creature. In Victor's stable, Joe finds his car, with a sealed nuclear drive that requires no fuel. On it is mounted a swivel gun, with which Joe plans to destroy the monster. When the monster and his mate emerge and engage in a grotesque mating dance, however, Joe watches in horrified fascination, unable to fire, while the monsters couple and then vanish. When Victor proposes making a third monster to kill the first, Joe shoots him dead and burns the tower. He then takes over Victor's role and pursues the monsters in a hunt to the death across a bleak frozen wasteland created by a spreading rupture in time-space. Finding the monsters outside a vast citadel across an icefield—the last refuge of humanity—Joe shoots them both with tracer bullets from his swivel gun, killing first the female and then the attacking male. Then, anticipating a possible attack from the fortress, Joe waits "in darkness and distance"; the novel thus concludes with the same words as *Frankenstein*.

The Characters

Except for Joe Bodenland and a few minor characters, the characters in *Frankenstein Unbound* come either from *Frankenstein* or from actual history. Aldiss' portrayals of Byron and Shelley correspond to the image one has of them from their life and works. A novelist takes a certain risk in re-creating great writers and inventing dialogue for them; the danger is that the fictional portrait will fall flat and the dialogue be far beneath the writers' own style. Yet Aldiss succeeds brilliantly in making Byron and Shelley seem authentic; he endows the former with sardonic wit and the latter with eloquent idealism and nervous mannerisms. As for Mary, she is described as "fair and birdlike, with brilliant eyes and a small wistful mouth" and an irresistible laugh. Joe Bodenland finds in her a warm, generous affection, and in making them lovers, Aldiss may be indulging in a vicarious love affair with the founder of science fiction.

Aldiss takes liberties with the characters of *Frankenstein*, however, since he places them in an alternate world where they can assume a life of their own. Thus, Victor Frankenstein and his associates are far less sympathetic than in the original. In *Frankenstein Unbound*, Victor is less the noble hero of sensibility stricken with remorse for the horrors he has brought to his friends and family and is far more a morose, sullen individual, alternately wallowing in self-pity and subject to fits of megalomania. His fiancée, Elizabeth, and friend Clerval, both admirable in *Frankenstein*, are here presented as cold, arrogant, and hostile. Neither is killed by the monster, though they both are in the original.

The monster itself, far from looking hideous, is beautiful in a terrifying sort of way; the features are not quite human but resemble a helmet face painted on a skull; the monster looks "like a machine, lathe-turned." Aldiss' monster is less guilty than that of Shelley; he has killed William and caused the death of Justine, but he does not murder Elizabeth and Clerval. Thus, dying, he can legitimately cry that no fury he could possess could match that of Bodenland.

Bodenland is perhaps the least fully developed character in the novel. Though he is the narrator, the reader does not get a vivid image of him; one never even learns what he looks like. An intruder into this world, he serves mainly to alter the action and to engage in Platonic dialogues about the role of science, the nature of mankind, and the course of history. His thoughts tell more about the Shelleys, Byron, Frankenstein, and his associates than about Bodenland himself. Once stuck in the world of 1816, he ceases to think about his own world or his lost family; he simply plunges into the Frankenstein drama, driven by a boundless curiosity and compulsion to get involved. In one sense, he is the conscience of the novel; able to foresee the future consequences of Frankenstein's work, he tries to "wreck the *fatalism* of coming events." In another sense, he becomes corrupted, so that toward the end, he realizes that he has "lied, cheated, committed adultery, looted, thieved, and ultimately murdered." When he kills Victor and then takes over his role to pursue and destroy the monsters, he becomes as deadly as they, and the dying monster accuses him of not knowing compassion.

Themes and Meanings

Like *Frankenstein*, *Frankenstein Unbound* explores the effects of science upon society and examines the role and responsibility of the scientist. Whereas Mary Shelley wrote at the beginning of the Industrial Revolution, Aldiss writes from the perspective of the nuclear age and can evaluate the scientific developments of the intervening centuries. Much of the novel consists of debates over this issue among Bodenland, Byron, and the Shelleys, or between Bodenland and Frankenstein. Bodenland considers Frankenstein "the archetype of the scientist whose research, pursued in the sacred name of increasing knowledge, takes on a life of its own and causes untold misery before being brought under control." A legacy of Frankenstein's folly, in Bodenland's view, is overpopulation and technological warfare. In his defense, Victor argues, "Truth was everything to me! I wanted to improve the world, to deliver into man's hands some of those powers which had hitherto been ascribed to a sniveling and fictitious God." When Bodenland argues that "scientific curiosity by itself is as irresponsible as the curiosity of a child. . . . You have to accept responsibility for the fruits of your actions," Victor disclaims such responsibility; it is no fault of his if a corrupt society misuses his discoveries. Similarly, whereas Shelley has unbounded faith that science will liberate humanity, like Prometheus unbound, Mary insists, "Our generation must take on the task of thinking about the future, of assuming towards it the responsibility that we assume towards our children. There are changes in the world to which we must not be passive, or we shall be overwhelmed by them."

In a letter to Mary, Joe enumerates the improvements between her era and his in medicine, public health, the growth of social conscience (thanks in part to the Victorian novelists) resulting in an end of child labor, debtors' prisons, and better treatment of the mentally ill and the elderly. "On the one hand, there is the sterility of machine culture and the terrible isolation often felt by people even in overcrowded cities; on the other, there is a taking for granted of many basic rights and freedoms which in your day have not even been thought of."

Another issue is religion. Rejecting a "fictitious God," Frankenstein finds life to be a purposeless pestilence; he must therefore put humanity in control of an otherwise meaningless universe. Bodenland has never been religious, but upon seeing Justine's face upon the body of the monster's mate, cobbled together from cadavers, he believes that Victor has committed blasphemy.

And to say as much . . . was to admit religion, to admit that life held more than the grave at the end of it, to admit that there was a spirit that transcended the poor imperfect flesh. Flesh without spirit was obscene. Why else should the notion of Frankenstein's monster have affronted the imagination of generations, if it was not their intuition of God that was affronted?

In his own century, Bodenland finds that Organized Religion has been replaced by Organized Science, allied with Big Business and Government and with "no interest in the individual—its meat was statistics! It was death to the spirit." Such is the victory of the "Frankenstein mentality." In Shelley's day, there was still a chance that the head and heart might have marched forward together, but the head has triumphed.

Critical Context

Concurrently with *Frankenstein Unbound*, Aldiss was working on *Billion Year Spree* (1973), a history of science fiction, which he published the same year as the novel (1973). It opens with a chapter on Mary Shelley and considers *Frankenstein* to be the first science-fiction novel, the "origin of the species." Calling *Frankenstein* "the first great myth of the industrial age," Aldiss finds that it "foreshadows many of our anxieties about the two-faced triumphs of scientific progress" and "the disintegration of society which follows man's arrogation of power. We see one perversion of the natural order leading to another. *Frankenstein* is loaded with a sense of corruption. . . ." *Frankenstein Unbound*, even more so, has this sense, and it is Mary Shelley's concepts that Aldiss explores in more depth in his novel.

It is at the same time a gloss on *Frankenstein*, to which it is also indebted for its structure. Both begin as epistolary narratives and then shift to the first-person narrative of the protagonist. During the course of *Frankenstein Unbound*, Joe analyzes Mary, her milieu, and the characters, episodes, and ideas of her fiction, and she herself tells him the circumstances under which she began her work, while Victor later summarizes for Joe the experiences of the monster during the period in which he was abandoned and before he killed William.

Up to the point at which Mary has not yet completed the novel—the point at which Victor has promised to make the monster a mate—Aldiss follows the outlines of Mary Shelley's novel, though he alters the characters in it; thereafter, he feels free to change the course of events, as Bodenland interferes with them. Though Joe complains that his recollections of the novel were obscured by travesties of it on film, Aldiss borrows from the James Whale films *Frankenstein* (1931) and *The Bride of Frankenstein* (1935) the title of Baron Frankenstein, the details of Victor's laboratory in the tower of a ruined castle, and the image of villagers with torches who might come to burn it, though they never do.

Frankenstein Unbound is not only a science-fiction novel but also to some extent a historical novel, as Aldiss re-creates in some critical detail the world of 1816 before he alters it with slips in time and space. In contrasting the world of 2020 with the Romantic era of the early nineteenth century and the developments between them, Aldiss shows considerable historical awareness.

Besides the innumerable film sequels, there are several forgettable novelistic sequels to *Frankenstein* by inconsequential authors. Aldiss, one of the preeminent British science-fiction writers, has not written a sequel but has entered the novel and created an alternate-universe version of it that enables him to explore in more depth the themes and meanings that Mary Shelley originally raised.

Sources for Further Study
Aldiss, Brian W. *Billion Year Spree: The True History of Science Fiction*, 1973.
Hall, H. W. Review in *Library Journal*. XCIX (August, 1974), p. 1988.
Rogan, Helen. Review in *Time*. CIV (August 5, 1974), p. 84.
Shelley, Mary. *Frankenstein: Or, The Modern Prometheus*, 1818.

Robert E. Morsberger

THE FRENCH LIEUTENANT'S WOMAN

Author: John Fowles (1926-   )
Type of plot: Historical novel
Time of plot: 1867-1869
Locale: Lyme Regis, London, and Exeter, England
First published: 1969

Principal characters:
CHARLES SMITHSON, the protagonist, an amateur paleon-
tologist and a gentleman
ERNESTINA FREEMAN, Charles's fiancée, the beloved daughter
of a wealthy industrialist
SARAH WOODRUFF, the "French lieutenant's woman," a fallen
beauty who becomes Charles's obsession
MRS. POULTENEY, a sanctimonious hypocrite who runs a
boardinghouse
SAM FARROW, Charles's surly valet
UNCLE BOB, Charles's rich, titled, and eccentric relative
whose estate he expects to inherit
DR. GROGAN, a freethinking physician

The Novel

A playful, self-conscious narrative voice situates the opening of *The French Lieutenant's Woman* in Lyme Regis in 1867. Charles Smithson and his fiancée, Ernestina Freeman, are walking beside the bay when they encounter a mysterious woman known locally as "The French lieutenant's woman," because of the foreign sailor who has jilted her. Charles becomes fascinated by this enigmatic figure, whose real name, he learns, is Sarah Woodruff. His fascination soon develops into a romantic obsession, one that will overwhelm the complacencies of his privileged existence.

Because of her scandalous background, Sarah is a pariah. Yet Charles, a baronet's nephew, and Sarah, an impoverished former governess, meet several times in clandestine trysts. They eventually, and awkwardly, make love. Charles feels compelled to break off his engagement with Ernestina, an action that provokes litigation by her indignant father and resentment by his valet Sam, who hopes to marry Ernestina's maid Mary. When Charles writes a letter to Sarah asking her to marry him, Sam fails to deliver it.

Sarah vanishes, and for the next twenty months, Charles travels the world desperately seeking her. Fowles in fact offers three separate conclusions to the plot he has contrived. In one, Charles fantasizes that he never sees Sarah again and that he marries Ernestina. In the other two, he finally discovers Sarah in London, living with the Pre-Raphaelite poets and painters. *The*

French Lieutenant's Woman does not so much conclude as simply halt; its author refuses to constrain the freedom of his characters or to deny his readers the exercise of their own imaginations.

The Characters

Charles Smithson's rather ordinary name is appropriate to his portrayal as a conventional Victorian gentleman who, because of his encounter with Sarah, undergoes a radical transformation. As an amateur paleontologist and an advocate of Charles Darwin's new theories, Charles is a bit of a freethinker, but only in the socially sanctioned manner of his feckless mentor, old Dr. Grogan. When Charles does genuinely challenge the codes of his place, time, and class by courageously embracing the outcast Sarah, he is ostracized and dispossessed.

Sarah Woodruff is less a fully developed character than an absence onto which Charles and others project their fears and fantasies of the feminine. Her name suggests the kind of wildness, the passionate self-assertions, that Victorian repression was not entirely successful in subduing. She is a vivid counterpoint to Ernestina Freeman, whose last name mocks the respectable young woman's conformity to her community's dour attitudes. Yet the character who most embodies the sense of late nineteenth century England's social constraints, its embodiment of duty and guilt, is Mrs. Poulteney, a hypocritical despot who, in a public display of charity, lets the homeless Sarah live with her but then will not let her live.

John Fowles, however, is less interested in fully rounded characterizations than in providing through these people a sense of the past and in developing his themes of human servitude. He is also intent on challenging novelistic conventions of realistic characterization and on championing the freedom of characters from their authors as much as the freedom of individuals from social custom. To that end, he is forever intruding into his narrative in such a way as to remind the reader that these are, after all, fictional creations. Fowles himself even appears briefly within the story, mingling with his characters in such a way as to confound ordinary distinctions between author and artifice.

Themes and Meanings

The possessive in its title points to the theme of emancipation that pervades *The French Lieutenant's Woman*. Fowles has fashioned a richly detailed evocation of a particular time and place that happen to precede the period in which he was writing by exactly one hundred years. *The French Lieutenant's Woman* is not only a historical novel, providing a convincing excursion back into mid-Victorian England, but also a novel very much about history, about the relationship of the individual to the forces of a particular time and of time.

In providing a confrontation between 1967 and 1867, two moments he por-trays as possessed by remarkably similar preoccupations, Fowles is intent on providing a double liberation: from the claustrophobic confines of his fictive 1867 and from what he sees as the parochialism of 1967. Most of *The French Lieutenant's Woman* is deliberately set in the Wessex area that Thomas Hardy used a century earlier in naturalistic novels portraying the individual as a helpless victim of vast, indifferent forces. Fowles's novel is a throwback to earlier literary styles in its chattiness and in its fatalistic mechanisms. As a pseudo-Victorian novel written in 1967, it seeks to transcend the residual tyr-anny of Victorianism.

As omniscient, and irreverent, narrator, Fowles flaunts his independence of space and time, his ability to move freely back and forth through history and into and out of the fictional world. *The French Lieutenant's Woman* is filled with footnotes, epigraphs, and authorial commentaries that make the work seem almost as much a treatise as a narrative. At one point, the author expresses a desire to introduce a baby carriage into his story, though he admits that they were not to be invented for another decade. A profusion of self-conscious anachronisms as well as references to twentieth century figures such as Henry Moore, Alain Robbe-Grillet, Marshall McLuhan, and Jean-Paul Sartre defy historical sequence and assert the kind of freedom, for the author and for his readers, that is sadly lacking for the characters imprisoned in the novel's Victorian world.

Its playful movements into and out of particular contexts prevent the nov-el's readers from being stranded in either 1867 or 1967. Its imagination sets readers free, not only of the social constraints of a particular era, but also, through the novel's mockery of its own fictional devices, of the conventions of literature. *The French Lieutenant's Woman* remains open-ended. "It is only when our characters and events begin to disobey us that they begin to live," proclaims the author, who delights in the possibility that he will lose control of his own fictional creation. The novel's final words leave Charles by him-self, to contend on his own with "the river of life." The rivers that Fowles celebrates are not frozen. Declaring war on stasis, *The French Lieutenant's Woman* is a moving experience in its allegiance to movement, in and out of fixed points in time and in and out of the illusions of fiction.

Critical Context

The French Lieutenant's Woman was enormously successful. It attracted the favorable attention of critics and scholars, and it remained on the best-seller lists for more than a year. It was also, in 1981, adapted into a somewhat less compelling film, directed by Karel Reisz and starring Meryl Streep and Jeremy Irons.

Fowles's third published novel, *The French Lieutenant's Woman* reworks the theme of his first book, *The Collector* (1963), which explores the notion of woman as Other and the misguided attempt to possess, in the name of love, another human being. In its emphasis on game-playing and fictionalizing as a means of defining personal identity, *The French Lieutenant's Woman* also echoes *The Magus* (1966), while it anticipates *Daniel Martin* (1977), which is explicitly about a writer, and *Mantissa* (1982), which is about a writer and his muse. *A Maggot* (1985) is another sophisticated historical romp, this time into the eighteenth century, but it does not surpass the achievement of *The French Lieutenant's Woman*.

With his Victorian tour de force, Fowles established himself as a preeminent figure in contemporary English fiction, one who is both a stylistic virtuoso and a thinker worth studying. Though turning to the past as the setting for *The French Lieutenant's Woman*, Fowles clearly aligns himself with those who, like Alain Robbe-Grillet or John Barth, are committed to innovation, to renovating the novel form. Fowles has sometimes been attacked for stylistic indulgences, for exacerbated self-consciousness, and for a preoccupation with form at the expense of content. At least in the case of *The French Lieutenant's Woman*, however, his bravura flourishes are an integral part of his accomplishment. The novel is a lively exercise in and exorcism of what Fowles presents as the deadening experience of Victorianism.

Sources for Further Study
Huffaker, Robert. *John Fowles*, 1980.
Loveday, Simon. *The Romances of John Fowles*, 1985.
Olshen, Barry N. *John Fowles*, 1978.
Thorpe, Michael. *John Fowles*, 1982.
Wolfe, Peter. *John Fowles, Magus and Moralist*, 1976, 1979.

Steven G. Kellman

FRUITS OF THE EARTH

Author: Frederick Philip Grove (Felix Paul Greve, 1879-1948)
Type of plot: Historical chronicle
Time of plot: 1900-1920
Locale: The prairies, approximately fifty miles south of Winnipeg, Manitoba
First published: 1933

> *Principal characters:*
> ABE SPALDING, the protagonist, who embodies the essence of
>   the pioneering spirit
> RUTH SPALDING, his wife
> CHARLIE SPALDING, his favorite child, who is accidentally
>   killed
> JIM SPALDING, his remaining son, who leaves the farm for the
>   city
> MARION SPALDING, his daughter, who leaves the farm to settle
>   in Winnipeg
> FRANCES SPALDING, his other daughter, who exemplifies the
>   values of the new generation, youth and fast living
> NICOLL, a neighboring farmer, a close friend of Abe Spalding

The Novel

The original title of *Fruits of the Earth* was "The Chronicles of Spalding District." Although the publishers were probably correct in suggesting the richer, more suggestive title, the original one best describes the nature of the realistic plot of the novel. The work offers a chronological record of Abe Spalding's career, beginning with his arrival on the bare prairie, on which he is eventually to build a vast farmhouse and barns. Abe's career is followed step-by-step to the peak of his economic success while, at the same time, there is a continuing revelation of why his great achievement is flawed.

The story, in fact, can easily be divided into two parts, a division the author himself uses to give shape to his material. Part 1, "Abe Spalding," delineates the courageous, determined pioneer. Abe is shown as a man of epic proportions, a "giant in the earth," a man capable of combating and, to a degree, of overcoming the forces of nature and society which oppose his success. Much of the focus of this first part is on revealing that Abe had to be dominant, at times even rigid, to be able to withstand the adversities nature and society sent his way. Repeatedly, Abe is shown as having the single-minded preoccupation necessary for building a substantial farm in a vast, empty plain.

Part 2, "The District," traces what happens once Abe has used his tremendous resources to give shape and order to the environment. In effect, by demonstrating through will and determination that the land is arable, he has prepared the district for culture and civilization. This second section, however, stresses that singleness of determination is inadequate in the face of the varied and complex demands which will be placed on the world he created. The farm itself will, it is repeatedly suggested, decay, just as the grand and awesome structures of Egypt and Rome and Greece have decayed and fallen into disuse. In part, failure is inevitable, for no human achievement can withstand either the continuing forces of nature or the equally rapidly changing needs, wants, and desires of civilization. The novel begins to take on a tragic tone as it increasingly becomes clear that Abe's heroic features are diminished in these circumstances. Once the environment is tamed, the pioneer's task is done. He lives throughout most of the second half of the book as an anachronism. Ironically, he cannot settle down to enjoy the fruits of the earth for which he labored so magnificently.

The tragic fate of the pioneering spirit is made convincing and realistic in the novel by the author's recording of the gradual collapse of Abe's family. Abe's favorite son, whom he hoped would carry on in his work, is accidentally killed at the moment when Abe's fortunes are at their peak. Abe's remaining son, Jim, is attracted to the city. Addicted to machinery rather than to farm life, Jim becomes a mechanic in Winnipeg. Abe has no success with his daughters, either. Marion also leaves farming to live in Winnipeg, and Frances, his remaining daughter, finds life on the prairies too tedious to tolerate. Frances is revealed as a young woman totally absorbed by the youthful culture of fast-paced living. The novel closes with the twilight of Abe's hopes: The society he helped to create, he realizes in the end, has become too complex for him. His singleness of mind has fostered a complex social network with which he cannot cope.

The Characters

Because *Fruits of the Earth* is built so obviously around the central and dominating protagonist, a clear understanding of that character will show how the minor characters act as complements or foils to his all-important qualities. Abe Spalding may be counted among the most important creations of Canadian literature dealing with the pioneer spirit. He is given near-tragic dimensions, for he embodies the indomitable singleness of spirit required to combat nature, a singleness which also limits him from full participation in the society to which he gives birth.

Abe represents the duality which haunts so much of Canadian writing. On one hand, he is the striking, admirable individual of heroic stature who can, and does, overcome nature, at least in the immediate sense. He builds where there was nothing before him and therefore earns the reader's respect and admiration. Moreover, he is an intelligent man who becomes, gradually, fully aware of his dilemma: He can build the foundations for a society, but he cannot sustain it.

Frederick Philip Grove is particularly masterful in his method of gradually allowing his protagonist to gain insight into his own flaw. Employing a third-person narrator, he usually describes the successes and failures of his main character from an exterior point of view; in crucial scenes, however, he allows the narrative voice to merge with the consciousness revealed, thereby giving a powerful and clear sense of the inner feelings of the protagonist. Particularly memorable is the presentation of Abe's insight into the impermanence of his own creation: "The moment a work of man was finished, nature set to work to take it down again." Just as nature—the weathering process—gradually begins to erode his house the moment it is completed, so society and culture begin to erode the singleness of purpose used to give a basis to the District of Spalding. The gradual process of decay represented by nature, and the inevitable winds of change represented by social forces, will gradually and inevitably disperse and erode the single force that gave shape to the whole. A tremendous measure of sympathy is accorded Abe by the end of the book.

Themes and Meanings

If the original title, "The Chronicles of Spalding District," best describes the structure of the novel, the new title, *Fruits of the Earth*, best suggests its theme. The title phrase is drawn from the Bible, specifically Mark 4: "You are lost if you forget that the fruits of the earth belong equally to us all, and the earth itself to nobody."

The biblical passage reminds readers of the central flaw of Abe's character. He thinks only in terms of building a new community; he pays little heed to the fruits of his labor, and when he does, it is too late. The theme, however, is not to be viewed as a pessimistic one. In *Fruits of the Earth*, man is shown as capable of being a "giant in the earth." The heroic quality of man, however, has its limitations. Determining how the fruits of labor will be divided among the community which earns them must, in Grove's view, be central, not secondary, to the human endeavor. Grove, however, does not shy away from a realistic portrayal of the ironic, possibly tragic, circumstances of mankind. Often those best capable of creating the new order are also the very people least capable of giving it direction, order, and stability.

Critical Context

Fruits of the Earth is recognized by many critics as a work not only central to Grove's career but also central to Canadian literature. The year after its publication, in fact, Grove was awarded the Lorne Pierce Medal by the Royal Society of Canada to honor his contribution to Canadian letters.

The novel is, in later criticism, particularly admired because of its effort to demythologize the image of the pioneer. Grove gives heroic stature to the pioneer, but he does not refrain from bringing that heroic stature into realistic focus. The achievements of single-mindedness deserve full credit and acknowledgment, Grove suggests, but the consequences of that single-mindedness should not be oversimplified or overlooked. Heroic strength, determination, and endurance cannot, without foresight, create a sustained community. Thus, Grove's work functions as a kind of criticism of a culture which often lacks vision.

Finally, Grove's effort to demythologize the Canadian past is particularly crucial because it makes him one of the key writers who introduced social realism to Canadian literature. Although, in the past, his writings were too frank, too open, too harsh for the popular taste, which preferred less exacting and less problematic versions of the pioneers, Grove's prairie realism has gradually won respect and recognition. His works are considered by most critics to be some of the best and most forthright literature dealing with the idealism and the disillusionment of the pioneer period.

Sources for Further Study
Nause, John, ed. *The Grove Symposium*, 1974.
Spettigue, Douglas O. *FPG: The European Years*, 1973.
Stobie, Margaret R. *Frederick Philip Grove*, 1973.
Sutherland, Ronald. *Frederick Philip Grove*, 1968.

Ed Jewinski

FULL MOON

Author: P. G. Wodehouse (1881-1975)
Type of plot: Romantic farce
Time of plot: The 1940's
Locale: A country estate in aristocratic Great Britain
First published: 1947

Principal characters:
CLARENCE EARL OF EMSWORTH, the patriarch of Blandings
    Castle
COLONEL WEDGE, his brother-in-law and a guest at Blandings
    Castle
VERONICA WEDGE, the colonel's daughter
FREDDIE THREEPWOOD, the earl's son
TIPTON PLIMSOLL, the American suitor of Veronica and
    Freddie's "rival"
GALAHAD THREEPWOOD (UNCLE GALLY), a trickster and
    matchmaker for the young lovers

The Novel

Blandings Castle, a well-used setting for P. G. Wodehouse's comic novels, is an aristocratic country estate overseen by the venerable but hopelessly absentminded Earl of Emsworth. Once again, it is the stage on which a cast of unwittingly ironic, self-consumed characters roam from social gathering to social gathering and plot both romantic and business couplings among the British aristocracy and the American nouveau riche.

A guest of his brother-in-law, Lord Emsworth, Colonel Wedge ponders with his wife, Hermione, what will happen to his attractive daughter, Veronica: "the dumbest beauty" listed in the social register. Veronica was once engaged to her cousin, Freddie Threepwood, Lord Emsworth's son, but Freddie instead married the wealthy daughter of an American dog-biscuit manufacturer, becoming one of his father-in-law's chief ambassadors for the company.

This rather placid setting is upset, however, by the arrival of Tipton Plimsoll, a rich young American whose father owns the chain of Tipton Stores, a lucrative retail outlet in the United States. Freddie has brought Tipton to the estate in the hope that he could convince him to carry his line of dog biscuits exclusively in his stores. Meanwhile, with Colonel Wedge's complete endorsement, Tipton falls madly in love with Veronica.

After accidentally discovering that Veronica and Freddie were once betrothed, Tipton undermines the normally peaceful castle in a series of uproarious events in which he mistakenly attributes to Freddie a secret devotion to Veronica. The tranquillity of the castle is further threatened by a subplot in which Prudence, Colonel Wedge's niece, is forced to call off her marriage to her beloved Bill Lister. Midway through the novel, Blandings Castle is in utter turmoil over the triangles created by the competing and thwarted lovers.

All is saved, however, when Galahad Threepwood, "Uncle Gally," intervenes with a series of wildly ingenious, quite improbable, but ultimately successful schemes to reunite both sets of young lovers. In the end, each lover is paired off with an appropriate partner, and Blandings Castle returns to its rightful, complacent state.

The Characters

The plot of *Full Moon*, filled with Wodehouse's trademark schemes and counterschemes, completely overshadows its cast of stock characters. The Blandings estate had been used serially in at least twelve previous novels and many more after that. Consequently, Wodehouse wrote *Full Moon* for a group of readers who needed no introduction to the propensities and predicaments of its protagonists and antagonists. In this, he indeed seems to have been the precursor of the "situation comedy," creating a hunger in the public for the next round of adventures for a familiar crew of eccentrics, ne'er-do-wells, and young lovers.

Wodehouse populates *Full Moon* with distinctively snobbish, slightly anti-intellectual characters often laden with colorful, preposterous names. "Freddie Threepwood" and "Tipton Plimsoll" exemplify his penchant for calling attention to the pretentiousness of the ladies and gentlemen of high society. Their improbable surnames accentuate the frequent silliness of the social situations into which Wodehouse places them; they invite the reader to treat their actually minor travails as major trials with mock-heroic seriousness.

The fulcrum of the story is, nevertheless, the endearing Lord Emsworth, an increasingly senile country gentleman—a widower who has nothing better to do with his time than observe the tribulations of his fellow gentry and raise prize pigs and pumpkins. He is utterly self-effacing, bossed about by his sisters and their spouses and offspring, yet always somehow in the middle of an adventure. Wodehouse never patronizes this elderly gentleman, however, and is clearly charmed by his aloof perspective above the commotion of relatives all about him.

As gentle as Wodehouse is in mocking the foibles of the aristocracy, he is merciless in his parodying of obstinate American businessmen and their cocky sons "on tour" of the British Isles. American "efficiency" and paranoia are satirically focused in Tipton Plimsoll, the stereotypical brash American, fond of tweaking the social etiquette of British society while pursuing what he wants at all cost.

In the end, with few exceptions, Wodehouse's characters manifest no depth and reflect no serious development. The Lord Emsworth of a 1910 novel has neither aged nor matured by his appearance in a 1950 novel. They serve as counters and placeholders amid the comic situations and predicaments created by Wodehousian wit.

Themes and Meanings

As in most of his comic novels, the chief appeal of *Full Moon* is the intricacy of Wodehouse's plotting: mannered intrigues perpetrated by eccentric characters that result in a light comedy of errors, punctuated by misconstrued intentions and farcical situations. Thus, the "theme" of any Wodehousian novel may be summarized in this way: All's well that ends well. In *Full Moon*, a number of characters—naïve, pretentious, or both—lose their way, stumble further, and then regain their composure (and their dignity) by the end of the story.

These recoveries are nearly always engineered by some eccentric, scheming background character interested in seeing that young love is requited, that justice is served, and that the household returns to its dubious normality. In Wodehouse's popular Bertie Wooster novels, this eccentric role is played out by his valet, the gentlemen's gentleman, Jeeves. In *Full Moon*, the trickster and practical joker is Uncle Gally, without whom (as well as despite whom) none of the principals in the story would have settled with his true mate.

It would be a mistake, then, to find in *Full Moon* anything other than an anachronistic, lighthearted treatment of aristocratic romance. As one critic has observed, the success of Wodehouse's comedies "depends upon the convention that nothing has changed since about 1905."

Critical Context

Full Moon is one of several novels in the Blandings cycle, all set at Blandings Castle and all carefully plotted in Wodehouse's cinematic style. It thus represents a fair sampler of Wodehouse style and substance. His plots are ingenious and uproarious, his dialogue crisp, direct, and genuinely amusing, his endings predictably happy. His novels thus meet a general audience's appetite for genteel romantic comedy occurring within absurdly pretentious social settings.

One Wodehousian literary trademark that *Full Moon* exhibits in an extraordinary manner is the masterful use of the elaborate simile. Whether he is describing Lord Emsworth's affection for his prize pig ("He could hear her deep, regular breathing, and he was drinking it in as absorbedly as if it had been something from the Queen's Hall conducted by Sir Henry Wood") or the courtship of young lovers ("Tipton Plimsoll, feeling as if some strong hand had struck him shrewdly behind the ear with a stuffed eelskin, stared bleakly at this lovers' reunion"), Wodehouse deftly uses this figure of speech to heighten the reader's sense of his character's eccentricities. As many critics have observed, few twentieth century writers have come close to Wodehouse's skill in employing the simile to capture the buffoonery of snobbish characters.

Wodehouse wrote nearly fifty "adult" novels, earning praise from such disparate sources as George Orwell and Evelyn Waugh. In 1939, he received an honorary doctorate from Oxford University, and many of his contemporaries regarded him as a modern Oscar Wilde. Among critics of Wodehouse, there is hardly a middle ground: He is regarded either as one of the most amusing English-language humorists in the twentieth century or one of the most predictable and, thus, redundant writers ever to achieve public success.

Sources for Further Study
Donaldson, Frances. *P. G. Wodehouse: A Biography*, 1982.
Hall, Robert A., Jr. *The Comic Style of P. G. Wodehouse*, 1974.
Usborne, Robert. *Wodehouse at Work to the End*, 1977.
Voorhees, Richard J. *P. G. Wodehouse*, 1966.
Wind, Herbert W. *The World of P. G. Wodehouse*, 1972.

Bruce L. Edwards, Jr.

FUNERAL GAMES

Author: Mary Renault (Mary Challans, 1905-1983)
Type of plot: Historical novel
Time of plot: 323-286 B.C.
Locale: Greece, Egypt, and Asia Minor
First published: 1981

> *Principal characters:*
> ALEXANDER THE GREAT, the Macedonian Conqueror
> ALEXANDER IV, the son of Alexander and his wife, Roxane
> ANTIGONAS, a Greek general under Alexander
> ANTIPATROS, the regent of Macedon in Alexander's absence
> BAGOAS, a Persian eunuch, who is devoted to Alexander
> EURYDIKE, the wife of King Philip
> KASSANDROS, a Macedonian leader and regent, the son of
>   Antipatros
> KLEOPATRA, the sister of Alexander
> MELEAGER, a Greek officer and leader of the common
>   soldiers
> OLYMPIAS, the mother of Alexander
> PERDIKKAS, a regent under King Philip
> PHILIP ARRIDAIOS, declared KING PHILIP and known as
>   PHILIP III, Alexander's half brother
> PTOLEMY, a Macedonian officer and the founder of the
>   Egyptian dynasty
> ROXANE, the Bactrian wife of Alexander and mother of
>   Alexander IV
> STATEIRA, the Persian wife of Alexander and daughter of
>   Darius

The Novel

Beginning with the year 323 B.C., *Funeral Games* chronicles the disintegration of Alexander the Great's empire following his death in Babylon at age thirty-two. Although it is generally believed that he died of a fever, the novel suggests that he was poisoned at the hands of Iollas, the brother of Alexander's enemy, Kassandros. As he lies dying in the palace at Babylon, he is too ill to name a successor. Before his death, he manages only the ambiguous gesture of giving his ring to Perdikkas, the ranking commander among those on the scene.

The Macedonian custom being for the army to decide the succession when none is designated, the soldiers assemble to deliberate the question. They face a difficult decision because Alexander has left no descendants, though he has left two pregnant wives, Roxane and Stateira, whose children will have a claim to the throne. Another claimant, Alexander's half brother Philip Arridaios, is mentally retarded and afflicted with epilepsy. Nevertheless, the common soldiers support him, largely because of his resemblance to his father, Philip II; they name him king, despite the opposition of Perdikkas. After some struggle and confusion, it is agreed that Philip will bear the title "King of Macedon," at least until Alexander's children are born; actual power, however, remains with Perdikkas, designated as regent.

This arrangement is imperiled when Meleager, an opponent of Perdikkas, gains the King's signature on a document charging Perdikkas with treason. Having been forewarned, Perdikkas takes his cavalry outside the city and lays siege. Following overtures designed to patch up matters, Meleager emerges from the city with his followers onto the plain, where a ritual sacrifice to the gods has been arranged to promote concord. After the ceremony, Perdikkas, his force in battle formation, seizes thirty of Meleager's followers, binds them, and has them trampled underfoot by a charge of elephants as a lesson to other potential traitors. Meleager, abandoned and shunned by his terrified followers, is assassinated in the temple where he seeks refuge, leaving Perdikkas without a rival.

Yet among the claimants to the throne, the rivalry intensifies. Roxane, Alexander's Bactrian wife, sends a letter bearing Alexander's seal to his Persian wife Stateira, summoning her to Babylon. Believing the summons to be from Alexander, she sets out in the company of her sister Drypetis, widow of Alexander's closest friend, Hephaistion. Shortly after their arrival, Roxane poisons them and compels Perdikkas to conceal the bodies. Thus, when Roxane's child is born, it is the sole descendant of Alexander. Thereafter, Roxane seeks to assure that her son Alexander IV will prevail over King Philip, who enjoys the army's support.

Philip's hand is strengthened when Eurydike, who has been betrothed to him by Alexander, travels to Babylon and marries him, in the hope that they will produce an heir for the Macedonian empire. Eurydike, however, becomes more a nurse and guardian than a wife. Furthermore, her bold attempts to encourage Philip to demonstrate leadership are thwarted at critical times by awkward displays from Philip that remind all who observe him of his unfitness for rule.

The return of Alexander's body to Macedon is delayed for more than a year while artisans craft a magnificent bier, adorned with gold. Before departing for Egypt, Ptolemy convinces Bagoas, the Persian favorite of Alexander, that the tomb should be in Alexandria, not in Macedon. He reasons that contentions for the honor of burial among Perdikkas, the Macedonian regent Antipatros, and Alexander's mother Olympias may lead to civil war. When Perdikkas takes his army to Sardis, Ptolemy, with assistance from Bagoas, diverts the procession bearing the bier and takes Alexander's body to Egypt. To punish the treachery of Ptolemy, Perdikkas turns his army toward Egypt; yet by the time he arrives, he finds Ptolemy well prepared. Perdikkas encounters defeat in an initial skirmish, and a disastrous river crossing causes the loss of two thousand lives. Having lost confidence in Perdikkas, the leading commanders slay him and make their peace with Ptolemy, leaving him secure in Egypt.

Perdikkas is succeeded by less able regents, and Eurydike seizes the opportunity to draw part of the army under her command. She faces defeat after Olympias, Alexander's mother, joins the force supporting Roxane and Alexander IV. After Eurydike's soldiers refuse to fight, she and Philip are captured, and Olympias has the couple put to death following a brief imprisonment.

Subsequently, Olympias' tyranny turns many against her. When Kassandros besieges her stronghold at Pydna, numerous followers defect, and he eventually takes the city. He arranges for a vengeful mob to stone Olympias to death and later poisons both Roxane and Alexander IV, leaving the remnant of Alexander's empire under his command.

The novel concludes with an aged Ptolemy, having ruled successfully in Egypt, talking with his son about Alexander, after completing a biography of his revered leader.

The Characters

Of the novel's thirty-eight characters, thirty-five are based upon historical personages. Mary Renault freely expands upon her sources, adding motivation, speeches, and conflicts in order to develop both the characters and the narrative. Two factors, however, limit the depth of characterization within the novel. First, the large number requires that few characters are memorably detailed or well-rounded. The novel does little to demonstrate development of character over theme. Second, for most characters, the motivations and conflicts are the relatively simple ones of power, assertiveness, and self-advancement. Idealism, vision, and deeply emotional experiences are absent. With but few exceptions, notably Eurydike, the women characters are either fully mature or aged. Even Eurydike—bold, attractive, possessed with aplomb and a quick intellect—seeks to establish a Macedonian dynasty primarily to settle grudges against Alexander for the death of her father. She marries the simpleton Philip Arridaios only with this purpose in mind.

Few characters rise above the crime, violence, cruelty, and ruthlessness that mark the plot. Those who do are endowed with memorable human qualities or cling to some ideal. Ptolemy views with disapproval the excessive violence of Perdikkas but is powerless to prevent it. He returns to Egypt, where he rules with magnanimity, gaining the loyalty of the Egyptian people. His piety toward Alexander persists, and in the end, his wisdom enables him to place the events of many years into perspective.

Insofar as piety and loyalty are concerned, the Persian boy Bagoas represents another memorable example in the novel. He reads the thoughts of the dying Alexander and afterward remains devoted to his memory. In matters of policy, he thinks not of himself but of Alexander.

Perhaps the most poignant characterization is that of Philip Arridaios, the essentially harmless and childlike half brother of Alexander. Renault details his activities, such as arranging his collection of rocks on the floor, with subtlety and tact. Manipulated first by Meleager, then by Eurydike, he faces public meetings that confuse and bewilder him. Left to his own preferences, he would rather remain under the care of his devoted servant, Konon. Unwittingly, he becomes a helpless and pathetic pawn in struggles beyond his understanding and dies at the instigation of Olympias. When Renault shifts the point of view to him, as she often does, his limited understanding, perplexity, confusion, and childlike trust are affective and memorable.

Themes and Meanings

The overriding theme of the novel is the disintegration of an empire when the forceful spirit that created and sustained it no longer survives. Following the death of Alexander, as each subordinate fends for himself and attempts to salvage whatever he can, the empire dissolves amid rivalries, jealousies, renewal of old grudges, hatred, violence, and treachery. The title reflects a grim irony: The funeral games are the disruptions and destructiveness of those Alexander left behind.

Critics have pointed to the conflict in Renault's Greek novels between the Apollonian ideals of reason, grace, and moderation and the Dionysian spirit of destructiveness and disorder. In *Funeral Games*, the Dionysian spirit is loosed with a vengeance. The barbarous violence instigated by Perdikkas, when he has the elephants trample his enemies in full view of the army, signals its onset; from that point, the Dionysian spirit reigns.

A major motif, perhaps the novel's most pervasive motif, is death through poisoning. The aged Queen Sisygambis, mother of Darius, recalls that in the reign of King Ochos, poisoning was common practice. In the narrative, Iollas poisons Alexander at the instigation of Kassandros, Roxane poisons Stateira and Drypetis, and Kassandros poisons Roxane and Alexander IV. Afterward, he attempts to poison Alexander's memory and reputation by suborning Greek historians to defame him. The numerous deaths, many by treachery and stealth, form a fitting complement to the narrative of a disintegrating empire.

As a strong counterbalance to the prevailing violence and disorder, the book constantly reminds the reader of Alexander and his extraordinary achievements. Although he appears only briefly and does not speak, his deeds, words, and accomplishments are recalled by numerous characters. The novel gives Ptolemy the final words about him, and because Ptolemy has been successful while others have wrought havoc and chaos, his perspective forms the most reliable account. Explaining why no one could replace Alexander, he reflects, "All those great men. When Alexander was alive, they pulled together like one chariot-team. And when he died, they bolted like chariot-horses when the driver falls. And broke their backs like horses, too." He concludes that they were right to consider Alexander divine, for he had helped them perform miracles while he lived: "He was a man touched by a god; we were only men who had been touched by him; but we did not know it." Ptolemy assumes that his own good fortune came as a result of the piety he demonstrated in building Alexander a splendid tomb.

Amid destruction and decay, Alexander's memory serves as a reminder of vanished greatness. Other reminders are the magnificent temples, city walls, towers, gates, and memorials that Renault amply describes. In the absence of noble ideals, deep emotions, and great deeds, these monuments stand as testimony that, in a better time, noble deeds had occurred among civilized men.

Critical Context

Mary Renault's final novel represents an appropriate conclusion to her series of eight novels dealing with Greek themes. In addition to these, she produced a biography of Alexander in 1975. Of the historical novels with a Greek setting, three—*Fire from Heaven* (1969), *The Persian Boy* (1972), and *Funeral Games*—deal with Alexander's career and empire. Renault appeared captivated by Alexander's enigmatic character, bold leadership, and genius in achieving the loyalty of his followers.

In *Funeral Games*, the narrative structure is episodic, arranged by sections for each year of the plot in the manner of a chronicle. The accounts of the plot's early years are longer and more complicated than those for later years, and several years during the action are omitted. The style is both simple and arresting, and the novel flows smoothly, shifting gracefully from an omniscient narrator to a limited character point of view.

Critics have found numerous flaws in Renault's art, particularly in her oversimplified characters and her use of anachronisms. Anachronism in this novel is minimal, but the characters are so numerous and the plot so complicated that few characters are well-rounded or well developed. Renault's work bears comparison with Robert Graves's series of historical novels, *I, Claudius* (1934). While the two novelists' efforts to recapture a lost world are perhaps equally serious, Graves develops his narrative in much greater detail, and his characters evince more substantial development as individuals. Renault relies more heavily on the historical events themselves to hold the reader's interest.

Sources for Further Study

Adams, P. L. Review in *The Atlantic*. CCXLIX (January, 1982), p. 87.

Brunsdale, Mitzi M. "Mary Renault," in *Critical Survey of Long Fiction*, 1983. Edited by Frank N. Magill.

Burns, Landon C., Jr. "Men Are Only Men: The Novels of Mary Renault," in *Critique*. VI, no. 3 (1963), pp. 102-121.

Cooke, Judy. Review in *New Statesman*. CII (November 20, 1981), p. 22.

Dick, Bernard F. *The Hellenism of Mary Renault*, 1972.

Ricks, Christopher. Review in *The New York Times Book Review*. LXXXVI (January 17, 1982), p. 7.

Wolfe, Peter. *Mary Renault*, 1969.

Stanley Archer

G.

Author: John Berger (1926-   )
Type of plot: Historical fiction
Time of plot: The late nineteenth century through the beginning of
    World War I
Locale: Italy, England, and Trieste
First published: 1972

> *Principal characters:*
> G., the protagonist, a modern Don Juan
> LAURA, G.'s mother, the offspring of American and British
>   parents and the mistress to Umberto, G.'s father
> BEATRICE, Laura's cousin and guardian of the young G., who
>   initiates G. into sex
> JOCELYN, Beatrice's brother, who assists in G.'s initiation into
>   violence
> MARIKA, G.'s mistress in Trieste, a Hungarian married to a
>   prominent Austrian banker
> NUŠA, a Slovene girl whom G. attempts to seduce

The Novel

Despite its assertive subtitle, "A Novel," John Berger's *G.* hardly seems a novel at all. Many of its pages are taken up with reports about historical events contemporaneous with the narrated fictional incidents in the life of the hero, and many more are occupied with the narrator's reflections upon his own task as a writer: the difficulties he faces in telling the story, knowing how the plot will come out, grasping the innermost springs of his invented characters. The formal problem presented by this text is symmetrically opposite to that of Berger's earlier novel, *A Painter of Our Time* (1958). There, the events of the narrative were largely presented by the narrator who told the story of the life of his painter friend Janos Lavin, while Lavin's journal provided the occasion for philosophical reflection upon politics and art. In *G.*, it is the narrator who talks incessantly about the theoretical problems that are inherent in aesthetic production, while the protagonist simply acts out the life of a modern Don Juan, for all the reader knows without the slightest self-awareness of what he is doing or where he is headed.

The novel opens prior to G.'s birth, with the rivalry between Esther, the wife of G.'s father, Umberto, and Laura, Umberto's mistress and the mother of G. While Laura greatly desires to have Umberto's child, she is unwilling to have that child reared by his father—nor is she prepared to be a proper parent herself. She thus allows G. to be reared by her cousins Jocelyn and Beatrice in rural England. The former initiates G. into violence by taking him hunting, the latter into sex. G.'s seduction by Beatrice is the result of a peculiar concatenation of circumstances, the most fully revealed of which involve Beatrice's own past as the wife of a British officer posted to Africa (where Beatrice goes mad). The encounter will in turn send G. off on a long string of amorous encounters, all illicit and many involving physical danger to himself (which G. seems to relish). The comparison between G.'s career as a lover and that of his mythical namesake, Don Juan or Don Giovanni, is made explicit throughout the novel, not least in the spectacular finale of G.'s death.

After Beatrice's seduction, the scene shifts from rural England to a small town in the Italian Alps, and the time moves ahead some eight years to 1910. The context involves the attempt by a flier, Chavez, to traverse the Alps by air. While Chavez is successfully making the crossing—only to crash upon arriving in Italy—G. seduces Camille Hennequin, the wife of a prominent French businessman. The husband subsequently attempts to avenge himself by shooting G., who is wounded but recovers in the same hospital where Chavez is dying nearby. G.'s ostensible lack of regret over the death of his friend Chavez disgusts their American compatriot Weymann, and the entire episode ends with G.'s reflections upon his now lost mistress Camille, marooned in Paris, and with Chavez accorded the funeral honors of a hero.

The long final section of the novel takes place in Trieste in 1914. Then under the domination of the Habsburg Empire, the city is a crossroads of European culture and politics, including among its population a large number of Slovenes as well as Italians. G. attempts to seduce a young Slovene named Nuša, at the same time that he is carrying on with the wife of an Austrian banker. G. bribes Nuša to attend a formal ball with him by offering to obtain a forged passport for her political-conspirator brother. She consents, and when the two appear at the ball, the banker correctly construes this as a direct insult to him (he knows about his wife's infidelity but is content to allow it as long as she remains discreet). More important for the action, however, G.'s mistress Marika is outraged and attacks Nuša with a horsewhip. Driven from the ball, G. and Nuša are eventually arrested by the Austrian police, interrogated separately, and released. G. makes good on his promise and delivers the passport on the day Italy declares war on Trieste. Caught up in the anarchic violence of the crowd, G. is recognized by a group of Slovene patriots who believe him to be a traitor. He is carried off, knocked unconscious, and dumped into the Adriatic to drown. The novel closes with a description of the sea at sunset, the line of the horizon compared to the edge of a curtain ending a dramatic performance.

The Characters

The reader is given information about several of the characters, including many minor ones (such as Nuša's brother Bojan, who appeared in 1915 in a Marseille police file under the false name issued to G. on the forged passport obtained from the British Foreign Office), but the only character who matters profoundly is G. himself. Everyone else is, as it were, simply a vector that intersects with and deflects the path of G.'s life.

In another sense, however, the real "hero" of this novel is the narrator, whose voice insistently interrupts the narrative to discourse on the poetics and aesthetics of the novel, on the course of European history both contemporaneous with the action and distant from it, and on the problems of representing in language the lived experience of a human consciousness. The narrator is at once assertive, knowledgeable, and authoritative, and strangely vulnerable, confused, unsure of the progress of his own narrative.

There is, however, yet a third "character" in this novel, one that possesses none of the self-conscious sophistication of the narrator, still less the implacable will of G. What emerges with a force and a determinate shape all its own is the march of modern European history, gathering momentum through the fervor of the Italian Risorgimento up to the nationalist rebellions of the Slavic peoples that will provide the proximate cause of World War I. *G.* is not only about the titular hero and his amorous adventures in the opening years of the twentieth century; it is, and perhaps more powerfully, about the emergence of historical forces and movements which will rip apart the last vestiges of the *ancien régime* in Europe and open up, if only briefly, the road to Socialist emancipation. How history unfolds, in a progressively coherent pattern visible only at those moments when it has crystallized into global trends that dominate all action and perception, this is the authentic subject of *G.* The novel portrays the emergence of the modern world in the conflagration of interimperialist war.

Themes and Meanings

Berger himself has written with great lucidity about the significance of aesthetic, scientific, and political achievements in early twentieth century Europe. He has dubbed this epoch "the moment of cubism," praising it for its revolutionary projection of new human perspectives, the first since the triumph of humanism, Galilean mechanics, and visual perspectivism during the Renaissance. *G.* itself has been compared (by David James in the essay cited at the end of this article) in its formal experimentation to analytical cubism in painting. The comparison is surely apposite. Berger's essay was published in 1969, only three years prior to the publication of this novel, and Berger was almost certainly continuing the same itinerary he had sketched in the essay when he chose to write a historical fiction about the period.

The problem set by cubism in the visual arts is the relationship between the perspective of the individual observer upon an event or a phenomenon and the complex structural determinations which are necessary for the phenomenon to come into existence. While European art since the Renaissance had tended to privilege the individual viewer in presenting the world as if it could be comprehended from a single point of view, cubism shattered this visual plane by presenting one and the same object from different vantage points, thus producing an object of representation which no single observer occupying a given position could possibly behold. The implication is that the nature of reality is not accessible from any single perspective; it can only be constructed or, better, analyzed by subjecting the object of investigation to a series of distinct observational experiments which are then synthesized in the single intuition of the visual figure. In the famous portraits done by Pablo Picasso and Georges Braque between 1907 and 1914, the distortion of the figures derives not from some brutal or misanthropic desire to disfigure the human form (as the more simple-minded defenders of traditional representational art have believed) but from the conviction that authentic objectivity demands such a multiplication of perspectives.

In the novel, this conviction is shared by the narrator, who tries tirelessly to incorporate different perspectives on the character and actions of G. On a higher level of generality, Berger himself is attempting to account for the distinctive trajectory of European history during the nearly half century from 1870 through 1914, by positioning his protagonist in a variety of national, temporal, and political contexts, allowing G.'s loves to give the appearance of coherence to a narrative that is less about him than about the time and the structures of history and society into which he is born and out of which he passes at the novel's end. The effect is to give the reader less the portrait of a person, a so-called well-rounded character (as, say, Honoré de Balzac or Charles Dickens or George Eliot might have done) than to present an analytical cross-section of the various forces and events that coalesced to produce a new conception of human being and living during this crucial period in European history.

Critical Context

G. is undoubtedly Berger's most ambitious and probably his most successful novel. It incorporates and synthesizes the obsessive themes of the early fiction: alienation, the relationship between art and politics, the difficulty of sustaining vital, life-giving aesthetic forms under an increasingly reified regime of daily life. In addition, it is the culmination of the more than fifteen years during which he worked as one of the liveliest and most penetrating art critics in the English-speaking world. Finally, it marks a kind of terminus for the modernist novel in English, for it is difficult to see how anyone could go further than Berger has down the road of a fiction that self-consciously reflects upon its practice and the problems of narration as an aesthetic mode. By comparison, *The French Lieutenant's Woman* (1969) or the later novels of John Barth are child's play—one might even say childish.

As Wyndham Lewis once said of James Joyce's *Ulysses* (1922), G. is less a revolutionary work (in the aesthetic or formal sense) than it is a terminal moraine. *G.* marks not only a terminus in the formal possibilities of the English novel but also a kind of cul-de-sac for Berger himself. His subsequent nonfiction works, the collaborative books with the Swiss photographer Jean Mohr, the art criticism, and the mixed mode of *Pig Earth* (1979) have proven thus far poorer achievements by comparison with *G.* This is not to say that Berger's career has reached its own end point, merely to observe that the historical moment of revolutionary possibility which Berger himself located in the epoch of cubism has not found its contemporary analogue in any of the arts—at least not in the so-called First World. If one takes Berger's conclusions about the relationship between the artist and the determining force of history seriously, it should come as no surprise that John Berger has not been able to surpass the achievement of *G.* The trajectory of contemporary history itself will have to present artists such as Berger with the material and the impetus to go beyond the moment of *G.*'s revolutionary realism.

Sources for Further Study

Caute, David. "What We Might Be and What We Are: The Art of John Berger," in *Collisions: Essays and Reviews*, 1974.

James, David. "Cubism as Revolutionary Realism," in *The Minnesota Review*. N.s. XXI (Fall, 1983), pp. 92-109.

McMahon, Joseph H. "Marxist Fictions: The Novels of John Berger," in *Contemporary Literature*. XXIII (Spring, 1982), pp. 202-224.

The Minnesota Review. N.s. XXVIII (Spring, 1987). Special Berger issue.

Robbins, Bruce. "Feeling Global: John Berger and Experience," in *Boundary 2*. XI (Fall, 1982/Winter, 1983), pp. 291-308.

Michael Sprinker

THE GAMES WERE COMING

Author: Michael Anthony (1932-   )
Type of plot: Social realism
Time of plot: From January to April during a year in the early 1950's
Locale: The town of Marabella and the city of San Fernando in southern
    Trinidad, British West Indies
First published: 1963

> *Principal characters:*
> LEON SEAL, the protagonist, a competitive cyclist in his early
>   twenties
> SYLVIA, his girlfriend
> DOLPHUS SEAL, his preadolescent brother
> FITZ SEAL, Leon's father and trainer
> MAY, a friend of Sylvia

The Novel

Two events not only reveal but also contribute to the central conflicts in the novel: the Southern Games (including the fifteen-mile Blue Riband cycling race) and Trinidad's most important annual event, its colorful and hedonistic Carnival. These two events are to be held only weeks apart, and for the first time, Leon Seal turns his back on Carnival and single-mindedly prepares to win the race which will establish him as one of the country's cycling stars.

Under his father's guidance, he quits his job at the Pointe-à-Pierre oil refinery and avoids any activity which might strain a muscle or weaken his body. Accepting the popular mythology, he decides to abstain totally from any physical involvement with his devoted girlfriend, Sylvia, during the several months of his training. Leon's carefully calculated regimen and his iron discipline are coolly and rationally directed toward the goals of heroic action and personal glory; Leon's assumptions concerning the people close to him and the importance of his quest, however, fail to take into account the feelings and needs of Sylvia, who is in love with him but has little real interest in cycling. Intellectually she accepts her diminished position in Leon's life, but emotionally she is hurt and confused by his treatment of her.

Leon further complicates the situation by sexually arousing Sylvia during the occasional visits he permits her, only to turn away from her abruptly with a show of his self-control. The situation leads Sylvia to reassess her relationship with Leon and to question her own social and moral views. Frustrated and resentful, she is forced to conclude "Bicycle is his woman!" and consider other options. Mirroring and contributing to her inner turmoil is the general excitement building in the population as Carnival approaches with its loosening of inhibitions and its invitation to bacchanalian abandon.

Sylvia is gradually drawn into an affair with her employer, Imbal Mohansingh, and becomes pregnant. She seeks help from her friend May in obtaining an abortion but is refused. She decides to take May's advice and pretend that the baby is Leon's. May urges Sylvia to forget her troubles and enjoy the Carnival: "This is Trinidad. And you young, and you ain't dead yet!" Yet, as often happens in the novel, the external world reflects the psychological or moral state of the characters: "In the street all the calypsoes were twisted into obscenities and were on the lips of young and old alike."

Sylvia persuades the unsuspecting Leon to promise that if he wins the Blue Riband race he will marry her immediately, but she knows that Leon is fully capable of putting her off for another year if his goal is not achieved. The tension of the entire novel becomes focused on the last chapter and the expertly controlled account of the fifteen-mile race on which ride the fortunes, for better or worse, of the central characters. The novel's last sentence indicates that Leon has indeed won the race. Yet Michael Anthony's skill in creating characters who live in the imagination forces the reader to speculate on the true nature of that victory for both Sylvia and Leon.

The Characters

Although the physical action of the novel centers on Leon's preparation for the Blue Riband bicycle race and his eventual triumph, the novel's most important and interesting developments take place within the mind and heart of Sylvia. Leon simultaneously values and pities Sylvia for her seeming lack of a personality independent of his own; "she was always cool, always easy, always pliable to his will." It is a view with which Sylvia herself concurs; her enforced loneliness and the boredom of her job, however, cause her to become more reflective and self-aware. At twenty-one, she leads a life of slightly prudish respectability, but her growing friendship with the disreputable May and her consciousness of the hypocrisy which often lies beneath the veneer of Trinidadian propriety lead her to recognize her own potential for coarse thoughts and immoral behavior.

Sylvia's heightened awareness of Carnival and her liking for the melodies of calypsoes whose lyrics she considers "vile" and "almost all immoral" reflect the moral ambiguity which soon leads to acquiescence in her seduction by Mohansingh, a married man. Sylvia's decision to trick Leon into accepting Mohansingh's baby as his own is not only an act of desperation and retribution but also an admission of moral weakness and the acceptance of a sense of debased self-worth.

Leon's quest for glory illustrates an aspect of the importance of sport in preindependence Trinidad, a poor country where opportunities for respectable members of the working class to distinguish themselves were severely limited. Leon's participation in cycling is predicated on an obsessive will to win and not on enjoyment of sport for its own sake. He is proud of his strong body and is willing to endure pain to turn it into an efficient instrument of his ambition, but the constant monitoring, massaging, and observation of his physique verges on the narcissistic; in his own way, he is every bit as preoccupied with the flesh as any Carnival reveler. Leon feels some shame for his treatment of Sylvia. Naïvely oblivious to the changes he has caused her to undergo, he believes her still to be "simple and good. . . . Perhaps more like a faithful dog than like a woman." Although he looks forward to the ecstasy of making love to Sylvia, he feels that "the real ecstasy" will be in winning the race.

Contained within Leon's wish to isolate himself from the undisciplined mob of vehicles which could wreck his bike and from the Carnival crowd which could sap him of his strength and weaken his resolve is not only a desire for calculated and ordered activity but also an element of disdain for the ordinary man. In the race he shows that he is no team player; his drive for preeminence is totally selfish in its aims. Paradoxically, in the elaborate ritual of proving his manhood and identity, he denies an important part of his own humanity and irreparably damages the life of the woman who once loved him.

Anthony has an unusual talent for providing even minor characters with a roundness and psychological depth which breathes life into them. Dolphus Seal, Leon's younger brother, is a wholly believable little boy despite his obvious functions within the novel's schematic design. Because the attentions of the adults are focused on Leon, Dolphus is left alone to weigh the modes of life represented by the different activities surrounding the Southern Games and Carnival. Sometimes Dolphus tends, like Leon, to see the events as discrete and mutually exclusive, but more often he synthesizes them naturally as one reminds him of the other. Anthony is best known for his skillful depiction of the minds of children and youths; it is through the filtering consciousness of Dolphus—as in the long and lyrical passage where he tries to decide between being a cyclist or a steelband musician—that the most evocative details of both the games and Carnival are presented.

Leon's father, Fitz Seal, is a reserved man in his early fifties who, his wife Melda informs the children, once was a drinking, dancing Carnival man. He has since reformed and settled into the responsible yet less exciting role of husband and father. His values of order and discipline have been passed on to Leon, for whom he serves as trainer and through whom he vicariously pursues some of the dreams of his youth.

May acts as a catalyst for Sylvia's change in personality. She has two or three illegitimate children and has had several abortions. At first, Sylvia simply dismisses May as being beneath her socially and morally, but as her own life becomes complicated she turns to May for help and advice. May is not simply a "good-time" girl but also a victim to a common West Indian pattern of life and attitudes toward women. May resents Sylvia's initial innocence and air of propriety. Despite some feelings of sympathy, May experiences a vindictive satisfaction when Sylvia is brought down to her level.

Themes and Meanings

The principal themes in the novel are best summed up by the "two fevers" contained within Dolphus: the attraction of the Southern Games, with its emphasis on discipline and hard work in an ordered striving for perfection, and the seductive allure of Carnival, whose spirit is, even for a young boy, "robust, carefree, [and] cruel." The need to resolve the conflict between the two attitudes toward life represented by the games and Carnival is universal, but it is also of particular relevance to the individual lives of Trinidadians and to the life of the nation itself: In Trinidad, Carnival has become institutionalized for economic and political as well as social reasons. In *The Games Were Coming*, Leon represents individual ambition and personal austerity carried to excess, while May illustrates the tragic consequences for those who live for today only to count the cost when the masquerade is over. Clearly, a balance is needed for the well-being of individuals as well as nations. As the case of Sylvia shows, however, the balance must be real and not based on a fragile morality or on social values which put a premium on the appearance of order and propriety while individual and public corruption flourish, fitting material for the calypso and the sly remark.

The frequent repetition of the phrase "the games were coming" as well as the many references to the approaching Carnival are structuring devices used to create tension, but the words "games" and "Carnival"—which refer to the abjuring of flesh—also have ironic possibilities for the lives of the central characters, especially Leon and Sylvia.

Critical Context

Michael Anthony was born of Afro-Caribbean ancestry in the remote Trinidadian village of Mayaro. He published poems in local newspapers before moving to England in 1954. Encouraged by the success of fellow West Indian writers Samuel Selvon and George Lamming, he began to produce more poems before being urged by V. S. Naipaul to concentrate on fiction. He had several short stories published or broadcast by the British Broadcasting Corporation and embarked on the novel *The Year in San Fernando* (1965), which was not published until after *The Games Were Coming*. He has published more than a dozen other books of fiction and popular history, including the novel *Green Days by the River* (1967) and the collection of short stories *Cricket in the Road* (1973). In 1968, Anthony moved to Brazil before returning in 1970 to Trinidad, where he received his nation's highest civilian award, the Order of the Humming Bird, for his achievement in literature.

The Games Were Coming is characterized by a limpid, unaffected prose style which is deceptive in its surface simplicity. By exploiting the full range of language—from dialect to standard English—available to the West Indian writer, Anthony is able to convey the world and thoughts of his dialect-speaking characters to the reader in a manner which feels natural and unmediated despite the sophisticated technique required to accomplish it. Because Anthony never treats the details of Trinidadian life as exotic, the novel is also impressive for its sensitive and authentic presentation of West Indian characters on their own terms.

Sources for Further Study

Barratt, Harold. "Michael Anthony: A Critical Assessment," in *Bim*. XVII, nos. 66 and 67 (1983), pp. 157-164.

Niven, Alastair. " 'My Sympathies Enlarged': The Novels of Michael Anthony," in *Commonwealth Essays and Studies*. II (1976), pp. 45-62.

Ramchand, Kenneth. *An Introduction to the Study of West Indian Literature*, 1976.

Smyer, Richard I. "Enchantment and Violence in the Fiction of Michael Anthony," in *World Literature Written in English*. XXI, no. 1 (1982), pp. 148-159.

Douglas Rollins

GAUDY NIGHT

Author: Dorothy L. Sayers (1893-1957)
Type of plot: Mystery
Time of plot: From June, 1934, to May, 1935
Locale: Oxford and London, England
First published: 1935

Principal characters:

HARRIET VANE, a thirty-two-year-old writer of detective fiction, an honors graduate of Shrewsbury College in Oxford

LORD PETER DEATH BREDON WIMSEY, a forty-five-year-old amateur sleuth who is in love with Harriet

LETITIA MARTIN, the dean of Shrewsbury College

HELEN DE VINE, a new research fellow at Shrewsbury College

MISS HILLYARD, a history tutor and a feminist

MISS LYDGATE, Harriet's former tutor, a specialist in English prosody

ANNIE WILSON, a "scout" or maid at Shrewsbury who is widowed with two children

The Novel

Ten years after she is graduated from Shrewsbury College, in Oxford, Harriet Vane accepts the invitation of a classmate, Mary Stokes Attwood, to return for an annual celebration, the "Gaudy." While at the college, she finds a scrap of paper blowing around the quadrangle; on it, she finds a crudely drawn picture of a naked woman stabbing a figure in academic dress. Later, on her way back to London, a message flutters from her gown: "YOU DIRTY MURDERESS. AREN'T YOU ASHAMED TO SHOW YOUR FACE?" The words have been formed with letters cut from newspaper headlines.

Harriet thinks no more of the picture and assumes that since she was accused of murdering her lover, Philip Boyles (as recounted in Dorothy Sayers' *Strong Poison*, 1930), the message is a personal attack. Several months later, however, Dean Letitia Martin asks Harriet to return to Shrewsbury, because many similar notes have been appearing on campus. In addition to these hateful letters, vandalism has become a problem. The manuscript of Miss Lydgate's study of English prosody has been mutilated, gowns have been burned in the quadrangle, and library books have been torn.

Reluctantly, Harriet accepts the task of trying to find the person who is responsible for these bizarre occurrences. Despite her careful records of each episode and her attempts to catch or at least discourage the vandal, she cannot identify or apprehend the perpetrator. Members of the faculty begin to suspect one another, and only adroit maneuvering by the college and university administration prevents a major scandal.

Unable to solve the mystery herself, Harriet at last turns to Lord Peter Wimsey. Lord Peter had unraveled the circumstances of Philip Boyles's death and had thus saved Harriet from the gallows. For five years, he has dutifully been proposing marriage to Harriet every three months, but she has consistently refused, fearing the loss of her independence. As they work together on this case, though, she discovers that he neither bullies nor protects her. When they realize that the vandal may become violent, Lord Peter buys Harriet a dog collar to guard her from strangulation and teaches her some fundamentals of self-defense. He does not, however, discourage her from pursuing the solution to the mystery. Nor does Lord Peter reveal to her the name of the culprit after he examines her evidence; he trusts that Harriet is sufficiently intelligent to arrive at the answer herself.

At the end of the book, two puzzles are solved. Lord Peter reveals that Annie Wilson, one of the college "scouts," or maids, is the culprit. Six years earlier, Helen De Vine had been provost of Flamborough College, in York. There she showed that Arthur Robinson had suppressed information contradicting the argument of his M.A. thesis. As a result of her actions, Robinson had lost his degree and his teaching job. Later, he killed himself in despair. Annie had been his wife, and she had sought to avenge herself on Helen in particular and on the whole body of women scholars generally. The note that Harriet had found had been intended for Helen; their gowns had lain next to each other, and Annie had mistaken them in the dim light. Annie had hoped that the newspapers would cover the strange occurrences at Shrewsbury, create a scandal, and cause the closing of the relatively young women's college.

The other puzzle concerns Harriet's feelings toward Lord Peter. Having seen that he is not a domineering, pampered aristocrat who would take away her career, she agrees to marry him.

The Characters

At age thirty-two, Harriet has had to fight her way to success. An honors student in literature with a scholarly bent, she had decided to leave the academy to become a popular writer. Her works sell well, but she has narrowly missed hanging for the supposed murder of her lover, her reputation has been damaged—while Annie Wilson's note was not intended for her, other letters of the same ilk do trouble her—and she is uncertain of her future. Should she return to the quiet world of Oxford? Should she surrender her career and independence and accept Lord Peter's hand and an ample income?

In Harriet, Dorothy Sayers creates a semiautobiographical figure whose ambition, history, and doubts mirror her creator's. Sayers had no Lord Peter pursuing her, but in other respects the similarities, including appearance, are striking.

Sayers had introduced Harriet in 1930 so that she could marry off Lord Peter and be rid of him. Just as Sir Arthur Conan Doyle tired of Sherlock Holmes, Sayers wanted to free herself of her popular detective. Before she could allow Harriet and Lord Peter to marry, however, she had to humanize her airy and often pompous aristocrat. In this novel, she accomplishes that goal. As always, Lord Peter is brilliant. An honors student in history as Harriet is in literature, he discovers in a week what has eluded Harriet (and the entire Shrewsbury faculty) for months. As always, too, he is attractive to women. Everyone at Shrewsbury is curious about Lord Peter before he appears and is enchanted by him once he arrives. His wealth, generosity, and wit also remain unchanged.

Harriet does discover other characteristics, though. He is not a shallow player with words but a serious scholar, as much in love with Oxford as she is. She realizes that his mind is keen, keener than hers, in fact. She also learns that he is not simply skating on the surface of life, using his wealth as a shield from reality. Repeatedly, he travels to European capitals, where he works long weeks to preserve the fragile peace. Despite his self-deprecating dismissal of himself as an amusing man who smooths ruffled feathers, she recognizes that the foreign office, and Lord Peter himself, take his role very seriously indeed. Further, she sees that his seemingly impregnable ego is vulnerable: He wishes that he were younger and taller, and his easy dismissal of Harriet's repeated rejections masks a deep pain. Sayers thus transforms Lord Peter from a puppet to a real person, whom readers can appreciate and whom Harriet can marry.

Around these two central figures revolve many lesser ones. Each of the dons at Shrewsbury has her peculiarity. Miss Lydgate is forever revising her manuscript; to get it to press Harriet must finally disregard all efforts at last-minute changes. Miss Hillyard unceasingly complains about men. Various students, too, appear to advance the plot but are no more developed than this necessity demands. Gerald Wimsey's automobile accident gives Harriet an excuse to communicate with his uncle, Lord Peter. The youthful Reginald Pomfret serves as a foil to Lord Peter, and his misadventures provide some clues about the vandal. Yet only Annie Wilson rivals Harriet and Lord Peter as a well-rounded character. Shadowy throughout the novel, in her final confrontation with the female dons whom she abhors, she exposes the pain she has lived with since her husband's disgrace and death. Though Sayers does not condone her actions, she does permit the reader to sympathize. Hence, instead of punishing Annie by sending her to jail, Sayers places her under psychiatric care and holds out the promise of rehabilitation.

Themes and Meanings

In "Gaudy Night," an essay about her detective fiction, Sayers said, "By choosing a plot that should exhibit intellectual integrity as the one great permanent value in an emotionally unstable world I should be saying the thing that, in a confused way, I had been wanting to say all my life." To determine whether any of the dons might be responsible for the vandalism at Shrewsbury, Lord Peter engages them in a conversation on the subject of intellectual integrity and discovers that not one would sacrifice that quality for personal gain or emotional satisfaction. Lord Peter replies that "if it ever occurs to people to value the honour of the mind equally with the honour of the body, we shall get a social revolution of a quite unparalleled sort." Further, as Sayers told Charles Williams, "I do not know whether we can be saved through the intellect, but I do know that I can be saved by nothing else."

Annie Wilson acts as she does because she lacks that respect for intellectual integrity. Neither she nor her husband could understand why Helen De Vine would interfere with a man's livelihood simply because he suppressed a piece of evidence. Driven by her emotions rather than by her reason, Annie is willing even to kill to get revenge.

Sayers does not reject emotion. At the end of the novel, Miss De Vine concedes that while she acted properly when she exposed Robinson, she was remiss in failing to alleviate the hardships her actions caused. Lord Peter and Harriet, too, recognize the need for a balance between head and heart. Shortly before Harriet accepts Lord Peter, they attend a performance of the Bach double violin concerto. Sayers chooses this piece intentionally, for it expresses the kind of life Lord Peter and Harriet will lead. Each musician is independent, yet the two violins must play together to make the music come alive. The violinists also resemble reason and emotion, each providing counterpoint to the other, yet both blending to produce harmony.

Critical Context

Although a student nearly kills herself after receiving some thirty poison-pen letters, and although both Harriet and Helen De Vine narrowly escape being murdered, *Gaudy Night* lacks a corpse. Some fans of mystery therefore have criticized the book as false to the demands of the genre. Sayers, however, regarded this as her best detective novel, and readers were undeterred by the absence of death. Within two months, the book went through six printings and had sold forty thousand copies in Great Britain alone.

Gaudy Night is the author's most successful effort at fusing the novel of manners with the mystery. Her leading characters assume lives of their own and are not mere marionettes to be manipulated for the sake of the plot. She had admired the mysteries of Wilkie Collins and Charles Dickens precisely because they transcended the simple detective story, and in *Gaudy Night* she successfully emulated them. Her knowledge of and respect for academic life allow her to create a vivid portrait of the joys and perils of that world; if the threat of death is remote, the dangers facing the women of Shrewsbury are only slightly less catastrophic. They confront the loss of mutual trust, so essential for any community to exist, and they come close to losing their newly won right to have a women's college at all.

Having offered this tribute to academia, Sayers soon abandoned detective fiction, writing only one more Wimsey novel, *Busman's Holiday* (1937). She had always regarded herself as a scholar, and in her later years she turned to serious drama, research, and the translation of such classics as Dante's *The Divine Comedy* (c. 1320) and *The Song of Roland* (c. 1100). Before leaving the genre that had ensured her fame, however, she created a masterpiece showing what the mystery could achieve.

Sources for Further Study
Brabazon, James. *Dorothy Sayers: A Biography*, 1981.
Gaillard, Dawson. *Dorothy L. Sayers*, 1980.
Hone, Ralph E. *Dorothy L. Sayers: A Literary Biography*, 1979.
Tischler, Nancy M. *Dorothy L. Sayers: A Pilgrim Soul*, 1980.

Joseph Rosenblum

GENTLEMEN IN ENGLAND
A Vision

Author: A. N. Wilson (1950-   )
Type of plot: Satire
Time of plot: 1880
Locale: Victorian England
First published: 1985

> *Principal characters:*
> HORACE NETTLESHIP, a Victorian geology professor who has lost his faith in God and man
> CHARLOTTE NETTLESHIP, his troubled wife, who is searching for balance in the midst of family upheaval
> MAUDIE NETTLESHIP, Horace and Charlotte's daughter, who is coming of age without a compass
> LIONEL NETTLESHIP, Horace and Charlotte's son, who is seeking a spiritual purpose in his life
> TIMOTHY LUPTON, a bohemian artist who inadvertently exposes the emptiness of the Nettleship home
> WALDO CHATTERWAY, Charlotte's old friend, a social gadfly who helps arbitrate the family turmoil

The Novel

Geologist and volcano expert Horace Nettleship has long ago lost his inherited Christian faith; the world to him seems "an infinitely empty, infinitely extensible accident." Unwilling to confront or debate her husband's negative affirmation of faith, Charlotte retreats from him psychologically, consumed by the task of leaving "footsteps on the sands of time by embroidering cream-jug covers or writing letters, or managing the servants."

They speak only in public, their lack of intimacy extending from the bedroom to the dinner table—where they converse only with their daughter, Maudie, and never with each other. Into this static household one morning comes the promise of release, or, at least, diversion; Maudie receives two letters: one from her brother, Lionel, who declares his desire to become a priest, and another from her godfather, Waldo Chatterway, who announces his return from self-imposed exile on the Continent.

When Waldo, or Marvo, "the marvelous bore," arrives, he becomes the catalyst for a series of events which signal both the coming of age of Maudie and the spiritual maturity of Lionel. He brings with him not only a sprightly, unsettling worldliness unknown to this staid and barren home, but also Timothy Lupton, the living embodiment of unbridled sensuality and forbidden passion.

The remainder of this complex satire of the crumbling Victorian ethos evolves as a tragedy of errors which focuses on the further disintegration of the Nettleship marriage and the loss and recovery of innocence in the Nettleship children. Charlotte mistakenly interprets Lupton's passion and attention as affection for her. Looking for sympathy and liberation, she earnestly confesses to Lupton, "when you are married, it is like living in a house where almost all the cupboards and rooms are locked up for ever." Lupton, however, is infatuated with Maudie and finds Charlotte's tragic pose and underlying sexuality "spiritually unbecoming," since "naked passion . . . is something nightmarish and ugly." Horace, meanwhile, rummaging inside and out for his lost manhood and fearing cuckoldry, rapes Charlotte in his futile search for renewal.

These events reveal to the Nettleship children for the first time how fractured and unnatural their family relationships have been, further convincing them of their need to remain devoted friends to each other. The narrative proceeds to its ironic conclusion as Horace falls down a flight of stairs, emblematic of his fall from grace, injuring his ankle; he is thus unable to accompany Charlotte and Maudie on holiday, a vacation designed to relieve the "sea-lion bark," or consumptive cough that Maudie has developed. Thus resigned to fate, Charlotte sighs, "There is plenty to *see*, heaven knows, in England." Lionel resolves to become a priest, his life now "subsumed in the farce of a broken ankle."

In the novel's last scene, one finds Maudie and Lionel on the proverbial Dover Beach, speculating about whether the tide is going out or coming in. It is coming in, they conclude, and as they "squeal with childish merriment," they regain a kind of faith and achieve a kind of rebirth, retrieving a humanity that had been detached and trampled upon in the death of their parents' marriage.

The Characters

Gentlemen in England depicts a post-Darwinian Britain which has lost its faith in a Supreme Being fully in control of His created universe. This loss is exemplified most dramatically in the lives of the geologist Horace Nettleship and the painter Timothy Lupton, but it is just as true of Charlotte Nettleship's life.

Through his geological research, Horace, the unhappy atheist, has helped "shed the last vestiges of credence in Archbishop Ussher's theory that the world had been fashioned at a precise date in 4004 B.C." His speciality is volcanoes, but he confines his potency to his scholarship. An aunt "had told him at a formative age that it was injurious to the constitution if one's back touched a chair," hence he must never relax his guard or he might fall into a genuine and thus "improper" relationship with others.

Charlotte and Horace can find nothing to talk about for fifteen years, and when Nettleship eventually uncovers Charlotte's buoyant but misspent desire for Timothy Lupton, he assaults her in an attempt at self-affirmation. Actions speak louder than words, and, in this case, such actions solemnly ratify Horace's public break from faith of any sort. Lupton, who seemingly had no faith to lose, is apparently disgusted by Charlotte's innocence in all this; the novel's narrator comments, "only innocents commit adultery; of all sins it is the one which suggests the most optimistic capacity to alter the status quo. She actually thought her life could be improved!"

The result of this pervasive human apostasy is the death of marriage and the demise of the family as a stabilizing institution in society. Charlotte comes to represent a generation of daughters, mothers, and wives who lived lives of quiet desperation in touch with the world, if at all, only through their fathers, husbands, or children. She reminds herself, "We must make our pleasures at home," and thereby resigns herself to a hollow, shadowy existence on the periphery of human life.

Themes and Meanings

In the absence of a compensatory faith even in mankind itself, a secondary faith arguably derived from faith in God, A. N. Wilson's characters lose their ability to navigate a hostile world with lasting, meaningful relationships. Neither science nor art can fill the vacuum left by the impotence of a church whose incessant message is fidelity and perseverance.

Wilson himself has commented that the novel's subtitle, "A Vision," has great significance for understanding its setting and theme. Because the novel clearly emulates the trappings of a traditional Victorian novel, Wilson suggests that he added the subtitle to "establish the right mood by giving the book an old-fashioned touch." Moreover, Wilson points out, there is, as in many Victorian novels, an actual apparition in the story, and this focuses the reader's attention on "how we see the phantom world," or the supernatural realities constantly at one's elbow but constantly eluding one's senses.

In the novel's climactic scene, Wilson offers his readers an ironic reaffirmation of the faith that Matthew Arnold once declared would be displaced by poetry and literature but lingers still. Lionel, turning finally to the life of the spirit and discarding the life of the flesh, and Maudie, her innocence about the world still intact, make contact with that world of phantoms at Dover Beach.

Critical Context

Gentlemen in England is preceded in the Wilson canon by seven acclaimed novels, two of which, *The Sweets of Pimlico* (1977) and *The Healing Art* (1980), have won for him international literary prizes. Wilson is also the author of three well-received biographies of British men of letters and a monograph on Christianity, *How Can We Know?* (1985). The latter volume helps amplify Wilson's clear intention to imbue his fiction with the haunting impact of religious faith or its absence upon British culture.

Gentlemen in England thus takes its place among these works as another of his carefully stylized inquiries into British sensibilities at the end of the twentieth century. Whether set in the present libertarian age or in the seemingly repressive Victorian period, Wilson's texts aim to expose the thin veneer of unacknowledged nihilism within which contemporary culture operates.

In this, Wilson's themes and styles of narrative often resemble those of such American writers as Saul Bellow and Walker Percy, and as well such British writers as Evelyn Waugh and Kingsley Amis. While neither as sober as Amis and Bellow, nor as comic as Waugh and Percy, Wilson stands beside them as a conservative advocate for restoring a moral, even religious, voice to modern letters.

Sources for Further Study
Library Journal. Review. CXI (February 1, 1986), p. 95.
The New Republic. Review. CLXCI (March 17, 1986), pp. 37-38.
The New York Times Book Review. Review. XCI (March 9, 1986), p. 7.
Time. Review. CXXV (March 17, 1986), p. 81.
The Wall Street Journal. Review. CCVII (April 8, 1986), p. 28.

Bruce L. Edwards, Jr.

THE GINGER MAN

Author: J. P. Donleavy (1926-   )
Type of plot: Picaresque comedy
Time of plot: The late 1940's
Locale: Dublin and London
First published: 1955, expurgated; 1963, unexpurgated

Principal characters:

SEBASTIAN BALFE DANGERFIELD, the protagonist, a twenty-seven-year-old American student of law at Trinity College, Dublin

MARION, his English wife

KENNETH O'KEEFE, an American and a former Harvard student

LILY FROST, one of Dangerfield's mistresses

MARY, another of Dangerfield's mistresses

CHRIS, yet another of Dangerfield's mistresses

The Novel

Sebastian Balfe Dangerfield and his English wife, Marion, together with their infant daughter, Felicity, are living in Dublin. Supported by the G.I. Bill and nominally a student of law at Trinity College, Sebastian idles away his time in a continuous spiral of drink, seduction, and deception. He finances his rakehell exploits by sponging on the gullible, stealing or pawning whatever is movable, and conning whomever he can, using his posh accent and college scarf as reference. His wild pranks range from the humorous to the outrageous: fetching home a sheep's head for dinner, engaging in a furious pub brawl and a hilarious chase among Dublin's streets, seeing excreta falling through the ceiling in one lodging, hacking through the sewer line in another, even, at one point, attempting to smother Felicity. The cumulative effect of these escapades and the neglect of his daughter (she suffers from rickets) is to wear out the patience of his wife, who finally leaves him for her parents in England. Undeterred by his progressively straitened circumstances, he seduces his tenant, the naïve and timid Miss Frost (a frustrated, early-middle-aged florist's assistant) and carouses among the denizens of Dublin's bohemia, all the while gleefully eluding a former landlord, Egbert Skully.

His closest companion is a fellow American, Kenneth O'Keefe, who is preoccupied with schemes for the surrender of his virginity, without success. His letters to Dangerfield on his failures with women (and men) in Ireland and France punctuate the story of the hero's debaucheries until O'Keefe finally returns to the United States. Thus the plot of the novel is a loose string of harum-scarum adventures of the irrepressible Sebastian as he awaits his father's death and his own substantial inheritance. Before this happens, he leaves Ireland for London; there, he is pursued by Mary, one of his conquests, for whom he has developed a genuine affection—an inconvenient sentiment, given his overriding commitment to self-gratification.

As hilarious as these adventures are, they are less memorable than the lusty, blasphemous, vibrant imagination of Sebastian as he reflects on the world around him: the seedy side of Dublin life viewed from a material, sensual, American perspective. Much of the novel is taken up with a highly energetic, irreverent, deliciously articulate interior monologue, as Sebastian mentally skewers the shambling, penurious, vacuous Irish he encounters. His occasional bursts of protest—wildly, absurdly violent—often frighten him into a sense of his own futility and doom.

As befits a picaresque novel, the plot is episodic, alternating between domestic scenes, interludes with O'Keefe, and accounts of Sebastian's three liaisons, with Chris, Mary, and Lily Frost. The narrative is highlighted by several savagely humorous scenes: an uproarious pub brawl, the seduction of Miss Frost, Sebastian's trashing of Skully's house, Sebastian's ride home in the train with his penis exposed. Indeed, one of the achievements of this novel is its scabrous black comedy. Even in the midst of its wildest humor, however, the reader is reminded of the stark reality behind the fun—of Dangerfield's starving baby, Miss Frost's ruined reputation, the wanton waste of intelligence, money, and property.

The Characters

Sebastian Balfe Dangerfield is a brilliantly realized character, urbane, witty, evidently handsome, and resourceful. He is also truly demoniac: the consummate rogue, confidence man, and iconoclast. Behind his flair and verve, however, lie a desperate nihilism and a compelling sense of futility which are occasionally expressed in self-destructive violence. This rootless Don Juan, this American abroad, sees himself as an undeserving outsider, denied access to the social status he desires (his favorite word is "dignity"). Thus, his infantile, frustrated search for unearned security finds its expression in a bawdy mockery of his every human contact and in fantasies of power and vengeance verging on the mythic.

Dangerfield is based on an actual person: Gainor Crist, an alcoholic bohemian from Dayton, Ohio, who was a contemporary of Donleavy at Trinity College. Some of the minor characters are based on native Dubliners of the same era, including playwright and author Brendan Behan.

Both Dangerfield and O'Keefe are versions of the Irish-American type, drawn into a love-hate relationship with both cultures. If Dangerfield is an alazon from classical comedy, O'Keefe derives from the comedy of humors, driven by two prevailing forces: the search for sex and a perverse attachment to Ireland. Marion is a stereotypical Englishwoman, with her lexicon of English and prejudices against the Irish and the lower orders.

The minor characters are stereotyped in the manner of Dangerfield's perception: the Trinity College Anglo-Saxon snobs, the servile shopkeepers who give them credit, the genteel Protestant old ladies, the materialistic parish priests, and the lonely women searching for love. The novel is more original in its portrayal of MacDoon, Clocklan, Mary, and Malarkey, all living outside Eamon, De Valera's pious, official Catholic Ireland. These denizens of Dublin's Catacombs form a counterculture which transforms the familiar ethos of the Irish pub into a mythical underworld of Celtic abandon.

Themes and Meanings

In the picaresque tradition, this novel projects an anarchic view of the world. Sebastian sees Ireland from the outside and shows no understanding of or sympathy for the values which give Irish life its meaning. His response to this nihilistic perception is withdrawal into cynical, uncompromising selfishness, and maniacal laughter and sadism. Yet the dash and imaginative frenzy of the protagonist and the sheer exuberance of the narrative style buoy up an essentially dismal view of the human condition.

Sebastian takes nothing seriously. He is a man of impulse, ready to seize on any immediate opportunity. Like him, the plot is made up of occasions for quick, cynical, superior laughs at the expense of the dull, earnest natives. The conclusion of the plot, with Dangerfield's undeserved inheritance, is similarly arbitrary. In a world without meaning, things can turn out for the best just as easily as the opposite.

Beneath all the high jinks, evasion, and good fortune, however, lie a number of dark-veined motifs: Dangerfield is constantly haunted by fears of madness and death. While he flails at the pious hopes of his Irish acquaintances with bawdy and blasphemous invocations, he is constantly pursued by feelings that he is himself sinking into a hopeless chaos. His only positive response comes in flashes of wit or verse, his poor attempt to emulate the aristocrat, whose position he feels is his rightful inheritance, one which would insulate him from the discomforts and obligations of ordinary life.

Critical Context

The Ginger Man is J. P. Donleavy's most admired work; his later novels appear less spontaneous, more mannered than this original success. Indeed, upon its appearance, the novel ran the gauntlet of angry censors, a situation which delayed its unexpurgated publication and led to lengthy litigation. Donleavy's dramatization of the novel in 1959 renewed the controversy over its blasphemy, so that it was banned in Ireland for some time.

The Ginger Man originally appeared during the "Angry Young Men" movement in British drama and fiction in the late 1950's. Indeed, it shares many elements with the works of writers such as Kingsley Amis and John Osborne, expressing through eloquence, invective, and violence the sense of disenfranchisement, rebellion, and misogyny that characterized such writers. Still, *The Ginger Man* is distinct from the works of those writers in its lack of political and social content and its deeper pessimism. In many ways—its stream-of-consciousness narrative, its use of locale, the precision and beauty of much of its language, its biting humor—*The Ginger Man* shows Donleavy to be a disciple of James Joyce.

Sources for Further Study

Alsop, Kenneth. *The Angry Decade: A Survey of the Cultural Revolt of the Nineteen-Fifties*, 1958.

Hassan, Ihab. *Radical Innocence: Studies in the Contemporary American Novel*, 1961.

Hicks, Granville. Review in *Saturday Review*. XLI (May 10, 1958), p. 10.

Malcolm, Donald. Review in *The New Yorker*. XXXIV (October 25, 1958), p. 194.

Masinton, Charles G. *J. P. Donleavy: The Style of His Sadness*, 1975.

Podhoretz, Norman. *Doings and Undoings*, 1964

Ryan, John. *Remembering How We Stood: Bohemian Dublin at the Mid-Century*, 1975.

Time. Review. LXXI (June 2, 1958), p. 88.

Cóilín Owens

THE GIRL GREEN AS ELDERFLOWER

Author: Randolph Stow (1935-   )
Type of plot: Symbolic realism
Time of plot: The early 1960's
Locale: Suffolk, England
First published: 1980

> *Principal characters:*
> CRISPIN CLARE, the protagonist, twenty-five years old, who
> has returned to his ancestral home after suffering an illness
> in the tropics
> ALICIA CLARE, his forty-three-year-old widowed cousin
> MARCO (MARK) CLARE, Alicia's nineteen-year-old son
> MIKEY CLARE, her six-year-old son
> LUCY CLARE, her ten-year-old daughter
> AMABEL, a spritelike seven-year-old friend of the Clare
> children who seems to be able to communicate with
> spirits
> JIM (JACQUES) MAUNOIR, a priest from North America
> MATTHEW PERRY, an old schoolfellow of Clare
> A FOREIGN-LOOKING GIRL, who in some ways corresponds to
> the imaginary "girl green as elderflower" of the title

The Novel

Crispin Clare awakens in an old house in Suffolk, the home of his ancestors, to which he has returned to recuperate from a serious but unspecified illness (the reader later learns that it was malaria, which eventually provoked attempted suicide). Looking out his bedroom window, he sees a world covered with snow, while on his wall hangs a painting, done by his widowed cousin Alicia Clare, showing the same view on a beautiful summer's day. Although it is winter and freezing in the cottage, it is also a morning suffused with "the new year's astonishing first white light," and although Clare is still ill, he ruminates in his half-waking state that "the doing" (of what, the reader is not told) "might even be the rebeginning of his health." Trying to recapture the fever-dream of the night before, he is forced fully awake by the ringing of the downstairs phone. It is Mikey and Lucy, Alicia's two younger children, inviting him over to see what their Ouija board has been "writing" for their friend Amabel.

Thus begins *The Girl Green as Elderflower*, a novel in which little happens in the way of external action, yet which takes its main character through a process of healing and renewal, as he comes to grips with his past and integrates it with the present. The novel is structured accordingly: The first two-thirds is titled "January"; the last third is broken into three brief sections titled "April," "May," and "June." The narrative proper (limited to Clare's point of view, somewhat depersonalized by being rendered in the third person) consists of outwardly unremarkable events—Clare's playing with the children, his accompanying Alicia's oldest son, Mark, to the pub, his renewed acquaintance with an old school chum—which nevertheless gain the force of drama in revealing deepening layers of the central character's (and, to some extent, other characters') inner life. This level of the narrative alternates with three discrete symbolic folktales, of Clare's own invention, whose characters correspond directly with their real-life counterparts (Clare usually gives them the same names). It is clear that Clare's writing is self-therapy, perhaps connected with "the doing" of the novel's opening paragraph. Stow thus allows the reader insight into his central character by allowing Clare's thoughts and feelings about his real world—past and present—to surface through the symbolism of his private folktales.

Shortly after the novel's opening scene, Clare arrives at the home of his cousins Clare, where he engages in the Ouija-board game with the young, inscrutable Amabel. They contact a twelfth century sprite named Malkin, who speaks to them at first in Latin and then specifically to Clare, in the tropical language of his recent past, Kulisapini. The spirit now identifies itself as Clare himself, and says, in Kulisapini, that Clare has already died. This revelation sends Clare into a sprawling faint, yet the children and nineteen-year-old Mark seem less astonished by the apparently supernatural event than they are concerned for Clare.

After recovering from his faint, Clare and Mark go to the local pub, almost colliding with a foreign-looking girl on her way out as they are entering. Mark's polite attempt to make contact is rebuffed by her silence as she continues on her way, and his hurt and angry reaction is the first of several responses by various characters to this elusive figure and/or her fictional counterparts.

In the pub, Mark asks the pubkeeper who she is, and he is directed to an American, "Jim" (Jacques Maunoir), with whom she entered. While Mark looks Jim over and rejects him as "too old to matter" (it is clear that Mark leans toward homosexuality, as do several other characters in the novel), excusing himself to play darts with the "gypsy-looking" Robin, Clare and Jim get acquainted over drinks. Initially reserved, they soon warm to each other, and Jim explains that he had found the girl walking in the snow and offered her a ride and a drink; she had said little and left soon. The reader is treated to another flash of insight into Clare as he suddenly recognizes the civilian-garbed man as a priest and believes that he is an official sent to check up on him. The insight is only partial; Jim is, indeed, a former priest who has rejected his calling in search of a new identity and place, but Clare's paranoia has caused his irrational fear—which Clare himself, recovering his composure, momentarily realizes. Presently, Clare and Mark leave the pub, taking their leave of each other in the snow at Clare's gate. Clare ends his evening reading from a Latin text about the twelfth century Malkin and then writing his own story about her.

Thus the first (untitled) subsection of "January" ends, followed by the subsection titled "Concerning a fantastic sprite (*De quodam fantastico spiritu*)," which is Clare's fairy tale explaining the phenomenon of Malkin. Except for a fairy-tale-like beginning ("In the time of King Richard. . ."), Clare's narrative is remarkably realistic, even anachronistically so, especially the children's dialogue; in fact, a major part of the action consists in Malkin's psychokinetic manipulation of a Monopoly game. The distinction between past and present is further erased and their connection underscored by the appearance of Jim-Jacques as a priest who interviews the mother who abandoned Malkin, imploring her to take the child back to her bosom and thus restore her from the power of the witches who transformed the infant into a sprite. In this and the other quasi folktales by Clare, the line between past and present, mundane and magical, is fuzzy indeed.

In the next subsection, the reader is returned to the real-life narrative, in which Clare receives an unexpected phone call from an old schoolfellow, Matthew Perry, who arranges to visit Clare on the following Saturday. Clare meets his old friend at the train station, and they renew their acquaintance on the three-mile hike from the station to Clare's house. Perry reveals that he has remained homosexual (it is implied that he was homosexual when he and Clare were friends during their youth), and when they stop to rest, Clare, attempting to find matches to light Perry's cigarette, discovers in his coat pocket a Tarot card, the Fool (le Mat, also known as the Wild Man), which Perry claims as his own. Clare relinquishes the card with little thought as to the significance of the incident. That night, as neither can sleep, Perry further reveals that he is a Jew and, despite his homosexuality, will probably, according to his father's wishes, marry a Jewish girl someday. He then asks Clare to tell him what happened. The reticent Clare eventually reveals the details of his illness and the psychological state which led to his attempted suicide, and he ends weeping on Perry's shoulder. On the next day, Perry departs, telling Clare that he, Clare, has done *him*, Perry, good.

The final subsection of "January," titled "Concerning a wild man caught in the sea (*De quodam homine silvestri in mare capto*)," is the second of Clare's fictions, this one concerning a merman (though in all parts a man) caught by King Henry the Second's fishermen and called the Wild Man. The story is clearly meant to correspond to Perry's visit in the preceding subsection, and like Clare's story of the sprite, it conflates past and present by injecting into the folktale a modern transistor radio. The tale relates how the innocent, loving, and noble merman forms a bond with one John (Clare's counterpart) but is abused by the king's men. The merman escapes to the sea, waving what appears to the humans to be an obscene gesture—even those who loved him are offended. When the merman returns eventually, even John spurns him. Yet when John, as punishment for being absent without leave, is flogged and is thrown into the dungeon (where the merman has been kept), the merman nurses him and finally carries him to his home in the sea. Clare closes this story with the merman's silent underwater howl on realizing that John has drowned.

The last third of this short novel begins with the six-page section "April," in which Clare receives two pieces of correspondence: One is a letter from Jim, now in Maine, in which he reveals that he, too, writes for therapy and that he is teaching. The other, with an Iranian stamp, is from Perry and contains the Hanged Man card; Perry's inscription on the back of the card reads, "*Your card = Resurrection.*" Later that day, Mark asks Clare to let him use his house as a meeting place for him and a girl. During the day, Clare is forced to hear the sexual exploits of Robin with, it so happens, the very girl whom Mark is finally unsuccessful in seducing—the foreign-looking girl of the opening section. Clare and Mark end the day by drowning their sorrows in whiskey.

In "May," Clare's story "Concerning a boy and a girl emerging from the earth" is told. The children of the title, named Michael and Amabel, are from another world and have skin and hair of varying green hues. The boy wastes away, despite the best efforts of his earthly discoverers to nurse him, uttering in his own language the words "Green home." The girl lives but is raped by a lascivious boy and becomes lascivious herself, seducing various men and telling each a different story of her origins. Only the priest refuses her, nevertheless asserting that he loves her as a child of God. Years later, when she is on her deathbed, no longer "green as elderflower" but now white and the widow of Matthew the pedlar, the priest prays for her: "For no man is lost, no man goes astray in God's garden; which is here, which is now, which is tomorrow, which is always, time and time again."

"June," the final section of the novel, consists of but four pages which include a letter to Clare from Perry containing a ribald personal anecdote and the news that Jim may reenter the priesthood. Clare reads the letter as he tends the bar at the local pub, then falls into a light sleep in which Alicia/Amabel (the girl green as elderflower) speaks to him in Kulisapini. As he is about to approach her, he is jarred awake—by Alicia herself. He pours a drink for them as he tells her that he has landed a teaching job, explains the twelfth century myth of Malkin, and chats with her about Jim. The novel ends with a toast as he notices "a few flecks of green" in her eyes.

The Characters

Crispin Clare, the central character, is in transition, moving from sickness to health, attempting to connect past and present, to integrate a fragmented and confused self into a whole, healthy human being. In many ways he is opaque: From the context of the real-life narrative, he himself says little to cast light on his own thoughts and evident traumas; indeed, for one who is recovering from serious mental illness, he seems, on the surface, strangely quiet, unassuming, "normal." It is only in brief moments of action—the faint during the Ouija-board game, the paranoia during the first meeting with Jim—that the reader suspects the troubled mind beneath the almost passive exterior, and it is only with Matthew Perry, in the middle of the night, that Clare can confront his painful past. That he is recovering by the novel's end is made evident not only by the fact that he has secured a teaching position but also in Stow's hints that past and present, imagination and reality, are beginning to merge into a unified whole.

Other characters in the novel face similar challenges to the self, but they function primarily as foils to, if not projections of, Clare. Clare's nineteen-year-old cousin, Mark, like Clare is entering a new phase of his life (adulthood) and is undefined sexually. Jim Maunoir, the priest who has lost faith in his calling, appears, near the novel's end, to be about to return to the priesthood—to have found himself. Matthew Perry, who arouses a negative response in Clare by revealing his homosexuality ("Oh Jesus. I thought you'd have grown out of that") and who surprises him by declaring that he is Jewish ("You! Ah, come off it, Matt"), is in many ways the integrated, self-accepting, nurturing self that Clare both seeks and denies. "Made lonely by strength," like Clare's Wild Man, Perry is a sort of positive life force, surfacing from Clare's past to sustain him in a dark hour. Also like Clare's Wild Man, Perry, as a Jew and a homosexual, risks persecution by society. The Clare children, Lucy and Mikey, not only serve to engage Clare in a family/communal life but also help to heal him by re-engaging him in the innocence of the past (Stow's interest in children emerges not only in his fiction for adults but also in the children's book *Midnite*, 1967).

The elusive "girl green as elderflower" is embodied in many characters, both in the real-life narrative and in Clare's fiction: Amabel, who, like Clare, is an outsider who observes others and is associated with the spiritual world; the foreign-looking girl, who says little but evokes the interest of Jim, Clare, Mark, Robin—with varying results; and in turn the "girl emerging from the earth," who grows into the lascivious, and love-starved, "girl green as elderflower," whose story of herself differs for each man who comes in contact with her. In a sense, the "girl green as elderflower," whatever her identity, seems to be the thing-sought-after that will bring unity and wholeness to the seeker. That Clare ultimately is able to see "a few flecks of green" in the eyes of Alicia, the widow with children—the survivor of loss who yet nurtures new life—suggests the final, hopeful, identity of his symbol with real life.

Themes and Meanings

The Girl Green as Elderflower is a novel about healing, the search for identity, rebirth, resurrection: Clare Crispin's, specifically, but also that of other characters: Jim Maunoir, Mark Clare, and Matthew Perry have all suffered loss or confusion of identity and all seek reintegration with and acceptance by themselves and others. In one sense, the "girl green as elderflower," another lost child seeking love, stands as a symbol for them as well as that which they seek.

Accordingly, primary motifs in the novel include the contrast between winter/white (death/dormancy) and summer/green (youth/renewal); between the past (Clare's especially, figured forth in his illness, characters such as Matthew Perry, the land of his ancestors, the ancient texts which form the springboard for his fictions) and the present; between youth/innocence and age/experience; between the magical and the mundane; between reality and the individual's imaginative reconstruction of reality.

That Clare, in his writing and ultimately in his real life, is beginning to reconcile these seeming opposites speaks to the essentially positive note on which the novel ends. That Clare's road back to health is buoyed by his relationships with others—Perry, Jim, Alicia, the children—speaks to Stow's belief in the healing powers of community.

Critical Context

The Girl Green as Elderflower represents a rebirth not only for Clare but also for Stow himself: Along with *Visitants* (1979), *The Girl Green as Elderflower* marked Stow's rebirth as a published writer, after a hiatus of a decade.

The novel, like much of Stow's fiction, leans heavily on symbolism (Stow is in the tradition of Patrick White in this regard), here to the point of allegory. It also reasserts themes that concerned Stow in earlier fiction: the individual's search for spiritual identity, for an integration of past and present experience in an effort to achieve wholeness. Such is the struggle of the old man Heriot in *To the Islands* (1958, revised 1982), of the boy Rob Coram in *The Merry-Go-Round by the Sea* (1965), and of Rob's cousin Rick Maplestead—who, like Clare, is fighting to heal himself after a traumatic experience (in Rick's case, the atrocities of World War II). The theme of man exiled from his spiritual self is expressed in *Visitants* as the confrontation between Western and native South Pacific cultures.

The Girl Green as Elderflower is thus a transitional work, one that reaffirms Stow's preoccupation with the dichotomies of experience and looks forward to their treatment in another novel set in Suffolk, *The Suburbs of Hell* (1984).

Sources for Further Study

Goodwin, Ken. *A History of Australian Literature*, 1986.

Hassall, Anthony J. *A Strange Country: A Study of Randolph Stow*, 1986.
Kramer, Leonie, ed. *The Oxford History of Australian Literature*, 1981.

Jane Schwabenland

A GIRL IN WINTER

Author: Philip Larkin (1922-1985)
Type of plot: Psychological realism
Time of plot: Sometime in the mid-1930's and early 1940's
Locale: A provincial town in England and a village in south Oxfordshire, England
First published: 1947

Principal characters:
 KATHERINE LIND, the protagonist, a foreign girl visiting and later living in England
 ROBIN FENNEL, her teenage English pen pal
 JANE FENNEL, his sister
 LANCELOT ANSTEY, the librarian at Katherine's place of work
 MISS GREEN, a junior library assistant

The Novel

A Girl in Winter is divided into three parts. The main action, in parts 1 and 3, takes place on a winter Saturday in the life of Katherine Lind, a twenty-two-year-old wartime refugee from an unnamed European country. The second part is a flashback to a three-week summer holiday which Katherine had taken in England six years previously.

Katherine, from whose point of view the story is told, has been in wartime England for nearly two years and has secured a routine job in a public library. The work is far below what her intelligence and education merit, and she is constantly irritated by her boss, the self-educated, boorish, and pompous Lancelot Anstey. One morning, as the novel opens, Katherine is eagerly awaiting a letter from her former pen pal, Robin Fennel. She has not seen him for six years, since the time, when they were both sixteen-year-old schoolchildren, that he had invited her to stay with his family in England. She is asked to accompany a junior employee, Miss Green, who is suffering from a toothache, to the dentist. On returning to her rooms later, she discovers the letter from Robin, who is now in the army, saying that he will be calling on her that very afternoon. Katherine is alarmed by this, however, and leaves the house without leaving any message for him.

The second and longest section of the novel flashes back to Katherine's first taste of England, when she had stayed at the Fennels' house in a village in Oxfordshire. Her visit was neither an outstanding success nor a great failure. Robin's parents were kind and solicitous, but as for Robin himself, she never managed to penetrate beyond his courteous, precocious, self-confident exterior. He did not seem to express much interest in her, beyond the demands of politeness, except for an impulsive and clumsy kiss bestowed on the eve of her departure. For a few days she had fallen in love with him and attempted to draw him out, but her feelings only made her miserable. She was puzzled by his attitude, but it turned out that it had not been Robin's idea to invite her, but that of his sister Jane, a rather aimless, sarcastic girl, nine years their senior, whom Katherine did not particularly like.

Part 3 returns to the present. Katherine recalls how she quickly lost touch with the Fennels following her visit and then dwells on her current loneliness, isolation, and pessimism regarding the future. She has developed a tendency to idealize the past. She calls on a Miss Veronica Parbury to return a handbag which she had picked up by mistake, and in conversation she discovers by chance that Miss Parbury has received a marriage proposal from Lancelot Anstey. Miss Parbury intends to turn down the proposal, however, because she is fully occupied in caring for her invalid mother. Returning to work, Katherine is rebuked by Anstey for lateness, but she gets her revenge by alluding to his affair with Veronica.

When Katherine returns home after work, she finds Robin on the doorstep, slightly drunk. They quickly catch up on the important events in each other's lives since they had last met, but they soon find that they have little to say to each other. To her, he seems like no more than a chance acquaintance, and she can do no more than extend an impersonal hospitality. When he asks her if he can stay the night, she refuses, but he persists and eventually she agrees, feeling indifferent to the proposition and agreeing only because she thinks it an "unimportant kindness" which would quickly be forgotten. The novel ends with them asleep in bed together, but there is no sense of closeness between them.

The Characters

The chief interest of the novel lies in the development of the two main characters, Katherine Lind and Robin Fennel, since with the exception of the superb sketch of the self-important, wordy, unpleasant Lancelot Anstey, Philip Larkin does not lavish much attention on his minor characters.

The distinguishing characteristic of Katherine is that she is alone. This is partly a result of her foreignness, of which she is continually aware. She is forced to do the odd jobs at the library that no one else wants, which only emphasizes "that she was foreign and had no proper status there." There is more than one hint that the English do not take kindly to foreigners in times of war.

The shock of her removal from her own country reinforces her isolation as she refuses to make friends. She resolves not to trust or to love, although in the past her happiness came from her relationships with other people. Now she believes that her strength must come solely from herself, but she cannot avoid the realization that her life has become like "a flat landscape, wry and rather small." She has temporarily managed to convince herself that her meeting with Robin will change all that.

The events of the day force her into a modification of her attitudes. When she accompanies the wretched Miss Green, she feels protective and generous, happy at once more having someone who depends on her. Her happiness is also, however, a result of the expectations she holds for her renewed contact with Robin. Later in the day, when she talks with Miss Parbury and learns of her relationship with Anstey and of her invalid mother, Katherine senses "the undertow of people's relations, two-thirds of which is without face, with only begging and lonely hands." She cannot forget Miss Parbury's selflessness in placing her mother's welfare above her own.

When she returns to work and finds a telegram from Robin saying that he is not coming, the vain hope she was entertaining, that her life could dramatically change for the better, is suddenly destroyed. Yet her eventful day has left its mark. She seems to realize that human beings do owe something to one another, merely by the fact of being fellow travelers. Although she now cares little for Robin, when he turns up unexpectedly she can think of no reason to deny him the pleasure which she has power to bestow. The fellow traveler has a right to her tenderness. She, at least, has found a serenity which he cannot touch, whatever happens. It is quite unlike her behavior as an adolescent, when she carelessly reached out to him with her emotions, or how only a few hours previously she had eagerly awaited his visit. The lovemaking between them is merely a transient act; it carries no obligations and will soon be forgotten.

Robin Fennel's growth is from certainty to uncertainty. Like that of Katherine, it involves a loss of comforting illusions. As a sixteen-year-old, there was an easy confidence in his judgments. Katherine noticed that he acted "as if he had long ago made up his mind about her," and she also observed that his movements were "always beautifully finished and calm." It seemed as if he had an "almost supernatural maturity [which] suggested that he drew on some spiritual calm." Not only did he have his career planned out in advance, but he also knew at what age he wanted to marry.

He is now an adult, however, and all this has changed. Physically restless and mentally on edge, Robin is in a state of "perpetual unease" and attempts to disguise his discomfort under a false and irritatingly jocular manner. When Katherine questions him about his career, he replies, "Everything's so uncertain." He has grown accustomed to making no plans for his activities further than a week ahead. The war, he complains, has "broken the sequence," yet he no longer cares much about the future. In refuting her reason for refusing to sleep with him—that it would be meaningless—he reveals a nihilism which would have been quite foreign to the sixteen-year-old: "I don't see that anything means very much. I spend all my time doing things that don't matter twopence. So do you."

Themes and Meanings

The main theme of the novel is that the human capacity for creating illusions must be overcome before there can be any true wisdom. It is better to see life clearly, even if the vision is dark, than to bathe in the rosy light of illusions: Katherine's realization toward the end of the novel that life "had shrunken slightly into the truth" is worth more than all of her previous false hopes.

The recurring motif of the journey, ironically employed, reinforces the theme. As Katherine gets on the bus early in the novel, she feels "a momentary flicker of pleasure, as if she were entering on a fresh stage of some more important journey." The motif is taken up later, when she reflects that the day has become so odd that "it was beginning to resemble an odyssey in a dream," and at the close of the novel, the strongest link she feels with Robin is "that they were journeying together." The meaning of the term, however, has changed. The journey is no longer seen to possess significance or even to be a journey at all in the conventional sense. It is only a series of disconnected and fortuitous events which two people might by chance share momentarily.

The other recurring motif, with strong metaphoric overtones, is that of the cold winter weather. The first chapter is devoted entirely to the winter setting: Villages are cut off, and many people are forced to remain in their rooms, shut off from one another. Significantly, what little light the morning brings seems to come from the snow itself. This setting is contrasted with the description of summer with which the first chapter of part 2 begins. Katherine arrives in England at the climax of a week of superb weather; it is as if the days "were progressing towards perfection." Yet the sunshine promises only to disappoint, since this episode is marked by a series of defeated expectations on the part of Katherine, particularly her belief that she can make real contact with Robin.

This pattern continues in the first chapter of part 3, which is also devoted entirely to the landscape. There is nothing romantic about it. The snow is dirty and makes the scene "dingy and dispirited." The dark and heavy atmosphere, not yet discharging itself in snow, suggests the buildup of tension, the pregnant weight inside the mind of the protagonist. Significantly, when Katherine and Robin have reached their rapprochement, the snow begins to fall once more, a reflection of their emotional release.

The link between mental states and the landscape is made explicit in the richly poetic, and ambiguous, prose of the final paragraph. As the lovers sleep, the falling snowflakes seem to gather in their minds into a "vast shape that might be a burial mound, or the cliff of an iceberg." Their dreams crowd into the shadow of this shape, "full of conceptions and stirrings of cold, as if icefloes were . . . going in orderly slow procession, moving from darkness further into darkness." Yet this does not bring sadness, but rather, inner peace.

The dream, at least, expresses the truth, and "against this knowledge, the heart, the will, and all that made for protest, could at last sleep."

Critical Context

Larkin wrote only two novels, *Jill* (1946) and *A Girl in Winter*. After these, he devoted all of his attention to poetry. *A Girl in Winter* has much in common with the earlier novel. Both deal with isolation and the building up and breaking down of illusions. Like Katherine Lind, John Kemp, the hero of *Jill*, is a stranger in the society in which he finds himself, the upper-class undergraduate world at Oxford which will not accept him. He also has to cope with radical discontinuity in his life, and he, too, indulges in a fantasy world, although to a far greater extent than does Katherine. When his illusions fail to stand up in the light of the real world, he reflects "how little anything matters. . . . See how appallingly little life is," phrases that are strikingly similar to the conclusions reached, respectively, by Robin and Katherine.

Larkin held a low opinion of his own novels, but critic John Bayley has described *A Girl in Winter* as "one of the finest and best sustained prose poems in the language," a view which is not difficult to justify. It is valuable, among other things, for its conciseness, its concern for detail, and its convincing exploration of the feelings of a woman of delicate sensibility. It also looks forward to many of the concerns expressed in Larkin's poetry: the need for honesty and for realistic self-knowledge, the difficulty of obtaining intimacy in relationships, the oppressive nature of time (in the novel Robin cannot stand the ticking of Katherine's watch), and the cheerlessness of life.

Sources for Further Study

Martin, Bruce. *Philip Larkin*, 1978.
Motion, Andrew. *Philip Larkin*, 1982.
Petch, Simon. *The Art of Philip Larkin*, 1981.
Timms, David. *Philip Larkin*, 1973.

Bryan Aubrey

GIRL, 20

Author: Kingsley Amis (1922-   )
Type of plot: Comic realism
Time of plot: The late 1960's
Locale: Greater London
First published: 1971

> *Principal characters:*
> DOUG YANDELL, the narrator and coprotagonist
> ROY VANDERVANE, the protagonist, a composer, conductor,
>   and eccentric
> KITTY VANDERVANE, his wife
> PENNY VANDERVANE, his daughter by a former marriage
> SYLVIA MEERS, Vandervane's teenage mistress
> VIVIENNE "VIVY" COPES, Yandell's mistress
> GILBERT ALEXANDER, Penny's West Indian lover
> HAROLD MEERS, Yandell's editor and Sylvia's father

The Novel

Music critic for a London newspaper, narrator Doug Yandell has just left the office of his priggish editor, Harold Meers, when he receives a call from Kitty Vandervane, the wife of his friend, Roy, a composer, conductor, and ne'er-do-well celebrity. Arriving at the Vandervane home, he learns from Kitty that Vandervane has taken still another mistress, this one even younger than his others. She urges Yandell to help Vandervane, to save him from the irreparable ruin that would ensue if her fifty-seven-year-old husband decided to run off with his latest mistake.

The "mistake" is Sylvia Meers, the Girl 20—though she is actually only seventeen—the daughter of Yandell's editor, Meers, a philistine who already despises Vandervane as he does all artists whom he does not appreciate or understand. As for Vandervane himself, he readily admits his infatuation with Sylvia. He unashamedly explains that he finds her youthful sexuality a healthful tonic, exciting, stimulating, renewing.

The narrator, too, is no stranger to purely sexual relationships. He shares Vivienne Copes, his mistress, with "another bloke" about whom Vivienne is tactfully reticent; Yandell is also in love with Vandervane's daughter, Penny, who has taken Gilbert Alexander, a black West Indian, as her lover.

With these relationships clearly defined, the story moves quickly. Vandervane convinces Yandell to help him, not in Kitty's meaning, but in supplying him with access to Yandell's apartment, where he and Sylvia can pursue their lovemaking. Additionally, Yandell finds himself lending a semblance of respectability to the affair by accompanying Penny on a double date with

Vandervane and Sylvia. After a madcap evening ("the night of the favour") at a pub and then at a wrestling match, the couples separate. Penny gives herself to Yandell, but only on condition that they never become intimate again or see each other except as acquaintances.

Over the next few weeks, the narrator becomes more involved with Vandervane's creative life as well, attending his conducting sessions and learning with some dismay that Vandervane has planned to lead a rock concert at which he will play one of his own compositions, *Elevations 9*, a sexual pun. Meanwhile, Sylvia's father, Harold Meers, has discovered the relationship between his daughter and Vandervane. Inviting Vandervane and Yandell to dinner, he gloats over his knowledge and threatens to publish an exposé which will ruin Vandervane's reputation. Vandervane is blasé, irritatingly cavalier, taunting the editor to follow through on his threat.

Yandell voices these concerns to Vivienne, but she, while sympathetic, brings him along on a visit to her father, who understands his daughter's sexual appetites and enjoys an evening of philosophical and cultural conversation with Yandell, this latest of "Vivy's" men.

The climax of the book is Vandervane's performance of *Elevations 9*. Despite Yandell's objections and the narrator's attempt to sabotage the concert by greasing Vandervane's bow, Vandervane is brilliant. In a hilarious scene, Vandervane plays his Stradivarius with passion and skill while the rock group, Pigs Out, accompanies him on the bongos. After the concert, as Vandervane and Yandell are leaving, a gang of toughs attacks them, breaking Vandervane's Stradivarius and knocking Yandell unconscious.

Recovering, Yandell pays a last visit to Vandervane and learns that Vandervane and Sylvia have indeed decided to run off, Meers's blackmail threat notwithstanding. Meers, in fact, has already fired Yandell for his part in the affair. In a final twist, Yandell also discovers that he has lost Vivienne; she has decided to run off with "the other bloke," who is revealed to be Gilbert Alexander, Penny's former lover.

When Yandell meets Penny in the final scene, he remarks how much happier she appears now that all relationships have been either severed or consummated. Penny responds that she has gone on to hard drugs and that, indeed, they are "all free now."

The Characters

On one level, Roy Vandervane seems nothing more than a melodramatic comic embodiment of the male in middle-age crisis. His taking a girl one-third his age without regard for reputation and decorum is a contemporary redaction of the great Romantic artist-cad who took what he wanted because the world had to pay that price for his art. As his name suggests, Roy Vandervane is a vain, regally uncaring man who pursues his own needs, indifferent to moral values or societal obligations.

Yet Vandervane's sexual wanderings, comic as they often are, reveal a desperation, a frenzy that comes close to tragedy. Sex for him, as he tells the narrator, is not simply a renewal of a jaded appetite, but a kind of freedom from the mediocre as well. Vandervane knows that he is growing old, knows that his relationship with Sylvia is scandalously obscene, but his own spirit of respectability, which forces him to use comic euphemisms such as "Christian gentleman" for vulgar expletives, seeks release from his wife, family, and second-rate artistic pretensions. What Roy realizes more cogently than anything else is that his art is as conventional as his life. His attentions to Youth are attempts to begin life afresh, to be recognized, even adulated.

As for Kitty, she is the true melodramatic heroine, the comic study of the injured wife. She shows what Yandell calls her "paraded bravery" when she implores the narrator to help Vandervane, and she attempts to maintain an aggrieved dignity when she confronts Sylvia, only to get herself entangled in an undignified brawl. Kitty is, in sum, respectably dull.

Respectability of sorts also characterizes the position of Doug Yandell, the narrator. His seeming stability as hack critic on a minor newspaper, and his reputation for being judicious and fair-minded, make Kitty's choice of him as ambassador to her husband apt yet ironic: Yandell's personal relationship with Vivienne is itself only tenuously respectable. He amorally accepts her being shared by another man and has no intention of marrying her; he is even fearful that she might one day expect marriage as the price of her fidelity. He lusts after Penny, secretly admiring her body each time they meet. Ironically, he can muster the proper chagrin at Vandervane's conduct yet is himself something of a moral coward, unable to make a commitment to a belief or to a spiritual value. He surprises Vivienne, for example, by his casual admission that he leads his life from day to day without much belief in immortality.

Penny Vandervane leads the same kind of life, a slow, daily drift toward the undefined. She is neither happy nor unhappy but exists in a humorless, loveless relationship with her West Indian boyfriend out of the simple human need for connection with someone or something. Her one-night affair with Yandell is not an affirmation of passion but a preemptive act to destroy the need for any deeper feelings. As she tells him: "Talking soft is not part of the contract." This trend leads to her ultimate lapse into mind-distorting drugs.

A mindless sexuality is all that characterizes Sylvia Meers. One of the most unattractive characters in all of Amis' fiction, Sylvia is representative of the grossest elements of the Youth movement of the 1960's and 1970's. Iconoclastic, insensitive, irresponsible, Sylvia—despite the Romantic evocations of her name—is the very antithesis of Romance, an ironic foil to Vandervane's attempt to escape the reality of growing old. Clearly anti-Establishment, she is, for all of her sexuality, a sort of neuter, committed only to the cause of uncommitment.

Finally, Vivienne Copes is the most appealing woman in the novel. Caring, sympathetic, and tactful, she has a sense of decency and morality, but her decision to take up with Penny's former lover shows that, like all the other characters, she, too, has lost her footing in the slippery world of unstable relationships.

Themes and Meanings

Girl, 20 is a comic indictment of contemporary society's spiritual bank-ruptcy, of a world not so much of immorality as of amoral unbelief. Center-ing on the witty insouciance of the narrator—who leers at his best friend's daughter while he tries to save this same best friend's reputation—the novel depicts contemporary life in roughly the same terms as a Restoration comedy of manners portraying the way of the world. The novel is, in fact, highly suggestive of that courtly form of drama in which men and women engage in witty verbal combat as a prelude to love, in which love is really only sex and in which sex is the final preoccupation of all that worldly wit and wisdom.

As in Restoration comedy, sex in *Girl, 20* is the controlling fact of life, the matrix of human behavior. Yet the comedy is also too deep for laughter. Sex, the ultimate act in a healthy relationship, is for the characters in this novel a purely physical experience, not an ultimate act but a final one. It is an act that does not consummate love but signals desperation—a frenzied escape from age, from mediocrity, from responsibility, from commitment. "We're all free now," says Penny in the last line of the book. Yet that freedom is not a liberty of spirit, but an estrangement, a disconnection, a dissolution of all meaningful relationships.

Critical Context

Like his first novel, *Lucky Jim* (1954), Kingsley Amis' ninth, *Girl, 20*, draws on contemporary manners, pointing out their comic shallowness and the grim pathos of their implications. *Lucky Jim* pilloried the educational establishment, showing the hypocrisy, the priggishness, the ultimately dehu-manizing aspects lurking behind a façade of respectability and staid cultural norms.

Girl, 20's ambience is the superficial world of pop culture, of boutiques, discos, rock groups and lowbrow entertainment. Unlike earlier novels, how-ever, *Girl, 20* is more cynical, less affirmative in tone. Amis' playfully poetic language is richly descriptive, often breezily colloquial, as in his earlier work, but the humor of *Girl, 20* is bleaker, the laughter drawn not so much from a sense of fun or even outrage as from a sardonic view of life, a pessimism about the human condition. The book is evidence of the growing seriousness in Amis' work, a sense of bitterness unrelieved by energetic horseplay or wholesome comedy.

Sources for Further Study

Caplan, Ralph. "Kingsley Amis," in *Contemporary British Novelists*, 1965. Edited by Charles Shapiro.

Cooper, Arthur. Review in *Newsweek*. LXXIX (March 6, 1972), p. 77.

Gardner, Philip. *Kingsley Amis*, 1981.

The New Yorker. Review. XLVII (February 5, 1972), p. 102.

Rabinovitz, Rubin. *The Reaction Against Experiment in the English Novel, 1950-1960*, 1967.

Sheppard, R. Z. Review in *Time*. XCIX (February 7, 1972), p. 88.

Edward Fiorelli

A GLASS OF BLESSINGS

Author: Barbara Pym (1913-1980)
Type of plot: Comic realism
Time of plot: The mid-1950's
Locale: London and its environs
First published: 1958

Principal characters:

WILMET FORSYTH, the protagonist and narrator, a beautiful
and aimless woman in her thirties

RODNEY FORSYTH, her husband, a civil servant

SIBYL FORSYTH, Rodney's mother, a prosperous widow

ARNOLD ROOT, a professor, Sibyl's regular companion

MARY BEAMISH, an unmarried contemporary of Wilmet

MARIUS RANSOME, a handsome clergyman

ROWENA TALBOTT, Wilmet's best friend

HARRY TALBOTT, Rowena's husband, a thriving businessman

PIERS LONGRIDGE, Rowena's ne'er-do-well brother

The Novel

A Glass of Blessings begins and ends in one place, at the Anglo-Catholic church of St. Luke in the select West London neighborhood called Holland Park. As the novel opens on the feast day of St. Luke, Wilmet Forsyth notices her old acquaintance Piers Longridge at the church she has recently started attending. The story ends approximately a year later. Wilmet, now firmly established in the "charmed circle" of regular members, comes back with her fellow parishioners from seeing Father Marius Ransome instated as a suburban vicar and turns her thoughts and steps toward her husband, Rodney, in their new flat.

The time between these two events is a period of change and growth for Wilmet. As she is first seen, Wilmet is a privileged but idle woman. Beautiful, elegant, and perceptive, she is married to a good and successful man some years her senior. They have no children and live stylishly with his widowed mother. Apart from her war years in Italy, where she met Rodney, Wilmet has never done anything, largely because she has never needed to do anything. Now, after years of comfort, she has grown restive. Feeling the need to exert herself, Wilmet half deliberately and half accidentally enters into new experiences.

First is her growing involvement with the Church, that arena of choice for so many Pym heroines. Initially reserved, Wilmet gradually makes the acquaintance of the parishioners and their three clergymen: the epicurean rector amusingly named Father Thames, the more priestly if less courtly Father Bode, and Father Marius Ransome, a handsome newcomer in whom Wilmet takes a romantic interest which she vaguely sees as altruistic.

Besides taking Wilmet beyond the sphere of her household (both Rodney and Sibyl are agnostics), this connection with St. Luke's strengthens her ties with a long-standing acquaintance, Mary Beamish. Miss Beamish, earnest, dowdy, unselfishly devoted to good works, and shackled to a demanding elderly mother, is both a foil and a reproach to Wilmet, who largely because of this contrast holds her in mild dislike. Yet church events, the quartering of Marius Ransome in the Beamishes' flat, and old Mrs. Beamish's death, draw the two women together. Wilmet becomes something of a confidante to Mary. She chooses a dress for her unsophisticated friend and sympathizes as Mary, rich and bereaved, seeks a new focus for her unselfish energy—first as a novice in a convent, then as housekeeper in a retreat house, finally as wife and chief parish helper to Marius Ransome. The reader sees this match coming from far off (the Christian names and the verb "marry" absurdly underline the outcome), but Wilmet, self-deluded, seriously misreads the evidence, just as she fails for a long time to understand how deep and rewarding her friendship with Mary has become.

Wilmet is equally inaccurate in understanding the depth of her relationship to Rowena Talbott, her husband, Harry, and her brother Piers. Rowena may be Wilmet's "best friend," but their intercourse appears to be superficial. What truly interests Wilmet for much of the story is the admiration offered by Harry, "love" she will not accept but cannot bring herself to discourage. Yet more romantic potential seems to inhere in Wilmet's growing, if episodic, friendship with Piers, a night-school instructor in Portuguese and an editorial proofreader. Occasional strolls, lunches, and phone calls encourage Wilmet, who does not have the luxury of worrying over reliable Rodney, to fret about Piers's disorderly life: his drunkenness, his moodiness, and his unprofessional behavior. Wilmet fancies "improving" Piers and cherishes the illusion that she has indeed reformed him, until an invitation to tea at his flat discloses the truth, that a different love, a handsome if "common" young man called Keith, has made the difference in Piers's life.

When Marius, Harry, and Piers are no longer romantic possibilities, Wilmet is thrown back on her old life with Rodney—but with a difference. Yet another marriage takes place. Sibyl and Professor Root join hands. Again the reader sees the event coming through a sequence of clues that Wilmet ignores. Once Sibyl marries, Wilmet and Rodney must leave their comfortable groove. Literally, they must find new lodgings; emotionally, they must learn to rely on each other's companionship, for throughout the novel both have seemed, if in different ways, closer to Sibyl than to each other.

The Characters

A Glass of Blessings is, along with *Excellent Women* (1952), the only first-person narrative among the novels Barbara Pym published during her lifetime. Like the earlier book, it focuses on the one character rather than on a group or community, though to be sure a wide range of characters is seen and judged through Wilmet's eyes.

If *A Glass of Blessings* departs from Pym's prevailing narrative convention, so Wilmet Forsyth is unusual among Pym heroines. First, she is a married woman, though marriage for Wilmet is a comfortable confinement, an arrangement that permits her worst qualities, idleness and self-indulgence, to flourish. Wilmet is similarly handicapped by two other positive gifts of fortune, beauty and taste, that Pym seldom grants in abundance to her heroines. In Pym's novels, such women as Wilmet, Leonora Eyre in *The Sweet Dove Died* (1978), and Prudence Bates of *Jane and Prudence* (1953) consider their beauty sufficient in and of itself to gain for them the romantic regard of men. Miss Bates makes an incidental appearance in *A Glass of Blessings* as the passively attractive "other woman" whom Rodney takes to dinner, if not to bed. Wilmet, in much the same manner, considers the admiration of men nothing less than her due. The novel's sequence of events teaches her two important points: that men can love less lovely women (or, in Piers's case, other men) and that feminine friendship and the solid affinities of marriage are more important to her life than is the romance she wants to receive from Piers, Harry, and Marius.

Though Wilmet is a clearly imperfect character, readers are not inclined to dismiss or dislike her, for she is a touching mixture of self-knowledge and self-deception, a sometimes shrewd and sometimes blind student of human behavior, and a highly imaginative observer of life's small and great spectacles. Deft at seeing what people are like, Wilmet is less successful at understanding how they feel about one another. The discerning reader therefore accepts much of what Wilmet has to say about traits of character but resists some of the conclusions she draws about those qualities.

The characters surrounding Wilmet are at once schematic and credible. Pym succeeds in giving even the most minor bit players, such as Miss Limpsett, the contentious proofreader of Greek at the publishing house where Piers works, at least a suggestion of roundness. Yet all the lesser characters exist to be compared and contrasted with Wilmet and with one another. For example, of the three chief men in this phase of Wilmet's life, Rodney, Harry, and Piers, Rodney and Harry resemble each other in being successful and independent bourgeois men, stouter and less dashing than when Wilmet first encountered them in Italy. Yet while Harry pays Wilmet the court she demands, though it is homage of a heavy-handed and ultimately unacceptable sort, Rodney takes her for granted, as she does him. Piers, only a few years junior to Rodney and Harry, has remained more boyish in looks, in worldly situation, and in attitude. He attracts Wilmet because, like Harry, he admires her (in a purely aesthetic way, it turns out) and because, unlike Rodney, he "needs" her (or so she thinks until she discovers the true nature of his needs). Wilmet's three principal female friends also balance one another. Rowena, beautiful like Wilmet, is unlike her in being fully and busily involved in domestic life: house, husband, children, community. Mary, though dowdy, self-denying, and "splendid" in the way of good works, shares Wilmet's religious interests—and her tastes in poetry, a sign of true affinity in the Pym world. Sibyl may be a bluff and unadorned old woman, a freethinker, do-gooder, and intellectual, but she nevertheless believes much as Wilmet does on many matters, her empathy being most clearly revealed in the fond but patronizing way that both women treat Rodney.

Themes and Meanings

The key to *A Glass of Blessings* is found in the words of the title, a phrase from George Herbert's poem "The Pulley," quoted and applied to Wilmet's life by Mary and Marius toward the end of the novel. Beautiful Wilmet, throughout most of the story, has been living her life in the spirit of a romantic heroine, as if she were a young single girl looking for love and the one relationship that would crown and validate her existence. Yet Wilmet is already married and no longer in her first youth. Her year of sometimes agreeable and sometimes botched relations with Piers, Harry, and, to a lesser extent, Marius Ransome finally shows Wilmet how much she has to value in Rodney, a man who notices what she notices, likes what she likes, and lives as she lives. Wilmet also sees that the male regard she has wanted all for herself belongs to others as well, to the beautiful (Rowena and Keith) and the less beautiful (Mary and Sibyl).

The love of men is not life's only crown, though; Wilmet's glass contains more blessings than simply that. Besides marriage, there are ordinary friendships with women and, indeed, with men, as Wilmet's cameo appearance with Piers and Keith in Pym's next novel, *No Fond Return of Love* (1961), makes clear. There is the life of the Church, with its festivals and duties. There are the other gifts Wilmet has enjoyed all along but never properly valued: a comfortable home, good clothes, money, a lively mind. These blessings, by no means the exclusive property of the young and lovely, are the redemption, not to say the transformation, of mundane life for the person wise enough to cherish them.

Critical Context

The novels Pym published through the 1950's up until the start of the 1960's achieved sound if unspectacular critical, popular, and financial success. In the 1960's and 1970's, they fell into neglect until mention by Lord David Cecil and Philip Larkin in *The Times Literary Supplement*'s list of "most under-rated writers of the century" brought about a Pym revival to which the author herself contributed by returning to fiction-writing after years of silence.

The critical fortunes of *A Glass of Blessings* have risen along with those of Pym's work as a whole. As noted above, it was exceptional for Pym to employ first-person narration (indeed, early drafts of *A Glass of Blessings* were written in the third-person). Critical discussion of the novel has focused on the narrator and central character, Wilmet Forsyth; Robert Emmet Long, for example, who regards *A Glass of Blessings* as "the most psychologically elegant of Pym's novels," describes Wilmet as "the most stylish of her heroines."

Sources for Further Study
Benet, Diana. *Something to Love: Barbara Pym's Novels*, 1986.
Long, Robert Emmet. *Barbara Pym*, 1986.
Nardin, Jane. *Barbara Pym*, 1985.
Pym, Barbara. *A Very Private Eye: An Autobiography in Diaries and Letters*, 1984.

Peter W. Graham

THE GO-BETWEEN

Author: L. P. Hartley (1895-1972)
Type of plot: Romance
Time of plot: 1900, with framing chapters that take place in 1951 or 1952
Locale: Chiefly at Brandham Hall in Norfolk, England
First published: 1953

Principal characters:

LEO COLSTON, the protagonist and first-person narrator, a
schoolboy visiting a friend at Brandham Hall in 1900
MARCUS MAUDSLEY, Leo's friend at Southdown Hill School
MARIAN MAUDSLEY, Marcus' older sister, eventually Lady
Trimingham
HUGH, VISCOUNT TRIMINGHAM, the impoverished owner of
Brandham Hall, eventually Marian's husband
TED BURGESS, Marian's lover, a farmer on the Brandham Hall
estate
EDWARD, the eleventh Viscount Trimingham, in fact the
grandson of Marian Maudsley and Ted Burgess

The Novel

The narrative structure of L. P. Hartley's *The Go-Between* develops out of
the discovery by Leo Colston, the novel's protagonist and first-person narrator, of a diary he kept while visiting his schoolmate Marcus Maudsley at
Brandham Hall in 1900. The diary, come upon in 1951 or 1952 in a box of
mementos preserved by his late mother, prompts Leo to recall his life at
Southdown Hill School prior to his visit to the Maudsleys in July and August.
The prologue to the novel details these memories; the epilogue shows Leo
returning to Norfolk to fill in gaps in his memory of the nineteen days he
spent at Brandham Hall and to determine the degree of his personal responsibility for the catastrophe which occurred there on his thirteenth birthday.

Leo's diary for 1900 is the key to the action of *The Go-Between*. Encouraged by his use of magic to defeat the school bullies Jenkins and Strode, Leo
arrives in Norfolk half convinced of his ability to bend events to his will. He
also arrives with a personal cosmography, derived from the figures of the
zodiac printed inside the cover of his diary, to which the adults at Brandham
Hall appear to conform. Identifying Marcus Maudsley's older sister Marian
as the Virgo figure in the zodiac, Leo allegorizes the conflict between Marian's fiancé, Hugh, Viscount Trimingham, and her lover, Ted Burgess, as a
struggle between Sagittarius and Aquarius.

Dubbed Mercury by the adults who use him as messenger, Leo is ambivalent about both men. Trimingham, the aristocratic but impoverished owner of Brandham Hall, is a heroic figure, scarred during military service in South Africa. Burgess, a tenant farmer on the Viscount's estate, is the father figure Leo has lacked since the death of his own father in 1899, showing him how to fire a rifle and binding his knee after he cuts it while sliding down the farmer's strawstack. Leo is attracted to both men, and he is unsure as to which he would prefer to win Marian Maudsley. His dilemma is complicated by the fact that at age twelve going on thirteen, he himself feels a half romantic, half sexual attraction to her.

Aware that Marian and Burgess are using him to arrange meetings, Leo senses that his duties as go-between are morally suspect. His uneasiness comes to a head when Marcus Maudsley tells him that Marian's engagement to Lord Trimingham is about to be announced. Leo thinks that his efforts have betrayed the Viscount, and he resorts to magic to separate Marian and her lover. The spell Leo plans involves uprooting a gigantic *Atropa belladonna*, a deadly nightshade, but while wrestling with the plant to secure leaf, berry, and root for use in his spell, Leo is knocked to the ground and symbolically defeated. This struggle with the "beautiful lady" sets in motion the train of events which climax on the afternoon of his thirteenth birthday, with Leo's discovery of Marian and Ted "together on the ground, the Virgin and the Water-carrier, two bodies moving like one."

Ted Burgess shoots himself; Mrs. Maudsley, Marian's mother, has a mental breakdown. Leo himself suffers an emotional collapse and, but for discovery of his diary for 1900, would have continued to repress the experience. Having relived the events of his nineteen days at Brandham Hall through the pages of his diary, Leo returns to Norfolk to piece together his recollections. In the village church, he finds memorial tablets for the ninth Viscount Trimingham, who had died in 1910, and for a son born in February, 1901, and killed in battle in France in 1944. Outside the church, Leo meets a young man who reminds him of Ted Burgess; Edward is the eleventh Viscount, and his appearance accounts for the parentage and birth of the tenth Lord Trimingham.

Edward explains that his grandmother Marian is alive, and Leo visits her, reluctantly accepting her request that he act to reconcile her grandson to the facts of the past and to assure Edward that he does not live under the spell of a curse. "Tell him," she says to Leo, "that there's no spell or curse but an unloving heart. You know that, don't you?"

The Characters

Leo Colston is Hartley's most fully rendered protagonist. He is also the only one to tell his story in the first person. Presenting his story from the dual perspectives of 1900 and 1952, the elder Leo comments reflectively on the experiences narrated directly by his thirteen-year-old self. In Leo's character, Hartley treats the problem of moral responsibility, the central concern of his fiction. He also deals with the topic of the past's effect on the present. When Leo was thirteen in 1900, his ignorance of the facts of life, not merely those about human sexuality, made him unfit for moral insight. The elder Leo's Proustian effort to recapture past time enables him to perceive moral significance. In token of his capacity to judge and to act, Leo is able to visualize the façade of Brandham Hall for the first time in more than fifty years.

He is also able to see that Marian, Ted, and Lord Trimingham were neither demigods nor callous manipulators of his childhood self. He recognizes that all three were genuinely fond of the boy he once was. They did not seek to hurt him. Leo faces the fact that he conspired in his own deception, by viewing events through the romantic screen of a personal allegory. Hartley's treatment of these characters stresses both the subjectivity of young Leo and the potential in the three adults for the heroic attributes he assigns them. The tragedy of the love triangle derives from the fact that they fail to rise to the roles assigned them in Leo's personal drama.

The pivotal relationship is that of Leo and Marian Maudsley. She prompts him to enter the world of his imagination by buying him a green summer suit and playing a flirtatious Maid Marian to his Robin Hood. The bicycle she purchases as his birthday gift is also green. Hartley's description of the grounds surrounding Brandham Hall stresses their lush vegetation. Yet Leo fails to recognize the potential for evil embodied in the *Atropa belladonna* in a ruined outbuilding. The plant, looking like a woman standing in a doorway, recalls the sexual temptation of young Robin in Nathaniel Hawthorne's "My Kinsman, Major Molineux." Like so many of the male protagonists in Hawthorne's stories, Hartley's Leo is an innocent who walks through a moral wilderness in which the forces of good and evil struggle for his soul. In its association with Marian Maudsley, the belladonna represents sexual initiation, the attraction of lust, and the corruption of innocent love.

Yet the equation is more complex than that. In his relationships with Viscount Trimingham and Ted Burgess, Leo faces a choice between models of male behavior. Frightened by his own sexual feelings, he rejects Ted and both the passion and the love the farmer feels for Marian. He affirms the sterile code of the gentleman embodied by the scarred, perhaps symbolically impotent, Viscount.

Themes and Meanings

Hartley's romance, like those by Hawthorne, has a level of moral significance. When Leo pauses at the church near Brandham Hall, having visited the Trimingham family graves, he prays for all involved in the drama enacted in 1900, including himself. In effect, he forgives their unthinking treatment of him and accepts responsibility of his unwitting betrayal of them. As Marian tells Leo at the end of *The Go-Between*, there is no curse except an unloving heart. The tragedy of Leo's adult life, rectified by his acceptance of Marian's request that he talk to her grandson, Edward, is that he did not know that the highest expression of love is self-sacrifice.

In *The Go-Between*, Hartley explores the spiritual emptiness of England during the first half of the twentieth century. His treatment of Leo rejects the nihilism of so much twentieth century fiction and suggests that spiritual rebirth can be found within the framework of institutional Christianity. Like his books *The Hireling* (1957) and *Facial Justice* (1960), this novel demonstrates Hartley's repeated emphasis on the transcendent values. The motifs suggesting the Christian framework are not imposed upon Leo by the narrative; he interprets them for himself. As a result, his account of spiritual regeneration is convincing as a personal experience and persuasive as a metaphor for a process in which Hartley would like to believe.

Critical Context

Perhaps Hartley's best novel, *The Go-Between* was awarded the Heinemann Foundation Prize in 1953. A film version by Joseph Losey, from a script written by Harold Pinter, won the Grand Prize at the Cannes Film Festival in 1971. The novel argues for the existence of a spiritual dimension to life and for a moral imperative, in the tradition of E. M. Forster, to connect oneself with its will.

The moral, even political, conservatism of Hartley's position, expressed most clearly in the essays collected under the title *The Novelist's Responsibility: Lectures and Essays* (1967), has its most aesthetically convincing representation in *The Go-Between*. By placing control of the story in the hands of Leo Colston, Hartley eliminates the intrusive narrational commentary characteristic of some of his other novels. Here he manages, through a narrator-protagonist who is nearly simultaneously an adolescent boy and an elderly man, both to dramatize the conflict between good and evil, which is his recurring subject, and to set it within a convincing social context.

The nineteen days Leo spends at Brandham Hall in 1900 represent a major change in the class structure of England. Ironically, the aristocratic Viscount Trimingham, the traditional military leader, is forced to turn to the middle-class Maudsleys for the capital and the wife he needs to maintain his status, in the bargain accepting as his own son the child of a farmer.

Sources for Further Study

Atkins, John. *Six Novelists Look at Society*, 1977.
Bien, Peter. *L. P. Hartley*, 1963.
Bloomfield, Paul. *L. P. Hartley*, 1970.
Hall, James. *The Tragic Comedians: Seven Modern British Novelists*, 1963.
Jones, Edward T. *L. P. Hartley*, 1978.

Mulkeen, Anne. *Wild Thyme, Winter Lightning: The Symbolic Novels of L. P. Hartley*, 1974.

Webster, Harvey Curtis. *After the Trauma: Representative British Novelists Since 1920*, 1970.

                                                                Robert C. Petersen

GOD ON THE ROCKS

Author: Jane Gardam (1928-   )
Type of plot: Psychological realism
Time of plot: The 1930's and after World War II
Locale: Northeast England
First published: 1979

> *Principal characters:*
> MARGARET MARSH, the eight-year-old protagonist
> ELINOR MARSH, her mother
> KENNETH MARSH, Margaret's pious father
> TERENCE MARSH, her baby brother
> CHARLES FRAYLING, a bachelor who once hoped to marry
>   Elinor
> BINKIE FRAYLING, his spinster sister
> ROSALIE FRAYLING, the invalid mother of Charles and Binkie

The Novel

The action of *God on the Rocks* involves a small number of characters, who at the beginning of the story are leading quiet lives, seemingly no longer emotionally involved with one another. Elinor Marsh, who was once engaged to Charles Frayling, lives the restricted life of the Primal Saints, devoted to her strict husband Kenneth Marsh, who disapproves of her previous association with the wealthy Frayling family. Charles and Binkie Frayling live their separate lives in Dene Close; Charles is a retiring, sexless English teacher, Binkie a housekeeping spinster who pays occasional duty calls to the mother whom they both hate. Rosalie Frayling, too, is isolated at the beginning of the story, confined to her bed at the old Frayling home, which she has turned over to mental patients as a gesture of spite toward her disappointing children.

Directly or indirectly, it is Margaret Marsh, the eight-year-old protagonist, who brings together the lives of these characters. Because Margaret feels neglected after the birth of her brother, Terence Marsh, she is taken to Eastkirk, where she wanders off to the old Frayling estate and eventually meets Rosalie. On another expedition made for Margaret's sake, Elinor resumes her relationship with Charles and Binkie and therefore breaks out of the narrow world of the Primal Saints. At the end of the book, it is Margaret's disappearance which sends her father out in a storm to rescue her, a mission which costs him his life.

While the adults around her are roused to action by their encounters with one another, Margaret herself is discovering the world, observing the approaching death of Rosalie, watching the casual mating of the maid and a stranger, catching the suppressed feeling between her mother and Charles, analyzing such different characters as the mad artist, Edwin Drinkwater, and Binkie, who is far less sure of herself than she appears.

As the novel progresses, Margaret sees the old patterns break up. Elinor gravitates toward Charles, and Kenneth is overcome by lust for the blowsy maid. At the climax of the novel, after catching Kenneth and the maid together, Elinor runs to Charles and sweeps him into bed, Margaret disappears, and Kenneth is drowned. In an epilogue, placed when Margaret is twenty, the reader learns that Charles has moved to Australia, Elinor has married the Anglo-Catholic priest, and Binkie remains alone, still concealing some of the secrets to which she is party. Only Margaret, though taller, and the maid, though older, remain essentially unchanged.

The Characters

Jane Gardam's perceptive young girl protagonists are generally the brightest and the strongest characters in her novels. To this rule, Margaret is no exception. In a world where the adult characters drift on the currents of circumstance and passion, Margaret observes, pursues her own interests, and preserves her own independence. Whether she is climbing a tall tree, exploring a private estate, or crawling up a cliff to save herself from drowning, Margaret has control over her emotions and her destiny.

Although Margaret's mother must define her own life by adopting her husband's causes, she admires her daughter's strength. Recognizing the fact that the adults in the book all attempt to enlist Margaret's loyalty and to blur her judgment, Elinor notes, "She has a better brain than all of them. . . . She sees straight and clear. She's strong as a lion. . . . She's the child his mother should have had, poor feeble Charles."

Although she loves Charles, Elinor realizes that he is weak. Despite his own love for Elinor, Charles could not resist his mother's threats and broke off the engagement, hoping for an inheritance which his mother later refused. As Margaret sees, Binkie, too, is weak, fearful of illness, consumed by hatred for her mother, wasting her Cambridge education. Charles himself views Elinor as shy and self-conscious, a hometown girlfriend who was easy to forget when he was at Cambridge, now a dowdy matron. Only when Elinor makes her hysterical descent upon Charles does he see her as a different person, one with force and confidence, one who is something of a threat to the sexless schoolmaster.

Realizing that she has driven away her own children, Rosalie blames her bossiness on the permissiveness of her own mother, who allowed young Rosalie to marry a man whom she did not love. If Rosalie had been as strong as Margaret, however, she would not later have let the mysterious wounded captain depart from her life. When her emotional survival was at stake, she did not climb the cliff to safety.

The weakness of the adults around Margaret is typified by Kenneth. Despite his pious pronouncements and his assumption of the role as family priest and lawgiver, the little bank manager not only attempts to seduce the maid whom he has been converting but also goes so far as to justify himself while he does so. His heroic death cannot make up for his consistent hypocrisy, but at least it leaves his children an inheritance of pride.

Themes and Meanings

When Kenneth Marsh's lifeboat ends up on the rocks, the metaphor applies not only to the preacher who could not control his emotions enough either to resist temptation or to think out a rescue plan but also to all the characters in the novel who find themselves on the rocks because they lack the wisdom and the practicality of Margaret Marsh.

If one does not understand one's own motivations and those of others, one will be at the mercy of chance. Thinking back on her own relationship with Charles, Elinor recalls a few patronizing words from his mother which caused her to go to Cambridge for a visit, an impulse which drew her toward Kenneth, like her an outsider in that rarefied society, and another impulse which caused her to accept Charles's proposal, "looking astonished at herself." For Charles, marriage to Elinor had seemed the easiest way to escape his mother, but like Elinor, Charles was drifting, ignorant of his own weakness, ignorant even of the fact that he did not really love Elinor.

The weakness which is evident in most of the adult characters in *God on the Rocks*, then, derives from a lack of discipline. They may have studied the Bible, like Kenneth, or mastered the subtleties of language, like Charles, but they have not observed themselves and others in order to become wise, and they do not think before they act. Clearly, their weakness is not a mere fact of human nature, for Margaret sees and reasons, and Margaret survives, emotionally, intellectually, and physically. Although the fecklessness of her characters accounts for much of their charm, although their impulsiveness results in delightful comic scenes, it is clear that Gardam's sensible and wise young Margaret is the standard by which other human beings should be measured.

Critical Context

Although Gardam's books are often cataloged as publications for children or young adults, they have attracted many adult readers, who see in their wit, their psychological perception, their subtle symbolism, and their frenzied comic explosions the proof of a considerable writing talent. In many of Gardam's works, such as *Crusoe's Daughter* (1985) and *The Summer After the Funeral* (1973), the heroines compare themselves to fictional characters, with the result that the sophisticated reader has an even richer field of associations and parallels suggested by the novels. In *God on the Rocks*, Gardam has substituted for the literary allusions a complex system of religious symbols, from the garden and the serpent to the rocks of the title and the ineffectual lifeboat of Kenneth Marsh. While young adults are attracted to Gardam's heroines, who are so much brighter than the dim-witted adults with whom they must live, the increasing popularity of her books among adult readers is clearly a result of the depth of meaning below the seemingly simple surface.

Sources for Further Study
Duffy, Sister Gregory. Review in *Best Sellers*. XXXIX (November, 1979), p. 277.
Kirkus Reviews. Review. XLVII (August 1, 1979), p. 873.
Listener. Review. C (October 19, 1978), p. 518.
New Statesman. Review. XCVI (October 13, 1978), p. 479.
Observer. Review. October 8, 1978, p. 30.
The Times Literary Supplement. Review. October 13, 1978, p. 1141.

Rosemary M. Canfield-Reisman

THE GOLDEN NOTEBOOK

Author: Doris Lessing (1919-   )
Type of plot: Realism
Time of plot: The early 1940's, 1950-1956, and the summer of 1957
Locale: London and South Central Africa
First published: 1962

Principal characters:
ANNA FREEMAN WULF, the protagonist, a writer
MOLLY JACOBS, an actress, Anna's best friend
TOMMY JACOBS, Molly's only son
ELLA, a fictional character whom Anna creates
SAUL GREEN, an American, one of Anna's lovers

The Novel

A woman writer struggling toward living an authentic life in the modern world is the focus of action for this complex novel. As the novel opens, Anna Freeman Wulf has written a commercially successful novel based on her experiences as a young woman during World War II in South Central Africa, in a country called Southern Rhodesia. Now living in London on the royalties from this novel, Anna cares for her thirteen-year-old daughter, Janet. In her role as mother, Anna finds emotional stability and meaning; some of the best scenes in the book involve Anna and her daughter. Meanwhile, Anna writes continually in her notebooks to explore the larger meaning of her life and of her writing.

Anna keeps four separate notebooks; the entries in these notebooks occupy more than three-quarters of the total novel, and they are responsible for the complex structure of the book. The blue notebook is a diary of the daily events of her life; the red notebook is concerned with politics; the black notebook is concerned with her previous life in Africa and with her professional life as a writer; and the yellow notebook is for initial drafts and ideas for stories. Entries from all four notebooks are interspersed among the sections of ongoing action of the fictional present, the summer of 1957. Those sections by themselves constitute a short novel in which the dramatic interest revolves around Anna's life and her relationship with her friend, Molly Jacobs. A few years earlier, Anna and her daughter Janet had shared a house with Molly and her son, Tommy; Anna now lives a half mile away, but the two women maintain their close friendship.

The nature of this friendship is one of the central subjects of the novel: Both women are divorced, and both are committed to rearing a child while living a life which is outside the traditional boundaries of society. They are both members of the Communist Party of Great Britain, and both believe in the nonmaterialistic values of a life-style which leaves them open to experiences in the world. Both women sense that their friendship is one of the key factors which enables them to survive in this life-style.

One central event in the "Free Women" sections is the attempted suicide of Tommy, which leaves him blind. In part, Anna and Molly blame themselves for the incident, and Tommy plays upon this guilt, controlling their lives in a manner which they deeply resent but feel powerless to change. The notebook entries enable Anna to explore this suicide attempt from a number of perspectives. In her blue notebooks, her diary, she re-creates her relationship with Tommy and analyzes it directly. In her yellow notebook, she is in the process of writing a novel called "The Shadow of the Third." Although Anna is never able to finish this novel, progress on it is important to her own development as a person. In this novel, the protagonist, a writer named Ella, is writing a novel about a young man who commits suicide. Anna is able to explore her thoughts on the actual suicide attempt by Tommy through the fictional suicide in her character Ella's novel.

This situation is only one of the many parallels between Anna's life and the fictional life of her protagonist Ella. Like Anna in her relationship with Molly, Ella lives with another woman, Julia. The mutual support which the women find in this friendship is a parallel development of the sisterhood theme explored in the relationship between Anna and Molly in the "Free Women" sections. Another parallel is also crucial to Anna's development toward living an authentic life; like Anna, the fictional Ella falls deeply in love with a man who finally leaves her after their intense relationship. After her lover leaves her, Ella feels herself changing in ways which she cannot control. She becomes less self-confident, less mentally independent. In writing Ella's story, Anna discovers that she herself has been more profoundly affected by her lover's leaving her than she previously realized. Like Ella, after the loss of her lover, Anna becomes depressed and loses her feeling of self-confident independence.

Long passages of the blue notebook, Anna's diary, involve a rigorous self-analysis, which leads to the self-knowledge Anna must have to live a meaningful life. One of the most important areas of that self-knowledge evolves from Anna's recognition that she is not experiencing the events in her life with sufficient emotion—she is closed off from her own feelings. She therefore places herself under the care of a psychoanalyst, Mrs. Marks, or Mother Sugar, as Anna calls her. Mrs. Marks tells Anna that she is suffering from a writer's block, which keeps Anna from doing her best work. Although Anna denies this conclusion at the time, she does sense that her life is fragmented, and that she is not emotionally free to feel as she should.

The action moves toward a climax when Anna rents a room in her flat to an American writer, Saul Green. The two writers engage in an intense love affair which emotionally transforms Anna. She moves through a painful psychological barrier as her old fragmented life dies—with symptoms that indicate she is undergoing a nervous breakdown—until a new self emerges that is capable of writing. In that breakdown, Anna experiences powerful visions of the world, and of her place in the world, which are lyrically compelling. Symbolically, her transformation is completed when she moves from writing in the four separate notebooks—an indication of her fragmented life—to writing in one notebook, the golden notebook, which contains the essence of her now-integrated self.

The Characters

One of the most completely realized characters in modern literatuie, Anna Wulf represents the New Woman. Although she believes that she is emotionally fulfilled in a love relationship with a man, she does not rely on a man for her position in the larger society. Doris Lessing's achievement is in tracing the development of such a woman from her early twenties to her mid-thirties. Part of that development is an honest portrayal of the character's sexual identity. As a young woman, Anna was not fulfilled sexually in her relationship with a young Communist in Africa. It is only after she has moved to London and has established a relationship with Michael, the lover who eventually leaves her, that she feels sexually fulfilled. Significantly, it is after Michael has left her that she feels her identity undergoing a crisis.

In addition to having a lasting, meaningful relationship with a man, Anna feels the need to make a commitment which will give meaning to her life. Joining the Communist Party is one attempt at making that kind of commitment. A sensitive, highly intelligent woman, Anna longs to bring social justice to the world, and she believes that the Communist Party is the most effective avenue toward achieving that goal. As a girl in South Central Africa, she witnessed the terrible results of racial discrimination, and she wants to do something to change it.

Yet Anna discovers that the Communist Party is not finally the avenue she must follow; it contains inner paradoxes which will not allow her the freedom to experience a more subjective, individual meaning—a meaning she believes she must develop in order to live an authentic life. It is only in her writing, in her art, that she can achieve that sense of meaning. When she turns to the golden notebook, she begins to write the "Free Women" sections of the novel, and thus moves toward the possibility of an integrated, meaningful life.

Anna's relationship with Molly Jacobs allows Lessing to explore the concept of sisterhood, which in the novel becomes a necessary aspect of the New Woman. Both women derive mutual support from their relationship; it enables them to face the loneliness of being without men, to endure the resentment of those people who fear nontraditional life-styles, and to survive the emotional blows of life—such as Tommy's suicide attempt. Through it all, the two women communicate their inner lives to each other as they share in the bonds of friendship.

Lessing's insight into the sisterhood relationship between modern women is matched by her exploration of the relationship a woman has with a man. Although the male characters are all viewed through the eyes of Anna, they have the kind of depth and complexity which makes them alive for the reader. The character Michael, Anna's lover in London, fulfills Anna's emotional needs; it is only after he leaves her that she realizes how essential he was to her independence. And it is only after her relationship with Saul Green, the neurotic American writer, that Anna is able to break through to a rich emotional and creative life.

The African setting in the black notebook presents a different cast of characters, both colonials and young English servicemen who are stationed there for the war. Willi Rodde is a German refugee who leads the local Communist Party which Anna joins, and he is Anna's unsatisfying lover; Paul Blackenhurst is a young flier from the British upper classes with whom Anna falls in love. Lessing's lyrical treatment of the African landscape contains some of the best writing in the novel.

Anna's novel, "The Shadow of the Third," presents yet another gallery of characters in the London setting. Although Anna and her protagonist Ella share many characteristics, Ella is a distinct character in her own right. Her lover, Paul Tanner, is a doctor who is married and has a family, and, like the character Paul Blackenhurst in the African setting, he is a witty, charming man.

Themes and Meanings

Lessing develops the central theme of the fragmentation of modern society through Anna's emotional "breakdown." In this painful psychological experience, Anna breaks through the false patterns which society has created in her, patterns that have resulted in her fragmented life. She moves through the self's false dichotomies and divisions to a "self-healing" which enables her to share fully in another's life—Saul Green's—and to have that other share fully in hers.

The individual dichotomies which Anna must overcome are developed in the separate notebooks, with a different emphasis in each. In the red notebook, the tensions between the two political ideologies—Communism and capitalism—are explored; in the black notebook, the tensions between two races, the white imperialist and the black African native; in the yellow notebook, the tensions between male and female; and in the blue notebook, the tensions between Anna as an artist and Anna as a person. Each represents a different aspect of Anna, a different fragment; it is these separate fragments which society has created in her that break down and dissolve into a new self in the healing process. With her new, integrated self, Anna enjoys a rich emotional life that enables her to create as an artist—an integrated life symbolized by the golden notebook.

In a preface to the novel, Lessing discusses this central theme; she believes that, in general, the novel, or "stories," teach the social ethic. They contain the "intellectual and moral climate" of an age. That intellectual and moral climate also is reflected in other important themes of *The Golden Notebook*. In the African setting, the injustice of racial discrimination which arises from the economic and cultural dichotomy between white and black is one such theme. In the London setting, the intellectual as well as the emotional relationship between Anna and Molly generates another, the theme of sisterhood. The moral climate of the novel also is reflected in the very character of Anna. In her psychological action to resolve the tensions that those dichotomies have created in her, she triumphs over the destructive forces of division and thus asserts the individual's ability to achieve meaning itself.

Critical Context

The rich texture of the intellectual and moral climate created in *The Golden Notebook* makes it one of the most important novels of the post–World War II era. Critics not only have praised the ambitious scope of the novel, with its various themes and settings, but also have hailed it as a remarkable accomplishment in aesthetic form. The technically complex structure—with the various notebooks contained in the separate narrative of the "Free Women" sections—generates the novel's content: Subject and structure thus complement each other in a formalist manner, and the work is fully integrated.

Although the novel is essentially realistic in approach, Anna's preoccupation with words—and with how words create a fictional reality—gives a metafictional dimension to the work. This aspect of the novel is further developed in the tension between the main story line and the fictional world which Anna creates in her novel, "The Shadow of the Third." Common to both Anna and her fictional character Ella in "The Shadow of the Third" is the theme of a young woman seeking her identity in the modern world. It is a theme Lessing also develops in the early volumes of the Children of Violence series, through her protagonist Martha Quest. The character of Anna and her struggles to live an authentic life outside the stereotypical roles which have been reserved for women was an inspiration to feminist critics, and *The Golden Notebook* remains a classic of the women's movement. Another subject which occupied Lessing in her early work was the African setting, with its theme of racial discrimination. That theme is the focus of her popular first novel, *The Grass Is Singing* (1950), and it also appears in *Martha Quest* (1952), the first volume in the Children of Violence series.

Although Lessing was to turn away from the African setting and her focus on the identity of modern women in her later novels, she continued to explore the theme of the breakdown in *Briefing for a Descent into Hell* (1971)—in that novel, through a male protagonist. The theme also appears in Lessing's short fiction: In "To Room Nineteen," one of the most widely anthologized short stories in modern literature, the quest for individual identity ends in the suicide of the protagonist Susan Rawlings. Anna's triumph in overcoming the fragmentation of modern society in *The Golden Notebook* is made with great effort and pain; as the death of the protagonist in "To Room Nineteen" illustrates, the individual cannot always be so successful. For Lessing, however, the integral vision that the individual finally may achieve is the one element that can bind the world and make it whole. It is a self-healing not only of the individual but also of society itself. Only a major novelist of Lessing's stature is capable of sustaining such an ambitious theme.

Sources for Further Study

Brewster, Dorothy. *Doris Lessing*, 1965.

Draine, Betsy. *Substance Under Pressure: Artistic Coherence and Evolving Form in the Novels of Doris Lessing*, 1983.

Knapp, Mona. *Doris Lessing*, 1984.

Schlueter, Paul. *The Novels of Doris Lessing*, 1973.

Singleton, Mary Ann. *The City and the Veld: The Fiction of Doris Lessing*, 1977.

Ronald L. Johnson

THE GOOD APPRENTICE

Author: Iris Murdoch (1919-   )
Type of plot: Domestic realism
Time of plot: The 1980's
Locale: London
First published: 1985

Principal characters:

EDWARD BALTRAM, the protagonist of the novel, who is full of
guilt over causing his friend's death
STUART CUNO, Edward's half brother and the good apprentice
of the title
HARRY CUNO, Stuart's father and Edward's stepfather, who is
carrying on an affair with Midge McCaskerville
THOMAS MCCASKERVILLE, a psychiatrist who is treating
Edward

The Novel

The Good Apprentice incorporates many of the themes and techniques
that are found in other Iris Murdoch novels. There is, first of all, the debate
and dramatization of the ethical problem of "the good"; there is the theme of
the role and place of the artist in the late twentieth century; there is the dou-
bling and pairing of characters and the switching about of lovers and relationships; there is, finally, the qualified happy ending of this brilliant and typical
Murdoch novel.

The novel begins with a moral and ethical problem: Edward Baltram gives
a friend a hallucinogenic drug in a sandwich, leaves him sleeping while he
visits a girl for a few minutes, and returns to find that his friend has jumped
to his death through a window. Edward is crushed; everything he has lived
for is now meaningless. A family friend, Thomas McCaskerville, who is a
psychiatrist, is treating Edward, but there is no indication of improvement or
change. Searching for some relief, Edward accepts a fortuitous invitation to
visit his father, Jesse, at his house in the country.

Edward's half brother, Stuart Cuno, is not looking to relieve guilt but has,
instead, apprenticed himself to the good. He has given up sex, renounced his
brilliant academic career in mathematics, and is thinking of doing some sort
of slum work. His problem is the opposite of Edward's; neither one, however, seems to be able to have any success in dealing with these very different
problems. Edward is constantly depressed, and Stuart does more harm than
good in his clumsy attempts at goodness.

Edward does not manage to see his father at Seegard, Jesse's eccentric
country home, but he is welcomed by Jesse's wife and Edward's two half sis-

ters. It is a pastoral setting and an artistic one, and it begins to draw Edward out of himself and his problems. He takes long walks in search of the sea but finds instead the girl he had visited on the night of his friend's death, Sarah. Through her, Edward manages to get in touch with Brownie, his dead friend's sister. Brownie acts as an antidote to the hate and guilt that Edward feels; the possibility of her love may drive out the hate.

Stuart, who is in search of someone to help, visits Edward at Seegard and sets into motion a switch of lovers. His father, Harry, and Midge McCaskerville (whose husband is treating Edward) stumble upon Seegard after miring their car in the mud; they try to conceal their identity and relationship, but Stuart and Edward recognize what is happening. Midge, however, then transfers her love from Harry to Stuart. Stuart is appalled and rejects her offer of love, and Thomas McCaskerville finds out about the affair between Midge and Harry. The love quadrangle seems unresolvable, and everyone is miserable. Thomas is angry and sulking; Harry is furious about Midge's betrayal and Stuart's role in it; and Stuart's plans to become a good person are sidetracked, while Midge is upset with everyone.

Edward is removed from most of the misery brought on by the love quadrangle as he continues his search to be reunited with his father at Seegard. The obstacle to that reunion is Jesse's madness; he is kept under lock and key by his wife and daughters, and although Edward hears strange sounds that he connects with Jesse, he is frustrated in his attempts to make contact with him. Finally, father and son meet while Edward is talking with Brownie. Jesse asks if Edward has been forgiven by Brownie, and when Edward says that he is not sure, he says: "Then I forgive you." Edward declares his love for his father and adds, "You could do everything for me, you could make me all over again." Jesse has "forgotten it all," however, and is incapable of doing what Edward asks. Edward must remake himself and not hand over the job to someone else.

A short while later, Jesse gets out of Seegard and drowns in the nearby river. Edward sees him in the water but thinks that it is only a hallucination. After arguing with his sister and Jesse's wife, he sets out for London to find Jesse. He returns shortly thereafter and discovers Jesse's body and takes his ring as a sign of their continuing connection. Both Edward and Stuart reach a low point here; Edward is accused of bringing nothing but death and misery to others by Mother May, Jesse's wife, and Stuart is seen as the source of all the trouble by Harry. "You've done nothing but cause trouble, pain and strife, that's what your good intentions amount to." At this low moment, however, the novel begins to change; in the last chapter, "Life After Death," the forces of life, love and renewal, overcome the death that began the novel and the suffering that pervades it.

What brings about a change in the mood of the novel is not individual effort or self-help but people helping one another; Stuart appeals to Brownie's mother to forgive Edward, and Edward helps Midge see that her feelings for Stuart are false. Both characters must pass through a moment of crisis, however, before they can alter their situations. Stuart feels "as if he were banished from the human race," but he suddenly has a revelation when he sees a mouse very much at home under the tracks at a train station; he is filled with a "peaceful joy" as he realizes that he has a place in the universe. Edward's revelation is more subtle. When he receives a letter from Brownie telling him that she is to marry someone else, he falls into despair, feeling that he is "dead." When he puts on his father's ring, however, he begins to see more in life. He now thinks of simple survival, of other women he can love, and, perhaps, even of writing about his experience and transmuting the pain into art. Finally, he says, "Anyway I'll try to do some good in the world, if it's not too difficult, nothing stops anyone from doing that." With his recovery, Midge and Thomas are reunited, Harry has published a novel and, thus, has found his place, and he and his sons drink to "the good things in life."

The Characters

Edward Baltram moves from despair to hope in the course of the novel. What brings about this change is not so much his own efforts but the efforts of and contact with others. For example, Thomas McCaskerville works behind the scenes to bring Edward to Seegard, while Stuart helps the mother of the boy Edward has inadvertently killed to forgive him. In addition, the appearance of such characters as Brownie and Jesse helps Edward return to a more normal perception of the possibilities in life. Edward must, however, make that last step by himself; when he does so, he becomes, in perhaps a truer sense than Stuart, an apprentice to the good. Furthermore, when he thinks of becoming a writer and using his experiences, he unites the advice of Thomas, the role of his father, Jesse, and the example of his stepfather, Harry.

Stuart Cuno is something of a stereotyped character; he is so earnest about becoming good that he creates misery and disruption wherever he goes. His concept of goodness has something of the abstract about it. It is only at the end of the novel, when Stuart finds a specific outlet for his attempts to do good, that he becomes a force for good. He is to become a teacher of small children in order to "give them an idea of what goodness is, and how to love it."

Jesse Baltram has many of the traits of the great artist; he lives an unconventional life, he loves many women, and his art is ignored or unappreciated. Jesse, however, is now only the shadow of his once-heroic self. His madness and infirmities reduce him to a near-childish state. Even in that reduced state, however, he can reach out, touch, and change others. The few words he speaks to Midge and Stuart alter their lives, and his forgiveness begins to bring about some important changes in Edward. His death is as romantic and mysterious as one can imagine; it is similar to the death of Percy Bysshe Shelley or that of George Gordon, Lord Byron. After his death, "Jesse lives" begins to appear on walls in London. In a curious way, then, Jesse embodies many of the aspects of the great artist even though he has lost the ability to create.

Themes and Meanings

The dominant theme of *The Good Apprentice* is, clearly, the search to discover "the good." The major characters in the novel, Edward and Stuart, are closely involved in this ethical search, although Edward's search is less direct than that of Stuart. The presence of such a theme in Murdoch's fiction is not accidental; she has written about the subject a number of times, notably in *The Sovereignty of Good* (1970). The two qualities she singles out as prerequisite for the good to exist are "[first] the ability to perceive what is true, which is automatically at the same time [second] a supression of self." Stuart's renunciation of sex and his announced intention of doing good seem nearly a parody of Murdoch's description of the good; his egotism and lack of contact with others ensure that his search will go astray. In contrast, Edward's self has been nearly obliterated by his guilt, and he can begin to "perceive what is true" in the real world after an initial period of distortion. Another aspect of the good in the book is love; Murdoch equates love with both selflessness and the perception of reality, and so the affair between Harry and Midge is not one of love, nor is it remotely connected with the good, since it involves an affirmation of self above everything else.

Critical Context

The Good Apprentice was Iris Murdoch's twenty-second novel, and, not surprisingly, it shares some of the important characteristics of the earlier ones. First, *The Good Apprentice* has the social detail and realistic surface as well as the complex plot typical of Murdoch's fiction. Her novels often have surprising twists, suspense, sudden reversals, and what one critic has called "the eventual subsidence of emotion in a general feeling of justice." Another noteworthy aspect of Murdoch's novels is the intellectual or philosophical dimension: Murdoch was for many years a professor of philosophy, and her first published work was *Sartre: Romantic Rationalist* (1953). From the beginning of her career, her novels have been concerned with such philosophical issues as power and freedom and, above all, the good. Since her eleventh novel, *The Nice and the Good* (1968), the problem of finding the good in the modern world has been a primary concern of her fiction. *The Good Apprentice* clearly reflects Murdoch's interest in dealing with this ethical problem in fiction in the characters' search for the good and in the dialogue about how and where it is to be found.

The critical response to *The Good Apprentice*, like that to most of

Murdoch's novels, has been mixed. Harold Bloom noted the typical complex and comic plot and the philosophical element, but he had doubts whether "the comic story and the spiritual kernel can be held together by Miss Murdoch's archaic stance as an authorial will." Howard Moss's review was more favorable, but he did not like being "told so schematically and so often that the 'good' exists." Gillian Wilce called the novel a "moral soap opera," but she also noted Murdoch's great theme: "the human inclination to go on struggling not just for meaning but for, well, goodness."

Sources for Further Study
Baldanza, Frank. *Iris Murdoch*, 1974.
Bloom, Harold. Review in *The New York Times Book Review*. XCI (January 12, 1986), p. 1.
Byatt, A. S. *Degrees of Freedom: The Novels of Iris Murdoch*, 1965.
_____. *Iris Murdoch*, 1976.
The Christian Science Monitor. Review. LXXVIII (September 3, 1986), p. 22.
Dipple, Elizabeth. *Iris Murdoch: Work for the Spirit*, 1982.
Hague, Angela. *Iris Murdoch's Comic Vision*, 1984.
Moss, Howard. Review in *The New York Review of Books*. XXXIII (June 12, 1986), p. 39.
Saturday Review. Review. XII (June, 1986), p. 74.
Time. Review. CXXVII (January 6, 1986), p. 89.
Wilce, Gillian. Review in *New Statesman*. CX (September 27, 1985), p. 30.

James Sullivan

GOOD MORNING, MIDNIGHT

Author: Jean Rhys (Ella Gwendolen Rees Williams, 1894-1979)
Type of plot: Psychological realism
Time of plot: 1937
Locale: Paris
First published: 1939

>   *Principal characters:*
>   SASHA JANSEN, the protagonist, a middle-aged woman
>   shattered by the pain of her past experiences
>   ENNO, her former husband, who loves her and leaves her
>   twice
>   RENÉ, a gigolo
>   MR. BLANK, a former employer
>   A TRAVELING SALESMAN, unnamed but central to the action of
>   the novel

The Novel

Prior to her writing of *Good Morning, Midnight*, Jean Rhys published four books—a volume of short stories, *The Left Bank and Other Stories* (1927), and three novels, *Postures* (1928; published in the United States as *Quartet*, 1929), *After Leaving Mr. Mackenzie* (1931), and *Voyage in the Dark* (1934). After the publication of *Good Morning, Midnight*, twenty-seven years elapsed before her next novel, *Wide Sargasso Sea* (1966), an imaginative re-creation of the life of Rochester's mad wife, based on characters created by Charlotte Brontë in *Jane Eyre* (1847). Critics often say that the female protagonists in Rhys's previous novels culminate in *Good Morning, Midnight*. If so, then Sasha represents the essence of a typical Rhys protagonist: a woman afraid, lonely, poor, whose life patterns are worked out in seedy hotels and bars and transitory affairs with men in a patriarchal society whose boundaries are defined by male values and class consciousness.

Sasha Jansen was married once to a charming but unemployed man named Enno (an anagram for "none"?). Enno is sure that money will turn up some way or another if he and Sasha are married and are living in Paris. He insists that Sasha leave all the worrying to him, and so, the world becomes *now* for Sasha, one big beautiful romance from which only lifelong happiness can result. Enno, however, does not find work and cannot find money. Poverty is not what Sasha bargained for: "I didn't think it would be like this—shabby clothes, worn-out shoes, circles under your eyes, your hair getting straight and lanky, the way people look at you. . . . I didn't think it would be like this."

Then, after accusing Sasha of not knowing how to love, Enno leaves for three days; at this time, she becomes sure that she is pregnant. On the fourth day, he is back and she believes she loves him even more deeply. Life is not a fairy tale, however, especially for young women without monetary means to care for themselves. After the birth and death of an infant son, Enno leaves again, as Sasha really always knew he would. At this point, her life begins to go to pieces.

She returns to London, where a small annuity keeps her from starving and provides a series of rooms in which she lives. She spends her time trying to drink herself to death, a condition Sasha likens to drowning in a large, dark river. Then, a friend rescues her by providing some extra money for a trip to Paris, which is to be an attempt at rejuvenation.

Paris, however, is too painful. There, Sasha's life exists in two separate worlds on two different time planes, past and present, and events from one time interweave with those from the other time. Characters from her memory come to mind and become actual substance, and people in her present mirror people in her past. To complicate further this replication of times and experiences, past and present, Sasha separates herself into two parts: the part that is world-weary and filled with despair and the part that still has not realized that happiness is illusory for an impoverished and unmarried but sexually active woman in a sexist society on the brink of World War II. Sasha's separate selves have conversations with each other and one will sometimes create films in her mind, of scenes such as, for example, a married woman who envisions herself in a whitewashed room dressed seductively and watching for the expression of a man's face when he turns to see her. Yet all is not well:

> Now he ill-treats me, now he betrays me. He often brings home other women and I have to wait on them, and I don't like that. But as long as he is alive and near me I am not unhappy. If he were to die I should kill myself.

If Sasha rejects her "film-mind" as any way to exist, she rejects also what others have offered—Mr. Blank, for example, an employer from her past who treated her like an idiot or like a spoke in the machine of his operation, and René, who also calls her stupid because she will not play his game on his terms. René is a counterpart character to Enno, and both René and Enno are embodied in Mr. Blank.

René is a gigolo who mistakes Sasha for a moneyed woman, but even when he finds out the limited extent of her finances, he continues to pursue her to feed his ego and to satisfy his physical needs (food as well as sex). One part of her plays his games, stopping only at providing sex; the other part of her continually turns him away, refusing to play the role he has outlined for her.

In the brilliant concluding section of the novel, Rhys brings together all aspects of the duplicated characters. The events, seeming more like they are happening in dream or hallucination, play themselves out as they must, given the initial assumptions of the situation. Sasha allows René into her room as he is still imploring her to allow sex because it would make her feel so much better, but once again, she pulls back. The cerebral part of her rejects his fancy, and she insists that he leave. He does leave, and immediately the "feeling" part of her wants him back. She rushes to the door and finds him waiting in the dark hallway, and once again they go through the same charade. He tries to force her into submission and suggests that gang rape might be what she needs. Once again, she rejects him, deflating his ego by telling him that he can have money without "servicing" her.

He does take some money and he leaves, but she jumps up immediately to determine how much he has taken and finds that he has taken only a token amount. The feeling part of her emerges dominant once again, and she wishes him back. She plays in her mind the events of his returning, and while she imagines his return, she removes her clothes, unlocks the door, gets into bed, and waits for him to return. The door opens and a man appears as though she has willed his presence, but the man is not René. He is, rather, another variation of all the men who have attempted to use her for sexual and crassly material purposes. Her night visitor is the traveling salesman, who has throughout the novel taken her for a prostitute and now simply wants to take his turn.

The Characters

The only fully developed character in the novel is Sasha, from whose point of view the story is told. Since Sasha is troubled, at times almost schizoid, her perceptions sometimes seem vague and dreamlike, sometimes hallucinatory and distorted, and sometimes lucid with pristine clarity. In addition, characterization is effected by tone and style. The precariousness and numbness that Sasha feels, for example, is exemplified in her need to order her life into small bundles, a need impressed upon the reader by Rhys's use of a sentence structure whose staccato arrangements of clauses and phrases make the point as much as the words do. "I have been here five days. I have decided on a place to eat in at midday, a place to eat in at night, a place to have my drink in after dinner. I have arranged my little life."

Each day Sasha awakes, dresses, chooses a restaurant for her food, takes her Pernod at a café, goes to a cinema or does some other carefully planned activity (buys a hat or goes to her hairdresser), speaks only if spoken to, and goes to sleep at night with the help of a sleeping potion. Men approach her and to some she responds, but she knows that she must always be careful. Each man wants something from her, wants to use her in some way. She must be careful about the places she frequents and the streets she walks because at any time she can be plunged back into memories of painful times or, even worse, of happy times that gave way to grief.

All the men in the novel are variations of one another, and though no one is fully developed, when they are taken all together, there emerges a psychosexual picture of male dominance in a patriarchal society which denies its women individuality, intelligence, and the ability to define themselves in terms of themselves.

Mr. Blank is symbolic of them all. He is the manager of a dress shop in which Sasha once worked. The dress shop is filled with mannequins, women dressed up like dolls, acting like automatons, and the shop itself is a maze of fitting rooms, showrooms, and downstairs offices, dozens of tiny rooms, and stairs and passages that do not lead anywhere but merely go up and down and around. Mr. Blank's treatment of Sasha turns her into an unthinking machine, and because he throws her into a panic, she finds herself on an unending chase that is similar to the haphazard scurrying of a rat in a maze. Later, she cries for a long time for herself, for an old bald woman she has recently seen, and for all the defeated people in the world. Still later, she is angry, and in her mind she addresses Mr. Blank, admitting to him that he does represent authority and leadership in society and that she is only an inefficient and somewhat damaged member of that society. He has the right, she says, to cut off her legs, but not the right to ridicule her afterward because she is crippled. He does not, she insists, have the right to despise those whom he exploits, though that is the right he most desires.

Themes and Meanings

At this point the novel concludes, but not without one of the most controversial endings in modern literature. Sasha opens her arms to this man whom she detests, seemingly allowing both parts of herself to merge into a unity, and she utters the words, "Yes—yes—yes. . . ." The words undeniably call to mind the conclusion of Molly Bloom's famous soliloquy in James Joyce's *Ulysses* (1922), and because they do, many critics have allowed Joyce's interpretation of Molly's needs to direct their own responses to Sasha's words. Since Molly's series of yeses are usually considered to be totally affirmative of the life force and fertility cycles that guarantee continued rebirth, most critics of Rhys's novel interpret Sasha's series of yeses as affirmative, also signaling her willingness to accept love where she can find it. It is, however, quite possible to read Sasha's yeses in another way and to recognize that a merger of the two aspects of Sasha's character can be accomplished by an acceptance of reality. The yeses may simply mean that Sasha now realizes and accepts what life is. The two parts of her mesh to discover that this traveling salesman is all that there is. Life exists without dreams and illusory hopes.

Critical Context

After publishing *Good Morning, Midnight*, Jean Rhys dropped out of view and was nearly forgotten as a literary artist, but with the publication of *Wide Sargasso Sea* and the reissuing of her previous books, including hardback and softback editions in the United States, Rhys's skills and talents were once more brought to the attention of readers in both countries and led some critics to call her the best living English novelist. Her fictions became the subject of serious critical study resulting in several scholarly books and many articles. Her importance rests on her skills and modernist novelistic techniques, where form not only shapes but also dictates meaning; on her use of wasteland images and existential themes similar to those of such major modern writers as James Joyce, Ernest Hemingway, William Faulkner, Virginia Woolf, and the early T. S. Eliot; and on her unsparing rendering of the plight of women in a society in which their roles are secondary to those of men, anticipating the concerns of many women writers of the 1970's and 1980's. Rhys was a female voice speaking in a text that in 1939 needed decoding, a text the implications and complexities of which did not begin to be understood until more than thirty years after the publication of her early works and are still subjects of critical contention and admiration.

Sources for Further Study

Davidson, Arnold E. *Jean Rhys*, 1985.
Gardiner, Judith Kegan. *Good Morning, Midnight: Good Night, Modernism*, 1984.
Rhys, Jean. *The Letters of Jean Rhys*, 1984.
Staley, Thomas F. *Jean Rhys: A Critical Study*, 1979.
Wolfe, Peter. *Jean Rhys*, 1980.

Mary Rohrberger

THE GOOD SOLDIER

Author: Ford Madox Ford (1873-1939)
Type of plot: Domestic tragedy
Time of plot: From the last few years of the nineteenth century through 1913
Locale: Nauheim, Germany, and the country near Branshaw Teleragh, England
First published: 1915

Principal characters:

JOHN DOWELL, the narrator, a wealthy American who looks after his wife while she is treated for heart disease at fashionable European spas

FLORENCE DOWELL, his wife, who feigns heart disease to stay in Europe to pursue her romantic and social goals

EDWARD ASHBURNHAM, a wealthy English landholder, captain in the British army, and "comforter" of vulnerable women, the "good soldier" of the title

LEONORA ASHBURNHAM, his wife, who repeatedly saves her husband from what she perceives to be financial and moral ruin

The Novel

The Good Soldier is a novel about the differences between appearance and reality—and about human willingness to see events in a light that best suits the viewer, regardless of how accurate that vision may be. John Dowell calls his narrative "the saddest story I have ever heard"; perhaps the saddest aspect of the story is Dowell's own unwillingness to see through the fine veneer covering the faults of his wife and friends.

The narrator sets his story up as a fireside conversation, a confession delivered in private to the reader. As the novel opens, Dowell is trying to come to terms with new and disturbing discoveries about his wife and Edward Ashburnham, both now dead, and about how thoroughly he had been deceived by appearances when they were alive. The story of the nine-year relationship of the Dowells and the Ashburnhams is revealed in fragments, and this is not surprising, considering that the import of the events of that relationship is only now becoming clear to the narrator, who was a part of the relationship from the beginning. The reader gets pieces of the puzzle, not in chronological order, but as Dowell remembers them and as their significance becomes apparent to him. Reading *The Good Soldier* becomes a process of discovery, along with the narrator, and it is not until the very end of the novel that one seems to have all the facts.

John and Florence Dowell first meet Edward and Leonora Ashburnham at the health resort in Nauheim, Germany. They are seated together for dinner one evening, and that is the beginning of their long, and seemingly idyllic, relationship. To John Dowell, the Ashburnhams are quintessential English gentry: Edward is a captain in his army regiment, a landowner, a philanthropist, and a gentleman of refinement; Leonora is a woman of beauty and accomplishment, the perfect partner for her husband. Edward has returned with Leonora from army duty in India because of his health. The Dowells are also in Europe for health reasons. Both Edward and Florence are in Nauheim because they have "hearts"; that is, they suffer from heart conditions. The two couples meet every summer at the spas in Nauheim, where they lead lives of leisure and dignified reserve. They travel together in Europe and become close friends. Dowell, however, notes in the first paragraph of the novel that, despite how well people think they know one another, they quite possibly do not know one another at all. When he makes this observation, the narrator reveals one of Ford's major themes—for the ideal relationship that Dowell sees for nine years turns out to be built on deceit and intrigue.

The narrator does not find out the real nature of the people who are close to him until after the death of both his wife and "the good soldier." Florence dies, seemingly of her heart condition, during their stay at Nauheim in the summer of 1913. Dowell observes her running back to the hotel, and her body is found on her bed, her hand clutching a vial of what appears to be her medicine. Edward and Leonora return to their estate in England, and the narrator returns to America to administer the estate of his deceased wife. He then receives separate notes from both Edward and Leonora, asking him to come to visit them. Dowell makes the trip to England, only to find Edward's health much deteriorated; in fact, during the American's stay at Branshaw Teleragh, his host, the wealthy landowner and "good soldier," commits suicide. With her husband dead, Leonora Ashburnham reveals to the narrator the story he tells in his self-styled fireside conversation. She tells him the truth, unaware of Dowell's blindness to what has gone on around him for nine years. The perfect English country gentleman he had known as Edward Ashburnham was really a man with a weakness for vulnerable young women—in fact, for nearly any woman but Leonora. His inability to resist other women was matched only by his inability to manage his money properly. What Leonora had assumed Dowell knew, and what proves most shocking to the narrator, was that one of Edward's affairs, a quite lengthy one, had been with Florence, and that Florence did not die of a heart attack but rather killed herself at the thought that she was losing her lover to a younger woman, Nancy Rufford. Neither Edward nor Florence had suffered from heart disease at all. These astonishing revelations, mixed with the narrator's recollection of a variety of episodes from his life with Florence and with the Ashburnhams—recollections in a new and sordid light—form the narrative that Ford provides through the character John Dowell.

The Characters

The narrator, while detailing the moral weakness of Edward Ashburnham, is careful to point out that the man has the noble qualities that make him "the good soldier." He is, in fact, a benevolent administrator of his large estate. Branshaw Teleragh has a number of tenants, families who have lived under the protection of the Ashburnhams for centuries. Edward is sincerely concerned with their welfare; against his wife's objections, he remits their rent during difficult years and sees that they have the things they need and want. When Edward's concern for a visibly distressed young servant girl on a train leads him to provide comfort with an embrace and a kiss, he discovers, perhaps unwittingly at the time, a source of closeness and concern that his increasing estrangement from Leonora is denying him. A series of affairs (including the one with Florence) that both he and his wife find humiliating saps him of self-respect and of money. When he falls in love with his ward, Nancy Rufford, his disgust and self-hatred finally lead him to cut his own throat.

During the course of his deterioration, Edward always maintains the façade of the country squire; he is the perfect officer in his regiment, the perfect host, the perfect friend. The façade, however, hides the soul of a tortured man within. The strain of trying to live his life as he believes it should be lived—as lord of his estate and of his tenants—coupled with the refusal of his wife to support him in his life's role, destroys Edward Ashburnham, both morally and physically.

Though Edward must bear responsibility for his actions, Leonora is not without blame in this tragedy that is "the saddest story." She is the third of seven daughters of an upper-middle-class Irish Catholic family that has fallen into financial difficulties. Her marriage to Edward was arranged, primarily by the two mothers, who were anxious to see that their children married well.

From the beginning, it is a marriage strained by conflicts. Having been reared in a home where the budget was very tight, Leonora is horrified at Edward's cavalier way with money. Moreover, Edward is a member of the Church of England, and Leonora is crushed when she learns that no agreement was struck before the marriage to ensure that her children would be reared as Catholics. The thought that her babies might be damned without the blessing of the Church weighs heavily on Leonora's mind. Her increasing interference in Edward's management of Branshaw Teleragh, and to a lesser extent her religious concerns, make Leonora a distant and cold wife and Edward a puzzled and resentful husband. Within a very few years, the Ashburnhams speak to each other only in public, as a thing necessary to maintain appearances.

In Florence Dowell, the author creates a fascinating mirror in which to view Edward. Like Ashburnham, Florence has a weakness for extramarital liaisons, but she has none of the redeeming qualities of "the good soldier." She marries John Dowell as a way to get to Europe to continue her affair with a reprehensible character known only as Jimmy. She also has dreams of becoming the mistress of some great English estate. Once in Europe, she feigns heart disease, and a doctor tells the Dowells that Florence must remain on the Continent because a voyage back to America might prove fatal. Florence uses the illness as an excuse to bar her husband from her bedroom, and John is reduced to the role of nurse for an invalid, a role which he fills until Florence dies. It is through Florence that the Dowells and Ashburnhams meet in 1904. Florence observes Leonora in the act of cuffing Maisie Maidan, Edward's current love interest. From that moment, Florence has Leonora in her power. She becomes Edward's new lover and eventually makes a misery of the lives of both Ashburnhams. Florence sees Edward as her way to become mistress of an English estate. She does not, however, anticipate his tiring of her. When Edward falls in love with Nancy, Florence perceives that she is losing her hold over the Ashburnhams and kills herself. Like Edward, she was unfaithful, but unlike him, she was a moral desert, cruelly dedicated to advancing her own ambitions at all costs.

The narrator, John Dowell, is a paradox. He is at once the least interesting and the most fascinating character in the novel. He tells the story of his own gullibility, and the reader is moved to pity him. At the same time, however, how can one like or respect a character who is so ridiculously credulous? For nine years, just beneath the surface of very respectable gentility, a scandal of moral degeneration took place, and Dowell, an observer of these events, was unable to see them for what they were. The narrator's calm acceptance of the facts, once he has them, also undercuts reader sympathy for his plight. Though his marriage to Florence was not arranged, as the Ashburnham union had been, there is no real passion between Dowell and his wife; in fact, the narrator is not sure that he wants to marry. He does, however—despite cryptic warnings from Florence's relatives that there is something wrong with the girl. Florence marries only to use the well-to-do Dowell; he is her ticket to Europe and a reunion with her lover, Jimmy. Though Florence soon tires of Jimmy, she continues to use the narrator to legitimize her movements in polite society. On the night that she dies, Florence is not simply heartbroken at the loss of Edward Ashburnham; she fears that her past relationship with Jimmy has been revealed to her husband. It has been, but Dowell is not perceptive enough to realize what he has been told—nor does he seem to care that his wife may not be the kind of woman he assumed she was from the beginning. Leonora thinks of John Dowell as a child. The reader can only think of him in a similar fashion. He is a man unwilling to deal with reality, living out his life in the shadow of Edward Ashburnham, the robust "good soldier," and being nursemaid to a faithless and cruel woman. He refuses to see the corruption around him until it is thrust undeniably before him. These qualities that make him both bland and fascinating are qualities around which Ford Madox Ford hinges his major themes.

Themes and Meanings

The possibility for vast discrepancies between form and content, between reality and appearance, is the major theme in Ford's novel. The story is set among the upper class of Europe: the places they frequent, the things they do, the very tenor of their lives. It is an idealized setting, the picture of perfection. Ford, however, exposes a seamy undercurrent to this beautiful life. Beneath the carefully fashioned exterior of Edwardian society, real people live, people with desires and prejudices, people who hate and are cruel. The "good soldier," for all of his kindness and good manners, is, after all, an adulterer and something of a wastrel. Florence, for all of her show of gentility, is but a scheming social climber with no morals. Leonora is long-suffering and gallant, but she is also cold and unfeeling as she slowly destroys her husband's sense of self. And the narrator, though kind and trusting, is ineffectual and unwilling to face reality.

John Dowell is thus the author's vehicle for illustrating the folly of seeing things as one wants them to be, rather than as they really are. In this, he is representative not merely of a particular character-type or of a particular social class but rather of Europe itself: decadent, complacent, oblivious to impending catastrophe. Ford would have readers know that refusal to deal with things as they are, however painful that reckoning may be, can only lead to greater suffering. That is why John Dowell's is "the saddest story."

Critical Context

Ford Madox Ford was a prolific writer, both of fiction and of criticism. He founded several literary reviews and was an important editor. *The Good Soldier* is considered to be the best of his novels. In fact, Ford himself labeled it as his best work. He began to write it on his fortieth birthday, December 17, 1913. A dedicated craftsman, Ford consciously set out to put into *The Good Soldier* all that he knew about writing. His mastery of plot, characterization, and especially point of view show that he knew much. He had originally intended to call the novel "The Saddest Story," but his publisher recommended against that title; the year of its publication, 1915, was a grave time as the "sad story" of World War I spread across Europe. Pressed to come up with a different title, Ford impulsively chose *The Good Soldier*, a decision he always regretted; though the title fits the story of Edward Ashburnham well, the author did not want his novel confused with a story of the war. Along with the tetralogy *Parade's End* (1924-1928), often known as the Tietjens novels (for their main character), *The Good Soldier* stands as the high point in Ford Madox Ford's career.

Sources for Further Study

Cassell, Richard A. *Ford Madox Ford: A Study of His Novels*, 1961.
Leer, Norman. *The Limited Hero in the Novels of Ford Madox Ford*, 1966.
Lid, R. W. *Ford Madox Ford: The Essence of His Art*, 1964.
Ohmann, Carol. *Ford Madox Ford: From Apprentice to Craftsman*, 1964.

Michael Crane

THE GOOD TERRORIST

Author: Doris Lessing (1919-   )
Type of plot: Social realism
Time of plot: The 1970's
Locale: London
First published: 1985

> *Principal characters:*
> ALICE MELLINGS, the protagonist, the "good" terrorist who
> acts as housekeeper to the group
> JASPER, her boyfriend, who thinks of himself as one of the
> leaders of the group
> FAYE,
> ROBERTA,
> PAT, and
> BERT, the other would-be terrorists who share the same
> commune
> PHILIP,
> JIM,
> MARY, and
> REGGIE, the other nonterrorist members of the commune

The Novel

The Good Terrorist focuses on the lives of a loosely knit group of vaga-
bonds and would-be terrorists who share a commune in contemporary London. As the novel opens, the members of the group set out to make their
newfound "squat" habitable and to keep it from demolition. Their first task
is to restore the plumbing and to dispose of the many buckets of excrement
which have accumulated in the eight months since the house was condemned
and its lavatories were filled with cement. As the novel ends, several months
later, the group has dispersed; those still left in the commune go their separate ways following (despite their bungling) a successful car bombing which
kills five people, including one of their own.

The leaders of the commune belong to a small splinter group, the Communist Centre Union (CCU), which seems to embrace all the popular causes
and seeks alliance with the Irish Republican Army (IRA). Clearly amateurs,
they drift from one abandoned house to the next, living off their unemployment checks, occasionally spending a day demonstrating as if on holiday, or
calling a late-night meeting to plot future protest activities. Though they
yearn to be arrested so they may be taken seriously as terrorists, in fact they
prove themselves to be quite incompetent and harmless until the tragic
ending.

During most of the novel, the group's political agenda occupies far less of their time and attention than the more mundane tasks of fixing the house, foraging for money, and working through their complex relationships with one another. The stakes begin to rise, however, as the "real" terrorists next door take an interest in some of their activities. These shadowy figures are led by a Comrade Andrew, who pretends to be an American but looks like Vladimir Ilich Lenin (at least according to Alice). When he disappears, two former members of his household join the commune and persuade the others to help them build bombs according to a terrorist manual. After a disappointing practice run which causes little damage and is blamed on hooligans, they pick their target—the busy street in front of a fancy hotel during rush hour. This time they succeed, in spite of an apparent malfunction in the timing mechanism. The public is outraged at the monstrous murder of innocent people and blames the IRA because of an anonymous phone call actually made by Alice. The IRA denies any involvement and vows revenge on the group which perpetrated such a heinous act in its name. Ironically, the CCU has now earned the enmity of the very revolutionaries it had hoped to impress.

The Characters

At the center of the commune is Alice Mellings, the "good" terrorist, who cooks, cleans, and steals from her friends and parents to keep the house going. It is Alice who negotiates with the Council and the police to keep the house from demolition, who persuades a plumber to help them fix pipes, and who does most of the heavy work involved in repairing the house.

Alice is a stocky thirty-six-year-old who sometimes looks like a clumsy twelve-year-old, sometimes like a fattish woman of fifty, but never her own age. She has been to college but has no interest in doing anything with her education. Instead, for the last fifteen years, she has been moving from house to house with Jasper, the boyfriend who perpetually abuses her. Jasper enjoys kicking her ankles and squeezing her wrists until he hurts her, all the while letting her look after him and complaining that other people exploit her. Alice seems to live for those moments when Jasper confides in her or allows her to show her affection for him. Her greatest fear is that Jasper will move his sleeping bag to another room (not that he ever allows her to touch him), or that he will not return from a night spent cruising the homosexual bars with money she has provided.

Alice goes through the novel on an emotional roller coaster of sorts. After two days of running from one government office to another, of scrubbing the walls and floors of the house, almost single-handedly saving it, she glows in the praise of her friends. A few moments later, she is in tears, left alone to continue the drudge work while the group goes off to a demonstration.

Alice's relationship with her mother is a particular source of ambivalence and emotional turmoil. She constantly berates her mother for her middle-class values, then begs her for money and approval. Alice literally becomes hysterical when she learns that her mother has sold her house, yet she cannot seem to understand that it is largely her own fault that her mother could not afford to stay there. Alice's mother had tried to protect Alice from becoming another "all purpose female drudge" who would spend years "staggering around with loads of food and cooking it and serving it to a lot of greedy-guts." During their final meeting, she laughs bitterly in acknowledgment of her failure and Alice's self-deception.

The commune as a whole is held together by Alice's mothering, with each character representing a certain sociological type and also acting as a foil to help reveal Alice's personality. Jim, a black man who has been in and out of trouble for years, has lived in the house for about eight months when Alice and Jasper arrive. Alice adopts him, helps him find a job at her father's factory, then unwittingly becomes the agent of his further victimization as he is fired: blamed for a theft she herself committed. The plumber-repairman, Philip, whom Alice persuades to help fix up the house in exchange for squatter's privileges, is constantly being underpaid or cheated by his employers. Too weak to do the jobs for which he is hired, he ultimately dies utterly alone, with only Alice to attend his funeral. Mary, the Council clerk to whom Alice appeals to stop the house's demolition, is simply looking for an inexpensive place to live. She and her boyfriend, Reggie, are approved by the group because they are good liberals who wear "Save the Whales" stickers and attend Greenpeace rallies. Pat, the most competent activist and perhaps the sanest member of the group, befriends Alice while her boyfriend, Bert, and Jasper are in Ireland trying to make contact with the IRA. Later, she moves out, apparently having been recruited for serious terrorist training. Faye, the most fragile member of the group, depends on her lesbian relationship with Roberta to keep her from self-destructive depression. When Roberta must leave to visit her mother in the hospital, Faye cuts her wrists and is rescued by Alice, who stays by her side night and day until Roberta returns. It is Faye who sets the timing mechanism on the bomb, presumably committing suicide in the process.

By the end of the novel, Jim, Philip, Reggie, Mary, Pat, and Faye are all gone. Roberta goes back to her mother, Jasper and Bert go off to find a new house, and Alice is left alone to face the consequences of their actions.

Themes and Meanings

The novel seems primarily an analysis of female victimhood; Alice is the typical daughter who rebels against her mother and then grows up to be exactly like her. It is also about female masochism and the inability of women to walk away from men who abuse them and offer nothing in return for years of care and devotion.

At first, Alice seems deserving of the reader's sympathy. Certainly she is the hardest worker of the group. Though the others criticize her for caring more about fixing up the house than for their political causes, the sincerity of her feelings is never in question; again and again she is moved to tears by the injustices of her world. Yet Doris Lessing's portrait constantly emphasizes the excessiveness of her responses: "her heart full of pain" at the sight of such a beautiful house left "unloved," hysteria—to the point that Pat must shake her to stop her sobbing—over a bird's nest that crashes to the ground.

Alice may very well see herself as an unloved child who has been kicked out of her home, but the evidence suggests that her parents have always cared for and even indulged her. At thirty-six, she has no more control over her emotions than does a sixteen-year-old. Unfortunately, it is not simply herself she hurts: Alice's naïveté and indiscretion, in combination with her childlike need for approval and love, are ultimately to blame not only for her mother's plight but also for the murder of innocent people. It is Alice who first approaches Comrade Andrew, acting as if she knew all about him. He tries to seduce her and then to bribe her, yet when crates of guns are delivered to the commune, she makes no connection between the money she has accepted and this contraband.

Alice enjoys the "practice" bombing but becomes hysterical minutes before the car bomb is set to go off. She actually calls the "Good Samaritans" to warn them, but when asked for the bomb's location she cannot bring herself to give the exact address. Alice, the "good" terrorist, thinks back on a wonderful evening spent spray-painting trains as one of the happiest nights of her life without fully comprehending how such fun could lead to the violence in which she is now implicated. Though Lessing keeps the reader in the dark about the real identity of Comrade Andrew and the other presumably authentic terrorists or spies who attempt to exploit Alice, she makes it clear that Alice's silly conversations with them endanger her both friends and the public. The last image of the novel is of a woman alone, clutching her teacup, looking like a nine-year-old as she waits "for it to be time to go out and meet the professionals."

As the above discussion indicates, the plot of the novel is complex and often confusing. Like many of Lessing's works, *The Good Terrorist* can best be understood as a psychological case study set in an interesting sociological and historical context. The backdrop for this particular case study is a grimly realistic portrait of terrorism and its agents. Though it is never entirely clear whether Lessing blames Alice and her friends for being so incompetent and obstructing the work of the real revolutionaries such as the IRA, or whether she sees terrorism as the product of just such adolescent game-playing, she makes terrorism seem all the more alarming because it is so haphazard. Presumably, Lessing chooses not to reveal the identity of the so-called professionals because she wants the reader to focus on the psychological rather than the political sources of terrorism. Alice is quick to assume that her next-door neighbors are Soviet agents without any real evidence to support her assumptions. Her horror of reading anything but newspapers is proof of her own limited perspective and may be Lessing's harshest indictment of middle-class, "knee-jerk" liberalism. The social injustices that move Alice to tears are real, but certainly there is little hope that she and her friends can do anything to improve the society which they profess to hate.

Critical Context

The Good Terrorist represents a shift in Lessing's work away from her later quasi-mystical science fiction to the realism of earlier novels such as the "Children of Violence" series (1952-1969). Lessing's realistic novels and short stories are filled with characters—usually women—who do not have the strength of personality or intelligence to break out of the drab, monotonous existences that threaten to smother them. Alice Mellings may be Lessing's most pessimistic portrait of a woman who is victimized not only by society's expectations for her but also by her own stupidity.

The novel also reflects Lessing's increasing pessimism about the possibility of making the world a better place. The young writer who came to London from Rhodesia hoping to find less prejudice and exploitation has long been disabused of any faith in the future. Many of Lessing's critics complain about her drab and graceless prose and the almost awkward attention to detail. There are some, however, who see such a style as appropriate to the grim reality she seeks to portray and praise her ability to force the reader to attend to her themes rather than to her words. There is little disagreement about the distance Lessing establishes between narrator and character; readers are discouraged from developing any sympathy for Alice Mellings and her friends. *The Good Terrorist* is not a novel to love; rather, it represents an interesting stage in the work of this prolific and controversial writer. It remains to be seen whether Lessing will return to science fiction out of sheer despair at the world she knows at first hand, or whether she will continue to play the prophet of doom.

Sources for Further Study

Bell, Pearl. "Bad Housekeeping: *The Good Terrorist* by Doris Lessing," in *The New Republic*. CXCIII (October 28, 1985), pp. 47-50.

Donoghue, Dennis. "Alice, the Radical Homemaker," in *The New York Times Book Review*. XC (September 22, 1985), p. 3.

Lardner, Susan. "A Kind of Dryness," in *The New Yorker*. LXI (October 14, 1985), pp. 136-140.

Jane M. Barstow

THE GORMENGHAST TRILOGY

Author: Mervyn Peake (1911-1968)
Type of plot: Fantasy
Time of plot: A mythical present
Locale: The castle of Gormenghast and the surrounding countries
First published: 1967: *Titus Groan*, 1946; *Gormenghast*, 1950; *Titus Alone*,
  1959

> *Principal characters:*
> TITUS GROAN, the heir to Gormenghast
> LORD SEPULCHRAVE, his father
> COUNTESS GERTRUDE, his mother
> LADY FUCHSIA, his sister
> DR. PRUNESQUALLOR, the physician to the family
> STEERPIKE, a devious and ambitious servant
> BELLGROVE, the headmaster of the castle school
> JUNO, Titus' lover

The Novels

   Titus Groan, the first book of *The Gormenghast Trilogy*, may well be the only work in English literature whose most striking character is a building—the building being Gormenghast Castle, the immensely old and inconceivably huge ancestral home of the Groans. The story of Titus, the Seventy-Seventh Earl of Groan, is one that takes an extraordinarily long time to get under way. *Titus Groan* starts with Dr. Prunesquallor delivering Countess Gertrude's baby, Titus, and by the end of the book, Titus is only one year old. The hundreds of pages between the first and last paint a detailed and loving description of the setting, Gormenghast Castle, and its principal inhabitants.

   Gormenghast is a place absolutely isolated from the world of the reader: No one in the story knows or much cares what is happening outside their own time-bound society. Gormenghast, for as long as anyone can remember, has been ruled by the dictates of the Ritual, a code of behavior that prescribes the daily conduct of the castle's inhabitants, particularly that of the reigning Earl. Titus will much later rebel against the stifling demands of the Ritual. That is in the future, however, when the story begins.

   The plot of the first book begins with the introduction of Steerpike, an apprentice cook when he first appears, a villain whose will shapes the early story. Unlike the other characters, Steerpike has a genuine ambition. It is small at first—to escape the domination of Swelter, the head cook—but it soon grows until he dreams of taking complete command of the castle. After escaping from Swelter's dominion, Steerpike discovers a possible center of power in this fragmented society: He wins the trust of the feeble-minded sisters of Sepulchrave, the twins Cora and Clarice. These witless old maids are members of the Groan family, yet simpletons he can manipulate. Through them, he plots to set fire to Sepulchrave's library when the family gathers for a ceremonial; he plans to rescue the Earl and the heir from the fire to advance himself further in their affections. The arson goes as scheduled, and Sourdust, the master of Ritual, dies in the fire. Steerpike realizes that the position is one of central importance in the castle, but to his dismay, Sourdust proves to have a son, Barquentine, who assumes the post. Steerpike then attaches himself to Barquentine as his apprentice.

As this summary shows, the plot of the first book is largely the story of Steerpike's ambition. There are, however, a number of subplots, principally the rivalry between the head cook, Swelter, and Sepulchrave's devoted valet, Flay. The story of their mutual hatred provides the ending for this first part of the trilogy. In a climactic duel, Flay kills Swelter; Sepulchrave banishes his servant from the castle and then disappears himself. The first book closes with the proclaiming of the infant Titus as Seventy-Seventh Earl of Groan.

The second book, *Gormenghast*, begins with Titus at seven. Unlike his father, Titus has had no childhood postponement from the demands of the Ritual. From his earliest years, Barquentine, master of Ritual, orders and limits his daily existence. Barquentine has no particular affection for Titus: The old man's only loyalty is to the Gormenghast Ritual and to the duty that he serves harshly and exactingly. Under Barquentine's control, Titus yearns for the freedom simply to do what he likes.

One of the main contrasts between the second book and the other two is that *Gormenghast* provides much more humor, chiefly through the subplot of Titus' school and its masters. The headmaster, Bellgrove, and his associates are grotesques—characters exaggerated to the point of comedy in their appearances and actions. The story of Titus' schoolboy adventures is accompanied by the romance of Bellgrove and Irma Prunesquallor, the doctor's sister. Yet this comedy is superimposed on the sinister backdrop of Steerpike's continued plotting.

From the moment of his burning the library, Steerpike is linked with fire. It is his principal tool, and the image with which he is most often associated. In the first book, in an odd foreshadowing of a later event, old Sourdust catches some hairs from his beard in a door. Unable to unlock the door and free himself (which would break the Ritual), Sourdust cuts off the trapped hairs and, to remove them from the door, sets fire to them. Again, an interpolated story in the second book speaks of a hollow-cheeked youth setting the beard of his master aflame. Still later, the reader is told of Steerpike not that he has several hours "to kill," but that he has several hours "to be burned." Steerpike's fire, his ambition, begins to take strange forms: His domination over Cora and Clarice has degenerated into a desire for gratuitous cruelty. Telling them that there is a plague in the castle, he imprisons them in their apartment, keeping them half starved and making them literally crawl for his amusement. Eventually, in their desperation they try to kill him, and the attempt enrages Steerpike against the hierarchy of the castle, moving him to action.

He goes to Barquentine's room, determined to kill the old man, no longer content to wait for him to die. In the struggle that follows, Steerpike sets Barquentine's beard and clothes ablaze, but the old man seizes Steerpike in a deathgrip. Steerpike manages to jump from the window, still clutched by Barquentine, and the flaming pair fall into the castle moat, where Steerpike finally drowns Barquentine. Although badly injured himself, Steerpike manages to convince everyone that he has been burned trying to rescue Barquentine, and he finally achieves his ambition, becoming master of Ritual. When he recovers, scarred by his burns, he realizes that Cora and Clarice have starved to death, locked in their rooms.

Through all these events, Titus has been growing, and growing restless. In his play in the surrounding forests, Titus becomes acquainted with Flay, who has been living in the wilderness near the castle since his banishment, and Flay communicates his own suspicion of Steerpike to Titus. Flay's warning adds to the dissatisfaction that Titus had focused on Steerpike, who, as master of Ritual, dominates Titus' life. Steerpike, meanwhile, has set himself a new conquest, the seduction of Fuchsia, but this time he overreaches himself. Flay, in a moment of prescience, foresees some evil about to occur and returns to the castle. In the company of Titus and Dr. Prunesquallor, Flay follows Steerpike to the room in which lie the bodies of the twins. There, the three attempt to arrest Steerpike, but he murders Flay and escapes to hide somewhere in the enormous castle.

Steerpike's flight is aided by a torrential rain that floods the region, turning the castle into an archipelago that can be explored only by boat; as Titus begins to take control of the plot, the images of fire give way to those of water. The unthinkable is happening: Gormenghast itself is changing, its former mountainlike solidity becoming a cluster of islands and inlets. The shape of Gormenghast is said to resemble the island of Sark, and a special allusion occurs when the characters refer to a part of the castle called "Little Sark." The images of water, however, are not entirely life-bringing: Fuchsia, genuinely in love with Steerpike, is stunned by the revelations about him. In a moment of solitary inattention, she loses her footing and drowns in the floodwaters. Caring nothing about Gormenghast but thinking that Steerpike has killed Fuchsia, Titus tracks down Steerpike and kills him in a flooded room. With the death of this former prime mover of the plot, Titus no longer has anything to hold him to the castle. He loathes the Ritual, and his sister, to whom he was closest, is dead. He tells his mother that he is going and, despite her prediction that he will return, leaves Gormenghast.

The third book, *Titus Alone*, follows the picaresque adventures of Titus on his own in a society as unusual in its own way as was that of Gormenghast. Although some critics have suggested that Mervyn Peake's failing health affected his writing of the third part, there is no abrupt change in characterization or handling of plot to suggest that its writer was unable to do what he wanted. Peake's depiction of the city's underground (in both a figurative and a literal sense) is especially powerful, as well written as anything in the first or second books. Even the familiar symbol of Gormenghast Castle frequently appears: To Titus' chagrin, people in the city he finds think that Gormenghast is a myth, and Titus finds himself doubting his own sanity as he begins to wonder if Gormenghast really exists. The presence of Gormenghast, however, like a gigantic sleeping animal, is largely replaced by another menace: the omnipresent surveillance to which Titus believes himself subjected. In strong contrast to the solitude which was characteristic of Gormenghast, privacy is now hard to secure. Small flying machines observe the actions of the inhabitants of the city, and Titus himself is hounded by a mysterious pair of uniformed, helmeted figures, apparently agents of the shadowy government.

If the earlier books were the story of Titus' youth, this is the story of his young manhood; of his first love, Juno; of his first involvements with equals in society. Again in strong contrast to the unchanging castle of the early books, *Titus Alone* presents a picture of a changing political scene. For the first time, Titus finds centers of authority—Law and Police—outside himself and finds that they can be masters as uncompromising as the Ritual. Titus finds himself jailed as a vagrant, thinking of his mother's prophecy that he will return to Gormenghast, but still as changeable as water. He is paroled into the custody of Juno, a woman of substance in the city. She loves him and for a time he returns that love, yet his restlessness causes him to leave her as well. After all the adventures that follow, Titus escapes from the oppressive, stifling city and flees into the countryside. Eventually, he comes in his wandering to a place he knows: a ridge from the other side of which he could see Gormenghast. His world does exist, and with the knowledge that he is sane, he no longer has any need to return. He therefore turns away without crossing the ridge and coming in sight of the castle itself.

The Characters

As has been suggested earlier, Peake draws his characters as grotesques. It is no surprise that an artist should provide strongly visual presentations of his characters, presentations aided in most editions by illustrations by the author. Many of these characters remind the reader of the "humour" characters of seventeenth century English drama, people so exaggerated in one respect or another that the quirk becomes the personality of the character.

The main characters are highly individualized, each isolated in his or her own private world: Lord Sepulchrave, lost in his melancholy, mopes from one

Ritual requirement to the next. Titus' mother, Gertrude, lives in her rooms surrounded by the only creatures in the world that she loves: hundreds of birds (who come when she calls) and a host of pet white cats. His teenage sister, Fuchsia, spends her days playing in an attic gallery stuffed with discarded odds and ends. There is little interaction in the usual novelistic sense because the characters so seldom meet: Gormenghast offers sufficient room, both metaphorically and literally, for its dwellers to stake a claim and in which to preserve their own separate identities. Numerous descriptions of the castle depict it as an enormous structure, with wing after wing extending to the horizons, and in its vast expanse, each character is free to pursue an individual goal, no matter how odd. The desire most frequently expressed by the characters is a desire to be let alone.

Even the more minor characters are individualized to the point of caricature: Take, for example, Barquentine, who not only has a withered leg but also is so stunted that he stands only half normal size, or Dr. Prunesquallor, whose foppish manner and nervous laugh allow the reader to identify his speeches even without attribution. The names of the characters aid this method: In book 3, two characters associated throughout with animal images are the political revolutionary Muzzlehatch and his daughter Cheeta.

Flay, the majordomo, is all sharp angles and points; his knees crack like pistol shots with every step (at one point, when Flay wants to move silently, he even muffles his knee joints). His adversary, Swelter, is a character as soft and as formless as the dough he kneads. It is not surprising that most of the characters, guarding their own individuality so jealously, are preoccupied with their own desires, subordinated only (for all but Steerpike and Titus) to the traditions of Gormenghast. The castle gives them at least this: the opportunity to be themselves in whatever unorthodox directions their whims lead. Titus never perceives this unusual coupling of freedom with restriction: What is sustaining to the others circumscribes him, and he must leave the castle to appreciate what it had offered.

Themes and Meanings

The Gormenghast Trilogy is the title customarily given to the three major literary productions of Mervyn Peake—*Titus Groan, Gormenghast*, and *Titus Alone*—but there are problems with both "Gormenghast" (a title Peake himself never intended) and the generic classification of trilogy. Titus' ancestral castle, Gormenghast, figures as the setting for only the first two books, but Titus himself appears in all three, the only character to do so. Whatever statement the work makes has more to do with Titus' desire to free himself from dependence on and domination by others. The three romances are much more the story of Titus himself, his infancy, his growing up, and his assertion of his own independence, than of the castle. The critic John Clute argues that a better title would be "The Titus Groan Trilogy," for certainly a main theme of the work is the search of the adolescent for self-definition, rather than acceptance of a definition imposed from outside, whether by tradition as in books 1 and 2, or by society, as in book 3.

Yet it would surely be a mistake to think of Peake's romances as books written to illustrate a thesis, for even the word "trilogy" is inaccurate: Peake probably had no overall design for the work. He was working as an artist and book illustrator when he was drafted into the British army in 1940. In the cramped conditions of army life, it was impossible for him to paint, but he could write, and it was then, in those unlikely conditions, that he began to write the first volume. The second and third followed in time, and in the 1960's, as Peake's health declined toward his tragic end, he even began to write a fourth volume, only a few pages of which survive, which presumably would have followed Titus' life even further.

Although the work was not planned as a whole, it is consistent in its themes. Those themes—freedom from restriction and the sustaining yet also stifling nature of tradition—were certainly ones that Peake must have felt keenly, especially as one of the most inept soldiers ever to wear a British uniform. Although these ideas never intrude, they are often voiced by Titus, especially at points of tension in the works.

Critical Context

The author of *The Gormenghast Trilogy* spent much of his life ignored by the critics and tastemakers in several branches of art, despite his facility as a poet, a writer of prose, a painter, and a book illustrator. It was a life hampered by the irregular and insecure place of the artist in society, by the conflicts of nations, and by common mortality.

Yet it was not dull; Peake's life was itself much like a romance, filled with the color of exotic places and with an often bizarre humor. He was born in the city of Kuling in China, where his father was a medical missionary, and he lived there until he was eleven. Some readers have suggested that Peake derived his conception of Gormenghast at least in part from his recollections of this early period. The Peakes were frequent visitors in Hankow, the capital of the province, where foreigners lived in a walled compound surrounded by Chinese workshops that produced fine porcelain. The resemblance between the castle of Gormenghast with the village of the Bright Carvers huddled against its walls and the compound in Hankow surrounded by the porcelain-makers is striking. The resemblance is there, however, only in general, because there is nothing particularly Oriental about the detail of the setting of Gormenghast, its inhabitants, or those who cluster around its walls. The Bright Carvers, artists though they are, show nothing characteristically Chinese in their way of life, their names, or their pursuits.

Whatever influence Peake's childhood in China had on his work, it may have ultimately had a malign effect on his life: In 1917, Peake contracted a

viral disease epidemic in China, one that may have been the remote cause of
the nervous condition that struck him years later at the height of his production. Peake's childhood was largely a pleasant one, however, even amid the
turmoil of the Chinese political situation. In 1923, the family returned to
England, where Peake was enrolled at Eltham School. Six years later, he
began the course of study at the Royal Academy School in London. Never
much of a student and perhaps uncomfortable with the regimen of the Royal
Academy, he left before completing the course and joined an artists' colony
on the island of Sark in the English Channel. He was to return again and
again to Sark, and his affection for the place showed in his writing.

In the years that followed, despite the restrictions of postwar shortages,
Peake established himself as one of the foremost book illustrators in England. He wrote a play and published several books of poems and collections
of drawings before developing a condition in 1957 that was first diagnosed as
a nervous breakdown. By 1960, it was clear that Peake had something more
lasting, perhaps an affliction such as Parkinson's Disease, but one that developed decades after the original infection. He suffered increasingly from
lapses of attention, shaking, and an inability to concentrate. He would begin
a sketch for a book illustration and, while drawing, forget what he was
depicting. At last, his wife was no longer able to care for him, and in 1964 he
began four years in nursing homes that ended with his death in 1968.
Ironically, it was during the last stages of his illness, when he was less and less
in touch with the world, that *The Gormenghast Trilogy* was published in pa-
perback in the United States, an event that led to the work's becoming a cult
favorite.

Peake, as a devoted husband and father, as a man with a wide circle of
friends, was certainly not Titus. He was not a crusader for political causes
and certainly no champion, in the ordinary sense of that word, of individualism. Yet there was something almost medieval in his unconcern with material
possessions or for the rules of bureaucracy. As a man who honestly did not
know that one had to be licensed to drive a car, he exhibited something of
the spirit of Gormenghast's inhabitants. He lived, almost unthinkingly, that
freedom to be oneself, even to the point of eccentricity, that his characters
showed in abundance. In a world that has never shown much tolerance
toward individualists, the popularity of his work is a good sign.

Sources for Further Study
Batchelor, John. *Mervyn Peake: A Biographical and Critical Exploration*,
    1974.
Gilmore, Maeve. *A World Away: A Memoir of Mervyn Peake*, 1970.
Watney, John. *Mervyn Peake*, 1976.

Walter E. Meyers

GOSSIP FROM THE FOREST

Author: Thomas Keneally (1935-   )
Type of plot: Historical chronicle
Time of plot: November, 1918
Locale: Berlin, Germany, and Compiègne, France
First published: 1975

Principal characters:
MATTHIAS ERZBERGER, a German politician and the leader of the German peace delegation
MARSHALL FOCH, the leader of the Allied delegation
MAXIME WEYGAND, Foch's Chief of Staff, a member of the Allied delegation
COUNT ALFRED MAIBERLING, a friend of Matthias Erzberger and a member of the German delegation
ADMIRAL ROSSLYN WEMYSS, a British member of the Allied delegation
GENERAL DETLEV VON WINTERFELDT, a member of the German delegation who is married to a Frenchwoman

The Novel

In the autumn of 1918, the war started to go very badly for Germany and her allies. Not only were they beginning to be defeated in the field, but also the armed forces were refusing to obey orders and alarming acts of rebellion with Socialist and Communist overtones were erupting throughout the country. The end was drawing near, and steps were being taken to provide for the belated abdication of the Kaiser and the peaceful transition of power to a republican government. A cease-fire had to be arranged quickly, not only to save lives on both sides but also to halt the complete disintegration of the German state.

This novel, based loosely on the historical record, traces the Germans' journey through the lines of battle to the conference, the preparation of the two delegations, and their meetings in a railway carriage in a forest clearing near the town of Compiègne, a few miles north of Paris.

The delegations, surprisingly small, and narrow in their representative range, are what interest Thomas Keneally most. The Allied group is thoroughly dominated by its chairman, the French Marshall Foch, who is confident that he can "will" the Germans to accept severe terms. He is accompanied by Maxime Weygand, who is hardly more than a messenger boy for Foch, and by two English naval officers, Admiral Rosslyn Wemyss and Hope, who are intent on one thing: destroying the German army.

The German quartet is somewhat more colorful. Matthias Erzberger, their leader, is not a military man but a politician who has been trying to get Germany out of the war for some time, and he sees his appointment as a punishment for his failure to support the war effort. He will bear the stigma of having signed away Germany's freedom. His delegation is not much help. Count Alfred Maiberling, a last-minute substitute, is a self-pitying drunk and looks as if he is having a breakdown. General Detlev von Winterfeldt, who is suspect in his own profession because of his marriage to a Frenchwoman and his affection for France, thinks that he can, with his intimate knowledge of the French sensibility and his skill in the French language, win concessions from the Allies, and he is determined to play a central part in the negotiations. The naval representative, Vaneslow, is deeply distressed, knowing instinctively that the German military and merchant fleet will be a prime target of the Allies in settling terms for the treaty.

The chaos of their nation, reeling on the edge of political and social anarchy, makes everything difficult for the German group, and its leader, Erzberger, is in constant fear that if their mission is known, they may be assassinated before they reach France. His recurring dream of defending himself from gunmen with an umbrella does not make things easier for him; moreover, the fractious nature of his committee, their difficulties in simply getting through the lines, and the cool reception they meet suggest that things will go badly. In the minds and dreams of all the German participants, they are on a mission which is likely to prove disastrous.

The Allies have similar doubts and suspicions, but they, at least, are in the position of power, and their struggle lies in their variant ideas on how much pain and unmitigated punishment can be imposed on the Germans as well as on the question of who is to rule at the conference table. The British pair, Wemyss and Hope, do not entirely trust Foch, and the French, in turn, make it clear that they consider the British presence to be superfluous. Foch intends to force formidable terms down the Germans' throats, and he does, satisfying the British demands at the same time.

Some minor adjustments are made to the swingeing demands for reparations, but they are hardly sufficient to meet the German plea (and warning) that the obligations forced upon them will destroy any chance of Germany's recovery from the ravages of war. The Allies, shortsightedly, reject any consideration of the long view; the treaty makers, who will formalize the terms later (at Versailles), can worry about that problem. The Germans sign, aware of the fact that they have no choice and also that they will hardly be received at home with much honor.

Erzberger resumes his political career, but his nightmare with the umbrella will eventually come true.

The Characters

This novel is a combination of three forms: fictional narrative, documentary, and drama, with the occasional intrusions of a fulsome, theatrical inter-locutor who has a hand in shaping an ironic point of view.

The characters are less important than the nature of the action, perhaps not surprisingly so, given the historical importance of the signing of the cease-fire agreement in November of 1918. That event, however, is seen in the context of the personalities involved, and Keneally has used biographical materials from the real lives of the participants as well as fictional embellish-ments on the same to flesh out the dramatic implications of the brief, chilly confrontation which was to end World War I.

Most of the characters function within the ambit of stock typology, but Keneally allows them, through the use of personal rumination and dreams, to be modestly individual within their functions as representatives of the mili-tary and political sensibilities. Count Maiberling, for example, has a thrust-ing, lively personality which is interesting in itself, and his friendship with Erzberger goes beyond any use that is made of it in the workings of the Ger-man peace delegation.

Erzberger is the most obvious exception to stock characterization. Coming from modest peasant stock and having established a reputation for second-guessing the mad chauvinism which has pitched Germany into the tragic mess of the war, he is always aware of his singularity, always questioning his right to be in command, and constantly nagged, waking and sleeping, by the fact that he may have fallen into a trap laid for him by the old ruling classes of Germany who are using him to do the dirty work. Much of the novel is committed to his point of view, his anguish and uncertainty. If Maiberling reveals the suicidal aspect of the German dilemma, Erzberger is used to ex-plore the conscience of the common man cleaning up, as best he can, after the carnage of the military disaster, the last grand gesture of the old class-ridden Junker Germany—or so Erzberger hopes.

There is similar density in the portrait of Foch, though his character is less fully explored. Foch is the mystic theorist of the French military, jeered at by many for his metaphysical musings, his intellectual approach to battle, and his violent quarrels with the politicians. He is revealed as a vivid example of the obsessed military ego, acting out the fitting role of a punishing Jehovah, deaf to pleas for forgiveness, and seeing his role as the vindication of his entire career.

Themes and Meanings

The central meaning of this novel rests upon simple historical facts which the reader must bring to the novel: that the peace treaty imposed upon the German allies (the Treaty of Versailles in 1919) followed the basic outline established at the cease-fire conference at Compiègne, and that, in destroy-ing the economic as well as the military strength of Germany, it unwittingly sowed the seeds for the rise of Fascism in Germany—for World War II.

Erzberger and his small group of beaten men are, if unable to tell the long future, prescient enough to know that what is demanded of them will do damage which they cannot entirely assess. The natural, righteous indignation of the Allies, intensified by the excesses of the military ego, leads to the imposition of penalties on the Germans which seem consistent with the necessity to make the Germans pay for the horror of a war that should not have happened and that turned out to be the greatest nightmare, at that time, in the history of warfare. The path to further destruction, a further generation down the line, is laid by men who, for one reason or another (sometimes because of a psychological quirk, professional prejudice, or xenophobic suspicion), are determined to take the proverbial pound of flesh.

The fact that Erzberger (ironically the one politician in the group), a decent man who earlier proved his credentials by attempting to get Germany out of the war, makes it clear that Germany cannot take care of its most fundamental bread-and-butter needs is of no interest to the Allies. Germans started the war and are, it follows, liars, attempting to get off easily.

Significantly, the Allies refuse to give the Germans any time to prove otherwise; each, in his own way, wants only to exercise that arbitrary power which he despised in Germany's pursuit of military conquest. Germany sought to avenge the death of the trivial Archduke Ferdinand; it is the Allies who achieve such an act of vengeance, and for the French it is particularly sweet, since they remember the shame of their treaty of Versailles of 1873, imposed on them after their defeat in the Franco-Prussian War.

Nothing is straightforward, nothing is learned; man continues to play the fool. Adolf Hitler took that same railway carriage back to Berlin in the triumph following the fall of France in the 1940's. *Gossip from the Forest* illustrates the way in which man, in his pettiness, vanity, and rancor, never seems to learn—never, this novel suggests, wants to learn.

Critical Context

An Australian by birth, Keneally, whose career began at home and who has continued to live in and to write extensively about Australia, has on several occasions written novels which explore non-Australian themes. Among these are some which are directly or indirectly based upon historical events. Keneally often employs the historical novel, a genre which has a rather dubious reputation, as a vehicle for exploring serious themes with considerable aesthetic care. He has written a novel about Joan of Arc (*Blood Red, Sister Rose*, 1974) and another about the American Civil War (*Confederates*, 1980), and he has won the important Booker Prize for *Schindler's Ark* (1982; retitled *Schindler's List* in the United States), a carefully researched novel about the perverse exploits of a German national who saved the lives of Jewish workers during World War II.

Keneally's use of history, if in a fictional setting, is usually as accurate as he can make it, given the exigencies of the fictional form, and *Gossip from the Forest* can bear close investigation in its use of the facts and its portrayal of the actual participants in the Compiègne meetings. Only Maiberling is entirely fictional. Count Alfred von Oberndorff was, in fact, the fourth principal in the treaty affair, and he appeared in the British edition of the book, but there was an objection raised by the surviving Oberndorff family to the portrayal of the man, for which Keneally apologized in a letter in *The Times Literary Supplement*. He did, however, claim that the representations of Erzberger, Foch, Weygand, and others were accurate and that the flaws in the Oberndorff portrayal were caused by a lack of accessible research material.

Sources for Further Study
Burns, D. R. *The Direction of Australian Fiction: 1920-1974*, 1975.
Burns, Robert. "Out of Context: A Study of Thomas Keneally's Novels," in *Australian Literary Studies*. IV (1969), pp. 31-48.
Geering, R. G. *Recent Fiction*, 1974.
Keneally, Thomas. "Doing Research for Historical Novels," in *Australian Author*. VII, no. 1 (1975).

Charles H. Pullen

GRATEFUL TO LIFE AND DEATH

Author: R. K. Narayan (1906-   )
Type of plot: Magical realism
Time of plot: The late 1930's
Locale: Malgudi, in Southern India
First published: 1945, in Great Britain as *The English Teacher* (U.S. edition, 1953)

> *Principal characters:*
> KRISHNA, the English teacher
> SUSILA, his wife
> LEELA, their young daughter
> THE FRIEND, a spiritualist who can contact the dead
> THE HEADMASTER, an eccentric friend and teacher of Leela

The Novel

In his autobiographical memoir *My Days: A Memoir* (1974), R. K. Narayan declared that *Grateful to Life and Death* was the most autobiographical of all of his novels, very little of it, in his account, being fiction. This statement must immediately arouse doubt, if not skepticism. One can see how the start of the book, with its quasi-satirical picture of the protagonist, Krishna, teaching at Albert Mission College, could be drawn from Narayan's memories of his own schooling at the Lutheran Mission School in Madras and the Maharaja's Collegiate High School in Mysore. Furthermore, the pivotal event of the book, the death of Krishna's wife, Susila, is very clearly based on the tragic death of Narayan's own wife, Rajam, from typhoid, in June, 1939—a bereavement which left him, like his fictional hero, with a young daughter to rear on his own. What is harder to accept—though there is something close to a direct assertion by Narayan of its truth—is the last part of the book, in which the hero succeeds in establishing closer and closer contact with his dead wife, culminating in a transcendent moment of union and joy. Can this be credited? To ask a question more relevant in literary terms, does Narayan succeed in anything but an autobiographical way in unifying what appears to be a series of different threads of his hero and first-person narrator's experience?

At first sight, one has to answer no to the last question. The mood of *Grateful to Life and Death* keeps changing unpredictably. The first sections are of a familiar comic type. Krishna, like many other junior teachers in novels such as Charles Dickens' *Nicholas Nickleby* (1838-1839) and Bernard Malamud's *A New Life* (1961), finds himself in an ill-run establishment with a foolish head, and he takes revenge by not preparing for classes and complaining ineffectively to anyone who will listen. The joke is partly that his superiors are so insufferably petty (Brown, the Principal of the College, flies into a rage because one boy has spelled "honour" without a *u*), and partly that Krishna is so inept in his protests, his ineffective resolutions, and his general attitude. The mood changes when Susila arrives with her baby to join her husband, becoming one of tender domesticity, in which Krishna appears much more likable. The mood changes again when Susila contracts the illness which kills her, described in the novel in a long and slow section oscillating between hope and despair. Yet again, after her death, the mood shifts, though this time the effect achieved is almost surreal: Krishna not only goes through a set of psychic experiences with regard to Susila but also contracts a relationship with his daughter's teacher, a man who is convinced that he knows the date of his own death, and who insists on being socially dead, to his wife and children, even when that date is past. In a final coda, Krishna resigns from the almost forgotten Mission College (in which Brown, the principal, has suddenly become reasonable and likable) and breaks through to full contact with his wife.

There is no argument which will make a completely integrated structure out of this novel, though there are certain thematic connections. Probably Narayan's own statement that this is how things happened to him is the simplest explanation, in which case *Grateful to Life and Death*—dedicated to his dead wife—could be seen as a "therapeutic" novel. The novel is distinguished above all, however, by its overt statements about loneliness as the inescapable factor of human life, though one must note that these statements are strongly denied by almost all the novel's events and relationships. The novel turns on a devastating sense of loss, contrasted with an even more powerful belief in the strength of love.

The Characters

Central to the novel is the relationship between Krishna and Susila, seen (in life) as total opposites. Krishna is glib, talkative, and inept. He loves to explain books to people, except in those hours when he is paid to do so, and always has an elevating sentiment to turn into poetry. Yet he has no perseverance, is bullied by everyone, and cannot so much as get his wife's belongings off a train without feelings of inadequacy, camouflaged by authoritativeness. In contrast, his wife is quiet, a slow reader, a careful manager who runs a household on one hundred rupees a month (then about twenty dollars) and still has money, time, and energy to spare. The love between these two opposites is entirely credible and beautifully presented.

After Susila's death, there is a danger that all other characters will become mere tools and reflections of the central figure, Krishna, who is too absorbed by his own feelings to notice others. This does seem to happen with "the friend," an unnamed and unexplained figure who sends the hero a note one day to say that he is in touch with Krishna's dead wife, and from then on does little but conduct experiments in automatic handwriting. Quite soon the friend has virtually disappeared as a character; one notes only the results of the handwriting. The novel is saved partly by the growing prominence of Krishna's daughter Leela, in whom he comes to recognize something of the grace and good sense of her mother, and partly by the intriguing figure of "the headmaster," her teacher. This latter character is indeed best explained as a double, or analogue, of Krishna himself. The headmaster shows the same practical ineptitude as Krishna, but by his idealism, he draws Krishna in to such an extent that the hero resigns his college post and goes to teach for the headmaster at a quarter of his former salary. Whereas Krishna's marriage is ideally happy, however, the headmaster's is a total failure; yet the headmaster escapes from it, not by his wife's dying, but by insisting that he himself is dead, an action which in India at that time was acceptable and, even as an ascetic practice, mildly approved. His rise from misery to serenity parallels and guides Krishna's but at the same time remains unpredictable, amusing, governed by the character's own wayward individuality.

Grateful to Life and Death contains a large cast of subsidiary characters, most of them—like the Dr. Shankar who insists on treating Susila for malaria when she has typhoid—variants on the theme of amusing, or infuriating, impracticality. All remain firmly subordinate, however, to the narrator. Just as the headmaster shows how life can be continued, or restarted, with new vigor and meaning after symbolic death, so the others—doctors, housebuilders, colleagues, and relatives—play their parts by reflecting aspects of Krishna's own character, whether negative (vagueness, indolence, indecision) or positive (humility, tolerance, warm affection).

Themes and Meanings

Rather as in E. M. Forster's *A Passage to India* (1924), another classic of Indian life, there is at the heart of *Grateful to Life and Death* an event which takes place in the dark, with only one character present, which is never fully explained to the reader but which nevertheless appears to carry immense, quasi-symbolic force. What happens in *Grateful to Life and Death* is that Krishna and Susila go to look at a house they are thinking of buying. It appears to them absolutely ideal, even having over its gateway creepers of jasmine, Susila's favorite flower. They decide to buy it. It will be called Jasmine House. It will be the flowering place of their love. As the men discuss the contract, however, Susila vanishes. She has gone to a lavatory in the backyard and been trapped in it. When Krishna frees her, she is sick and horrified at the squalor of the place; the vendor explains that passersby know that the house is empty and foul it beyond description. She also seems, in that half-hour, to have contracted her fatal disease, for she is never well again.

The juxtaposition of beauty and horror is very striking, as is the fact that Susila can never explain what has affected her mentally. It seems as if she has in some way "fallen out of" the bright, cheerful, comic, real world which she has inhabited until then, and come upon some other, eternally present, awareness, as real metaphysically as her previous world. One danger, after her death, is that Krishna will undergo a similar experience and follow her into despair and termination; the description of his reaction to her funeral pyre suggests that he is very close to taking that path.

He is saved by spiritualism, automatic handwriting, and a vision of his wife from beyond the grave, and many readers will find this much less credible than the powerfully invoked horror of the fly-ridden yard behind the jasmines. Narayan indeed plays on the reader's skepticism, quite often presenting spiritualist failures—his wife's spirit at the start cannot, for example, remember, or cannot successfully transmit, even the name of their child—as also a sequence of vague explanations from the friend which seem to be of a deliberately maddening kind. Still, successes slowly outweigh failures. Susila's spirit directs Krishna to a sandalwood box full of keepsakes about which he knew nothing. She seems to know what he is thinking. Slowly she calms his feelings of regret and remorse. As Krishna undergoes his psychic development, seated in the friend's garden, he often sees some distance away the twinkle of funeral pyres at the open-air cremation ground where he burned his wife; yet these visions change, over the course of the novel, from being macabre to being comforting, even friendly.

In the novel's final scene, Krishna finds Susila sitting beside him on his bed, more beautiful than ever, scented with jasmine. They talk for a few moments, and then a cock crows for dawn—a traditional signal in folktales for the ghosts to fade and return to their own place. Susila indeed rises as if to go, but what could be a scene of further unbearable loss is made instead, through the symbolism of sunrise, a moment of hope and new beginning, as if Krishna were sure now that he will never lose Susila again. It is odd that only a few pages before, Krishna has declared, as if giving the novel's moral, "A profound unmitigated loneliness is the only truth of life." This statement appears to be completely contradicted by the novel's ending. Yet perhaps it is not. Loneliness may be the truth of life. In death, however, Narayan expects a compensatory union.

Critical Context

Grateful to Life and Death is the fourth of Narayan's novels, none of the preceding three having attracted much attention and all four having been printed by different publishers. After 1945, though, Narayan's career became much better established. It may not have been *Grateful to Life and Death* which caused this change: The novel—suggested above to have had therapeutic properties for the author—marks the end of Narayan's first phase of writing and the beginning of his maturity.

As a novel, *Grateful to Life and Death* resembles several highly conventional types, such as the "campus novel" seen from the perspective of a junior instructor, or the novel centered on a moment of incommunicable horror. Its main achievement, however, is to resist the gravitational tug of these modes and to persist in its own line of development, from youth to maturity, from love to loss and back again. The novel also combines a characteristically Indian challenge to Western views of reality with elements of humor and self-deprecation taken from the very mainstream of the English novel.

Sources for Further Study
Naik, M. K. *The Ironic Vision: A Study of the Fiction of R. K. Narayan*, 1983.
Ram, Atma, ed. *Perspectives on R. K. Narayan*, 1981.
Sundaram, P. S. *R. K. Narayan*, 1973.
Walsh, William. *R. K. Narayan: A Critical Appreciation*, 1982.
_____, ed. *Readings in Commonwealth Literature*, 1973.

                                                                              T. A. Shippey

THE GREAT PONDS

Author: Elechi Amadi (1934-   )
Type of plot: Social morality
Time of plot: 1918
Locale: Nigeria
First published: 1969

Principal characters:
OLUMBA, the main warrior of Chiolu village
WAGO THE LEOPARD-KILLER, the main warrior of Aliakoro
  village
IKECHI, a young Chiolu warrior
EZE DIALI, the chief of Chiolu village
EZE OKEHI, the chief of Aliakoro village
ANWUANWU, the dibia (shaman) of Abii village
IGWU, the dibia of Aliakoro village

The Novel

War and its effects define the plot of *The Great Ponds*. The war is fought between the village of Chiolu and the village of Aliakoro over fishing rights to Wagaba Pond, one of the ponds alluded to in the title of the novel. Thirty years prior to the time of the story, Chiolu warriors won a battle with those of Aliakoro, and since then members of Chiolu have claimed Wagaba Pond and fished in it without hindrance. Aliakoro villagers, however, have begun to poach in the pond, and Chiolu sends a war party to catch the poachers.

Olumba, the main Chiolu warrior, heads the party. They catch two poachers and almost a third, Wago the leopard-killer, the chief Aliakoro warrior.

The conflict soon escalates. In the first major battle, Ikechi, a young Chiolu warrior and Olumba's protégé, kills his first opponent and is initiated into the company of his colleagues. Aliakoro wins the next battle, however, with the aid of the Isiali village, whose warriors kidnap four Chiolu women, among them Oda, Olumba's pregnant youngest wife, and Chisa, Eze Diali's daughter, whom Ikechi wants to marry.

Beyond working out the ransom for several of those taken by both sides, the highly ritualized conferences between Chiolu and Aliakoro (conducted by the chiefs and elders of each village or their delegates, with input from warriors such as Olumba and Wago) fail to solve the issue of Wagaba Pond. The war becomes so serious that no one in either village is safe and the daily routine in both deteriorates.

Chiolu and Aliakoro belong to the Erekwi clan, and the other villages that constitute the clan come together to keep the war from spreading and to bring an end to it. They set up a peace conference between the warring villages, at which Olumba, offering himself to the ritual whereby property disputes are commonly settled, swears by Ogbunabali, the god of night, that Wagaba Pond belongs to Chiolu. If Olumba is alive in six months, the pond will indeed belong to Chiolu. If he dies during this period, Aliakoro's claim to it will be honored.

From this point onward, the novel focuses on Olumba. His village insists that he remain inactive and more or less in his compound. Though he takes great pains not to omit any kind of worship that might help him (which he is wont to do anyway, since he is a profoundly religious—if not superstitious—man), his anxiety begins to wear him down. Events conspire against him as well. While dislodging a hornets' nest from a palm tree in his compound, he is badly stung and suffers a severe fall. Anwuanwu, a more powerful dibia or shaman than Chiolu's, is engaged to save his life. Though he succeeds in doing so, he has to be called in again when Olumba falls violently ill from a spell put on him by Igwu, the dibia of Aliakoro. Igwu has unwillingly performed this powerful and (since Olumba's oath forbids such intervention) illegal spell, mostly because Wago has intimidated him and his fellow villagers. With Anwuanwu's help, Olumba survives this, too. His household, however, causes him further worry. Nchelem, his young son by Oda, his kidnaped wife, falls ill because he misses his mother. Nyoma, Olumba's senior wife, and after her Wogari, his middle wife, also become seriously ill. This illness spreads through the village and through Aliakoro and the entire district as well. Aliakoro calls the disease "wonjo," and many die from it. Olumba loses Nyoma and his daughter Adada and contracts the disease himself. No family in the village is unaffected by it, and some families die out from it.

It is to this tragic state of affairs that Oda and Chisa finally return. The Isiali village sold them to slave traders, but their masters died in the epidemic. Chisa has been raped, and Oda's male baby was born dead, which Olumba reads as a further sign that he has been cursed. The return of Eze Diali's daughter and Olumba's wife is a cause for rejoicing in Chiolu, but the celebration is short-lived. The epidemic—which is the worldwide influenza epidemic of 1918—continues, and to make matters worse, Olumba is attacked one night by Wago disguised as a leopard. Ikechi and several other warriors save him and wound Wago; Wago is found the next day, dead in Wagaba Pond.

This event ends the dispute over the pond in the worst possible way for Chiolu and, presumably, Aliakoro. As Eze Diali points out from the evidence, Wago has committed suicide in Wagaba Pond, and this means that no one may fish there again. Both sides have lost the conflict, and the only winners have been pride, stubbornness, and ruin themselves.

The Characters

Olumba and Wago the leopard-killer dramatize in *The Great Ponds* the pride of the warrior temperament and the lengths to which it can go. Both behave as though not only the progress of the war but also the welfare of their villages depend on their personal efforts. Olumba assumes the entire burden of Chiolu's claim to Wagaba Pond by making himself the target of divine intervention for six months. Wago, on the other hand, defies the divine and spoils the moral integrity of his village by forcing its dibia to perform a spell against Olumba's life. Olumba, at least, as his strength ebbs and his household crumbles, learns humility and a compassion for his wives that he did not have before. Moreover, his bravery is tested and deepened in a new way, for he must battle mental illness—a "voice" that is in him but seems apart from him that continually tells him that his efforts to survive are in vain. Wago, it appears, succumbs to such a "voice," for his open attack on Olumba and his subsequent suicide in Wagaba Pond suggest that he has lost his mind completely.

Like Olumba, Ikechi, the young Chiolu warrior, learns through adversity to temper his pride. He also learns, by helping to represent his village in diplomatic missions and by traveling to locate the missing women, the frustration and complexity engendered by the war. When Chisa, the chief's daughter, finally returns, Ikechi has matured. Though his father is on the point of death, he is able to comfort Chisa, accepting the fact that she has been raped and that her high spirits have been broken.

Eze Diali and Eze Okehi, the chiefs of Chiolu and Aliakoro, respectively, are a study in the inability of tribal elders to settle the conflict. Despite their skill in negotiation, their moderation, and the respect accorded them by their people, they are bound by parochial interests and tradition so thoroughly that breaking new ground in solving their common problem is beyond their imagination. The intervention of their fellow chiefs helps, but their solution, based on superstition, leaves the matter in nonhuman hands, and so fails. In fact, the system that Eze Diali and Eze Okehi represent is so brittle that they lose control in the face of the unexpected: Diali cannot keep Olumba from harm, and Okehi cannot stop Wago from essentially taking over Aliakoro. A sign of both chiefs' weakness is the illness to which both fall prey at one time or another in the story and the influenza epidemic that decimates their villages.

The most colorful characters in the novel are the dibias, or shamans. Through their divinations, spells, and medicine, they exert an extraordinary power over the villages they serve. The most powerful dibia in the story is Anwuanwu of Abii. His "magic" is the most far-reaching and successful. He is able to diagnose and counter the spell Olumba is under, for example. He is much in demand beyond his village, and because of his power and reputation, he holds himself above the war. He seems to be somewhat amused by it, indeed, and he does not let it either hurry or fluster him. Igwu, the dibia of Aliakoro, having less power than he and harassed by Wago, faces a moral dilemma. If he does not put the deadly spell on Olumba as Wago and the village want him to do, he will fail his village. If he does employ the spell, he will fail himself and his calling. His pride and exasperation lead him to choose the latter; confronted by Wago's cynicism and afraid to lose face in his village, he is unable to rise above the pressures of the war and thus contributes to them. If Anwuanwu is too powerful to be drawn into the war, Igwu is not powerful enough to avoid being drawn into it. The least powerful of the dibias in the story is Achichi of Chiolu. He serves his village without compromising its moral integrity, partly because he is unable to do so as a mediocre dibia and partly because he has accepted his lack of talent and power without resentment.

Themes and Meanings

The Great Ponds stands—intentionally, it seems—as an allegory of full-scale, modern war insofar as its cause is small, its conduct all-consuming, and its end (which reminds one of the probable effects of a nuclear war) a defeat for both sides. In addition, both sides feel justified in waging it.

The novel underscores the irony of such a war in that the people of Chiolu and Aliakoro are decent and likable. Wago is an exception; he represents the kind of military mind that in its xenophobia loses perspective and in its egomania destroys itself and corrupts the cause it serves. All in all, war is pictured as a monster that devours the well-intentioned but nearsighted people who create it.

The divine is also a conspicuous element in the novel. It is not only consulted and used by both villages in their daily life but also appealed to by them in their conduct of the war. The use of "God is on our side" to justify bloodshed is as much alive here as it is today. Indeed, any ideal relying on superstition, tradition, and emotion may substitute for the divine in supporting warfare, and *The Great Ponds* strongly suggests this.

The irony built into this aspect of the novel relies on the physical—one might say the objective—essence of war. War produces injury and death irrespective of the ideals of those involved in it. What accompanies (and, in effect, ends) the war in this case is a virus—a physical reality which no amount of religiously oriented conjuring or justification is able to stop. Thus Elechi Amadi makes his point that war is first a moral madness and last—and most of all—a physical evil.

Critical Context

Elechi Amadi's interest in playwriting appears in the emphasis on dialogue and setting in *The Great Ponds*. The novel suggests his background and interests as well. He was a captain in the Nigerian Civil War, he has been an educator, and he has had an avowed interest in religion, having coauthored a prayer-book and hymnal in Ikwerre, his native language. His sophisticated view of the complexities and psychology of war owes something not only to his firsthand experience but also to his travels in Europe and the United States and to the fact that he is a political independent. That his works are set in his homeland gives them an authentic ring, and that he focuses on the pressures brought to bear on traditional habits of thought shows his concern with, as he has put it, "gods . . . matter. . . life's purpose (if any), and man."

Sources for Further Study
Emenyonou, E. *The Rise of the Igbo Novel*, 1978.
Library Journal. Review. XCVIII (June 1, 1973), p. 1842.
The New Yorker. Review. XLIX (January 21, 1974), p. 84.
Niven, Alastair. *The Concubine: A Critical View*, 1981. Edited by Yolande Cantu.
Publishers Weekly. Review. CCIII (March 19, 1973), p. 61.
Spectator. Review. CCXXIII (September 20, 1969), p. 374.

Mark McCloskey

THE GREEN MAN

Author: Kingsley Amis (1922-   )
Type of plot: Ghost story
Time of plot: The late 1960's
Locale: Fareham, in Hertfordshire, and Cambridge, some twenty miles away
First published: 1969

> *Principal characters:*
> MAURICE ALLINGTON, the narrator, the innkeeper of The
>   Green Man
> JOYCE, his second wife
> AMY, his daughter by his deceased first wife
> DIANA MAYBURY, the wife of Allington's doctor, with whom
>   Allington conducts an affair
> DR. THOMAS UNDERHILL, one of the ghosts who haunt The
>   Green Man
> "THE YOUNG MAN," a character not otherwise identified,
>   seemingly an apparition of God

The Novel

The Green Man is the story of a haunting and an exorcism. Its action takes place in The Green Man, an English pub not far from Cambridge, which harbors at least three apparitions: the harmless and ineffective ghost of Mrs. Underhill, allegedly murdered by her husband by supernatural means some time in the 1680's; Dr. Thomas Underhill himself, a malignant ghost still trying to cause harm from beyond the grave; and the Green Man, a spirit (or force) which can take physical form from trees and bushes and so carry out the murderous wishes of its director. Yet although all these "facts" have been made clear and accepted by the end of the story, they are at the beginning naturally no more than allegations, faced by the deep skepticism of characters and at least a majority of readers. The main difficulty of the novelist writing a ghost story in the late twentieth century is to persuade his audience that superstitions from the past can coexist with a well-imagined and realistic present.

Kingsley Amis achieves this in several skillful and unexpected ways. To begin with, the "real world" is always strongly present in the novel. While Maurice Allington grapples with ghosts and visions, he is always simultaneously coping with a demanding job (taking bookings, pacifying staff, checking and collecting deliveries) and with a sequence of personal crises (mainly the death and burial of his father, but also a withdrawn teenage daughter and a second wife who is reluctant to act as a business partner and stepmother). Weird events, then, are firmly embedded in prosaic context.

Allington, the narrator, furthermore reacts to the hauntings in much the same way as he reacts to everything else, with strong feelings of frustration. The frustration in this case is caused by the fact that he cannot assemble any proof of any of the events that happen. At least a dozen times in the book Allington sees a ghost or undergoes a supernatural experience of one kind or another—the way in which these are varied and built up to a climax being one of the novel's major successes. Yet the event is never unequivocally shared by any other person. Allington's increasingly desperate attempts to find some tangible proof, some object which will guarantee that he is telling the truth, both make the reader aware that Allington is not a fanciful character and raise the interesting question of what can be considered "proof" of any subjective experience.

Surrounding the main protagonist is a whole set of doubtful and skeptical characters, whom Amis allows to be won over slowly to Allington's side. Preeminent in this role is Lucy, his daughter-in-law, called to The Green Man for the family funeral. She is trained in philosophy, and on several occasions refines and comments on Allington's accounts. It is a good stroke to make her and her father-in-law hostile to each other not only over ghosts but also temperamentally; this means that as Lucy starts to concede, out of sheer intellectual honesty, that her father-in-law could be telling a sort of truth and cannot be instantly disproved, the reader takes this as a genuine admission. Other minor and major characters in the novel take on similar roles. Yet there is no doubt that appearances always remain against Allington. A final complication to a plot based on the incommunicability of experience is that Allington is well on the way to becoming an alcoholic. At least three of his ghost sightings coincide closely with drunken blackouts. He admits to having nonsupernatural hallucinations. One of his major fears, throughout the novel, is that he is not seeing ghosts at all but is going mad.

All these tensions give credibility and complexity to a plot based on the notion that a man nearly three centuries dead is trying, not exactly to come back, but to reenact former sadistic pleasures by taking over a weary, middle-aged innkeeper who might be expected to be full of his own concerns. A final surprise in *The Green Man*, though, is that Allington and Underhill are connected by more than coincidence.

The Characters

There is in a sense only one fully realized character in *The Green Man*, and that is the narrator. Since he tells the story, the reader tends naturally to side with him, amused by his repeated furies over careless staff, boring conversations, and tedious television programs. Events, though, start to turn against Allington quite soon, and especially over sexuality. Allington is highly sexed, by reputation and in fact, and early in the novel succeeds in seducing Diana Maybury, his doctor's wife, a woman he quite clearly despises. The reader may go along with his own feelings of delight and triumph on this occasion; but doubts begin to surface as Allington goes straight on from this success to try to organize an "orgy" involving himself, his wife, and Diana simultaneously, and perhaps with even more force as the reader comes to realize that Allington has no insight into Diana's psychology at all. She hates her husband; everybody else remarks that this is obvious, yet Allington has never noticed. He is very good, in short, at persuading other people, very bad at observing them. Although he appears sympathetic, is he not in fact a cynical manipulator?

If so, that may be one reason why the evil Underhill has decided to exert pressure on him rather than on any previous owner of the house. Underhill's psychology is revealed through a diary which Allington locates and reads in a college library at Cambridge University, and it is based first on a desire to survive after death but second on a preoccupation with sexual experiment, leading easily to sadism. Allington is not a sadist, but he is an experimenter. He also has a teenage daughter, who seems to be a further reason for Underhill's interest. The climactic division and opposition between Underhill and Allington comes when the latter, who has retrieved an image from Underhill's coffin which can call up the demonic Green Man, realizes that all this has been aimed at his daughter, lured out of her bed at night for the Green Man to kill and Underhill to watch. Allington immediately rebels, but even after he has drawn off the Green Man and saved Amy, he is uneasily aware that what he thought was a kind of scientific inquiry may in reality have been prompted by motives not far removed from Underhill's vicious sadism and his own sexual experimentation—a sort of excited curiosity.

Allington in the end remains difficult to judge. There is much to be said against him. He is a drunkard, a womanizer, a habitual deceiver with little interest in others; his first wife had good reason to leave him, as does his second, Joyce, at the very end of the novel. On the other hand, he feels guilt over the deaths of his first wife and his father (neither in any way his fault), means well, is capable of kindness, and is also totally determined when it comes to resisting Underhill and the Green Man and getting rid of them both via exorcism—a process in which he has, once again, and this time perfectly forgivably, to use his old skills in manipulation and deceit. The characters round him, it should finally be said, all like Allington, however clear they are about his failings. In better circumstances, one believes, he might be a better man.

Themes and Meanings

The major themes of *The Green Man* are death and religious belief. At the start of the novel, Allington has no belief at all in any kind of personal immortality—a feeling made more painful by the death of his father. His slowly growing conviction that Underhill is still there, still affecting events from beyond the grave, however, forces him to think again; if he is wrong in believing that there is no life after death, perhaps he is wrong also in his connected belief that there is no God. The thematic center of *The Green Man* is, accordingly, Allington's interview with the "young man" who appears to be God.

This interview takes place just before the novel's narrative climax (when Underhill tries to kill Amy). It ought, in a way, to be a turning point: Before it, Allington has failed at virtually everything, from conducting his orgy with Joyce and Diana to persuading people of his sanity. After it, he possesses a crucifix-talisman which even checks Underhill for a moment, and he should have the satisfaction of knowing that he has been recruited by a higher power to carry out a specific task. Nevertheless, the incident is anything but reassuring. To begin with, the "young man" fits conventional notions of God rather badly. He is very powerful but not omnipotent; otherwise, he would be able to destroy Underhill himself. As it is, he is restrained by his own concept of "rules," one of which is avoiding personal involvement. Furthermore, the "young man" clearly does not want worship; indeed, the reason he wants Underhill destroyed is that the existence of ghosts might start people believing once more: He regards Underhill as a "security risk." Amis' "God" is in fact playing a complex game with people and is anxious only that it should be played fairly. From time to time, he comes down, as it were, to stand among his own chess pieces, either as Christ, or it may be as Satan. Yet he seems at best morally neutral, certainly not benevolent, marked in his interview with Allington above all by curiosity, faint annoyance, and perceptible hints of cruelty. The "young man," in short, is very like both Allington and Underhill—a manipulator, but raised to a very much higher power.

This eerie picture dominates the worldview of *The Green Man*. In this novel, many things are faced which are omitted from supposedly more realistic novels: fear of death, fear of age, fear of pointlessness, regret over one's lasting inability to take back mistakes. None of these is removed by the interview with "God." In the world the "young man" has created, all the fears above are intrinsic, sensible, and not to be removed by religious belief. The one assurance given to Allington—that there will be a life after death—seems to be no reassurance at all, given the chilling personality of the Creator with whom he must expect to be reunited. It is difficult to tell how seriously Amis intends all this, outside the artificial confines of a "ghost story." Yet the view of life which Amis offers, via Allington, is at least recognizable to everyone who has started to grow old.

Critical Context

The Green Man can be seen in one way as a late example of the "ghost story," a subgenre brought to perfection, in many opinions, in the tales of M. R. James (1862-1936). Amis' novel shows several resemblances to these, not least in its grasp of period detail and in its careful setting of one major scene within a college library. (James was provost of King's College, Cambridge, and frequently used his immense knowledge of paleography in his fiction.) It is a great technical achievement to have added to this framework at least three elements quite alien to the "Jamesian" story, namely sexuality, individual characterization, and skepticism.

The point of doing this can, however, only be grasped in terms of Amis' own development. In this context, *The Green Man* shows Amis' increasing disenchantment with political themes, his alienation from the highly politicized scene of the late 1960's, and his conviction that the truly serious concern of the novel ought to be one's ability to develop and hold a personal philosophy in the face of organized disbelief and the erosion of all moral standards.

That is Allington's success. He does win through to a kind of creed, even after his interview with the "young man"; he recovers his daughter, both physically and emotionally. The major achievement of *The Green Man* is to rescue conviction from the jaws of skepticism, fear, and nihilism. It may usefully be compared with several other novels by Amis on the themes of age, death, and deity, particularly *The Anti-Death League* (1966), *Ending Up* (1975), and *The Alteration* (1976).

Sources for Further Study

"Drunk and the Dead," in *The Times Literary Supplement*. October 9, 1969, p. 1145.
Gardner, Philip. *Kingsley Amis*, 1981.
Salwak, Dale. *Kingsley Amis: A Reference Guide*, 1978.

T. A. Shippey

GUERRILLAS

Author: V. S. Naipaul (1932-   )
Type of plot: Satiric realism
Time of plot: Sometime in the 1970's
Locale: An unnamed Caribbean island
First published: 1975

> *Principal characters:*
> PETER ROCHE, who was once a revolutionary hero in South
>   Africa and is now a perpetual refugee working for an
>   international firm
> JANE, Roche's mistress
> JIMMY AHMED, a romantic black revolutionary
> MEREDITH HERBERT, a local politician who becomes a minister
>   after the troubles on the island
> HARRY DE TUNJA, a local businessman and friend to Peter,
>   Jane, and Meredith
> ADELA, a servant to Peter and Jane
> BRYANT, a local orphan who lives in Jimmy's commune

The Novel

Based loosely on V. S. Naipaul's nonfictional essay "Michael X and the Black Power Killings in Trinidad," the action of *Guerrillas* recasts the story of postcolonialism in terms of the relationships between four people on a disturbed West Indian island. The novel opens with a sentence whose tone, eerily out of place, recalls that of other nineteenth century English stories whose ideology creates an ironic subtext: "After lunch Jane and Roche left their house on the Ridge to drive to Thrushcross Grange." Peter Roche is a man who has gained respect, employment on the island, and press coverage for his first book as a result of his reputation "as someone who had suffered in South Africa." He works for an American bauxite company (once associated with the slave trade) from which he gets secondhand machinery to support his association with Jimmy Ahmed, a Black-Chinese radical leader. It is to Jimmy's commune, Thrushcross Grange, that he drives Jane at the start of the novel. Jane is a white female version of what Naipaul elsewhere called a "mimic man," a person who has mindlessly and inattentively learned to mimic what she hears in print and words. Living vicariously through others, she follows Roche to the island only to be progressively disappointed by his lack of power and authority. She starts, thoughtlessly, a sexual affair with Jimmy that ends only with her brutal rape and murder at the end of the book.

The action of the novel results from the unexamined and unacknowledged consequences of the apparently innocent "drive" to Thrushcross Grange. For Jane and Roche, the visit is the start of the disintegration of their fragile relationship. For Jimmy, meeting Jane is the start of a fevered imaginary encounter with a deranging object of ambivalent desire that he translates into a fictional Clarissa in the hysterically romantic novel he is in the process of writing. For Bryant, one of the poor local youths who lives in the commune, it is the start of his sexual betrayal by Jimmy.

The novel alternates between chapters that depict the action from the perspective of each of the major characters, who view, with varying degrees of insight, the political, racial, and economic problems of the island. The cold journalistic eye that reports the action of the first chapter contrasts with the frenzied confessional yearnings of Jimmy's fictional self in his letters and novel and with the brilliant chapter in which Meredith interviews Roche on radio. The action of the novel begins with illusion in the possibility of revolutionary change, disperses itself into a cloudy uprising, and ends with a grotesque rape-murder. As the epigraph to the novel, written by Jimmy, suggests, political actions built out of mindless slogans result in personal, communal, and political chaos: "When everybody wants to fight there's nothing to fight for. Everybody wants to fight his own little war, everybody is a guerrilla." The sequence of action reflects Naipaul's conviction that politics is but the extension of human relationships and that the corrupt fantasies that sustain neocolonialism must necessarily be expressed in the corruption of the private relations that engender such fantasies. At the end of the novel, Roche knows that Jimmy has murdered Jane, escapes the island concealing evidence of her existence, and, in the process, necessarily denies connection, knowledge, or memory of her.

The Characters

Peter Roche has in his own way been a "guerrilla," a white man who has written a book about his torture and imprisonment by the South African government; he now sees himself, however, as a man without a function who undermines himself daily. His involvement with Jimmy's idea of a revolution based on land, a fantasy agricultural commune, is exposed by the end of the novel to be as ephemeral as his relationship with Jane. The irony of his present job as a public relations officer for Sablich, a firm that was once involved with the slave trade, suggests the discrepancy between the ideals of his autobiography and the reality of his daily life. Chapter 13, in which Meredith interviews Roche, is the crucial chapter in this respect, revealing the emptiness beneath Roche's illusions of himself as a revolutionary on the side of the local blacks. In fact, as the interview suggests and as Roche has earlier admitted to Jane, the driving force in his personality has not been the revolutionary's desire to subvert the establishment but rather the need of the colonial personality to identify with the oppressor rather than the oppressed. In admitting his acceptance of authority, Roche blames the educational system that subjected him to a kind of humiliation that conditions colonizers to revere order, power, and the group, and to fear the alien Other.

Jane, the white upper-middle-class woman educated on fantasies of class, power, and race, is compelled to face her own duplicity and lack of identity in relationships on the island. Her relationship with Roche duplicates the falsehood and dependency of a depraved colonial relationship: It is dependence without responsibility, action without historical memory, and a bond based on illusion and fantasy of the power of the Other to protect and provide a reason to be. Her relationship with Jimmy is entered into with a characteristic thoughtlessness and indifference to consequences. Because she becomes a symbol of the white world that Jimmy desires and loathes, she becomes both a victim and a scapegoat for what the colonial oppressors have done to the oppressed.

Jimmy Ahmed, the vacuous, central "guerrilla" of the novel, is a character created by the verbal adulation of a European press. Celebrated in England as a radical black leader, Jimmy is a nightmare vision of the victimized, marginalized, excluded man (Heathcliff in the subtext of the novel) who empowers himself through subjecting others to his personal, political, and sexual demands. Jimmy's mental baggage, like the interior decor of his house, is made up of the refuse of colonial education: "The furniture was also English . . . of a kind seen in the windows of furniture shops. . . . On the fitted bookshelves a number of books . . . stood solidly together: The Hundred Best Books of the World. . . . It was a room without disorder." So, too, his ordered dreams are made up of packaged, meaningless revolutionary clichés and slogans:

> All revolutions begin with the land. Men are born on the earth, every man has his one spot, it is his birthright, and men must claim their portion of the earth in brotherhood and harmony. In this spirit we came an intrepid band to virgin forest, it is the life style and philosophy of Thrushcross Grange.

The pathology of his demented relationship to his fictional "Clarissa" is duplicated by all the other personal, social, and political relationships in the novel.

Themes and Meanings

The major themes, reflected in the action, characters, and images of the story, concern the crippled personalities of those marginalized by history—the "guerrillas" of the title. Naipaul's central idea about postcolonial society is its inability to create an identity apart from inflated rhetoric, play-acting, nostalgia for a nonexistent past, false hopes, and "tribal causes." "People with causes inevitably turn themselves off intellectually," he has said in an interview with Charles Michener for *Newsweek*. The island was once a part of the British Empire, and in spite of its apparent rejection of Imperial rule, it yet mimics the old patterns of life, symbolized most ironically in the name Jimmy chooses for his commune and in the furnishings of his house, his mind, and his art. The violent sexuality of the novel may be interpreted in political terms: As Naipaul has elsewhere suggested, "the politics of a country can only be an extension of its idea of human relationships." Hana Wirth-Nesher sees Jimmy's murder of Jane in terms of political allegory, reading it as suicide, with his native self taking revenge on the European-colonial self that he both needs and rejects. The local politicians on the island think that they have won independence, but they have only to look at "the pink haze of bauxite dust from the bauxite loading station" to know that the economic powers running the island are not substantially different from those which dominated it in the colonial era.

Critical Context

The first of Naipaul's novels to win acclaim in the United States, *Guerrillas* is the most bitter of a series of novels he has written about the contemporary history of the island of his birth, Trinidad. Like his later novel *A Bend in the River* (1979), *Guerrillas* had its inspiration in reality, in the Trinidadian Black Power cult figure Michael X, who killed a white woman. It is one of Naipaul's darkest, most complex studies of politics, history, postcolonial traumas, and individual identity, a brilliant examination of the problem of identities made marginal by culture, history, and economics, and of the terror of reforming identity in exile.

Sources for Further Study

Gurr, Andrew. *Writers in Exile*, 1981.

Hemenway, Robert. "Sex and Politics in V. S. Naipaul, " in *Studies in the Novel*. XIV (Summer, 1982), pp. 189-202.

King, Bruce. *The New English Literatures*, 1980.

Lim, Ling-Mei. *V. S. Naipaul's Later Fiction: The Creative Constraints of Exile*, 1984.

Wirth-Nesher, Hana. "The Curse of Marginality: Colonialism in Naipaul's *Guerrillas*," in *Modern Fiction Studies*. XXX (Autumn, 1984), pp. 531-545.

Zohreh T. Sullivan

THE GUIANA QUARTET

Author: Wilson Harris (1921-   )
Type of plot: Mythic realism
Time of plot: The twentieth century, after the colonization of Guyana
Locale: Guyana
First published: 1985: *Palace of the Peacock*, 1960; *The Far Journey of Oudin*,
   1961; *The Whole Armour*, 1962; *The Secret Ladder*, 1963

Principal characters:
Palace of the Peacock
THE DREAMING I, the narrator
DONNE, a European conquistador, captain of the crew
CAMERON, a descendant of Scottish and African grandparents
SCHOMBURGH, a man of German and Amerindian descent
VIGILANCE, a black-haired Indian, the lookout
CARROLL, a Negro boy, a singer
WISHROP, the "inspired vessel" into whom they all poured the
   desire to hate "whatever they had learnt to hate"
JENNINGS, the one who looked after the boat's engine
MARIELLA, an old woman who represents the folk, the land,
   the Mission, and all other objects of the crew's quest
THE CREW, a collection of men of various racial mixtures

The Far Journey of Oudin
OUDIN, a mysterious figure who appears out of nowhere
RAM, an Indian moneylender who covets other people's
   property
MOHAMMED, a third-generation Indian whose grandfather
   immigrated to Guyana, the eldest of his father's children
HASSAN and KAISER, Mohammed's younger brothers
RAJAH, a cousin of Mohammed and his brothers
MOHAMMED'S FATHER, the youngest of his father's children,
   who inherits the large estate acquired by his father

The Whole Armour
ABRAM, a patriarchal old man who lives alone in a cabin near
   the coast
CRISTO, a fugitive, accused of murder
SHARON, a virgin and a femme fatale
MAGDA, a prostitute, Cristo's mother and a friend of Peet
PEET, a selfish man, Sharon's father and the self-appointed
   representative of the community

MATTIAS, Sharon's new fiancé, the son of a wealthy
 Portuguese man

The Secret Ladder

FENWICK, the protagonist, a surveyor in charge of the crew, a
 man of mixed racial origins
POSEIDON, the antagonist, an ancient African who is the
 leader of a community of Negroes
JORDAN, the storekeeper of the camp and the keeper of the
 money
BRYANT, a Negro who adopts Poseidon as his grandfather
WENG, a tough Chinese foreman, a hunter and marksman
CHIUNG, an illiterate night reader, attacked by Poseidon's
 men while wearing Fenwick's hat and cloak

The Novels

In *The Guiana Quartet*, Wilson Harris transforms the history and landscape of his native land into myth. By allowing the creative imagination to
travel backward and forward through time, he examines the history and landscape of his country in the hope of finding the true identity of his people (and
the people of the Caribbean in general) and the potential for future development. The journey, moreover, becomes a quest for "the essential unity within
the most bitter forms of latent and active historical diversity," as Harris himself puts it. It is indeed a quest for a vision of the true essence of life and
nature.

Palace of the Peacock, the first novel in the sequence, begins with a dramatic scene dreamed by the narrator, in which a horseman, riding at breakneck speed, is shot. The shot seems to affect the dreaming narrator by pulling him up and stifling his "own heart in heaven." The rider dies, with a
"devil's smile," and the horse, "grinning fiendishly," snaps at the reins. The
old woman Mariella, whom the explorer, Donne, has treated as a useless
creature and ruled "like a fowl," has killed the horseman, her captor and
tormentor; she then frees his chickens and controls them by feeding them.

Before the dreaming narrator fully awakes into the fictional past, he meets
Mariella, who tells him of Donne's cruelty and shows him evidence of it. He,
in turn, observes and strokes the beauty she has managed to preserve in her
thighs. Awaking in full, he is caught between the poetic vision inspired by
Mariella and his predominantly materialistic perception of Donne. He cannot
understand the cracks that have begun to appear within the "monument of
conquest" that his own admiring self and Donne himself have constructed.
As the novel progresses, however, it becomes clear that the relationship
between the narrator and Donne represents the dialectical forces within the
self—that is, between the popular and the mundane elements of human

nature and behavior and the transcendental possibilities inherent in them. The tension of the novel is derived from the struggle between these two opposing forces.

The main part of the novel, however, presents the details of a seven-day journey which Donne and his crew make upriver into the Guyanese jungle. Each of the four books into which the twelve chapters are divided seems to emphasize a significant stage of the crew's symbolic journey through introspection and reflection to a vision of new potentialities and the possibility of rebirth.

After the first day of the journey beyond Mariella, from whom the folk had fled, the dreaming narrator is interrupted, and a journey through the "straits of memory" unfolds through a third-person narrative voice. Touched by the presence of an old Amerindian woman whom they have taken with them as a guide, they are beset by all the old guilts and insecurities; they also, however, begin to perceive a blurring of the differences between themselves and their captive, between the conquerors and the folk. The landscape itself functions on the symbolic as well as the realistic level.

On the seventh day, after the wrecking of the boat and the apparent deaths of the crew members, the voice of the dreaming narrator returns to present the "inapprehension of substance" to the reader. Completely freed from the materialistic perspective of Donne, his dreamed twin brother into whom he was previously absorbed, he now sees through his truer spiritual eye.

To present the final vision to which the dreaming principal and the journey itself have advanced, Harris resorts to the medium of music: the harmony that enfolds all the elements of diversity. Peacock and palace, soul and flesh, savannah and forest, time and eternity, illusion and reality, the material and the spiritual are all presented as one entity. The crew, having lived through the challenge of second death, have realized the insignificance of conquest and wealth, which previously obsessed them. Consequently, they can envision the possibility of rebirth and spiritual fulfillment. Moreover, the formation of a true community, comprising all the various elements of the history and personality of Guyana, is perceived as a distinct possibility.

Like *Palace of the Peacock*, *The Far Journey of Oudin* functions on both the realistic and symbolic levels. Also like the first novel in the sequence, *The Far Journey of Oudin* involves the dreaming principal. This time, however, the narrative is not controlled by a single point of view (either first-person or third-person); instead, the plot is developed through a shifting point of view. The burden of synthesizing and assimilating the separate pieces of the author's vision of life is left to the reader.

The novel begins with Oudin's death, which he experiences as a dream—a dream of the cyclic process of life, of planting and reaping, of beginnings and endings. He, however, realizes that "his labour of death" has come to an end.

His dream is shattered by a scream from his wife, Beti, as she discovers his dead body. At this point, however, the moneylender Ram (hence the world of reality) enters the scene, and a flashback to the events that preceded Oudin's death begins.

The owner of a large estate (inherited from his father, despite the fact that there were two older sons in the family) finds himself increasingly disappointed with his three sons and hands over nearly all of his possessions to a half-witted son, whose mother (the father claims) was "an out-side woman . . . dead in childbirth." Outraged, the brothers, led by the eldest, Mohammed, and their cousin Rajah conspire against their half brother and murder him. Ram, who has been gradually building himself into a powerful figure through theft and other illicit means, covets Mohammed's land. To fulfill his plans, Ram enlists Oudin (who has appeared out of nowhere) to accept employment on Mohammed's land. Oudin's appearance becomes a curse for Mohammed, whose wife loses the "manchild" he hoped would become his heir and wastes away to death. This marks the apparent ascendency of Ram and the downfall of Mohammed, whose brothers and cousin eventually die. Eventually, Mohammed himself dies. This economic struggle between Ram and Mohammed, however, is not the main concern of the novel.

The bulk of the novel depicts each conspirator's confrontation with the reality of his deeds and his eventual death. The reader is allowed to witness the most intimate details of the life-in-death the conspirators subsequently experience. The journey through their past which they undertake after their deaths leads to the possibility of second birth. First, however, they must free themselves of all of their earthly encumbrances—of the consciousness of their material selves.

The last part of the novel deals with Oudin's journey through the forest—a hazardous flight through the "heart of darkness." He must make this journey before he can fulfill his covenant of bringing light to those in darkness. After three encounters, he begins to enjoy greater awareness of the meaning of things. As is destined, he and Beti, Rajah's daughter, return home and live as man and wife for thirteen years.

The novel comes full circle, returning to Oudin's death and Beti's discovery of his body. Oudin becomes a part of the spiritual harmony that transcends all diversity. Beti, recognizing her freedom, defeats Ram's intentions, bears Oudin's child, and thereby fulfills the promise of new life for nature and the community.

The next novel in the quartet, *The Whole Armour*, superficially reads like the script for a modern television melodrama. In a land haunted by the presence of a man-eating tiger, jealousy, hatred, and lust combine to initiate acts of violence and even murder. The familiar convention of the chase—the pursuit of a suspected murderer by the police—adds a dimension of excitement to a story that already involves hideouts, prostitution, and assumed identities. Beneath this deceptive surface, however, there is an elaborate symbolic structure woven of myth and biblical allusions; the novel's title alludes to Saint Paul's injunction (in the Epistle to the Ephesians) to "put on the whole armor of God."

Sharon (whose name literally means "the beautiful flower in the midst of the jungle") is the femme fatale, the dragon-lady who breathes the flame of passion into the hearts of young men. In their struggle to possess her, these young men resort to murder. Cristo (possibly a modern Christ or Antichrist), the son of the prostitute Magda (a name that recalls Mary Magdalene and/or Madelaine), is a fugitive from justice. He, the latest in a cycle of lovers, flatly denies the charge of killing Sharon's previous lover.

Abram, a kind of father figure (reminiscent of the biblical Father Abraham), is persuaded by Magda to shelter Cristo in his isolated cabin. The unexpected death of the old man moves Magda to suspect that her son has murdered him. Consequently, she brings him back to the scene and forces him to switch clothes with Abram's jaguar-mutilated and festering body. She then persuades him to flee toward the far regions of the Venezuelan border. Before he leaves, he confesses to the murder of Abram, an act he actually did not commit. In so doing, he accepts his portion of communal guilt, even as Abram had earlier accepted responsibility for fathering him—something that was impossible.

By the end of the first book of the novel, "Jigsaw Bay," the author has already revealed the pieces of the puzzle of community which must be reintegrated into a meaningful whole. The death of Abram, who, in his struggle to protect his home on the crumbling foreshore, isolated himself from the community, foreshadows the end of the old ways and promises a new beginning in the figure of Cristo. The Christlike figure, victimized by a community that longs to see his mother suffer for her prostitution, assumes the role of savior of the very community that ostracizes him, thereby replacing the patriarchal figure that Abram was.

Book 2 not only announces the eagle of salvation but also warns of the appearance of false prophets. The reader witnesses the exposure and striking down of all those who presume to be leaders, at a wake organized by Magda forty days and nights after the "death" of Cristo. The forces of community which were to be rallied "into an incestuous persona and image of alliance" become angry and drunk while the music pulsates. The selfish Peet (reminiscent of Saint Peter), already a failed leader, fails in a drunken attempt to seduce Magda, who splits his head open with his own boot. Moreover, he is unable to comprehend the implications of the vision of Abram's death that rises out of it. Frustrated and drunk, he accidentally wounds Mattias, his daughter Sharon's new escort. The crowd, driven to a frenzy by Peet's ravings about his daughter's rape, tramples Mattias to death. Mattias' cry of death coincides with Sharon's cry of ecstasy mingled with pain, as she becomes over-whelmed by Magda's seductive presence. Moved by the revelation of her fa-ther's attempted rape of Magda and by Cristo's letter, she resigns her role of virgin-temptress.

The title of Book 3, "Time of the Tiger," and the epigraphs from William Blake and Saint John of the Cross draw the reader's attention to the dialectics of change, which involve the forces of both destruction and creativity, as well as to the dialectics of life, which involve time and eternity. The death of Mattias and the emergence of a new Sharon are indeed part of the dialectical process of the novel.

The final section of the book, "All the Aeons," presents the resolution of all the apparently disparate elements. Sharon responds to Cristo's summons and joins him in the dark forest, where they consummate their love. Through the richness of language, Harris describes the "sacramental union" of man and nature, as the landscape not only witnesses but also participates in the act. Sharon, the virgin-temptress, now becomes a devoted lover and pregnant mother, thereby fulfilling the promise of fertility inspired by her name.

In keeping with the myth of regeneration, Harris reveals the details of Cristo's experience of forty days and nights in the forest. Through an ordeal that recalls the temptation of Christ, Cristo has been initiated into the mysteries of life and death; he now understands the inevitable cycles of change within eternity. Moreover, in confronting the dark mysteries of the heartland, he has gained the imaginative freedom to relive and reassess not only his personal, immediate past but also the more distant past of his country's history. As in *Palace of the Peacock*, a dreamed reunion with the folk opens up new avenues to salvation and regeneration. Not only has Cristo encountered and defeated the tiger of death, but he has also assumed the tiger's identity himself, thereby transforming destructive energy into a creative life force.

No longer afraid of the illusions of death and enjoying a heightened consciousness, Cristo reveals to Sharon the revolutionary process by which the community must be saved. It is they who must teach their parents; they must become "the first potential parents who can contain the ancestral home." Their parents, the "problem children," must forget the fables of the past and recognize the diverse elements from which the community has been derived; they must, most of all, recognize the importance of the land to their survival, the fertile heartland that they so long neglected in their determination to salvage life through a continuous struggle with the encroaching sea and the river floods.

Cristo, at the end of the novel, dreams the destruction of time and envisions his betrayal in the future by his unborn child. As he learns of the death by suicide of Peet and recognizes Magda's regression into a second childhood or senility, he is prepared to surrender to the police. These developments do not bother him, for he knows that he will eventually wear the "whole armour" that transcends "the elements of self-division and coercion."

The last novel of *The Guiana Quartet*, *The Secret Ladder*, is, as the author himself points out, the least fantastic of the four. Book 1, "The Day Readers," depicts the arrival of Fenwick and his crew from the world of light and civilization. They initiate their plans for "reading" the river Canje, in the hope of eventually controlling the flow of water to the flatlands. Book 2, "The Night Readers," introduces the mysterious and primitive forces of a dark, ancient world who oppose the scheme. Book 3, "The Reading," reveals the resolution of the opposing forces. At the end of each book, the significant incidents are recapitulated.

The author moves the reader backward in time, through seven days, in order to re-create a positive vision of life and community—the seven days evoking the creation myth of Genesis. Dramatic tension is provided by the conflict between the forces of rationality and those of irrationality, between the representatives of modernity and those of elemental existence. Again, landscape is used as "the cradle of history"; it is the "prime agent" in Fenwick's transformation. The antagonist, Poseidon, the ancient African leader of the folk, is reflected in the landscape, even as the landscape is mirrored in him. Like the Greek god, he represents not only the control of the water but also the equilibrium between the land and the water. As in *Palace of the Peacock*, the river plays a formative role. In fact, the dinghy in which Fenwick travels the Canje is named after the novel, thus confirming the relationship between the two novels. The drama unfolds not only on the river but also along its banks; the meeting of the savannah and the forest in this area symbolizes the dialectic of season and eternity.

Thus, *The Secret Ladder*, like its predecessors, functions on both the realistic and the symbolic levels. The elements of realism, however, do seem to be more clearly portrayed than in *Palace of the Peacock* and *The Far Journey of Oudin*. Like *The Whole Armour*, the novel is a successful blending of the two modes of writing: the realistic and the poetic/symbolic.

The Characters

Conscious of the cry of futility uttered by some Caribbean writers, Harris has argued that there is a historical stasis by which their sensibility has been affected. To help them escape this "prison of history," he suggests that the breach between the "historical convention" and the "arts of the imagination" in the Caribbean should be repaired. Consequently, Harris rejects the Anglo-European "novel of persuasion," which "consolidates" character, in favor of a "vision of consciousness" through which the personality of the West Indian can be expressed.

A discussion of Harris' approach to characterization must take into consideration this fictional principle. Harris resorts to the poetic-symbolic language of mythmaking in order to subvert the linear shape of time. He also resorts to several superrealistic devices in the shaping of his novels and, consequently, in the portrayal of his characters. By using such devices as dreams, visions, fantasies, and hallucinations, he allows his characters to transcend the limitations of time and space. As they live in the fictional present, they also carry the burden of the past with them. Such is the case, for example, in the portrayal of Donne and his crew in *Palace of the Peacock*. Because of the incestuous nature of community, as Harris sees it, the characters not only resemble or reflect one another but also are incorporated into one another's personalities. The individual members of the crew share Donne's identity.

Harris, moreover, resorts to the twinning of characters. In *The Far Journey of Oudin*, there is an uncanny resemblance between Oudin and the murdered half brother, between Mohammed and Kaiser, between Mohammed and the sacrificial bull, between Kaiser and the Negro woodsman, between Hassan and the round-faced fisherman. In *The Whole Armour*, as well—although the distinctions between the characters are not as blurred as in the first two novels—Harris uses the twinning technique: Abram and Cristo, through the switching of clothes and, symbolically, identities, suggest the paradox, or rather the dialectic, of youth and age, life and death. Later, Abram is reflected in Peet, reminding the reader of the biblical Father Abraham and Saint Peter. Other pairings here include Magda (prostitute) and Sharon (virgin), both of whom at some time in the novel play the role of the cruel priestess who destroys men; Mattias and Cristo, men of different classes, rivals for Sharon's love; and Abram and Magda, the figurative father and mother of the community, to which Cristo, a modern Christ, comes with the promise of salvation. Harris even extends this twinning technique beyond the narrative proper by using biblically derived names for his characters—Abram/Abraham, Peet/Peter, Magda/Magdalene, Cristo/Christ—and in this manner suggesting in his own characters the significance of their biblical counterparts/antitheses. In *The Secret Ladder*, the pairings are of opposites: Fenwick, the leader of the crew, the man of science and technology, versus Poseidon, both a farmer and a fisherman, the leader of the folk, who opposes the forces of modernity; Bryant, the spiritual grandson of Poseidon (who, ironically, accidentally causes his "grandfather's" death), versus Jordan, the force of conformity, order, and discipline. As in the other novels in the sequence, these opposites are resolved in a dialectic: Fenwick eventually purges himself of all conflicting forces that nearly throttled him, emerging as a figure of the new equilibrium into which all that both he and Poseidon represent has been absorbed. Such *dedoublement des personnages*, popular in Romantic literature, becomes in *The Guiana Quartet* vital to Harris' mythmaking.

Harris also recognizes landscape as a most important factor in the shaping of character—particularly character *qua* mythic archetype. Throughout the quartet, characters and landscape often mirror each other: The old Arawack woman in *Palace of the Peacock*, who rides the boat with the crew, is an example of this. In *The Whole Armour*, Sharon is identified with the land in her ultimate fertility/pregnancy as well as in the literal meaning of her name ("the beautiful flower in the midst of the jungle"). In *The Secret Ladder*, Poseidon, the African leader, is identified through his mythic namesake with the sea and, accordingly, is reflected in the landscape even as it reflects him—his eyes, for example, appear to Fenwick to be "a bottomless gauge and river of reflection."

Themes and Meanings

In these novels, the myth of El Dorado, which has been associated with the futility of life past and present in the Caribbean and Guyana, becomes a window through which the author and his readers enjoy a "vision of consciousness." To discuss Harris' *The Guiana Quartet* in terms of the various elements of the conventional novel is most difficult and, in fact, inadequate, since the author himself rejects the "novel of persuasion" as unsuitable for the Caribbean writer. Instead, he attempts to visualize the fulfillment of the Caribbean personality through the principle of creative mythmaking.

Palace of the Peacock shows how a genuine confrontation of one's past can result in the cleansing of the doors of one's perception, the reintegration of the disparate elements of personality and of the community, and a realization of the potentiality for new beginnings and rebirth. The dreaming narrator, by confronting the illusions of his past and his fear of death, eventually understands that he is not only a part of the crew but also part of a larger unit, mankind.

The Far Journey of Oudin deals with the question of inheritance and the quest for an heir in a particular community. This community represents the community of both Guyana and of the world in general. The search for an heir, therefore, takes on biblical and mythological dimensions. The quest becomes one for a positive force which will counteract the decadent and self-destructive conditions of community and landscape that threaten to become ossified. The novel, therefore, deals with a community in transition.

Oudin's flight through the forest, after the abduction, is also a symbolic flight through his heart of darkness. Like Conrad's Marlow, Oudin must run the gamut of introspection, self-awareness, and self-acceptance before he can experience true self-fulfillment. Only then can he understand his role as a revolutionary and a man of destiny. Like the knights of the grail legend, he must make the hazardous journey to the Castle Perilous before he can discover the grail of meaning which will restore fertility to the barren land and sterile community of the impotent Fisher Kings. While Oudin succeeds, the others fail because they cannot free themselves of their earthly encumbrances—from the consciousness of themselves. The novel, therefore, deals with the theme of regeneration and rebirth. Through second death, Oudin becomes part of that spiritual harmony that transcends all diversity.

The Whole Armour is indeed a novel of salvation and regeneration. At the commencement of the novel, the fictional community wears the "dark mantle of unexpurgated violence" and murder. The region has gained a name for "irresponsibility, subversion and feud." Such a blind, materialistic community must eventually collapse; it must fall victim to the seeds of self-destruction contained within it. Yet it is out of its own crumbling heart that the forces of liberation and redress will emerge. It is Cristo, the son of a prostitute, who is destined to fulfill the role of savior. It is his son with Sharon, once the virgin-temptress but now the Earth Mother, who will usher in a new community.

Before Cristo can fulfill the role of savior, he must first accept his lot of human guilt. He must confront the tiger of death and of fear, experience the shattering of his ego, and envision the true nature of the self—the diversity which exists within the unity of his self. He must accept the paradoxes of life and nature. The community itself must also experience the shattering of its security and recognize the illusory nature of its past—the nothingness out of which the regenerative force will eventually arise.

Once Cristo achieves his heightened consciousness, after his journey through the heart of darkness of the forest, he recognizes the boon that must be delivered to his community. Yet even as he has been regenerated through the sacrifice of Abram, he knows that his death must be an inevitable stage of the community's regeneration. Consequently, when he anticipates his future betrayal by his son, he understands that it will only be a confirmation of the ongoing dialectic of change—of life and nature. The prospect of surrendering to the police does not frighten him, as it does his aging mother, for he understands the transcendence of earthly life that he will enjoy once he puts on the "whole armour" of God—once he is freed from the burdensome trappings of his earthly material life.

In *The Secret Ladder*, Fenwick, faced with the reading of the river of time—of mounting "an introspective ladder," descends to the lowest rung of the "ladder of conscience" and experiences a cleansing of his perception. Previously blinded by his dreaming scientific eye, he could not understand the struggle for survival in which Poseidon was engaged. He could not perceive the spiritual essence that transcends the dead material present. Eventually, however, he becomes aware of the brash self-confidence and arrogance that possessed him, finally enjoying a vision of the ultimate truth of life and art. By recognizing his true ancestral roots and the paradoxes of life and nature, he receives new life. Once again, Harris invokes the theme of rebirth through a confrontation with the chaotic past and the terrifying forces of life.

Through an imaginative exploration and probing of myth, an extension of the past that has become ossified into disturbing puzzles, Harris invites his readers to witness its liberation and blossoming into a newer, more meaningful vision. The defeat which Poseidon and his men seem to suffer at the end of the novel is not the end of anything. The cycle of change, in Harris' mythic vision, is a never-ending process. Mutability is inevitable in life and nature.

Critical Context

Although he is not widely known in the United States, Wilson Harris is highly regarded by scholars of Caribbean literature, and he is frequently mentioned as a candidate for the Nobel Prize. *The Guiana Quartet*, comprising his first four novels, remains by far his best-known work, but it does not exhaust his achievement; rather, it should be seen as an invitation to a richly ambitious oeuvre, establishing the themes which he has gone on to explore in more than a dozen subsequent books.

All of Harris' works—including collections of essays such as *Tradition, the Writer and Society* (1967) and *The Womb of Space* (1983)—are animated by his conception of language as a vehicle for the exploration of consciousness. In *Tradition, the Writer and Society*, he rejects the "apparent common sense" of traditional fiction, calling instead for a "concept of language... which continuously transforms inner and outer formal categories of experience." The significance of Harris' fiction, its striking originality, lies in his dense, poetic language, shaped by what he has called a "logic of potent explosive images."

Sources for Further Study

Drake, Sandra E. *Wilson Harris and the Modern Tradition: A New Architecture of the World*, 1986.

Gilkes, Michael. *Wilson Harris and the Caribbean Novel*, 1975.

James, Louis, ed. *The Islands in Between: Essays in West Indian Literature*, 1968.

Maes-Jelinek, Hena. *Wilson Harris*, 1982.

Moore, Gerald. *The Chosen Tongue*, 1969.

Ramchand, Kenneth. *The West Indian Novel and Its Background*, 1970.

Van Sertima, Ivan. *Caribbean Writers: Critical Essays*, 1968.

Lorris Elliot

THE HANDMAID'S TALE

Author: Margaret Atwood (1939-   )
Type of plot: Antiutopian fantasy
Time of plot: The future, late in the twentieth century
Locale: Cambridge, Massachusetts
First published: 1986

> *Principal characters:*
> OFFRED, the protagonist and narrator, a Handmaid
> THE COMMANDER, a high-ranking official of the Republic of
>   Gilead, Offred's master
> SERENA JOY, the Commander's wife, a onetime television
>   evangelist
> NICK, the Commander's chauffeur, later Offred's lover
> LUKE, Offred's husband before the revolution
> OFGLEN, another Handmaid, a member of the underground
> MOIRA, a friend of Offred in college, a rebel

The Novel

In the late years of the twentieth century, Protestant Fundamentalists, with the tacit approval of the military, have assassinated the president and the Congress, suspended the Constitution, and established the Republic of Gilead. Under the new regime, women have no rights: They cannot hold jobs, they are not permitted to have money or property, and they have no public role. Since the birthrate has fallen, men in high positions, if their own wives are barren or are past childbearing, are assigned "Handmaids" from a pool of trained women who have already borne children. The only function of a Handmaid is to conceive and bear her master's child, based upon Rachel's command to Jacob in the Bible: "Behold my maid Bilhah, go in unto her; and she shall bear upon my knees, that I may also have children by her." Fertile women who refuse to become Handmaids are killed, sent to illegal but officially tolerated brothels, or sent to the "Colonies," to work on toxic-waste disposal. Handmaids are deprived of their names and are known only "of" their masters' names: Offred, Ofglen, Ofwarren, and so on.

Offred's story covers a spring and summer during which she fails to conceive a child by the Commander. Her only duties during this period are to shop daily for groceries in state-controlled stores and to present her body at regular intervals for nonerotic sexual intercourse with her master; in these episodes the Commander's wife, Serena Joy, is present, holding Offred between her knees. In the Republic of Gilead, sex is officially sanctioned only for the purpose of reproduction. Handmaids are required to wear long, red dresses, veils, and wimples; they can communicate with one another or with other people only about the necessities of life.

Because there is so little to occupy her time, Offred has plenty of opportunity to think about her past life, especially about the daughter who was taken from her and given to an official's family to be reared, and about Luke, who was probably killed when they unsuccessfully tried to escape to Canada. On her shopping trips, she and Ofglen must go together; a Handmaid cannot pass the frequent checkpoints alone. They make a regular practice of passing "The Wall," where the bodies of those hanged for crimes against public morality or the state are suspended from hooks as warnings and examples; Offred looks for Luke on "The Wall," but she has not found him. Because of the boredom and degradation of their lives, Handmaids are tempted to attempt suicide and are therefore denied access to sharp objects or any other possible means of ending their own lives; if they misbehave, however, they may be hanged by the state.

Serena Joy hates Offred for usurping part of her wifely role, although she remains ignorant, for a time, of the illegal private meetings between Offred and the Commander, during which they play Scrabble or other games, and during which the Commander allows Offred to read forbidden magazines from earlier times such as *Vogue*, *Mademoiselle*, or *Ms*. Anxious that there be a child, Serena Joy arranges a single clandestine and illegal meeting between Offred and Nick, the Commander's chauffeur, hoping that this will result in the conception of a baby. Offred continues to go to Nick's room, in secret; although she believes that she is betraying Luke, she cannot resist her reawakened sexuality. In the end, Nick helps her try to escape.

Escape has become a necessity. With Ofglen, Offred has attended a required public ritual, a "Salvaging," at which two Handmaids and a Commander's wife have been hanged for unspecified crimes. This ritual has been followed by another, a "Particicution," in which the gathered Handmaids are encouraged to tear limb from limb a man they are told is guilty of rape. Ofglen is observed kicking him in the head to render him unconscious before the other women get to him; she whispers to Offred that he was a member of the underground. Ofglen hangs herself before she can be arrested, but as her companion, Offred is sure to be suspected and questioned. Nick arranges for what he tells her is a false arrest by men who will help her escape. The narrative ends as they take her away.

The Characters

Because Margaret Atwood's purpose is to provide as much detail as possible about her imagined new country, the characters in *The Handmaid's Tale* are not provided with strongly individualized personalities. Offred reports on her experience in detail, but she has been an ordinary person before the changes brought about by the religious revolution. The daughter of an activist in the women's movement, she has gone to college, worked at a clerical job, and fallen in love with Luke, a married man; after his divorce, they marry and have a daughter. After their attempt to flee, Luke disappears, the daughter is taken from her, and Offred is sent to a school run by "Aunts," who train the surrogate-mothers-to-be in their new responsibilities.

The Commander is at first a menacingly shadowy figure, but he becomes more human as he invites Offred to participate in forbidden intimacies. He tries to win Offred's affection, since he gets none from Serena Joy, and he does so by offering Offred forbidden enjoyments: skin lotion, access to books and magazines which were supposed to have been destroyed, and information she is ordinarily denied. As she perceives, he wants to make her his mistress, an outdated conception in this society. In the end, he dresses her up in a skimpy costume and takes her to a former hotel in Boston, now a brothel for the powerful and for foreign visitors, where he shows her off and tries to make love to her. He mistakenly believes that he is too powerful to be subject to the puritanical rules of the society, and he indulges in his desire to make more personal his relationship with Offred; as an epilogue shows, he is sure to be purged soon after Offred's departure from his household.

Serena Joy is a bitter woman. Before the revolution, she had occupied an important position as a singer and lecturer, urging women to be subservient and to stay at home; now that her message has become law, she has lost her status, and with no children to occupy her, she spends her time tending her garden and consorting with other officials' wives. She is cruel to Offred, and even when she seems to act kindly in preparing to arrange the tryst between Offred and Nick, it is clear that she refuses to see Offred as a person.

The other characters are less developed. Ofglen is no more than a whispered voice giving Offred information and some hope, before she gives herself away and commits suicide so that she will not betray others when tortured. Moira is a defiant friend from college days who escapes from the Handmaids' training center and winds up in the brothel. Janine is a Handmaid who tries to escape by denying the reality of the present; she becomes Ofwarren, bears a child which is in some way unsatisfactory and which is "shredded," and completely loses touch with the world. Rita and Cora are "Marthas," servants in the Commander's house, older women beyond childbearing age who might wish to sympathize with Offred but cannot risk being shipped to the "Colonies." All these characters function to demonstrate the grievous restrictions imposed on women in Gilead.

Themes and Meanings

Atwood's central intention is to provide a warning about the danger of turning back the clock to a time when women were wives and mothers and no more. In *The Handmaid's Tale*, she has constructed a fable which shows how dangerous it would be to deny women the opportunities for independence which have come in the last few centuries: gainful occupations, free choice in love and other personal matters, and political and economic power. To remove these rights for the sake of a religious ideal would be to depersonalize women.

Atwood points out that such a change could be accomplished only with the cooperation of a large number of women. The "Aunts" and the officials' wives are essential to the new order. They accept their roles because to refuse them would mean torture and death. Yet their acceptance means that those in charge need not worry about a concerted resistance by women to these changes. Like all dictators, the officials use force, but they also use members of oppressed groups to control others in those groups.

The society depicted in *The Handmaid's Tale* is most immediately menacing to women, but Atwood makes it clear that the threat is not limited to women. Any group in a society can be effectively controlled only if the entire society is subject to strictly applied rules. Men in this society may seem to have more freedom than women, but in fact they, too, have been deprived of virtually all the rights and privileges which have come to be taken for granted in the Western democratic nations. In Gilead, men must serve the state as "Guardians" who enforce the rules but who have no civil rights and are denied access to women. Some men serve as soldiers in the interminable wars against enemies, such as the Baptists in Tennessee, or as "Eyes," spying on everyone for those in control. As the Commander shows, even those in authority have much power but find little satisfaction in it. A society which oppresses a large segment of its population oppresses everyone; it is mostly men who are hung like meat on "The Wall."

Atwood is not completely pessimistic. An epilogue to *The Handmaid's Tale* reports on a conference of historians 150 years after the events of the narrative, at which the narrative is discussed. It is clear from the discussion that Offred escaped, at least long enough to make a tape recording of her story; her ultimate fate is not known. Her escape, and the fact that the historians represent a more humane society (disturbingly, this society seems too complacent, as though there is no recognition that another revolution can always happen again), confirm an article of Offred's faith: Even the worst of times will pass, although the individual may not survive to see the better days to come. Yet Atwood's warning is that even the best of societies can be overthrown.

Critical Context

Like all of Atwood's previous novels, *The Handmaid's Tale* provides a feminine perspective on social issues, although this is the first of her novels to project contemporary tendencies into the future. In choosing such a projection, Atwood makes her contribution to the growing literature of antiutopias, of which the most famous modern examples are George Orwell's *Nineteen Eighty-Four* (1949) and Aldous Huxley's *Brave New World* (1932). Such fictions deny the optimism of Sir Thomas More's *Utopia* (1516) and subsequent works which see the future as having resolved the social and economic dilemmas of the present and which present blueprints for a more just society.

Antiutopias, in contrast, take elements of the author's society and show how those tendencies, if followed to their conclusions, would lead to far less just societies. It is Atwood's achievement in *The Handmaid's Tale* to have taken the emphasis on the "proper" role of women as preached by certain Protestant Fundamentalist ministers and by such supporters as Phyllis Schlafly, showing what kind of lives women could expect to lead if that "proper" role were forced upon all women by a theocratic government. Atwood is also concerned to show that such repression would have disastrous effects on all members of such a society, men as well as women, rulers as well as ruled. Like Orwell and Huxley, Atwood is also concerned about the ways in which modern technology might be used in achieving and enforcing dictatorial rule: When the new repression begins, computers are used to deny women access to their bank accounts and to cancel their credit cards, an easy way of ending their economic independence.

Atwood's warnings about the future set her apart from other feminist writers who have written novels projecting more equality for women, developing from gains made by the women's movement. While she is not entirely pessimistic, suggesting that in the very long run such gains may come, Atwood is aware that social changes provoke a backlash which may cancel any gains, at least in the short run. Like other antiutopian novels, *The Handmaid's Tale* uses exaggeration of certain tendencies to make its point more powerfully.

Sources for Further Study

Ehrenreich, Barbara. Review in *The New Republic*. CXCIV (March 17, 1986), p. 33.

McCarthy, Mary. Review in *The New York Times Book Review*. XCI (February 9, 1986), p. 1.

Sage, Lorna. Review in *The Times Literary Supplement*. March 21, 1986, p. 307.

Stimpson, Catharine R. Review in *The Nation*. CCXLII (May 31, 1986), p. 764.

Updike, John. Review in *The New Yorker*. LXII (May 12, 1986), p. 118.

John M. Muste

HARLAND'S HALF ACRE

Author: David Malouf (1934-   )
Type of plot: Impressionistic realism
Time of plot: From early in the twentieth century to the mid-1980's
Locale: Southern Queensland, Australia
First published: 1984

> *Principal characters:*
> FRANK HARLAND, an artist
> PHIL VERNON, a personal friend of Harland
> WALTER NESTORIUS (KNACK), a Polish antiquarian
> AUNT ROO, Phil's aunt

The Novel

Against a broad sweep of Australian twentieth century history, Frank Harland, an artist, lives a life that is emblematic of that country's evolving social identity, even though he remains an outsider, set apart by his calling.

Harland lives on the fringes of society but seeks an artistic identity rooted in society—more specifically, in his sense of family. A family-tied, worldly undertaking symbolizes that spiritual pursuit: From the early decades of the century until his death in the 1980's, Harland quietly buys up the farmland that had been worked by his forebears until, during the nineteenth century, it was lost at a card table. That loss dispossessed those ancestors and, in a sense, all the Harlands who came after.

Only occasionally, as Harland's renown increases, does the reader hear of his land purchases. They betoken his gradual acquisition of a spiritual, artistic landscape. From youth, Harland has endowed his ancestry with a modest kind of mythical quality, and by the time he dies, he has supplemented this with a personal artistic mythology that he has constructed through his life and work.

Harland lives most of his life on the road, gathering impressions of Southern Queensland. Then, approaching death, he is content to inhabit a series of rough-hewn enclosures on an almost uninhabited island. Yet the half acre of the title does not refer specifically to the small plot of sheltered land of his last days, which is repeatedly wracked by violent storms, nor does it necessarily describe Harland's ancestral farmland. Rather, it is the small patch of identity that Harland carves out against the steep odds posed by a world hostile to beauty.

After an apprenticeship with a graphic artist, and with the coming of the Great Depression, Harland takes to the road. He adapts, spiritually as much as physically, to that life, submitting to enormous economic hardships in pursuit of art. Yet he contends that the purpose of life is, simply, to seek happiness. Misery, he says after living through it and witnessing from afar the devastation of Europe by war, is too easily attained.

He befriends the family of Phil Vernon, who is a youth when he meets Harland just after World War II. That connects him with a broad familylike group of people from many sectors of Australian society. The family suffers tragedy and personal ruin. Harland is often driven to return to a state of virtual homelessness, which appears to be a state suited to him. His development into an itinerant, ascetic artist was foreshadowed during his childhood, described at the beginning of the novel. His father, for example, is renowned for his tall tales and daydreaming.

Before he dies, Harland tries to patch the tattered fabric of his family. Yet it is the artistic drive that is most powerful. He is content to fight the elements as he paints in his rough-hewn shelters. In this way, he returns to the influence that has been as great as family and society: the land. Like his father's tales, then, his art is "woven out of his life, out of the countryside and the past of their family."

The Characters

Frank Harland is a curious character. His extraordinary impressionistic art demonstrates how sharply but obliquely he sees the land and people around him. Yet he is also reticent, self-effacing, and uncomfortable in social settings. Moreover, he is in every way unsophisticated. His simplicity is, however, an illusion: He is a supremely disciplined artist of profound cultural engagement. He lacks a milieu such as the fine salons and galleries of Europe, but between stints of isolation, he cultivates people of widely varied social backgrounds: tramps on the railroad, families such as Phil Vernon's, surfers who happen upon his island, whoever crosses paths with him.

Harland is, in fact, so steeped in the everyday world of Southern Queensland that he appears never to enter so alien an institution as an art gallery. He never frames his canvases, and he sends his work, through an agent he appears never to address personally, to Sydney, which during most of the twentieth century was Australia's closest approximation to an artistic capital.

Elements in the characters of many of Harland's relatives and acquaintances bring into sharper focus his much more fully developed artistic sense and serve to emphasize how great his sacrifice is. Several, such as his father, the teller of tall tales, have artistic qualities or aspirations. Phil Vernon's Aunt Roo longs for a life in the theater and, until she attains it, designs her less glamorous existence as an ongoing spectacle, complete with massive fits of melodrama. Two characters provide the sharpest counterpoints to Harland: Phil Vernon and Knack.

During his life, Knack, a pseudonym for Walter Nestorius, has been a philosophy student, a soldier, a black marketer, a playboy, a fugitive, and a refugee. During the time Harland knows him, he is an antiquarian living in

Brisbane, a port of call for United States military personnel and refugees fleeing war-torn Europe. He embodies experience that is beyond Harland's reach because it is so far removed from Australia's history and culture. While Harland is a student of the land and its people, particularly of society's fringe-dwellers, Knack, himself a fringe-dweller, is learned: He is trained academically and as a musician. He is an impressive speaker. He has lived through events that shock Harland when he sees them on wartime newsreels.

Knack is nevertheless the character most similar to Harland emotionally and in sensibility. He is the inverse of Harland. He is driven from his homeland by war and persecution and expresses himself in torturous, impassioned playing on the piano. Harland chooses exile primarily as a necessary condition of his calling and creates art that, despite its nonrealism and rough appearance, is controlled and considered.

If Knack is a dark version of Harland, Phil Vernon is the lighter, socially adapted version. He shares the older man's keen eye for artistic detail, and he eventually becomes Harland's adviser in legal and other worldly affairs. Yet, unlike Harland, Phil is firmly rooted in a middle-class life-style, even though he does not in all ways toe the family line.

Themes and Meanings

David Malouf clearly intends that Harland should stand as a personification of his country's artistic and cultural growth from meager beginnings. It is a growth that is both based on, and divergent from, its roots in European cultural history. Malouf establishes this opposition at the very beginning of the novel when he describes the plot of land that the Harlands lost: "Named like so much else in Australia for a place on the far side of the globe that its finders meant to honour and were piously homesick for, Killarney bears no resemblance to its Irish original." Harland advances beyond this slavish cultural attachment by an art that carves out a "half acre" of native life and a spirit that augments his country's meager cultural heritage.

Harland's Half Acre provides a glimpse of the social history of Australia during this century. It is regularly punctuated by powerful events in Australian and world politics and society. The Great Depression propels Harland into a life on the road. World War II introduces him to Knack, the intellectual Polish antiquarian and refugee from Nazism who expresses for Harland both the overwhelming suffering and superior cultural wealth of Europe. With the increasing affluence in Australian society in the 1970's, Harland's paintings appeal to investors as tax shelters, and his name becomes fashionable.

The events in Australian and global twentieth century history are primarily a backdrop, however, to the particular lives of the novel. In several cases, these are marred by deaths, suicides, and personal ruin, events which are small-scale reflections of larger world and national events. Twice Frank's faith in life is shaken by suicides—first by Knack, then by a nephew whom he has reared—that derive from a loss of hope.

Malouf suggests that the artist dwells perilously close to this same chasm. To attain the artistic vision he seeks, Harland must spend his life with "those who were outside." The Harlands' dispossession from the land prefigures Frank Harland's destiny to join the dispossessed. Yet even when "outside," Harland is confronted with the relative security of Australia and the challenge it presents to those seeking a vision of the human condition. The burden of history personified by Knack astounds Harland. It shows him that his own conception of art and life is circumscribed by the isolation, infancy, and innocence of Australia.

Harland, so married to his land and its people even though he remains an outsider until his death, represents an Australian artistic, and social, identity which is divergent from that of Europe and which is, Malouf suggests, viable and vital. The novel gains in stature from Malouf's ambitious undertaking to make this connection. Yet the almost programmatic way in which he does so can also be seen as the novel's greatest weakness.

Critical Context

Malouf deals in this novel with themes that he has addressed in earlier fiction and poetry: exile, belonging to the land or to a society, and hopelessness that is expressed through suicide. For example, an earlier study of an artist separated from his society is *An Imaginary Life* (1978). It recounts the life of the Roman poet Ovid and describes his achievement of a spiritual communion with the region along the Danube River, where he has long been exiled. In *Johnno* (1975), the title character and a friend nicknamed "Dante" leave Australia in search of identity. Harland, in contrast, is utterly steeped in the genius of his own locale. Yet he, too, ponders at times the rich historical and cultural heritage of Europe that Australia lacks.

Johnno and *Harland's Half Acre* have other elements in common. Like two characters in the later book, Johnno commits suicide through despair and emotional instability. This second characteristic is one he shares with a number of the minor characters in *Harland's Half Acre*.

Both novels also include carefully drawn evocations of Southern Queensland at earlier times in this century and of the characters' family lives. With this technique, Malouf places his characters in social contexts that suggest some of the prevailing characteristics of the Australian national identity. He suggests that the foremost characteristic of those who have tried to shape that identity has been an urge to escape the incipient society long enough to reorient it and refine it.

Malouf does this most ambitiously in *Harland's Half Acre*. Often the cogs of his grand construction grind audibly, but the work was greeted as the strongest to that point in his career.

Sources for Further Study

Adams, Phoebe-Lou. Review in *The Atlantic*. CCLIV (October, 1984), p. 126.

Gorra, Michael. Review in *The New York Times Book Review*. XCI (October 14, 1984), p. 9.

Hamilton, K. G., ed. *Studies in Recent Australian Fiction*, 1979.

Jose, Nicholas. "Cultural Identity: 'I Think I'm Something Else,'" in *Daedalus*. Winter, 1985, p. 311.

Waldhorn, Arthur. Review in *The Library Journal*. CIX (September 1, 1984), p. 1687.

Peter Monaghan

HARRIET SAID

Author: Beryl Bainbridge (1934-   )
Type of plot: Psychological realism
Time of plot: Mid-twentieth century
Locale: Formby, England
First published: 1972

> *Principal characters:*
> THE FIRST-PERSON NARRATOR, a thirteen-year-old girl
> HARRIET, her fourteen-year-old best friend
> PETER "TSAR" BIGGS, a fifty-six-year-old businessman who
>   falls in love with the narrator
> MRS. BIGGS, his wife

The Novel

The action of the novel takes place in an extended flashback that covers the summer holidays of two young teenage girls: the unnamed narrator and her friend Harriet. The narrator tells a dispassionate story of how she and her friend destroy the self-effacing Peter Biggs, whom they have named "Tsar." The choice of this name highlights their childish romanticism and ignorance. The summer for them is no innocent rite of passage into young womanhood but rather the working out of their twisted need to control and destroy those adults who get in their way.

The narrator has returned from her year at boarding school, where she was sent because her behavior was so unruly. Like her friend Harriet, she is wise beyond her years, but she lacks the necessary maliciousness to act on her desires without the prodding of Harriet. When Harriet returns from her holiday in Wales, the two girls take an interest in the life and activities of Peter Biggs and his wife. Capitalizing on Biggs's friendliness toward her earlier in the summer, Harriet begins—with an almost scientific detachment—to engineer ways for the narrator to be thrown together with him.

Harriet is the real troublemaker. She has already experimented with the power of her sexuality in her flirtations with the Italian prisoners of war interned in Formby as well as with a young man she met while on holiday. She subtly forces the narrator to entrap Biggs by alluding to "something" she did with that young man but that she cannot bring herself to talk about "just yet." The two girls have kept a diary chronicling their sexual coming-of-age. Harriet dictates; the narrator transcribes. Biggs becomes the focus of their information gathering and the target of their experiment.

Early in the novel, the two girls spy on Biggs and his wife as they make love in their front parlor. The girls are discovered, and their nosiness only adds fuel to Mrs. Biggs's already growing suspicions that these two children are at least acting improperly toward her husband, if not actually trying to seduce him. The knowledge that Biggs's wife "knows" about their intentions provides Harriet with a perfect rationale for first disliking her and later feeling no remorse for what eventually occurs.

Goaded by Harriet's inferred sexual initiation, the narrator follows Biggs on his walks to the seashore and allows him to express his unhealthy attraction to her, first verbally, later through a kiss, and finally sexually. Harriet, in a fit of jealousy, provides the two with the needed opportunity by locking Biggs and her friend in the parish church one night. Then, when they learn that Mrs. Biggs will be away for several days, the girls invite themselves over to Biggs's house. Harriet cruelly derides his affection for her friend as the sign of a weak man. At this point, the narrator turns away from Harriet but not from Biggs. Believing that the more worldly-wise Harriet has already lost her virginity in Wales, the narrator gives hers to Biggs one night on the beach.

Harriet has, however, misled her friend; she retains her virginity and is shocked that the narrator gave hers away so casually. Later, just before the narrator is due to return to school, the two girls return to Biggs's house. When he goes out to buy cigarettes, his wife unexpectedly returns. Trapped in the house, Harriet concocts a perfect solution: She makes the narrator knock Mrs. Biggs out—but the force of the blow kills, rather than stuns, her. The story concludes with Harriet telling the narrator that they will return home and tell their parents that they saw Mr. Biggs murder his wife. After all, they are only children, they cannot be held accountable.

The Characters

The narrator is a curiously weak individual. She allows herself to be driven by her friend Harriet to commit acts of increasing anger and violence, yet on her own she acts passively and as one would expect a thirteen-year-old girl to behave. Her curiosity about sex and the power of her sexuality is not unusual, nor are her shallow infatuation and fantasizing about the much older Peter Biggs. Even a diary such as the two girls keep is unremarkable for girls in early adolescence. Beryl Bainbridge captures a thirteen-year-old's personality well in her use of the first-person narrative and presents an accurate picture of the girls' parents and of the Biggses as seen through adolescent eyes. In some ways, the narrator is the dullest character in the story, acting primarily as the medium through which Harriet's plans are carried out.

Harriet's, on the other hand, is truly a frightening personality. The anger she feels toward adults, and toward men in particular, is apparent in her behavior toward her father and Biggs, not to mention the Italian soldiers or the young man with whom she had some sort of physical relationship earlier that same summer. Her relationship with her father is stormy, reflecting the tempestuous nature of her parents' marriage. Thus, her behavior toward the men in the novel could be explained as her attempt to control or dominate men, all of whom represent her moody, explosive father. Her use of her sexual attractiveness to tease interested males rather than to satisfy them—as she did with Douglas Hind, Biggs's houseguest—demonstrates her anger at, or hatred of, men. At fourteen—one year older than the narrator—she is the dominant figure in this friendship, and she controls the narrator in much the same way that she controls everyone else, by virtue of her angry will. Perhaps her attitude concerning love best expresses her nature: She tells the narrator that, "at thirteen there is very little you can expect from loving someone but experience." Now she can also add killing to her list of experiences.

Peter Biggs is a pathetic man of fifty-six. He is a mousy, little white-collar worker married to a fat harpy. For his entire life he has allowed himself to be told what to do, so it is hardly surprising that he surrenders so easily to the flirtations of the two girls. He has been married for thirty years to a woman who won their house in a raffle; he married her because the house needed to be occupied. Over time, Mrs. Biggs has grown fat and angry; she dominates her husband with the bulk of her aggressive will as well as with her greater size. The scene in their parlor in which she forces him to have sex with her exemplifies the way in which she has overwhelmed him. Something in the narrator's youthful sexuality arouses Biggs, and he is too weak to turn away from an obviously destructive attraction. His weakness not only causes his wife's death but also enables Harriet to pin her murder on him.

Themes and Meanings

This novel is a study of teenage sexual curiosity and male mid-life crisis. Yet it is also more than simply another Lolita story. The most frightening aspect of this book is its low-key portrayal of the angry, destructive Harriet, who, it must be remembered, is responsible for the destruction of both Peter Biggs and his wife, and for the actions of the narrator. Like other fictional characters before her, Harriet is a bad seed, and she exerts her evil influence on all who come in contact with her. Yet the reader sees her only through the eyes of the narrator, who seems merely to report what went on during that one summer vacation. The detached tone of the narrative flattens the action and makes the horrific nature of the events more frightening because they are related so matter-of-factly.

As a coming-of-age novel, *Harriet Said* certainly gives the reader a chilling glimpse of adolescent anger translated from the fantasy world of girlish dreams and diaries into a real-world scenario, with terrible consequences. That it is told as an extended flashback adds to the disturbing nature of the entire narrative, since the voice telling the story is clearly older now but certainly no more aware of the perniciousness of the events of that summer than when they were actually happening. The novel concludes by circling back to its first chapter, in which the narrator described how she and Harriet screamed and cried as they accused Peter Biggs of murdering his wife.

In healthy adolescents, sexual curiosity and an exploration of the power that it can afford them are certainly normal. Bainbridge, however, makes it clear that these two girls are aberrant; she shows the reader what can happen when sexuality becomes a weapon, as it does not only for Harriet and the narrator but for Biggs's wife as well. Mrs. Biggs is a metaphoric black widow who consumes her husband by the sheer force of her will, a woman whose dominance is expressed both in the inequity in their size (she outweighs him by a considerable amount) as well as by her demands for physical attention, which Bainbridge graphically illustrates in the parlor love scene witnessed by the two girls.

This novel consistently portrays the main female characters as physically, emotionally, and sexually domineering while at the same time presenting its male characters as weak (Peter Biggs) or brutish (Harriet's father). The powerful women in this novel have learned to use sex as a weapon; Harriet and the narrator become so proficient in this regard that they destroy both Biggs and his wife, cause havoc in their respective families, and will undoubtedly never be able to relate to a male in any healthy way. They are able to relate only to each other, giving this book faint lesbian overtones.

In the four main characters, Bainbridge also explores the theme of dominance and submission. The two relationships—between Harriet and the narrator and Biggs and his wife—resemble each other in one important way: In both pairs there is a dominant and a submissive partner. Harriet clearly controls the actions and responses of the narrator and is certainly to blame for the other girl's destruction. The same may be said of Mrs. Biggs. Considered from a psychoanalytic perspective, *Harriet Said* explores the unhealthy results of such unequal partnerships as well as the pathology of the master-slave relationship. Furthermore, there is some indication that Harriet dominates the narrator because she wants to possess and control her in the same way that she causes the narrator to ensnare and control Biggs.

Critical Context

Harriet Said resembles Bainbridge's other novels in its careful examination of psychological motivation, jealousy, and the results of an unhealthy sexual tension or preoccupation. Like many contemporary British novels—Alan Sillitoe's *The Loneliness of the Long Distance Runner* (1959) or John Braine's *Room at the Top* (1957), for example—this book focuses on working-class characters trapped in the backwaters of industrialized England, people who would ordinarily fade into a crowd. It is exactly this "invisible" person who affords Bainbridge the perfect means by which to shock her readers. Her fiction could be described as domestic horror because it focuses on unassuming people only to reveal the startling, and frequently frightening, hostilities hidden beneath their weak exteriors. In Bainbridge's novels, the everyday world is transformed into one of terror when a character's repressed anger erupts and destroys the entrapped victim. In this regard her interests parallel those of such contemporary writers of horror fiction as Thomas Tryon, Peter Straub, and Stephen King, who, like Bainbridge, focus on the banal somehow transformed into the horrifying.

As a *Bildungsroman*, Bainbridge's novel treats themes similar to those in J. D. Salinger's *The Catcher in the Rye* (1951) or Rita Mae Brown's *Rubyfruit Jungle* (1973). Like the main characters in both of those books, Harriet and the narrator are adolescents at odds with a world which they perceive to be ruled by stupid, repressive adults. All these characters are misfits who refuse to be socialized; they are also streetwise survivors. What distinguishes Harriet and her friend from Brown's or Salinger's adolescent rebels is the form that their rebellion takes: They murder or otherwise destroy the adults who block their way. In this respect, *Harriet Said* may be compared to Thomas Tryon's *The Other* (1971), whose young protagonist kills not only his alter ego (his identical twin) but also any adult who tries to make him take responsibility for his actions.

Sources for Further Study
Godwin, Gail. Review in *The New York Times Book Review*. LXVIII (September 30, 1973), p. 38.
Ms. Review. III (December, 1974), p. 39.
The New Yorker. Review. XLIX (October 29, 1973), p. 49.
Wimble, Barton. Review in *Library Journal*. XCVIII (November 1, 1973), p. 3280.

Melissa E. Barth

THE HEALERS

Author: Ayi Kwei Armah (1939-   )
Type of plot: Historical fiction
Time of plot: 1873-1874
Locale: The Asante empire area and Cape Coast of Ghana
First published: 1978

> *Principal characters:*
> DENSU, the protagonist, a twenty-year-old young man who
> has to choose between aspiring to a local kingship and
> joining the ascetic healers
> DAMFO, the leader of a community of healers and a mentor to
> Densu
> ABABIO, initially Densu's guardian, a corrupt local court
> official and later a local king
> ARABA JESIWA, the mother of the murdered crown prince and
> a friend to Densu
> AJOA, Densu's beloved, the daughter of Damfo
> ASAMOA NKWANTA, an Asante general
> SIR GARNET WOLSELEY, a British general
> CAPTAIN GLOVER, a vain British military freebooter

The Novel

In his desire to do justice to his tale, the narrator, the "story-teller," of the events of the novel, invokes the arts of eloquence from a long-revered tradition of African masters of narrative. Convinced of the urgency and importance of his tale, the narrator must remind himself, through the invocations, that discipline in storytelling is a paramount factor that he must not forget. The main task of the narrator is to show how the events of the twentieth year in the life of the protagonist, Densu, serve to illustrate aspects of the larger society. There is a focus on a specific historical time, during which critical changes occurred as a result of internal political and spiritual conflicts exacerbated by British colonial incursions into the Asante empire.

The novel opens with the notation that a brutal murder has occurred and that the protagonist, Densu, is involved in this event. Murdered is Appia, the crown prince of Esuano, and also believed murdered is his missing mother, Araba Jesiwa. The action flashes back to the period just prior to the murder, the festival season of the chosen-year ceremonial games of competition in the town of Esuano. Densu and his age-group, young men passing into manhood, compete in several athletic and mental skills. In the past, these games were regarded as cooperative rituals of wholeness. Now, however, the festivals have a strong emphasis on individual competition, which Densu believes promotes fragmentation and division. Densu, who dislikes aimless and disruptive conflict, reluctantly competes, and his overall skills are superior. Appia is declared winner of the games, however, when Densu compassionately refuses to kill a tethered pigeon in the final shooting competition.

Two forces pull at Densu. One is his manipulative guardian, Ababio, who, out of self-interest spurred by greed for power, wants Densu to aspire to royal service and even to the local kingship. Ababio would hope to be *de facto* ruler, with Densu as a figurehead. The other force pulling at Densu is his own inclination to become a healer, to get far away from court life and join Damfo's community of simple-living healers in the eastern forest.

The action catches up with the present with Appia's murder, and as a result of Ababio's machinations, Densu becomes the prime murder suspect. Densu knows too much of Ababio's desires, and Ababio has schemed to have Densu killed in a trial-by-ordeal: Densu must drink a poisonous potion as a test of his guilt or innocence.

After escaping from Ababio's trap, Densu joins Damfo in the forest. Densu had gone to Damfo earlier, but Damfo sent the young man back to town to spend a year contemplating whether he was sincerely resolved to cast his lot with the ascetic healers. Now, events have propelled him rather quickly back to Damfo. In this period, the love of Densu and Ajoa blossoms.

Damfo has two key patients to restore to health. One is Araba Jesiwa, whose four limbs are broken, whose speech is lost, and whose mind has strayed—all as a result of having witnessed Appia's murder and having been beaten herself. She has been a kind mentor to Densu and a longtime patient and friend of Damfo. After several months, her bones heal, but her speech is elusive. Damfo's other patient is Asamoa Nkwanta, the Asante army chief general, who is in acute depression because his favorite nephew has been treacherously killed by a spiteful court rival. Asamoa Nkwanta's leadership is needed because the Asante army is in disarray without him and because the English forces are threatening the Asante empire.

Damfo succeeds in getting Asamoa Nkwanta to recognize some of the flaws in Asante society. For example, the holding of slaves and the sacrificial slaying of slaves are Asante practices which are at core disrespectful of life. If Asamoa Nkwanta, with his respected influence, can be brought to enlightened awareness, then there is more of a chance for progressive changes, "healing" changes, to occur in the society.

One critical obstacle to unity is the royalty. Some lesser and rival kings, eager for money and gin, collaborate with the English interests. The Asante royal family itself betrays Asamoa Nkwanta rather than risk a diminution of its influence should the Asante general defeat the English and thus become even more popular among the people. The royalty, jealous wielder of power, is not ready for generous healing. The Asante king has sent word to General Garnet Wolseley that the king's quarrel is not with white men, only with black men, but the English forces do not relent. They sack the city of Kumase, and the royal family is forced to flee.

Densu has a new trial, under English jurisdiction, and he is proven innocent when Araba Jesiwa, regaining her speech, testifies and implicates Ababio, now king of Esuano, in the murder of her son, Appia. Ababio, who shamelessly cast his lot with the English, is bound over to be tried by them for murder.

The final scene of the novel expresses an ironic development. General Wolseley is returning to England in triumph after his incursion into Kumase. By their imperial machination, however, the English have unwittingly effected a "gathering of the tribes" of black people. The English have brought blacks from various parts of Africa and the West Indies, albeit in the service of colonial conquest, to Cape Coast, and the novel closes with these curiously gathered people participating in a communal dance. Present colonial conquest has not doused the healing impulse seeking unity.

The Characters

Densu observes his society and has uneasy feelings about its aims and his place within it. He is on the threshold of setting his course in life, and he finds no comfort in the direction his manipulative guardian, Ababio, would have him take. Ababio would have Densu, with his talents and resourcefulness, court power by serving Ababio and the white men. In Densu's view, Ababio is a betrayer and a predatory user of the people. Densu, orphaned when an infant, consistently is able to refuse the promises of power which his wily guardian dangles before him. Densu chooses to pursue the path of inspiration and of healing, rather than that of manipulation. Densu wants to be true to his convictions, and the work of the healers genuinely intrigues and attracts him. To be drawn into the governing system as it is then constituted would be tantamount to enlisting in the forces of manipulation and exploitation. To join Damfo and the healers would offer the opportunity to promote unity of body, of mind, and of society.

Densu's strength of conviction, along with Damfo's gentle support, sustains him throughout trying perils and crises of spirit. Near the end of the novel, Densu is offered the kingship of Esuano, but he refuses it. He is free in mind and enlightened; he believes his energies will be better spent in working at the dream of black unity rather than serving as an instrument of a shortsighted status quo.

Damfo, the healer, is a man with a farsighted agenda. He is able to heal the physical and psychological impairments of individuals. He can lead individuals to see the truth of themselves in their predicaments. His great goal, however, is again to bring together black people in unity. The achievement of this goal may take centuries, but the more the people accept the truth of kinship, the greater the possibility of the goal being attained. "Ebibirman," the unified community of black people, of wholeness, is the aim of the healers.

Asamoa Nkwanta's illness presents a special challenge for Damfo. The Asante general is in deep depression because his favorite nephew has fallen victim to a shameful societal practice that the general has never opposed. At a king's death, some slaves and other unfortunates are stalked and killed at night in order that the murdered victims might serve the dead king as slaves in the underworld. One of the princes, out of a private hatred, takes such an opportunity to murder Asamoa Nkwanta's nephew.

Damfo's dilemma is that he sees the royals as corrupt exploiters, and Asamoa Nkwanta serves the royal family; thus, will the healing of Asamoa Nkwanta abet royal manipulation? The dilemma is resolved in part by Damfo's leading Asamoa Nkwanta to question some of the corrupt practices of the society and to admit that the present regime is exploitative of the people. Healed in mind and in attitude, Asamoa Nkwanta is equipped to exercise keen judgment in the service of his people. After he reunites and readies the army to repel the English invasion, however, he is betrayed by the royal family and rivals when, rather than see him emerge as a strong influential victor, the king attempts to negotiate a truce with the English.

Ababio is the epitome of a fully corrupt manipulator. He early and consistently puts his greed before all other interests. He wants to acquire and wield power, and although he becomes king of Esuano through his treachery, he remains a slave to his aspiration for power. Blatantly he admits that he will serve as a lackey to the whites, because then his own power will be secure, he believes. It is the white man, however, who administers his final condemnation.

From a distance, the figure of the British general, Sir Garnet Wolseley, an actual historical personage, casts a long shadow over the scheme of events of the novel. What is shown more directly is the process and results of Wolseley's campaign. The English forces—whites, Africans from other parts, and black West Indians—relentlessly move against the Asante, who are weakened by internal dissension and lack of concerted resolve. Wolseley's mechanically authoritative administration of the campaign is contrasted with a closer portrait of Captain Glover, a vain freebooting officer who exacts exaggerated deference from his black charges. The Africans are able to manipulate him by pretending to cater to his vanity. Wolseley's military action succeeds and in spite of the looting and theft by white soldiers in Kumase, Wolseley's imagined honor accompanies him back to England.

Themes and Meanings

Healing has the lofty and worthy aim of achieving black unity, which would allow a healthy society and all of its members to flourish in an environment of mutual respect and fulfillment. Damfo assumes the realization of such a development to be far in the future, but he recognizes that seeds of its attainment must be sown persistently and nurtured by each generation.

Early in the novel, Densu recognizes two groups in the world around him: inspirers and manipulators. He sees many manipulators (Ababio is a blatant one), and he dislikes them; he sees few inspirers (Damfo is a refreshing one), and these he loves. The methods of the manipulators—force, fraud, deceit— grow increasingly abhorrent to Densu. The inspirers, through the use of their healing and creative efforts, offer him a welcome alternative. The health of the present and future of black people is something Densu can advance by serving as a healer.

There is considerable disunity in the times. Disunity within the individual is illustrated in the cases of Araba Jesiwa and Asamoa Nkwanta, both of whom are healed. Also apparent is large-scale group disunity of the people who are scattered in mind as well as geographically. Rulers, for whom the welfare of the society should be paramount, become lost and destructive in their jealous greed for power. There is danger from within the society when loss of mutual regard occurs and when foreign oppressors are able to take advantage of and further promote disunity among blacks.

Critical Context

Ayi Kwei Armah subtitles *The Healers* "an historical novel," and he chooses as his framework a specific and vital event—the 1873-1874 Second Asante War when the British penetrated to the heart of the Asante empire. This event is portrayed in an expansive fashion from an Afrocentric view. The novel examines intricate elements of Asante society, in full-dimensional detail. In *Two Thousand Seasons* (1973), which covers a long stretch of a thousand years, Armah cannot present as consistently colorful details as he can in *The Healers*, which treats a brief period of high intensity.

Around the documented events and personages (for example, the war it- self, and General Wolseley, and the Asante king, Kofi Karikari), the author utilizes his fictive skills to present a vision which humanizes the action. The dynamic potential of the Asante is noted, but also exposed are weaknesses which negate the potential. Still, in spite of disruptive shortcomings, hope is not extinguished; the dream of the healers, of the awakening and unification of the people, remains alive.

Sources for Further Study
British Book News. Review. June, 1980, p. 373.
Fraser, Robert. *The Novels of Ayi Kwei Armah*, 1980.
New Statesman. Review. XCIX (March 7, 1980), p. 362.
The Times Educational Supplement. Review. April 18, 1980, p. 22.
World Literature Today. LIV (Spring, 1980), p. 246.

James H. Randall

HEAT AND DUST

Author: Ruth Prawer Jhabvala (1927-   )
Type of plot: Philosophical romance
Time of plot: 1923 for Olivia's story, 1975 for the framing story
Locale: The towns of Satipur and Khatm, India
First published: 1975

Principal characters:

ANNE, the main character and narrator of the framing story, about twenty-eight years old

INDER LAL, Anne's landlord, who works as a bureaucrat in the Department of Disposal and Supplies, about twenty-five years old

RITU, Inder Lal's wife, in poor health and uneducated; her husband is embarrassed by her in the presence of foreigners

INDER LAL'S MOTHER, overprotective and proud of her son's "official" status

MAJI, a friend of Inder Lal's mother, a widow "said to have certain powers," a "holy woman"

CHID (CHIDARRANDA), a young Englishman from the Midlands who has converted to the Hindu religion, undertaking a pilgrimage to the holy cave of Amarnath

DOUGLAS RIVERS, a dedicated civil servant working in Satipur in 1923, overworked to the point of neglecting his wife

OLIVIA RIVERS, his wife, who, out of boredom, frustration, and neglect, spends rather too much time with the Nawab, the Prince of Khatm

MR. CRAWFORD, the British Collector and chief officer at Satipur in 1923

BETH CRAWFORD, his wife, bright, brisk, cheerful, and sophisticated

MRS. MINNIES, an artist, also "cheerful and undaunted" by India

MAJOR MINNIES, her husband, another old India hand with more than twenty years of service, appointed political agent "to advise the Nawab and the rulers of some adjacent states on matters of policy"

DR. SAUNDERS, the medical superintendent at Satipur in 1923

JOAN SAUNDERS, his wife, a slovenly, disagreeable woman, distrustful and fearful of her Indian servants, whom she considers "devils"

THE NAWAB, the local ruler at the Palace of Khatm, married,
but separated from his mentally disturbed wife; a "manly
and strong" manipulative character, shrouded in mystery

THE BEGUM, the Nawab's mother, in her fifties in 1923; she
presides over Olivia's abortion after Olivia becomes
pregnant by her son

HARRY, a "weak" Englishman, not in good health, who is
friendly with the natives and has been the Nawab's
constant houseguest for more than three years

KARIM, the Nawab's nephew, who lives in a Knightsbridge flat
in London with his wife Kitty in 1975; though the Nawab's
heir, he is a prince without a kingdom

DR. GOPAL, the latter-day successor to Dr. Saunders as
medical superintendent in Satipur

The Novel

Heat and Dust tells two stories in two time frames: 1923, before the end of
British colonial rule in India, and 1975, as a relative of the earlier colonial
rulers returns to India to investigate a mysterious family indiscretion. The
main narrative line tells the story of Olivia Rivers, a woman who "had gone
in too far" probing the exotic "mysteries" of the Orient, seduced by the "oriental privacies" of India and, in the opinion of the ruling British community,
corrupted by them. Years after his retirement, one of the colonial characters,
Major Minnies, publishes his memoirs, described as "a monograph on the influence of India on the European consciousness and character"; this description neatly summarizes the intent of *Heat and Dust*.

The frame story is narrated by Anne, the granddaughter of Douglas Rivers by his second wife, who goes to Satipur to unravel the mystery of her
grandfather's first wife, Olivia. Like Olivia, the narrator is seduced, reliving
in a later cultural and political context Olivia's experiences in "the other
dimension," forbidden territory for British colonials.

Olivia Rivers travels from England to Satipur early in 1923 to join her husband Douglas, a dedicated colonial officer. The story primarily concerns
Olivia's difficult adjustment to life in India, particularly the provincial and
isolated attitudes of those who live in the colonial enclave of "the Civil
Lines," as the British residential area was called. The British administrative
class maintains itself in cultural isolation from the Indian population, but
Olivia, partly out of curiosity, partly out of sheer boredom, takes particular
interest in a local prince, the Nawab, and his circle of friends, who are more
entertaining and amusing than her husband's British friends.

A turning point occurs when Olivia declines to accompany two of the
colonial wives, Mrs. Crawford and Mrs. Minnies, to Simla on an extended
vacation to escape the summer heat of Satipur. This chaperoned vacation

would have kept Olivia occupied and out of mischief, but she prefers to stay at home, ostensibly to be with her husband. She dearly wants to have a child but finds her overworked husband preoccupied with his official duties. First out of boredom, later out of fascination, Olivia turns to the Nawab for company and attention. A sensual relationship eventually develops with the Nawab, who seduces and impregnates Olivia, partly, one suspects, out of spite for the English. Knowing that the child's color will betray its parentage, Olivia decides to have an abortion. Indian midwives induce a miscarriage, but when Olivia is taken to the colonial hospital, Dr. Saunders recognizes the work of the Indian midwives. The now disgraced Olivia escapes from the hospital and goes to the Nawab's palace, never to return to Douglas, her husband. Concurrently, the Nawab is usurped by the British because of his complicity with local robber bands, and Olivia elopes with him to a mountainside village in the Himalayas, where she continues to live in isolation until her death, never returning to England.

A secondary story, used as a narrative framing device, links the main characters of the two time frames. Like Olivia, the narrator, Anne, becomes involved with an Indian lover, her young landlord in Satipur, Inder Lal, who is married and who also, like the Nawab, lives with his mother. Like Olivia, the narrator gets pregnant, but unlike Olivia, she does not have the child aborted. Like Olivia, she goes to live in the Himalayas after leaving Satipur.

Olivia and the female narrator are clearly intended to be parallel characters, as the narrator follows Olivia's geographical progress across India, from Satipur and Khatm to "the small town of X" in the Himalayas, where Olivia chose to live out her days with the Nawab after deserting her husband. The narrator does not have a husband to abandon, however, and leaves Inder Lal behind in Satipur. She is not dominated by the mores of an artificial colonial enclave, as was Olivia, and she is therefore more fully liberated.

The Characters

The characters of *Heat and Dust* are carefully designed and arranged to counterpoint and reflect one another, and this artful arrangement of characters is one of the novel's most impressive achievements. Douglas Rivers, for example, is the very model of a "proper Englishman" in India: ambitious, absolutely dedicated to Indian service, but absolutely aloof from the Indian population he serves and the native culture of the country to which he has been assigned. His opposite is the "weak" Harry, the Nawab's three-year houseguest, infirm of body and spirit, contaminated by Indian indulgence, and either unwilling or unable to extricate himself from the Nawab's influence, even though he apparently wants to return to England. Olivia is Harry's female counterpart, caught between two worlds and two cultures and strongly influenced by the Nawab's charm and charisma. Since Douglas clearly "did not like Harry," he could only be horrified by full knowledge of his wife's behavior and attachment to the Nawab.

Mrs. Crawford and Mrs. Minnies are strong and "proper" official wives, determined to be "bright and cheerful," and, like their husbands, aloof from Indian life and culture. Their counterpart is the sick Mrs. Saunders, who lives in fear of being molested by her Indian servants. Like Harry, she is "weak" and sickly, but her weakness draws her to European rather than Indian standards. She lacks the strength and the willpower to be "cheerful" about her lot. She despises India.

In the framing story, Chid is the equivalent of Harry, caught between two cultures, but ultimately bound to return to England. Just as Harry lives off of the Nawab and his family, so Chid is taken care of by Inder Lal's family, since the Nawab, representing India under imperial rule, is clearly counterpointed by Inder Lal, representing India after imperial rule. Inder Lal holds an official position that carries prestige, even if he lacks the power and assurance of the Nawab, and even if he is intimidated, as the Nawab was not, in the presence of Europeans. Inder Lal is the new man of the new India and shares the Nawab's sexual charm. Grouped together, Inder Lal's mother and her friend Maji, the "holy woman," constitute the latter-day equivalent of the Begum, the Nawab's mother, and her retinue.

The most striking chronological counterpoint is between Olivia and the narrator. Jhabvala was able to retell the story in the motion-picture version which she scripted from her novel in 1983 for director James Ivory and producer Ismail Merchant. In the motion-picture version, Anne, the narrator, is drawn even closer to Olivia, who becomes the narrator's great-aunt, rather than the first wife of her grandfather. In the novel, Beth Crawford is the narrator's great-aunt. Beth's sister Tessie comes to Bombay in September of 1923, after Mrs. Crawford returns to Satipur from Simla, and after Olivia has eloped with the Nawab. Tessie meets Douglas and later marries him after his divorce from Olivia.

The narrator of the novel, a relative of Beth Crawford, then, is able to assimilate the experience of India much more fully than her great-aunt could have done under colonial rule. She is open and sensitive to Indian ways, like Olivia before her, but she is also more liberated than Olivia, following the same progression of events, but determined to have her child while also pursuing spiritual perfection in the Himalayas. The film version suggests that the narrator is the very reincarnation of Olivia, which would be possible if the framing story were set during the 1980's, as in the film, instead of ten years earlier. This later revision, which carries authorial force since Jhabvala herself reinvented the story for the screen, is suggested when, at the end, Anne looks into the window of Olivia's mountain bungalow and sees Olivia with the Nawab at her piano; the woman behind and the woman reflected in the window then merge into one, transcending the simple parallelism of the novel.

Themes and Meanings

Heat and Dust is especially effective as a novel of social criticism. Jhabvala brilliantly captures the nuances, tensions, and frustrations of Westerners living under stress in an alien setting, artificially maintaining a facsimile of an English country village with its manners and traditions. It is appropriate that the British residential area should be called "the Civil Lines." The British are superficially "civil" toward the local population but remain socially aloof and, among themselves, disdainful.

The British ruling class is marked by its smugness and condescension: "like good parents they all loved India whatever mischief she might be up to." When Olivia speaks in defense of the Indians' right to practice their traditions, her countrymen "sportingly discussed her point of view as if it were one that could be taken seriously." Dr. Saunders, who is openly hostile to Olivia and considers any sensitivity towards Indian culture as a sign of weakness, condemns the Indians for their "savagery and barbarism." Most of the English characters are more tolerant than Saunders and his wife, who are extreme cases, more openly frustrated and less practised at veiling their hostility and contempt for India. The usual tolerance is a part of the colonial image and a consequence of conditioned civility. The "proper" Englishmen, such as Douglas, Crawford and Minnies, will be protected by their smugness and strength of character. It is no wonder the Nawab delights in spiting them.

This theme is best expressed through the character of Major Minnies, who realizes that there are many reasons for loving India: "the scenery, the history, the poetry, the music, and indeed the physical beauty of the men and women." Major Minnies adds, however, that it is "dangerous for the European who allows himself to love [India] too much" and warns that the "proper" Englishman "has to be very determined to withstand—to stand up to—India."

The successful European will know, like Beth Crawford, "where lines had to be drawn, not only in speech and behavior but also in one's thought." Olivia does not know where to draw the line, however, and that is her "weakness." Major Minnies explains that this "weak spot is to be found in the most sensitive, often the finest people." Hence, only the insensitive can succeed in India by English standards.

Finally, the major theme of *Heat and Dust* is cultural transformation, a process for which only the most determined of the sensitive are qualified. India is not a healthy place for Olivia's friend Harry, who languishes in the Nawab's entourage and who is unable to extricate himself from the Nawab's influence. Only after the prince's fall from power is Harry free to return to his mother's flat in Kensington.

The Nawab and his immediate relatives are ultimately seduced and destroyed, ironically, by Western values and creature comforts. As a prince, he lives beyond his means. For profit, he allows bands of thieves to terrorize his province, the price of his being able to stay at Claridges while in London. While Olivia stays in India, the Nawab spends much of his time in London, glutting himself on pastries, and, later, in New York, where he dies in the Begum's Park Avenue apartment in 1953. As Harry remarks after seeing the prince in London, "The Nawab was quite changed."

The Nawab's relatives are further contaminated by the Western world. Before going to India, the narrator visits the Nawab's nephew and heir, Karim, and his wife, Kitty (who, despite the cute Western name, is descended from Indian royalty), at their Knightsbridge flat. Karim and Kitty's circle of London friends, all of them transplanted Indians, tell stories of their debauched relatives who "had been involved in scandals in London hotels," or, like the Nawab, "had been deposed for some frightful misdemeanour, had squandered away family fortunes, had died of drink, drugs, or poison administered by illegitimate brothers." Such corruption and debauchery, for these transformed Indians, is a matter of nostalgia, not of shame: "Those days had their charm," they conclude, witlessly.

Only the strongest-willed characters, such as Olivia and her latter-day counterpart, can survive the transformation with integrity. Harry is seduced by Indian indulgence and the personal charm of the Nawab. In the framing story, Chid is seduced by Hindu spiritualism, but his transformation is superficial and incomplete. Chid is unable to cross over into what Major Minnies calls "the other dimension."

"We Indians are fit to live here," Dr. Gopal tells the narrator: "But no one else." Clearly, Chid is not physically "made to live the life of an Indian holy man." Yet Dr. Gopal's speculation does not apply to Olivia, who not only manages to cross into "the other dimension" but even manages to take her piano along, up the Himalayas to a transcultural community that includes a German Buddhist and "two ex-missionaries who had tried to start a Christian 'ashram.'" Both Olivia and her latter-day counterpart do manage both to pass through the "heat and dust" of the lowlands and to climb to a higher plane of spiritual existence. Because the times have changed (presumably for the better), the more liberated narrator is able to rise to these heights with her child, and that fact would seem to indicate both hope and spiritual progress.

Critical Context

The imagined experience of two European women in India has biographical significance for the novelist. Ruth Prawer Jhabvala was born in 1927 in Cologne, Germany, where her grandfather was a cantor in the city's largest synagogue. In 1939, her family emigrated to England. After earning a degree in English literature from London University (Queen Mary College), she met and married an Indian architect, Cyrus S. H. Jhabvala. In 1951, they moved to New Delhi, where they reared three daughters. Since 1955, she has written eight novels set in India, including *Heat and Dust*, which won the prestigious Booker Prize in England. She has also written screenplays for ten theatrical films, most of them for James Ivory and Ismail Merchant. Her filmscript for *Heat and Dust* won the British Academy Award for Best Screenplay.

Ruth Jhabvala's work has been compared to that of E. M. Forster (there are obvious situational affinities between *Heat and Dust* and *A Passage to India*, 1924), Anton Chekhov, and Jane Austen. Her portrait of British society transplanted to India of the 1920's often reads like a comedy of manners, though Jhabvala's focus is upon women after marriage, rather than upon the manipulations leading up to the married state, and her sensibility is far removed in time and spirit from Austen's.

"I never had to deal with India," the novelist told Bernard Weinraub, who interviewed her for *The New York Times Magazine* and who described "heat and dust" as "her metaphor for the disease and squalor" she found surrounding her in India. "Heat and dust" is also surely a metaphor for passion and mutability in the novel. Olivia is sexually frustrated during the "hot" summer and wonders why, for all of his strength and manliness, Douglas has not got her pregnant. She says, "I don't know what's wrong with me." Douglas answers "it's the heat. No Englishwoman is meant to stand it."

At the same time, the title obviously connotes disease, squalor, and poverty in India. "Once you start seeing the poverty, you don't see anything else," the novelist told *The New York Times*, adding that the "terribly hot summer" of 1974 when she wrote *Heat and Dust* "was the last summer I spent in India." She has since settled in New York and divides her time between New York and Delhi.

Sources for Further Study

Gooneratne, Yasmine. "Irony in Ruth Prawer Jhabvala's *Heat and Dust*," in *New Literature Review*. No. 4 (1978), pp. 41-50.

Pradhan, N. S. "The Problem of Focus in Jhabvala's *Heat and Dust*," in *Indian Literature Review*. I, no. 1 (1978), pp. 15-20.

Rani, K. Nirupa. "India in the Fiction of Ruth Prawer Jhabvala," in *Commonwealth Quarterly*. III, no. 9 (1978), pp. 112-127.

Shahane, Vasant A. *Ruth Prawer Jhabvala*, 1981.

Souza, Eunice de. "The Blinds Drawn and the Air Conditioner On: The Novels of Ruth Prawer Jhabvala," in *World Literature Written in English*. XVII (April, 1978), pp. 219-224.

Weinraub, Bernard. "The Artistry of Ruth Prawer Jhabvala," in *The New York Times Magazine*, September 11, 1983, p. 64.

Williams, Haydn M. *The Fiction of Ruth Prawer Jhabvala*, 1975.

James M. Welsh

HER PRIVATES, WE

Author: Frederic Manning (1882-1935)
Type of plot: Social realism
Time of plot: 1916
Locale: Somme and Ancre in northern France
First published: 1929, in Great Britain as *The Middle Parts of Fortune: Somme and Ancre, 1916* (U.S. edition, 1930)

>   *Principal characters:*
>   BOURNE, a private in the Westshire regiment
>   SHEM, a Jewish private
>   CHARLIE MARTLOW, a young private

The Novel

Set on the western front during a period of several weeks in the middle of World War I, the plot of *Her Privates, We* involves much frenzied and destructive action, yet little happens in the sense of purposeful change. Bourne, a private in the Westshire regiment, is first seen lost in the trenches after an attack, on which he reflects while drinking some whiskey he has discovered. Its owner, a junior officer named Clinton, arrives to claim it; later, Clinton is blown to bits during a working-party up the line at night, his last words being that he knew that he would "get it" there. Meanwhile, Bourne and his buddies, Shem and young Charlie Martlow, who met by chance after a battle and stuck together, engage in survival tricks which include getting sufficient water for washing, purchasing food and drink from the French, and coping with the absurdities of military life. Bourne deals with a wide variety of situations and people. Against his wishes, he is assigned to work in the orderly room as a typist (though he does not type), and there he observes petty meanness and devious manipulations: He is glad to be ordered back to infantry duty. While on parade, several troops are killed by what is at first thought to have been a German bomb; then suspicion grows that it was a British shell. When a corporal tells a Frenchwoman who has offered accommodation that it is "cushy," she is outraged and knocks him down. Recognizing that she has mistaken that Hindustani word (meaning comfortable) for "couchez," Bourne manages to appease her. At the request of a French girl, he writes in English to a young English soldier with whom she has fallen in love. Bourne, Shem, and Martlow are sent to a signals section. Since the orders for their transfer have not been processed, they hide in a loft to avoid what they regard as useless training for an attack. Bourne, who is particularly generous about sharing the food parcels he receives, is furious when the merchant at the Expeditionary Force Canteen, which has been funded by public donations, refuses to sell him food because he serves officers only. After a tense period of waiting, during which they endure the ordeal of being shelled, the Westshires go over the top of their trenches, get through the barbed wire, and engage the Germans in close combat. Early in the attack, Shem is wounded in the foot and crawls back to the British trenches, but Martlow has the back of his head blown off, his blood oozing onto Bourne, who has rushed to him. Maddened by Martlow's death, Bourne kills several Germans. After the attack diminishes, he receives a lance corporal's stripe as a prelude to being made an officer, a promotion he had repeatedly declined. Before his departure, he is pressured into participating in a night raid. The raiders destroy a German machine-gun post but, when almost safely back, Bourne is fatally shot in the chest and is dead by the time he has been carried back to the British trenches.

The Characters

Although *Her Privates, We* is not written in the first person, Bourne's activities and consciousness dominate the point of view. Like the author, Bourne is Australian, or so one infers from several pro-Australian comments he makes, as well as this reflection: "He felt curiously isolated even from them [the Westshires]. He was not of their county, he was not even of their country, or their religion, and he was only partially of their race." This difference helps to give him a detached perspective on those around him, though he is throughout a sympathetic observer, aroused to anger only by meanness, malice, and the dodging of responsibility. He shares the frontline soldiers' scorn for those "parasites behind them pinching the stores." His attitude toward senior officers who are safely insulated from the horrors of the trenches is seen in the sardonic reflection: "Presently arrived magnificent people on horseback, glancing superciliously at the less fortunate members of their species whom necessity compelled to walk." Because of his education and ability to influence others, he is identified as one who should become an officer, a move he repeatedly rejects because before enlisting he had no experience in dealing with men and after serving in the ranks he believes that he belongs with them. He comes to agree with the assessment of him as a man who

> looked at a question upside down and inside out, and then did exactly what the average man would do in similar circumstances. . . . He experienced a quite futile anxiety as to whether he were doing the right thing, while he was doing the only possible thing at that particular moment; and it troubled him much more in the interval before action.

Bourne's nature thus contains some attributes of Hamlet and of Everyman.

Shem is a shadowy figure. Bourne describes him as a cynic and a materialist who nevertheless gave up a safe job in the Army Pay Office in England for the trenches in France. Martlow jokingly refers to Shem's Jewish "prudence" in not offering to pay for the drinks, while acknowledging that if the others are broke Shem will pick up the bill.

Martlow, the son of a gamekeeper, is a down-to-earth lad, who stubbornly holds onto his resentments, yet "is full of generous impulses." Martlow casually sat beside Shem and Bourne after a battle, by which chance encounter their comradeship was formed. They were three people with nothing in common: nothing, that is, except that necessity which bound them together. Elsewhere, Bourne observes that comradeship may involve an intensity that friendship never touches: "At one moment a particular man may be nothing at all to you, and the next minute you will go through hell for him.... The man doesn't matter so much, it's a kind of impersonal emotion, a kind of enthusiasm, in the old sense of the world.... We help each other [because] we are all in it up to the neck together, and we know it."

Around these three characters, Frederic Manning provides a full range of other privates, noncommissioned officers, junior officers, and even a captured deserter. Civilians, including several women, necessarily are in secondary roles, but they are usually presented in memorable vignettes.

Themes and Meanings

No matter how fully Manning may depict character in the case of Bourne or others, he stresses the ultimately unknowable element in each personality. In this connection the word "mystery" occurs often, and at the end the survivors of the raid in which Bourne is killed sit silently, "each man keeping his own secret."

Another recurrent theme is that of the will, individual and collective. One elaboration on the former occurs in the first chapter: "The function of our moral nature consists solely in the assertion of one's own individual will against anything which may be opposed to it." It is through exercising one's moral conscience that one asserts one's individual freedom.

Bourne meditates in chapter 9 on the collective will, in connection with the stoicism and capacity for endurance of the French peasants, that people understand "that war is one of the blind forces of nature, which can neither be foreseen nor controlled." Still, taken collectively, "the violence and passions of man become...an impersonal and incalculable force, a blind and irrational movement of the collective will, which one cannot control, which one cannot understand, which one can only endure...."

Another device which adds a dimension to the novel's realistic reporting of the brutality and stupidity of war is Manning's use of epigraphs. His title uses the bawdy witticism exchanged between Hamlet and Rosencrantz and Guildenstern: "On fortune's cap we are not the very button.... Then you live about her waist, or in the middle of her favours?... Faith, her privates we." In addition, each of the eighteen chapters has an epigraph from works by

William Shakespeare; many of these from *Henry IV*, Parts I and II, and *Henry V*, thereby invoking the struggles and fears of British soldiers in a glorified past.

Critical Context

Manning, born in Sydney, Australia, in 1882, had settled in London and published books of poems and essays before World War I broke out in 1914. He promptly enlisted in the British army and survived the kind of trench warfare depicted in his novel, the work for which he is remembered. He died in London in 1935. Eleven years later, his authorship of *Her Privates, We* was made public.

Her Privates, We was one of the wave of novels about World War I that appeared about ten years after it ended. It bore no author's name, only the serial number of a private in the British army, and its unexpurgated first edition as *The Middle Parts of Fortune: Somme and Ancre, 1916* was privately printed in small numbers, facts which helped to make it something of an underground classic. It soon drew favorable comments from writers of such diverse tastes as Arnold Bennett and Ezra Pound. Ernest Hemingway called it "the finest and noblest book of men in war that I have ever read. I read it over once a year to remember how things really were." T. E. Lawrence declared, "No praise could be too sheer for this book. . . . Its virtues will be recognized more and more as time goes on."

Sources for Further Study

Dutton, Geoffrey, ed. *The Literature of Australia*, 1976 (revised edition).

Jones, Joseph, and Johanna Jones. *Australian Fiction*, 1983.

Kramer, Leonie, ed. *The Oxford History of Australian Literature*, 1981.

Murray-Smith, Stephen. "The Manning Revival," in *Australian Book Review*. October, 1964, p. 229.

Ramson, W. S., ed. *The Australian Experience: Critical Essays on Australian Novels*, 1974.

Christopher M. Armitage

THE HISTORY MAN

Author: Malcolm Bradbury (1932-   )
Type of plot: Social satire
Time of plot: The fall semester of 1972
Locale: The fictional Watermouth University in Watermouth, England
First published: 1975

Principal characters:

HOWARD KIRK, a professor of sociology at Watermouth
  University
BARBARA KIRK, his wife
HENRY BEAMISH, a friend of the Kirks and Howard's
  colleague
MYRA BEAMISH, his wife
FLORA BENIFORM, another sociology colleague
MOIRA MILLIKIN, another sociology colleague
MISS ANNIE CALLENDAR, a member of the English
  Department
FELICITY PHEE, a student and sex partner of Howard
GEORGE CARMODY, a traditional student

The Novel

In mock-epic and mock-sociological style, *The History Man* satirically explores the rituals of a contemporary social phenomenon, at its height in the early 1970's: the unstructured life, whose deliberate lack of form becomes the new structure of things. Defined by its Freudian-Marxist context, human nature is, in Malcolm Bradbury's words, "a particular type of relationship to the temporal and historical process, culturally conditioned. . . ." Howard Kirk, joined by his wife, Barbara, is the full embodiment of the postmodernist man, with his new self-consciousness. At the basis of this mode lies the abandonment of traditional sexual, familial, and professional (academic, in this case) mores.

The epicenter of events, Howard, a professor of sociology at Watermouth University, makes things happen to himself and to those around him—or, in his own terms, *allows* them to happen. These "happenings," a term used by Bradbury in the narrow sociological definition of the protest generation of the 1960's, form the loose plot of the novel. Happenings occur at two parties held by the Kirks', one at the beginning and the other at the end of the fall term. All the remaining action radiates from these central events. To their parties the Kirks invite friends, colleagues, students, and strangers, in the hope of generating spontaneous happenings that will destructure existing feelings, attitudes, and relationships. Howard practices his beliefs to the hilt.

In lesser degrees and with varying results, most persons in his orbit find the new rituals exhilarating. Others, however, are less than satisfied, and some are even devastated in the end. The desolation experienced by the two persons at one time closest to Howard finds expression in the smashing of a window, at the first party by Henry Beamish and at the second party by Barbara. The first "accident" goes unnoticed by most of the guests; the second occurs even more quietly at the novel's end. On this last note Bradbury ends his sociological romp through the sexual and intellectual promiscuities of the new man in the new academia, which has little in common with the Oxford-Cambridge, or Redbrick, university traditions of England.

The new rituals include Howard's sexual exploits with Flora Beniform, an Earth Mother figure whose sexual appetite matches Howard's in its lustiness; Felicity Phee, a student starved for sexual gratification from her academic idol; and Miss Annie Callendar, the prim English Department faculty member who loses all inhibitions by the end-of-term party.

The freedom of the new sexual rites is echoed in Howard's intellectual life. He conducts his seminars in the freewheeling style of his amorous exploits. He demolishes a traditional student, George Carmody, whose conventional views and behavior run counter to Howard's. When Carmody threatens Howard's status by appealing a failing grade to higher university officials, Howard beds Annie Calendar, who knows of the Carmody case and is a potential defender of Carmody. Academic abuse extends to campus activities, such as the rumored engagement of a racist speaker on campus. Ironically, the scientist dies the night before his controversial appearance.

Between October 2 and December 15, 1972, the dates of the two parties, the events of the novel fictionalize a generation of social change. The references at the beginning and end of the novel to Richard Nixon's running for the presidency of the United States and then to his victory suggest that the tawdriness of the larger world has infected even those people who protest against it.

The Characters

Born and reared in the North of England, Howard Kirk has made his way up the educational and, consequently, social ladder in a class-conscious society. From his working-class origins, via grammar school and Leeds University, he has moved to the newest of higher educational institutions, the University of Watermouth, to the south of Leeds. The university may very well be like that at which the author himself teaches, the University of East Anglia in Norwich, Sussex. Having been graduated with a "first," the English version of the American summa cum laude, Howard energetically and grittily patterns personal and academic life after the liberation sociology of the 1960's. With unprincipled ferocity, he beds colleagues, colleagues' wives, and students, applying the new religion as well to the classroom, department meetings, and other campus activities. With Machiavellian cunning, he seduces minds and bodies indiscriminately, encouraging all who come within his periphery to follow him into the brave new world.

As he enjoys his latest conquest, Miss Callendar, she murmurs, "Historical inevitability," and he responds, "Marx arranged it." Sociological justification for every experience becomes Howard's uncompromising principle. It takes on Rabelaisian proportions in his liaison with Flora Beniform, who outplays Howard in his own game by doling out her favors only at her convenience. Otherwise, Howard manipulates the most prim of female colleagues or the most sex-starved of students, all in the name of a higher consciousness to which the new man is called. Indeed, the title of Howard's book is *The Coming of the New Sex.*

His wife, Barbara, at first an approving partner in the "onward transactions of the historical process," experiences an increasing uneasiness and, finally, desperation. Unlike Howard, she is not graduated with a "first." Her sexual emancipation—in fact, both of their sexual liberations—begins innocently, with Hamid, a dark-eyed Egyptian student, whose purpose, Howard later rationalizes, "was to establish intimacy between the male parties . . . because of his culturally determined view of women." Barbara and Howard constantly refer to this catalyst for their new lives as the "Hamid strategy."

The strategy determines even their choice of a dilapidated home in a derelict section of Watermouth—the result of the powerful feeling of liberation. Barbara's sexual rebirth takes her to London for "shopping" weekends, during which she enjoys a liaison with an actor. Eventually the affair ends, and at the Kirks' second orgy, she puts her hand quietly through a window glass, hardly interrupting the saturnalia around her. Despite her liberation, evidenced in the confidence with which she greets guests with questions about which type of contraceptive they have brought, she is unable to divest herself of her social and moral origins as easily as can Howard. When she falls into her increasing fits of depression, he recommends a party, a Valium, participation in a demonstration (a "demo"), shooting a soldier, or bedding a friend.

Most negatively affected by the current sociological fashion are Henry and Myra Beamish, friends of the Kirks from their graduate school days at Leeds University. No longer having much in common, the Beamishes and the Kirks see one another only at the parties. As a result of her first taste of the new freedoms, Myra drinks more, talks in frenzied excitement, and announces her intention to leave Henry. Henry, like Barbara, injures himself as he breaks a window at a party.

Other characters represent significant "advanced" living patterns, Moira Millikin, Howard's unorthodox colleague and unmarried mother, always carries her baby to class, "where it gurgles and chunters as she explains the gross national product. . . ." Arriving behind Moira at the last party are the

Macintoshes, each "bearing a baby in a carrycot." Miss Callendar ("Annie" now) has discarded her prim dark suit and literally let down her hair. Melissa Todoroff, a visiting faculty member from New York, berates Howard for neglecting her and talks incessantly of the radical movement (in Berkeley, Columbia, and Vincennes).

Only George Carmody, the student who dares to wear a university blazer and to complain to the administration about Howard, joins the Beamishes as outsiders to the new consciousness.

Themes and Meanings

When John Osborne's Jimmy Porter in *Look Back in Anger* (1956) was graduated from a Redbrick university in the bleak midlands of England, he had no outlet for his energy and intellect except as operator of a sweets stall and as angry tormentor of his wife and of a good friend who lived with them. His articulate but raw anger gave a name to the British antihero of the 1950's. From the same background, Howard Kirk, nearly a generation later, is no longer the angry young man but an aggressively intolerant academic bully who manipulates the societal changes of the 1960's to his personal and professional advantage. Determined to make the historical process work for him, he transforms the anger of an earlier generation into cunning manipulation. Self-consciously, he and Barbara deconstruct traditional social and academic patterns.

The larger theme of the novel involves the additional tier to the English higher education system that universities such as Watermouth represent. Bradbury devotes pages to descriptions of the modernist architecture, determined by one Millington Harsent, radical educationalist, former political scientist and vice chancellor. Harsent suffers from an "Edifice Complex," especially the style of the futurist architect Jop Kaakinen. The social science building is a high glass tower, and its rooms are "stark, simple, repetitious, each one an exemplary instance of the others." Their standard furniture includes "one black-topped Conran desk; one grey gunmetal desk lamp; one plain glass ashtray," and the like. Every year new buildings, new paths, new stretches of water multiply endlessly. This demotic and democratic institution contrasts with what only ten years ago was "a peaceful, pastoral Eden, a place of fields and cows . . . with the turreted Elizabethan mansion now screened from sight by the massive constructions. . . ."

Joining this architectural parade into the future are the faculty, who "ceaselessly innovate, plan, design new courses . . . and new reasons for trips to Italy. . . ." Students "sit on the tiled floors of the corridors, their backs against the wall, their knees up, their hands holding, or spilling, plastic cups of coffee, obtained from an automatic vending machine next to the life shaft." Democracy and technocracy complete their reign with the advent of the new Computing Centre, which "began work by issuing a card with a number on it to everyone on campus, telling them who they were, an increasingly valuable piece of information."

With corrosive effect, Bradbury uses sociological jargon to satirize itself, as characters comment on the new mores in marriage, sex, and education. Most participate self-consciously, playing out their historical inevitability. According to Howard, the new lawmaker, a person is defined in his sociopsychological center.

Critical Context

From Frederic Raphael's famous contemporary work *Glittering Prizes* (1976), about the lives of Cambridge-Oxford dons, to plays about seedier institutions such as the second-language school in Simon Gray's *Quartermaine's Terms* (1918) or the University of London in Gray's *Butley* (1971), academia, still the major definer of class in England, has been the subject of many dramas and novels since World War II. Having written his first novel, *Eating People Is Wrong* (1959), about the Redbrick university of the 1950's, Bradbury continues the tradition in *The History Man*.

Reviewers have mentioned the strong physicality of Bradbury's style, particularly the endless lists of objects. George Steiner mentions the Homeric quality—lists and catalogs—and concludes with a comparison of Bradbury with Henry James, referring to the "density of convention, the same alertness to the flick of intonation." The long lists of the furniture of the Kirks' home, of the food served at the parties, of the separate routines of the Kirks as they prepare for a party, of the viciously detailed dress and general behavior of the guests, of the fashionable language—all these serve to create a thick textural tone of objects and language, at times providing subtle insights and at other times overwhelming with their sense of mass.

Hilary Spurling writes that she "cannot help feeling that inside this fat catalogue of very superior goods a thinner, sharper and altogether more disconcerting novel is struggling to get out." The novelist Margaret Drabble sees the novel as immensely readable, and if it is about ideas, those ideas "are embodied in closely observed details—an apron, a chair, a conference room, an umbrella, 'an old party handbag from the days when there were party handbags.'"

Bradbury's angle of vision is that of a disengaged sociologist creating a fictional world, utopian according to the modern impulses flowing from the radical-liberal actions of the 1960's. It is bluntly obvious that he does not approve of this new world. In his use of the present tense, he progressively removes himself from the people about whom he writes. They are around him but not of him. He describes the characters as he does the buildings, with clinical detachment: ". . . the Kirks are, of course, enormously busy people, with two full lives, and two separate diaries," and "the Kirks are, indeed, new people."

American novels on academic life by writers such as John O'Hara, Saul Bellow, John Updike, and Joyce Carol Oates are many. One of these, Oates's *Unholy Loves* (1979), emphasizes the private lives, with the satiric thrust subordinate to the individualization of characters. Bradbury's vision, however, evokes the sterile world of Eugène Ionesco in part and, in part, the gigantism of a François Rabelais or a Federico Fellini.

Sources for Further Study

Bradbury, Malcolm, ed. *The Novel Today: Contemporary Writers on Modern Fiction*, 1977.

Drabble, Margaret. Review in *The New York Times Book Review*. LXXIV (February 8, 1976), p. 3.

Spurling, Hilary. "Campus Mentis," in *The Times Literary Supplement*. November 7, 1975, p. 1325.

Steiner, George. Review in *The New Yorker*. LII (May 3, 1976), p. 130.

Susan Rusinko

THE HOBBIT
Or, There and Back Again

Author: J. R. R. Tolkien (1892-1973)
Type of plot: Quest fantasy
Time of plot: A mythical past
Locale: Middle-earth
First published: 1937

Principal characters:
BILBO BAGGINS, a hobbit, the hero of the tale
GANDALF, a wizard
THORIN OAKENSHIELD, a dwarf, proposer of the quest
GOLLUM, a corrupted hobbit
THRANDUIL, an Elven-king
SMAUG, a dragon, guardian of the Lonely Mountain

The Novel

Perhaps exactly how *The Hobbit: Or, There and Back Again* came to be written will never be settled. J. R. R. Tolkien himself said that inspiration for the beginning of the story came to him one day when, in the midst of grading examinations, he found that a student had turned in a blank sheet of paper. On that sheet, Tolkien wrote, "In a hole in the ground there lived a hobbit." He said that names always suggested stories to him, and that he immediately wanted to find out what hobbits were. Tolkien's children also recall hearing parts of the story told to them at bedtime; some version of *The Hobbit*, perhaps incomplete, was probably in existence before 1932, when it was seen by C. S. Lewis, then a fellow professor with Tolkien at Oxford.

Whatever the immediate spark, the story that resulted was a fresh version of an age-old plot, the quest. At the very start of the story, the reader learns what hobbits are: a smaller, shyer, home-loving race related to humans; a race living in a far-distant mythical past on a world both like and unlike Earth. The central character, the young hobbit Bilbo Baggins, seems typical of his people at the beginning, content to live a quiet and unexciting life in his cozy dwelling. From the beginning, however, the story sounds a note of mystery: Gandalf, a wizard whose powers are only hinted at, has seen in Bilbo a taste for adventure and a capacity for heroism.

Gandalf knows that the dwarf Thorin Oakenshield plans a return to the Lonely Mountain, the former home of his people. Long ago, the dwarves (Tolkien's famous spelling of the plural form) had been driven from the mountain by a dragon who has converted it into a secure lair. What the dwarves need is a burglar, someone who can penetrate the lair and scout its defenses, and Gandalf (without informing Bilbo) tells Thorin that Bilbo is just the hobbit for the job. Thus, at the beginning of the story, Thorin and his band of followers show up at Bilbo's hole and sweep him away on the quest.

Although Bilbo shows some initial reluctance, Gandalf had judged him rightly. Bilbo sets out with the dwarves and steps into a larger world. As the band travels to the Lonely Mountain, they encounter situations that increase in danger. They are threatened by trolls and captured by goblins. During the latter episode, Bilbo gains a crucial possession and meets an important character. While lost in the goblin caverns, Bilbo finds a ring and not long afterward encounters its owner. This character is Gollum, a loathsome, solitary figure, dwelling in darkness and ruled by his greed for a magical ring. Not knowing that he has lost the ring, Gollum regards Bilbo as an intruder and is ready to kill him when Bilbo challenges him to a game of riddles. With the ring in his possession, Bilbo is more than a match for Gollum and, in an act that will later be important, spares Gollum's life and escapes from the caverns. The adventures continue, but now Bilbo is growing to fit his role. Thorin's band is seized by giant spiders and imprisoned by elves, a race long suspicious of dwarves, but the dwarves are delivered from each of these dangers by Bilbo's imagination and daring (qualities he himself had not suspected he possessed). Eventually, they reach their destination.

Once again, Bilbo proves equal to the task, and by now he is rather enjoying being a burglar. He single-handedly enters the mountain lair, manages to confuse the dragon, and escapes with a piece of treasure from the hoard, an act that leads directly to the climax of the story. Discovering the theft, the dragon suspects someone from Dale, a nearby town inhabited by humans, and he flies out to punish the thief. During the devastation that follows, Bard, a hero from the town, kills the dragon with an arrow. In the meantime, Thorin, Bilbo, and the band of dwarves reenter the mountain caves, and Thorin prepares to establish the seat of his kingdom there. As the climax approaches, forces are gathering to contest Thorin's claim to the dragon's treasure: The humans of Dale, the wood-elves from the forest of Mirkwood, and a reinforcing army of dwarves kindred to Thorin dispute who has a right to the treasure. This quarrel is postponed by the arrival of a force of wolves and goblins, and a general mêlée follows, one which Bilbo sees as the futile result of greed and in which he takes no direct part. Although the wolves and goblins are defeated, the victory costs Thorin his life. Before he dies, though, Thorin realizes that his greed has killed him and that the treasure is large enough to share. After the dwarves, elves, and humans have come to a friendly settlement, Bilbo returns home with the memories of his trip and with the ring.

The Characters

Surely one reason for the success of *The Hobbit* is the skill with which

Tolkien blends a mixture of elements long familiar from fairy tale, legend, and folklore with absolutely original elements. The characters are a good example of this technique: Thorin Oakenshield and his companions, as dwarves, are almost familiar figures; the characteristics that they exhibit— suspicion, a love of gems, skill at mining and delving—are the characteristics long associated with dwarves. Consider the dragon who guards the Lonely Mountain: Although Smaug is an especially acquisitive and cunning dragon, such are traits characteristic of the dragons of legend. The dwarves and the dragon—even a wizard such as Gandalf—place the reader in a familiar context and arouse in the reader's mind the expectations consistent with stories of heroic fantasy. To this context, Tolkien adds original characters, ones who will not only fulfill but also exceed the reader's expectations. Chief among these are the hobbits, Tolkien's chief contribution to mythology and probably his most enduring one.

When Stanley Unwin was considering *The Hobbit* for publication, he took the normal step of sending the manuscript to a reader for evaluation; the reader, however, was unusual: It was his ten-year-old son, Rayner. That the hobbits—Bilbo in particular—caught Rayner's imagination is no surprise: Bilbo's small stature and relative youth make him a hero likable to children. The hobbits as a race enjoy comfort, eating, and drinking, and the pleasures of a secure home—all pleasures accessible to children. Their vices, too, tend to be those of children, chiefly greed and quarrelsomeness. Yet they act in adult affairs and in their actions can well represent something more: Tolkien later claimed that the limited imagination and great courage of the hobbits were traits of the ordinary Englishman, traits which he had the chance to observe under the stress of World War I.

Whether children or Tommies, the hobbits have a deeper dimension: They are capable of moral choices, and one of the most successful characters of the story is one who later proves to be of central importance, Gollum. When he appears, Gollum is so repellent a character that he seems at first to be another species entirely from the wholesome hobbits. As the reader hears his story, however, it becomes quite clear that Gollum's vice, his overwhelming lust for his precious ring, is only a fault of the ordinary hobbit carried to the extreme.

One may see Bilbo and Gollum as a contrast: Both, perhaps, show a bit more daring than the ordinary hobbit, and both find themselves subjected to temptations outside the ordinary. Both are similar in this, too, that although their adventures in *The Hobbit* form a satisfying story with a beginning, a middle, and an end, that story will be seen from a more profound perspective in *The Lord of the Rings* (1954-1955). The depth of Gollum's lust for the ring and the height of Bilbo's heroism in renouncing it will be appreciated in their full dimensions only later when, with the maturity of years, the children who read *The Hobbit* will turn to its adult sequel.

Themes and Meanings

J. R. R. Tolkien, a devoted and believing Roman Catholic, did not avoid giving his works a moral dimension; he most surely would have been bored by fictions that lacked one. It is not difficult, therefore, to find that in *The Hobbit*, characters make choices that count, that they are held accountable for their behavior, that the good characters value mercy, and that a benevolent providence shapes the characters' ends.

Bilbo's kindness in sparing Gollum can only be fully appreciated in *The Lord of the Rings*, when Frodo, Bilbo's nephew and the trilogy's protagonist, will even more explicitly pity Gollum, an act which indirectly saves Frodo's own life. Bilbo rejects the temptation of the dragon's treasure, an act which keeps him safe in the final battle. By contrast, Thorin's refusal to compromise leads eventually to his death. One can also better understand the real heroism of Bilbo at the start of *The Lord of the Rings*: Of all the characters in either story, only Bilbo freely surrenders the ring to another in a peaceful situation after calm reflection.

Tolkien's heroes always have significant moral choices to make: They always value mercy over power or possessions. They pass the test. If they are rescued in the final, almost hopeless crisis, that providential intervention comes with a sense of justice, a sense that life is not meaningless or hostile to human values. One could forcefully argue that the hobbits are Tolkien's parable of the theme that the meek shall indeed inherit the earth.

Critical Context

Although Tolkien's scholarly work was well-known by 1937, *The Hobbit* made him famous as a writer of fiction. There was no contradiction between the activities that gained for him these two very different reputations. From his youth, Tolkien had been fascinated both by languages and by the great cycles of folktales—for example, the Arthurian legends or the Norse Eddas—that embodied the imagination of a people. He was later to complain about the lack of such a cycle for the English (he considered the stories of Camelot too much a mixture of British, Celtic, and Continental sources to qualify), and he yearned to give his own country a heroic cycle of legends set in a secondary world. Moreover, he knew from his studies and later from helping to compile the *Oxford English Dictionary* that the history of a language is the history of a people. He was convinced of the close connection between a language and its literature.

From his youth, he delighted in constructing mythical languages, and while still an undergraduate, he began to compose stories that embodied those languages. The stories that make up *The Silmarillion* (1977) were certainly begun before his service in World War I, and, although he did not live to see their publication, they were always his first love.

The grand mythos of which *The Silmarillion* was only one part might have remained a father's bedtime story had not Tolkien been a regular member of the Inklings, the literary circle gathered around C. S. Lewis at Oxford University between the World Wars. As the circle of people who knew of *The Hobbit* grew, the work came to the attention of publisher Stanley Unwin, who accepted the book for publication. The popularity of the work in both Great Britain and America prompted Unwin's request for a sequel, leading eventually to *The Lord of the Rings*. When Tolkien wrote *The Hobbit*, he was not beginning a story or creating a setting anew: On the contrary, he was placing the tale within a larger framework, a history of thousands of years. It was a history he already knew intimately because he had been working on it for more than twenty years.

The Hobbit differs from his *The Lord of the Rings* and *The Silmarillion* in being explicitly written as a children's book, but as a specimen of its type it is in no way inferior to them, either by itself or as an episode in the greater saga of the end of the Third Age of Middle-earth. If the narrator of *The Hobbit* seems intrusive at times or seems to be talking down to his audience, one must remember that styles change, even the styles of children's books. The proper comparison for *The Hobbit* is not to Tolkien's works intended for adults but to the works of his contemporaries intended for children. The book's audience must be considered as well: Until children find the narrator's presence oppressive, it seems pointless for adults to complain.

Although Tolkien may have preferred other stories of his own, stories with a greater range of human emotion, no story of his has carried more readers on the first stage of their journey to Middle-earth than has *The Hobbit*, and although those readers may be young, they seem to develop a taste for the trip.

Sources for Further Study

Green, William H. "The Four-Part Structure of Bilbo's Education," in *Children's Literature*. VIII (1979), pp. 133-140.

Nitzsche, J. C. "The King Under the Mountain: Tolkien's Hobbit," in *North Dakota Quarterly*. XLVII (Winter, 1979), pp. 5-18.

Shippey, T. A. *The Road to Middle-Earth*, 1983.

West, Richard C. *Tolkien Criticism: An Annotated Checklist*, 1981.

Walter E. Meyers

THE HONORARY CONSUL

Author: Graham Greene (1904-   )
Type of plot: Political realism
Time of plot: The early 1970's
Locale: A port city in northern Argentina and, briefly, Buenos Aires
First published: 1973

> *Principal characters:*
> DOCTOR EDUARDO PLARR, the protagonist, a physician
> CHARLES FORTNUM, the British Honorary Consul in
>   Argentina
> CLARA FORTNUM, his wife, more than forty years his junior
> LEON RIVAS, a former priest turned revolutionary
> DOCTOR SAAVEDRA, a novelist of minor reputation
> COLONEL PEREZ, the chief of police

The Novel

In Graham Greene's *The Honorary Consul* a group of Paraguayan revolutionaries attempt to kidnap the American ambassador to Argentina. By mistake, however, they seize Charles Fortnum, the British Honorary Consul, who has accompanied the Ambassador on a visit to some ruins in the north. Much of the action of the novel deals with the consequences, for various individuals, of the bungled kidnaping.

The novel opens in a small river port in northern Argentina on the Tuesday evening of the kidnaping. Doctor Eduardo Plarr is anxious. Because of a complex of reasons, not the least of which is the hope of freeing his father from political imprisonment in Paraguay, Plarr has been induced to provide the revolutionaries with precise information about the Ambassador's movements. The revolutionaries are led by Plarr's old school friend, a former priest named Leon Rivas. When, after the kidnaping, Plarr is called to Rivas' camp to provide medical assistance, he recognizes Fortnum and alerts Rivas to the mistake. Unfortunately, Fortnum also recognizes him.

Plarr argues for the Consul's release on the grounds that he is not important enough to be useful to the revolutionaries' cause. Fortnum is not an official member of the diplomatic corps because he is not a real consul. Plarr points out: "An Honorary Consul is not a proper Consul." Rivas rejects Plarr's appeal because kidnaping the wrong man is better than kidnaping no one; the revolutionary followers of El Tigre would be "discouraged if nothing happened. . . . Even the kidnapping of a Consul is something."

Plarr's desire for Fortnum's release is not uncomplicated. Fortnum's wife, Clara, is Plarr's lover, and she is pregnant with his child. Plarr would prefer to leave responsibility for Clara and the child to her cuckolded husband than to take it on himself. ("Fortnum would make a better father for the child than he would.") Moreover, unless Fortnum is released while he is still drunk, he could implicate Plarr in the kidnaping plot as well as endanger Rivas and the Paraguayan revolutionaries, for whom Plarr has some feeling.

The day after the kidnaping, Plarr visits Fortnum's house outside the city to see Clara and finds Colonel Perez there. The chief of police has come to tell Clara that her husband's car has been found in the Parana River near Posadas. Plarr realizes that he implicates himself with the excuses he offers Perez for his own visit. Later that day, the radio broadcasts the official news about Fortnum's kidnaping along with the kidnapers' demands. Ten political prisoners held in Paraguay are to be released and flown to either Havana or Mexico City; the kidnapers will wait for four days, until Sunday midnight, for the authorities to agree to their terms; if there is no agreement by that time, Fortnum will be killed. Back at Rivas' camp, Fortnum attempts to escape and is wounded in the foot.

Plarr flies to Buenos Aires the following morning to interest Sir Henry Belfrage, the British ambassador, in Fortnum's plight. After the usual courtesies, Belfrage tells Plarr that his only hope is to enlist the support of the press. That evening, Plarr invites Doctor Humphries, an English teacher, and Doctor Saavedra, a novelist, to sign a letter on behalf of Fortnum to the papers from the newly formed Anglo-Argentinian Club. For different reasons, both men refuse. In an excess of machismo, however, the psychological principle which dominates his novels, Saavedra offers to exchange himself for the Consul. Disheartened, Plarr returns to his flat, where Perez finds him to tell him that his father was killed trying to escape a Paraguayan prison more than a year before. Plarr realizes that he has been misled by Rivas.

Summoned to Rivas' camp for the last time, Plarr overhears Fortnum dictating a final letter to Clara and finds himself jealous of the Consul's capacity to love. Later Fortnum will overhear Plarr speaking with Rivas and learn that Plarr is the father of Clara's child. While the kidnapers wait for their deadline to pass, Perez's men surround their camp. Attempting to save the lives of both Fortnum and Rivas by bargaining with Perez, Plarr steps out of the hut and is shot. Rivas comes out after him to face his own death. Fortnum survives to take up his life with Clara and their soon-to-be-born child.

The Characters

Graham Greene has created a carefully poised series of juxtapositions which allow him to develop individual characters in terms of a central concern of the novel: personal and political commitment. Rivas, the former priest who is now a revolutionary prepared to kill, has a capacity for belief which contrasts with Plarr's lack of belief. The strength of the love which Fortnum, an elderly drunkard whose first wife left him, feels for the new wife he found among the prostitutes of the local brothel is an ironic measure of Plarr's own cynical and egotistical rejection of such love.

Like so many of Greene's heroes, Plarr is an isolated man. His father was an English political activist in Paraguay, who left his wife and young son in order to face the dangers of his life alone. Although he does not remember his father, Plarr still misses him. Love is something the son has learned to find in brothels, and his experiences with women have made him highly suspicious of emotional involvement. His medical training has exaggerated his cynicism, imparting to him an air of clinical detachment.

Yet Plarr does not lack empathy for the suffering of others. He is a physician who treats the poor, although he says that he does so only because he thinks it is something his father would have liked him to do. In his conversations with Rivas about the Church and God, Plarr often means to goad him but finds himself moved by the spectacle of his old friend driven from the Church and into rebellion by his compassion and sense of justice. Rivas himself suffers his separation from the Church with anxiety and remorse. He is repulsed by the violence which his new life as a revolutionary demands and feels genuine sympathy for Fortnum, his intended victim. When Rivas agrees to say a final Mass before the police close in, he acknowledges that he is condemned to belief in spite of his revolutionary ideology.

Plarr pejoratively describes his feeling for Clara as an "obsession." On the last night he spends with her, Clara declares her love for him, but her declaration repels him. He remembers his mother offering him her love: "Something was always asked in return: obedience, an apology, a kiss which one had no desire to give." Yet the obsession with Clara persists.

It is not until Plarr listens to Fortnum's letter to Clara that he understands the depth of feeling the Consul has for his wife. Fortnum loves Clara as a father loves a child. (Indeed, Fortnum has assumed the role of a loving and forgiving father with Plarr and Rivas as well.) Although he is in peril of losing his own life, Fortnum's principal concern is for Clara and the baby she is carrying. His love for her is unashamedly sentimental: "He was not crying now for himself. The tears were for Clara and a few of them for Fortnum's Pride [his Jeep], both left alone and defenceless." That Plarr is capable of feeling jealous of Fortnum's love is a testament to his own rekindled humanity, for such jealousy is an implicit recognition that love counts for something in the world.

By the end of the novel, cracks have begun to appear in the apparently impassive surface of the emotional wall Plarr has constructed around himself. His growing concern for Fortnum is itself in marked contrast to the indifference of those in power to the Consul's fate. Rivas, Clara, and Fortnum all make claims on Plarr's sense of responsibility. It is these claims which impel him toward the final act of commitment, the heroic action in which he gives his life to save the lives of the others.

Themes and Meanings

When Plarr says to Fortnum, "Caring is the only dangerous thing," he is obliquely announcing the major theme of *The Honorary Consul*. Like his spiritual predecessors, Fowler in *The Quiet American* (1955) and Querry in *A Burnt-Out Case* (1961), Plarr allows himself to become involved in spite of his declared policy of noncommitment. He is capable of intellectually rejecting love as "a claim which he wouldn't meet, a responsibility he would refuse to accept, a demand." Yet the ironies of the plot, as well as the development of his own character, push him toward a final and tragic action in which love is both the motivation for and the vehicle of self-knowledge.

With the examples of Fortnum and Rivas before him, Plarr comes to understand that in a politically promiscuous world the absence of faith is not only to be decried but also to be remedied by acts of love. That these acts may include kidnaping and political murder testifies to the complexity of the central dilemma which the novel explores.

Plarr has spent much of his life searching for a father whose compassionate heroism caused him to desert his family. Ironically, through his involvement with Clara and his subsequent concern for Fortnum and Rivas, Plarr finds himself fighting for the same cause for which his father died. Unwilling to let Fortnum and Rivas die, he chooses to act. In making his self-sacrifice, he demonstrates that caring is indeed a dangerous thing. Yet in a faithless world, it is also the only course open to the man of compassion.

Critical Context

It is generally agreed that Greene's first mature period of development coincides with the religious novels which include such titles as *Brighton Rock* (1938), *The Power and the Glory* (1940), *The Heart of the Matter* (1948), and *The End of the Affair* (1951). To a lesser extent, *A Burnt-Out Case* is part of this group in which Greene's understanding of Catholicism emerges as a significant narrative force. With the appearance of *The Quiet American*, Greene announces a new direction in his fiction: The vision is outward-looking, and its focus is more squarely on the public world of international politics than it is on the varieties of religious faith. Along with *The Honorary Consul*, the major political novels which follow are *The Comedians* (1966) and *The Human Factor* (1978).

The Honorary Consul is an important book in Greene's career because, better than any other, it brings into a unified whole the two predominant themes of his mature fiction, religion and politics. The narrative vehicle of the novel, a politically motivated kidnaping directed by a deeply religious man, allows Greene to combine moral issues with a serious examination of the political as well as the spiritual role of the Catholic Church. This book is about political commitment by men of varying degrees of religion. It is a credit to Greene's skill as a dramatic writer that such weighty concerns as he is manipulating never tear through the fictional fabric of the novel and erupt into pure polemic. The inanities of contemporary religious and political debate are dramatized in genuinely human terms as Plarr, Rivas, and Fortnum argue life and death in their hut while the police move ever closer.

Sources for Further Study

Kulshrestha, J. P. *Graham Greene: The Novelist*, 1977.

Leigh, David J. "The Structure of Greene's *The Honorary Consul*," in *Renascence*. XXXVIII (Autumn, 1985), pp. 13-24.

Sharrock, Roger. *Saints, Sinners, and Comedians: The Novels of Graham Greene*, 1984.

Smith, Grahame. *The Achievement of Graham Greene*, 1985.

Spurling, John. *Graham Greene*, 1983.

Richard Butts

THE HONOURABLE SCHOOLBOY

Author: John le Carré (David John Moore Cornwell, 1931-   )
Type of plot: Suspense
Time of plot: The early 1970's
Locale: London, Hong Kong, Tuscany, Thailand, Laos, Cambodia, and
   Vietnam
First published: 1977

> *Principal characters:*
> GEORGE SMILEY, the chief of the British Secret Service
> JERRY WESTERBY, one of Smiley's personally recruited and
>   developed agents
> DRAKE KO, a Hong Kong millionaire who is the trustee of his
>   beloved younger brother's Russian gold account
> LIZ WORTHINGTON, the beautiful blonde British mistress of
>   Drake Ko
> NELSON KO, Drake's brother, of whose existence few are
>   aware
> PETER GUILLAM, Smiley's assistant and protégé
> CONNIE SACHS, a Russian specialist and Secret Service
>   archivist, previously retired but brought back to work
>   by Smiley

The Novel

   John le Carré's novel *The Honourable Schoolboy*, the second in the Karla
trilogy, centers on the attempts of George Smiley, chief of the British Secret
Service (or the "Circus" as it is known to insiders), to restore confidence in
the Service by tracking down and capturing Nelson Ko, a Chinese official
long ago recruited by the Soviets. Within five years, the "Dolphin Case," as it
has come to be known, has become a legendary problem for new Circus re-
cruits. The nostalgic and ironic tone of the novel is partially created by the
narrator, who attempts to explain objectively the failure of this operation. As
in a tragedy, the narrator indicates from the first that something crucial went
badly awry, and le Carré's use of foreshadowing grows as the novel moves to
its climax. Even the narrator is at a loss to explain or blame anyone for the
eventual tragic outcome. Although some historical facts may be ascertained,
the key characters' motives, and hence the final mystery, remain ultimately
unfathomable.

   The overarching plot line of le Carré's complex novel traces the actions of
George Smiley to rebuild and revitalize the British Secret Service after the
defection of its chief, Bill Haydon, to Russia. Smiley must reestablish credibility both with the English Intelligence Committee (to regain funding) and

with its American "Cousins," the Central Intelligence Agency (CIA). Smiley and his researchers therefore backtrack through files in London to discover when, where, why, and about what Haydon had undertaken cover-up activities. In Circus lingo they are "taking a back-bearing," determining Moscow's priorities and knowledge gaps by discovering what information its agent Haydon most thoroughly destroyed.

When they first find and trace cover-ups of large Russian gold payments which are found in a Hong Kong trust account, Smiley sends one of his personally groomed agents, Jerry Westerby, undercover as a journalist to Hong Kong, to flush the trustee, Drake Ko, a Hong Kong millionaire. Thus, part of the operation takes place in London, while the other half is conducted in Hong Kong and Southeast Asia. The ultimate goal of both facets of the operation is the same: the apprehension of Drake's younger brother, Nelson Ko, the man the Russians believe to be worth so much gold. He is in possession of details of all of China's military capabilities, especially those of its navy.

While Smiley, in London, is forced into an alliance with the CIA because of the British agency's lack of funding, Westerby finds himself in an ad hoc arrangement with Asian-affairs journalists and suspects in the Orient. When the capture of Nelson Ko is about to occur, Smiley and company, with CIA representatives, journey to Hong Kong to be present at the "kill."

The second important strand of the plot line concerns Jerry Westerby's archetypal journey into the wilderness on a modern Arthurian quest. Set primarily in Hong Kong, Westerby's journey takes him through Thailand, Laos, Cambodia, and Vietnam during the last chaotic days of the American war in Vietnam. Each place he visits reinforces the sense of the decay and doom of Western civilization's efforts in the Asian jungle. Westerby often finds himself isolated and adrift, simply waiting for orders from London and, hampered by the loss of the local intelligence networks destroyed by Haydon, unwilling to trust the few channels that remain. He finds himself in love with a fair lady— Liz Worthington, Drake Ko's mistress—and empathizing with Drake's love for his brother. Westerby's movements and interviews finally precipitate the plan of escape from China for Nelson Ko, exactly as Smiley has hoped.

When cleared for return to London, however, Westerby's own sense of honor conflicts with his vow of obedience to the British Service and Smiley, his friend and tutor. Too many "innocents" have been killed in this operation, and Westerby believes that his responsibility is to stay. His return to Hong Kong to save the distressed Liz and Drake brings about the true crisis of the novel. Westerby pays with his life, and Smiley pays with his career: He never returns to Circus headquarters. Smiley has been betrayed by a secret pact between some ambitious Parliamentary leaders in collusion with the Americans, who whisk Nelson Ko to Langley, Virginia, for the glory and honor of the CIA. Yet the Americans' intelligence coup is offset by their failure to control events in Southeast Asia. As one disillusioned army officer,

Major Masters, comments sardonically, "the United States of America has just applied to join the club of second-class powers." The notions of honor, duty, country, and obedience are left empty and meaningless. The big bang of le Carré's conclusion is deliberately presented as a despairing whimper.

Le Carré's masterful blending of flashbacks and recollections, of simultaneous actions occurring in London and in Asia, and the tone and perspective of the narrator lead the reader through the myriad conspiracies with clarity and without ever breaking the strands of suspense.

The Characters

To the villagers in Tuscany, where he makes a failed attempt to write a novel, Jerry Westerby is "the schoolboy"; as the son of a titled press baron, he merits the designation "honourable": thus the novel's ironic, oxymoronic title. It is a title which gains in suggestive power as the action unfolds. Like a schoolboy, Westerby quite often carries a booksack, invariably stocked with works by T. E. Lawrence, Joseph Conrad, Ford Madox Ford, and Graham Greene—all writers who knew the heart of darkness within man and the failures of romantic idealism. Westerby is a schoolboy also in the sense that he is a product of Sarratt, the Circus' training school for field agents. Throughout the novel, Westerby is simply a "Sarratt man," obediently carrying out orders, always reviewing in his mind what he was taught at Sarratt before taking action. His schooling covers all contingencies until the final scenes, when his sense of remorse for the deaths he has inadvertently caused conflicts with his feelings of loyalty toward Smiley.

Smiley, on the other hand, is rather professorial: eccentric, unfathomable, solitary. He appears in control of the entire operation until he learns that he has been betrayed. Ironically, Smiley does not realize the degree to which Westerby suffers precisely because their despair stems from the same root: loneliness.

In some ways, George Smiley, in his sixties, and Jerry Westerby, fifty-three, the protagonists of this novel, are both "honorable schoolboys." Smiley, the thinker and idealist, and Westerby, the practical man of action, together define what is best in the English character. Both aspire to the love and loyalty of a woman but fail; both are loyal to their country and its Secret Service, never questioning the price paid. In addition, the two men truly care for each other.

The difference in the width and depth of their intelligences, however, and the lack of direct communication over a long, pressure-packed time period eventually create a morass of misperceptions. By the end, Smiley can no longer anticipate or understand Jerry's actions, and Jerry cannot trust that Smiley's directives will be carried out. Le Carré's narrator repeatedly points out that no one ever completely understands Smiley's inner workings, but everyone seems to assume that Jerry Westerby is easy to understand until it is too late. As in Greek tragedy, each man's strengths eventually betray him and others.

One of le Carré's greatest gifts is to present the reader with a world of believable and memorable minor characters. None is a stereotype or caricature. Some, like Charlie Marshall, the half-Chinese, half-Corsican ace pilot, are talked about by others but reveal themselves primarily in long monologues. Old Pat, Westerby's third stepmother, has only one short scene, mostly in dialogue, to establish herself. Craw, the old Australian journalist and Circus agent, recalling past services for the British, appears brusque and cynical, but his underlying compassion is revealed in a scene with Phoebe Wayfarer, a neurotic, but occasionally useful, low-level agent he has trained and developed over the years. The British missionary, his daughter, and Liz Worthington's husband and parents all reveal themselves as they speak of others.

Themes and Meanings

Le Carré is concerned with at least two major themes in this novel. The first concerns the destruction of the British Empire and Western civilization. On one level, echoing Joseph Conrad, he shows entropy and decay in the colonial cities of Asia. The jungle, reclaimed by animals and animal-like men, reaches closer and closer, reinforcing the "heart of darkness" theme suggested by Westerby's books: Man's greed and lust for power have helped return the region to the chaos of wilderness it once was. In addition, le Carré alludes to and even quotes from Arthurian legends in which Arthur's kingdom is destroyed from within, not without, by the Knights of the Round Table, who ignored their dreams and broke their vows of loyalty and obedience. Yet the Arthurian legends left hope that Arthur and Camelot would come again, that new order always replaces the old. Toward the end of the novel, echoes of Alfred, Lord Tennyson, abound: Smiley thinks of the Grail quest and Westerby even thinks of himself as Liz's Galahad.

Cast into a modern, nonheroic mode, George Smiley is the Arthur figure, an idealistic intelligence loved and admired by all of his loyal knights and his unfaithful wife. He believes in serving his country and wishes to rebuild his Round Table to its former preeminence. His faithful and favorite knights— Jerry Westerby; Peter Guillam, his "tight-mouthed cupbearer"; and the corrupt Sam Collins, a field agent previously expelled from the Service—are instrumental in the destruction of the order, although neither Guillam nor Westerby ever intended such a conclusion. In addition, le Carré introduces specific historical facts that emphasize that no new order can be established which will bring back the values of the past. The British Parliamentary leaders are ambitious and greedy; the Americans, demoralized by their loss in Vietnam; the Royal Colony of Hong Kong, with few exceptions, has never been assimilated and is soon to be returned to mainland China. Le Carré's settings—crumbling and deserted buildings, war zones, the omnipresent rain and fog of London, Southeast Asia, and Hong Kong—reinforce the sense that it is all over for England.

The second theme concerns the honor of the individual and the knowledge gained on the archetypal journey. Smiley and Westerby, after a lifetime of secret service, learn of the evils brought on individuals by choices and actions they made to achieve good goals. Westerby, the man of action, feels personally responsible for the deaths which have followed his path; he believes that he cannot deny personal responsibility and simply walk away from what will happen to the Ko brothers and Liz Worthington after the Service catches Nelson Ko and the others are left to bureaucracies that care little for the fate of individuals. George Smiley, the thinker, learns this same truth and something more from all the betrayals of the story. The enemy, he says, is no longer clearly identifiable: "Today, all I know is that I have learned to interpret the whole of life in terms of conspiracy."

Critical Context

The Honourable Schoolboy is the second volume of a trilogy John le Carré has written tracing the postmodern history of the British Secret Service. George Smiley, a minor character in *The Spy Who Came in from the Cold* (1963), became the Western world's most famous and believable spy in *Tinker, Tailor, Soldier, Spy* (1974). *The Honourable Schoolboy* seems to end his career, but *Smiley's People* (1980) gives him one more chance to win against his rival, Karla, of the Russian KGB.

The first and third books in the trilogy form a pair: Both center on the Circus, on England, on Smiley's quest for Karla. These elements are significant in *The Honourable Schoolboy* as well, but this middle book offers a different perspective. The canvas is wider; much of the action takes place in Asia, and it is not so narrowly restricted to the shadow world of espionage. The title character is not Smiley but rather Jerry Westerby. Thus, *The Honourable Schoolboy* anticipates le Carré's attempt in *The Little Drummer Girl* (1983) to work in an entirely different milieu.

Sources for Further Study

Ansen, David. Review in *Newsweek*. XC (September 26, 1977), p. 84.

Binyon, T. J. Review in *The Times Literary Supplement*. September 9, 1977, p. 1069.

Burgess, Anthony. Review in *The New York Times Book Review*. September 25, 1977, p. 9.

Finger, Louis. Review in *New Statesman*. XCIV (September 23, 1977), p. 414.

James, Clive. Review in *The New York Review of Books*. XXIV (October 27, 1977), p. 29.

Lewis, Peter. *John le Carré*, 1985.
Monaghan, David. *The Novels of John le Carré*, 1985.

Ann Reynolds

HOTEL DU LAC

Author: Anita Brookner (1938-   )
Type of plot: Psychological romance
Time of plot: The early 1980's
Locale: Lake Geneva, Switzerland, and London
First published: 1984

>   *Principal characters:*
>   EDITH HOPE, the protagonist, a successful writer of romantic
>   fiction
>   DAVID SIMMONDS, a London auctioneer, her lover
>   GEOFFREY LONG, a prosperous businessman, her former
>   fiancé
>   PHILIP NEVILLE, the owner of an electronics factory
>   MADAME DE BONNEUIL, an elderly countess
>   IRIS PUSEY, an elderly, wealthy widow
>   JENNIFER PUSEY, her daughter
>   MONICA (LADY X), a young woman married to a titled
>   Englishman

The Novel

Everything in *Hotel du Lac* is seen through the eyes of Edith Hope, a diffident and unassuming writer of popular romantic fiction who is staying in a hotel of former splendor beside Lake Geneva, apparently against her will. She has been temporarily banished from London in some kind of disgrace. The hotel, the few guests who are lingering on to the end of the season, and the events which have led to Edith's reluctant vacation are described in an elegantly written third-person account of her thoughts, reminiscences, and observations and through the long and loving letters she writes to David Simmonds, a married man with a family, with whom she has been having a clandestine affair.

The letters are full of wryly amused accounts of her fellow guests and their behavior, but she makes only cursory references to her encounters with Philip Neville, a cool and immaculate businessman who has recently turned up at the hotel. Not until the end of the novel is it revealed that none of the letters had been posted.

The only other guests are an elderly aristocrat, Madame de Bonneuil; the beautiful but painfully thin Monica, "Lady X," with her little dog; and the rich, glamorous, elderly widow Iris Pusey and her voluptuous daughter, Jennifer Pusey. Through her observations of these women, Edith tries to come to grips with her own emotional dilemma, which is revealed in gradual stages.

Although Edith loved David and was never happier than when ministering to his insatiable lust for food, she had been depressed by the infrequency of his visits. After meeting Geoffrey Long, a prosperous but very boring businessman, at a party given by her matchmaking neighbor, Penelope Milne, she had drifted into a marriage engagement with him, lured by the security and domesticity which he could offer and David clearly could not.

In one of the engaging sad-and-comic passages which now and then break through the restrained surface of the book, Edith recalls the scandal she caused on her wedding day, when she changed her mind at the last minute and drove right past the waiting groom and guests at the registry office. Her friends had been deeply shocked, and Penelope had packed her off to Switzerland to be out of the way until things cooled down at home.

A strange and disturbing relationship develops between Edith and Mr. Neville. He is able to plumb the depths of her fragile and uncertain soul with calculated cruelty. She is dumbfounded when he asks her to marry him.

"I am proposing a partnership of the most enlightened kind," he tells her. "A partnership based on esteem. If you wish to take a lover, that is your concern, as long as you arrange it in a civilised manner," and he claims the same right for himself. For him, the marriage will provide an efficient hostess and an intelligent companion who will not humiliate him or make demands on him. For her, he tells her candidly, it represents the final chance of a secure and comfortable future. The alternative, he warns, is a gradual descent into loneliness, boredom, and triviality.

Edith, remembering the unsatisfactory nature of her affair with David, recognizes the harsh logic of his argument. After a night of introspection, she writes a farewell letter to David telling him she is going to marry Mr. Neville. This, however, like the rest of the letters, is never posted.

Throughout the novel, Edith has been puzzled by Jennifer, whose sexually provocative presence is at odds with her apparent joy in devoting her whole life to her mother. In the penultimate page of the book the mystery is solved. Mr. Neville, she realizes, has been spending all of his nights with Jennifer. Suddenly aware that the marriage contract that has been proposed would provide the husband with license but the wife with humiliation, she tears up the letter to David and drafts a telegram to Penelope.

The final sentence of the novel, in which she changes the wording of the telegram from "coming home" to "returning," is a poignant indication of her uncertain future.

The Characters

The book is essentially about Edith Hope; she is the only character whose mind is fully explored. The reader can evaluate her as she at first sees herself, as she believes her friends see her, as Mr. Neville sees her, and as she eventually sees herself in the light of her experiences at the hotel.

Despite Edith's unassuming and self-effacing persona, she privately believes that she has inherited her father's strength of character; by the end of the book, however, she is not too sure. Having suffered emotional neglect from her mother, she yearns for love—for the kind of domestic love she has experienced in little snatches with David, but with the security which Geoffrey had offered. Although she rejects feminist aspirations, she wants to be a free and equal partner within the romantic framework which she envisages. The unfolding of her character is full of ambiguities and contradictions which are presumably intentional; Edith is a person to argue about rather than to judge.

All the rest of the characters are presented through her own constantly changing perceptions of them. They are vividly, even grotesquely, visualized, but not deeply analyzed; they exist as grist for the mill of her introspection, helping her to confront her own emotional problems through negative example.

Madame de Bonneuil, who seems at first to be a rather gross bourgeoise, turns out to be a desperately lonely aristocrat who has been ruthlessly turned out of her splendid mansion across the lake by her son and his arrogant wife. Monica looks like a bored, high-born sophisticate but is in fact a fortune hunter who has succeeded in marrying a titled Englishman and is now in danger of losing him. She is suffering from a nervous eating disorder (she surreptitiously passes most of her food to her dog), which has affected her reproductive functions. Sir John has sent her to the hotel with orders to pull herself together sufficiently to bear him a son and heir; otherwise he will boot her out. Money is her main motivation in life.

Edith is particularly fascinated by Mrs. Pusey and her daughter, who spend most of their time shopping for expensive clothes and jewelry. They make themselves the center of attraction wherever they go. Edith, watching them, has constantly to update their ages, and at Mrs. Pusey's birthday party, the description of which is one of the tragicomic highlights of the novel, she learns that the glamorous old lady is seventy-nine. Mrs. Pusey, whose main motivation is the acquisition of beautiful things, surrounds herself in a cozy and complacent glow of self-delusion, especially with regard to her not-so-faithful daughter, Jennifer.

The most difficult character to come to grips with is Mr. Neville (significantly, he is rarely referred to by his first name). He is a literary device rather than a full-blooded personality, a devil-figure tempting Edith with the cold, cynical logic of his doctrine of self-interest. His taste in food, clothing, and possessions is impeccable, his manner imperturbable. The only time he betrays a little emotion is when he describes the breakup of his marriage and his determination never again to undergo such a humiliating experience. As with Geoffrey Long, Edith's other rejected suitor, his greatest fear is of being made a laughingstock before his friends.

Geoffrey and David, the men in Edith's London reminiscences, are more familiar in type. Geoffrey is a staid, traditional businessman, who was very close to his mother until her recent death, which freed him for matrimony. He is clearly seeking a mother-substitute. To Edith, he represents security without romance.

David is an altogether warmer and more romantic person, the stuff of Edith's dreams. She knows in her heart, however, that he has been enjoying the best of both worlds: an amiable wife, lovely children, and a comfortable home as well as an intelligent and loving mistress he could visit at leisure. The fact that he makes no effort to contact her during her "exile" in Switzerland consolidates her doubts about him and convinces her that she must think of her future life without him.

Themes and Meanings

The novel explores several interrelated themes in a teasing and tentative manner, with many flashes of witty insight but with no attempt at final resolution. Brookner's novel is mainly about loneliness, and in particular about the loneliness of women, symbolized to an extreme by the rejected and unloved Madame de Bonneuil.

"My idea of absolute happiness," Edith tells Mr. Neville "is to sit in a hot garden all day, reading or writing, utterly safe in the knowledge that the person I love will come home to me in the evening. Every evening," she adds, thinking ruefully of David's infrequent visits. Her loneliness springs from her knowledge that for her this will always be an unfulfilled dream. "In my books," she says, in a recollected conversation with her agent, Harold Webb, "it is the mouse-like girl who gets the hero. The tortoise wins every time. This is a lie, of course. In real life, it is the hare who wins."

Allied to the loneliness theme is a disconsolate inquiry into how women should behave. In a one-sided conversation with Monica, Edith expresses disgust with women who are "complacent consumers of men," constantly expecting privileges and rewards. She suggests that feminists should direct their attacks at this kind of woman, rather than at men. Brookner is, in fact, very explicitly distancing herself from feminism.

Edith's wistful rejection of modern values and her nostalgia for the past are symbolized by the faded elegance of the hotel, which was built in a more confident and serene era, and which, in the period of Edith's stay, is at the end of its season.

The nostalgia theme is reflected in the meticulous style of the writing and in several literary allusions. Henry James is singled out as an author "precious" to Edith, and Mr. Neville, on the surface, is very much a Jamesian character. A Chekhovian flavor tinges many of the descriptions and is personalized, again on the surface, through Monica, the lady with the little dog. A mention of Colette in the text finds an echo in the verbal twist of the final sentence—a true sting-in-the-tale Collette-ism. Edith's pride in being frequently told that she resembles Virginia Woolf—another literary allusion, and a kind of running joke throughout the book—is twice punctured, comically by Mrs. Pusey and cruelly by Mr. Neville.

Critical Context

The award of Britain's most prestigious literary honor, The Booker Prize, to Brookner in 1984, for *Hotel du Lac*, met with a mixed reception from the critics. Those who favored the selection praised the novel for its classical style and form and for the sensitivity and wit of its perception.

Others, while admiring the technical qualities of the book, thought that it was rather lightweight in comparison with the other short-listed novels, and some complained that the judges, by making a safe and traditional choice, had failed to encourage experiment and innovation. The novel was broadly accepted as Brookner's finest work to date, with a tighter structure and firmer sense of purpose than before.

Brookner's protagonists are usually lonely, fastidious women who watch life from the sidelines, envying and yet despising women with fewer scruples who achieve their own kind of success. Several, like Edith in *Hotel du Lac*, are writers who dream out their lives through their novels, but Edith is more resilient than her forerunners. The open ending of *Hotel du Lac* indicates plenty of difficulties ahead but suggests that Edith has already found the inner strength to make difficult decisions about her future.

Written in a period when feminist writing was in the ascendancy, *Hotel du Lac* is a deliberate retreat from, and a gentle challenge to, the prevailing mood among women writers in the early 1980's.

Sources for Further Study

Hardy, Barbara. Review in *The Times Literary Supplement*. September 14, 1984.

The New Yorker. Review. LX (February 18, 1985), p. 121.

Tyler, Anne. "A Solitary Life Is Still Worth Living," in *The New York Times Book Review*. XC (February 3, 1985), p. 1.

Nina Hibbin

A HOUSE FOR MR. BISWAS

Author: V. S. Naipaul (1932-   )
Type of plot: Comic realism
Time of plot: The first half of the twentieth century
Locale: Trinidad
First published: 1961

> *Principal characters:*
> MOHUN BISWAS, the protagonist, a poor boy whose ambition
>   is to own a home
> SHAMA TULSI BISWAS, his wife
> SAVI BISWAS, their older daughter
> ANAND BISWAS, their older son

The Novel

When Mohun Biswas died of heart trouble at forty-six, jobless and penniless, leaving a wife, four children still in school, and a three-thousand-dollar mortgage on a poorly constructed house, it might seem that he was a failure in life. In his own eyes, however, Mr. Biswas was triumphant. Not only had he won one of the two great battles of his life (his wife, Shama Biswas, had finally learned to put her husband and her children ahead of the family into which she was born, the enormous Tulsi clan), but also he had bought his own house on his own land, thus providing a place for his family to be a family. In the prologue to the novel, V. S. Naipaul reveals Mr. Biswas' sense of satisfaction with his achievements, while at the same time realistically describing the house of which he is so proud. The story then moves backward in time to the birth of Mohun Biswas and proceeds chronologically, concluding with his funeral.

Mr. Biswas, as he is called throughout the novel, was born in a mud hut on a sugar estate, born backward, with a sixth finger, and thus obviously ill-fated from birth. His asthmatic father put all the children to work as soon as possible, and he was delighted when this luckless boy got an opportunity to make some money tending a calf. Unfortunately, the boy lost the calf, which drowned, and his father drowned diving for the frightened and missing boy. Thus, early in his life, Mr. Biswas had caused the death of his father and the breakup of the family. After he left the mud hut, he was to be homeless and alone for thirty-five years, wandering from place to place and changing from occupation to occupation. That odyssey is the story line of the novel.

The first jobs by which Mr. Biswas tries to secure his future are dismal failures. His apprenticeship to a pundit leaves him with a permanent stomach problem, caused by his being forced to eat seven bananas as a punishment for having taken two from the pundit's bunch. The resulting nervous stomach and constipation prevent his being able to function in the strict religious timetable, and he leaves in disgrace. The second job procured for him by a well-to-do uncle is in a rumshop run by the uncle's brother. Unfortunately, the manager, who steals regularly from the business, accuses Mr. Biswas of theft and beats him. This time, Mr. Biswas quits, resolving to find his own work. When an enterprising friend employs him as an assistant sign painter, his life is destined to change, for the job takes him to Hanuman House and to the Tulsi family, which lives there, and against whom he is to fight a life-long battle for a spouse loyal to him, not to them, and for a house which is his, not theirs.

At the beginning of his campaign against the Tulsis, Mr. Biswas is at a distinct disadvantage. Having been indiscreet enough to pass a love note to young Shama, he is bullied by the family into a marriage which brings him no dowry, no house, and no job. Stuffed into a room in Hanuman House, Mr. Biswas is given no respect, either by his wife or by the relatives who also inhabit the house. Although he has a roof over his head, he feels homeless. Although he is married, he feels alone. Angrily, he retaliates by insulting the family members, spitting at them from his window, even throwing food on them. Inevitably, he is beaten and finally sent with his pregnant wife to live in a shack which functions both as home and shop. At this point, the pattern is set which is to rule Mr. Biswas' home life for years. Whenever he quarrels with Shama and whenever she is about to give birth, she returns home, sometimes for months. Meanwhile, he has no one with whom to share his worries, and his children grow up hardly knowing their father. In their six years at the shop, Mr. Biswas fails dismally, at last alienating the community when he employs a lawyer to collect the overdue bills. As a sub-overseer at another family project, he is the innocent victim of a quarrel between owners and laborers. His dog is killed, his son Anand Biswas is terrified, and the house he has built is burned.

Finally, Mr. Biswas moves to Port of Spain, becomes a journalist, and for a time feels like the head of his household, even though he shares a house with his mother-in-law and her remaining son. Gradually, however, the Tulsis take over, parking lorries in his rose garden and generally assuming ownership, as they have done no matter where Mr. Biswas has lived. There is another attempt to build a house, but this time Mr. Biswas nearly burns down his own house. Back go the Tulsis and Mr. Biswas to the Port of Spain house, which is now filled with family members who have suddenly decided that they must be educated in city schools. Even though he becomes a Community Welfare Officer and buys a car, Mr. Biswas is still at the mercy of his wife's family, as he discovers when his mother-in-law evicts him to ready the house for her son, who is returning from England, and brings him back into a single room. Desperate, Mr. Biswas imprudently buys a poorly built, overpriced house, a purchase which will keep him in debt throughout the rest of his short life and leave his family without a penny but which enables him at last to claim his wife, his children, and his identity. While the novel's prologue had suggested that the Biswas family would lose the house, at the end of the book the older daughter, Savi Biswas, returns to Port of Spain to earn a living for the family. Although the Tulsis make their usual destructive raid when they gather for Mr. Biswas' funeral, the ramshackle house does not fall before their onslaught, and ironically, after the funeral the Biswas family goes back to Mr. Biswas' house, which is now empty.

The Characters

One of V. S. Naipaul's achievements is his ability to create characters who are irrational and eccentric, yet thoroughly believable and sympathetic. Usually, whether he writes in the first person or in the third person, he presents his narrative through the eyes of a single character, in this case Mr. Biswas. Usually, too, the novel involves gradual development of understanding, even a gradual initiation into life.

In this novel, Naipaul details the growth of Mr. Biswas, first a dreamy child, too young even to feel guilt for his father's death, then an innocent boy, whose desire for a girlfriend leads him into the Tulsis' trap, finally a long-suffering husband and father, endeavoring to "claim" his own wife and children. Like many of Naipaul's protagonists, Mr. Biswas has tragic possibilities. Although life seems determined to destroy him, or at least to submerge him in his wife's family, he always fights back, whether by insulting them or by defying them. No matter that the defiance is useless, that his children finally keep the names which the Tulsis gave them rather than those Mr. Biswas had chosen, or that his wife inevitably finds an excuse to return to her family whenever he has taken her and the children away from them, it is the little man's determination which makes him admirable. If he wins only to die, that too is tragic.

One of Mr. Biswas' problems is the kind of woman he married. So much a part of her family is Shama that she constructs her entire life on their pattern. Keeping house, she relies on Tulsi recipes; pregnant, she imitates Tulsi behavior. As Naipaul comments, "there was no doubt that this was what Shama expected from life: to be taken through every stage, to fulfil every function, to have her share of the established emotions. . . . Life, to be full, had to be this established pattern of sensations." To a woman so programmed, Mr. Biswas is not a person but a generic husband, and his desire for a separate identity is incomprehensible. She is happiest when in the midst of a family, acting out the roles which she sees her sisters acting.

There are a number of characters less fully developed, yet clearly recognizable, from the inconsistent pundit at the beginning of the book to the self-important, briefly Communistic doctor near the end. Yet Naipaul's skill in revealing character without making explicit comments can be illustrated by the scene at Green Vale when Shama is once again about to leave her husband. For the first time, Anand stays with his father. Puzzled, Mr. Biswas assumes that Anand wanted crayons or some other material object, but Anand denies such motivation. He stayed, he says, angry at himself and at his father, "Because they was going to leave you alone." The complexity of emotion suggested by Naipaul's words, the pity and love of Anand for his father, and Anand's anger with himself for feeling pity and anger with his father for inspiring it do not need further explanation. The boy's character is consistent. At the end of the novel, Anand both wishes and does not wish to come home; finally, he does not.

Themes and Meanings

In *A House for Mr. Biswas*, Naipaul presents two sharply opposing views of life. For the Tulsi family, life is immersion in a community, which governs behavior and prescribes emotions. There is no need for a separate identity in the Tulsi household. Children squabble, husbands and wives quarrel, people move in and out, but everything remains the same. All the Tulsis eat the same bad food on ordinary days, the same lavish food on holidays. All the Tulsis move to a new area at the same time. All the Tulsis develop a passion for education at the same time. Their insistence on conformity is illustrated by their observation of Christmas; all the children receive the same presents, which they break at about the same time.

Although he has never formulated his view of life, from the moment of his unusual birth Mr. Biswas has thought for himself and made his own decisions. It is unfortunate that so often they have been disastrous. Had he not been so busy contemplating the fish, he might not have caused both the calf which he was supposed to watch and his own father to drown. Later, every time he strikes out for himself, whether in building or buying a house or in managing a store, he seems to make the wrong decision—not one which a fool makes but one which could just as well have been right. If he had never become a sign painter, he would not have become involved with the Tulsis; if it had not rained, he would have inspected the poorly built house more carefully. Between destiny and the Tulsis, he seems to be doomed. Even his attempt to make Christmas a special occasion for his children fails. Impulsively, he spends all of his money on a dollhouse for Savi, his oldest child; once again, however, things go wrong. Anand is upset, and because his father has no more money, he must wait until the next payday for his present; the Tulsi tribe is upset, and therefore Shama is upset; finally, Shama destroys the dollhouse in order to placate her family, upsetting Savi and infuriating Mr. Biswas.

Yet if one would be an individual, clearly one must imitate Mr. Biswas, rather than his wife. His ambition to own something derives not from an acquisitive instinct but rather from a creative desire. If he died, Mr. Biswas thinks early in the novel, nothing of him would remain. Nowhere has he been more than a guest; nothing would cause people to remember him. Occasionally he tries to write a story but always he abandons it. At last it is the house which he knows will outlast him. Admittedly, he must settle for less than the ideal—not immortality, but a few years. Still, that is better than being nothing but a carbon copy, like the Tulsis.

Critical Context

A House for Mr. Biswas is the final book in Naipaul's Trinidad group, including *Miguel Street* (1959), *The Mystic Masseur* (1957), and *The Suffrage of Elvira* (1958). Although they are too masterful to be called apprenticeship novels, they do have a zest for life and a comic tone less evident in the later works, both fiction and nonfiction, whose theme is frequently that of the destruction of social order in the postimperialistic world, along with the resulting displacement and violence.

This novel is also significant in that in the foreword to the 1983 edition, Naipaul called it his "most personal book, created out of what I saw and felt as a child," including "some of my funniest writing." Mr. Biswas, Naipaul comments, is a man like his own father, attempting to make something from his simple life last. In the complex and troubled Anand, it may be supposed, Naipaul may have placed both his own capacity for sympathy and his artistic detachment.

Sources for Further Study

Gurr, A. J. "Third-World Novels: Naipaul and After," in *Journal of Commonwealth Literature*. VII, no. 1 (1972), pp. 6-13.

Hamner, Robert D., ed. *Critical Perspectives on V. S. Naipaul*, 1977.

McSweeney, Kerry. *Four Contemporary Novelists: Angus Wilson, Brian Moore, John Fowles, V. S. Naipaul*, 1983.

White, Landeg. *V. S. Naipaul: A Critical Introduction*, 1975.

Rosemary M. Canfield-Reisman

HOUSE OF ALL NATIONS

Author: Christina Stead (1902-1983)
Type of plot: Intrigue
Time of plot: The early 1930's
Locale: Paris and its suburbs, London, and Amsterdam
First published: 1938

> *Principal characters:*
> JULES BERTILLON, a mercurial director of the private bank run
>   by the Bertillon brothers
> WILLIAM BERTILLON, Jules's older brother and a lesser
>   partner in the family bank
> CLAIRE-JOSÈPHE, Jules's wife, a beautiful and socially
>   cultivated heiress
> MICHEL ALPHENDÉRY, a Communist intellectual and the
>   bank's exchange expert
> ARISTIDE RACCAMOND, a client's representative who attaches
>   himself to the Bertillon brothers
> MARIANNE, Raccamond's calculating and vindictive wife

The Novel

House of All Nations is a fictional tale dependent on the dramatic events of economic history to substantiate its fantastic plot. At the center of the novel is the Banque Mercure, ostensibly run by the Bertillon brothers. The brothers' official, legal responsibility for the bank's mysterious but apparently successful inner workings, however, exists more in the minds of the institution's clients than it does on paper. As Jules says, "It's easy to make money. You put up the sign BANK and someone walks in and hands you his money. The façade is everything." The petty European aristocrats, South American plantation profiteers, and American businessman who deposit at the bank and rely on its stock-exchange services are continually buoyed by the profits they see themselves making thanks to the financial wizardry of the enigmatic but gracious Jules Bertillon. Yet, while the men who make these fortunes and the bank which helps them flourish share a penchant for the trappings of elegance, as demonstrated in the clients' refined manners and the plush atmosphere of the bank, they also share less glamorous common attributes. The private matters of neither the institution nor those it serves can withstand close inspection.

In this realm of precarious financial stability, where a façade of substance and reliability is carefully maintained, Jules Bertillon reigns over all. Everyone in the bank—employees, clients, even his brother William—thinks that Jules is the driving imagination and creative presence maintaining the bank's solid position during the dangerous storms of the 1930's global financial climate. It is Michel Alphendéry, however, who is the true genius: While Jules's urbane, expansive personality draws in clients and their capital, Michel, when markets fluctuate, juggles the discrepancies between the bank's apparent and actual position, recorded in numerous hidden account books.

As Jules, using the bank clients' funds for capital, recklessly plays in the gold and commodities markets, Michel covers the losses "on the books." Michel reconciles these dishonest practices with his personal politics by cynically acknowledging that the inescapable corruption of the system that his work supports will inevitably cause its own downfall.

Aristide Raccamond insinuates himself into the chaotically disorganized bank administration, hoping to recover recent personal financial losses and promote himself as a client's representative through his association with the bank. Jules overlooks his superstitious misgivings about Aristide's recent involvement with a failed competitor and takes Aristide into the bank, despite a premonition that the "customer's man" brings bad luck.

Jules never takes the business of his bank too seriously. When reverses in the global financial community portend the bank's failure, Jules, encouraged by Claire-Josèphe and with Michel's help, siphons his clients' funds into bank accounts abroad. He thus ensures his family's future security. Aristide, however, discovers the plan, and he and his wife try to blackmail the Bertillons. The Raccamonds fail not only because the Bertillons have prepared for every eventuality but also because the malicious and potentially damaging rumors they spread about the Banque Mercure and its directors do not convince any of its clients or employees, who have been utterly seduced into loyalty by the enigmatic and charming Jules. Their admiration for him remains intact, even after the abrupt disappearance of both the Bertillons and the bank's entire capital. After some mourning over their lost income, the poseurs of Continental high society, along with the bank workers whom Jules exploited and the financiers he duped, transform their memories of Jules into a legend. He is remembered as the gracious charlatan who was clever enough to deceive anyone—even other professional deceivers.

The Characters

None of Stead's characters, with the possible exception of Michel, invites the reader's sympathy; they are not intended to do so. While Jules seems to charm everyone and even wins the grudging respect of his enemies, he manages this only by withholding a complete and genuine representation of himself from any one individual. The narrator grants a complete view of Jules's numerous weaknesses, mistakes, and character flaws from the reader's perspective only. The reader sees Jules, and the other characters, from a privileged position, comprehending their foolishness and errors in ways which they cannot. Hence, William's unquestioning trust for his brother becomes a confidence based not on filial love but on his sense of inadequacy, compared with Jules's glittering self-confidence. William not only defers to Jules's superior business sense; he shirks his own responsibilities. Claire-Josèphe's vocal concern for her children's future is a convenient guise for expressing a genuine fear originating in self-interest, and not the parental conscience which she employs as its vehicle. Jules's family circle is composed of characters whose veneer is only slightly more superficial than his own. Moreover, he never claims that the bank's practices are ethical; he simply never discourages the clients from assuming that they are. Jules deceives perfectly within his circle, exposed through the narrator's unrelentingly critical and ironic examination.

Although the reader is encouraged to recognize the Bertillons as the high-class con artists that they are, their practices are not as unsavory as those of the Raccamonds—at least the Bertillons have style and do not concede the criminal nature of their financial ruses. They accept that dishonest business is the only sort of business and assume that their clients think as they do, unlike the physically unattractive Raccamonds, who possess neither elegance nor the means to create its semblance. The Raccamonds' brand of criminality is more noxious than that of the Bertillons, for the Raccamonds claim to be motivated by the clients' interests, not their own, when attempting to blackmail the bank. Their pretense to moral obligations in the world of finance is as false as Jules knows such obligations are. Stead maneuvers her characters to transgress the limits of conventional morality repeatedly as they reiterate her message: that those conventions, like other social conventions, are simply a quite useful commodity in the world of high finance.

The exchange of these commodities, however, is not easily effected. The traders must always be deeply invested in the system itself. Michel's character is an utter contradiction—his constant generosity and good humor coexist with an unflinchingly ruthless economic strategy. His commitment to working within the world of high finance seems opposed to his political beliefs, but his investment in the bank is marked by a sense of the futility of all capitalist endeavors. He sees the frequently brutalizing effects of capitalism on the members of its ruling class as inevitable. His cynicism is different from Jules's in that his faith lies elsewhere—in the eventual demise of an unapologetically exploitive system. Yet Michel's love of Jules is genuine, and unlike the others, he sees beneath Jules's flattering mask. In a world distinguished by corruption and greed, Michel is Stead's evidence that something in human nature is ultimately redeemable and morally worthwhile.

Themes and Meanings

Although Stead's narrative provides some information about the personal lives and backgrounds of virtually all of more than one hundred major and minor characters, these individual stories are fragmented, and their details are delayed and discontinuous. Marginalizing these characters' personal histories reinforces concern with the Banque Mercure, the central preoccupation of their—and the reader's—consciousnesses. Stead constructs a mercilessly cutting social satire exposing the inherent corruption of a system in which the sole ethic is a drive to accumulate and maintain wealth. Ironically, while each character suffers from the disease of conspicuous consumption thriving under capitalism, the collective nature of their fate carries specifically Marxist political implications.

The overall ironic gesture of Stead's project in *House of All Nations* is, nevertheless, more skillfully carried out than that called for by a purely political agenda. Stead's discourse on finance seems to assume that the reader's knowledge of the inner mechanisms of high finance is as sophisticated as her own. Still, a frequent sense of mystification is deliberately introduced: The reader is enjoined to comprehend the powerful structures of global economics by deciphering the jargon of the people who manipulate those structures. Knowing them in their own language is the first step toward subverting them.

Critical Context

House of All Nations was the third novel in Stead's long and prolific literary career. Inspiration and material for the novel came while Stead, an Australian, worked in a Paris bank while living with William J. Blake, the Marxist economist whom she eventually married. While the themes present in *House of All Nations* chronicle an important period of Stead's growing political awareness, the novel is not as intimately autobiographical as her later work, particularly *The Man Who Loved Children* (1940), her fourth and most critically acclaimed novel.

House of All Nations is notable for its exquisitely complicated plot and its skillful indictment of the relationship between individual and collective greed. The later brilliance of Stead's narrative technique is practiced and refined in this novel. After producing *House of All Nations* and in addition to her more autobiographical and domestic emphasis, Stead created a number of female protagonists rivaling Jacques Bertillon in their ambition and adventurousness. Later women characters, such as Teresa in *For Love Alone* (1944) and the title character of *Letty Fox: Her Luck* (1946), face uniquely female challenges and represent the author's specifically feminist political concerns.

Stead's political sentiments, out of favor in the McCarthy era, are partly responsible for the unavailability of some of her work in the United States during that period and some years after. Given the renewed interest in the feminist and political ideology that Stead's work espouses, much of it was republished and made widely available in the years preceding her death in 1983.

Sources for Further Study
Gold, Michael. Review in *Daily Worker*. September 8, 1938.
Lidoff, Joan. *Christina Stead*, 1982.
The New Yorker. Review. XIV (June 11, 1938), p. 71.
Strauss, Harold. "A Novel of Frenzied Finance," in *The New York Times*. LXXXVII (June 12, 1938), p. 2.
Time. Review. XXXI (June 13, 1938), p. 73.

Mollie A. Brodsky

THE HOUSEHOLDER

Author: Ruth Prawer Jhabvala (1927-   )
Type of plot: Comedy of manners
Time of plot: The late 1950's
Locale: New Delhi, India
First published: 1960

Principal characters:
>PREM, the protagonist, a young Hindi teacher at Khanna
>   Private College
>INDU, his wife, who is expecting their first child
>RAJ, his friend, a low-level bureaucrat in the Ministry of Food
>HANS LOEWE, a young German and Prem's friend, who is
>   seeking enlightenment
>MR. KHANNA, the headmaster of Prem's school
>SOHAN LAL, an older teacher of mathematics at the school
>THE SEIGALS, Prem's carefree landlords

The Novel

In the opening pages of the novel, the third-person omniscient narrator introduces Prem, struggling to maintain an illusion of dignity and beset with anxieties over how he will manage the family's affairs. His marriage with Indu was arranged, according to Hindu custom, by his mother after his father's death. He is in his first year as a Hindi teacher at Khanna Private College, a school for boys of wealthy families who need additional study before they can be accepted into better colleges. Although he has been married for a few months, Prem regards Indu as a stranger; she does little that suits him, and he is critical of even her visits with the Seigals, his upper-middle-class landlords who live in an apartment below his own modest quarters. Prem, characteristically lacking self-confidence, sees himself as a failure as both a husband and a teacher.

Prem defines his role as husband as only that of material provider. Embarassed by sexuality and Indu's increasingly visible pregnancy, he thinks of the anticipated birth only in terms of higher salary, lower rent, or both. His bumbling, comic attempt to request a raise from Mr. Khanna, the aloof overbearing headmaster, ends without Prem having even made the request. When Prem attempts to ask the Seigals for reduced rent after the baby arrives, he suffers the same result: Prem cannot ask for what he wants, because he does not know what it is that he really wants. Isolated from his fellow teachers and indifferent to classroom discipline, Prem is befriended by Sohan Lal, a mentor figure, who has been a householder for much of his life. Lal's response to the anxieties and responsibilities of family life, however, has been to adopt lower-middle-class living standards and periodically to visit a local guru, whose message, ironically, is the renunciation of mundane, material life—including that of the family. The message is anything but relevant to Prem. Trying to assert himself as a disciplinarian in order to impress Mr. Khanna and hoping to avoid what he perceives as the humdrum routine of Lal's life, Prem reports several students who harass young girls passing the school. When he is confronted by Mr. Khanna's inaction (he is afraid of losing the boys' tuition), Prem retracts his accusations. Whatever Prem sets out to do, he seems destined to fail.

In the midst of his anxiety, Prem meets a young German, Hans Loewe, who sees Prem as a stereotype of Indian spiritualism. While Hans questions him about the philosophical virtues of Hinduism, Prem reports the material progress of independent India. Shortly after his new friendship with Hans, Prem accompanies Lal to the guru's temple, the top floor of an old house. While Prem is moved by the guru's happiness and devotion, the impression is fleeting. Completely isolated (even his weekly meetings with his friend Raj at the cinema have ended), Prem is forced to confront conflicting loyalties to his wife and to his mother, who plans to visit at the same time that Indu plans to return home, a plan that Prem has forbidden to no avail. To make matters worse, Prem has been invited to a tea party at his school—an occasion whose importance he vastly overestimates—and he expects Indu to accompany him.

When his mother arrives, Prem's household becomes engulfed in silent tension. His mother gives the couple little room for privacy, and Indu withdraws further into herself, remaining silent much of the time, weathering the mother's snide comments and retiring to bed earlier than usual. As his mother, a self-pitying busybody, apologizes for Prem's bad marriage, Prem himself comes to appreciate Indu more than ever before. In fact, he begins to fall in love with Indu, although he is still unwilling to defend her from his mother's criticism or notice that she delays her trip in order to go to the tea party with him. Resuming his friendship with Raj, Prem finds himself warming to the idea of being both husband and father, a householder.

At the Khannas' tea party, Prem is fascinated with Indu's beauty, but his enthrallment gives way to embarrassment as Indu gobbles up sweets and ignores the condescending insults of Mrs. Khanna, the domineering, arrogant voice of power behind the scenes at the school. Desperately hoping for the chance to impress his colleagues at the party, Prem remains oblivious to Mrs. Khanna's shabby treatment of his wife; he leaves the party still dreaming of the perfect profound statement but without having uttered much more than a word. The next day, once again sensing his failure, Prem contemplates the guru's call for renunciation of desire and ambition and for a life of devotion, *bhakti yoga*. After once more attempting and failing to ask for lower rent, Prem begins to sense that much of his life is illusion, or *maya*, as the guru had suggested. He is jerked back into reality, however, by his mother's relentless martyrdom and Indu's departure for her parents' home.

In Indu's absence, Prem's mother pampers him as if he were a child. The very contrast in his mother's attitude and his own sense of failure as an adult drives Prem deeper into his frustration. During his mother's visit, however, Prem develops a genuine love for Indu: He writes angry letters and an explicit love letter but then destroys them. After another visit to the guru during which Prem realizes that devotion to God can also be devotion to Indu and the householding stage of his life, a halfhearted attempt to secure a new job in Raj's office, and receiving a letter from Indu, Prem realizes that he enjoys the household pressures. He begins to feel confident that he can accept responsibility, and stronger for the realization, he writes to Mr. Khanna requesting a raise.

When Indu arrives home, Prem acts quickly, writing his sister in Bangalore in order to arrange for his mother to visit his sister upon her request. Indu and Prem discover new intimacy in their sexuality, and Prem senses, perhaps for the first time, that they do belong together. Once more overcome by timidity, however, he asks his mother to request the reduction in rent, which fails when she insults the Seigals before asking them. After his mother leaves for Bangalore, Prem and Indu fall more in love than ever. The sense of belonging fortifies Prem anew: he argues with Mr. Chaddha, the pretentious history teacher with whom he shares a classroom, after Mr. Chaddha has insulted him in front of his students. As a result, Prem is threatened with dismissal, but he accepts the threat stoically, realizing that lower rent (when Prem finally does make the request, the Seigals ignore him) and a higher salary will not be possible.

Happy simply to have his job, Prem's depression abates more rapidly than it might have in the weeks before Indu's return. A visit to the guru, a chance encounter with Hans while he visits his friend Raj, and the recollections of his own wedding while attending that of Lal's daughter all lead to Prem's growing satisfaction with his responsibilities. When Hans visits him at the college before returning to Europe, Prem realizes that his best friend is Indu. He delights in pleasing her by inviting Raj and his family to dinner. With his confidence in both her and himself thus expressed, Prem beams with pride when Raj accepts the invitation. As the novel closes, Raj compliments Prem on Indu's cooking, symbolizing Prem's newfound comfort and pride in his role as head of household.

The Characters

Ruth Prawer Jhabvala's characterization achieves a balance between the round character, who seems fully human in psychological development, and the flat character, who represents types or ideas pertinent to the action. Not even Prem, who is the most fully rounded character in *The Householder*, is developed sufficiently for readers to believe that they know him well. Yet even a seemingly flat character such as the guru is given sufficient dialogue to escape the predictability of stereotype. Jhabvala peoples her novel with characters who are individualized but also capable of representing various types in modern Indian society. Furthermore, by using both European and Indian characters, Jhabvala establishes cross-cultural relations as well as dissecting the manners of middle-class urban India.

Hans Loewe represents the naïve European who believes that everything, and everyone, in India is gifted with spiritual wisdom. He befriends Prem, apparently one of the first people he meets, with a fierce determination to achieve enlightenment as soon as possible. Although Hans lasts only a few weeks in India, he is there long enough for his flattery of Prem to have its ironic consequences, for it is Hans who first renews Prem's interest in his own religion's spiritual legacies. By the end of the novel, his shallow approach to any sort of discipline is enough to convince Prem that friendship, with Indu or Raj, is much like the discipline of householding.

Kitty, who runs a poorly kept boardinghouse that caters to wandering Europeans and who rents Hans a room, is representative of the expatriate European who has been in India long enough to develop a jaded, cynical attitude toward both India and Indians, whatever attitude toward spiritualism remains. While she tolerates Prem for the sake of her roomer, she is downright crude and condescending toward her servant. Kitty is a British holdover from colonial India; when Prem accompanies Hans and her to a party, Kitty and several other snobbish women share their disdain for Indians "by birth" and declare their superiority spiritually by claiming to be Indian "by conviction." The irony is not lost on Prem, and he leaves the party quickly and quietly. He prefers his own confusion to their willed ignorance.

In Jhabvala's portrait of middle-class urban India, she offers a cross section of ordinary life. Raj and Lal represent young and old householders, respectively, who bear the daily struggle to make ends meet with quiet resolve. Although Raj is sometimes sullen and always quick to allow Prem to pay the bills on their outings and Lal flirts with renouncing his family life as less than godly, both characters offer role models to Prem. Through their friendship, Prem comes to discover the pleasure of mundane responsibilities and to build the confidence necessary to fulfill them.

On the other hand, Jhabvala presents characters who signify the materialistic corruption of some upper-middle-class Indians. The Seigals are wealthy enough to enjoy frequent parties and indulge excessively in whiskey, contrary to Hindu custom, while nearly ignoring the riotous nightlife of their son Romesh Seigal. Despite their comfortable standard of living, however, they seem oblivious to the needs of their young tenants, refusing even to negotiate a lower rent. Mrs. Khanna is bored by her husband's academic façade and spends her time inflating the price of the teachers' lunches and gossiping about illicit affairs. Mr. Khanna and Mr. Chaddha represent characters whose self-righteousness far exceeds the illusionary status of their positions. Prem's responsibilities seem far more sincere and serious than their pretentions of wealth and status.

Jhabvala's characters avoid falling flat because of the settings in which they live and act. Readers come to know characters as much from her vivid descriptions of place as from narrative exposition. Street scenes are vibrant; the visual appearance of rooms is fully described with well-selected details; the activity at the cinema and in the tea shop is wrought with vitality. Prem's school and his apartment become places in which one could walk around with familiarity. In *The Householder*, class, nationality, and setting are so intricately linked that the characters seem never to be out of place, even when, as in the case of Prem's mother, they are awkwardly placed for comic effect.

Themes and Meanings

Jhabvala's dominant theme is the difficulty of reconciling traditional belief with contemporary life in modern India. The householder is the traditional third stage of four in Hindu philosophy. The other three stages are: the child, who must learn patience and love from the model of the family and who delights in his innocence; the student, who expands his knowledge and learns to accept a disciplined existence; and, fourth, the recluse, who, leaving family and friends behind, must pursue a solitary path toward spiritual growth. As a householder, Prem is not yet ready to relinquish his student life, which was secure and at which he was very good; he fears his marriage because it demands that he consider others beside himself. He is tempted by the guru's appeal and Lal's example to leap to the fourth stage, but, ironically, it is both the guru and Lal who indirectly assist him in realizing the devotion that is a necessary discipline for a healthy household.

Complicating the theme is the further conflict between materialism and spiritualism. Prem teeters on extremes: when he is materialistic, he is obsessed with ambition and status but rendered helpless by the obsession; when he is spiritual, he is relieved of his worries but unable to repress his growing love for Indu. His sense of failure comes, ironically and comically, from his failure to see that householding teaches a balance between material and spiritual concerns, the patience to develop self-discipline into genuine and intimate devotion, and the vulnerability required to establish meaningful friendship with one's spouse and one's peers.

Another complicating factor of the theme is the cross-cultural relationship between Hans and Prem. Through the clipped speech of Prem as he tries to be proper and impressive and the mindless chatter of Hans as he tries to use Prem to gain instant enlightenment, Jhabvala suggests that people can provide insight not only about their own cultures but also for those in another culture. Hans seems to miss completely the experience of India that is before him, but he does assist Prem, if only implicitly, to recover a deeper sense of his own religious values. In turn, Prem teaches Hans that one cannot easily grasp another's cultural values, particularly if one seeks to do so through stereotypes. In short, cross-cultural experience helps one to understand one's own culture by revealing the differences between it and others. Prem is more deeply Hindu for having succumbed temporarily to Hans's flattery.

Critical Context

Born Jewish in Nazi Germany, educated in England, a resident for much of her adult life in India, Ruth Prawer Jhabvala seems especially well suited to offer a detached yet intimate picture of ordinary life in modern Indian society. Jhabvala's first six novels, of which *The Householder* is the fifth, all seek to establish a thorough social documentation of postindependence India. With insight equally perceptive from both English and Indian perspectives, her fiction offers the same balance that she brings to her characters. Like Henry James, she focuses her craft on recording the rapidly changing culture of a society at a major turning point and on the consequent interior changes in the people of that society. Like Prem, the India of *The Householder* (and of Jhabvala's other five domestic comedies) is undergoing a major transition during its first decade as a Western-style democracy. Jhabvala's achievement is in demonstrating that West and East can inform each other, yet do so without destroying the cultural integrity of either one.

Sources for Further Study

Asnani, Shyam K. "Jhabvala's Novels—A Thematic Study," in *Journal of Indian Writing in English*. II, no. 1 (1975), pp. 38-47.

Gooneratne, Yasmine. *Silence, Exile, and Cunning: The Fiction of Ruth Prawer Jhabvala*, 1983.

McArthur, Herbert. "In Search of the Indian Novel," in *The Massachusetts Review*. II (Summer, 1961), pp. 600-613.

Shahane, Vasant. *Ruth Prawer Jhabvala*, 1976.

Williams, Haydn M. *The Fiction of Ruth Prawer Jhabvala*, 1973.

Michael Loudon

THE HUMAN AGE

Author: Wyndham Lewis (1882-1957)
Type of plot: Dystopian fiction
Time of plot: Eternity
Locale: Third City and Matapolis, cities of the afterlife
First published: 1955: *The Childermass*, 1928; *Monstre Gai*, 1955; *Malign Fiesta*, 1955

> *Principal characters:*
> JAMES PULLMAN (PULLEY), a great writer of satiric fiction
> when he was alive
> SATTERTHWAITE (SATTERS), Pullman's "fag" (a boy who runs
> errands for an upperclassman) when they were at the same
> British public school
> THE BAILIFF (THE OLD BAILEY), who controls entrance into
> Third City, where he has limited political power
> THE PADISHAH, the ineffectual angel who is the ruler of Third
> City
> SAMMAEL (THE DEVIL), who rules Matapolis
> HYPERIDES, the leader of the right-wing opposition to the
> Bailiff in Third City
> MANNOCK, Pullman's friend in Third City
> DR. HEINRICH SCHLANK, Pullman's friend in Matapolis
> DR. HACHILAH, who runs the Punishment Service in
> Matapolis
> ALECTRYON and
> POLEMON, disciples of Hyperides

The Novels

Although *The Human Age* is described as a trilogy, the first book was written in 1928, long before the other two were conceived, and Wyndham Lewis left still another volume in the series ("The Trial of Man") unfinished at his death in 1957. *The Childermass* is different in form and tone from the later volumes; it has virtually no plot, adopts an unsympathetic attitude toward its characters, and is more political than theological in its theme. It contains some of Lewis' most impressive descriptive prose, and its opening lines immediately reveal to the reader the hallucinatory vividness of his painter's eye:

> The city lies in a plain, ornamented with mountains. These appear as a fringe of
> crystals to the heavenly north. One minute bronze cone has a black plume of

smoke. Beyond the oasis-plain is the desert. The sand-devils perform up to its northern and southern borders. The alluvial bench has recently gained, in the celestial region, upon the wall of the dunes.

After publishing the first section of *The Childermass*, Lewis intended to go right on to its second and third sections, but he said that the need to make a living prevented him from continuing such a difficult work for a limited, highbrow audience. In 1951, however, a successful television dramatization of *The Childermass* led to a commission for its continuation and subsequent adaptation for radio.

With its long dialogues and otherworldly setting, *The Childermass* is well suited for dramatization. It falls roughly into three parts: a series of discussions by James Pullman and Satters about the strange land to which they have been ferried after their deaths; their wanderings over its shifting space-time terrain; and their observations of the Bailiff holding court outside a city which they are told is "Heaven." The discussions are all one-sided and didactic, because Satters, although he died an old man, is mentally a schoolboy and appears as his true mental age in the afterlife. Satters is repeatedly called Pullman's "squire." Thus Pullman and Satters are one of the many "doubles," inspired in part by Miguel de Cervantes' Don Quixote and Sancho Panza, that fill Lewis' fiction.

Pullman the intellectual lectures Satters the average sensual man about matters such as the way their past lives influence their present condition, the nature of the inhabitants of the plain (who live in foxholes), and the way its scenery shifts as if it were projected on a cinema screen. Lewis' characteristic satiric targets, such as the twentieth century concern with appearing youthful, the decadent styles of writers such as Gertrude Stein and James Joyce (Pullman physically resembles the latter), and homosexuality (Pullman becomes Miss Pullman for a while), are all discussed by this pair. When they begin roaming over the plain, Lewis' attitude toward what he calls the "time philosophy," a doctrine in which the solid, spatial world of three dimensions is dissolved in a relativistic world of space-time, is dramatized as they enter zones which represent seventeenth and then eighteenth century England. Lewis reveals his opinion of the thoughtless brutality of the average man when Pullman and Satters meet a miniature version of Thomas Paine and Satters squashes him underfoot while Paine struggles to escape his grasp.

The final third of the novel takes place outside the "so-called Yang Gate," where the Bailiff interrogates those who wish to enter "Heaven." The court is like a Punch and Judy show, with the hunchbacked Bailiff playing Punch and with minor roles played by "puppets" with names such as Alf, Barney, and Harold. The Bailiff is a spokesman for the "time-philosophy," and he is challenged by a commonsensible Scotsman named Macrob, who accuses him of being a Red revolutionary. As in a puppet show for children, the insults and violence grow until Macrob pulls the Bailiff's nose and is beaten to death by one of the Bailiff's thugs. Criticism of the Bailiff is nevertheless continued by a character known as Hyperides, who has an aggressive band of followers and who counters the Bailiff's relativistic time-philosophy with a doctrine— clearly influenced by Fascism—that asserts the value of tradition and authority. Hyperides' disciple Alectryon argues with the Bailiff about the legitimacy of homosexuality, but a disciple named Polemon poses the question for debate with which the book ends: "So the battle for the reality can be joined at once for the idea of reality. Who is to be *real*—this hyperbolical puppet or we? Answer, oh destiny!" The debate about which side best represents the "real" world is postponed while the Bailiff returns to his "citadel of Unreality," and Pullman and Satters move away into the unreal "nowhere" of their ghostly existence.

Had the work been continued in the 1920's, Lewis would probably have continued the ponderous debates between the followers of the Bailiff and those of Hyperides. In the 1955 *Monstre Gai*, fortunately, elements such as plot and character displace the static dialogues and descriptions of the earlier work. The "gay monster" of the title, derived from Voltaire's epigram that we prefer a lively monster to a bore, is the Bailiff. Pullman has convinced a ferryman to carry them across a body of water from the plain to the steps of the city. They regret their boldness, however, as they are left exposed to the desolation and cold outside the city walls. The Bailiff has not yet entered, however, and as he does he notices the two newcomers and asks Pullman to visit him at his headquarters. Pullman and Satters enter the city with the Bailiff, experience the return of bodily sensations, and stop to rest at one of the impressive city's many cafés. There they meet a man named Mannock, who recognizes them as newly entered citizens and offers to help them until they can be settled.

At first, the city its inhabitants call Third City seems a utopia. It is ruled benignly by the "Padishah," who represents God's power. Its citizens have no need to work, are comfortably housed and fed, and entertain themselves by shopping or with discussions in the cafés. Lewis reveals the true nature of the city slowly and suspensefully as Pullman's intellect analyzes and explains it for the obtuse minds of Mannock and Satters. It is in fact a dystopia that is reminiscent of the world of George Orwell's *Nineteen Eight-Four* (1949), which, like *Monstre Gai*, is also a satiric version of the welfare state of post–World War II England. The inhabitants are supported by an authoritarian system that nourishes their bodies and degrades their minds. Moreover, as in a modern big city, only certain classes of inhabitants are comfortable; the city has impoverished sections where dangerous youth gangs (one of which Satters joins for a short time) victimize the citizens. Worst of all, as Pullman at length learns, there is a ghetto where all the women (a medieval contempt for the daughters of Eve motivates the rulers of the afterlife) are imprisoned under appalling conditions which foster the vice and crime from which the Bailiff profits.

Third City thus expresses Lewis' negative opinion of British socialism. Yet the theological dimension of this fiction is still more important than the political. Third City is a kind of Purgatory or Limbo for souls who are unsuited for Heaven or Hell. Yet no purgation, as T. S. Eliot has observed, occurs there—as it should in an orthodox Christian Purgatory. That is Lewis' point: Christianity has become so decadent that even its supernatural institutions have lost their meaning. There is no hope for Pullman's purgation, although Third City's theological basis allows Pullman to use his experiences there to help him understand the morality of his life on earth. He makes a harsh judgment on his past life when he attends a political rally in which Hyperides, who has entered the city with his followers, the Bailiff, and a spokesman for the Catholic faith named Father Ryan all present their views. Pullman, who was born a Catholic and educated by the Jesuits, believes that he should respect the otherworldly view that man should turn from earthly ambitions and think of saving his own soul. Yet Pullman, whose fame as writer has given him entrée to the circles of both the Bailiff and the Padishah, is fascinated (as Lewis himself was) by political power. Pullman sees no hope in supporting the Padishah. The ruler of Third City is too bored with this decadent Purgatory and indeed with mankind itself even to control the Bailiff's rackets. The Bailiff may be a monster, but he is a gay one, and his sincere appreciation of Pullman as a writer and observer of human life flatters Pullman and makes them useful to each other. Pullman enjoys the luxuries with which the Bailiff provides him and sticks with him even after he assassinates Hyperides.

Yet the Bailiff's days of influence in Third City are numbered. The women in the ghetto revolt and kill the police chief, and a brutal retaliation provokes the Padishah to move against the Bailiff. The Bailiff must flee to his home planet, and Pullman and Satters accompany him to a planet known as Matapolis, light-years away.

If Third City is a decadent Purgatory, the Matapolis of *Malign Fiesta* is a decadent Hell. The name is a combination of the Greek word for city, *polis*, and the Latin word *mactus* (which is also the root of *matador*), for "sacred" and "sacrifice." Once again, the reader learns about the nature of this city slowly as Pullman himself penetrates its structure. The Bailiff tells him that Matapolis is primitive compared to Third City but not unpleasant. Pullman learns from the Bailiff's mother that Matapolis is a Punishment Service ruled by Satan, who uses the Hebraic name Sammael. Pullman is terrified when Sammael calls him in for an interview. Instead of treating him like a "sinner," however, the Devil shakes hands with Pullman, explains that he punishes mankind only as a favor to God, and arranges a tour of the Punishment Service for Pullman.

Pullman survives his terrifying visit to the chief torturer, Dr. Hachilah, and Sammael is impressed with his self-control and insight into human nature. Taking him further into his confidence, Sammael explains that he (like the Padishah in Third City) has become bored with the role God has given him as "Satan." There was never any battle between God and the Devil: Sammael simply left Heaven when God insulted the angels by creating man. Now he sees that neither the angelic nor the human nature is satisfactory. Men are short-lived and foolish (this Puritan detests women and anything to do with human reproduction), but he must admit that they are more intelligent and enterprising than angels. Sammael therefore proposes a "Human Age" in which the angels will mate with humans (sex being a necessary evil) to create superior beings over which Sammael will rule. Pullman fears that God will stop this obvious challenge to his authority, but Sammael assures him that he is God's equal and that divine power cannot span the immense distance between Heaven and Matapolis.

Thus convinced, Pullman uses his intellectual gifts and human insight to assist Sammael's plan by founding a university, in which Pullman is assisted by the great physicist (saved from the Punishment Center) Dr. Heinrich Schlank, and by establishing an information-gathering system. (The Bailiff is rescued from being punished for his mistakes in Third City in order to help establish a spy network.) The main step in the "humanizing" process is the "malign fiesta" of the title. A huge entertainment is staged for the angels and human women in order to excite the long-atrophied sexual instincts of the angels. Despite some violence, the fiesta is a huge success, and the "miscegenation" of the human and the angelic proceeds.

Pullman knows that his actions are wrong, but he feels a fatal attraction to Sammael's energy and intelligence. He is terrified when messages reach him, apparently from God, telling him of his wickedness. Nevertheless, he has cast his lot with Sammael, even though he becomes convinced that the Devil is mad with pride. At the end of *Malign Fiesta*, he learns that Sammael is not only a madman but a liar as well. A huge host of God's angels appears over Sammael's headquarters, having easily traveled the distance that the Devil claimed was unspannable. Pullman is swept up by two "White Angels," who say that no harm will come to him, and the book comes to an end as he is carried away.

The Characters

As in any satiric or dystopian fiction (Orwell's *Nineteen Eighty-Four* or Aldous Huxley's *Brave New World*, 1932), the ideas and action of the fiction are more important and the characters less important than they would be in a traditional novel. Satters, in particular, is too mindless to have a developed character and exists merely to give Pullman someone to lecture. Most of the characters are nothing more than representatives of satiric concepts:

Mannock and Satters represent the small-minded average citizen; Hyperides, the Fascist leader; the Padishah, the weak, ineffective liberal statesman; Drs. Hachilah and Schlank, politically irresponsible intellectuals. Only Pullman, the Bailiff, and Sammael have characters that are of interest in themselves. Even the Bailiff and Sammael, however, are recognizable stock types, political manipulators common in Lewis' fiction, and they are characterized from the outside with satiric disapproval rather than from the inside with sympathy. Pullman alone is a fully developed character, and fortunately he is portrayed with autobiographical intensity. In one scene of *Malign Fiesta*, Pullman observes Satters trying to write a story and asks him what he is learning about himself. It has never occurred to Satters that he might learn something about himself by writing fiction, and Pullman dryly comments that he sees what kind of author Satters is. The incident shows the reader that the moral agonies that Pullman experiences as he is drawn into evil plans reflect Lewis' own thoughts, while in his seventies, on the meaning of his literary career.

Themes and Meanings

The collective title of Lewis' three books, *The Human Age*, identifies their common theme. Although Lewis was drawn to Christianity only late in his life, he always believed that there must be values that transcend the relativistic human world. This position was a philosophical one that at most would assert the existence of eternal principles or a divine mind and not a personal God. Thus, in the first book of the sequence, *The Childermass*, Lewis satirizes both the relativistic liberalism of the Bailiff and the merely human authoritarianism of Hyperides. Divine authority is necessary, and so Pullman is wrong to help the Bailiff and Sammael challenge that authority. Witnessing the political rally in *Monstre Gai*, Pullman, addressing himself, admits to himself that "the role which had been yours on earth was essentially diabolic." When alive, Pullman believed that his life expressed a disinterested love of art; in the afterlife, he learns that he had deceived himself. Pullman reflects to himself that in this strange afterlife, "as in my own case, you would find yourself involved with a powerful demon, whereas on Earth he would merely be dear old so-and-so, a rich patron of the arts, or a go-ahead publisher."

Pullman dimly understands his guilt in Third City, but he is truly remorseful only when he finds himself in a plot to attack the Divine by establishing a Human Age. Pullman now learns something about himself. Although the pessimistic and satiric works Pullman once wrote may have been great art, the man who wrote them led a coldly intellectual, selfish life that after death aligns him with the diabolical. Can he nevertheless be saved? A personal sense of God's reality, and not merely a philosophical or theological conviction, enters the work when Pullman comes to believe that, despite man's wickedness, "God values man" and that he can still pray for salvation. The issue of whether he deserves redemption would presumably have been the subject of a fourth volume that Lewis had barely begun at his death, "The Trial of Man."

Critical Context

The Human Age was highly praised on publication for its ambitious range and themes and was compared to the satire of Jonathan Swift. Yet the work contains many inconsistencies. For example, Lewis' characterization of his angels, some treated comically and some with reverence, suggests that Lewis was merely toying with a theological system that needs the intellectual commitment of a John Milton to present convincingly. The relationship of God to the world that the work presents is especially weak. The reader learns that Satan is lying when he claims that he is God's equal. If he was lying, however, and if as Pullman concludes "God values Man," why did God tolerate Satan's sadistic treatment of man? The basic problem here, and the one from which all the others spring, is that although Lewis uses a Christian framework (embellished with Gnostic doctrines), and was even drawn to the Christian religion late in his life, the spirit of his work is far from Christian. Satan is condemned for trying to do exactly what Christians believe Christ has done: join the divine with the human. It is doubtful that Lewis could have solved such problems in the proposed fourth book. In the existing manuscript pages (at Cornell University), God is introduced as a character—a kindly, intellectual gentleman who makes polite conversation. It was difficult enough to take the Devil seriously when he was presented by Lewis as a witty, urbane politician, but introducing God as a character is an artistic error, and one might well imagine that Lewis abandoned the manuscript for that reason.

Despite its structural and thematic weaknesses, *The Human Age*, especially the second and third books, ranks high in the Lewis canon for its creation of what is perhaps his most memorable character after René Harding of *Self Condemned* (1954). Lewis also ranks high among authors of dystopian fiction for the vividness of his imaginary world and the satiric sharpness of the way it comments on the reader's own world. Lewis indeed surpasses many writers of dystopias by avoiding the essaylike expositions employed by writers even as skillful as Aldous Huxley and instead introducing the reader to his fictional world by stages as the main character learns about it himself. For the depth of characterization of its protagonist and the descriptive brilliance of many of its scenes, it is one of the finest satiric fictions of the post–World War II era.

Sources for Further Study
Chapman, Robert T. *Wyndham Lewis: Fictions and Satires*, 1973.
Jameson, Fredric. *Fables of Aggression: Wyndham Lewis, the Modernist as Fascist*, 1979.

Kenner, Hugh. *Wyndham Lewis*, 1954.
Pritchard, William M. *Wyndham Lewis*, 1968.
Wagner, Geoffrey. *Wyndham Lewis: A Portrait of the Artist as Enemy*, 1957.

Timothy Materer

I FOR ONE ...

Author: Frank Sargeson (1903-1982)
Type of plot: Psychological realism
Time of plot: Mid-twentieth century
Locale: New Zealand
First published: 1952

Principal characters:
  KATHERINE, a schoolteacher who is single and living with her
    mother
  DR. HUBERT NOCK, an American psychologist
  KATHERINE'S MOTHER, who is recently widowed
  HILDA JAMES, Katherine's half sister by her father
  HELEN, Hilda's daughter

The Novel

I for One . . . is written as a series of diary entries kept by Katherine, a schoolteacher, over the course of the five months following her father's death. Katherine seems to be in her thirties and lives at home with her mother. The death of Katherine's father has left both women curiously unaffected, except that it has caused Katherine to take up her diary again after a ten-year hiatus. Katherine is disturbed by her mother's apparent stoicism and believes it to be the product of a denial of the terrible loss. She is shocked, then, to discover that her mother is, in fact, relieved at the man's parting, that she had loathed him for years. This is the first of many occasions on which Katherine displays a naïveté which both disturbs her and remains her great comfort.

On a rare social outing, Katherine is introduced to Dr. Hubert Nock, an American psychologist who captivates her with his fine manners and interesting conversation. Katherine finds one of his stories particularly moving, a story about a boy who was extremely nearsighted. Not until the boy grew older did people recognize the true nature of his problem, which was easily corrected. Previously, they had thought him simply dull-witted. With his sight corrected, for the first time in his life the boy was able to gaze out into the world, "lost in the wonder of it all." The clear implication is that Katherine herself suffers from a kind of myopia, a failure to see reality clearly.

A relationship seems to develop between Katherine and Hubert. He, however, is often away for reasons of work, if the reader is to believe what he has told Katherine. On one occasion during his absence, Katherine reminisces about her first love, a boy she had befriended as he convalesced in the local hospital. She had been introduced to him by a nursing friend and felt an immediate pity which she mistook for love. When the boy recovered and departed without any declaration of affection, she was heartbroken. The memory causes her to question once again the nature of her innocence.

Katherine travels to visit her nursing friend, Else, during another of Hubert's absences. Else shares a house with two old ladies, sisters—one a spinster (Miss Drake), the other separated from her husband (Mrs. Ellis-Thomas). Else is away, so Katherine visits with Miss Drake, who, in the course of the conversation, describes how her sister pitifully awaits the unlikely return of her wicked husband. Inviting Katherine to a window to view a man across the way who is obviously shiftless and unkind, she explains how her sister insists that clean linen be kept out in case her husband, a man not unlike the one in view, should return. The wizened old woman makes light of this, expressing the opinion that her sister should be grateful to be rid of "bad rubbish."

Disconcerted, Katherine leaves in a rush, convinced that the old woman is crazy. Her emotional response is the same as what she had experienced when her mother had offered similar sentiments. For the moment, she wants to believe in love, and although she no longer lacks for examples of love gone wrong, she excuses Hubert when he fails to call for a long while, asking for no explanation.

Something more of Katherine's character is revealed when she invites one of her students, a girl named Katie Willis, home for tea. Katie is a painfully shy girl, very like what one might imagine Katherine to have been when she was younger. Katie has failed her exams at school, and her mother is sorely disappointed. Katherine explains that although Katie has failed one set of exams, she remains an attractive girl with a wonderful talent for art. She is able to draw highly emotive pictures. When one of these pictures is shown to Katherine's mother, she is noticeably unimpressed. The similarity to Katherine with her journal is unmistakable. In both instances, self-expression is more private than public and goes unappreciated. Katherine has sympathy for the younger girl but cannot recognize the parallels with her own situation.

One day while walking, Katherine encounters two strange girls who give her an envelope. Inside, she finds a lewd message addressed to her. Not so shocked by the content of the message itself, Katherine is more disturbed that such a foul thing should be addressed to her. Selected as a target for some of the nastiness of the world, Katherine finds her vulnerability disquieting.

Hubert continues to make only rare appearances, begging off frequently because of a mysterious illness. Not wishing to doubt him, Katherine accepts his word; in fact, her admiration for him grows. She writes in her diary, ". . . he is so fully adult and reliable that I can't help being reminded of father." The nature of her attachment is thus revealed. In a later entry, Katherine writes, "If only one could have a home of one's own and stay there forever, content always to attend to all the little tasks that have to be done without ever wanting to put one's foot on the street outside. Nothing could go wrong then." Katherine continues, however, "It is only when we meet people, and because we meet them, that things go awry." Katherine then meets Hilda James, her half sister.

In meeting her half sister, Katherine is forced to confront the conflict between her image of her father as a near-saint and the reality of his irresponsible life. In a parallel discovery, she soon learns that Hilda is the wife of her beloved Hubert, the reason for his frequent and prolonged absences. Katherine crumbles.

Only after a week of recovery under the care of Hilda's daughter, Helen, does Katherine come to accept that the world in which she has believed was in fact a sham. Her mother, long a protector and guardian, reveals a bit of the truth when, touched by her daughter's sad confession, she feels compelled to share some of her own past. She tells of how she met Katherine's father (who, at the time of their meeting, was a married man) and risked everything to run away with him; she recounts tales of cross-country trips and motels. Later she attempted to put off the inevitable divorce. All this comes as a revelation to Katherine, and her reaction is one of instant relief, as if a great burden had been lifted. She sheds her misconceptions like an outgrown skin and, like the nearsighted boy of Hubert's story, looks out into the world with a new sense of exhilaration and wonderment.

The Characters

I for One . . . is told through Katherine's diary entries and thus is restricted to her outlook. Katherine's character is for this reason not so eccentric as might at first appear. She calls herself to rather harsh judgment throughout the novel, doubtful of her perceptions, skeptical of her assessments, and leery of her ability to survive change. Such is not extraordinary. Stated simply, Katherine has a well-developed intellect, but by virtue of being overprotected, only now is she coming of age emotionally. Katherine's parents lived unconventional and turbulent lives. Clearly, they wanted something more stable for their daughter. In creating a secure environment, however, they fostered in Katherine a false sense of life and love as they normally occur, leaving their daughter naïve to the ways of the world.

The strength of Katherine's character shows in her instinct to write. Writing is her method for consolidating a sense of her developing self and beginning the struggle to emerge as a healthy individual. A diary gives her freedom to reflect, to speculate, to study, or to debate without challenge. It allows her to maintain, even in the looming shadow of her parents, an independent identity free from constraint.

Still, Katherine must get beyond writing. She ponders the ultimate worth of writing herself at one point, asking, "Can it be that when we feel we live, really and truly live, we become impatient with what is merely on paper?"

Yet, she also understands that, in the early stages of her growth, such questions come to light only in the process of writing. The answers, as well, are clearly defined only when she can work them out on paper. In the end Katherine's developed self does emerge. She rids herself of unnecessary shame, dumps the surplus from her vast stores of humility, and, unlike T. S. Eliot's Prufrock, enters the world triumphantly.

There is some temptation to classify Katherine's mother and Hubert as villains in the story, but that would be both inaccurate and unfair. Katherine's mother, after all, does what comes naturally to most parents, and the implication of Hubert's occupation as a psychologist is that he may have been trying to assist Katherine. He offers romance. His deception, although ungentlemanly, passes in this world, and as Katherine admits, he was the first to ask her to defy convention and live for herself.

Themes and Meanings

I for One . . . is in some degree reminiscent of classic stories such as Sophocles' *Oedipus Tyrannus* and, from the feminist perspective, the poetry of Sylvia Plath. It is a story of self-discovery in the manner of Sophocles' play, depicting the discomfort, horror, relief, and joy of discovering one's place in the cosmos. The novel depicts a dogged pursuit of truth. It finds the key to identity not in one's innocence but in one's honesty.

Sargeson's novel is the portrait of a young woman smothered under the legacy left at her father's death. So much remained to be learned of him, so much to be revealed of his life. In much of her poetry Sylvia Plath complains that her overbearing father died prematurely, before she had a proper opportunity to confront him as an adult and do away with misconceptions and undue influences. Just as much of Plath's poetry is addressed to her father, so most of Katherine's diary is part of a process of toppling her own Colossus, of laying to rest the great myths enshrined at her father's death.

Critical Context

Frank Sargeson has been credited with giving New Zealand literature new life. The path he cleared was for the return home of many expatriates who, as he did, had fled the vast separateness of life which they had perceived in New Zealand for what was hoped to be the rich intellectual life of England and Europe. What Sargeson discovered and encouraged others to recognize was that, as New Zealanders, they could not deny the unique nature of life in their island nation, nor could they write of it in borrowed forms and language. Sargeson wanted to set himself and his countrymen to writing about New Zealand life in a more familiar idiom.

The early years of Sargeson's career were marked by his success as a writer of short stories. An avid reader of the works of Nathaniel Hawthorne and Mark Twain, Sargeson observed how effectively one might approach the heart of a culture or region by way of its curious rather than respectable characters. What emerged was a fiction that seemed to peer at New Zealand life from the dark corners and lonely hearts of the nation. There was no self-conscious posing, nor was an accommodation made for overseas readers. In short, what Sargeson began was the self-examination of the psyche of a small nation, with little regard for what a larger audience might think.

Sargeson's earliest stories are like parables. He wrote about his waiflike protagonists with insight and concern, often using them to deliver some thinly disguised message. Later stories obtain the oblique perspectives and rich characterization while becoming less didactic.

When Sargeson began writing novellas and novels, he brought his short-story skills with him. His longer works are almost invariably episodic or picaresque. Some of the novels suffer for this. *I for One* . . . , however, does not. As a story told through a series of diary entries, an episodic narrative is not only inevitable but preferable. The narrative device works especially well because Sargeson is able to maintain his fictional female's point of view credibly throughout.

After *I for One* . . . Sargeson began to experiment in drama, with limited success. He continued writing fiction as well, and his themes remained essentially the same. Although he produced a satire of some note in *Memoirs of a Peon* (1965) and a disturbing examination of human nature in *The Hangover* (1967), few among his longer works rival the masterly craftsmanship and intuitive understanding of *I for One* . . . .

Sources for Further Study
Copland, R. A. *Frank Sargeson*, 1976.
King, Bruce Alvin. "New Zealand: Frank Sargeson and Colloquial Realism," in *The New English Literatures: Cultural Nationalism in a Changing World*, 1980.
Rhodes, H. Winston. *Frank Sargeson*, 1969.

Robert J. Helgeson

I LIKE IT HERE

Author: Kingsley Amis (1922-   )
Type of plot: Social satire
Time of plot: The mid-1950's
Locale: London and Portugal
First published: 1958

> *Principal characters:*
> GARNET BOWEN, a free-lance writer
> BARBARA BOWEN, his wife
> BENNIE HYMAN, a publisher and sometime employer of
>   Garnet Bowen
> WULFSTAN STRETHER, a novelist and recluse

The Novel

Garnet Bowen, formerly a journalist, now a part-time reviewer and essayist with ambitions to be a dramatist, lives somewhat hand-to-mouth, supporting his wife and three young children, hoping for something more permanent in the literary trade. He is equally elated and deflated by a commission for an article on European travel which will pay well but obliges him to go to the Continent. Bowen hates leaving London, and particularly despises anything to do with traveling in Europe.

His reluctance to go abroad is further eroded by the chance to make a bit of money and to ingratiate himself with Bennie Hyman's publishing firm, which he hopes may hire him on a permanent basis if he does a job for them in Portugal which is, by chance, the country his wife wishes to visit.

One of the publishing firm's oldest novelists, Wulfstan Strether, who supposedly stopped writing some time before, has mailed Hyman's company the manuscript of a new novel. The editor who had handled Strether's work has died, and no one in the organization is quite sure if the new novel is really by Strether. Bennie Hyman asks Bowen to visit Strether and, without Strether knowing what he is up to, try to decide if the man claiming to be the novelist is the real thing or an impostor.

Bowen, reluctantly, sets off to the Continent by car (his wife driving), and by sea to take up a house rental in Portugal, which proves considerably less than satisfactory. Bowen meets the putative Strether, who is pleased to entertain someone from the London literary world, but he is not easily manipulated into proving unknowingly that he is the genuine article. Bowen is unhappy about trying to catch Strether out, and Barbara, his wife (when she finds out what Hyman has talked Bowen into doing), is sharply critical of her husband for agreeing to such an underhanded task.

Along the way, Bowen, suspicious of Continentals and irritated by the day-to-day details of travel, looks with a sharp eye at the liabilities of being abroad and finds that, as he expected, the family is exposed not only to food that occasions intestinal revolts but also to bad plumbing, insects, flies, and off-and-on peculation. They manage to escape from their first, unpleasant lodgings through the kindness of Harry Bannion, a retired bank executive and full-time practical joker, who provides temporary accommodation. Bowen's mother-in-law, the subject of a running negative commentary by Bowen (kept conveniently to himself), takes ill back in Great Britain, and Barbara and the children return home.

Eventually Bowen winds up staying with Strether, who treats him with kindness and generosity but proves to be something of a pompous literary bore. Bowen, still unsure about whether Strether is bogus, and inclined to suspect him, decides that he will not tell Hyman anything. He would, however, like to know, and eventually, through two unrelated incidents, he does discover the truth—not only about Strether but also about himself and his long-held aversion to doing anything which is personally discomforting.

The Characters

Kingsley Amis is a satirist and as such is interested in using characters to make points about aberrant behavior (generally social, but not always so), most immediately exemplified by "types" rather than individuals. His characters have an obviously caricatured quality and are rarely, in this novel, seen as other than surface representations of certain exaggerated points of view.

Garnet Bowen is used as the commentator for this consideration of human and social foibles. By profession a writer, by personal inclination skeptical and wary, he is appropriately skilled in commenting upon everything (and usually does) with some aptly scarifying wittiness. This kind of character is the common focus of Amis' novels. Bowen is educated, intelligent, thin-skinned, and quick to respond to any pomposity or stupidity. He is, however, not lacking in eccentricity himself, and Amis uses Bowen's prejudices to mock that peculiar British disease, the disdain for foreigners over the water, a hangover attitude from the days of the old Empire. Bowen is a bundle of nerves, responding to the constant bombardments of normal social irritants with constant, witty verbal counter-punching which makes for much of the pleasure of the novel and which ranges from offhand swipes at popular singers (Frank Sinatra), architecture, red tape, and the beastliness of travel, to quirky in-jokes upon the state of modern literature. He is never without an opinion; indeed, it might be said that much of his character is opinions. He is, however, an unaggressive fellow, and he tends to keep to himself his disapproval, which Amis allows into the text in ways which are reminiscent of the "aside" in drama. Bowen talks continually to himself about what he sees; it is his response to the world which pervades the novel.

Other characters are seen through Bowen. Fortunately, given his natural inclination to social jaundice, he is fair-minded. Indeed, in the case of Oates, Bowen might be suspected of being not only reluctant to judge but downright gullible as well. It takes his wife, Barbara, to get him anywhere near irritation about the way Oates is cheating them.

There are only a handful of characters who are able to make a place for themselves, principally because they are so exuberantly larger than life. Bannion, the life of the party, is quite out on his own, beyond Bowen's usual ability to sum up a character satirically, and the Commie-hating American paranoid on the boat is an example of how Amis uses characters not to make plot, but to make fun of obsessive humans who are mad, if not legally certifiable.

Themes and Meanings

Satire can range from purposeful destructive dismemberment to genial finger-pointing, and Amis is quite capable of working along the line of tonalities from one end to the other, sometimes on the same page. He is, as is often the case with satirists, very quick, and he gives to his major character that same quickness to smell out the odors of sanctity, pomposity, venality, stupidity, and hypocrisy—but not, for Garnet Bowen, without a price. If Bowen is to reveal through his hypersensitive geniality an eye for the silly and the stupid, he is to learn that he, too, is not entirely free of untenable preconceptions.

He hates the idea of going to the Continent, not only because of all the trouble such a trip will occasion (which he keeps to himself in his long list of "bum" tasks) but also because he *knows* how bad it is over there, how dirty, how dishonest, how bothersome it will be—and all this turns out to be true. Yet it is Oates, a fellow Briton who cheats him, and whose toilet facilities nauseate the Bowen family. Much of what happens to Bowen is not particularly unpleasant at all, and his near-seduction by the beautiful Emilia is a bonus he could hardly have imagined.

It is, however, bothersome. Bowen has to make up his mind to act honorably in the matter of Strether, and is called upon to make an effort when Strether is hurt, to the point of actually driving a car, a task which he has carefully avoided for years. Amis is a commonsense author with not much truck for symbolism, but it is, perhaps, not unfair or excessive to suggest that Bowen's driving of that car is a sign of a man who has, for the moment, thrown in his hand with ordinary mortals. Strether's need forces Bowen to become involved; he cannot simply solve the problem with a witty comment.

Amis, for all his inclination to use his novels to shotgun targets of social silliness right and left, always explores, if modestly, the question of how and when enough is enough, how and when his main character, however determined not to get involved, invariably does, simply because, for all his disdain, he is an Englishman with a touch of gentlemanly responsibility about him.

Just as Bowen knows in his heart that he cannot expose Buckmaster if he discovers that he is not Strether, that it would simply not be the thing to do, simply not honorable, he also knows that he deserves nothing for helping him, deserves nothing for discovering that Strether is, in fact, the real thing. In a typically wry Amis ending, that is what he gets. The job which was to be his reward goes to someone else, someone considerably less deserving. Bowen is not surprised and, as usual, is not unpleasant about it (as Bennie Hyman knew he would not be), because for all his skepticism he is a nice man. His reward is not the blackmailer's girl but his own wife.

There is a second, lesser line of meaning which is connected to the string of literary jokes and anecdotes and to the Strether problem. The praise of Henry Fielding which results in Strether convincing Bowen of his authenticity lies at the center of Bowen's dislike of the pretensions of the great tragic novelists. Strether thinks that he is better than Fielding; he is, in fact, a bit of a down-market imitation of Henry James at his most flatulent. Manly common sense is what Bowen likes in literature—and, significantly, what he likes in life. Occasionally he gets it. His problem at the end is somehow to get it working in his own creative work.

Critical Context

There is a long tradition in English letters which can be traced back to Henry Fielding (whom, significantly, Bowen admires) which has produced some of the best satiric-comic work in the novel. The early twentieth century master was Evelyn Waugh; Amis is his successor and has been so since *Lucky Jim* was published in 1954. In 1986, his sixteenth novel, *The Old Devils*, won England's most prestigious literary award, the Booker Prize.

I Like It Here, Amis' third novel, is in several ways one of his slighter, least ambitious works in the genre. Based in part on his own visit to Portugal (part of an award for winning the Somerset Maugham Prize with *Lucky Jim*), it is a bit of a loose notebook of impressionistic experiences, clearly less structured than is usual. The intrusion of Salazar and Gomes with their contrasting comments upon the dictatorship of Salazar seems to be forced into the narrative, as if Amis felt something had to be said but was unsure of how to do it. Bowen may be a bit too normal, in fact, to do the kind of dirty work that other Amis protagonists might do on someone such as Salazar. Bowen has his moments of mild lunacy (the amusing set piece of mutual misunderstanding over Grim-Grin is one of these) and his "bum-bum" dislike of doing anything different reminds one, but only faintly, of the manic excesses of the wilder heroes in other books. This is one of Amis' calmer, nicer books, but the really frenetic energy is sadly missing. Bowen is simply too pleasant to beat up on the natives. The novel does, however, clearly show that Amis, for all his satiric instincts, expects his main characters to act decently in the long run.

Sources for Further Study

Amis, Kingsley. *What Became of Jane Austen? and Other Questions*, 1972.

Bergonzi, Bernard. *The Situation of the Novel*, 1972.

Gardner, Philip. *Kingsley Amis*, 1981.

Green, Martin. "British Comedy and the British Sense of Humor: Shaw, Waugh, and Amis," in *Texas Quarterly*. IV (Autumn, 1961), p. 217.

Charles H. Pullen

ICE

Author: Anna Kavan (Helen Woods Edmonds, 1901-1968)
Type of plot: Surrealist fable
Time of plot: The near future
Locale: A sequence of unidentifiable countries, probably in Northern Europe
First published: 1967

> *Principal characters:*
> THE NARRATOR, a former soldier, obsessed with a onetime love
> THE YOUNG GIRL, a pale and slight creature, continually
>   pursued by the narrator
> THE MAN SHE MARRIES, possibly to be identified with the
>   character below
> THE WARDEN, a blue-eyed man who repeatedly abducts and
>   hides the girl

The Novel

The scenario for *Ice* is familiar from a dozen science-fiction novels. A new Ice Age is coming, created seemingly by radioactive fallout from a nuclear explosion of some unknown type. As the glaciers extend, more and more heat is reflected back from the Earth, dropping the temperature further and setting up a disastrous downward spiral. Some populations react to this by fleeing south, which creates immediate resistance and sets up the conditions for further war, civil disturbance, and military dictatorships. In the developing chaos, one man searches frantically for his lover, hoping to take her to safety. This clichéd plot outline, however, does no justice to the individuality of *Ice*. As a science-fiction "disaster story," *Ice* is in fact inadequate and uninteresting. The nature of the original disaster is never more than vaguely specified; there is no concern for realistic political reactions; the author spends no time at all in trying to persuade the reader that her plot is even plausible. The science-fiction scenario is never more than a background and at times appears to lose realism altogether, becoming instead a metaphor for an exploration of an obsessive inner state.

The mind explored is that of the narrator, whose history very soon takes on the quality of a dream or nightmare. The reader is never at all sure where he is. He begins on a lonely road, in bitter cold, trying to reach the house of his love and her husband before nightfall. His account of this search, however, immediately becomes interspersed with a memory of a former visit in summer heat, only to fade very soon into a later stage, when the wife has left her husband and fled by sea into the thickening ice. He follows her to another country, possibly Norway, where she is hidden from him by the "warden" of the harbor town. As he finds his way to her, she and the warden escape again, across another frontier, to be pursued once more. Half a dozen times he comes up with her in different locations. Each time they are separated, until the end, when he and she are for once together and alone, in a car, driving in temporary security to yet another frontier.

Even this chaotic account of pursuit and loss does not convey the full disorientation of *Ice*, for another very strongly marked feature is the narrator's sudden plunges into accounts of events, usually involving the girl, which appear to be historical memory (such as the sack and pillage of the warden's town), pure myth (such as the sacrifice of the girl to a fjord-dragon), or macabre dream (such as the narrator's vision of an alien being). So pervasive are these shifts of scene that the reader soon loses confidence that any of the events narrated are actually meant to be happening at all. Sometimes they are identified as dreams; sometimes they contradict one another so clearly (as when the girl is shot, only to come alive again without explanation) that one cannot take them as straightforward narration of any kind.

The general effect is not one of sequential plot so much as of recurrent image, defined only by the obsession of the narrator. Again and again, he sees his frail, bruised, pallid love bound, raped, sacrificed, killed. Again and again, he pursues her in and out of frozen harbors. Several times he finds himself in an unknown labyrinth, seeking her, finding only her always-present protector, the man with the ice-blue eyes, always in a position of power and authority sufficient to keep the lovers apart. There is, it is true, a conclusion to the plot, as the girl for the first time turns on the narrator and abuses him for the cruelty he shows in always trying to "protect" her. They seem, for a moment, to reach an equal relationship in warmth and safety. Yet the gun in the narrator's pocket and the snowflakes driving into his car windscreen have been such recurrent images that even at the end they imply only further doubt and insecurity.

The Characters

It is almost fair to say that *Ice* has no characters. Certainly it is never clear how many there are. The girl's husband appears to vanish after the first two chapters, but his threatening behavior in those is so like that of the warden later on that it is tempting to identify them—especially as the warden reappears so often in different roles, places, and uniforms, always picked out, however, by his flashing blue eyes. Furthermore, as the novel progresses, the narrator becomes more and more uneasily aware that he and the warden are like each other, are perhaps identical twins. One cannot avoid the thought that they represent different fractions of the self, as it were an ego and an alter ego. Having gone so far—and remembering that the author of the book is female—one could even continue the thought and suggest that all the characters are fragments of one personality, the action of *Ice* taking place entirely in the mind.

Whether that is so, the following points can be made. There is something infantile about the girl. Though she is always perceived sexually, her thinness and paleness are insisted on to the point of morbidity. She is also until the very end invariably a victim, crushed by the men, trapped within walls of ice. She represents something thwarted but never quite destroyed—the "real me," perhaps, the person one knows one might ideally have been. The narrator always tries to free and rescue this persona but almost always finds himself provoked into furious cruelty by her flight or passivity; it is this which creates his uneasy fellow feeling with the ruthless and physically dominant "other" figure of the warden—a sympathy made stronger by the fact that the narrator, too, is a former soldier, employable by and useful to the warden in his many different roles of power. These two male figures represent, perhaps, different urges toward maturity, a state to be reached either by compulsion (via the warden) or by persuasion (via the narrator): except that the force of persuasion can never be trusted not to run amok and send the whole process back to the beginning once more.

Many other theses might be propounded. Are the three characters Id, Ego, and Superego? Are they Good Angel, Bad Angel, and Soul? Whatever the answer, several facts are clear: These characters are not "rounded"; they have no history; their motivations are perfunctory; they do not exist in their own right, but rather demand interpretation.

Themes and Meanings

The novel is dominated by two opposing images, the walls of ice and the singing lemurs. Both are introduced in the first chapter, the former with characteristic unreality. At this point, the narrator is driving along a lonely road in the dark, seeing only the hail and snow flashing through the head-lights to strike his windscreen. Then he looks sideways through a gap in the hedge, to see "for a moment . . . the girl's naked body, slight as a child's, ivory white against the dead white of the snow. . . ." What can the girl be doing, naked in a field in a snowstorm? If she were there, surely the narrator would stop? Instead, he describes in slow detail the way in which walls of ice close in on her, reach over her, set hard over her feet and ankles, climb up her body until all that is left is a black mouth open to scream. How, one wonders, could the narrator have seen all this from a moving car through a gap in the hedge? No answer is given. Instead, the reader finds six pages on his past infatuation and is then returned to the problems of his drive in the snow. The girl and the walls of ice have been a hallucination, though it proves to be a recurrent one.

By contrast, the narrator's other obsession lies in the study of a nearly extinct race of singing lemurs called the Indris, who live only in the forests of a remote tropical island. From time to time, he plays their songs; works on a monograph about them, to the total exclusion of his immediate surroundings; makes plans, always foiled, to visit them again. The Indris function as an image of Paradise, opposed in every way to the normal world of the narrator. They are warm, sociable, beautiful, and gentle. His world is frozen, harsh, individualistic, and cruel. It is difficult not to think that the lemurs represent mankind as it should be, the walls of ice human society as it is, constantly freezing and trapping individuals within unbreakable but transparent bonds.

Ice becomes in this view a study of alienation. This reading is confirmed by the book's overall inability to deal with characters in any way other than one at a time. Extensive conversations are rare until the last chapter. Groups of people together are invariably seen as hostile, often being reduced to gangs, uniforms, and armies. There exists a recurrent political fear of quasi-Fascist states, allegedly thrown up by the emergency but actually representing, it seems, the author's only model of an organized society. This alienation, the "freezing of the soul" within walls of ice, may be read as an attack on society. Yet even the narrator is uneasily aware that the freezing could come from within and be a product of his and his lover's inability to relate in any way other than obsessively to each other or to the people around them. In *Ice*, it seems that only the lemurs have solved the problem of mutual happiness. Humans are victims or exploiters. The narrator's quest for love turns easily to hallucination, or to sadism.

Critical Context

In reading this novel, one should not forget that Anna Kavan was for many years a heroin addict, and that she committed suicide very shortly after this book was published. The simplest way of reading it is to see it as an account of a disturbed personality trying to express fear of the outside world together with a desperate (if ultimately unsuccessful) ambition to break through to it, to come out of ice, entrapment, and mental confusion to a place in the sun. In this view, *Ice* would take its place as one of many modern documents of disturbed states, together with, for example, the poetry of Robert Lowell or Sylvia Plath, the fiction of William Burroughs or Franz Kafka.

To this view, however, two further dimensions may be added. One is that *Ice* remains a work of science fiction, which has been highly praised by Brian Aldiss, and has many points of resemblance to the futuristic visions of J. G. Ballard, especially *The Crystal World* (1966) and the short stories of *The Terminal Beach* (1964). The other is that *Ice* is clearly a work of the late 1960's, a period in which "consciousness-raising," often by use of drugs, became a cult activity believed to permit glimpses of a truth inaccessible to sober realists.

The achievement of this novel may be, accordingly, to have combined in one work three different forms of nonrealism: one personal, to do with the author; one generic, stemming from its science-fiction mode; and one ideological, dictated by its period. The three are fused in a highly characteristic style which moves abruptly from banality to bizarrerie and is animated by unforgettably surreal images.

Sources for Further Study
Aldiss, Brian. "Introduction," in *Ice*, 1973.
Aldiss, Brian, and David Wingrove. *Trillion Year Spree: The History of Science Fiction*, 1986.

T. A. Shippey

THE ICE AGE

Author: Margaret Drabble (1939-   )
Type of plot: Social chronicle
Time of plot: The mid-1970's, with flashbacks to earlier periods, especially the
    decade preceding the action of the novel
Locale: Yorkshire, London, other locations in England, and Wallacia, "a
    Balkan country well behind the Iron Curtain"
First published: 1977

> *Principal characters:*
> ANTHONY KEATING, one of the two protagonists of the novel,
>   a property developer threatened by economic collapse
> ALISON MURRAY, the other protagonist, Anthony's lover, an
>   actress who gave up her career to care for her daughter
>   Molly, who is afflicted with cerebral palsy
> LEN WINCOBANK, a zealous property developer, in prison for
>   fraud
> MAUREEN KIRBY, Len's secretary and lover, a survivor
> JANE MURRAY, Alison's older daughter, imprisoned in
>   Wallacia for killing two people in a traffic accident

The Novel

How does one behave when the age of faith is past and when economic recession undercuts one's efforts to create an earthly paradise? How does one make responsible choices in an Ice Age in which the innocent and guilty alike suffer catastrophe and where human endeavor too often seems futile?

For Anthony Keating, responsible conduct—if such is possible—seems to depend not so much on conscious choices as on an instinctive awareness of his kinship with all the vulnerable creatures of the globe. Anthony recognizes this kinship at the opening of the novel, when he identifies with a stricken pheasant floating in his pond. He correctly guesses that the bird has died of a heart attack, the same malady from which he is himself recuperating at his Yorkshire estate.

As Anthony buries the pheasant, he muses on the words of a friend: "*These are terrible times we live in.*" Thereupon follows a catalog of private and public woes. The friend, Kitty Friedman, has had her foot blown off and her husband killed by an arbitrarily placed Irish Republican Army (IRA) bomb. Anthony's lover, Alison Murray, is languishing in Wallacia, an anti-British, Eastern-bloc nation, where she is vainly trying to help her teenage daughter, Jane, imprisoned for killing two people in a traffic accident. Anthony himself and his partners in the Imperial Delight Company are facing possible bankruptcy, and Len Wincobank, Anthony's mentor in the property business, is in jail for trying to retrieve his fortunes by fraud. Even beyond Anthony's circle, "depression lay like fog" and "people blamed other people for all the things that were going wrong" without knowing "whose fault it really was."

The issue of fault and blame comes up repeatedly in the novel as Anthony and Alison and their acquaintances struggle to assume or deny responsibility for their lives. Kitty Friedman is nearly unique in her refusal to blame anyone for the tragedies of her life, but such saintliness is achieved only at considerable cost. Her defense against the perverse blows of chance is simply not to think about them, to deny the force of evil in the universe, to screen out the "black wastes" of suffering. The price that Kitty must pay for this strategy is the loss of the past, for she "dare[s]" not "think" of her own husband.

No more realistic than Kitty and much less good-natured is Linton Hancox, an anachronistic classics teacher and a failed poet, who blames dull students and unappreciative readers for the blighting of his promise. Similarly, Len Wincobank charges the "planning authorities" at Porcaster with causing his downfall. Tom Callander, an architect in prison with Len for taking bribes, attributes his misfortune to a disturbance in "the law of chance," an idea he has culled from a confused reading of Arthur Koestler's *The Roots of Coincidence* (1972). Maureen Kirby, Len's self-sufficient paramour, is unusual in regarding the drop in worldly status that she and so many others have experienced as a return to reality following the enjoyment of unearned gifts.

Anthony, for his part, is perfectly willing to accept responsibility for his fate. Indeed, he takes comfort in reflecting that "he had brought it on himself." Yet he fails to see the justice of the "punishments" doled out to some of his friends. What is the point of making the right choice if one may be killed by a bomb at any time?

While Anthony in Yorkshire reviews the choices of his recent past, Alison in Wallacia ponders her own choices and responsibilities as she works for the release of her daughter Jane. Had the fatal accident truly been accidental, or had Jane been unwittingly putting in her claim for the constant maternal attention she had been denied from age seven, when her sister, Molly, a victim of cerebral palsy, was born?

Alison's return to England in response to Molly's apparent need of her suggests that Jane may have a valid complaint. In a farewell meeting before Alison leaves Wallacia, mother and daughter are both resentful—Jane, of Alison's rejection of her in favor of Molly; Alison, of Jane's continued hostility and immaturity. In a speech that she should have made long before, Alison advises Jane to assume some responsibility for her life and choices, to stop blaming the accident of Molly's condition for all of her own misfortunes. Alison, however, makes a mistake: She turns from her daughter, closing her lecture with the words, "I wash my hands of you." At the very time that Alison tells her daughter that she must answer for her actions, she herself tries to sever her ties to that daughter. Alison works hard at being a good mother, but she forgets that she cannot will away her obligations any more than can Jane. It is not surprising that she feels a certain deadness upon her return to England.

Alison's deliberate compartmentalizing of her responsibilities works less well than Anthony's instinctive—even if sometimes reluctant—conservation of all the vulnerable creatures with whom he comes in contact. It is this innate generosity of spirit that enables Anthony to tolerate and even protect Tim, the pathologically confused servant and struggling actor sent along by Donnell Murray, Alison's former husband, to help with Molly; to accompany a friendless and drug-addicted woman in labor, whom he finds "squatting" in his empty London house, to the hospital; and, at great personal risk, to go to Wallacia to rescue the unsympathetic Jane.

When the British Foreign Office asks Anthony to retrieve Jane from a politically unstable Wallacia, he welcomes the call to action with amused self-mockery: "[W]ho am I to resist an appeal to a chivalric spirit that was condemned as archaic by Cervantes?" Yet if Anthony laughs at himself for his adherence to an archaic, chivalric code of conduct, he is nevertheless aware that the adoption of such a code when it is no longer enforced by society constitutes an act of self-definition. Looking at Jane's copy of *Antigone* as he sits trapped in a Wallacian airport, Anthony considers that "Antigone had gone out and died for a completely meaningless code." Yet he also sees that Antigone made a stand that cannot be ignored—because it was her attempt to preserve her individual integrity.

Like all choices made in the Ice Age, Anthony's choice is a gamble. On the one hand, it pays off in the reform of Jane, who at last emerges into adulthood, takes responsibility for her accident, and decides to become a nurse. On the other hand, it results in Anthony's imprisonment in a Wallacian camp, where, in his extremity, he explores "the nature of God and the possibility of religious faith."

Thus, Anthony consoles himself at the close of the novel. At the same time, the Ice Age recedes with the discovery of North Sea oil; with returning affluence, most Britons will regain their illusions of control over their own destinies, the IRA bombs and the victims of life's accidents forgotten for the moment. Alison alone remains suspended in a frozen, sterile world: "Britain will recover, but not Alison Murray."

The Characters

A gentle man who has difficulty making choices in a chaotic universe, Anthony Keating almost seems to welcome the external constraints imposed upon him. Reared in a cathedral city and educated at Oxford, Anthony, as the son of a clergyman-schoolmaster, is at first more eager to escape the expectations of his father than to establish his own identity. He marries young, lives by "his wits," and follows a friend's suggestion that he get a job writing for television. It is not surprising that Anthony finds "incomprehensible virtues" in Giles Peters, the friend who tells him what to do: Giles can make decisions.

Outwardly successful, Anthony gradually comes to recognize that his marriage is a failure and his job lacks challenge. Just as Anthony is "ripe for conversion, to some new creed," he meets "self-made" property developer Len Wincobank, who is devoted, "with a kind of blinkered faithful zeal," to rebuilding the face of England. Margaret Drabble's use of the language of religious experience is suggestive here. When the old faiths go by the wayside, energetic men such as Anthony will look for substitutes. In a society apparently ruled by chance, the preoccupation with property development and speculation, which is, after all, a form of gambling, seems appropriate.

Len's example inspires Anthony, with the help of Giles and his money, to form his own property development firm, the Imperial Delight Company. The name is inherited from an archaic candy factory purchased by the new partners but, nevertheless, indicates the significance of the venture. Although Anthony believes himself to be "a modern man, an operator, at one with the spirit of the age," his enthusiasm seems to belong to an earlier time, his "sense of empire" rather like that of a nineteenth century captain of industry. Characteristically, his greatest "pride" lies not, as in Len's case, in his plans for new buildings but in the "possession" of a defunct gasometer—"a work of art"—that will ultimately "have to come down." It is probably just as well that a heart attack removes Anthony from the scene of the action; even the sacrifice of a small elderberry tree to Imperial Delight's redevelopment plans is a source of regret.

The same instinct to preserve and protect manifests itself in Anthony's mission to rescue Jane. In assigning him that mission, the British Foreign Office makes possible still another conversion for Anthony, one that may be no truer objectively than the religion of property development, but which has the virtue, at least, of being consistent with his character. Indeed, his action springs from his own inner imperatives rather than from any consideration of rewards or consequences.

It is Alison who remains fixated upon the consequences of her choices and who fears that she is somehow responsible for all the evils that have befallen her family. There is the case of her older sister Rosemary, whose envy of Alison's greater beauty has always "made Alison feel guilty, sick." When Rosemary undergoes a mastectomy, Alison's guilt has something real to attach itself to: She cannot help but attribute the cancer to her resentment of Rosemary, much as a child may ascribe the death of a sibling to his own dark fantasies.

Alison's self-accusations do not end with her relationship to her sister but extend to what she defines as the central role of her life, that of mother. She wonders whether chance is the only element at work in producing her daughter Molly's affliction or whether she must suffer "the guilt of Molly's sacrifice" in a world that metes out "punishments for... unknown crimes." For Alison, it is an act of faith to believe that her daughter's condition really is an accident and not the intentional malevolence of a hostile universe.

Yet Jane's traffic accident, her continuing resentment of Molly, and her petulant claims on her mother's attention all exacerbate Alison's fears. Undeniably, Alison stands at the center of an ugly, repeating pattern of sibling rivalry: Jane is jealous of Molly, as Rosemary has always been jealous of Alison. The victim of so much "ill will" and disaster, Alison fears her own thoughts. In a vision that is both a fantasy of power and a nightmare of guilt, she sees, "a world where the will was potent, not impotent; where it made, indeed, bad choices and killed others by them, killed them, deformed them, destroyed them."

A less extreme reaction to misfortune than the angst of Alison or the conversions of Anthony is the cheerful pragmatism of Maureen Kirby, Len Wincobank's secretary and paramour. After Len goes to prison, Maureen gets a new job, builds a successful career, tries to be faithful to Len, but does not agonize too much when she decides that she cannot. Full of vitality and good humor, Maureen takes herself less seriously than does Alison; she acknowledges responsibility for her own actions but does not blame herself for all the misfortunes of her world.

Themes and Meanings

In Anthony's quixotic mission and in Alison's tortured self-questioning, Drabble raises the crucial, if unresolvable, issues of the novel: How much real choice do human beings have? Where does responsibility begin and end? In her exploration of these issues, Drabble gradually and somewhat tentatively reveals a link between respect for life in all its phases and the willingness to take responsibility for oneself and others. That respect is too often missing in Anthony's and Alison's worlds. Indeed, the Ice Age wasteland must be at least partly attributed to the egocentricity of its inhabitants. Terrible accidents do happen, and there is apparently no benign providence to set them right. It is equally clear, however, that too many people have made irresponsible, "anticonservationist" choices. Kitty is maimed not by accident but because someone deliberately planted a bomb, not caring who its victims might be. The property developers have crashed because they have risked too much on schemes of questionable social utility—and society, sometimes in the form of recalcitrant city planning boards, is making them pay the price. It is clear also that too many people—Jane Murray, Linton Hancox, Tom Callander—are so preoccupied with assigning blame to others that they

do not learn from their own mistakes. All recognize an atmosphere of petu-
lance and irresponsibility, but few recognize their own contributions to that
atmosphere. Anthony and Alison, for all of their inconsistencies, are able to
see—at least intermittently—the interconnectedness of things: "None of our
decisions is taken in isolation—if decisions we can call them."

Yet Drabble's universe is not a moralistic one in which the bad are punished, the good rewarded, and everyone gets what he deserves. Luck,
chance, and accident undercut the individual's sense of purpose and destroy
the illusion of control. Resilience may depend upon an acceptance of life's
uncertainties.

Critical Context

A prolific writer, Margaret Drabble has written a number of novels, a
biography of Arnold Bennett, and several stories and articles. She has edited
the fifth edition of the *Oxford Companion to English Literature* (1985), a
project that suggests the depth and breadth of her knowledge of English literary traditions. Her eighth novel, *The Ice Age* reveals her indebtedness to,
and creative use of, those traditions.

Like the Victorian novelist George Eliot, to whom she is often compared,
Drabble examines the conditions and consequences of moral choice in novel
after novel. Her protagonists struggle, if not to make the right choices, then
to accept responsibility for the choices they have made. In *The Ice Age*, however, the act of choice is threatened—perhaps more than in any previous
Drabble novel—by the individual's powerlessness to foresee consequences in
a world dominated by chance.

Drabble gives no universally applicable solutions to the problems she sees.
In an interview with Nancy Poland, she notes: "I have lots of questions. I
don't really pretend to have any answers so I am not a teacher. I am an explorer." *The Ice Age* explores alternative adjustments to depression and chaos
in the strategies or nonstrategies worked out by her various characters.

In moving from character to character, Drabble employs an omniscient
narrator reminiscent of those of her nineteenth century forebears, but
Drabble seems deliberately to exert less control over her fictional universe
than Eliot did over hers. At the opening of the last section of the novel,
Drabble's narrator announces to the reader, "It ought to be necessary to
imagine a future for Anthony Keating"—as if storytelling becomes more tax-
ing amidst the intransigent conditions of twentieth century disillusionment,
so that the narrator must struggle to imagine the remainder of the story. At
the end of the novel, the narrator proclaims that Alison's "life is beyond
imagining." The tidy resolutions of the Victorian novel are no longer possible
for the intelligent modern novelist. Drabble not only refuses to predict
Alison's future for the reader but also suggests that such a prediction, were
she to offer it, would be a falsification of experience.

Sources for Further Study
Creighton, Joanne V. *Margaret Drabble*, 1985.
Rose, Ellen Cronan. *The Novels of Margaret Drabble: Equivocal Figures*, 1980.
_____, ed. *Critical Essays on Margaret Drabble*, 1985.
Sadler, Lynn Veach. *Margaret Drabble*, 1986.

Linda Seidel Costic

ILLYWHACKER

Author: Peter Carey (1943-   )
Type of plot: Picaresque yarn
Time of plot: From 1886 to the mid-1980's
Locale: Victoria and New South Wales, Australia
First published: 1985

> *Principal characters:*
> HERBERT BADGERY, the aged narrator
> LEAH GOLDSTEIN, his friend and sometime lover
> PHOEBE MCGRATH, his sometime wife
> CHARLES BADGERY, his son

The Novel

Herbert Badgery, the narrator of *Illywhacker* and the patriarch of its three generations of Badgerys, claims at the outset of the novel that he is 139 years old. He also boasts that he is an inveterate liar. *Illywhacker* is the memoirs of this aged, but not too aged, mendicant. He describes a life of wandering about southeastern Australia, from adventure to adventure, from fib to fib.

The rambling style of his six hundred pages of reminiscence—tall tale after tall tale grafted onto other tall tales—matches the style of his life. His story begins in the early days of air travel. He ditches his unpredictable aircraft in a paddock near a church parking lot, where Phoebe McGrath and her parents have imagined that they are safely picnicking. Jumping from the plane, Herbert captures a deadly brown snake that threatens to bite him. When Phoebe asks why he has the snake in his hands, the only likely explanation he can quickly muster is an out-and-out fib—he says that it is a pet. The snake wriggles its way in and out of the narrative for many pages until, after Herbert has broken the family's trust by dallying amorously with Phoebe on the roof of the McGraths' farmhouse, the snake takes Phoebe's father's life—rather, he commits suicide with it.

This episode typifies, although it greatly simplifies, the complex, convoluted, comic style of Herbert's narrative. It also presents the kinds of thematic materials from which he will stitch together a case against his fellow Australians. He tells of fleeing beatings at ten and being taught survival skills by a Chinese merchant and magician; of what happens when he excuses his crash-landing by assuring Phoebe's father that they could make a better, Australian aircraft themselves; of his love for Leah Goldstein, a medical student prompted to become an exotic dancer by a confused dedication to Socialist causes; and of much more.

Herbert's memoirs are almost an allegory of Australian history. At every turning, Herbert refers to events of national significance but then quickly reverts to details of his own life. In national affairs, he sees lies, the greatest of them being that Australia is its own master. To salvage honor from the failure of national proportions, he spins his own, monumentally idiosyncratic pack of lies. He piles anecdote upon anecdote and follows every back road of his life, until eventually the reader realizes that Herbert has been doggedly defying the expectation that he will tie up the loose ends of his fragmentary, meandering narrative. For Herbert, diversity is the point. His memoirs are a celebration of the natural resources—the elements of his landscape worthy of being spun into a good yarn—that have been ill-used by his fellows.

Not surprisingly, then, the celebration is bittersweet. Herbert may see that his illywhacking beats his countrymen's bland, patriotic mush of lies anytime. He can know that an Australian automobile made by an American company which takes all the profits is in fact no Australian automobile at all. Yet he also sees that the belief that it is can persist anyway. When his son, Charles, builds a successful business—the Best Pet Shop in the World—its success depends on the readiness of foreign customers to purchase smuggled exotic Australian birds and reptiles. Herbert sees that such colonialism is inevitable. His own projects, however resourceful they are, are, after all, notoriously unsuccessful or inconsequential, too. In a final irony, as Herbert ends his narrative, he is an attraction at a bizarre human zoo that his grandson, Hissao, has established with Japanese backing.

The Characters

Herbert Badgery, the aged narrator of *Illywhacker*, warns his readers bluntly at the outset that "lying is my main subject, my specialty, my skill." He is assigned, by himself and others, a variety of names from his Australian vernacular—"ratbag," "illywhacker," and so on. Leah Goldstein explains this last term: An illywhacker is "a spieler" she says. "A trickster. A quandong. A ripperty man. A con-man."

Herbert's six hundred pages of anecdote, diversion, and fabrication describe a varied and colorful rascal's life. He is at once a nest-builder who can turn scraps into houses and an itinerant who wriggles along so quickly that even a ten-year stint in jail cannot slow him down. In a typical period of his life, he says, he wandered about Victoria "writing bad cheques when I could get hold of a book, running raffles in pubs, buying stolen petrol." Yet he is no malicious criminal and no ordinary rascal. His disdain of legal and social restraints and his fabrications are his ennobling defense against society's large-scale, demeaning lies that win easy, infuriating acceptance. As he says, lying is his main subject.

The lie of Australian independence is for Herbert the largest of all. It fuels his disdain for others and disappoints his vision of the rich potential in Australia's resources. He says: "I would rather fill my history with great men and women, philosophers, scientists, intellectuals, artists, but I confess myself incapable of so vast a lie." That, however, is a fib, too, for his people have their own stature. He makes a giant, albeit a giant of the mundane, of every farmer, immigrant, pioneer, and dreamer with whom he drinks a beer or whose daughter or wife takes his fancy. Yet, bathetically, every person in this rich, curious cross section of his young country, himself included, disappoints him.

When Herbert becomes a guest of the McGrath family, he quickly becomes enamored of the teenage Phoebe. After first seducing her history teacher, Phoebe seduces and marries Herbert. After several rooftop rendezvous, however, Herbert finds that Phoebe is as calculating as she is sexually precocious. She bears two children, then runs away with Horace, the itinerant poet, and Annette Davidson, her history teacher and lover, eventually to achieve, poorly and pretentiously, her ambition to become a poet.

When, as a young man, Herbert meets Leah Goldstein, she is the very exotic dancer of such numbers as the Emu Dance. She becomes Herbert's lover and then his friend. She took up dancing, Herbert learns, to emulate Rosa Kaletsky, an expelled member of the Soviet Communist Party whose son, an emotionally gnarled Party organizer, Leah later marries.

Charles, Herbert's son, achieves more fully than does his father the ambition to establish an Australian industry: He runs a pet shop that is, he believes, the best in the world. Half-deaf and hopelessly inadequate, Charles nevertheless prospers in business and provides for all the other Badgerys, Herbert included. Yet his success is tainted. Like Australia's economy, Peter Carey suggests, Charles's pet store succeeds only by pandering to American, Japanese, and European customers.

In considering Herbert's depiction of the characters in his life story, it is well to remember that he is pathologically and purposefully a liar. Late in the memoirs, a note from Leah Goldstein appears that accuses Herbert of distorting facts so as to portray cruelly both himself and others.

Themes and Meanings

In meandering through approximately ninety years of Badgery history, Herbert develops as many themes as he spins yarns. The more important, however, involve various forms of lying. As Herbert says, lying is his main subject.

The great Australian lie, according to Herbert, is the claim that Australians are their own masters. During his lifetime, they have accepted English, European, American, and finally Japanese dominion of varying kinds—colonialist, economic, cultural. In its persistent, sprawling diversity, the novel resembles a fantastically prolonged yarn that might be told at a country pub. Herbert cannot understand, however, why he sees everywhere Australians who complacently and indifferently undersell themselves and whatever is of value to them to the highest foreign bidder. This is not to say that the book is a political diatribe. Carey builds his case so gradually and unobtrusively that the book remains entertaining.

At the same time, a darker significance emerges. As the episodes of Herbert's yarn endlessly proliferate, his caustic larrikin's voice acquires a bitter tone. The humor has soured by the time Herbert becomes a withered old man. In retrospect, his opening words, "It is hard to believe you can feel so bad and still not die," can be taken literally, not simply as comic bathos.

Many other applications of lying, including fiction itself, are studied in the novel. Herbert's memoirs are, for example, a demonstration of distinctive Australian modes of mythmaking. The epigraph from Mark Twain suggests the central place of this aspect of the Australian psyche. Australian history, Twain said, reads less like history than "like the most beautiful lies."

Ultimately, lies and other varieties of deception and unfulfilled aspiration take a personal toll on Herbert. He is an odd man with little sense of humor or forgiveness. Yet because he acknowledges those shortcomings, the final, sad laugh is his.

Critical Context

In *Illywhacker*, Carey develops in depth the themes and style he introduced in *The Fat Man in History* (1974), a collection of short stories, and *Bliss* (1981), his first novel. One reason for the length of *Illywhacker*, however, is that in it Carey writes, far more fully than before, about his native Australia. The subject clearly compels him—for all of its length, *Illywhacker* appears not overlong, but bursting to expand.

In *Illywhacker*, as in his other works, Carey writes in a vigorous satirical style whose language is down-to-earth but whose structure is sophisticated. All of Carey's works feature rigorous attention to physical details. In *Illywhacker*, Herbert's infatuation with the ordinary—he tells, for example, why there are few things in the world more useful than a Hessian bag—has a clear thematic purpose. It suggests, for example, the way the pioneers and even recent citizens of the historically young country have been forced to eke out a living from whatever was at hand.

Black humor also is a constant feature of Carey's writing. In *Illywhacker*, Carey's dark satire has found an ideal vehicle in Herbert Badgery, who minutely inspects every event, person, and thing. The result is always humorous and generally satirical. Carey's, like Badgery's, is a mind that will not agree with polite society that certain things, such as bodily functions and trash, can be blithely ignored. Themes common in other works that also appear here include the nature of colonization, particularly at the hands of American cultural influence.

Sources for Further Study

Hutchinson, Paul E. Review in *Library Journal*. CX (August, 1985), p. 113.

Jacobson, Howard. Review in *The New York Times Book Review*. XC (November 17, 1985), p. 15.

Lewis, Roger. Review in *New Statesman*. CIX (April 19, 1985), p. 34.

The New Yorker. Review. LXI (November 11, 1985), p. 154.

Publishers Weekly. Review. CCXXVII (May 31, 1985), p. 47.

Peter Monaghan

AN IMAGINARY LIFE

Author: David Malouf (1934-   )
Type of plot: Historical romance
Time of plot: Approximately A.D. 8 to 18
Locale: Tomis, an outpost of the Roman Empire, between the Danube and
the Black Sea
First published: 1978

> *Principal characters:*
> OVID, the famous, exiled Roman poet
> THE CHILD, a wild boy adopted by Ovid
> RYZAK, the village headman
> HIS MOTHER
> HIS DAUGHTER-IN-LAW
> LULLO, his grandson

The Novel

For reasons which even Ovid seems not to know clearly, the poet, at the height of his career, is exiled from Rome to a small village in the wilds near the Black Sea. Although he is able to continue writing and to correspond with friends and relatives in Rome, he is faced with the possibility of spending the rest of his life in this primitive backwater where the natives, obviously ordered to take care of him, do not even speak Latin, and whose lives are spent working barely to survive. Eight months out of the year, the land is cold, and the village is threatened by packs of wolves or marauding barbarians. Ovid, unhappy and unused to taking care of himself, is a burden to the village. He is housed with the headman, Ryzak, and the headman's family.

Slowly, reluctantly, Ovid shakes himself out of his self-pity, busies himself with his writing, and starts to take an interest in the community, to learn the language, and to help in the communal chores. He also makes some attempt to civilize his surroundings by growing a few flowers and by trying to teach the grandson of the headman's family to speak Latin. He puts his life into some perspective, recognizing the appropriateness, in a sense, of his return to the country, for he was born in a rural part of Italy. He is less unhappy, realizing that these people, if ignorant and unimaginative, are not unkind. Ryzak, the old headman, becomes a close friend.

On the annual deer-hunting expedition, Ovid thinks that he sees something which looks like a child, and he is determined, if possible, to capture the animal. Over a period of a few years, the Child does in fact appear, becoming less and less timid and Ovid sets out food for him, and eventually, with the grudging permission of the community, Ovid does capture the Child. Bringing the boy into the village upsets Ovid's relationship not only to

Ryzak's immediate family but also to the tribal group in general. Ovid particularly fears the influence of Ryzak's mother, who has considerable power, and there is constant danger that the Child, who slowly responds to Ovid's kindness and instruction, may be killed.

On the death of Ryzak, Ovid realizes that he and the boy are not safe. They escape the compound, working their way north into the depths of the wilderness. The boy now leads and cares for Ovid, who, on their journey into the natural, uncivilized world, dies happily.

The Characters

It is helpful to be clear about what this novel is not doing or attempting to do. David Malouf is not attempting to portray the real Ovid. Indeed, little is really known about Ovid, save for that which can be guessed from his substantial body of work. What is known, however, suggests that he was not quite as romantic or deeply sensitive as Malouf would have him. The last of the great Augustan poets, Ovid is usually seen as the least profound of the group and, in many ways, closest to the high sophistication of Roman society. Malouf is aware of this, and his afterword to the novel is helpful in revealing his intentions for the Ovid of what is cheerfully admitted is "an imaginary life," taking for its basis a character whose response to adversity has lyrical and mystical implications which are not to be found in the work of the historical Ovid, whom Malouf perceptively calls "this glib fabulist."

The character who dominates this novel, and who is the sole speaker in the same, is a man of considerable range of feeling. The first-person narration allows for an intimacy which is enriched by the fact that Ovid is speaking directly to a later audience, to the modern reader, presuming that this record of his life will be read some centuries hence. This tale of exile, of the pain and suffering in both the physical and psychological sense visited upon the mature darling of high Roman society, is not seen by Ovid as meaningless, and the manner in which he responds to squalor and barren poverty is shaped with some propriety in poetic terms. Ovid may be in the wild ranges of barbaric danger, but his natural inclination is to make some sense of the world, however arbitrarily cruel it may seem. Self-pity is, as a result, refreshingly absent from his tale, and, from the start, he speaks candidly and simply to what he has been and what he must become if he is to survive.

Part of his attraction lies in his simplicity. There is no sense of the sophisticated literary figure mocking the natives, no sense that he despises them in their primitive ignorance. The language is straightforward, and, if sophisticated and intelligent, it has no satiric edge to it. This is probably the most successful part of the Ovid portrait.

The fact that Ovid is a poet is not forgotten, and the tale gathers lyric proportion on those occasions when the mystery of the Child is explored. This stylistic density is pleasingly strong in the prologue to the tale and reaches its aesthetic height in the last pages as Ovid and the Child work their way deeper into the wilderness to meet the waiting death of the poet. Ovid is appropriately seen as how he, as an artist, makes shape out of the chaos of his disgrace, how he makes art out of life, whether on the simplest level in growing flowers or on the more refractory level of how he makes friends in the obvious social sense or on the deeper metaphysical level.

What readers know of the others is what Ovid sees, and what he sees is often strongly touched by his magnanimity, his curiosity, and his willingness to give of himself. Ignorant and incoherent, living inside a timid animal sensibility, the natives, and later the Child, respond to the patient tenderness of Ovid and become more fully realized characters as he gets to know them and gets them to trust him. What readers know of them is seen through his eyes, but the eyes are so unjudgmental, so determined to see the best (while watching for primitive panic to flood back), that characters such as Ryzak and the Child achieve a weight which belies their atavistic silences.

Themes and Meanings

Ovid is chosen by Malouf, as he suggests in his afterword, because he stands in his high sophistication and civility between the barbaric animalism of the past and the ultimate refinements of our own time, when rationality and all that it stands for has come to fruition. Ovid is also chosen because his great work, the *Metamorphoses* (c. A.D. 8), explores the notion of fluid boundaries between the spiritual, the animal, and the human world.

Malouf offers an Ovid expelled from his civilized world and determined to construct another in its place, in ways which are to be read as examples of the admirable courage which man needs to tame his environment, and which Ovid sees as vital to all civilizations. It was thus, he believes, that Rome came to be the center of the world, and ultimately how a greater civilization will be achieved centuries later. If Augustus, the rational and efficient man, does not want the artist present, so be it. Ovid does not allow exile to destroy him as a poet, and he proves that he is not simply an effete darling of the Roman smart set.

Yet he goes further. In his attempts to civilize the village inhabitants and in seeking to draw the Child out of his animality, Ovid learns from them as well. His memory of the wild child of his early years, his imaginary playmate, leads him inexorably to the real thing, the boy brought up in the natural world, and as such, a step closer than the villagers to the world of spiritual experience.

His death, the final wandering into the heart of nature, led by the Child, and into a final unity of all time and all things, is an epiphanic moment of metaphysical metamorphosis far greater than any of the artistic imaginings he ever created. At that moment, he becomes, in a sense, pure poetry of a kind beyond art.

An Imaginary Life is a novel which can be easily read on several levels at the same time. At its most obvious, it is a clever tale of the last days of a great public man as imagined by a novelist who understands the poetic sensibility. The fact that what is known of Ovid is not really consistent with Malouf's portrayal must, however, circumscribe any acceptance of the tale as historically true.

It can also be read as a story about courage, about man at his best, rebuilding his life. In this novel, Ovid not only makes sense of defeat but also uses it to save himself and to help others to believe that there is more to life than survival. At the same time, he learns from the primitive about such survival and about human kindness and ignorance.

The title is appropriate, but the book could have been called "Metamorphosis" since it is about a man discovering the full range of human endeavor, from the high rationality of urban civilization at the one end to the spiritual mysteries and possibilities at the other.

If that is not enough, it is possible to think of the novel as a metaphor for the artistic process, for the way in which the artist uses technique, intelligence, and imagination to create the aesthetic object; in the process, as the novel demonstrates, the artist becomes that which he imagines, particularly in the creation of poetry.

Critical Context

Malouf came to the novel form somewhat later than to poetry, and there is an aspect of experiment in *An Imaginary Life* which suggests that it is not quite polished. This may be unfair, since a better appreciation of the work might lie in seeing it as somewhere in between fiction and poetry. Certainly the later passages are best read as poetry, redolent as they are with ambiguity and visual and oral densities.

It would be difficult to guess Malouf's nationality on the evidence of this novel, but he is, in fact, an Australian, and he has used variations on the themes of *An Imaginary Life* to deal with his own country. He is from Brisbane, and his 1975 novel, *Johnno*, is about that town, as is his most successful novel, *Harland's Half Acre*, published in 1984. In both of these works, Malouf brings the intelligent, disciplined man into confrontation with the savage, if, in the case of these novels, not quite so savage as the Child. The problem of how a man learns from that which is contrary to his own inclinations and training and of how it broadens him regardless of whether he likes it is clearly a constant in Malouf's work. In *An Imaginary Life*, the problem is explored in lyrically tragic terms; in *Harland's Half Acre*, that metaphysical aura is eschewed for a broader, realistic, and sometimes satirical look at how that civilization which Ovid imagined has not gone quite right.

Sources for Further Study

Eldred, Kate. Review in *The New Republic.* CLXXVIII (May 13, 1978), p. 36.

Kramer, Leonie, ed. *The Oxford History of Australian Literature,* 1981.

McNeil, Helen. Review in *New Statesman.* XCVI (September 15, 1978), p. 338.

Matthews, John Pengwerne. *Tradition in Exile: A Comparative Study of Social Influences on the Development of Australian and Canadian Poetry in the Nineteenth Century,* 1962.

Pollitt, Katha. Review in *The New York Times Book Review.* LXXVIII (April 23, 1978), p. 10.

Portis, Rowe. Review in *Library Journal.* CIII (March 1, 1978), p. 587.

Ramson, W. S. *The Australian Experience: Cultural Essays on Australian Novels,* 1974.

Charles H. Pullen

IN A FREE STATE

Author: V. S. Naipaul (1932-   )
Type of plot: Social criticism
Time of plot: 1954-1969
Locale: Bombay, Washington, D.C., the West Indies, London, and an
   unnamed African country, possibly Uganda
First published: 1971

> *Principal characters:*
>   SANTOSH, the protagonist of "One out of Many," an Indian
>   domestic
>   SAHIB, Santosh's first employer
>   PRIYA, an Indian restaurateur in Washington, D.C., who lures
>   Santosh away from his first employer
>   THE NARRATOR of "Tell Me Who to Kill," an unnamed West
>   Indian working in London to help his brother get an
>   education
>   BOBBY, the protagonist of "In a Free State," a white
>   homosexual civil servant who has emigrated to an African
>   country
>   LINDA, an acquaintance of Bobby, who shares a long car trip
>   with him

The Novel

   In a Free State is a collection of three stories: "One out of Many," "Tell Me
Who to Kill," and the title piece, "In a Free State." When the first story,
"One out of Many," begins, Santosh is in Bombay working for a middle-level
government official. When his employer is reassigned to Washington, D.C.,
Santosh faces the prospect of dismissal and having to return to his village in
the hills. Rather than face this loss of prestige and comfort, he presses his
employer to take him to the United States.

   He soon regrets coming to the United States, however, because in his new
home, Washington, D.C., he feels unsafe and out of place. Soon after he
arrives, he has an experience that will make it impossible for him to return to
India: He becomes aware of his own identity. Previously, he had been content to be a small part of his employer's presence, but—after lengthy scrutiny of his face in the mirror of his employer's bathroom to determine why
the maid finds him attractive (a question that would never have occurred to
him in Bombay)—he discovers that he is handsome, and his troubles begin.
He loses the ability to confide in his employer. The only Americans who
seem real to him are on television—which is where he usually sees them; the
$3.75 he earns per week is not enough to allow for social activity. He has a

romantic encounter with a black maid at the apartment building, but his attitude toward blacks (the *hubshi*), like all the attitudes he brings from Bombay, betrays him and, instead of solace, he finds only dishonor in his contact with her.

The misery of his life, coupled with his new self-awareness, makes Santosh susceptible to Priya, a restaurateur, whose talk and philosophy strongly attract him because they remind him of his life in Bombay. Therefore, he runs away from his employer and begins to work as a cook in Priya's restaurant. He is earning one hundred dollars a week and has his own room—an unimaginable extravagance—but, because of his complete lack of rapport with his surroundings, he soon realizes that he has only made his lot worse. He starts to think of Priya as his *sahib*: With Priya, however, the word is servile, whereas, with his old employer, the word *sahib* was part of his employer's dignity and therefore part of his own. He says, "Priya's dignity could never be mine; that was not our relationship." As his newfound freedom is lost, his desolation deepens. When Priya convinces him to marry the *hubshi* woman in order to get his citizenship, his desolation becomes absolute. He "closes his mind and his heart" to his new world and resigns himself to being alone forever.

In "Tell Me Who to Kill," the unnamed narrator is a member of an impoverished West Indian family who have pinned their collective hopes on educating the youngest and brightest son, Dayo. The narrator, after seeing that the immediate family cannot pay for Dayo's education, and that the extended family has no interest in doing so, borrows and saves enough money himself to send Dayo to study in London; he then comes to London himself to help look after him. In London, however, the brothers become alienated from each other as the narrator vainly urges Dayo to pursue studies in which he has no interest. Dayo spends his days loafing and smoking expensive cigarettes, yet makes just as much (or as little) progress toward ensuring a prosperous future as the narrator, who, having saved up two thousand pounds by working eighteen hours a day for four years, loses it all in a month when he invests in a curry shop that goes bankrupt. As the story ends, Dayo is getting married to an English girl—a marriage that the author intimates will be disastrous for him—and the narrator is too broken by his personal and financial losses to recover. His life in London is finished, yet he has nowhere else to go. He has word sent home to his family that he is dead, and as the story ends that is how the reader thinks of him.

The final story, "In a Free State," is equally pessimistic. In it, Bobby and Linda share a car ride from the capital, in the northern part of the African country, to the so-called Southern Collectorate, where Bobby works and where Linda will rejoin her husband. Ethnic rivalries within the country make this journey perilous because the president, whose politically and militarily dominant people control the north, has set up roadblocks to apprehend the king, whose weaker people populate the south.

The basic conflict between the two characters concerns their attitude toward Africa: Bobby, a homosexual who suffered a nervous breakdown at Oxford, has emigrated to Africa and plans to make it his home. "My life is here," he says. Linda has lived in the country for six years and considers it an exciting place for her and her husband to work, but she intends to go to South Africa, if it ever stops being "like a John Ford Western." Her attitude suggests that Europeans can never be accepted in black African society.

Conflict is implicit in their initial conversations, but their experiences during the two-day journey south dramatize it and prove convincingly that Linda is right. Bobby's claim of having made a new home is shown to be a pipe dream, both in his private life, when at the hotel where he and Linda stop for the night he misinterprets a young African's innocence for interest in a sexual encounter, and in his public life, when in a shockingly brutal scene he is beaten by the president's soldiers, who do not recognize Bobby's authority as a government official.

The story's final scene between Bobby and his houseboy, Luke—when Luke discovers that the president's men have very nearly beaten his employer to death—illustrates how insurmountable the distance is between Bobby and his would-be countrymen. The king's people are routinely beaten, imprisoned, and executed by the president's soldiers; Luke is a member of the king's people, yet when he sees what has befallen Bobby, he laughs and acts contemptuously toward him, rejecting out of hand the notion of fellowship between them. Bobby realizes that he will either have to leave or, by firing Luke, invoke the prerogative of the neocolonialists, whose culture he purports to reject. In either case, he perpetuates his status as outsider and, like Santosh and the narrator of "Tell Me Who to Kill," is lost.

The Characters

Santosh is at once the most likable and the least sympathetic of the three protagonists. His charming, unacculturated reportage of life in Washington, D.C., lends a comic air to the narrative which greatly adds to the story's richness. The reader is unlikely to forget, however, that Santosh has abandoned a wife and two children in India because he could not face the disgrace of returning to his village in the hills, and that even at the story's end, when he has nothing to look forward to except death, his motivation is his own prestige and comfort.

The narrator of "Tell Me Who to Kill," however, powerfully engages the reader's sympathies. His motives are entirely altruistic—to help his younger brother Dayo and his rural family. When the narrator must drop out of school, the great shame that he feels for perpetuating his family's poverty manifests itself in two ways: in an ambitious plan to help his dearly loved brother obtain a higher education, and in an overpowering, soul-destroying hatred, first toward his uncle's snobbish urban family and later toward the whites, whose seemingly impenetrable culture contributes to the defeat of his plan.

Bobby, like the other two protagonists, also has a trait which prompts him to expatriate; he is emotionally unstable, presumably because of English hostility to his homosexuality, as illustrated by his psychiatrist's wife's remark about having to take in "one of Arthur's young queers." Also, like the other protagonists, he searches for freedom in an alien culture but finds only loneliness and despair. He has great sympathy for his adopted countrymen, but his inability to understand them causes his every endeavor to fail.

Themes and Meanings

The devastating forces unleashed on these expatriate protagonists constitute a powerful argument to remain securely within the folds of one's own culture. Yet the lure of freedom and justice, along with the incessant siren song of the global media—American films figure prominently in each of the stories—make expatriation as irresistible to the discontented of the world as are the sandwiches thrown by tourists in the epilogue to the Egyptian desert children.

Once a character separates himself from his native land, his destruction is inescapable. The new culture changes him so that he is emotionally unable to return to the old, and at the same time he is alienated from his fellow expatriates—even Dayo and his beloved brother are set against each other. When, instead of life-giving freedom, the expatriate finds deadening anonymity, the initiative that led him to seek a new life degenerates into anomie.

In the first two stories, which are narrated in the first person, the narrator describes his own surrender. Santosh says, "I had never been free. I had been abandoned. I was like nothing. I had made myself nothing. And I couldn't go back." The narrator of "Tell Me Who to Kill" says, "My life finish." "In a Free State" is narrated in the third person, and Bobby's defeat is rendered dramatically when the president's soldier crushes Bobby's wrist beneath his boot and ". . . he could have cried then at the clear pure pain, the knowledge of the fracture, so deliberate, the knowledge that what had been whole all his life had been broken."

Despite the diverse histories of the three protagonists, they each begin in innocence—the loss of which is symbolized by loss of physical beauty and the experience of sexual shame. Santosh's once-handsome face becomes "pudgy and sallow," and he feels dishonored by his contact with the *hubshi* woman. Dayo, who had been "so small and pretty," soon has "a labourer's face," and his brother has a wet dream that leaves him "exhausted and dirty and ashamed." Bobby is disfigured by the African soldiers and, very early in the story, publicly humiliated when a young Zulu, to whom he had made advances in a bar, spits in his face in full view of the bar's patrons.

The protagonists inevitably fail to adapt to their new culture, and the punishment for their failure—loneliness, anonymity, and paralyzing despair—is unjust because, in V. S. Naipaul's pessimistic vision, it is unavoidable. An observer can either accept the injustice, as the narrator does in the prologue, or attempt to combat it, as he does in the epilogue. That the novel concludes with a man attempting to overcome the passive acceptance of injustice suggests that the author wants to weight this possibility more heavily in the reader's imagination. Nevertheless, the overwhelming force of the novel expresses, not the efficacy of resistance, but the ubiquity of defeat.

Critical Context

V. S. Naipaul's first novels, from *The Mystic Masseur* (1957) through *A House for Mr. Biswas* (1961), are set in Trinidad, his birthplace, and are considerably more optimistic than his later work. Naipaul has spent much of his adult life in England, the scene of *Mr. Stone and the Knights Companion* (1963), but the influence of widespread travels also appears in his novels. *The Mimic Men* (1967) reveals a less-than-hopeful worldview. Yet it is not until *In a Free State*, for which he received the Booker Prize in 1971, that Naipaul reveals the depth of his pessimism about mankind and its prospects—a pessimism which continues in *Guerrillas* (1975) and *A Bend in the River* (1979).

Born Brahmin Hindu, V. S. Naipaul was born in 1932. He has lived virtually his entire life in societies which were at best indifferent to Hinduism, and all signs of religion are conspicuously absent in his protagonists. Naipaul has no obvious literary antecedents, though some scholars see the influence of Joseph Conrad in his work, an insight he may be acknowledging, though not approving, when he has Bobby say, "You've been reading too much Conrad. I hate that book [presumably *Heart of Darkness*, 1902], don't you?"

Sources for Further Study

Hammer, Robert D. *V. S. Naipaul*, 1973.

Morris, Robert K. *Paradoxes of Order: Some Perspectives on the Fiction of V. S. Naipaul*, 1975.

Theroux, Paul. *V. S. Naipaul: An Introduction to His Works*, 1972.

Thomas J. DeKornfeld

IN THE CASTLE OF MY SKIN

Author: George Lamming (1927-   )
Type of plot: Bildungsroman
Time of plot: The mid-1930's to the mid-1940's
Locale: The fictional Creighton's Village, Barbados
First published: 1953

> *Principal characters:*
> G., the narrator-protagonist, who is portrayed from his ninth
>   birthday to the eve of his leaving Barbados in his seven-
>   teenth year
> G.'s MOTHER
> PA, the oldest villager, a repository of village lore
> MA, his wife
> MR. CREIGHTON, the colonial landlord
> MR. SLIME, a teacher, labor leader, politician, and banking
>   entrepreneur, who acquires management of the land
> TRUMPER,
> BOY BLUE, and
> BOB, friends of G.
> THE SHOEMAKER, an influential villager
> MR. FOSTER, an influential villager

The Novel

Told in the first person and the third person, this is the story of G., but it is also the story of Creighton's Village as it experiences major changes ranging from the break-up of the feudal colonial plantation system with its dominating white Landlord and Great House to a new age of labor unrest, an emergent black elite, and awakening nationalism. Richard Wright's introduction to the novel notes that the work is "a symbolic repetition of the story of millions of simple folk who . . . are today being catapulted out of their peaceful, indigenously earthy lives and into the turbulence and anxiety of the twentieth century."

The four boys (G., Trumper, Boy Blue, and Bob) at the center of the tale, with their experiences and with their own tales within the larger tale, serve for the reader as keys to the community. They share their sport and contemplations, but eventually their paths diverge when G., unlike the others, after succeeding at an examination, goes on to high school, with its aura of a different class: "The High School was intended to educate the children of the clerical and professional classes, while the village school served the needs of the villagers, who were poor, simple and without a very marked sense of social prestige." At this crucial point, some go to the left and others to the right, and once parted, most of them never really meet again. Thus, G. becomes more and more of an exile, alienated from both the urban high school and the village even as he tries to keep his feet planted in both worlds.

The novel exposes some of the impositions of colonial education. In the village school, the children learn many points of English history and ceremonially observe Empire Day and the Queen's Birthday. Yet, as the shoemaker, with his commonsense punditry, points out, they are taught nothing of Africa or Marcus Garvey, nothing of their own history as black people. Ironically, Trumper discovers black kinship away from home, when he spends time, through the contract-labor system, in the United States. Barbados, "Little England," prides itself as a shadow of big England, but as events progress, the villagers are shocked into realizing that their vassal security, under the colonial banner, is washed away.

Progress brings mixed blessings to Creighton's Village. Initially, the people see Mr. Slime as a deliverer from colonial restriction. He has promised them that blacks can own the land. With an ironic twist, the Poor Man's Penny Bank and the Help Your Brother Friendly Society, enterprises built to a great extent with the people's pennies, become the new "landlord" after buying the Creighton estate. Black elite major partners of the enterprise end up evicting some of the villagers from chosen plots of land. A relative stability of the stifled feudal order is overtaken by modern uprootedness and uncertainty.

The shoemaker, Mr. Foster, and Pa have to leave their homes. Pa—the revered eldest inhabitant, something of a village griot whose dream-memory encompasses African and island experiences—is to be sent to the Alms House to await death. Much change occurs. Displacement and dispossession gnaw at the people.

G. is not forced to leave, but he feels an inner compulsion to do so. On the eve of his departure from the island, he says good-bye to his mother, Trumper, and Pa. He is unsure of his future course (the village also is unsure of its course), but he has just had a deep conversation with Trumper, who, after his experiences abroad, has "found himself" and now has a confident though limited self-assuredness. G.'s concluding words stamp a telling link of passage: "The earth where I walked was a marvel of blackness and I knew in a sense more deep than simple departure I had said farewell, farewell to the land."

The Characters

G. emerges through adolescence to the brink of manhood with uncertainties within himself and before him, but he has become an individual willing to seek himself beyond his insular environs—beyond, in his case, the incomplete village of himself and into the broader world. He seeks some domain where he may feel comfortable and secure in being and showing his natural self. All along, he has given signs of his sensitivity and distinctiveness, but he has yet to find ease of mind about himself. As he is about to depart Barbados, he muses,

> When I reach Trinidad where no one knows me I may be able to strike identity with the other person. But it was never possible here. I am always feeling terrified of being known; not because they really know you, but simply because their claim to this knowledge is a concealed attempt to destroy you, . . . and thank God that's why they can't kill you. . . . They won't know the you that's hidden somewhere in the castle of your skin.

Much earlier, the reader gets a sense of the young G.'s wish to belong when he begins to notice distancing between himself and his boyhood friends. His educational path is one reason for this distancing; another is his ambitious mother's flogging-enforced admonitions to him about "the corner and the gang." Still, "Whatever was said or done, I knew what I wanted; and that was to be a boy among the boys." For a time he was one of them, but the oncoming years show him in further exile—to the extent that he believes that he has to hide himself within himself in order to preserve himself. Yet, he hopes for liberation.

Although he is in a state of uneasiness, G. is a keen observer. The people and the landscape become vividly alive through his reminiscences, which are charged with poetic aura by language and a revealing depiction of events. G.'s boyhood friends (Trumper, Boy Blue, and Bob), like most of the characters of the novel, are depicted largely through their own words and actions. They are shown in various activities: in school, having a momentous day at the beach, peeking in on a dance at the Creighton's, being caught up in a labor-strike riot. The boys reflect on life as they see it and on the village as their unique community. On occasion, they become juvenile philosophers weighing, in their own contexts, concepts of personality, systems of morals, and questions of history and politics. Some of their accounts are spiced with humor, yet there is an underlying seriousness about the boys' concerns.

Of G.'s friends, Trumper undergoes the most profound change. Boy Blue and Bob become members of the police force, but ironically Trumper becomes a member of a larger group: "the Negro race." He now has a focal center which gives him some comfort of identity. After working in the United States, in which he witnessed blatant racism and stalwart opposition to it, he says, "If there be one thing I thank America for, she teach me who my race wus. Now I'm never goin' to lose it. Never never." Trumper has new, astonishing assurance. He is no longer a shadowlike "Little Englander"; rather, his sense of himself now has firm direction. Once he said, in self-appeasing comfort, "Nothin'll ever change in the village"; now he has undergone a sea change.

Pa and Ma, the elderly couple who appear periodically, serve as a type of chorus in the novel. Through their dialogue (and later through Pa's musings after Ma has died), the reader gets an overview of the happenings in the village, including some historical reckoning of the passage of time. Pa's eventual displacement from his rented plot and his being sent to the Alms House are indeed sobering signs of change in the once stable society. Pa, the repository of village lore, is himself deposited in a moldy corner.

The other characters are woven meaningfully into the tapestry of the village, although some of them stand out in greater relief. There are the shoemaker and Mr. Foster, two commonsense men, informal village leaders, who also suffer the tremors of change. The shoemaker has taken some pride in Mr. Slime's nationalist advances, but Mr. Slime's black elite cronies, after buying out Mr. Creighton, evict the shoemaker from his plot. Mr. Foster, who once refused to abandon his house as a flood washed it away, now is forced to relocate.

G.'s mother's name is never revealed, but her persistent presence asserts itself, especially in the opening and closing sections of the novel. In the apparent absence of G.'s father (who never appears), she goads her son to achieve. She does not hesitate to flog him, to "roast his tail," but she also gushes into laughter with him as her affection at times bursts forth through her stern demeanor. As G. prepares to leave home, she dutifully warns him of the evils lurking out there in the world, but she is also resigned to and even supportive of his decision.

Lamming inobtrusively weaves in another character, or force: the Creighton family. Mr. Creighton and his family are prime representatives of the old colonial order which is changing as nationalist forces rise. Ma sees the Creightons, ruling from their Great House on the hill, as benevolent masters of the society. Pa sees the forces represented by Mr. Slime as righteous contenders for the Creightons' dominion. At a turning point of power, Mr. Creighton sells the land to Mr. Slime's consortium, but Mr. and Mrs. Creighton maintain a faded presence in the area by retaining their hilltop Great House.

An important character is the village itself. Lamming allows the village as an entity to tell its story through the actions and accounts of the inhabitants. Events of the times change its countenance over the years.

Themes and Meanings

Near the end of the novel, as G. and Pa are saying farewell to each other, Pa notes, "We both settin' forth tomorrow. . . . I to my last restin'-place, an' you into the wide wide world." G.'s leaving for his teaching job in Trinidad and Pa's entering the Alms House dramatically illustrate parting and change. Nurtured in part by Pa, G. now embarks on his own quest for meaning. At various times, G. is struck with the sad sensation that he is seeing "the last of something," and this feeling culminates in the ending scene with Pa. A focus on change is a feature of the novel, painful change suffered by displaced villagers and their world and apprehensive change affecting G. as the growth of his self-awareness within the insular community deepens his exile and alienation.

Another theme emerges from contrasting G.'s sense of himself as a "castle" protecting his inner self with other concepts of "castle" in the novel. Mr. Creighton's castle on the hill, for example, defines to some extent the social order over which it dominates—though its authority is succeeded by Mr. Slime's consortium. G.'s awakening artistic consciousness fashions an alternate central "castle" of definition which gives preserving autonomy. His perch is one of loneliness for the moment, but his situation gives him the opportunity to delineate himself, to view the outside world, and to try to become a conscientious relater of meaning. It is in relating to others that his life will assume real meaning.

Several of the villagers, with Pa as the chief example, are displaced, evicted from their familiar but tenuous groundings; for the time being, G. has refuge in the expedient and firmer "castle" of himself, from which he may be able to sally forth with confidence.

Critical Context

Lamming himself has noted that *In the Castle of My Skin*, his first novel, is a key book in the literature of the English Caribbean. He thinks that its universal appeal is based on some connecting link between the readers' experience and that of the novel, since everybody ("or nearly everybody," Lamming says) has a childhood and an adolescence.

One notion of Lamming's work (also echoed by the author) is that all of his fiction constitutes a single, slowly unfolding story. In such a scheme, *In the Castle of My Skin* would appear first, with its focus on the growing-up phase, the first steps of a journey taken to seek fulfillment. The realization of the world seen through the boys in this work is followed in subsequent works by the wider experiences of characters in search of their own significance: in England as emigrants; in the independence-era Caribbean; in modern London; in a myth-hazed seventeenth century reverie in *Natives of My Person* (1972), in which the journey toward completion of self goes forward by making a complete return to the beginnings of "new world" experience linking Africans, Indians, and Europeans.

Sources for Further Study

Gilkes, Michael. *The West Indian Novel*, 1981.
Ngugi, James. *Homecoming: Essays on African and Caribbean Literature, Culture and Politics*, 1972.
Paquet, Sandra Pouchet. *The Novels of George Lamming*, 1982.

James H. Randall

IN THE TIME OF GREENBLOOM

Author: Gabriel Fielding (Alan Gabriel Barnsley, 1916-1986)
Type of plot: Psychological realism
Time of plot: The late 1930's
Locale: Predominantly England, sometimes Ireland and Wales
First published: 1956

Principal characters:
>JOHN BLAYDON, a boarding-school student
>VICTORIA BLOUNT, John's platonic love
>MELANIE BLAYDON, John's younger sister
>EDWARD BLAYDON, John's father, a Church of England
>minister
>KITTY BLAYDON, John's mother
>ENID BLOUNT, Victoria's mother
>GEORGE HARKNESS, a country landholder, Enid's lover
>MARSTON, classmate of John at the Abbey school
>DAVID BLAYDON, John's eldest brother, an Anglican minister
>MICHAEL BLAYDON, John's next older brother, a university
>student
>HORAB GREENBLOOM, a student at Balliol College, Oxford,
>later a private book publisher
>GILBERT VICTOR, headmaster at Rooker's Close
>JANUS "JANE" BOSCAWEN-JONES, a poet, Greenbloom's
>newest discovery
>LADY GERALDINE BODORGAN, the local chatelaine at Porth
>Newydd, Wales
>DYMPHNA UPRICHARD, an Irish schoolgirl, a houseguest of the
>Bodorgans

The Novel

John Blaydon notices Victoria Blount at a lawn party at the home of a neighbor, Mrs. Bellingham. Victoria is thirteen years old; he is slightly younger. Victoria remarks that they are so much alike that John might have been her brother. John, hopelessly infatuated, suggests that they slip away from the others. They go out by the lake to "see the swans," but Victoria insists that they go for a swim, even though they both have no bathing suits. When they plunge into the water naked, John realizes that he loves her, that "he would always love her; even when he was old enough to love people he would love her and go on loving her for ever—."

Suddenly, John hears her cry for help. He swims to where she was and desperately searches for her underwater; finally locating her white body, he pulls her to the shore, just as his sister Melanie and Tim, another guest, arrive on the scene, having come to look for him. John and Tim drag Victoria to higher ground, where John, sitting astride Victoria's unconscious body, proceeds to administer artificial respiration. While he is reviving the unfortunate girl, Mrs. Bellingham appears and immediately assumes that the adolescents have been engaging in sex. Fearing a scandal, however, she wants to keep the matter quiet.

When John and his sister return home, Melanie tells her mother everything. Mrs. Blaydon is outraged and interrogates John. She becomes convinced that intercourse did not take place, but she still finds the situation reprehensible, believing that her son's looking at Victoria's nakedness was bad enough. John explains that he saw Victoria without clothes but did not look at her. "If other people want to turn seeing into looking it's they who are wrong not me, isn't it?" he asks. Mrs. Blaydon has no answer. She leaves her son with feelings of guilt.

Back at his private boarding school, John cannot get Victoria from his mind. In order to see her again, he has asked his brother David to invite her to his wedding. John is overjoyed when he receives a letter from her, telling him that she accepts. John is also emotionally involved with Marston, another boy at his school, though Marston frequently makes fun of him. One night, however, Marston climbs into John's bed and begins to caress and kiss him. John struggles to free himself from Marston's grip and makes a commotion, which attracts the attention of the master, who has the boys put on boxing gloves to resolve their differences. The headmaster defers further punishment, allowing John to go to London to attend his brother's wedding.

John meets Victoria again but is anxious lest his mother embarrass her by making some sort of scene, as Mrs. Blaydon obviously does not like the mother of David's bride. Yet Mrs. Blaydon's antipathies do not prevent her establishing cordial relations with Victoria, and Mrs. Blaydon gives her consent for John to spend part of his holidays with Victoria and Victoria's mother.

The visit takes place at Danbey Dale, where George Harkness, a friend of Victoria's mother, has a farm. The two young people are left to themselves, and they arrange a picnic excursion to visit a nearby cave. When they reach one of the caverns, John makes a fire by which they will have their lunch. The sound of whistling, however, alerts them to the fact that they are not alone. A blond man, who had earlier spoken to Victoria, has followed them here. His presence makes the two young people uncomfortable, yet they still accept a ride from him back to the farm. When they arrive, Victoria realizes that she had failed to mail a letter of her mother's, and she accepts the stranger's offer to drive her to the post office.

When she fails to return home, the police are called. At first, they suspect that John had something to do with the girl's disappearance. Their investigation eventually takes them to the cave, where, not far from where John and Victoria built their fire, they discover Victoria's body.

Two years pass after the murder. John is still traumatized by the incident, especially since people will not allow him to lay it to rest. He is now enrolled in a different boarding school, Beowulf's, where he is known as the boy of the Danbey Dale Tragedy. The other students treat him as somewhat of an oddity; the headmaster would like John to leave and go to school somewhere else. John's isolation brings him closer to his brother Michael, who is a student nearby at Oxford. Michael is imposing on the generosity of a rich classmate, Horab Greenbloom, to whom he introduces John.

Greenbloom is Jewish, is immensely wealthy, has an artificial leg, and is impulsive. He seems to have an answer for everything, being particularly fond of quoting the philosopher Ludwig Wittgenstein, about whom he is supposedly writing a book. Greenbloom takes an instant liking to young Blaydon and proposes that they drive to London in his Bentley to go to the theater. He makes arrangements through his girlfriend Rachel, who lives there. The ever-restless Greenbloom finds the play boring and predictable, however, and is only too glad to leave before the end to return John to the boarding school to meet his curfew. Yet Greenbloom soon has a better idea: He will fly John and Rachel in his Dehavilland Moth to Paris. Michael is informed only after the boy is deposited in front of his residence at Oxford.

The trip to Paris is a fiasco. Greenbloom has no sense of direction and lands the plane in Ireland. Rachel is tolerant of such unpredictable behavior, but she tells John that he should go back to England by himself. John returns by ferryboat, but the whole escapade gets him dismissed from Beowulf's.

He is now enrolled at Rooker's Close, a private school for problem boys, where, to protect him from his past, he is known as Bowden. John, however, is still a loner and likes to spend his free time by himself. One afternoon, on the beach at the nearby resort of Worthing, he encounters the man who killed Victoria, recognizing him by the same whistled notes he heard in the cave. When John accosts him, the man tells him that he is crazy and manages to get away. Later that day at confession, John tells Father Delaura about the meeting, but the priest believes that John is mentally ill and so informs the headmaster of Rooker's Close. The headmaster takes John more seriously but does not want him to go to the police, because the headmaster fears that disclosure would engender bad publicity. Furthermore, he tells John that Rooker's Close may not be the most suitable place for him after all.

Two more years pass. John is now eighteen and attending a county school in Wales, where his parents live. He has just taken his final exams but fears that he might have failed. Greenbloom has drifted back into his life, having lived for the past several years in Paris. Greenbloom is vacationing in Angelsey with his protégé, an undiscovered poet named Janus Boscawen-Jones. Greenbloom is as opinionated as ever, now having abandoned Wittgenstein in favor of Jean-Paul Sartre, whom he claims to know personally. When Greenbloom discovers that John is depressed to the point of suicide, he offers to help him accomplish it.

Greenbloom, once responsible for providing John with so much reassurance, no longer has the influence over John he once had. John is now attracted to Dymphna Uprichard, whom he meets at the home of a local aristocrat. Dymphna resembles Victoria. John discovers that she intends to study at Trinity College in Dublin, where he himself wants to go. John appears to have worked through his sorrow, and he wants Greenbloom to know, but Greenbloom is ready to depart again from John's life.

The Characters

John's attempt to purge himself of guilt for the death of Victoria is constantly frustrated by an unfeeling and indifferent world. Most of the novel's characters hate children, especially the headmasters of the schools John attends. These educators, the black legend of Mr. Chips, are different from their Dickensian counterparts only in their preference for psychological, rather than physical, birching. Most of the other characters are similarly unsympathetic, being preoccupied with maintaining appearances and consistently indifferent to anything outside themselves.

John's mother, a source of authority and respect, is distant and threatening, believing that problems find their proper solution through a faith in God, an attitude that has little relevance to her son. John's only described encounter with the Anglican clergy—other than his relations with his minister father—ends disastrously. Father Delaura's lack of understanding and his hostility convinces John that it is impossible to achieve solace through the Anglican faith; "crossing himself for the last time," he hurries out of the church.

The sole person who seems to be interested in him is Greenbloom, an enticing neurotic with so much money he can pass as eccentric. Greenbloom, though, is as self-centered as everyone else, albeit more amusing and friendly. He convinces John that he is genuinely concerned about him. Consequently, in John's eyes, Greenbloom can do no wrong. Yet Greenbloom's irresponsibility—driving his Bentley at breakneck speeds, landing in Ireland instead of France, pretentious quoting from philosophers he does not understand—could only be genuinely tolerated by the likes of a lonely thirteen-year-old. Others can also overlook Greenbloom's demerits, but many of these are spongers who are attracted by his money. Even John's mother is after him to finance the construction of a rood screen in her husband's church.

For John to come of age, he must become independent of both his family and Greenbloom. When he is eighteen, he finally comes to the realization that he is disgusted with the entire adult value system, "if it were anything at all." He might apply the realization to himself, for it is difficult to make such an anxiety-ridden teenager appealing, no matter how many precocious things he has to say. John's rootlessness, his being bounced from one boarding school to another and the Weltschmerz following the death of Victoria, are reasons for pity, but not necessarily for concern. After years of searching and uncertainty, John finally manages to achieve a sense of worth. He bids an ambiguous *adieu* to adolescence, realizing that henceforth he can only count on himself, but at the same time rejoicing in the prospect of a new love to end his heartache. With such an ambivalent character, it is doubtful whether there can be success.

Themes and Meanings

Gabriel Fielding intended to depict love in all of its various directions, vagaries, and periods of life: love from childhood through adolescence and marriage, parental love, illicit love, sacred love, profane love. *In the Time of Greenbloom* falls short of this goal, but it covers much territory. In describing John Blaydon's trials and tribulations, Fielding includes a wide range of human experience. (He even manages to juxtapose two kinds of lust, as when John intrudes on the lovemaking of Victoria's mother and George Harkness at about the same time that Victoria is being raped and throttled.) John represents the honesty and innocence of youth versus the less-than-pure world of adults. It is obviously not wise to trust anyone over thirty and, judging from John's relationships with his fellow schoolmates, even those less advanced in years.

The protagonist's attempt to find meaning and understanding is handled episodically. The book skips from one scene to another, each possessing its own integrity, almost like a short story, albeit linked in the great chain of being which is John's life from late childhood to early manhood.

Victoria's death crushes him with prolonged guilt. "Can you tell me," he asks,

> why I feel that I ought to be forgiven for something I never did? Why do I keep thinking about it all the time? Why have I felt different since it happened? Was it wrong of me to love her? Is that why I go on and on like this? Will I never be the same again? Happy like other people?

Father Delaura replies, "These are difficult questions."

John cannot count on others to give him answers, and he becomes increasingly aware that they never will: "No one could ever effectively love or hate anyone else no matter how much they knew, no matter how great their love or their hatred might be, simply because everybody was fundamentally alone." Apparently, the final realization of Candide is still valid: It is necessary to cultivate one's own garden.

Critical Context

In the Time of Greenbloom, Fielding's second novel, is one of several to deal with the affairs of the Blaydon family. Its predecessor, *Brotherly Love* (1954), centers on the trauma John endures when his older brother David, whom he idolizes, has sex with a girl to whom John has become attached. Understandably, John thinks rather less highly of David than before. *Brotherly Love* was regarded as a promising first attempt. The critics were more effusive in their reception of *In the Time of Greenbloom*, some calling it "strikingly original," "expert at juxtaposing the bizarre and the grotesque," "surprising and delightful as a four-leaf clover in a bed of green carnations." Not all the praise was unqualified; the book was also judged confusing, the vision obsessive.

Although some of his later novels have been well received, *In the Time of Greenbloom* is widely regarded as Fielding's finest book. Fielding, at the time of its publication a physician practicing in southeast England, was so encouraged by the success of the book that he devoted less time to his medical profession and more to his writing. Eventually, he gave up the practice of medicine altogether, emigrating to the United States, where he combined a writing career with that of a university professor. In this early work, he established the major themes that have marked his later novels: man's relationship to God, his inherent weakness and fallibility, his moral shortcomings and feelings of guilt. Fielding, whose first published works were poetry, infuses his writing with a great lyrical style, but often there is a fine line between vitality and pomposity.

Sources for Further Study

Borello, Alfred. *Gabriel Fielding*, 1974.

Cavallo, Evelyn. "Gabriel Fielding: A Portrait," in *The Critic*. XIX (December, 1960/January, 1961), p. 19.

Havighurst, Walter. Review in *Saturday Review*. XL (June 29, 1957), p. 11.

Hogart, Patricia. Review in *Manchester Guardian*. June 19, 1956, p. 4.

Mallet, Isabelle. Review in *The New York Times Book Review*. June 23, 1957, p. 21.

The New Yorker. Review. XXXIII (June 29, 1957), p. 85.

Wm. Laird Kleine-Ahlbrandt

THE INIMITABLE JEEVES

Author: P. G. Wodehouse (1881-1975)
Type of plot: Farce
Time of plot: The early 1920's
Locale: London, Hampshire, Gloucestershire, Roville-sur-mer (France), and New York City
First published: 1923

> *Principal characters:*
> BERTIE WOOSTER, an indolent, wealthy young Londoner
> JEEVES, his valet
> RICHARD (BINGO) LITTLE, Bertie's longtime friend
> AGATHA GREGSON, Bertie's fearsome aunt
> HONORIA GLOSSOP, Aunt Agatha's choice as Bertie's wife
> SIR RODERICK GLOSSOP, Honoria's father, a psychiatrist
> CLAUDE and
> EUSTACE, Bertie's twin cousins
> MORTIMER, LORD BITTLESHAM, Bingo's uncle and the source of his income
> ROSIE M. BANKS, the author of popular sentimental novels who becomes Bingo's wife

The Novel

Bertie Wooster's friend Richard "Bingo" Little is forever falling in love with a wide variety of women, and it is up to Bertie, with the aid of Jeeves, his valet, to promote or prevent these romances, depending on the suitability of the young lady. At the beginning of *The Inimitable Jeeves*, Bingo is infatuated with a waitress and wants Bertie to make his Uncle Mortimer, the source of his income, receptive to the idea. Jeeves suggests having Bingo read the uncle such Rosie M. Banks novels as *Only a Factory Girl*, in which "marriage with young persons of an inferior social status" is advocated. Bertie has to pretend that he writes the Banks novels to encourage Uncle Mortimer further. These machinations result in the uncle marrying his cook, previously Jeeves's intended. Jeeves has been plotting for this eventuality since becoming friendly with the waitress Bingo loves.

Bingo next falls for Honoria Glossop, but Bertie's domineering Aunt Agatha wants her nephew to marry Honoria. Deciding to get out of this jam without Jeeves's help, Bertie pushes Honoria's young brother into a pond so that Bingo can save the boy and be a hero in his beloved's eyes, but on his way to the pond, fickle Bingo discovers someone else. Bertie finds himself engaged to Honoria, who says that he must get rid of Jeeves. The valet conspires with Claude and Eustace, Bertie's prankster twin cousins, to convince

Honoria's father, Sir Roderick, a prominent psychiatrist, that Bertie is crazy.

Bingo dons a false beard and pretends to be a revolutionary to win the heart of gold-toothed Charlotte Corday Rowbotham. In the guise of an anarchist, he threatens the life of Uncle Mortimer, now Lord Bittlesham, to obtain fifty pounds to bet on his uncle's racehorse. Jeeves rescues Bingo from the unappetizing Charlotte by revealing Bingo's true identity to his rival for the lady's affections, Comrade Butt.

At Twing in Gloucestershire, Bertie, Jeeves, Bingo, Claude, and Eustace become involved in the Great Sermon Handicap, betting on which of the local clergymen preaches the longest on a specific Sunday. All but Jeeves, who backs a long shot, lose heavily. They next wager on the village school games, only to have their contenders sabotaged by a gambling acquaintance, the cunning Steggles. Jeeves proves more cunning by fixing it for the last of the group's favorites to win.

When Bingo finds a new love, Steggles accepts bets on the affair with the odds on Bingo's rival. At first outraged, Bingo bets on himself. He then takes charge of the village school's Christmas entertainment to prove himself worthy of the lady, but Steggles, with help from Bingo's own incompetence, turns the festivities into a riot. Jeeves is pleased, however, having bet on Bingo's opponent.

Finally, Bingo is in love with another waitress, and Bertie again has to pretend to be Rosie M. Banks. The waitress forces Bingo to marry her without his uncle's consent and when presented to Lord Bittlesham reveals herself to be the real Rosie M. Banks, having been working as a waitress as research for her next book. Jeeves persuades Bingo to explain it all to his uncle by saying that Bertie is "subject to hallucinations and generally potty." Deeply offended, Bertie decides to fire his valet, only to weaken in the face of Jeeves's superiority.

Woven among the Bingo episodes are three other adventures. On the French Riviera, Aunt Agatha wants Bertie to marry the sister of a Dorsetshire curate, but Jeeves exposes the pair as con artists and recovers Agatha's stolen pearls. In New York, Jeeves saves Cyril Bassington-Bassington from a career on the stage to spare Bertie more of Aunt Agatha's wrath. When Claude and Eustace are sent down from Oxford for spraying the senior tutor with soda water, Agatha arranges for them to go to South Africa, but both fall in love with the same actress and refuse to depart until Jeeves tricks them into going.

The Characters

Jeeves is the epitome of the tradition of brilliant servants to foolish masters which goes back to classical Latin and Greek literature. Jeeves displays the most perfect mind in fiction, superior even to that of Sherlock Holmes. As Bertie observes, "Jeeves knows. How, I couldn't say, but he knows."

Jeeves is not simply superbly intelligent; for P. G. Wodehouse's plots to work, the valet must have sources of information denied the other characters. He is always the only one to know what is truly happening. Unlike Holmes, Jeeves resorts to lying and bribery to achieve his ends. He is everything the perpetually naïve Bertie is not.

Bertie is upset when he overhears Jeeves describe him as "an exceedingly pleasant and amiable young gentleman, but not intelligent. . . . Mentally he is negligible—quite negligible." Bertie, however, is intelligent enough to rely on Jeeves's judgment in most matters, considering his servant "a sort of guide, philosopher, and friend." He possesses remarkable self-knowledge for such a ninny, agreeing with those who "look on me as rather an ass."

Despite all this, Bertie is an admirable character. Much of his behavior derives from a strict code of conduct, and while this code is that of the privileged late Victorian schoolboy, it allows him to be modest, gracious, and magnanimous. He is unfailingly willing to devote his time and money to assist his friends. Whenever he is hesitant about helping Bingo out of a scrape, all his friend has to do is remind him that they were at school together for Bertie to spring into action. He has perhaps been described best by George Orwell as a "sluggish Don Quixote"; he does not look for windmills but never declines to tilt at them when honor demands.

If Jeeves is Sherlock Holmes and Bertie his Dr. Watson, faithfully recounting all of their escapades, Agatha is Professor Moriarty, always popping up to bring new difficulties into her nephew's life. To Bertie, "she's a sort of human vampire-bat." Even worse, "She's the kind of woman who comes and rags you before breakfast." Aunt Agatha is not simply imposing in herself; she is constantly finding younger versions of herself, such as Honoria Glossop, to force upon Bertie: women who want to reform him, to improve his mind, to keep him from sleeping past noon and betting on horses.

All the other characters in *The Inimitable Jeeves* are the stock figures associated with this type of comedy. They are necessary primarily to create conflict and advance the plot and are rarely more than one-dimensional.

Themes and Meanings

A frequent criticism of Wodehouse's post–World War II fiction is that he continues to write about characters and situations from the 1920's. Other critics say that this objection is incorrect, that even in the 1920's Wodehouse was re-creating an anachronistic milieu: Since he did not live in England after 1914, he was always drawing on the Great Britain of his childhood. Even this interpretation is wrong, since the universe of indolent Bertie Wooster probably never existed anywhere but in Wodehouse's imagination.

The triumph of the Jeeves stories and novels is Wodehouse's ability to maintain a self-contained fantasy world. Wodehouse cowrote several successful musical comedies, and it is this theatrical environment which dominates his fiction. In the writer's own words, he is "making the thing a sort of musical comedy without music, and ignoring real life altogether." When Bertie says, "you would recognize the tune if I hummed it," the reader senses how appropriate it would be for the narrator suddenly to burst into song. The charm of Wodehouse's fiction is that it has so little to do with real life.

The main factor in making this musical-comedy universe without music come alive is Wodehouse's distinctive use of language. His combination of unusual metaphors, unexpected images, and twisted clichés results in a style of comedy unlike that of any other writer. The following exchange between Bertie and Jeeves epitomizes this brand of inspired silliness:

"In the spring, Jeeves, a livelier iris gleams upon the burnished dove."
"So I have been informed, sir."
"Right ho! Then bring me my whangee, my yellowest shoes, and the old green Homburg. I'm going into the Park to do pastoral dances."

The Inimitable Jeeves abounds in examples of Wodehouse's humor at its best. When Bertie reveals how Aunt Agatha has been duped by the con artists, her demeanor becomes "rather like that of one who, picking daisies on the railway, has just caught the down express in the small of the back." When Bertie asks for a pair of purple socks of which Jeeves strongly disapproves, the valet takes "them out of the drawer as if he were a vegetarian fishing a caterpillar out of the salad." When Cyril Bassington-Bassington is insulted, he begins "to get pink in the ears, and then in the nose, and then in the cheeks, till in about a quarter of a minute he looked pretty much like an explosion in a tomato cannery on a sunset evening."

Critical Context

The first Bertie and Jeeves book is *My Man Jeeves* (1919), which includes four Jeeves stories told by Bertie. *The Inimitable Jeeves* is thus the first book completely about these characters. In it, Wodehouse weaves eleven previously published stories together into a mostly unified narrative with the story of Bingo's marriage to Rosie bringing many of the various elements together. The first true novel in the series is *Thank You, Jeeves* (1934).

The Inimitable Jeeves introduces the pattern of Bertie getting into trouble, Jeeves getting him out, and the master then having to sacrifice an article of clothing the valet finds offensive: purple socks, loud cummerbund, spats in Old Etonian colors. Some other conventional elements used include Aunt Agatha's efforts to have Bertie wed, only for him to escape narrowly, and Sir Roderick Glossop's conviction that Bertie is mad. Bingo and Rosie Little appear in other works, as does Honoria Glossop. One unique feature in this novel is Jeeves's attachments to the opposite sex.

Wodehouse's fiction grows out of the English comic tradition of William

Shakespeare, Ben Jonson, the Restoration dramatists, Charles Dickens, Oscar Wilde, and Saki. Most twentieth century literary comedians writing in English owe some debt to Wodehouse: Evelyn Waugh, Anthony Powell, Kingsley Amis, and Tom Sharpe in particular. Yet no one approaches humor exactly as Wodehouse does, and *The Inimitable Jeeves* is characteristic of the best of this distinctive style.

Sources for Further Study
Donaldson, Frances. *P. G. Wodehouse: A Biography*, 1982.
Hall, Robert A., Jr. *The Comic Style of P. G. Wodehouse*, 1974.
Morris, J. H. C., and A. D. MacIntyre. *Thank You, Wodehouse*, 1981.
Voorhees, Richard J. *P. G. Wodehouse*, 1966.

Michael Adams

AN INSULAR POSSESSION

Author: Timothy Mo (1953-   )
Type of plot: Historical satire
Time of plot: The early 1830's and 1840's, including the outbreak of the Opium
    War and Great Britain's colonization of Hong Kong
Locale: Canton, the Macao Peninsula, Lin Tin Island, and Hong Kong
First published: 1986

> *Principal characters:*
> GIDEON CHASE, the protagonist, an American clerk and
>   eventually a scholar of the Chinese language
> WALTER EASTMAN, his mentor and colleague, a part-time
>   journalist and painter
> ALICE REMINGTON, Eastman's romantic interest, the niece of
>   an American company senior partner
> HARRY O'ROURKE, a drunken British painter and an elder
>   friend of Eastman and Chase
> FATHER JOAQUIM RIBEIRO, a confidant and tutor of Chase
> PEDRO REMEDIOS, a pirate adventurer and collaborator in
>   Chase's journalistic investigations

The Novel

Presiding over the southern China trading world of *An Insular Possession* is the mighty British Empire, a rigid and notorious taskmaster of the native Chinese. In the century previous to the time of the novel, the Chinese wielded a precarious upper hand over the British: The empire's gluttonous demand for tea indebted it to these chief suppliers of the commodity, and it paid in pounds of silver. The solution to Great Britain's damaged economy lay in creating a viable trading commodity. The Empire turned to its largest colony, India, sent its laborers into the poppy fields and, subsequently, by increments and stealth induced in the Chinese an opium addiction that surpassed even the British taste for tea. In short order, England found itself not only breaking even on the trade but also filching enough silver from the Chinese to operate the government in India. As the novel begins, however, the trading network is in another stage of transition. The native bristles under the heavy hand of the foreigner, yet must be fed by it; the foreigner tightens the grip on his vicious monopoly before it dissipates.

The struggle for dominance embroils combatants and bystanders alike, most notably the American traders of the Meridian Company in Canton. Yet in the midst of the turmoil, the Americans declare their own innocence and even a higher calling. Trading precious silver for innocuous silks and porcelain, they disdain the illicit opium trade and pride themselves as harbingers of culture bent on drawing China into the greater world of civilized nations. The bravado—and the sanctimony—of this upstart country is epitomized by Walter Eastman, a brash twenty-four-year-old senior clerk and dilettante painter, and Gideon Chase, a junior clerk of seventeen and willing protégé of his idol, Eastman. While the Chinese suffer, Eastman and Chase pass idle days drinking fine bottles of claret and amusing themselves with a production of Richard Brinsley Sheridan's *The Rivals* (1775) on the neighboring peninsula of Macao, the social mecca where wives and children are comfortably billeted. Their weighty culture is never wasted on the Chinese, and their concern for the natives is, similarly, a passive, intellectual fancy.

The irony of the Americans' arrogance is emphasized when the Meridian senior partners find their own company in financial straits and resort themselves to the opium trade. Although apparently outraged, Eastman and Chase remain at their posts. Eastman, having secretly won the heart of Alice Remington, the niece of a Meridian senior partner, will not jeopardize his romance with an impassioned resignation; Chase refuses to abandon his colleague and mentor. When Eastman's affair is discovered, however, his employer dismisses him on the grounds of insufficient means. Only the climax of the novel, the outbreak of the Opium War, can cover Eastman's disgrace. At the urging of Chase, he starts a newspaper to rival the pro-British *Canton Monitor*, cleverly turning his humiliating dismissal into a bold, principled gesture in support of the exploited Chinese.

As publishers of *The Lin Tin Bulletin and River Bee*, Eastman and Chase reach a new height of moral indignation, documenting the war while it teeters between cautious strikes by the Chinese (the destruction of a cache of opium on Lin Tin Island) and decimating victories for the British (the obliteration of entire landscapes by the ironside steamer *Nemesis*). The war marks a crucial division in the relationship of Eastman and Chase: Although both men recognize their previous hypocrisies and their tacit sanction of a trading network founded on "enrichment (for the few) and enslavement and degradation (for the many)," Eastman, as writer, remains segregated from the Chinese, while Chase, as investigator, nurtures a growing empathy with them. With aplomb, then, Eastman attacks the savage British exploits but derives, in truth, more pleasure from the insults bandied between himself and the conservative editor of the *Canton Monitor*, a verbal repartee that leads ultimately to a duel with pistols not unlike the climactic scenes of *The Rivals*. Chase, on the other hand, witnesses among other atrocities the degrading rape of two Chinese women by a band of Indian soldiers and, under the guidance and tutelage of friends Harry O'Rourke and Father Joaquim Ribeiro, begins to study the complexities and guarded secrets of the Chinese language. It is this latter, supreme effort which finally distinguishes Chase, for in their language he finds the soul of the Chinese people, that "insular possession" which may not be traded or crippled by the foreigner.

The end of the Opium War draws the conflict of nations to another temporary peace. The Chinese are partly compromised from within by an emperor himself profiting on the opium trade, yet they succeed in pushing the British a step farther downstream to Hong Kong Island. Through gratuitous violence, the British, for their part, prove their conceit that might makes right and satisfy themselves with fortifying the new island possession. Eastman and Chase, in contrast, may no longer coexist. The ostensible purpose of their newspaper—eliminating the opium trade—is abandoned in the new tide of blind conservatism, and with it the ostensible relationship of mentor and protégé must be relinquished as well. By the end of the novel, the static, perennially superficial Eastman is easily surpassed by Chase, the true protagonist, whose newfound possessions combine sharp intellect with probing sensitivity. Two such disparate men will naturally part company as will, it seems, two such incompatible nations.

The Characters

If the comic irony of *An Insular Possession* precludes identifying with Timothy Mo's characters, they are nevertheless fascinating for their intellectual prowess and dramatic flair. Most subtle among them is certainly Walter Eastman. In a moment conniving to charm the socialite Alice Remington, directing a cast of temperamental amateur actors, eliciting the pity of staunch British patriots for the beleaguered Chinese, disparaging his journalistic rival with the most artful gibes, and perceptively arguing the merits of Impressionist art even while developing techniques of the new daguerreotype, he is an imposing intelligence—detached, perhaps so versatile as to be spread too thin, but a master showman. His diversity is appropriately conveyed through a variety of stylistic devices: The narrative is eclipsed by theatrical script, newspaper extracts, letters, and diary entries that illustrate Eastman's felicity in assuming a persona to suit any occasion. Ultimately, however, his stagecraft is not meant to be deceptive but defensive. His nose somewhat eaten away by smallpox, his pate balding, he is reputed to be the ugliest man in Canton. If he is, then, conceived by Mo as essentially comic, it is because he wishes his compatriots to perceive him as such. Lacking the commodity of beauty, he trades on his wit.

Gideon Chase, however, emerges from the novel more fully realized and empathetic. With both his parents deceased, he arrives in Canton for the second time, hoping to secure a position with the American trading company. When the slightly older Eastman takes a patronizing interest, he latches on to the surrogate father, eager to learn from him, willing to defer to him in all matters. Typically, Eastman leads Chase through the labyrinth of fine wines, offers the boy his first cheroot, teaches him the conventions of love, and imbues in him a heady respect for the Chinese. Yet Chase's coming of age eventually shapes the novel. When Eastman finds himself dismally unemployed,

Chase rescues him with the inspiration of *The Lin Tin Bulletin and River Bee*, even providing a salvaged printing press. When Eastman's editorializing draws near pomposity, Chase reprimands him. Step by step, Chase's naïveté and humility evolve into a compassionate authority, precisely because he enters the foreign world as a child. The Chinese language, a matter of indifference to the didactic Eastman, is inherited by Chase as by all infants of the culture and hence becomes the perfect metaphor for his growth. By the novel's end, Chase chooses for his parent not Eastman but China herself.

Acting as a buffer for the Americans is the sixty-two-year-old Briton Harry O'Rourke. For the most part dispensable to the plot, he becomes an often wise though curmudgeonly sounding board for the two young anarchists. He has seen enough of the world in India and China to appreciate and even encourage their idealistic assaults; as a legitimate artist brilliant with impressionist landscapes, he inspires their creativity. Yet O'Rourke's character, in the last analysis, is a contrivance, an opportunity for Mo to comment on British despotism. Thrasonical, drunken, cowardly, O'Rourke fled responsibilities to family and debtors in India to live parasitically among the Chinese. Capable of manipulating landscapes into art, he fails miserably with portraits, which require empathy with the subject. He is, finally, the archetypal Briton, capable of dispassionately molding a foreign landscape to fit his vision, but eventually despoiling it for the natives and deserting the travesty once its usefulness has passed.

In a similar vein, Mo's minor characters often remain loose threads in the fabric of the novel yet testify to his comic invective. Alice Remington, once the central love interest, vanishes from the pages after spurning Eastman, but her letters wryly accent the irony of her life in Macao: Following lengthy passages devoted to plays, parties, and romantic interludes, a postscript briefly announces the start of the Opium War. The free trader and part-time corsair Pedro Remedios, usefully employed by the British during the Opium War, is convicted and executed by order of the magistrate for the pirating which in war had been a service but in peace became a crime. Finally, the kindly Jesuit priest Ribeiro, sympathetic to the Chinese, takes his exercise in the form of painstakingly rolling boulders up and down the seashore; his Sisyphean efforts, it seems, embody the only righteous plan of action for the moral man: to persevere.

Themes and Meanings

The central theme of *An Insular Possession* is captured in the description of the southern China trading route, the Macao Roads, which begins the novel. Lifeline of the region, "the river succours and impedes native and foreigner alike; it limits and it enables, it isolates and it joins." The paradoxes of the river reflect its unpredictability: Passages once unobstructed are, suddenly, impeded by boulders and sand bars; into the firm margin of the mainland, peninsulas are carved overnight and later break away to form islands; the navigable, single river becomes many rivers, unchartered. Like its waterway, Canton, too, passes swiftly through stages of transition: Once a home to Muslims, it was invaded by the current natives, only subsequently to be seized by the British and again reprised by the Chinese. Both trading route and trading town suggest that reality itself, far from a fixed, objective fact, is a mutable entity, a panorama in constant flux.

The novelist and his characters strive, therefore, to determine the most reliable, accurate means of interpreting their fickle world. Following a successfully vanquished insurrection in Canton, for example, the town's natives surprise their captors by rising again, abducting hostages trapped in the trading houses. The conservative *Canton Monitor* interprets the attack as a clear sign that the Chinese are unruly, immoral, and willful, and must be taught, through utter destruction, obedience to the queen. In response, Eastman argues that the attack was instigated by Indian sepoys, a clever British ploy to provide justification for slaughtering the Chinese. Both interpretations, however paradoxically, are true, for each is a matter of perspective. Yet the editors accuse each other of blind falsehood, because their faith in their own perceptions denies the possibility of alternatives.

Mo raises the theme to a conscious level in his characters through Harry O'Rourke. As one of the original Impressionists, O'Rourke marks the transition in art from strict attention to realistic detail to subjective interpretations of the world. His art concentrates not on portraying the world but rather on the impressions the world makes on him. Rejecting this innovation, Eastman challenges O'Rourke with the newly invented daguerreotype, which he believes, in providing factual representations of the world, will replace the pictorial arts. Yet upon operating the newfangled machine, Eastman must admit that it fails to record the world objectively. The variables of light exposure and framing render the photographer as much an interpreter as the painter, and Eastman finally accepts O'Rourke's theory that life, after all, will imitate art. When he finds himself dueling with the *Canton Monitor's* editor, as he had so recently dueled with an actor in *The Rivals*, Eastman requires no more convincing on the subject.

The outcome of these investigations into the nature of reality is consistently paradoxical. Reality is absolute, Mo suggests, but it is not universal: For any individual, there is a single reality, but for the next individual that reality may well differ. Ultimately, this theme serves the novel's purpose by explaining Great Britain's chief failure in building her empire. Rather than peacefully coexisting in this foreign world, Great Britain hopes to dictate reality for all of its people, bringing her government and galas and drawing-room chatter, imposing her values with the force of an ironsided steamer.

Critical Context

An Insular Possession, Mo's third novel, broadens the scope of his previous work, rendering the multifaceted world through a collage of forms, but
maintains the essentially comic perception of divergent characters and cultures at odds with each other, the ramifications of a British Empire spread
too far. Like his second novel, the critically successful *Sour Sweet* (1982), it
was shortlisted for the Booker Prize, firmly establishing Mo as a major British Commonwealth novelist.

Like the modern British novelists of the first half of the twentieth century,
Mo implicitly condemns the British exploits of the Victorian period. Born of
rampant egotism, Great Britain's colonization depended on breaking the will
of foreign nations and eventually dissipated the strength of the mother country herself, making it, in retrospect, difficult to justify. Yet Mo consistently
steers clear of pontifical accusations himself; drawing his social commentary
from sardonically etched characters in fundamentally improbable circumstances, he conceives this historical era as a grand, if somewhat regrettable,
farce. To this end, he chooses the postmodern path of viewing the past from
a contemporary perspective. As in John Fowles's *The French Lieutenant's
Woman* (1969), Mo's narrator has the benefit of hindsight. As it does for
other novelists in the postmodern movement, the mollifying distance of time
provides Mo new solutions to the problem of resurrecting a culture from the
ashes of an empire.

Sources for Further Study
London Review of Books. Review. VIII (June 5, 1986), p. 20.
Listener. Review. CXV (May 8, 1986), p. 25.
New Statesman. Review. CXI (May 9, 1986), p. 27.
The Observer (London). Review. May 11, 1986, p. 24.
The Spectator. Review. CCLVI (May 10, 1986), p. 36.
The Times Literary Supplement. Review. May 9, 1986, p. 498.

Peter Juzwiak

INTENSIVE CARE

Author: Janet Frame (Janet Paterson Frame Clutha, 1924-   )
Type of plot: Social criticism/science fiction
Time of plot: The twentieth century and the unspecified future
Locale: New Zealand, London, and Melbourne
First published: 1970

Principal characters:

> TOM LIVINGSTONE, the protagonist of part 1, a World War I veteran, a controller of fires, and a dreamer
>
> CISSY EVEREST, Tom's "dream girl," a nurse who tended him during his recovery from his war wounds
>
> NAOMI WHYBORN, one of Tom's daughters, a victim of cancer and the writer of nostalgic letters
>
> PEARL TORRANCE, Tom's other daughter, a huge social worker serving "battered children"
>
> LEONARD LIVINGSTONE, Tom's brother
>
> PEGGY WARREN, a notoriously "loose" woman with designs on Tom
>
> COLIN TORRANCE, Tom's grandson, an accountant and murderer
>
> LORNA KIMBERLY, the woman Colin Torrance loves and kills
>
> COLIN MONK, the mathematics professor in charge of implementing the Human Delineation Act
>
> MILLY GALBRAITH, a retarded young woman and victim of the Human Delineation Act, the narrator of most of part 3

The Novel

Intensive Care, though divided into three official parts, actually consists of two stories which occur years apart and which are tenuously connected only by a pear tree on Tom Livingstone's property in Waipori City, New Zealand. The first story, encompassing parts 1 and 2, chronicles the events experienced by three generations of the Livingstone family; the second part, which occurs sometime after a nuclear war (it is set during King Charles's reign—perhaps it is the not-so-distant future), describes the implementation of the Human Delineation Act, which involves the classification, for economic benefit, expediency, and convenience, of people as either Human ("normal") or Animal (the old, weak, deformed, retarded, or even politically suspect), with the Animals being "deathed."

Since Tom was born at the turn of the century, his life represents the twentieth century, with its illusory dreams, bitter disappointments, elevation of technology over humanity, and replacement of family by impersonal institutions. Through a disjunctive narrative, multiple narrators, and a mixture of prose and poetry, Janet Frame depicts a man whose dreams destroy him. While recovering in England from war wounds, Tom meets and falls in love with his nurse, Cissy Everest, and then returns, like a dutiful husband, to his wife in New Zealand, where he leads a dull life working in the furnace room of a factory. Because he cannot rid himself of his dream about Cissy (he never gives up the photograph of them at Stoke Poges), he "turns off his valve of feeling" for Eleanor, his wife, distances himself from his children, who leave the home as soon as possible, and finds meaning in tending the "Flame," until his job is eliminated by progress in the shape of a machine. As soon as his wife dies, sixty-year-old Tom travels to London to find his "dream girl"; after he breaks his leg, he is sent to Culin Hall, a "recovery unit," where he finds her dying of cancer. When she fails to recognize him, thereby denying his existence ("his whole life had been built upon the memory of her"), he suffocates her and returns to New Zealand. He meets Peggy Warren, who resembles Cissy, and is about to marry her when he dies suddenly of a stomach ulcer.

Part 2 begins with an abortive relationship between Peggy and Leonard, Tom's brother, who, like Tom, is sent to a "recovery unit," where he does not belong. "The slender affirmation" of his existence is threatened when the "bond" between Peggy and him is broken, and he dies soon after being dismissed from the recovery unit. Leonard dies "rejected, negated, extinguished"—the "extinguished" suggesting the fire which went out for Tom as well. Frame establishes a pattern that extends from Tom to his brother and then to Colin Torrance, Tom's grandson, who repeats his grandfather's pattern: Colin, the calculating accountant, leads a life like Tom's before he, too, decides that his wife is not in his "dream" and forsakes his family for another woman. Pearl, his mother, asserts that Colin and her father were "the same"; like his grandfather, Colin has the "craze, the recklessness." Unfortunately, Colin's dreams (like Tom, he dreams that his wife is dead) lead him to duplicate his grandfather's crime of killing his "dream woman," but he also kills her parents and himself.

In part 3, Frame seems not only to tell a different story (while the setting is the same, the characters are different) but also to change from realism to science fiction. Colin Monk and Milly Galbraith narrate events that occur after the devastation of the North Island in a recent nuclear war, which has destroyed much of the world's vegetation. For expediency and convenience, the Human Delineation Act is enacted to separate people into two groups, "normal" Humans and the "numerous freaks of humanity," the Animals. Colin Monk, the computer professor, supervises the classification and must deal with those people who attempt to save their loved ones whom they suspect will be classified as Animals. Molly, who is "doll-normill" and a likely Animal, describes the approach of Classification Day by juxtaposing political events such as the use of American mercenaries to pacify the population and domestic scenes involving her cat and the Reconstructed Man, Sandy Monk, Colin's twin brother. Finally, the symbolic pear tree on the neighboring Livingstone place is cut down, and that event is followed by Classification Day and, ironically, by her birthday. After Milly and the other Animals are "deathed," Colin Monk resumes the narrative and recounts the "backlash," as nostalgia for the Animals leads to a reversal in which "the deformed, the insane, and the defective" become "the new elite," and he fears that he may himself be killed.

The Characters

Intensive Care is appropriately titled, for Frame's characters are victims in need of care for their physical, mental, and emotional wounds. The "recovery units," however, serve only as way stations between birth and death, and their first consideration is "the smooth running of the whole ward," not individual patients such as Tom or Leonard. Tom is a "war case," a man who cannot relinquish his gas mask or his nightmarish dreams; Leonard is also affected by the war, which does not bring him the family about which he dreams. Cissy becomes the Cissy Everest Cancer Doll, and Tom's daughter Naomi Whyborn, who also suffers from cancer, slowly loses one body part after another. In a sense, she resembles Sandy, the Reconstructed Man, whose doctors gave him everything except "care." Ironically, not even the apparent winners are safe, as Colin Monk's case indicates. The man who worships numbers because of their "cleanness"—and thereby resembles Colin Torrance, the accountant—and who believes that he has been "freed from guilt" finds that his "only hope" is to assume the identity of his twin brother, Sandy, "they myth, the Reconstructed Man."

Colin Monk's family has been killed at the end of the novel, which concerns the destruction of families by dreamers who reject reality for illusion. Because he cannot forget the War and cannot acclimate himself to his family, Tom tends the Flame "like a father or a lover," expending his energies and emotions on his job, not on his real family. (In his "dream" he is married to Cissy and has two idealized daughters, Cissy and May.) Naomi, who seems to have been most victimized by her father's neglect, is driven to reconstruct her childhood, to portray it in glowing terms ("our life was one of happiness and calm"), and to deny reality. Yet she cannot repress her real feelings, which surface in her account of the suicide of Donald Parker, a classmate whose death she blames on her father. Her letters pose the question reflected in her married name, "Why born?" Pearl, who is less reflective, suffers nevertheless, for she sees her behavior reflected in Colin Torrance's flight from her; her work with "battered children" ironically reflects her own treatment as a child.

The only positive family portrait Frame provides is of the Galbraiths, who are predictably classified as Animals to be destroyed. Ironically, it is the humanity, compassion, and caring of Milly's parents, their "human" qualities, that probably account for their classification as Animals—Humans seem, if Colin Monk's case is typical, to be concerned with conformity, theories, and machines (as landscapers and gardeners, the Galbraiths are more "natural"). Although Milly is, according to official "tests," "oughtistick" (autistic), her narration reveals her to be the moral center of the novel: She is both sane and human. Through Milly's misspelled words and her "unintentional" verbal irony, Frame conveys her view of a futuristic world gone mad.

Themes and Meanings

Although part 3 exists in the future, it is the past that informs that future and the present. Illusory dreams, romantic or bureaucratic, lead to destructive behavior, and part 3 is the logical, even inevitable, result of part 1. The sheep in the slaughterhouse beside Tom's cement factory are the soldiers in World War I, representing the past, the docile New Zealanders waiting for Classification Day represent the future. The parallels between the futuristic Human Delineation Act and Adolf Hitler's Holocaust are suggested by the use to which the Animals are to be put as slave labor and as raw material for shoes and lamp shades. (In fact, Milly's diary is reminiscent of a similar diary written by Anne Frank.) The Holocaust (with its association with burning) is itself related to the fire motif that runs through the story in Tom's "Flame" and metaphorically in the English recovery unit, "Culin" (kiln or furnace) Hall, where Tom's dreams are destroyed.

As Frame points out, "All dreams lead back to the nightmare garden," which is associated with Milly's "hisstree," a misspelling that also connotes the mythic fall from innocence. While Frame's characters are hardly innocent, they can repeat the fall as they sink to lower depths as they ironically believe they are progressing. This degradation is tied to the relationship between people and vegetation, most of which has been destroyed by the time part 3 begins. The pear tree serves as a symbolic touchstone for "man's inhumanity to man," for it survives nuclear war only to be cut down just before Classification Day, the culmination of inhumanity. In part 3, the green Taeri plains of part 1 have become the site of mass graves and of the "factrees" Milly mentions. The "fact trees" are a grim reminder of the replacement of nature by expedient machines (the world's real forests have also been replaced by artificial ones). To illustrate the perversion of nature, Frame uses Milly's "botannykill," which suggests the destructive mission of the scientists. After Classification Day, Colin Monk believes that there will be a "blossoming of the economy" through the use of "primary products" ("human Animals"); the factories do indeed produce a "new brew of blood and rose syrup" and the ingredients necessary for the "freshly fertilized garden" of the factory comanager Dora Nightshade. That Frame intends her readers to relate the various "gardens" to the original Garden is clear from

Sandy Monk's comment: "And you [Milly] and I are aloan, the golden man and the doll-normill woman, Adam and Eve in the bottanykill gardens."

References to killing and death pervade *Intensive Care*, which presents a bleak picture of the destructive power of well-intentioned dreams. The physicians are "meddykill" (meddle-kill) doctors, and the mathematicians who implement the Human Delineation Act are from the "Euniversity," with the "eu" prefix serving ironically. The professors who retreat from feelings to the safety of "numbers" rely on a "new one-question multiple-answer instant I.Q. gauge" and a "Central Computer" that gives each person a "primary judgment" at birth and a secondary, final judgment at five years of age. Rather than determining one's educational future—for Frame has only extended current testing practices—the test consigns its failures to death. Interestingly, the acronym for Human Animal Decision Enquiry Services is HADES.

Critical Context

Like the rest of her work, Janet Frame's *Intensive Care*, her eighth novel, depends upon the active participation of her readers, who must cope with her verbal virtuosity, multiple narrators, psychological complexity, and a blend of history and mythology. *Intensive Care* is a mixture of styles: The first two parts contain both poetry and prose, which functions as a key to understanding the poems; the third part, with its Human Delineation Act, reads like the science fiction of George Orwell, who described another dystopian society of the future, and the social satire of Jonathan Swift, whose *A Modest Proposal* (1729) comes to mind. In *Intensive Care*, Frame, despite the "limited" New Zealand setting, describes the macroworld of the present and the future. Here, as in *Daughter Buffalo* (1972), Frame seems more affected by her experiences in the United States: The American troops used to pacify a civilian population that its own government cannot control surely has its inspiration in the Vietnam War. Although she is by birth a New Zealand novelist, Frame has been established, through her work, as an international novelist, one whose work rivals James Joyce's in its density and complexity.

Sources for Further Study

Evans, Patrick David. *Janet Frame*, 1977.
Ferrier, Carole. "The Rhetoric of Rejection: Janet Frame's Recent Work," in *South Pacific Images*, 1978. Edited by Chris Tiffin.
New, W. H. "The Frame Story World of Janet Frame," in *Essays on Canadian Writing*. XXIX (Summer, 1984), pp. 175-191.
Rutherford, Anna. "Janet Frame's Divided and Distinguished Worlds," in *World Literature Written in English*. XIV (April, 1975), pp. 51-68.

Thomas L. Erskine

THE INTERPRETERS

Author: Wole Soyinka (1934-   )
Type of plot: Social realism
Time of plot: The early 1960's, soon after Nigerian independence
Locale: Lagos and Ibadan, Nigeria
First published: 1965

> *Principal characters:*
> BANDELE, a professor of history at the University of Nigeria
> at Ibadan
> EGBO, a clerk in the Foreign Office, heir to a village chiefdom
> BIODUN SAGOE, a newspaper reporter for the *Independent*
> *Viewpoint* in Lagos
> KOLA, a painter and a lecturer in art
> SEKONI, an engineer, later a sculptor
> KOMOLOLA DEHINWA, Sagoe's fiancée, a clerk in the Civil
> Service
> JOE GOLDER, a homosexual, quadroon American singer and a
> lecturer in African history at the University of Nigeria at
> Ibadan

The Novel

   The Interpreters has no central plot; it is instead a sequence of dramatic scenes and lyric descriptions that follow a chronological line, interrupted by periodic flashbacks and recollections, during the rainy season in Nigeria from May through July. The action shifts from Lagos and the university city of Ibadan to the back country and lagoons outside populated areas. The main characters are university graduates, who have studied and traveled abroad and have just returned to Nigeria because of the country's newly obtained independence. These intellectuals, interpreters of the new Nigeria, are trying to find their way within the new political structure, within a society dominated by confusion, insensitivity, social climbing, and corruption. One thing that holds the novel together is the gradual movement of the interpreters—Bandele, Egbo, Biodun Sagoe, Kola, Sekoni—toward an awareness of their situation.

   The first story that Wole Soyinka introduces is that of Egbo, the grandson and heir of a tribal chief and warlord. His dilemma is whether he should return to the old village and assume his powers and privileges (including polygamy) or abandon them and adapt to the new Nigeria. By delaying his return (he does make one abortive trip toward his home country), he in effect chooses to remain in the present, though the alternatives plague him throughout the novel. The dilemma is compounded by another: Should he remain with his mistress, Simi, a nationally famous courtesan with whom he forms an intimate relationship early in the novel, or abandon her to commit himself to a university student, a feminist, who is pregnant with his child and who challenges the moral prudishness of the university elite? The old African society, which Egbo has forfeited, has a social structure permitting him to keep both. The new society demands that he make a choice and, at the same time, declares unacceptable the two women he would choose. The novel leaves him in a state of frustration.

The second story to take shape is that of Sagoe, a reporter for a Lagos newspaper and an amateur philosopher. In addition to his relationship with his fiancée, Komolola Dehinwa—a comic, romantic sparring of intellectual equals—Sagoe participates in a picaresque sequence of curious adventures: a visit to a cemetery where he watches two funeral processions; an encounter with an evangelical preacher, Lazarus; indecorous, even zany, confrontations with respectable society; and an accidental meeting with Joe Golder, which provides psychological material for an entire chapter. What holds these adventures together is not the development of plot or even of character but of common motifs.

A third story, which extends over a large portion of the novel, especially the second half, is that of Lazarus, who is not a main character but who attracts the attention of all the interpreters. Sagoe first sees Lazarus, an albino, in a battered hearse leading a bedraggled funeral procession to a cemetery. When Sagoe steals a wreath from a rich procession to place it on the poor one, Lazarus marks him as a moral man. They meet again while watching a market crowd chase a thief. Lazarus eventually transforms that thief into an acolyte and has plans for him to be his new apostle, replacing the one who has died. In hopes of winning Sagoe and his interpreter friends over to his religion, or perhaps simply to get publicity for it, Lazarus tracks Sagoe down. He informs him and the other interpreters of his history; he shows them newspaper clippings as evidence that he died and came back to life. Since the interpreters have recently lost their close friend, Sekoni, and are intrigued with notions of rebirth, they accept Lazarus' invitation to a church service. There they see the marketplace thief, renamed Noah, apparently converted to the new faith. The interpreters are not convinced of Lazarus' resurrection or of Noah's conversion, but Kola is fascinated enough to ask both Noah and Lazarus to sit for his painting of the Yoruba pantheon. Lazarus' story ends disastrously when the homosexual Joe Golder intimidates Noah into jumping off the balcony of his eighth-floor apartment.

Such incidents as these make up the novel. They bring together the various interpreters who interact and respond to contemporary situations, learning about themselves and exposing follies in contemporary Nigeria. They do not, in mere outline, do justice to the artistry of Soyinka. His is a sensitive portrayal, though difficult to follow, of a lost generation. None of the stories ends with any assuredness of success. In the final pages the characters seem suspended in time.

The Characters

Rather than develop one protagonist, Soyinka paints a picture of an entire society in a wide variety of settings, not only the professional class that receives primary attention but also a few people on the fringes of polite society—an evangelical preacher, a courtesan, and a thief. In a sense, Soyinka divides the characters into two groups, the observed and the observer, though the observers themselves, the interpreters, must submit to the closest scrutiny.

Among the observed are the colleagues of Bandele at the University of Nigeria and their professional acquaintances. Theirs is a superficial world that Soyinka describes in a comic mode. Were they the only subjects of the novel, it would be a comedy of manners. The observed, however, are not only those who insist on Victorian manners and morals, those who hypocritically lecture on the "merel terpitude" of the young, or who, like Dr. Lumoye, exchange abortion services for sexual favors, but also more appealing characters. Lazarus, though a misguided evangelist, is both dignified and sympathetic, one of the false prophets that the moral chaos of modern Nigeria has created. Joe Golder, far from being a comic figure, contains within himself the conflict between the old and new cultures. As a quadroon American, he is descended from Africa. He has rejected Western society but, looking more white than black and not having been reared in Africa, he is homeless there as well. As a homosexual, he is alienated from society and from himself. In his conversation with Sagoe, Golder goes through a series of self-revelations, obviously repeated numerous times to different men, which, along with the "fastidious air" of his apartment, expose his lack of depth. He is, as he says in his favorite song "a motherless child," cut off from his roots. This void torments him and results in self-pity and, paradoxically, in an elevation of the self to a sense of superiority. He belongs nowhere, but for that reason, even though he is not one of the African interpreters, he represents a feeling that they all have. Their past, too, appears inaccessible and irrelevant to the modern situation.

Soyinka uses the interpreters to explore serious psychological and practical problems facing the honorable few in Nigerian society. Soyinka looks at them from the inside. Sekoni is a high-strung, withdrawn genius, thwarted by the authorities in his efforts as an engineer; turned sculptor, he is regarded by the others as an uncanny, though stuttering, medium of sacred truths. His death, while accidental, seems a tragic loss and changes the mood of the novel. As painter of the pantheon, Kola knows that Nigeria must return to its cultural heritage but seems to have confused Yoruba and Christian myths and is unsure of himself as an artist and as a man. His behavior toward

Faseyi's English wife, Monica, has false touches of a Western romantic love. Sagoe, as attractive as he is in his role as social rebel, is still a child in his continual conflicts with Dehinwa, in his antics at social gatherings, and in his final, comic plan to unite southern and northern Nigeria by exchanging Lagos "night soil" (human feces as fertilizer) for Hausa donkeys and human labor. He is a frustrated writer without a subject or an audience. He promises, however, to abandon his Philosophy of Voidancy (a Platonic evacuation of the bowels) when he and Dehinwa get married. Egbo, according to Kola, has the hidden power to accomplish great things, but he does not have artistic talent. His success must be in the world of human affairs, yet his strength is dissipated by his dilemmas. He cannot go beyond his personal problems to achieve anything practical. In what looks like a Freudian analysis of character, Soyinka places all Egbo's energy in the libido, not as yet sublimated into civilizing activities.

If anyone is the leader of the group of interpreters, it is Bandele; he speaks with the authority of the elders in ancient society, but the voice will not carry weight in modern Nigeria. Even at the end of the novel, when he finally decides to break with an increasingly unacceptable social hypocrisy, he cannot change anything; he can only shock by issuing a curse, accusing the elite of eating their own children to save themselves.

The comic presentation of character, which permeates much of the novel, has underlying it a satiric intent that darkens the mood. Among the observed, the figures of Joe Golder and Lazarus loom larger than the comic portraits; they belong to a serious or even tragic novel rather than a comic one. As for the observers, at the beginning they are a cohesive unit, enjoying life in one of many drunken get-togethers at a Lagos nightclub. By the end they are a sober, somber assortment, drifting apart, at odds not only with society but also with one another.

Themes and Meanings

Everything in *The Interpreters* suggests that Nigeria in the early 1960's is in transition: the comic but dangerous characters futilely holding on to the manners of Victorian England; the interpreters in suspension, seeking themselves and their roles in the body politic; the oppressive, seemingly interminable rainy season; the unsifted mixture of traditional and contemporary corruption; the death and rebirth motif that promises hope but is temporarily manifest in false forms; the open-endedness of the novel, which promises change rather than mere repetition.

Transition is a state of confusion and paralysis; no established code sanctions behavior. Egbo, for example, is lost because he is caught between two worlds, neither of them clearly offering a value system according to which he can function. He attempts to return to traditional Yoruba mythology, but it is a completely private process until he shares it with the stranger girl during one intimate night of love. During his childhood, his Christian guardians had beaten him for praying to heathen gods. Such worship was "apostasy"—a word repeated often enough in the novel to qualify as a key to the central theme. Kola describes it as "an absolute neutrality," the hardest thing in the world to paint. Later, Egbo and Kola debate its meaning and determine that there are two types of apostates, Christ and Judas. The one heroically breaks new ground by declaring an old code defunct or by reinterpreting it; the other, merely for the sake of immediate gratification, betrays an accepted belief. The difficulty lies in knowing what the true codes are and hence who the heroes are.

Soyinka presents three artist-interpreters—the writer, Sagoe; the painter, Kola; and the sculptor, Sekoni—who face the task of discovery. Sagoe gets no further than an article on Sekoni that becomes a pawn in a cover-up, a proposed article on Lazarus that has little chance of uncovering any truth, and a Philosophy of Voidancy that he has sworn to abandon by the end of the novel. Kola attempts to re-create in one painting the entire Yoruba pantheon but encounters numerous difficulties, among which are his own inadequate talent and conceptions and the paucity of adequate models in contemporary society. At one point, he thinks that he has found the perfect model for Esumare, the rainbow that will complete his picture, in the acolyte-thief, Noah. Yet he eventually acknowledges that Noah is "simply negative," an absolute neutrality, and an "unrelieved vacuity."

Hence, he changes his mind; Noah becomes the apostate servant who rolls the stone down the back of Obatala, causing the original fragmentation of the world. His next model for Esumare, Lazarus, proves similarly inadequate, at least according to Egbo, who harshly criticizes the painting. Egbo objects to the rainbow itself as a resolution. It would seem that Kola has allowed his evangelist model to influence his composition, by imposing a Christian solution onto the problems of contemporary life. As Egbo says, "He has made the beginning itself a resurrection. This is an optimist's delusion of continuity." Egbo, with his close ties to traditional society and myth, prefers Ogun, the warrior-god in Yoruba myth, as the god of resolution. Hence, also, his objection to Kola's representation of Ogun. After Ogun had built a bridge joining earth to the gods, he became drunk and slaughtered his own soldiers in a bloody massacre. Using Egbo as his model, Kola has chosen to depict this moment of Ogun's ultimate shame. In fact, Kola has perhaps accurately reflected the contemporary scene but wrongly turns to the ambiguous symbol of the rainbow, instead of to Ogun's victory, as a paradigm for recovery.

The artist that has best perceived the obligation facing the interpreters is Sekoni. His sculpture, *The Wrestler*, has its origin in a simple brawl in a nightclub during which Bandele had wrestled a waiter and bound him with a rope. The waiter seems to represent the treacherous servant who caused the original fragmentation of the world. In binding him, Bandele desperately tries to maintain wholeness. The sculpture reminds them of their Yoruba heritage, the original dissolution of order, and the struggle necessary to restore it. The novel may finally argue that apostasy is a blind obedience to alien codes and that the true "apostate" reinterprets the old tradition, essential African values, in the modern setting.

Critical Context

The novel, though a Western form, has proved to be a flexible medium for Soyinka and other African writers. In using it to reflect his perception of African life, Soyinka has created structures uniquely his own. Both *The Interpreters* and *Season of Anomy* (1973), his second novel, range from farce and social satire to psychological realism, romance, symbolism, and myth. In Soyinka's case the range derives its justification not only from the complexity of African life but also from his specific cultural context, the Yoruba mythology in Western Africa, specifically the god Ogun, whose mythical story makes him both creator and destroyer, both protector of the weak and drunken murderer. Such contradictory, paradoxical qualities in one god suggest to Soyinka the complexity of the human makeup and of human actions, and hence the variety of modes appropriate within one unified work. One finds similar mixes in Soyinka's drama.

One particular aim of Soyinka is to carry over into the novel what in his drama is a literary adaptation of communal ritual. Soyinka stresses its importance not only by its noticeable absence in *The Interpreters* and by its presence in *Season of Anomy* but also by the representations of the communal experience itself, insofar as that is possible in a narrative form. In *The Interpreters*, the five men who form the close-knit group of intellectuals are an unsuccessful substitute for what is lacking in the community at large. In *Season of Anomy*, Soyinka creates a whole community, Aiyéró, that possesses the old communal spirit and practices its rites. Much of the difficulty in Soyinka's style is its elusiveness, elliptical and imagistic qualities that convey a mysteriousness and a cultishness, a hidden presence that never quite reveals itself. To the Westerner encountering Soyinka's world, the sensation of strangeness is not only unmistakable but also persistent, even after several readings.

That Soyinka has created literary works distinctively original and has furthermore succeeded in becoming an African voice of international significance, has been officially recognized by the award of the Nobel Prize for Literature in 1986.

Sources for Further Study

Bibbs, James, ed. *Critical Perspectives on Wole Soyinka*, 1980.
Jones, Eldred Durosimi. *Wole Soyinka*, 1971, 1983, 1987.

Laurence, Margaret. *Long Drums and Cannons: Nigerian Dramatists and Novelists*, 1969.
Moore, Gerald. *Twelve African Writers*, 1980.
_____. *Wole Soyinka*, 1971, 1978.
Palmer, Eustace. *The Growth of the African Novel*, 1980.

Thomas Banks

THE IVORY SWING

Author: Janette Turner Hospital (1942-   )
Type of plot: Romantic realism
Time of plot: The 1970's, with flashbacks to the 1960's
Locale: A small South Indian village near Trivandrum in Kerala State; Winston, a small town in the province of Ontario, Canada (a thinly disguised Kingston); and Boston
First published: 1982

Principal characters:

JULIET, the protagonist, a housewife and mother of two, who has abandoned work on her doctorate in history but is still trying, in a desultory fashion, to finish a book

DAVID, her husband of twelve years, a professor of Indian religion

JEREMY, Juliet's former lover from Boston

SUSAN, David's student, who has seduced him once in Winston

ANNIE, Juliet's younger sister

PREM, a young Marxist university student who befriends Juliet and becomes Annie's lover

SHIVARAMAN NAIR, Juliet and David's landlord

PRABHAKARAN, Juliet's servant, a flute-player, sweeper, and peon on the Nair estate

YASHODA, a defiant young widow living on the Nair estate

MATTHEW THOMAS, a Christian Indian who befriends Juliet and becomes Yashoda's lover

The Novel

Juliet provides the focus for the novel's two-pronged exploration of male/female and North American/South Indian interactions. Much of the novel relates Juliet's memories and her experience of events. She loves her husband and children but has hated her twelve years in the backwater of Winston; she now finds South India equally debilitating. She feels torn between her desire for action and her need for security. Her former lover Jeremy represents the political engagement for which she longs, while her husband David embodies the detached appreciation of the timeless world of art that she has learned to appreciate during the course of their long relationship. Her marriage has caused her self-image to suffer, but it has also brought her moments of joy and contentment. The year's sabbatical in India provides her with a new context in which to assess the state of her marriage and contemplate her future.

Her main charge against David is that he keeps only "one kind of evidence." His memories are not hers. He seems unable to see from her point of view and unable to hear her frequently voiced complaints—about Winston and now about India. Yet through their involvement with Prabhakaran and Yashoda, India changes both of them. They are able to apply the lessons they learn from their difficulties in understanding this foreign culture to their personal problems in communicating their differences. As a result, each learns a new tolerance for the other.

The novel opens with the mutual mystery that India and America pose to each other, symbolized in the encounter between Juliet and Prabhakaran: "They did not quite know what to make of each other, Juliet and the boy." It ends after the tragedy of his death in a futile attempt to protect Yashoda from an angry mob of Nair estate workers, who are convinced that her breaking of *dharma* caused the bad harvest on the estate. Juliet mourns him as a "lost child" but concludes from this tragic outcome of her attempt to befriend the two Indians that "it was, ultimately, fatal to careen between worlds." Their deaths enable her to leave India, and thus her husband, temporarily, and possibly permanently, behind. Their deaths enable her husband to acknowledge, for the first time, that Juliet will have to leave him to find herself.

Juliet's search for selfhood is mirrored in the complementary quests of her sister Annie and her friend Yashoda. Annie envies Juliet her stability; Juliet envies Annie her freedom. Neither can acknowledge the price the other has paid for what she has achieved, until Yashoda pays with her life for her attempts to imitate their shared Western defiance of tradition.

Prem is also educated by Yashoda's death. From a poor, lower-caste family, he feels nothing but contempt for the sufferings of this rich, upper-caste widow as she attempts to wrest her freedom from the men in her family. Only after her death can he see the parallels between Yashoda's struggle to resist the traditional authority which justifys her oppression as a woman and his own struggles on behalf of the oppressed poor and untouchables: "He knew now that there were other wrongs and other griefs besides hunger and poverty."

Everyone feels implicated in Yashoda's death. Yet her death releases no answers, only more questions that reveal the difficulty of determining a right course of action within the complicated territory of intercultural, interracial, interclass, and interpersonal relations. The novel's final chapter provides two tentative images of possible resolution. After the fire of cremation, Juliet turns to the ocean and to the idea that "somewhere all the world's waters meet." She cannot give David any verbal assurances, but the novel ends with their embrace: "They held each other, frail beneath the moon and the palms, and kissed timidly, as frightened children do." True to its title image of the ivory swing, the novel ends in suspension.

The Characters

The Ivory Swing is Juliet's book. Its rhythms are determined by her moods, its language by the exuberance of her imagination, and its events by her driving compulsion to act. The other characters are important only in relation to her or in the reflections they provide of her dilemmas. Juliet's energy and intelligence give the book its strength; both her self-pity and her self-indulgence define its limitations.

Despite the centrality of Juliet, Janette Turner Hospital's use of an omniscient narrator enables her to portray the thoughts of other significant characters at key moments, including those of David, Annie, Prem, Shivaraman Nair, and Matthew Thomas. These characters, while remaining subordinate to Juliet, take on individual lives of their own and enrich Hospital's portrayal of the complexity of moral decision-making in a crosscultural context. Particularly moving are Matthew Thomas' efforts to bridge the cultural gaps because Juliet's obvious outsider status reminds him painfully of his daughter Kumari's exile in Burlington, Vermont.

The glimpses into the other men's minds seem more perfunctory. They work to confirm Juliet's assessments rather than to reveal new insights into character. Chapter 21, recording David's visit to the Hindu temple, is narrated almost entirely from his point of view yet serves chiefly to confirm Juliet's view of her isolation, even employing the same metaphors for her entrapment that she uses elsewhere.

Significantly, the text never penetrates the thinking of Yashoda and Prabhakaran. They remain impenetrable, permanently "other," symbols more than individuals. Victims of their contact with Western ideas, they are portrayed in terms of traditional Indian myth, as Radha and Krishna.

Yashoda, in particular, seems unreal, as if to confirm the superstitious belief that she is a *yakshi*, a demoniac spirit "who takes the form of a woman of surpassing beauty to lure men to damnation." To remain pure, the holy man must kill her. Her characterization as *yakshi* dooms her to death, a conclusion the novel unwillingly confirms. Western notions of individuality and free will are brought into question through this characterization of Yashoda. To complicate her meaning, she has been named for the foster mother of Krishna, a role she takes in her relation to Prabhakaran. These contradictory roles define the conflict-torn and unpredictable widow. No one takes her seriously, unable to see beyond her beauty, which makes her seem unreal and inhuman to men and women alike. As *yakshi*, she threatens men's control over their sexuality and women's control over their men. As rebellious widow, she threatens the divine, natural, and social orders, all of which depend on her keeping her place. As foster mother to Krishna, she represents an ideal of harmony, an ideal that is fractured even as it is realized in her relation to Prabhakaran because their togetherness violates caste taboos. Yashoda is trapped by webs of tradition that do not touch Juliet, yet her dilemma reminds Juliet of the high price to be paid for trying to change the world, and, in particular, of the many obstacles facing any woman seeking self-realization.

Themes and Meanings

As the plot and characterization make clear, *The Ivory Swing* explores the rewards and costs of interpersonal and intercultural relations. Juliet and David both savor and suffer from "the mysterious incongruities of their lives." Any reaching out beyond the known, Hospital suggests, involves not only danger but also a compensating excitement—what her characters think of as "the Balboa syndrome," their metaphor for discovery.

Balancing the epiphanic moments releasing the couple into freedom—experienced on frozen Lake Ontario and on the warm Indian Ocean—are the moments of entrapment, when Juliet sees herself as a caged bird and David sees himself as the helpless victim of his passion and the passive partner in others' initiatives. Nature offers Juliet and Art affords David brief moments of respite from the tyranny of Society, but the novel insists that one cannot escape from social confrontations into a private peace.

Hospital's characters must defend and act on the values they cherish, and assume responsibility for the actions they take or fail to take. As a new young faculty wife in Winston, Juliet refuses to wear white gloves when asked to pour tea at a university reception. In India, also, when compelled to serve tea to the Nairs, she refuses to serve it in the proper Indian manner. Her refusal of the customary in both societies makes her a kind of rebel, but unlike Prem, she is a rebel without clear goals. She swings between the extremes of wanting acceptance and refusing its terms. The ivory swing is a beautiful work of art, but too expensive for David and Juliet. Torn between conflicting needs, they remain in suspension until Yashoda's death—imaged as a fall from the swing—frees Juliet's imagination to revise the metaphor. "We are like trapeze artists," she thinks. "It is a delicate act, full of balance and hazard." They are ready to take responsibility for their movements. No longer visualizing herself as a caged bird, Juliet becomes an artist, a human being who shapes the curves of her flight.

The mixed metaphors of caged nightingale, bird of paradise, falcon, flying human, of swing's flight and trapeze flight, and the intertwined references to the three carvings—of bronze dancing girl, sandalwood Krishna, and ivory swing—underline the hybrid nature of modern experience. Early in their relationship, David tells Juliet, "I think we live in different worlds and speak different languages." Yet Juliet is a self-avowed "hybrid." Like the novelist, she connects apparent disparities to reveal fresh and challenging congruities. This novel is as alive to cultural differences as it is to gender-determined expectations, but it offers the hope that a shared humanity can, with tolerance, bring opposites together.

Critical Context

The Ivory Swing won Canada's fifty-thousand-dollar Seal First Novel Contest in 1982 and was nominated in the United Kingdom for the Booker Prize. It was developed from the short story "Waiting," which won an "Atlantic First" citation when published in *The Atlantic Monthly* in 1978. An unusually mature and accomplished first novel, it introduces many of the themes that continue to distinguish Hospital's work: the pleasure and anguish of cross-cultural interaction, alienation and belonging, women's experience. The titles of two later works signal these thematic preoccupations: *Borderline* (1985) and *Dislocations* (1986).

Hospital's life, from her birth and youth in Australia to her settling in Canada, with sojourns in Boston, Los Angeles, and India, represents the mixing of cultures that animates her work. Her writing seeks to remind one of the multiple perspectives and levels of meanings implicit in any object or event, a purpose that strains against the predominantly realist mode of narration she chose for *The Ivory Swing*. The novel draws on its author's wide reading in the classics of English literature and in Indian fiction, newspapers, and magazines. Both contexts are built into the novel's construction of its own reality. There are moments when the juxtapositions seem forced and even heavy-handed, the symbolism strained or obvious, problems that cannot be fully explained by the novel's concern with drawing connections between jarring differences. Yet *The Ivory Swing* succeeds brilliantly in its evocation of mood and atmosphere, and in compelling attention to moral questions of responsibility that cannot be easily resolved.

Sources for Further Study

Grossman, Elizabeth. "*The Ivory Swing*," in *Ms*. XII (July, 1983), p. 21.
Hill, Douglas. Review in *Books in Canada*. XI (December, 1982), pp. 26-27.
Jackson, Marni. "Exiles in an Exotic Dream," in *Maclean's*. XCV (October 4, 1982), p. 72.
Library Journal. Review. CVIII (May 15, 1983), p. 1017.
Publishers Weekly. Review. CCXXIII (March 11, 1983), p. 77.

Diana Brydon

JACOB'S ROOM

Author: Virginia Woolf (1882-1941)
Type of plot: Impressionism
Time of plot: The last decade of the nineteenth century and the first decades of the twentieth century, concluding with World War I
Locale: Mostly England (Cambridge, London, and other areas) and some European countries
First published: 1922

> *Principal characters:*
> JACOB FLANDERS, the main character, a romantic figure in love with classical literature and culture
> BETTY FLANDERS, his mother
> DICK BONAMY, Jacob's friend
> CLARA DURRANT, a young woman who is in love with Jacob
> SANDRA WENTWORTH WILLIAMS, a married woman with whom Jacob falls in love

The Novel

The plot of this novel is not nearly as significant as its characterization, and the characters themselves are important for their thoughts, not their actions. Virginia Woolf focuses not on what happens around the characters but rather on what happens within them, most particularly the central character, Jacob Flanders.

When the novel opens, Jacob is a young boy living in the seaside city of Scarborough with his widowed mother and two brothers. These geographical and familial roots provide the youth with his first experiences of complexity, which foreshadow his subsequent struggles to deal with an increasingly complicated world. Though the seaside location is strikingly beautiful, it is not always peaceful and romantic; it is also attacked by powerful storms and hurricanes. Further, though Jacob plays childlike games near the water and finds childlike treasures on the beach, he also discovers unsettling objects, such as a cow's skull, with its ominous suggestions of change intruding into the changelessness of the sea.

Going to Cambridge in 1906, Jacob begins his pilgrimage forward and backward. He becomes immersed in the twentieth century, experiencing what he cannot identify—the modern sense of restlessness and sadness— and he attempts to escape into earlier centuries, proclaiming his disdain for what he perceives as the modern civilization and announcing his admiration for previous cultures, particularly that of the Greeks. As both a representative and a victim of the twentieth century, Jacob moves through many relationships, never satisfied with the women he meets, never concerned with the people he leaves behind as he pursues his quest for ideal beauty and happiness. He is the solitary Adam in a post-Edenic world of change, movement, and transience.

As he plunges into the twentieth century, Jacob is obsessed with the ideas and ideals of earlier times. In stating his disdain for modern literature, for example, he so influences one of his lovers that she forces herself to read *The History of Tom Jones, a Foundling* (1749), by Henry Fielding, mistakenly believing that her efforts to move back in time will endear her to Jacob. He does not realize the sincerity of her efforts, being so insulated and obsessed by his own attempts to make meaning out of the increasing chaos he observes around and within himself.

He buries himself within the British Museum, contemplating the mysteries of the past; he reads books such as the *Byzantine Empire*, looking for clues in that tome; he argues about the ideas of Plato and Socrates, believing that his statements will bring him closer to an illumination of those ancients' messages. Then he journeys beyond British places and literary spaces. He travels to Greece, seeking to connect with the past that had been inspiring him. What he finds, however, is that he cannot escape what surrounds and shapes him: the twentieth century, with its burdens of change, complexity, and pain. As the narrator puts it, "This gloom, this surrender to the dark waters which lap us about, is a modern invention." The twentieth century is real, too real, for Jacob, and he cannot escape its influence. He returns to it and to England, leaving behind him in Greece the first woman whom he loves, a married woman who remains as idealized as his notions of Greece.

When the novel ends, World War I has created "such confusion everywhere," as Jacob's mother laments. The confusion is reflected in Jacob's abandoned room. The modern Adam is gone, and his litter and letters remain. Has he committed suicide? Has he been killed in the war? Has he retreated into a self-imposed exile? What remains are his remains and the last words of the book: "a pair of Jacob's old shoes."

The Characters

Jacob Flanders is the focal point of this novel, a complicated character who is interesting not only because of his struggles to see and understand the world but also because he provides the reader with the opportunity to observe the other characters' way of seeing as well. The other characters see Jacob—and the world—from the outside and find it difficult to describe him. They frequently speak of his being "distinguished-looking," but they are unable to specify in what way. As the narrator puts it, "distinction was one of the words to use naturally, though, from looking at him, one would have found it difficult to say which seat in the opera house was his, stalls, gallery, or dress circle." In their attempts to describe him, some characters, such as Clara Durrant, who loves him, see him in sentimental terms, while others, such as Captain Barfoot from Scarborough, see him as simply likable but for no specific reason. In all cases, the characters see only Jacob's surface, never witnessing the complexity within.

Jacob himself tries to simplify the world and his role in it by a romanticized view of specific people and the specific time in which he lives, the twentieth century. Thus, he has an affair with Florinda, a prostitute, taking her word for it that she is a virgin, telling himself that she looks "wild and frail and beautiful . . . and thus the women of the Greeks were." His attempt to idealize Florinda, however, is short-lived, for her superficiality becomes apparent to him, forcing him to see the emptiness of his romanticizing.

Similarly, Jacob romanticizes Greece and Greek culture, both before he actually visits the country and as he tries to maintain his romantic views during his trip there. He discusses Greek culture with his friends, arrogantly believing "that they had read every book in the world" and then deciding "in favour of Greece." He assumes an equally arrogant view as he begins his journey to Greece, determining that "after doing Greece he was going to knock off Rome." Yet his romantic, reductionist attitude is challenged by a persistent sense of sadness that accompanies him whenever he attempts to glorify the past. What he senses is that the past is indeed past, that time changes all, and that he cannot escape into a vision that either romanticizes previous cultures or reduces the complexities of the present into a simplistic view of the past. In short, Jacob Flanders is forced to replace his innocence with adulthood, just as the simplicity of the premodern period is replaced by the complexity of the twentieth century.

Themes and Meanings

The novel begins and ends with letters, a symbol that conveys one of the principal themes of the book: communication attempted but never completely successful. Letters and conversations permeate this book, continually demonstrating the efforts which characters make to connect but the impossibility of actually doing so. Thus, Jacob writes letters to his mother, but she complains that these are missives "telling me . . . really nothing that I want to know." Conversations similarly reinforce the idea that people are conversing but not communicating, perhaps because the solitariness of people prevents anything more than superficial relationships. The omnibus is used to demonstrate this separateness, for people ride the vehicle, not as members of a community, but as solitary passengers intent on the stories within them, ignoring the stories within the people traveling next to them.

Yet the efforts to connect accumulate, like Jacob's letters found in his abandoned room. Why this persistence? The answer is one of the themes of *Jacob's Room*: "letters are venerable; and the telephone valiant, for the journey is a lonely one, and if bound together by notes and telephones we went in company, perhaps—who knows?—we might talk by the way."

Critical Context

One of Woolf's early novels, *Jacob's Room* reveals the writer's early efforts to experiment with stylistic and thematic concerns that characterize her later, more sophisticated books, such as *Mrs. Dalloway* (1925) and *To the Lighthouse* (1927). Unfinished sentences, seemingly disjointed scenes, stream of consciousness—these techniques suit the ideas of time passing and individuals observing that passage from their unique vantage points. If truth is thus subjective, then the writer's job is to suggest, not to announce, and that is Woolf's mode, which her narrator in *Jacob's Room* implies in a pair of sentences repeated, word for word, near the beginning and near the end of the novel: "It is no use trying to sum people up. One must follow hints, not exactly what is said nor yet entirely what is done." This is Virginia Woolf's novelistic technique and her philosophical orientation. She whispers hints; she never shouts proclamations.

Sources for Further Study

Fleishman, Avrom. *Virginia Woolf: A Critical Reading*, 1975.

Guiguet, Jean. *Virginia Woolf and Her Works*, 1965. Translated by Jean Stewart.

Marcus, Jane. *Virginia Woolf: A Feminist Slant*, 1983.

Naremore, James. *The World Without a Self: Virginia Woolf and the Novel*, 1973.

Marjorie Smelstor

JAKE'S THING

Author: Kingsley Amis (1922-   )
Type of plot: Comic realism
Time of plot: The mid-1970's
Locale: London and Oxford, England
First published: 1978

> *Principal characters:*
>   JAKE RICHARDSON, the protagonist, a professor of early
>   Mediterranean history at Oxford University
>   BRENDA RICHARDSON, his third wife, who is twelve years his
>   junior
>   GEOFFREY MABBOTT, the neighbor for whom Brenda deserts
>   Jake
>   DR. PROINSIAS ROSENBERG, the psychologist who treats Jake's
>   sexual dysfunction
>   EVE GREENSTREET, Jake's former mistress
>   KELLY GAMBESON, a member of the therapy group who is
>   infatuated with Jake

The Novel

At the age of fifty-nine, Jake Richardson has become concerned about his lack of ability or desire to perform sexually. His family physician refers him to a psychologist named Proinsias Rosenberg, who begins therapy using a number of techniques collectively called "inceptive regrouping" and an apparatus known as a "nocturnal mensurator." Jake is instructed to complete a questionnaire on his aberrant sexual proclivities, to use pornographic magazines for the purposes of masturbation, to write out a sexual fantasy, and to engage his wife in petting sessions described as "non-genital sensate focusing." The therapy fails. Reading through the questionnaire, Jake realizes that he has no aberrant sexual desires, although he is careful to give answers which will not identify him as a prig. The modern pornography he buys is too explicit for his taste and effectively decreases rather than increases his sexual desires. The fantasy he concocts in six drafts of literary effort is transparently disingenuous. Finally, the "sensate focusing session" with Brenda seems to be merely a series of mechanical operations which Jake sneeringly calls "a feel-up by numbers."

Rosenberg sends Jake to a psychiatric hospital which runs an experimental sexual therapy program. There, Jake is subjected to further humiliations. Naked from his shirttails to his socks, he sits before an audience of male and female medical students while the female doctor in charge of the program shows him a series of pornographic pictures and measures his sexual response. The experiment yields no new insights into his problem, but Jake's embarrassment at having his genitals exposed in public convinces Rosenberg that Jake is inhibited by the guilt and shame conferred by his "puritanical up-bringing." In yet another psychiatric forum, a group therapy workshop which Jake attends with Brenda, he is again asked to remove his clothes in public. He reluctantly complies with the request but declines to attend subsequent sessions. Brenda stays on, however, to receive therapy for her compulsive overeating.

When Jake returns to Oxford for the summer term, he finds his college overrun with angry women protesting against its sexist admission policy. The protesters verbally abuse him, send him a plastic phallus inscribed with the perplexing word "Wanker," and maliciously annotate the library copy of an article he wrote. Ironically, the moment he decides he probably is an anti-feminist at heart, the college Master asks him to advocate the protesters' position in debate at the next college council meeting. Despite his personal bias, he does an admirable job in the debate until he is challenged about his true feelings. Jake shocks the council by launching into a chauvinistic dia-tribe which concludes with the recommendation that women students "bug-ger off back to Somerville, LMH, St Hugh's and St Hilda's where they began and stay there."

Jake's outburst is partially the result of a hangover from the previous night's debauch. Jake met his former mistress, Eve, for dinner, drank too much wine, and later went to bed with her. To make things worse, after the college council meeting, Jake arrives back at his room to find another woman waiting for him. Kelly Gambeson, a member of the therapy workshop, has tracked Jake to his quarters at Oxford intending to seduce him. When Jake rebuffs her, she throws a frightening tantrum of the sort she earlier displayed in the one workshop session he attended. Although alarmed by Kelly's beha-vior, Jake feels for her a "genuine interest as opposed to the testosterone-fed substitute that had graced his sometime dealings with Eve," and when she later invites him to attend a weekend outing with the therapy group, he ac-cepts. During the weekend, Kelly stages a drug-assisted suicide attempt in a manner calculated to cause minimum harm to herself and maximum guilt in Jake. Her plan goes awry, however, when Jake fails to keep a midnight ren-dezvous; Kelly is in critical condition by the time her overdose is discovered. In dismay, Jake departs from the workshop a day early, leaving Brenda to stay on to the end of the weekend.

When Brenda returns home, she informs Jake that she is leaving him for Geoffrey Mabbott. A neighbor whom Jake despises for his lack of personal-ity, Geoffrey had been attending the workshop sessions and presumably courting Brenda while Jake stayed home. Jake takes a suite of rooms, aban-doning the house to Brenda and Geoffrey, and, within a few months, he is fairly well adjusted to his new life alone.

The Characters

At the beginning of *Jake's Thing*, Jake complains to his physician about what he believes is a simple sexual dysfunction. He even hints to the doctor that some sort of medication might set him straight. By the end of the novel, however, after a series of psychological therapies, Jake's problem is compounded tenfold. In the concluding chapter, when Jake is finally offered a physical remedy in the form of testosterone supplements, he is so utterly averse to women that he responds with a decisive "No thanks."

Jake Richardson belongs to an older generation of men who have conservative notions of sexual decency. Rosenberg may be correct in his assessment of Jake's puritanical "guilt and shame," but Jake resents having to apologize for attitudes which he considers natural and proper. Although Jake assures Rosenberg that he does not mind "exposing his genitals in public" for the purpose of therapy, Rosenberg's obsession with the topic of such exposure annoys him. Jake believes that there are physical and psychological matters which ought to remain private. It seems to Jake that Rosenberg's insistent theme of public pubic display is an analogue for the modern mania for psychoanalytic exposure. Jake particularly resents the moral hegemony of the mental health profession, and he despises its cant: "If there's one word that sums up everything that's gone wrong since the War, it's Workshop. After Youth, that is." Despite his resentment, however, Jake persists in his therapy, partly because of an old-fashioned respect for the authority of doctors and partly because of his concern for Brenda's happiness.

Jake's recent encounters with women convince him that he does not really like the opposite sex. He is offended and intimidated by the women who picket his college; he is utterly repelled by the overbearing personality of his former mistress, Eve; he is alarmed by Kelly's invasion of his privacy at Oxford; and he is demoralized by Brenda's accusation that he is the sort of man who is only interested in women for sex. Eve essentially repeats Brenda's accusation the morning after she and Jake make love. When he confesses his attitudes toward women to a homosexual colleague at Oxford, Jake admits that Eve and Brenda are right: "I'd really—only—wanted—one—thing. [Eve] told me so this morning and that's when I saw it. I don't even like them much." Two subsequent experiences, Kelly's nasty suicide attempt and Brenda's elopement with Geoffrey, persuade Jake that his antipathy is well-founded.

Themes and Meanings

Jake's "thing" is really three things. Initially, and most literally, it is his penis, the object of much therapeutic attention. Later, Jake's thing is his misogynistic attitude. Ultimately, however, Jake's thing is his cultural critique which lashes out at trendy ideology and its social repercussions.

As appalling as his misogyny may seem, Jake does not start out actively disliking women. When the reader first meets him, he still feels affection for his wife despite his lack of sexual interest. A series of bad experiences with women and the humiliations of his sexual therapy, however, combine to demoralize Jake. The misogynistic attitude he acquires derives not from a well-considered philosophy but from an embattled ego.

Without sexual desire, Jake lacks what Brenda calls the "ballast" needed to keep him steady in the world. So long as his sexuality had given him a sense of social belonging, he remained unaware of his isolation from the cultural mainstream. Sexual therapy, however, forces him to look critically not only at himself but also at the world around him, and he does not like what he sees. More to the point, Jake does not like what he hears. The language used in modern culture tends to alienate people from one another rather than help them to communicate, a phenomenon which he did not notice in the days when he was still able to communicate sexually. Now that he is no longer physically attracted to Eve, for example, he recognizes that her elegant chatter is really a form of egotistical abuse.

From different perspectives, Jake and Rosenberg share a concern with language. Jake agrees with Rosenberg's tenet that "words embody attitudes of mind," but he despises the psychologist's jargon and the attitudes it embodies. To Jake, such words as "Workshop" and "facilitator" bespeak a dehumanizing of culture, while to Rosenberg, they convey a moral neutrality which makes them more therapeutically efficient than traditional terms such as "organiser" or "leader." Too sophisticated to believe in the possibility of such linguistic neutrality, Jake realizes that the conflict between him and Rosenberg is essentially a conflict between the values of humanism and scientism.

In more intimate relations, Jake sees the dehumanizing of culture manifested in the depersonalizing of sex. He is emotionally repelled by the clinical anatomical detail of contemporary pornography and by the equally cold mathematical motions of the prescribed "sensate focusing" sessions he performs with Brenda. In the novel's ultimate irony, Jake realizes that his social relations (notably his relations with women) merely exacerbate his feeling of alienation; his own sanity requires that he quit therapy and abandon sex forever. After all his tribulations, it is hardly surprising that when his physician finally offers a pharmaceutical cure for his moribund libido, Jake declines.

Critical Context

Since 1955, when he won the Somerset Maugham Award for his first novel, *Lucky Jim* (1954), Kingsley Amis has been celebrated as a writer of comic genius who protects nothing from satirical scrutiny. Jake Richardson, the hero of *Jake's Thing*, Amis' fifteenth novel, is an elderly version of Jim Dixon, although Jake's enervation contrasts sharply with the optimistic energy the young Jim had exhibited twenty-four years earlier.

Jake's Thing satirizes aspects of culture which Amis explored before in such novels as *I Like It Here* (1958), which takes aim at social pretensions, and *Girl, 20* (1971), an attack on the liberal sexual mores and radical politics of the 1960's counterculture. In his portrait of Jake Richardson, a fifty-nine-year-old Oxford professor in failing health who is uncomfortable with the drastic changes in society since the last world war, Amis also draws on the theme of the incapability and isolation of old age which he developed in *Ending Up* (1974).

Although Amis has been careful in interviews to distinguish between his own views and those of Jake, clearly he likes Jake well enough to carry his essential spirit forward to *Stanley and the Women* (1984). Like Jake, Stanley Duke endures abuse from women and rejects the destructive nonsense of the psychiatric profession. Both novels exploit a motif which resounds in Amis' mature work: a growing impatience with the fashionable cant of contemporary culture.

Sources for Further Study

Gardner, Philip. *Kingsley Amis*, 1981.
Plimpton, George, ed. *Writers at Work: The "Paris Review" Interviews*, 1981.
Pritchett, V. S. "Upmanship," in *The New York Review of Books*. LXXX (May 17, 1979), pp. 12-13.
Wilson, Keith. "Jim, Jake, and the Years Between: The Will to Stasis in the Contemporary British Novel," in *Ariel*. XIII (January, 1982), pp. 55-69.

Beverley Allix

JILL

Author: Philip Larkin (1922-1985)
Type of plot: Bildungsroman
Time of plot: 1940
Locale: Oxford
First published: 1946; revised, 1964

> *Principal characters:*
> JOHN KEMP, the protagonist, a naïve young student at Oxford
> CHRISTOPHER WARNER, a sophisticated public-school graduate who shares a room with John Kemp
> ELIZABETH DOWLING, a friend of Christopher Warner
> GILLIAN (JILL), Elizabeth's cousin and John's ideal girl

The Novel

Jill is a novel of education, the familiar tale of a young man's entrance into the world. The main character, John Kemp, is young, inexperienced, and working-class, the exact opposite of the stereotypical Oxford student. The novel begins with John setting out for the uncertain world of Oxford in the war year of 1940. He immediately displays his immaturity when he throws away his sandwiches because he does not wish the others on the train to see him eating; soon afterward, he sees the others break out their lunches, so he is forced to suffer hunger as well as embarrassment.

When John arrives at Oxford, he finds that he is sharing a room with someone who is as unlike him as possible: Christopher Warner is middle-class, public-school, and supremely confident and sophisticated. Christopher is hosting a tea party using John's china when John arrives. Christopher is not interested in obeying the rules or conventions; he seems, instead, confident of his place in the world. He is not, however, the guide for whom John is searching to initiate him into the world; rather, Christopher ignores John, and John is tormented by the difference between his world and Christopher's. John cannot be like Christopher, but he cannot deny his attraction to his world.

John's early weeks at Oxford are spent reading and outlining books in the way his teacher at Huddlesford had taught him. He is lonely and isolated; his only acquaintance is a young man who is from the same class and background: Whitbread, a Yorkshireman. Whitbread is interested in doing the right thing, in getting on in the world rather than fitting in with a sophisticated set such as that of Christopher Warner. Whitbread is an amusing character; he speaks in clichés and is fiercely dedicated to his own self-interest. John is not willing to enter Whitbread's world, and he cannot penetrate Christopher's.

One day, John overhears Christopher describing him as a "scared stuffed little rabbit," and all of his hopes of becoming a part of Christopher's world are dashed. In the midst of his anger and shame, John devises a way to counter Christopher's attitude of superiority by inventing a sister at a public school, Jill. John leaves the letters he has written in Jill's name around the room for Christopher, and he now has a topic for conversation with him. John's stratagem does produce a change in Christopher's attitude; he returns the money that he has borrowed from John and begins treating him more as an equal than before. This creation, however, begins to go beyond the initial purpose of intriguing Christopher. John has a moment of recognition: "Suddenly it was she who was important, she who was interesting, she whom he longed to write about; beside her, he and his life seemed dusty and tedious." He writes a short story about Jill and then creates a diary of her daily thoughts. John has created his own world so that his problems in the real world no longer seem as important. His difficulties, however, return when he sees his creation come alive on the streets of Oxford.

John confronts his "Jill" and attempts to speak to her, but she rebuffs his approaches. He becomes obsessed with her and spends his time waiting for a glimpse of her. His difficulties become more complex when she is introduced to him as a cousin of Elizabeth and a member of Christopher's set. Her name is Gillian, and she refuses to be called Jill. John finally has a moment with her, and his invitation to tea is accepted. John dashes around making preparations for the party; he seems finally about to enter that dazzling world he has longed to be a part of. When Elizabeth arrives to tell him that Gillian is not coming and that she is too young to accept such invitations, he is crestfallen. He mopes around for a few days trying to drive the loneliness and isolation out until he hears that his hometown, Huddlesford, has been bombed by the Germans.

When John arrives at Huddlesford, he finds that everything is strange and unfamiliar because of the bombing and his own Oxford experience. He passes by his parents' house and is relieved to see that it is untouched. He returns to Oxford with a very different attitude: "It [Huddlesford] meant no more to him now, and so it was destroyed: it seemed symbolic, a kind of annulling of his childhood. . . . Now there is a fresh start for you: you are no longer governed by what has gone before." After his return, John notices a letter from Elizabeth to Christopher about a party to which she will bring Gillian. John burns the letters and the story he had invented for his Jill and is ready to enter the real world. He sees Gillian with the others and rushes forward to kiss her. Christopher responds by throwing John into a fountain, a very different kind of initiation.

The novel ends with John in the infirmary brooding over his experience. Again, he contrasts his real experiences with "Jill" to his created one, and he believes that they "interlocked" in the dreamworld if not in the real one. He then sees that the distinction is meaningless, since "love died whether fulfilled or unfulfilled." This perception is extended by John so that he sees that the apparent differences of all opposites are also unreal, and if that is so he is "freed from choice." John's parents arrive, and Christopher leaves for the larger world of London with Elizabeth; the opposites suggest a return to childhood and a new freedom. As John has perceived, however, these supposed opposites really mean the same thing: "What did it matter which road he took if they both led to the same place?"

The Characters

John Kemp is crammed with facts and prepared for the scholarship examination a year ahead of time by his teacher, Mr. Crouch. He is the wrong age, the wrong class, and at Oxford at the wrong time. His retreat into fantasy is a way of controlling reality by inventing a world. Reality, however, keeps imposing itself on John's defenses: Jill comes to life, his hometown is bombed, he is thrown into a fountain. He has left his home and past behind, but he is not yet a part of Oxford. His character is defined by these opposites, but rather than choose one over the other, he suddenly sees that the differences are only apparent.

Christopher Warner is a stereotypical Oxford "hearty"; he is public-school and middle-class and is interested only in drinking and playing sports. He seems to believe that he can exploit whomever he chooses. He copies John's English notes and essays, and borrows money from his cronies. Oxford seems to be a social playground to him rather than an intellectual experience. His move to London with a mistress at the end of the novel suggests an enlargement of his horizons and, in contrast to John, a perfect adaptation to his environment.

Gillian is a minor character, but she assumes a symbolic importance in the novel. She seems to be a typical middle-class schoolgirl with a natural desire to get closer to the Oxford world. The reader never knows what she is thinking, and she does not change. What changes is John's perception of her. She is inflated into the ideal by John and then reveals herself to be human and real.

Themes and Meanings

The main theme of *Jill* can be seen in John's rejection of the world of his parents and of Whitbread, and his beginning to find a place in the larger world. After his return from Huddlesford, he feels at home for the first time: "It felt nice to be back." Yet this movement into the larger world is both incomplete and subjected to the usual Larkin irony. For example, although John burns the letters and the story he has created about Jill, he becomes a romantic hero when he attempts to "rescue" Jill from Christopher. He has left behind forever his parents' world and his childhood, but his parents come to Oxford to visit him in his sickbed.

A related theme is expressed in the moment of revelation in which John perceives that there are no differences between "any pair of opposites." This revelation may be an example of what the Romantic poet John Keats described as "negative capability," the ability to accept mysteries or unreconciled opposites intuitively rather than attempt to resolve them analytically. John, who has been the center of every scene in the novel, suddenly disappears from it; he is left with his revelation, while the perspective shifts to the opposites—his parents and Christopher—that have figuratively pulled his life from one side to the other. While they go about their business, Christopher to London and his parents to Oxford, John seems somehow beyond both of them.

Critical Context

Philip Larkin wrote *Jill* after he was graduated from Oxford, so it is his first extensive literary work. It was published a few years later, in 1946, and another novel, *A Girl in Winter*, followed in 1947. Later, in a typically wry manner, Larkin said that he was to have the career of a popular novelist. "I'd had visions of myself writing five hundred words a day for six months, shoving the result off to the printer and going to live on the Côte d'Azur, uninterrupted except for the correction of proofs." He could never write that third novel, however, claiming that the reason was that he "didn't know enough about people." The reason was more likely that he discovered that his real gift was for poetry rather than fiction.

Larkin was one of the most important writers in a group that came to be known as "The Movement." The writers of The Movement—Donald Davie, Kingsley Amis, and John Wain, along with Larkin, are the major figures— insisted on clarity and precision in place of "emotional fervor and wounded sensibility." While they rejected Romantic excess, however, they also were against the obscurities of modernism and experimental techniques. *Jill* is an example of many of the tenets of The Movement in its traditional form, its detailed and precise style, and its persistent puncturing of Romantic illusions.

Larkin has stated that the publication of *Jill* "aroused no public comment." Yet, as critics have concentrated on Larkin's poetry, they have begun to discuss and comment more on *Jill*. Some of these critics, especially Simon Petch, emphasize the "working-class" elements in the novel, an important part of such novels as John Braine's *Room at the Top* (1957). Others, such as Bruce K. Martin, stress the theme of "disillusion," a theme that is prominent in Larkin's poetry. Perhaps the only negative comments are those that focus on Larkin's "poetic" and almost obsessive attention to details. This may be an indication that Larkin's appropriate form was poetry and not the novel.

Sources for Further Study
Martin, Bruce K. *Philip Larkin*, 1978.
Motion, Andrew. *Philip Larkin*, 1982.
Petch, Simon. *The Art of Philip Larkin*, 1982.
Timms, David. *Philip Larkin*, 1973.

James Sullivan

JOURNEY INTO FEAR

Author: Eric Ambler (1909-   )
Type of plot: Suspense
Time of plot: January, 1940 (early in World War II)
Locale: Istanbul, Athens, and Genoa
First published: 1940

> *Principal characters:*
> GRAHAM, the protagonist, an English engineer
> JOSETTE, a dancer
> BANAT, a Romanian assassin
> KUVETLI, a Turkish agent who is traveling as a business
> representative
> MATHIS, a French Socialist
> MOELLER (alias HALLER), a German agent

The Novel

The action of *Journey into Fear* occurs in Istanbul, on a voyage from there to Genoa, and in Italy during the day the protagonist, Graham, an English engineer, arrives there. In the early months of World War II, Graham has been sent to Turkey to arrange for the rearming of Turkish warships. The information he has acquired will be carried to England in his head, so the Germans, to delay Anglo-Turkish naval cooperation, must try to stop him. When he is almost killed by a man he later identifies as Banat, a German agent under the control of the Gestapo agent Moeller, the Turkish Secret Police put him on a small Italian steamer which will carry him to Genoa, where he will take a train to Paris.

On the ship he meets Josette, a French dancer; Kuvetli, a Turkish business representative; Haller, a German archaeologist; and Mathis, a Frenchman who constantly irritates his aristocratic wife with his arguments for socialism. The ship sails first to Piraeus. Graham tours Athens, and when he returns to the ship the man he knows as Banat has come on board. Graham confides in Josette, for whom, in spite of her husband, he is developing romantic feelings, and he feels secure because he has a revolver in his cabin. The gun is stolen, however, and that night, when Graham returns to his cabin, Haller, who is actually the Gestapo agent Moeller, is there. Moeller suggests that since the Germans only want to delay the rearming of the Turkish warships for six weeks, Graham need only take a "rest cure" in Italy for that time as their guest.

When Kuvetli informs Graham that he is a Turkish agent, sent along to protect him, they hatch a plan for Graham's escape. Kuvetli is killed, however, and Graham must confide in Mathis, the Frenchman, who lends him his own pistol.

Moeller and Banat take Graham in a car into the country beyond Genoa, and when it stops, Graham is informed that he is to be killed. He shoots Banat, leaps from the car, and shoots into the gas tank. The car explodes, and Graham gets back to Genoa, where the Turkish consulate, warned by Mathis, helps him get a train to Paris. On the train he meets Josette, rejects her husband's offer of renting her to him for a weekend in Paris, and returns the pistol to Mathis.

The Characters

Journey into Fear is essentially an action novel designed to create suspense. Eric Ambler makes Graham an ordinary man to make it easier for the reader to identify with him. Like any other ordinary man, he is unwilling to believe that his situation is as dangerous as it is. At the same time, Ambler makes it clear that Graham is a rather cold person, uncommitted to anyone. He and his wife married only as a matter of convenience, and Graham has got through life by standing aside from people and from events, an observer rather than a participant in the real problems of the world.

It is only when Banat boards the ship in Piraeus that Graham realizes how terrifying his situation is. Yet while Ambler is primarily concerned with events which build Graham's terror and are designed to carry the reader along, he also makes his characters believable. They are not fully rounded, but neither are they the kind of cutout figures who sometimes populate spy novels. Ambler's method is not to get inside his characters to show their complexity but to present them to the reader as persons who are not what they seem to be.

Josette, for example, appears first as a sophisticated, though rather weary, woman of the world, and Graham himself realizes that she is playing a number of roles, shifting from one to another like a dancer gliding through the movements of a dance. Later, she seems truly concerned with Graham's predicament, but she also seems to be less concerned with his welfare than with the lucrative arrangements she intends to establish in Paris with him if she can help to save his life. Finally, on the train, she reveals herself as a businesswoman whose deal has fallen through.

Mathis tells Graham that he became a Socialist during World War I, when he learned that a French official had ordered that iron mines captured by the Germans not be bombed, because he owned them. At the same time, he seems to be less concerned with the usual left-wing social concerns than with threatening to spout socialism in public as a means of keeping his conservative wife in line.

Mathis and Josette exemplify Ambler's method of creating characters who are not what they appear to be. Kuvetli seems to be an inconspicuous little man traveling as a salesman, but he is actually a secret agent and a devoted Turkish patriot of considerable courage who dies in the service of his country.

Moeller pretends to be Haller, a distinguished German archaeologist, and at first he seems very much a man of ideas altogether too civilized to care any-thing for the usual antagonisms of people whose countries are at war. Actu-ally, he has taken over the passport and identity of the real Haller, even mas-tering a detailed knowledge of ancient history to make the deception work, and he is a very calculating Gestapo agent who believes in nothing but the murderous ideology of the Nazis.

Ambler, in other words, is not concerned with characterization in the usual sense. That would get in the way of the action of the novel, which must be fairly rapid to heighten the suspense which is the novel's purpose. *Journey into Fear*, after all, fits the requirements of the genre of the novel of intrigue, the modern version of which Ambler helped to create.

Themes and Meanings

Journey into Fear reveals no theme as such. It is an "entertainment" in the sense that Graham Greene used the term to describe his own thrillers. The espionage novel is a kind of crime story on an international scale, and it em-ploys many of the methods of the crime story, which is itself a departure from the traditional detective story. The plot is not based on the question of the identity of a criminal but upon the psychology of the characters. The princi-pal character is not a brilliant detective who discovers the answer to this question but only an ordinary man to whom things happen. It does not resolve itself in terms of a string of clues which the detective follows to his conclusion; the plot is about the characters. The setting (the exotic world of Istanbul and a small Italian ship steaming through the Aegean and Medi-terranean in wartime) is important in defining the sinister environment of the novel. Graham's survival does not depend on his being able to solve a puzzle but on being able to analyze correctly the character of each of the people on board the ship. Indeed, there is no puzzle; it is Graham's predicament, the exotic situation, and the characters he meets that one remembers.

Though the novel fits exactly the requirements of a novel of intrigue and though Ambler's meeting those requirements is more important to him than the development of any theme, the novel is not without meaning. The world Ambler describes is that of the period in history when efforts to appease Fas-cism had failed and Europe was at war. It is the "phony war," however, of the winter of 1939-1940, when a certain degree of civilized behavior was still pos-sible and when the struggle against Fascism could still be understood in per-sonal terms. In the previous decade, civilized people wanted to believe that everyone else was civilized in spite of evidence that the most monstrous crimes were already being unleashed against humanity. *Journey into Fear* captures that time of moral ambiguity. Graham is a kind of allegorical repre-sentation of his English society, secure and self-satisfied at the outset, sailing through dangerous waters, attempting to find allies in a world in which he discovers that almost no one can be trusted.

Furthermore, the novel provides a chilling vision of the kind of amoral environment in which the enemies of democracy and freedom move. Moeller, pretending to be the most civilized example of German scholarship, an archaeologist and therefore a preserver of the traditions of civilization, is actually a Gestapo agent. He kills without remorse, almost without noticing that he has killed, because he is the willing instrument of a government that values the state and the gangsters who rule in its name more than it values the people whose interests it claims to serve. Ironically, his lackey Banat is almost less morally repugnant because he actually enjoys killing people and does not pretend to do it for any higher good. *Journey into Fear* is a useful reminder of what the world had become by the first winter of World War II and a convenient introduction to the moral environment in which the games of international politics have been played ever since.

Critical Context

Ambler's first novels of intrigue expressed his criticism of the international bankers and armaments manufacturers who he believed in the 1930's were responsible for international conflict. The evils faced by his protagonists were the greed and social irresponsibility of international economic forces, served by agents who were willing to commit any crime for the success of their employers. By the time Ambler wrote *Journey into Fear*, he was no longer convinced that the world's ills could be so easily explained. Here the evil is Fascism, and the enemy of his protagonist is Nazi Germany, represented by agents who just as ruthlessly serve a murderous state bent on domination of the world. When Ambler returned to writing novels of intrigue after World War II, they were less sensational than his early work and more despairing. *Journey into Fear* stands as one of Ambler's finest achievements in espionage fiction because it goes beyond the often simplistic political vision of his earliest novels while preserving the positive, even moral, attitude of those works.

At the same time, if the novel adheres to the requirements of the novel of intrigue, it goes far beyond that genre's limitations. It is written in a style that is appropriately spare, and it goes as far in characterization as it can in a work which depends for its success on action and suspense.

Sources for Further Study

Eames, Hugh. *Sleuths, Inc.: Studies of Problem Solvers*, 1978.
Lambert, Gavin. *The Dangerous Edge*, 1976.
Landrum, Larry, and Pat Browne, eds. *Dimensions of Detective Fiction*, 1976.
Panek, LeRoy L. *The Special Branch: The British Spy Novel, 1890-1980*, 1981.

Robert L. Berner

JOY OF THE WORM

Author: Frank Sargeson (1903-1982)
Type of plot: Tragicomedy
Time of plot: Mid-twentieth century
Locale: Rural New Zealand
First published: 1969

Principal characters:
JAMES BOHUN, a Methodist minister
JEREMY BOHUN, the eldest of James's two sons
QUEENIE QUELCH, James's second wife
MAISIE MICHIE, Jeremy's first wife

The Novel

After a year of working at odd jobs around New Zealand, Jeremy Bohun returns home to reestablish contact with his parents. Jeremy is feeling at loose ends generally, a state of mind that contrasts with his father's great self-assurance. His father, James, is a Methodist clergyman who takes it as his professional obligation to direct the lives of those around him. To this end, he reads endlessly from theological and classical tomes and as a result projects himself in what he perceives to be an erudite manner. To others he seems merely eccentric, out of date, and overbearing. The result of his dictatorial and rather archaic manner is that his wife has retreated into a shell while John, his second son, has left home disgusted with his father's senseless pontification, vowing never to return.

When Jeremy first walks into the kitchen of his parents' home after his long absence, his father mistakes him for John, his favorite, and greets Jeremy accordingly. This greeting comes as no surprise to Jeremy, knowing his father as well as he does, nor does his father's request that he return to a long-standing practice and read to him daily from Gibbon's *History*. In time, the old man hopes, this will create a bond of mutual intellectual curiosity between them.

Soon Jeremy relocates to a small town nearby, where he secures a position with the local government. Taken under the wing of his predecessor, Mr. Greenlee, in whose home he lodges, Jeremy learns the various aspects of his job and settles comfortably into a routine. Another boarder at the Greenlee home, Maisie Michie, captures his interest, and a love affair ensues. Without the knowledge of the Greenlees, who would never brook such behavior under their roof, Jeremy and Maisie begin sleeping together. Jeremy goes to some trouble to furnish a back room of his office suitably so that they can meet there as well. Jeremy's meager salary is not very conducive to his romantic interests, and he therefore begins what becomes a rather inglorious habit of stealing from the office petty cash.

As this is occurring, Jeremy's mother is slowly dying back home. James, feeling the part of the long-sufferer, has had the help of one of his parishioners, a middle-aged woman named Queenie Quelch, in seeing to the care and comfort of his failing wife. Queenie first became known to James when she had asked his help in investing five hundred pounds inherited from her mother. Being suitably flattered and using the best means at his disposal, James invested the money in what became a losing proposition. He later reminisces, to his own comfort and gratification, that on the occasion of entrusting her money to him Queenie may have lost five hundred pounds, but she gained a husband, for after the first Mrs. Bohun's departure from the world, James begins to woo the nurse for his second bride.

Father and son are married on the same day, and both seem destined for happiness. James goes so far as to question whether his first wife really understood him, while Jeremy's household becomes filled with robust little children. James proves exceedingly virile and active as an old man, but the treachery of self-absorbed intellectual curiosity returns to the Bohun men, who retreat into a realm of reading and conversation that supersedes what they presume to be the mundane demands of job and family. It is as if the pursuit of women animates both James and Jeremy, but following the pursuit it is the love of books that take over, a need for the rarefied atmosphere of cerebral indulgence. James justifies his study as requisite to his job. Jeremy, being more forthright, merely neglects his office duties.

Jeremy is eventually caught in his theft of petty cash: A government auditor easily discovers his dishonest manipulations. Unknown to Jeremy, Maisie approaches another local official, Joe Lavender, for help. She is prepared to offer anything to save her family the ignominy of her husband's crime yet finds her task easier than she had ever expected it could be. Upon reaching the Lavender household, she observes Mrs. Lavender dressed as her husband, carrying out his chores, and Joe dressed in his wife's clothes, doing the ironing. After some flustered embarrassment, Joe admits to Maisie that he and his wife do such a switch on occasion to "keep things fresh." To avoid the public ridicule and reproach that would follow exposure of this, Joe volunteers to pay back the sum stolen by Jeremy, thereby righting the situation for Maisie and her less resourceful husband.

James, meanwhile, decides that he and Queenie need a break from each other. He writes to apprise Jeremy of his forthcoming visit. Maisie is not happy, but Jeremy, surprised at his own reaction, is actually pleased with the prospect of seeing his father. When James does arrive, the two men sequester themselves for lengthy, esoteric discussions. Their insensitivity to the women is evident, as all household chores devolve on Maisie, who laments being "the family charwoman."

After a lengthy stay, James returns home on the train. Queenie fails to meet him at the station, and after searching for her without success, James calls on Jeremy to attend him. Jeremy does so and arranges for a temporary nursemaid to watch over his father, but when he returns he finds, to his own surprise, that Maisie has left him. The narrator interjects, "But after all, to what end had he read all those books—all those endless speculations about human experience, all those demonstrations of human behavior, all those emotions on paper, if he were not to be better equipped for coping when the testing time came?" He does manage. He manages by muddling through.

Christmas vacation arrives and Jeremy takes advantage of the holiday to visit his father. There he finds the old man under the care of an attractive widow, Mrs. Bonnie. Jeremy finds himself drawn to her but is kept in check by his uncertain marital status. Interestingly, James has similar designs on his nurse. When Maisie's remains are discovered in some barren country not far away, Jeremy is not sure whether to mourn or rejoice. In short order, he dispenses with the usual funeral arrangements, proposes to Mrs. Bonnie, and is married.

Left to his own devices, James embarks on a quest to find Queenie and his other son, John. After some six months, Jeremy is called to a small town where his father is in the care of the widow of a licensee. There James chooses to remain and there he dies. Jeremy returns home to continue with his latest interest, seminary studies, hoping to become a vicar. As a tag end to the story, Jeremy hears rumors of a man answering the description of John living a rather ordinary life somewhere in Latin America.

The Characters

James Bohun is an older man deceived by his own moderate intellectual gifts and physical virility (which he retains into dotage). As a Methodist minister, he believes that he should be able to keep his own life in order as well as the lives of others looking (or even not looking) to him for guidance. Perhaps to save God the trouble, or perhaps simply to make sure that things are done properly, James assumes a position of authority within his small world and becomes not only self-righteous but arrogant and pushy as well. Presuming on his own generous estimate of his gifts, his godly calling, and a trace of aristocratic blood somewhere in the family line, James strides through life aware of his triumphs but woefully ignorant of his shortcomings or the strengths of others. His character is consistent throughout the novel and similar to the emperor who paraded so proudly in his "new clothes."

Jeremy is an attractive character when the reader meets him, employed at a laborer's job, enjoying the company and admiring the philosophy of simple working men; upon returning home, he is put off by his father's unbecoming blend of arrogance and insensitivity. As time goes on, however, Jeremy loses this wholesome, commonsense perspective and becomes increasingly like his father. Jeremy is more reflective than James, yet, when it becomes apparent to him that he is duplicating his father's life, he seems unperturbed and willing to continue. Previously he had sought to comfort his mother for being married to such a man. That he is aware of what has transpired is evident in his letter to a friend that concludes the novel: "To you I will confess the chilling thought that sometimes occurs to me when I am in conversation—if my brother were to return to us, he might hasten to depart again immediately, under the impression of being misinformed about our father's being no longer amongst us . . .—perhaps I am much more his son than I ever imagined."

Maisie is the only female character who is given much of an inner life, and it flickers only briefly before she decides to leave Jeremy. Maisie proves her mettle as a loyal mate in approaching Joe Lavender. Receiving no such consideration from Jeremy, burdened with an ever-increasing family, and having spoken with a woman who warned her about the exploitive nature of men, Maisie considers her lot in life. She observes in what respects her life has been dominated by males, including Jeremy, James, and her sons, and concludes that she and her daughter must escape the sexist-religious-intellectual oppression.

Themes and Meanings

Joy of the Worm is a loose compendium of ideas on life, death, relationships, and erudition. This is a reflection of James's eclecticism to a large extent. One notion, however, predominates: that of the conflict between the world of intellect and the world of events and emotions.

James and Jeremy are convinced that their reading and learned conversations will place them in a realm above ordinary people. In believing this, however, they often fail to see how dependent they are on others to care for them. Only Jeremy has a brief insight into this when he says to Maisie, as if it will redeem him, "I am a scoundrel, but I am a scholar." For all of their lofty talk, he and his father become essentially irreligious and inhumane.

When the fleshly world threatens, both James and Jeremy rationalize their way clear of it: "In case [Jeremy] might at any moment lose control, find himself too much up against the crude facts not to be in his heart 'all mad with misery,' he employed the stratagem of deliberately toying in his mind with these crudities—until he had made the decision that the two limits of their range were the ghastly and the tedious: everything else could be tolerated. Like his father he tended to be an in-between kind of man. . . ." Both men are lusty and enjoy the material world, but they are also fearful of it and want to limit its consequences. To this end they distort their perceptions of it.

Like children, James and Jeremy are lovers of romances. They liken themselves to Don Quixote and Sancho Panza. Jeremy discovers the fallacy in this:

It was like Don Quixote and Sancho finding themselves confronted with the dead mule in the Daumier picture: there was the horrid appearing gap of blank paper that separated romance from necessary fact—but there would always be those who would refuse to accept the gap as such, insisting that it was there waiting to be filled with a proper and satisfying blend of imagination and necessity.

James and Jeremy fill the gaps with chatter. They satiate what Jeremy calls "the crude appetite for life," his euphemism for sex, but hide from the "crude facts," his euphemism for responsibilities, in the library. Sargeson is not anti-intellectual; rather he argues for an intellect that is vital, courageous, compassionate, and adult.

Critical Context

As one of Frank Sargeson's later novels, *Joy of the Worm* shows the cumulative effects of many of his previous works. It exhibits Sargeson's tendency toward picaresque and episodic plots in his longer works. As another in a series of perspectives on New Zealand life offered by way of offbeat or curious characters, it says something about human nature and proffers a powerful, if not altogether succinct, moral. The story continues Sargeson's exploration of the Puritan mentality that guided the formative spirit of early colonial New Zealand and that has remained to superintend much of New Zealand's contemporary life.

In these several respects, *Joy of the Worm* follows naturally the short stories, which garnered several literary awards, and novels such as *I Saw in My Dream* (1949), *Memoirs of a Peon* (1965), and *The Hangover* (1967). The elements present in *Joy of the Worm* are those same elements mentioned most frequently by observers as constituents of the "Sargeson world," a world presumably similar to that of Charles Dickens in the author's re-creation of his milieu with the irregular building blocks of perverse, eccentric, lonely, lost, intriguing people.

One critic has characterized Sargeson's writing as "imaginative realism," a phrase which accounts for the author's unique approach to his culture and the dual nature of his characters as both representative and real. Sargeson has been placed alongside Katherine Mansfield as one of the giants of New Zealand literature. He has been called a "father figure to virtually all modern New Zealand fiction," and critics have spoken of his "sheer dominance of his fictional scene." His international reputation is limited, in part as a consequence of his single-minded determination to create a literature of New Zealand without looking over his shoulder toward larger audiences.

Sources for Further Study
Copland, R. A. *Frank Sargeson*, 1976.
King, Bruce Alvin. "New Zealand: Frank Sargeson and Colloquial Realism,"

in *The New English Literatures: Cultural Nationalism in a Changing World*, 1980.

Rhodes, H. Winston. *Frank Sargeson*, 1969.

The Times Literary Supplement. Review. August 7, 1969, p. 873.

Robert J. Helgeson

JULY'S PEOPLE

Author: Nadine Gordimer (1923-   )
Type of plot: Social realism
Time of plot: The near future
Locale: South African bush country
First published: 1981

> *Principal characters:*
> BAMFORD SMALES, a Johannesburg architect
> MAUREEN HETHERINGTON SMALES, his wife
> ROYCE,
> GINA, and
> VICTOR, the Smaleses' preteen children
> JULY, also known as MWAWATE, the Smaleses' houseboy and
>   caretaker for the past fifteen years, now their protector
> MARTHA, July's wife
> DANIEL, July's erstwhile assistant

The Novel

Nadine Gordimer's novel *July's People* is a fictitious account of a black revolt in South Africa. In the novel the blacks in the South African police force refuse to arrest their own people, public services break down, and fighting erupts in the major cities, quickly spreading into the rural areas. Bloodshed engulfs the country. The rebels have prepared well. They have heavy caliber weapons and airplanes and help from the neighboring black states of Botswana, Zimbabwe, Zambia, Namibia, and Mozambique, as well as from Cuba and the Soviet Union. Everywhere their forces threaten the security of the white settlers.

Bamford and Maureen Smales, a liberal, white couple, flee with their three children from their home in a comfortable residential district of Johannesburg and find refuge in the mud and thatched hut village that contains the extended family of their black servant, July.

July then becomes their protector. He quarters them in one of the dwellings that had been occupied by his wife. She resents the eviction, thinking that the whites should seek help from other whites, but defers to the authority of her husband. The lives of the white visitors are transformed beyond their imagination. In the bush they have none of the amenities of their former existence: no electricity, no running water, no modern sanitation. Maureen believes that she is in another consciousness; "it pressed in upon her and filled her as someone's breath fills a balloon's shape." Time, as the family once knew it, begins to lose meaning. Desperate for outside news, the adults practically worship their radio, fearful that its batteries might give out. Yet the garbled transmissions they receive do not tell them the fate of their society and its chances of survival.

July at first seems a considerate host, taking a certain pride in showing off his white family, almost like a trophy, but it is obvious that the pleasure of the Smaleses' presence is beginning to wear thin. The Smaleses, increasingly isolated, try harder to adjust to their alien way of life. The children cope better than their parents, disturbingly so as they begin to play like black children, acquiring their language, adapting themselves to their customs. The youngest son, Victor, begins to forget how to read and does not miss his old comic-book heroes.

The Smaleses' material possessions, those that they managed to bring with them, are also falling away from them, including the small truck, the "bakkie," in which they made their escape. Bamford Smales had intended it for weekend bird-hunting expeditions. July manages to get his hands on the keys and does not give them back. Unable to drive before, he now learns from Daniel, a younger black who had once driven a truck for a dairy in Bethal. The Smaleses are disturbed, but realizing that they cannot exist without the goodwill of the blacks, they avoid a confrontation by going along.

Maureen attempts to maintain a semblance of independence. She volunteers to participate in gathering food for her own family, but her offer is rejected by July, who says that his women perform this sort of work. Bamford tries to establish status as a provider of meat by shooting some young wild pigs with his twelve-gage shotgun, but the amount provided is hardly sufficient to make much of a difference.

The white couple's sense of malaise is increased by the discovery that July's village is under a higher tribal authority, exercised by a district chief. The chief summons the white family before him. The Smaleses are alarmed that he might order them out of the village, but they discover that he is more concerned with protecting his own territoriality against the black rebels. He views the Smaleses as potential allies, asking Bamford to teach him how to use his gun.

Following the return to July's village, Bamford discovers that the shotgun and all its ammunition have disappeared. His wife suspects that July is the culprit, but she finds out that the real thief is Daniel, who has taken the weapon to join the rebels. Before the effects of this latest incident can be felt, a helicopter arrives. Maureen, obviously assuming that it brings news of the victory of the white forces, is ecstatic and runs toward the sound of its whirling blades with the desperate frenzy of one rushing toward salvation.

The Characters

The English-speaking Smaleses listen to the radio hoping for the best, but at the same time asking themselves whether they would even want to resume their former lives. They have never considered themselves part of the

Afrikaner society, have always deplored the apartheid system, and once contemplated emigrating to Canada. They view their relationship with the blacks, especially with July, as almost one of friendship among equals, and they shudder at the thought that it in any way resembles one of master and servant. It would never occur to them that their treatment of the natives might be a form of condescension and that they share part of the blame for the state of affairs between the races.

The Smaleses speak no other language but their own and are equally provincial in other ways. Their good intentions cannot make up for their naïveté and their lack of imagination. Despite the weeks of serious rioting in Soweto, Bamford downplays the impending crisis. He withdraws his money from the bank only after he has been alerted by a bank accountant for whom he once designed a house, and even then does so reluctantly in a state of "detached disbelief." The Smaleses are professional liberals. "They had always—from a distance—admired Castro, the bourgeois white who succeeded in turning revolutionary." Undoubtedly, there are other South African whites who share these sentiments, but in this emergency, they do not seem important enough to give protection even to each other.

Maureen struggles to remain true to her ideals. Yet she does not have the personality or the experience to relinquish her parental attitude toward blacks. By indulging July in his appropriation of the truck, she allows him to gain the upper hand. He works on her conscience by accusing her of not trusting him—her boy who worked for her for fifteen years. He further insists that even out here in the bush he be paid exactly as he was in town. Maureen does not dare demand the return of the keys but tries to make him feel guilty instead. She reminds him about the mistress he left behind in Johannesburg, "Where is she, in the fighting there? Has she got something to eat, somewhere to sleep? You were so concerned about your wife—and what does she think of Ellen?" The ineffective ploy does not work. July walks away, the keys still in his pocket. Maureen's character is flawed by her lack of understanding about the people whose interests she had presumed to foster.

Nadine Gordimer involves the reader in the Smaleses' struggle to adjust to their new way of life; she describes its adverse effect on their sex life, Maureen's efforts to adjust to a life without sanitary napkins, the attempts to retain dignity as European-style clothing becomes increasingly tattered. By contrast, Gordimer tells her readers less about July, allowing access to his thoughts rarely and then only insofar as he struggles to comprehend whites and their institutions. In his way, he is as isolated and dependent as the Smaleses. He cannot even decide for himself the fate of his Johannesburg bank account, the exact worth of which he does not know. Now that the fighting has started, he suspects that his passbook is no longer worth anything, but he does not know. Should he destroy it? "He needed someone—

he didn't know yet who—to tell him: burn it, let it swell in the river, their signatures washing away."

July's lack of direction and helplessness (at least outside his own native milieu) is confirmed by Maureen as she angrily tells him: "You want the bakkie, to drive around in like a gangster, imagining yourself a *big man*, important, until you don't have any money for petrol, there isn't any petrol to buy, and it'll lie there, July, under the trees, in this place among old huts, and it'll fall to pieces while the children play in it." The whites are equally unsympathetic in their judgment of the native chief, who they feel has done so little, and even betrayed, his own people. Thus, the races are defined by their relationship to each other.

Themes and Meanings

Except for wearing a new snap-brimmed hat, the district chief looks like many other rural blacks in cast-off European clothing, but he has "the sharp, impatient, sceptical voice of a man quicker than the people he keeps around him." He interrogates the Smaleses about the war: Who is blowing up the government? Why have whites lost control? What are the goals of the rebels? The chief views the black nationalists with greater trepidation than he does the white settlers because the black rebels might come and take away his land.

Bamford Smales cannot believe that the chief would shoot his own people. "You wouldn't kill blacks. . . . You're not going to take guns and help the white government kill blacks, are you? . . . You mustn't let the government make you kill each other. The whole black nation is your nation."

Bamford is referring to a black nation that does not exist, and probably never will unless, if European experience is any judge, there has been a wholesale butchery of blacks by blacks. A successful black revolt against white masters will only be a prelude to an eventual civil war among the blacks themselves. Bamford and Maureen are as badly prepared to help avoid this eventual tragedy as they are to meet the blacks on a level of true equality, which neither really wants anyway. Their rescue will only be a reprieve. If they can return to their home in the suburbs with its endless supply of toilet paper and soap and electrical energy, it will always be as strangers in an alien land, and their existence will be even more marginal and hopeless than before.

Critical Context

Nadine Gordimer was born in Springs in the Transvaal gold-mining district and reared, as she has put it, "on the soft side of the color bar." In a previous novel, *A World of Strangers* (1958), she writes about the polarity of the South African people and the impossibility of achieving any true racial harmony. The main character is an English engineer come to South Africa on special assignment. In time, he believes that he has a sense of belonging but only "as a stranger among people who were strangers to each other."

Apartheid is the one constant in the author's unhappy homeland, and almost all of her characters are infected by its disease. *July's People* reexplores this persistent theme but does not bore the reader by its repetition because of Gordimer's success in infusing her characters with drama and personality. The action is contained and fairly localized but well-defined. Her vision is disturbingly pessimistic, especially about the prospects for South African liberalism, depicted here as essentially sterile and irrelevant.

The book possesses a fine sense of irony mixed with vivid realism, enabling one to forgive frequent stylistic eccentricities. Gordimer makes South Africa more than simply an exotic setting for conflict, but a character in itself, a basic element in changing, establishing, and molding the lives of all its people. African and European cultures, although in constant conflict and largely incompatible, are nevertheless interdependent and inextricably linked.

Sources for Further Study
Haugh, Robert F. *Nadine Gordimer: The Meticulous Vision*, 1974.
Jacoby, Tamar. Review in *The Nation*. CCXXXII (June 6, 1981), p. 705.
Paton, Alan. Review in *Saturday Review*. VIII (May, 1981), p. 67.
Strouse, Jean. Review in *Newsweek*. XCVII (June 22, 1981), p. 78.
Tyler, Anne. Review in *The New York Times Book Review*. LXXXIV (June 7, 1981), p. 1.

Wm. Laird Kleine-Ahlbrandt

KANGAROO

Author: D. H. Lawrence (1885-1930)
Type of plot: Psychological realism
Time of plot: The early 1920's, in the period following World War I
Locale: Sydney, Australia, and the immediately surrounding area
First published: 1923

> *Principal characters:*
> RICHARD LOVAT SOMERS, an English writer
> HARRIET SOMERS, his wife, a strong-willed German
> JACK CALLCOTT, an Australian friend of Somers
> VICTORIA CALLCOTT, his wife
> BENJAMIN "KANGAROO" COOLEY, the leader of a reactionary
> political organization

The Novel

The dynamic marriage relationship between Richard Lovat Somers and his wife, Harriet, is the central concern of this novel. As with all the important marriages in the novels of D. H. Lawrence, it is a constantly changing relationship that alternates between being nourishing and life-giving to each individual, on the one hand, and being destructive and emotionally suffocating on the other. As is also typical of Lawrence, the relationship is characterized by a great intensity. At times, that emotional and spiritual intensity completely engulfs the individual selves of the characters, and they achieve mythic proportions.

Richard Somers is an English writer who has come to Australia to escape what he believes is the worn-out, spiritually restricting culture of Europe. The novel opens with the arrival of Richard and Harriet by boat from India, and it closes with their departure for the United States several months later; in that interval, Richard and Harriet experience the unique social and physical landscape of the Australian continent, an experience which changes them forever.

The novel's dramatic action begins with Richard and Harriet becoming acquainted with their neighbors, Jack and Victoria Callcott. The couples are curious about each other. Victoria is fascinated by Harriet, whom she views as a European lady, a person of sophistication and worldly knowledge. Harriet, in turn, responds to Victoria's open friendliness, finding in her a symbol of the larger Australia with its freshness and its cultural freedom. Yet it is the relationship between the two men that is more important to the novel's development. Richard finds in Jack the characteristics of the friendly, slow-to-anger Australian, the man who seems to be an individual beyond all else.

Jack, however, a veteran of the recent war, now belongs to a reactionary group which has ambitions of taking over the Australian government in a semimilitary movement. When Jack learns that Richard is the son of a workingman and that Richard views Western civilization as basically hampering to the individual, Jack becomes emotionally committed to Richard. Jack pledges his friendship and takes Richard to Benjamin "Kangaroo" Cooley, a successful lawyer who is the spiritual leader of the organization. Richard is fascinated by Kangaroo, an individual of remarkable intelligence who possesses a great, deep love for mankind.

Kangaroo has read Richard's writings on the flawed nature of democracy, and he invites Richard to join the organization, which is composed largely of Diggers, a name for veterans from the recent war. Yet Richard hesitates: Although he wishes to become a leader of men, to move in the world of action, he finally rejects the offer to join the paramilitary group because he cannot believe in its political purpose. When Jack learns that Richard will not join, a tension develops between the two men which mars their friendship.

As these events unfold along one line of the novel's action, Richard and Harriet concurrently explore Sydney and the surrounding area in their search for cultural freedom. Aided by the Callcotts, they find a house by the beach in a small township outside Sydney and move into it. There they experience what becomes the essence of Australia for them: Before them, beyond their porch, is the marvelously changing ocean, and behind is the vast bush of the continent, which holds a great dark freedom from the restrictions of civilization. Yet in that very freedom, their unconfined, civilized consciousness seems to turn on them, and their situation becomes oppressive. Although they discover a sublime beauty in the landscape, a vast beauty that in many ways finds its complement in the openness of the Australian people, both discover that they miss the infrastructure of European civilization. They also realize that they do value a civilized consciousness; they cannot undo what they are.

Although Richard could not commit himself to Kangaroo's reactionary party, he still wishes to become involved in the world of political action. He believes that he requires some vital activity beyond his marriage in order to retain his identity. Harriet is made resentful by this desire, but Richard is determined to pursue it, so he arranges a meeting with Willie Struthers, the leader of the Australian Socialist Party. Like Kangaroo, Struthers has read Richard's writings, and he asks Richard to do a newspaper for the party. Struthers believes that Richard, as the son of a workingman, could make a great contribution in educating the Australian masses. Again, Richard is tempted to move into the larger world of action, but once again he rejects the offer. Richard believes that the impulses which modern man obeys are misguided; he believes that the old impulse toward doing Christian good—as represented by the Socialist movement—is outmoded. The traditional forces that rule man must be rejected, he believes, for some deeper, undefined source, a dark god that is a life force beyond love.

One chapter in the middle of the novel's development which is essential in understanding Richard and Harriet's characters is a long, complex flashback in which their past is portrayed in England during World War I. The couple lived in rural Cornwall, and the description of the landscape and the people contains some of the best writing of the novel. Richard was outspokenly against the war; he was not sympathetic with the Germans but was simply against war in general—not only the actual killing on the front lines but also the brutalizing, regimenting effect of the war on English society. Because of Richard's antiwar sentiments, and because Harriet is German, the English authorities constantly harassed them. When the war was over, they left England in despair.

The climax of the novel occurs at a large Socialist meeting when the Diggers disrupt the proceedings, shouting down Willie Struthers in the middle of one of his speeches. In the riot which follows, Kangaroo is wounded, hit by a bullet in the stomach. Richard escapes with Jack, and afterward Jack tells Richard how exhilarated he feels: Jack relates that he was able to kill three men under the guise of the riot, and that the feeling this action gave him was better than making love to a woman.

Richard is revolted at Jack's disclosure, and he returns home a sick man physically and spiritually. For days, Richard wanders the beach; he realizes that something inside him—the desire to participate in the political world of action, to become a leader of men—has died. The wonderful beauty of the ever-changing ocean is in stark contrast to his lack of feeling inside. It is as if his soul has died.

The desperately ill Kangaroo requests Richard to come to him, and although Richard would rather not, he goes. In this meeting, Kangaroo requests that Richard love him in the spirit of brotherhood, that Richard commit himself totally to love. Richard tells him that he will think it over. A few weeks later, Kangaroo again calls Richard to him. Dying, Kangaroo once again asks Richard to accept him in the name of love. Richard, however, cannot, for he senses that there are forces beyond brotherly love that preclude his total acceptance of love. Since Richard cannot lie to Kangaroo, he must reject him.

After this rejection, Richard realizes again that something inside him has died—some ideal of what he was, some aspect of his identity. He also realizes that because of that inner death, he can no longer remain in Australia. Harriet and he sail for America toward an uncertain future. If something has died inside Richard, he at least has not committed himself to some false, larger authority which would destroy his central relationship with Harriet. In the future, it is possible for his soul, his identity, to be reborn in that relationship with his wife.

The Characters

Richard Somers is a highly autobiographical character. Lawrence wrote all but the last chapter of the novel during his four-month stay in Australia, and many of Richard's characteristics and concerns were those of Lawrence at the time. Like Lawrence, Richard is living in a relationship with a strong-willed but loving and supporting wife. Like the characters of Richard and Harriet, Lawrence and his wife were persecuted during World War I, and they fled England in despair. Also, and most important to the art of the novel, Richard Somers, like Lawrence, is a man filled with inner paradoxes. He values his relationship with his wife above everything, until those times when it threatens his own individuality. During those times, he finds that this close, life-giving relationship becomes emotionally stifling, and he feels the need to escape it in order to preserve his sense of himself. Such inner paradox in a character in a marriage relationship is typical of protagonists in Lawrence's other novels.

Richard senses the spiritually deadening aspects of contemporary Western civilization; he yearns for some kind of rebirth in man linked to a different concept of a godhead. In Lawrence's fiction, Richard stands out as a protagonist in his desire to move into the world of political action, to become a leader among men. By the end of the novel, however, Richard realizes that political action will not accomplish this goal. He comes to the knowledge that the achievement of a new man can be made only through an inner, spiritual conversion in each individual that is beyond the outer structure of politics.

Although the character of Harriet is drawn closely along the lines of Lawrence's wife, Frieda, she is not an idealized figure. Rather, she is an emotionally complex character who is as fully developed as Richard. She seems to have an instinctive knowledge of her husband, and she serves as his emotional touchstone in the world.

As in most of Lawrence's fiction, the love relationship is the central concern in this novel. The other characters outside that relationship, such as Jack Callcott and Kangaroo, achieve life only in conjunction with the principal characters, yet Lawrence's rendering of such characters is so powerful that their figures become fully realized to the reader.

Themes and Meanings

The spiritual nature of contemporary man is D. H. Lawrence's central theme, and it manifests itself in this novel through the marriage relationship between Richard and Harriet. With his genius for exploring the emotional lives of his characters, Lawrence portrays Richard and Harriet in their everyday world. The essential fact for Lawrence is that the everyday world can contain the most profound spiritual life. It is often the small moments, the seemingly unimportant daily event—a walk on the beach, for example, that contains the detail that blossoms into the spiritually significant episode. Lawrence is at his best in such moments, and during them his characters become as compelling as any in fiction and his prose achieves a lyrical intensity that few novelists have ever equaled.

On a more prosaic level, Lawrence explores the possibility for political action in the character of Richard. Richard's search for some worldly way to lead men toward a new definition of a godhead recalls Lawrence's own ambitions. Yet Richard fails in that search; he realizes that politically such an action is not possible. In the very writing of the novel, Lawrence seemed to be exploring for himself what was possible in the political world and what was beyond political remedy.

Critical Context

Critics have agreed that the novel is flawed as a work of art by Lawrence's long, didactic passages on the concept of some dark god. Lawrence begins to dramatize the exploration of this subject of the dark god in Richard's mind, but when Lawrence loses that dramatic focus, the material becomes simple exposition. At times, that exposition is fascinating in its own right for the nontraditional ideas it contains, but it is finally detrimental to the novel's form. While not quite equal to Lawrence's masterpieces, such as *Sons and Lovers* (1913), *The Rainbow* (1915), and *Women in Love* (1920), *Kangaroo* contains scenes and passages that are clearly the work of genius. The characters of Richard and Harriet achieve a fictional life of their own, and their relationship contains the inner dynamics of marriage as uniquely portrayed by Lawrence. Also, some of the most brilliant passages of description that Lawrence wrote are found in the novel. The passages on Cornwall and the indignities of military induction are among them, as are the evocations of the Australian continent and its people. Australians believe that many of these passages are among the best that have been written on the subject of their homeland.

Sources for Further Study

Draper, Ronald P. *D. H. Lawrence*, 1964.
Leavis, F. R. *D. H. Lawrence, Novelist*, 1956.
Niven, Alastair. *D. H. Lawrence: The Novels*, 1978.
Stoll, John E. *The Novels of D. H. Lawrence: A Search for Integration*, 1971.
Yudhistar. *Conflict in the Novels of D. H. Lawrence*, 1969.

Ronald L. Johnson

KANTHAPURA

Author: Raja Rao (1908-   )
Type of plot: Folkloric realism
Time of plot: c. 1931, just prior to Gandhi's "salt march"
Locale: Kanthapura, a typical village in the province of Kara, South India
First published: 1938

> *Principal characters:*
>
> ACHAKKA, the wise female narrator, a flexible Brahmin who joins the Gandhi resistance against the British
>
> MOORTHY, a young, pro-Gandhian Brahmin
>
> BHATTA, a *zamindar*, or landlord, and a clever anti-Gandhian opportunist
>
> PATEL RANGÈ GOWDA, a sturdy, fierce materialist, charitable to the poor but a terror to the authorities
>
> SASTRI, a poet and singer, honored by the Maharaja of Mysore
>
> BADÈ KHAN, a policeman who is not accepted by Kanthapurans and who seeks refuge on the Skeffington Coffee Estate
>
> RANGAMMA, a young advocate who holds her own in disputes with Bhatta and who inspires the villagers in their struggle against the British
>
> KAMALAMMA, Rangamma's sister
>
> RATNA, the fifteen-year-old widowed daughter of Kamalamma, a very "modern" villager
>
> SANKAR, an ascetic widower and a lawyer of integrity and humility

The Novel

Rather than being a traditional novel with a neat linear structure and compact plot, *Kanthapura* follows the oral tradition of Indian *sthala-purana*, or legendary history. As Raja Rao explains in his original foreword, there is no village in India, however mean, that has not a rich legendary history of its own, in which some famous figure of myth or history has made an appearance. In this way, the storyteller, who commemorates the past, keeps a native audience in touch with its lore and thereby allows the past to mingle with the present, the gods and heroes with ordinary mortals.

The story is narrated in flashback by Achakka, a wise woman in the village. She, like her female audience (whom she addresses as "sisters"), has survived the turbulence of social and political change which was induced by Mohandas K. Gandhi's passive resistance against the British government.

Achakka provides a detailed picture of the rural setting, establishing both an ambiance and a rhythm for the novel. It is clear that her speech and idiomatic expression are meant to express a distinctively feminine viewpoint—an extraordinary achievement for a male Indo-English novelist. Achakka quickly creates a faithful image of an Indian way of life, circumscribed by tradition and indebted to its deities, of whom Kenchamma, the great and bounteous goddess, is made the village protectress. She is invoked in every chapter, for the characters never forget that her power resides in her past action. It is she who humanizes the villagers, and their chants and prayers ring out from time to time.

The narrator establishes the parameters of the story within old and new legends. While Kenchamma and Siva are remembered for their marvelous feats and interventions in human affairs, analogies are sometimes drawn with contemporary figures—such as Gandhi—who serve to turn fact and history into folklore, and who provide the motive for political struggle. At the beginning, while there are simply rumors of Gandhi's activities, the villagers follow their customary routines. Then, Moorthy, a young, dedicated Brahmin, inspired by Gandhi, returns to Kanthapura to propagandize the cause of the Indian National Congress and Gandhi's *satyagraha* (truth-force) movement. The colonial masters (nicknamed "Red-men" for their ruddy complexions) are a palpable, tyrannical presence but are sensed only obliquely at the beginning via the mysterious passing policeman who is treated as a spy and who, consequently, seeks refuge on the Skeffington Coffee Estate run by a brutal gang-boss.

Moorthy does not immediately win favor. He is opposed by Bhatta, a reactionary who sneers at "Gandhi vagabondage," and by fellow Brahmins who are increasingly upset by Gandhi's acceptance of Untouchables. The caste system, so much a part of Indian history, is shaking apart under Gandhi's example, and the social pattern of Kanthapura—delineated by separate quarters for Brahmin, Pariah, Potter, Weaver, and Sudra—is disturbed by the progress being made by the Untouchables.

Even Moorthy's own mother is revulsed by his Gandhian precepts, and Moorthy brings matters to a head by eliciting Patel Rangè Gowda's help in starting a Congress group and encouraging the villagers to vow to speak only truth, wear no cloth but homespun *khadi*, and use all forms of passive resistance. This Gandhian nonviolence provokes a brutal response from the authorities, and the villagers are attacked by the police. Moorthy and advocate Rangamma are arrested as Bhatta is uncovered as a traitor and some Brahmins are deployed to stir fear among the villagers. Patel Rangè Gowda is dismissed from his hereditary office as village executive chief, and the villagers turn to the gods for help.

The radical change in the political nature of India, however, becomes apparent as the women stir into action. Rangamma, who always links Indian scripture to contemporary events, manages to inspire the womenfolk to dire deeds as the men are forced to hide in the jungles around the village.

After Moorthy is released from prison, the political crisis deepens, and the villagers' suffering increases. There is a sense that the issue is now more than mere politics. The world resembles a jungle in battle with itself, and only Gandhi transcends this tumult, for he is like a huge mountain, unvanquished by the confusion and violence. Moorthy suddenly finds himself less in sympathy with Gandhi and more attuned to Jawaharlal Nehru, the emerging modernist.

The villagers, however, remain faithful to Gandhi. Toward the end, when nothing can stop the women (in spite of horrendous casualties) from marching against the soldiers sent by the British, the change in the social and political nature of the country is profound. The women decide to burn down what is left of their village, rather than return to it. Life, they realize, can never be the same without their Moorthy, husbands, sisters, and children who have perished in the struggle. Yet the women also recognize that they are part of history on the march.

The climax of the novel is the great violence of chapter 18, with the men in retreat, the women in the vanguard of resistance, and the soldiers in unrelenting assault, wreaking devastation. The concluding section (chapter 19) brings the tale full circle, fourteen months later, where there is eager anticipation of *Swaraj*, or independence for India. Of the male heroes, only Patel Rangè Gowda returns briefly to Kanthapura, yet the villagers feel blessed by the goddess Kenchamma.

The Characters

The numerous characters in this novel demonstrate the sense of community that unifies the plot and gives substance to the political and social conflicts. There is a sense of teeming life, and because the larger question is not about an individual's fate but about a group destiny, Raja Rao's mode of characterization is impressionistic. Dialogue is kept to a minimum, and the focus encompasses both the masses in the background and certain salient figures in the foreground.

The female narrator is a medium for storytelling as well as a character in her own right, for she expresses her own radical nature and that of changing India. Though she tells the reader little directly of herself (she admits to owning seven acres of wet land and twelve of dry, it is clear from her mode of speaking that she is willing to accept fundamental social changes. Although she is respectful of Hindu tradition, she is not bound to old ways. She is caught up in all the turmoil, and her at times breathless narration expresses the excitement of the period as well as her own recognition of a movement that is leading to India's autonomy.

The conflict between acquiescence to time-honored tradition and resistance to old tyrannies is dramatically expressed in the two factions: the Gandhians and their foes. Moorthy is the prime representative of the modern Indian struggling with dignity for freedom. He is linked to Hindu traditions from the outset, for he is the youngest son of a pious mother and is called a "holy bull," implying that he is a specially marked character. So thoroughly Gandhian is he in his creed and practice that he scandalizes his own mother by his unconventional fraternization with the Pariahs, and he is willing to suffer rejection and violence in the name of his cause. Like his mentor, he exerts both a political and a spiritual force. Yet he eventually turns from Gandhi to Nehru in an abrupt recognition that saintliness is not necessarily synonymous with political wisdom.

Rao skillfully controls the focus of the novel by bringing forward subsidiary characters at particular moments when they can sharpen the conflicts. They are usually distinguished by a single facet of personality: Bhatta is known by his smiling, false charm; Rangamma by her eloquent disputatiousness; Patel Rangè Gowda by his ceremonious speech; and Dorè by his scoffing manner.

Because the crux of the novel is a struggle for independence, there are the adversaries of Gandhi and, hence, independence. Although these figures are not without their melodramatic evil, they are granted their moments of fair combat when they summon up all of their arguments against Moorthy. Such is the case with the old government man who appears at a nationalist gathering and presents his cunning rhetorical attack on the Gandhians.

Finally, then, *Kanthapura* achieves a sense of continuous agitation. Even when the government soldiers lay waste to the village, dispersing the men and slaughtering many of the women, there is no victory for the old political arrangement. The new spirit of India is on the move across the vast land, and the hearts of the survivors in Kanthapura beat like a drum, with the strength of hard-won freedom.

Themes and Meanings

The story shows the birth of new ideas in old India. The arguments against change—which in the Gandhian sense is a change of soul and not simply of caste or social function—are made forcefully by reactionaries who point to the disorder, corruption, and arrogance of pre-British rule. As the old government man puts it, the British have come to protect *dharma*, or duty. Playing upon raw fear in the populace, the antinationalists argue that reform will mean the eventual corruption of castes and of the great ancestral traditions.

Although this novel does not have the profound philosophical nature of *The Serpent and the Rope* (1960), Rao's most massive novel, its thrust is certainly didactic in that it glorifies the idea of revolt. It is surprising, indeed, that the author was not incarcerated for his views.

Critical Context

Although dense with expressions of Indian customs, epical history, politics, and religion, *Kanthapura* is unusual as an Indo-English novel because the female characters serve in the forefront of revolutionary struggle. In her concluding summary, Achakka expresses her belief that what has happened in her village is essentially positive. Things have changed irrevocably.

In form, *Kanthapura* is an extension of the Indian oral tradition, adapted to a Western language and genre. The extensive use of songs and prayers, allusions, and digressions, and the more limited use of proverbs and epic lists, or catalogs, contribute to the folkloric nature of the writing. Sometimes the pace is heightened by a piling-on of compound sentences at a breathless tempo, and the use of tales-within-tales promotes the sense of impromptu fabrication and immediacy.

Kanthapura is one of the earliest examples of the Gandhian novel: fiction that derives its moral force from the figure and precepts of the great political and spiritual leader. It is not simply an exotic tale of a vanished era but also a clever use of a colonial language to serve didactic ends. Like the early novels of Mulk Raj Anand, it is a deliberately moral fiction, but unlike Anand's work, it is not almost exclusively sociological in tenor. By providing detailed notes on Indian terms and allusions, Rao is able to extend the reach of his fiction, compelling Western readers to slow down their pace of reading, examine the network of mythological and historical associations, and note the analogies which he is drawing between secular history and sacred mythology.

Sources for Further Study

Guzman, Richard R. "The Saint and the Sage: The Fiction of Raja Rao," in *The Virginia Quarterly Review*. LVI (Winter, 1980), pp. 32-50.

Naik, M. K. "*Kanthapura*: The Indo-Anglian Novel as Legendary History," in *Journal of the Karnatak University*. X (1966), pp. 26-39.

Narasimhaiah, C. D. "Raja Rao's *Kanthapura*: An Analysis," in *The Literary Criterion*. VII, no. 2 (1966), pp. 54-77.

Verghese, C. Paul. "Raja Rao, Mulk Raj, Narayan and Others," in *Indian Writing Today*. VII (1969), pp. 31-38.

Keith Garebian

THE KAYWANA TRILOGY

Author: Edgar Mittelholzer (1909-1965)
Type of plot: Historical romance
Time of plot: 1616-1953
Locale: British Guiana
First published: Children of Kaywana, 1952 (U.S. edition, 1952); *The Harrowing of Hubertus,* 1954 (*Hubertus,* 1955); *Kaywana Blood,* 1958 (*The Old Blood,* 1958)

Principal characters:

KAYWANA, a Guianese woman of mixed Amerindian and English blood

ADRIANSEN VAN GROENWEGEL, a Dutch trader and Kaywana's lover

AUGUST VYFIUS, a Dutch trader and Kaywana's lover

WILLEM VAN GROENWEGEL, the son of Adriansen and Kaywana

AUGUST VYFIUS, JR., the son of August and Kaywana

LAURENS VAN GROENWEGEL, the brother of Willem

HENDRICKJE VAN GROENWEGEL, the daughter of Laurens

AERT VAN GROENWEGEL, the brother of Hendrickje

IGNATIUS VAN GROENWEGEL, the nephew of Laurens and the husband of Hendrickje

HUBERTUS VAN GROENWEGEL, the son of Aert

DIRK VAN GROENWEGEL, the great-grandson of Hendrickje

PATRICK BAXTER-HOUGH, the grandson of Dirk

The Novels

The Kaywana Trilogy comprises *Children of Kaywana, Hubertus* (later republished as *Kaywana Stock,* 1959), and *The Old Blood.* All three novels are set in British Guiana (modern Guyana), a South American territory which was inhabited by Amerindians before the first European settlers, the Dutch, arrived in the early seventeenth century. The action begins in 1616 and, over a period of almost three and a half centuries, traces the course of social, political, and economic events while the colony changed hands many times between Dutch, French, and British rulers, until it finally became British in 1802. Often, these changes were rapid and unexpected, as during the last two decades of the eighteenth century, when the colony changed from Dutch ownership to British, to French, back to Dutch, and finally back to British. The turbulence and instability created by these changes are fully reflected in Edgar Mittelholzer's accurate observation of purely historical episodes, and his invention of characters whose eccentric or unusual psychological features of personality seem to match the unstable conditions in which they live. The pattern in all three novels is to furnish scenes of authentic history as a milieu for characters engaged in unusual, romantic, and sometimes perverse relationships.

Children of Kaywana opens with the earliest Dutch attempts to establish trading posts and plantations in Guiana, or "The Wild Coast," as they called it then. The Dutch resist many attacks from Spanish, French, and British rivals, and are able to establish their administration over the whole country, comprising three counties—Essequibo, Berbice, and Demerara—by the middle of the eighteenth century. Yet there is no real stability, and they have to contend with riots among their own soldiers and unrest among the African slaves, who provide labor for their sugar and coffee plantations. The action of *Children of Kaywana* ends in 1763 with the detailed account of a full-scale rebellion led by two slaves: Cuffy and Akkara. By Mittelholzer's account, the rebellion gives rise to scenes of inhuman abuse and bloodshed. It is not that Mittelholzer alters history; rather, he supplements it with invented characters, relationships, and preoccupations that probably fulfill his own subjective expectations of past events as much as they objectively dramatize these events.

Hubertus records a similar version of historical events from the end of the 1763 rebellion to 1797, and *The Old Blood* continues Mittelholzer's account from 1797 to its conclusion in 1953. The events in *Hubertus* are relatively peaceful, although unrest among the slaves continues and erupts again in 1823 in *The Old Blood*. Gruesome scenes are once more in evidence. In suppressing the rebellion, the authorities leave black corpses dangling from temporary gibbets erected on the roadside. The heads of decapitated slaves are also left stuck onto posts by the roadside. Although quite credible within the distantly undemocratic atmosphere of nineteenth century West Indian slave society, the scenes of violence and brutality appear excessive in their variety, regularity, and intensity. When the slaves are emancipated in 1833, however, there is a period of relative calm under continuous British rule, until the dominance of plantation owners and their heirs is decisively broken by the introduction of elections based on universal adult suffrage in 1953.

Interwoven with the historical events are episodes in the biography of the van Groenwegel family. The original ancestor of this family is Kaywana, daughter of an Amerindian woman and an unnamed English sailor. Kaywana has children by two Dutch lovers, Adriansen van Groenwegel and August Vyfius. It is the descendants of these children who form the principal characters in the novels of The Kaywana Trilogy. The turbulence of their relationships among themselves and with others fully matches the turbulent atmosphere that surrounds plantation society, with its rigidly authoritarian structures and inhuman distinction between masters and slaves. Typical incidents involve rivalry, intrigue, mystery, threats, revenge, suicide, murder, and obeah, or black magic. Some sexual incidents strongly reflect a situation in which enforced repression frequently provokes unlicensed indulgence: hence the frequent examples of violation, incest, rape, seduction, masochism, castration, flagellation, and mutilation. The opening section of *Children of Kaywana*, aptly named "A Jet of Fire," sets the exact tone of the action that is to follow. Kaywana lusts after Adriansen and August, and she defies the medicine man Wakkatai, whom she suspects of poisoning her daughter. Her own daughter survives, but Kaywana kills Wakkatai's daughter in revenge. Later, both Kaywana and Wakkatai are killed in a battle between the Dutch and Amerindians. While the second novel concentrates mostly on the problems of one character, Hubertus van Groenwegel, it reflects the conditions of a society that is identical to the one seen in *Children of Kaywana*. In the third novel, however, Mittelholzer depicts the gradual erosion of this old plantation/slave society and its feudalistic mores, which are slowly overtaken by more democratic practices of the mid-twentieth century.

The Characters

The Kaywana novels contain more than two hundred characters, of whom less than half are directly connected to the van Groenwegel family. Despite the variety of individuals within the family itself, two types of characters are generally recognized: those who are strong or dominant, and those who are weak and passive. Most of the van Groenwegels exhibit a combination of these traits, but there is no doubt that the one most admired is the one embodied in the family motto: "The van Groenwegels never retreat," or "The van Groenwegels never run."

The tough, fighting spirit behind this tradition can be traced back to Kaywana, the matriarch of the clan. Her Amerindian name—"Kay" meaning "old" and "wana" meaning "water"—links her firmly to the society in Guiana and to its struggle for survival under harsh, chaotic, colonial conditions. This society in which the Dutch vie for power among themselves, among other Europeans, and among the Amerindians, breeds ruggedly individualistic and self-sustaining values. In struggling constantly against her own people, and against Europeans, Kaywana exhibits striking qualities of defiance, resolution, hatred, and revenge. Although passionately loyal to her lovers and blood relations, she is fiercely hostile to their enemies, as shown by her outlandish passion toward Adriansen and August, and fierce defiance of Wakkatai. Kaywana is a product of Guiana in the throes of colonial occupation. In these circumstances, she is bolstered by an almost fatalistic belief in the inherent cruelty of the natural order.

Of Kaywana's descendants, none expresses this belief more faithfully than Hendrickje, daughter of Laurens, and great-granddaughter of Kaywana.

Hendrickje is a good example of the inbreeding that exists among the van Groenwegels, encouraging family pride in the "old blood." On her mother's side, Hendrickje is descended from Kaywana and August, while on her father's side, she is descended from Kaywana and Adriansen. Another possible influence on Hendrickje is the fact that her grandmother on her mother's side is an African slave. The introduction of "impure" African blood into the family is a source of anxiety for later generations of van Groenwegels. In Hendrickje's case, her main attitude toward the family is pride in the strength of her van Groenwegel "fire blood." She frequently counsels her grandchildren to observe the family tradition: "Never surrender. Never retreat." Hendrickje has a reputation for unyielding defiance and aggression. She is totally intolerant of weakness, and one of her descendants describes her as "that cruel, arrogant, beautiful magnificent harridan—the queen of the van Groenwegels." Her reputation is supported by unspeakable atrocities which she habitually inflicts on her slaves and which are recorded in letters passed on to her descendants. Like her ancestor Kaywana, Hendrickje remains stubbornly defiant to the end, which is for her very bitter indeed: In the 1763 rebellion, the slaves gain their revenge, and hack Hendrickje to death along with several of her grandchildren.

As the main character in a novel whose original title was "The Harrowing of Hubertus," Hubertus undergoes extraordinary torment and inner turmoil because of the conflict he feels between the harsh family traditions that he has inherited and his belief in Christian compassion and selflessness. In the main, the conflict manifests itself through Hubertus' sexual longings, particularly for his female slaves. As he confesses, to satisfy his sexual desires is to offend God. Yet he feels that there is a "mad beast" in him which he has inherited with the "slime" of his family. To his mind, his family has saddled him with unrestrained lusts, and he envies his English wife for her restraint. Whether his opinion of his wife or of himself is totally or partially imagined, Hubertus remains a tortured portrait of guilt, self-pity, and masochistic inner self-flagellation.

Dirk van Groenwegel, who appears in *The Old Blood*, is the great-grandson of Hendrickje. Dirk is the last of the traditional, plantation- and slave-owning van Groenwegels. Radical changes take place during his lifetime. Unrest among the slaves increases sharply—partly, no doubt, as a result of the educational and preaching activities carried out among the slaves by missionaries from the London Missionary Society. The first big upheaval is the 1823 rebellion, which is quickly followed by the abolition of slavery in 1833. Dirk reacts to these changes with a mixture of anger and regret, consoling himself with nostalgic recollections of his "old blood" and with theories of heredity that exalt the persistence and toughness of the van Groenwegel family. Perhaps it is some of this toughness that enables him to survive the passing of the old feudalistic order and to face the emergence of a new society in which free blacks can buy plantations on which they were formerly slaves.

The minor characters in The Kaywana Trilogy are too numerous to mention, but two—the leaders of the 1763 slave rebellion, Cuffy and Akkara—deserve mention because they are today regarded as national heroes in independent Guyana. In *Children of Kaywana* they appear to be bloodthirsty and trigger-happy, interested mainly in revenge. Their desire for revenge is quite plausible in the circumstances, but as in so many of Mittelholzer's characters, plausible traits are presented in such extreme fashion that they often appear morbid, exaggerated, or excessive.

Themes and Meanings

The two principal themes that emerge from The Kaywana Trilogy concern politics on one hand and sexual behavior on the other. The political theme derives from the stern, fatalistic tradition of the van Groenwegels, which amounts to a belief in jungle justice or an amoral world order in which only the fittest survive. This belief is given as the motive behind many acts of sadomasochistic brutality, including Hendrickje's inhuman treatment of her slaves and the equally inhuman retaliation of the slaves during the 1763 rebellion. To some extent, the belief is justified by the raw, chaotic conditions during the early centuries of Guiana's settlement by Europeans. As Mittelholzer comments in his travel book *With a Carib Eye* (1958), these conditions encouraged cynicism and cruelty in plantation owners, who felt themselves completely at the mercy of the rivalries and decisions of metropolitan rulers in Europe, who either did not know or did not sufficiently care about local conditions and problems in their distant West Indian possessions. Consequently, the West Indian planters had to fend for themselves most of the time. This entailed a struggle for survival in which only the physically strongest, intellectually most cunning, and spiritually selfish could succeed.

The ethics of jungle justice that thus evolved dictated that weak, compassionate, or unselfish individuals were likely to be quickly eliminated in the fierce competition of plantation society. That is why the van Groenwegels despise or distrust what they regarded as softness and compassion, either in themselves or in others. Hendrickje, for example, plainly admits that life is blind, haphazard, and brutal: "There isn't any God. People are simply born anyhow, like the animals, and if they can fight their way through the world they get on. If they can't, they get beaten and die." Most of the action in The Kaywana Trilogy appears to vindicate such ethics.

Mittelholzer's sexual theme is linked to the ethics of jungle justice, and his sexual relationships invariably include elements of the same violence and brutality that are so greatly admired by the van Groenwegels. The most prevalent sexual relationships in The Kaywana Trilogy involve seduction, incest, rape, and other types of violation. If there are "normal" sexual relationships, they play a distinctly secondary role to those that involve violation or cruelty. Kaywana's unbridled lust leads her into acts of unfeeling destructiveness. The passionate nature and uncontrollable instincts which generate such destruction are passed on to her descendants, who regard sexual desire as the single most dominant motive in human behavior. Dirk van Groenwegel, eight generations removed from Kaywana, sees the sexual urge as "the driving force . . . behind all our actions and all our destinies," and he cites several of his ancestors whose lives are completely dominated by sexual desire, and who therefore feel justified in violating any code of morality that stands in the way of their indulgence.

Yet it is not entirely accurate to claim that Mittelholzer advocates the totally amoral doctrine of the survival of the fittest in either his political or his sexual themes. Although the harsh ethics of the van Groenwegels, and of plantation society in general, produce acts of savagery and levels of abuse, pain, and suffering that are utterly dehumanizing, the slave rebellions provoke such gratuitously cruel behavior, in both masters and slaves, that the validity of the doctrine inspiring this behavior appears contradicted if not negated. Jungle justice, in other words, is presented more as an angry denunciation of injustice bred by the plantation system than as a valid theory of human behavior. Similarly, Hubertus' distrust of the "mad beast" in himself suggests that he recognizes the destructiveness of unbridled sexual indulgence, despite his instinct for it. He reluctantly admits that "the flesh is not of necessity evil, yet to yield to its urges is to wound the spirit." The numerous examples of sexual violation in The Kaywana Trilogy should therefore not be regarded as advocacy of sadomasochistic sexual activity but rather as an angry display of the perversions to which people can succumb, in social conditions where there is insufficient respect for both individual liberties and social order.

Critical Context

The novels of The Kaywana Trilogy collectively represent Mittelholzer's most distinguished achievement in a writing career which produced twenty-five books, twenty-three of which are novels. These novels are set in various parts of the West Indies as well as in British Guiana. Some are set in England, to which Mittelholzer immigrated in 1950, and where he died by suicide in 1965.

The reconstruction of three and a half centuries of any nation's history would be a daunting task for most writers. For Mittelholzer, it was even more daunting because there were very few sources on the history of British Guiana when he was writing. His main source was J. R. Rodway's three-volume *History of British Guiana* (1891). It is a measure of Mittelholzer's distinguished achievement as a novelist that, out of such meager resources, he was able to incorporate innumerable characters and incidents, changes of location (within British Guiana), and different historical periods into a smoothly flowing, coherent narrative that both dramatizes history and provides entertaining action. As fictionalized history containing a rich variety of dramatic incidents, colorful or even perverse characters, and a narrative of most palatable fluency, the Kaywana novels constitute a rare and inspired feat of imaginative reconstruction. Since he had no local literary tradition on which he could rely for models or techniques, Mittelholzer's achievement is essentially that of a pioneer, blessed with a brilliant and fertile imagination, versatile writing skills, and prodigious energy.

Mittelholzer was the first novelist in the region of the English-speaking Caribbean to produce so many novels. He was also the first novelist to explore the history of his homeland in such scope and depth. Most important, Mittelholzer was the first novelist from the English-speaking Caribbean to consider seriously such universal themes as the nature of political organization and sexual behavior. If The Kaywana Trilogy reveals some imbalance in the presentation of these themes by focusing on their more lurid aspects, it is partly the result of Mittelholzer's having to supplement the dearth of historical sources with the prodigal inventions of a romantic imagination. In the process, he has also created three novels which are unsurpassed in West Indian literature for their combination of vividly reconstructed history with vigorously romantic action.

Sources for Further Study

Birbalsingh, F. M. "Edgar Mittelholzer: Moralist or Pornographer?" in *Journal of Commonwealth Literature*. No. 7 (July, 1969), pp. 88-103.

Guckian, Patrick. "The Balance of Colour: A Reassessment of the Work of Edgar Mittelholzer," in *Jamaica Journal*. IV (March, 1970), pp. 38-45.

Seymour, A. J. "An Introduction to the Novels of Edgar Mittelholzer," in *Kyk-Over-Al*. VIII (December, 1958), pp. 60-74.

Frank Birbalsingh

KEEP THE ASPIDISTRA FLYING

Author: George Orwell (Eric Arthur Blair, 1903-1950)
Type of plot: Social realism
Time of plot: The 1930's
Locale: London
First published: 1936

Principal characters:
GORDON COMSTOCK, the protagonist, an aspiring poet who
  works in a bookstore
ROSEMARY WATERLOW, his girlfriend
PHILIP RAVELSTON, a wealthy young friend of Comstock

The Novel

In *Keep the Aspidistra Flying*, a discontented and embittered young man, who believes that "all modern commerce is a swindle," attempts to drop out of the monetary system altogether. He refuses to advance himself in life, obstinately defying pressure from family and friends. He falls willingly into the mire of poverty and self-neglect, until he is trapped by circumstances into embracing the very values that he formerly despised.

Gordon Comstock is twenty-nine years old, is well educated, and comes from a middle-class background. As the novel opens, he is working as an assistant in a bookstore in London. It is a routine job, and he earns only two pounds a week, but he prefers it to his former position at the New Albion Advertising Company, in spite of the fact that he showed promise as a copywriter. He refers disparagingly to this as a "good" job and wants no part of it. He sees himself primarily as a poet and is very proud of his one published volume, which was well reviewed but little read. Having declared war on what he calls the "money-god," he wants to live by his own values, not those of a corrupt, materialistic system which grinds the life and spirit out of people.

Having declared war on money, however, he soon finds that money is all he thinks about. He does not find happiness having renounced the values that others live by. Forced to live in unpleasant lodgings, with a nosy landlady, he believes that others reject and despise him because of his poverty. He cannot relate to his amiable, moneyed friend Philip Ravelston on equal terms (he refuses even to go into Ravelston's apartment), and he even blames his poverty for the fact that his girlfriend, Rosemary, will not go to bed with him. Nothing seems to go right. When he and Rosemary manage to scrape together enough money to spend a day in the country, he is humiliated by a waiter at an expensive hotel and this ruins his attempt to seduce Rosemary later in the day.

His situation changes dramatically when he receives a check for fifty dollars from an American journal to which he had submitted one of his poems. He promises to himself that he will give half this amount—five pounds—to his sister Julia, since he has frequently borrowed from her in the past. The remainder, however, he is prepared to spend. He decides to take Rosemary and Ravelston out to dinner, but to the dismay of both his companions, he is needlessly and ostentatiously extravagant. Later, having become hopelessly drunk, he makes insistent and rough sexual demands on Rosemary in the street; she slaps his face and runs off. After further drinking, he meets two prostitutes, and he and a reluctant Ravelston take a taxi to a sordid hotel where Gordon attempts, but fails, to have sexual intercourse with one of the women. The next day, he awakens in a police cell and is charged with being drunk and disorderly, although he remembers nothing of his behavior.

This episode marks the central dividing point in the novel. Now Gordon's downward slide begins. He loses his job, and although he eventually finds a position at another bookstore, the pay is even lower, only thirty shillings a week. He is forced to take inferior lodgings, but Gordon no longer cares. In his defeated frame of mind, he actually wants to be dragged down to the depths; he finds himself admiring the world of tramps and beggars, an "underworld where failure and success have no meaning; a sort of kingdom of ghosts where all are equal." He believes that he can be freed from his distress only by having nothing in the world to call his own and no prospect of acquiring anything. He enjoys his own apathy and hopelessness.

Gordon is saved from total disintegration only by the loyalty of Rosemary. For some unaccountable reason, she sticks by him, and finally, out of pity, she becomes his mistress, an act which gives neither of them much pleasure. When she later comes to him and confesses that she is pregnant, he is faced with a choice: Either he can refuse to marry her and leave her to face the resulting social stigma; he can marry her and fail to support her; or he can marry her and reclaim his old job at the advertising agency, which is still available. After a day of deliberation, he chooses the last option: The thought of the growing baby has somehow reignited his spirit. The circular structure of the novel now becomes apparent: The couple settle down to enjoy the middle-class existence which Gordon had formerly rejected and despised. He finds that it is what he secretly desired all along.

The Characters

There is a strong autobiographical strain in George Orwell's portrayal of Gordon Comstock. Like Gordon, Orwell had a middle-class upbringing, which he resented, and was sent to a school where all the boys were richer than he. This experience shaped his later political attitudes. Like Gordon, Orwell had deliberately allowed himself to sink into a life of poverty (his *Down and Out in Paris and London*, published in 1933, is a record of his own experiences), and also like Gordon, Orwell had worked part-time at a bookstore (in Hampstead, London, in 1934 and 1935). The parallels, however, have a strict limit. Gordon is a far lesser figure than the real-life Orwell. Resentful, badly adjusted, and immature, Gordon soon alienates the reader, who can hardly be expected to sympathize with a man who so willingly embraces a job in which there is "no room for ambition, no effort, no hope." In fact, Gordon is so mentally disturbed that he often hopes for a war in which the whole of London will be destroyed by bombs. Yet, in spite of this, he is blessed with two friends who go to extreme lengths to help him, although he does nothing to deserve or encourage them.

The first of these is Ravelston, the easygoing, charming aristocrat who edits a left-wing magazine. He is based on Orwell's close friend Sir Richard Rees, who was in the 1930's the editor of the *Adelphi* magazine in London. Ravelston moves easily through the world because of his inherited wealth, and although he tries hard to escape his class origins and identify with the proletariat, he never succeeds in doing so. Gordon is extremely sensitive to the disparity in their incomes, and their friendship involves subtle rituals designed to conceal it; they have an unspoken agreement that whenever they meet they will do nothing that involves spending more than a small amount of money.

There is more to distinguish one from the other than money. Ravelston's kindness, gentleness, humility, and extreme tact make him a strong contrast to Gordon, with his selfishness and boorish manners. The contrast is also apparent in their relationships with women. Whereas Ravelston and his girlfriend, Hermione, bask in material comfort and languid sensuality, Gordon's sexual encounters with Rosemary are full of misunderstanding and frustration. Yet in Gordon's eyes it is money that makes the difference between sexual success and failure.

Rosemary's loyalty and her simple good nature make Gordon's cruel, unfeeling behavior toward her particularly unjustifiable. Rosemary is also from the middle-classes, but she accepts without question the social system which Gordon despises. Genuinely humble and fair-minded, lighthearted and yet full of common sense, she never puts pressure on Gordon to find a lucrative job, even when she is pregnant with his child. Yet simply by being who she is, she continually invalidates Gordon's philosophy. For example, her touching gesture at the end of their disastrous day in the country, when she thrusts a packet of cigarettes into Gordon's pocket and runs off before he can protest, shows what goodness is possible in someone who in Gordon's terms is enslaved by an inhuman system.

Themes and Meanings

"Don't you see that a man's whole personality is bound up with his income? His personality *is* his income." Gordon's complaint to Ravelston succinctly expresses one of the main themes of the novel. Orwell had already announced it in an epigraph at the beginning of the book, an adaptation of the famous chapter from Paul's letter to the Corinthians: "And now abideth faith, hope, money, these three; but the greatest of these is money." Money, not love, is the prerequisite for goodness and virtue, and Gordon, according to this theme, sinks into moral decay not because of any innate character weakness but because of his economic circumstances.

There are some symbolic elements in the novel, the most important of which is the aspidistra, a favorite plant of the English middle classes. For Gordon, it symbolizes the conventional, bourgeois life that he seeks to escape. The aspidistra in his room is sickly, and he has on many occasions tried to kill it, but "the beastly things are practically immortal. In almost any circumstances they can preserve a wilting, diseased existence." He even has to put up with one in his poorest lodgings. It, too, is dying. Yet in the penultimate chapter, symbolically set during the coming of spring, he notices that the aspidistra has not died after all and is actually putting forth new green shoots. As part of his *volte face* at the book's conclusion (the credibility of which strains the reader's imagination), he suddenly looks more favorably on the general run of lower-middle-class life. Although civilization rests on fear and greed, "in the lives of common men the greed and fear are mysteriously transmuted into something nobler." He now sees that the common folk are, in their own way, fully and tenaciously alive, and in a sudden thought realizes that "the aspidistra is the tree of life." His "conversion" even leads him to purchase an aspidistra himself, to put in the window of his and Rosemary's new, middle-class home. After his futile stand against the "money-god," he is now happy to find himself and his pregnant wife "bound up in the bundle of life."

Critical Context

Keep the Aspidistra Flying was Orwell's fourth book, and its major themes are also to be found in his other works from the same period. All are concerned with poverty and its debilitating effects on the human spirit and with Orwell's belief that there was something fundamentally wrong with the way human society was organized. *A Clergyman's Daughter* (1935) has the same circular structure as *Keep the Aspidistra Flying*: Dorothy Hare is forced to escape her middle-class background, she gains firsthand experience of poverty, and then finally returns to her former life with renewed vision. In *The Road to Wigan Pier*, which followed in 1937, Orwell reports on his own experiences of life with the working-class poor in northern England, and it is in this book that he first advocates socialism as a way of reforming society. Although Orwell's subject matter during the 1930's was always grim, he had not yet reached the pessimism of *Animal Farm* (1945) and *Nineteen Eighty-Four* (1949).

Orwell disliked *Keep the Aspidistra Flying* and refused to allow it to be reprinted or translated. He had only allowed it to be published in the first place, he said, because he needed money. There is no doubt that the novel has serious flaws; the plot is sometimes unconvincing, the symbolism is heavy-handed, and there are lapses in the presentation of character (in particular, Ravelston's failure to extricate himself from the encounter with the prostitutes, which is so unconvincing that it undermines the credibility of the whole episode).

The novel does at times possess considerable force, however, a force which lies in the honesty and directness of Orwell's writing. He is ruthless and unsparing in his portrayal of the sordidness of poverty, down to its smallest detail, and it is this which gives *Keep the Aspidistra Flying* a place in the tradition of the novel of poverty, a tradition which includes Charles Dickens (on whom Orwell wrote a perceptive essay), George Gissing (whom Orwell acknowledged had an influence on his own work), Honoré de Balzac, and the contemporary novelist and critic John Wain.

Sources for Further Study
Alldritt, Keith. *The Making of George Orwell*, 1969.
Lee, Robert A. *Orwell's Fiction*, 1969.
Meyers, Jeffrey. *A Reader's Guide to George Orwell*, 1975.
_____, ed. *George Orwell: The Critical Heritage*, 1975.
Woodcock, George. *The Crystal Spirit: A Study of George Orwell*, 1966.

Bryan Aubrey

KEPLER

Author: John Banville (1945-   )
Type of plot: Historical novel
Time of plot: 1571-1630
Locale: Central Europe
First published: 1981

Principal characters:
JOHANNES KEPLER, the protagonist, an astronomer
BARBARA (née MULLER), Kepler's unsuitable wife
REGINA, Kepler's beloved stepdaughter
TYCHO BRAHE, a mathematician and astronomer, Kepler's
    reluctant mentor

The Novel

Although essentially biographical in conception, *Kepler* deals with the great astronomer's productive period. This period covers the years from his exile from Graz in 1598 to his death in 1630. John Banville provides the reader with much of the relevant material concerning his protagonist's early years, but such material—primarily dealing with family and education—has an influence on Johannes Kepler's development, which he may be seen to spend his career revising. For the most part, however, background material is kept firmly in the background. Rather than presenting the story of the formation of Kepler's mind, the novel centers on the protagonist's struggle to preserve a mind of his own.

This focus has a number of distinctive effects on the shape and gist of the novel. First, it enables Banville to scramble and elide the chronology of Kepler's life. The best evidence of this approach is in the section "Harmonice Mundi" (named, like each of the novel's five sections, for one of Kepler's scientific treatises). The section consists of selections from Kepler's correspondence. By presenting them out of sequence, however, Banville lends them a thematic unity which would be lost in a more linear, and ostensibly more unified, manner. In addition, the deliberate shuffling of the correspondence is most telling in a section of the novel whose title is most evocative of harmony. Thus, Banville deftly uses his approach not only as a narrative novelty but also as a means of suggesting thematic concerns.

Another result of dwelling on the years of Kepler's maturity is that it places greater emphasis on his public than on his private life. In particular, the astronomer's employment by the Emperor Rudolph, which leads to his firsthand experience of the wreckage of Empire and the chaotic discord of history, places his scientific attainment in vivid perspective. Banville conveys his obvious admiration for his protagonist's intellectual achievements all the

more strongly by providing detailed contextual evidence for the sheer unlike-
lihood, and indeed foolhardiness, of undertaking any scientific work. The
author is at pains to point out the period's political turmoil and the traumatic
effects such events have on the idea of an ordered world. In addition, and
rather more pointedly, political chaos is suggested to be the result of the contemporary struggle for men's minds being waged between Catholicism and
Protestantism. This struggle, in the novel's terms, is between conflicting notions of who may authorize ideas of order, the mind of the individual or
traditional institutions.

The novel's emphasis on Kepler's public involvements has the effect of
placing him at a distance from his private life. Kepler's marriage to Barbara
Muller is unsatisfactory in virtually all respects, and his dissatisfaction is compounded by the deaths of several beloved children. In later years, the rift
between Kepler and his stepdaughter, Regina, resembles his marriage to
Barbara in its unnecessary yet evidently inevitable sadness. When, at length,
Kepler does find marital happiness with young Susanna Reuttinger, he
remains too harassed by financially defaulting patrons to take full pleasure in
his good fortune. Despite—or, perhaps, because of—the quality, and hence
the burden, of his visionary scientific gifts, Kepler remains a mere mortal in
matters such as love and death. As *Kepler* demonstrates with subtle insistence, it is all too typically human to carry out a revolution in how the world
is viewed while at the same time suffering inescapably from those blows to
the heart which nothing in the world can change.

The Characters

Kepler's stated appreciation of Albrecht Dürer's engraving titled "Knight,
Death and Devil" may be an acknowledgment of his own possession of the
qualities that he perceives in that work—"stoic grandeur and fortitude"—
but it is an incomplete guide to his overall personality. There is no denying
the astronomer's tenacity and his commitment to his vision of the heavens:
His seven-year obsession with the mathematical implications of his revolutionary insights dramatically attest these qualities. In addition, on the private
front, his moral courage in the face of repeated frustration and loss is
affectingly affirmative. As *Kepler* makes clear, however, what is most impressive about its protagonist is the range of his personality. There seems to be
no one Kepler, but rather a not particularly harmonious aggregation of traits
which are at once allied and conflicting. Given this makeup, Kepler provides
an interesting contrast with the other main characters in the novel.

What characterizes his wife Barbara, mentor Tycho Brahe, and employer
the Emperor Rudolph is a certain narrowness. It is as though all these personages have found a structure in the known world within which to shelter
their personalities. In Barbara's case—which is at once the most vulgar, the
least original, and the most difficult with which to deal—the structure is

money. For Brahe, rather more heroically, the structure is the epic of mathematical calculations ultimately published after his death as the Rudolphine Tables. These tables, as Kepler realizes in the process of seeing to their publication, are of incalculable value to mariners and the like. Yet they also signify essentially the opposite of Kepler's pathbreaking, extraterrestrial conceptions, for their reality depends on the effective suppression of the imagination.

Banville, with characteristically subtle wit, highlights the Emperor Rudolph's character by making it a blend of the main elements of the other two. Thus, Rudolph is both a skinflint and superstitious. Kepler is never paid in full for his duties as Court Mathematician, duties which in any case call less for his astronomical gifts than for his skill as an astrologer. Rudolph, in effect, is the worst of both the worlds made real in the limitations of Brahe and Barbara. Yet, irrationally but convincingly, it is Rudolph the unworldly to whom Kepler is faithful, rather than the new order which supplants him.

In contrast to the three main characters on whom he is dependent, Kepler possesses a personality which seems both unstable and to know no bounds. Assertive, vain, passive, intense, gullible, restless, he is at once immensely vulnerable and larger than life, larger, at any rate, than the life of his times. It is appropriate, therefore, that he seems ill at ease in the world of mundane structures of security, whether they be financial, exegetical, or otherwise.

Themes and Meanings

"I hold the world to be a manifestation of the possibility of order," Kepler declares to Brahe, introducing the main preoccupation of his story. In spite of political disintegration and tragedies in his personal life, Kepler steadfastly maintains his devotion to a harmonious cosmos. Indeed, the novel argues that such devotion is all the more necessary in view of the discordant ways of the world and the fact that so much of life seems to consist of breakdown and incompleteness. In a manner which perhaps belongs more to the twentieth century than it does to Kepler's age, the novel continually questions the possibility of meaning emerging from a world of chaos.

Kepler's adherence to the conception of a perfectly integrated universe is not, however, mere pious fidelity to an idea. Much of the novel's drama comes neither from the astronomer's being swept along in the unruly tide of contemporary historical events nor from enactments of the pain of intimate losses. The greatest drama is the result of Kepler's temporary, but nevertheless successful, abstraction of himself from the fallible human world in order to pursue proofs of harmony in the heavens. It is not that Kepler simply asserts a dogma of harmony and serene completeness but that he believes that such a condition can enter human understanding by means of his discovery of the necessary mathematical models. Part of his eventual triumph is not only his provision of persuasive mathematical data but also his demonstration that the necessity of his own compulsions could create a sense of the cosmos which might uplift and appease frail, fallen man.

In order to reinforce this dimension of *Kepler*, Banville provides an epigraph which is a quotation from the ninth of Rainer Maria Rilke's *Duineser Elegien* (1923): "Preise dem Engel die Welt," which translates as "Praise the world to the angel." In keeping with this sentiment, the novel contains a neatly distributed amount of wing, bird, and air imagery, which also serves to underline a sense of the freedom of mind and the compelling desire to reach beyond immediate contexts which Kepler insists on for himself. The epigraph serves also, however, to draw attention to Kepler's humanity by implying that the goal of his career is not to cross over to the side of the angels, but rather, since he cannot be a member of their exalted company, to vindicate the sufficiency of his own side to them.

The terms of Kepler's vindication may be appreciated in his capacity for undergoing and withstanding emotional pain, his general willingness to accept the erratic and uncertain course of his career (provocatively, the occasion of Kepler's death coincides with an uncharacteristic preoccupation with settling his financial affairs), and above all his readiness to tell the truth— particularly the scientific or demonstrable, irrefutable truth—irrespective of how powerful or antagonistic his skeptical listeners may be. To these qualities must be added one that is rarer than all three: Kepler's exemplary ability to believe in and affirm happiness and his gift for extracting it from the most mundane occasions, a gift which humanizes him by giving him an eminently praiseworthy and angelic disposition.

Critical Context

Kepler is the second volume in a loosely connected tetralogy of novels which dramatize the nature of creativity. The first volume was devoted to the astronomer Copernicus (*Doctor Copernicus*, 1976) and also followed a basically biographical approach. Subsequent volumes, however (*The Newton Letter*, 1982, and *Mefisto*, 1986), have challenged or made problematic that approach, and while confining themselves to the area of scientific creativity—that is, with creativity which affects man's view of his world, rather than his view of himself—they have avoided being typecast as fictionalized chapters from the history of astronomy.

Banville's tetralogy has a number of noteworthy features, among the most obvious of which is its ambition. To sustain a sense of such an elusive, and perhaps mystical, subject as creativity over an extremely wide time span (*Mefisto* is set in the twentieth century) is achievement enough. To convey that sense in a manner which changes from volume to volume and from age to age, as Banville does over the course of the tetralogy, has the effect of demonstrating an inevitable interdependence between unity and diversity. This central preoccupation enables Banville to sketch other, more weighty but less artistically amenable, concerns, such as the epistemological implications of existentialist philosophy.

Coincidentally, by means of the tetralogy, Banville has participated in the recent refurbishing of the historical novel, a direction which he might well have taken in any case, given the concerns of his earlier fiction. Like many contemporary historical novels, however, *Kepler* and its companion volumes view history through a decisively twentieth century lens, meaning that it is less concerned with the denouement of a particular historical phase or episode than with the norms and criteria of human experience released in the course of a given historical moment but achieving significance by outlasting that moment.

In a sense made familiar by the contemporary Italian novelist Italo Calvino, the thrust of Banville's work is to create a myth of creativity. Like Calvino, though using rather less experimental narrative strategies, Banville is drawn to science for his creative archetype, using the conventions of what may be considered real (which science implies) in order to propose alternative realities.

Banville's originality and distinctiveness may be all the better appreciated in the context of Irish writing, where his work is far removed from the prevailing tradition of pastoral depression and perilous individualism. His novel's deftly sophisticated narrative flair, his subtly witty sense of character, even his slight tendency to overwrite make his work a breath of tonic air to students of Irish fiction as well as contribute to his reputation as one of the more stimulating and readable young novelists writing in English.

Sources for Further Study
Campbell, James. Review in *New Statesman*. CCI (February 6, 1981), p. 21.
Irish University Review. XI (Spring, 1981). Special Banville issue.
McCormach, Russell. Review in *The New York Times Book Review*. May 29, 1983, p. 10.
Peters, Andrew. Review in *Library Journal*. CVIII (June 1, 1983), p. 1152.
Prescott, Peter S. Review in *Newsweek*. CI (May 2, 1983), p. 78.

George O'Brien

THE KEYS OF THE KINGDOM

Author: A. J. Cronin (1896-1981)
Type of plot: Religious idealism
Time of plot: Late nineteenth century to 1938
Locale: England and China
First published: 1941

Principal characters:

FRANCIS CHISOLM, the protagonist, a parish priest and
missionary in China

ANSELM MEALEY, Francis' childhood friend, who becomes a
bishop

BISHOP HAMISH MCNABB, Francis' friend and mentor, who
sends Francis to China

DR. WILLIE TULLOCH, Francis' childhood friend, an atheist

NORA BANNON, Francis' cousin, who was in love with him

AUNT POLLY, a loving relative and helper to Francis

MOTHER MARIA-VERONICA, Francis' assistant in China

ANDREW, Nora's grandson, taken in by Francis

MONSIGNOR SLEETH, who must decide Francis' fate

The Novel

Utilizing his great narrative powers and ability to show the panoramic side
of China, A. J. Cronin offers his view of the fulfilled religious life as exemplified by the mind and heart of Father Francis Chisolm, a Scottish Parish priest
who spends the greater part of his life as a missionary in China. The compli-
cations in the novel mainly arise for Francis, who, despite his powerful faith,
is a self-doubter and a believer in religious toleration.

Cronin begins the novel almost at the very end, when Francis, now an old,
worn-out man in his sixties, has returned to Scotland as a parish priest after
more than thirty years of being a missionary in China. He has taken on the
burden of rearing Andrew, the grandson of his childhood love, Nora Bannon, as no one else wants the boy, and Francis faces retirement at the hands
of his superiors in the Catholic Church, men whom he has failed to impress
despite his many years of loyal and dedicated service. Monsignor Sleeth,
Francis' immediate superior, is, at this point, all for forcing Francis' retirement.

The remainder of the novel, until the very end, is a flashback detailing
Francis' life. It begins with his childhood as the son of pious parents who die
because of their religious faith and love for each other. Francis then lives a
life reminiscent of the novels of Charles Dickens, filled with privation, poverty, and suffering at the hands of unsympathetic relatives until he is rescued

by Aunt Polly, his benefactor throughout his life.

Despite finding his vocation in the Church, Francis suffers much uncertainty, which makes his superiors think that perhaps he is not fit to be a priest. Bishop Hamish McNabb, however, the head of the seminary, finds in Francis a kindred spirit, and he encourages Francis to become a priest; it is McNabb who is instrumental in sending Francis to China as a missionary.

In China, Francis finds not the thriving mission he had been informed he would take over but only some ruins and "rice Christians," Chinese who have pretended to convert for material gain, and he must create a mission by himself with the help of no one. In saving the life of the son of the wealthiest man in the town of Pai-tan, Mr. Chia, Francis slowly begins to win at first the admiration of the Chinese and finally their belief in his religion. Cronin shows Francis practicing medicine (like others among Cronin's characters in his medical novels), although on a primitive level, showing how Francis manages to get converts not by prayer alone but by helping members of the community.

His success results in the Church's sending three nuns to assist him in teaching the children of the mission. These nuns are led by Mother Maria-Veronica, an aristocratic German, who at first looks down on Francis because he is not the smooth, polished priest she expected to lead a successful mission. She eventually learns to value and respect Francis' humble and Christlike ways, however, especially after meeting Father Anselm Mealey, Francis' childhood friend and a leader of the missionary society that sent Francis to China. In Anselm, Mother Maria-Veronica finds the worldly priest rather than the man dedicated to helping others.

The mission, under Francis' strong, courageous leadership, survives flood, famine, plague, bandits, and war; when, however, after many years, Francis is finally recalled home, he is seen by his superiors as a failure because he did not succeed in creating as many converts as they unrealistically had hoped. Ironically, these men have no firsthand knowledge of the sacrifices and hardships Francis endured to keep the mission going with little or no help.

The novel then returns to complete the opening section, wherein Monsignor Sleeth must determine Francis' future. In a dream, the Monsignor discovers that he is not the kind of man he has wanted to be and that Francis, a truly saintly man, has been wronged by him. In an almost totally unexpected way, the Monsignor changes his mind about retiring Francis and allows Francis to continue in the only life he loves, that of a parish priest.

The Characters

Father Francis Chisolm is, without a doubt, the most inspiring character in the works of A. J. Cronin. In Francis, Cronin has created what in demeanor and appearance would be a most ordinary human being, but Cronin also shows how little appearance means compared to the inner nature of the man of conviction who is determined to leave the world a better place. Francis' inspiration lies in a humble nature and in a total commitment to humanity, not to Church dogma or Church politics. Because he is lacking in surface conviviality, he is not seen as the real success he is by his superiors.

In addition to this, there is his religious tolerance, a lesson which he learned by the death of his parents: He chooses not to impose his religious faith upon those who are not receptive to it. This tolerance is best exemplified by his friendship with Dr. Willie Tulloch, a friend of Francis from childhood on. Willie, a physician, comes to assist Francis at the mission in China during a terrible plague and finally dies for his efforts. Francis' regard for Willie shocks Mother Maria-Veronica because Willie was always an atheist and dies unrepentant and unconverted.

Francis' tolerance is again seen with the coming of Dr. Fiske to the town of Pai-tan. Dr. Fiske, an American Methodist missionary, is regarded by some of Francis' flock as a rival whom they would drive away as an unwanted competitor for the souls of the people. Instead, Francis befriends Dr. Fiske and his wife; together they do much to help the lives of the people of the town. At the heart of Francis' faith is his respect for the faiths of others, for he sees many gates on the road to Heaven.

In the same spirit, Francis learns some of the wisdom of Confucius from Mr. Chia, who is impressed when Francis refuses to accept his conversion to Christianity for saving his son's life, considering it a forgery to God. When Francis must finally leave China, however, he learns that he has genuinely converted Mr. Chia by the example of his own life.

The other characters in the novel, except for Anselm Mealey, are seen only as they are involved with Francis. Francis' family and friends are, for the most part, seen favorably, but the priests, except for Bishop McNabb, are not. Anselm Mealey, Father Kezer, and Monsignor Sleeth especially are seen as precisely what priests should not be: egocentric, ungiving, and narrow in their faith.

The best example of what a priest should not be is Anselm Mealey, often Francis' chief antagonist. Attractive, personable, and worldly, Anselm is the antithesis of Francis in his great success in the Church, reaping all the material rewards forever denied to the quiet, humble priests, who are averse to tooting their own horns to advertise their piety. Francis from time to time marvels at Anselm's success and even, at times, envies Anselm, but there is no doubt as to the path Francis would choose, had he any alternative. Cronin's often-stated thesis that it is a hard life for idealists is seen in his ironic depiction of Anselm's successes. Francis has sought to emulate the life of Saint Francis, who loved poverty, and gaining the keys to the kingdom is the only success he would ultimately seek.

The novel begins and ends with Monsignor Sleeth, who at first finds Francis repulsive and wants to retire him. Sleeth is one of the novel's unattractive characters, and his change is not entirely expected, for he is boring, dogmatic, and cruel. It is his cruelty to young Andrew, whom he threatens to send to an orphanage, which finally brings a reversal in his character. Readers may find this change of heart hard to fathom, but perhaps Cronin is saying that in His wisdom, God has manifested Himself to protect and preserve one of His most devoted servants.

Themes and Meanings

The major idea behind this work is immediately revealed by its title. The keys of the Kingdom of Heaven must be obtained not only through the inner-directed love of God but also in total dedication to helping one's fellow human beings. Prayer alone cannot give salvation to man, for prayer alone is a meaningless activity without the reality of good works.

In addition, Cronin has presented in Francis the kind of priest who seems to be more in the ascendancy among men of the cloth in all faiths. Not content with dispensing pious platitudes, Francis seeks to involve himself in the total life of his flock, desiring to improve their lives both physically and spiritually. He is drawn to the poor as an act of faith in doing the work of God.

Francis also sees toleration as the highest virtue, and in this he foreshadows a certain degree of reconciliation between Catholicism and other religious faiths. In Francis, one finds an image of the human face doing the work of God.

Critical Context

At the time this novel was published, it was generally regarded as Cronin's greatest work. Published by the Book-of-the-Month Club, the novel received an enormous readership and was greatly acclaimed by an overwhelming majority of the critics, although there were some negative comments about the sentimental and often melodramatic elements that feature much of the plot.

Yet, though literary critics, for the most part, commented favorably, there was greater division on the part of critics found in religious publications. These critics found little evidence of orthodox Christianity in the novel and were dissatisfied with the kind of religious example offered by Cronin in the life of his protagonist. Catholic literary critics were also divided in their views of the work, many of them believing that Cronin had distorted the goals and motivations of the priesthood and that he had not drawn a sympathetic portrayal of the Catholic Church on the whole.

This claim is perhaps true, for it does seem that Cronin has drawn not so much a model for one faith but a model for all faiths, and this may be why this novel remains the most widely read of all of Cronin's offerings. Medical doctors, too, complained bitterly about Cronin's *The Citadel* (1937), one of his major novels dealing with some of the evils practiced by medical men. Because Cronin was a medical doctor himself, however, there was a general acceptance of his views on how medicine was being practiced. As he was never a priest, some of Cronin's critics, especially those writing for religious publications, believed that he had not been entirely fair to organized religion.

Nevertheless, *The Keys of the Kingdom*, because it depicts an inspiring journey in the spiritual life of a saintly man, continues to be enjoyed by many readers and is still regarded as Cronin's greatest novel.

Sources for Further Study

Adelman, Irving, and Rita Dworkin. *The Contemporary Novel: A Checklist of Critical Literature on the British and American Novel Since 1945*, 1972.

Cassis, A. F. *The Twentieth Century English Novel: An Annotated Bibliography of General Criticism*, 1977.

Salwak, Dale. *A. J. Cronin*, 1985.

_____. *A. J. Cronin: A Reference Guide*, 1982.

Temple, Ruth Z., and Martin Tucker. *Twentieth Century British Literature: A Reference Guide and Bibliography*, 1968.

Bernard Zavidowsky

KINDERGARTEN

Author: Peter Rushforth (1945-   )
Type of plot: Impressionistic realism
Time of plot: December 24-28, 1978
Locale: Southwold, a small English town
First published: 1979; revised, 1980

> *Principal characters:*
> CORRIE MEEUWISSEN, an accomplished musician, who turns
>   sixteen at the end of the book
> JO MEEUWISSEN, Corrie's eleven-year-old brother, who is an
>   excellent singer
> MATTHIAS MEEUWISSEN, the youngest brother at three years
>   old
> LILLI, the grandmother of the three boys

The Novel

Although the action of *Kindergarten* takes place over only five days during the Christmas holidays of 1978, the text is intercut with so much parallel and peripherally related material that the novel resonates with significance greater than that one might expect from the story of a family Christmas celebration. *Kindergarten* is about childhood, home, and sanctuary; more than that, however, it is about a close-knit family circle in the context of a larger, often hostile society that seeks to invade and destroy familial bonds.

The novel begins with an excerpt from the tale "Hansel and Gretel"—the episode in which Hansel and Gretel's stepmother suggests that the children be abandoned in the forest—and then immediately introduces Corrie Meeuwissen, the protagonist, as he prepares to celebrate Christmas with his younger brothers, Jo and Matthias, and their grandmother Lilli Meeuwissen. Celebration of any kind is difficult for the boys this year: Their mother is dead—gunned down in a terrorist attack in Rome nine months earlier in April—and their father is in the United States helping to raise money for the families of the other victims. Lilli has promised the boys "a traditional German Christmas," an event for which she has been preparing secretly for days, and when the three boys enter her dining room for the promised treat, they are stunned by the decorations: a glittering tree, Lilli's paintings, gifts, a spread of holiday sweets including a gingerbread house (which immediately reminds Corrie of Hansel and Gretel and the enchanted house in the forest), and hundreds of lighted candles.

During the festivities, Corrie suddenly realizes that Lilli's generous act is not the re-creation of a childhood memory for the amusement of three lonely boys. Being an artist, she has contrived a ceremony that she, being Jewish, knows about only from books. Corrie is overwhelmed by this evidence of his grandmother's love. He has known about his Jewish heritage (his mother was English, his father only half Jewish) for only two years; as the Christmas celebration proceeds, Corrie puzzles over the meaning of his Jewishness. During the events of the next four days, Corrie often allows his thoughts to wander as he thinks of happier times, occasionally about his mother's death, and sometimes about being Jewish. While a considerable portion of the novel describes Corrie's—and occasionally Jo's—recollections of happy family events, a still larger portion is devoted to Corrie's secret: He has discovered a cache of letters from German Jews to a former headmaster of Southwold School, the school now administered by Corrie's father.

On December 24, while in the school's music building rehearsing, Corrie succumbs to a long-suppressed curiosity and opens a small locked door in his favorite practice studio. Behind the door are boxes of letters and postcards from Jewish families in Nazi Germany from 1934 to 1939. The letters and cards beg for places for Jewish children at Southwold School, request news of children already enrolled there, and plead for more time to remit fees when the German government forbids the sending of currency out of the country. While Corrie is already fascinated by his Jewish ancestry and by the knowledge that his grandmother was a refugee from the Nazi regime, his interest in the letters is further sparked by two events. First, a week earlier, German terrorists took several dozen children hostage in Berlin, and they are still holding them; the ongoing saga of the children's ordeal, daily reported on television, is a constant reminder of their mother's death to Corrie and Jo. Second, in his initial foray into the files, Corrie finds a postcard from a Jewish boy of about his own age, thanking that long-ago headmaster for granting him and his younger brother a place at the school.

Many of the letters and cards are quoted in their entirety, showing the anguish of parents trying desperately to find a safe place for their children. Over the next four days, Corrie returns repeatedly to the file room to read more of the letters, stopping to conjure up faces for the people he has come to know through their pleas and their guarded descriptions of a Germany inhospitable to Jews, particularly the children. A number of parents sent photographs of their children, and as Corrie looks at their solemn faces, he is reminded of Hansel and Gretel, abandoned in the dark forest, and of the Berlin schoolchildren now in their second week of captivity.

All of Corrie's preoccupations are forced to a form of closure on December 28, his sixteenth birthday. He finishes reading the letters, and a commando raid on the Berlin school frees most of the hostage children. More important, his birthday gift from Lilli is a new painting, her first since her flight from Germany in 1939. She also reveals to the astonished boys a new collection of paintings, no longer illustrations of fairy tales but evocations of the Meeuwissen family in happier times. For the first time, Lilli shows the boys a photograph of her family, all lost in the Holocaust. Corrie recognizes the faces, immortalized as characters in Lilli's earlier works, and he wonders about the fate of those families whose letters he has read. As the novel ends, Corrie, once again off in his thoughts, recollects the final scene of a school play for which he composed the music.

The Characters

Peter Rushforth has created an unforgettable quartet of precisely delineated individuals made memorable through their thoughts and actions, their fears and preoccupations, their cherished possessions, and their unique relationships with one another.

Corrie, whose point of view informs *Kindergarten*, is an exceedingly talented sixteen-year-old, whose accomplishments include music composed for a production of a play by William Shakespeare, the organization of an Elizabethan consort, and an opera-in-progress. In addition, Corrie has a tendency toward introspection and analysis by allusion. In Corrie's mind, all events are interconnected with other remembered events, stories, snatches of poetry or song, and the news on television, and all experience somehow comments on and reflects family life and home. Corrie's favorite images in Lilli's German paintings are of rooms, snug and secure with their doors shut against the exterior world or connected with other rooms in the same house, the details of those other rooms visible through open doors but the whole still secure from the outer world. These rooms—remarkably similar in Corrie's mind to the two Meeuwissen houses, linked through a connecting sun lounge—connote the security of strong family ties and affection, contained by the doors shut against what he often thinks of as "the pressures of the outer world."

Known to people in the town as a quiet, polite boy who is taking his mother's death very well and helping his younger brothers cope, Corrie knows that he is more than the seemingly well-adjusted boy who smiles respectfully when he is greeted. He is "aware of depths within himself; little doors deep inside his head, doors that should never be opened." His slightly-too-intense sense of family, his preoccupation with certain fairy tales in which children are menaced by adults, his near obsession with both the fate of the Jewish children in the 1930's and the plight of the terrorist-held schoolchildren—all reveal an adolescent perhaps fearful of growing up and certainly aware that, in countless ways, life is hostile to childhood. He reads the letters from the files with a sense of foreboding, knowing that in 1939—the year Southwold School was forced to close—a door closed forever, shutting hundreds of children out of the safety and serenity that Corrie and his brothers enjoy.

Jo does not display any sort of obsessive traits; in many ways, he is an average eleven-year-old whose bedroom is decorated with Charlie Brown comic strips and family photographs, littered with schoolwork, clothes, books, posters, drawings, mobiles, and toys. Jo is no more average, however, than is Corrie. Precocious almost beyond belief—his speech is a combination of Shakespeare and the thesaurus, the books on his floor include *Kobbé's Complete Opera Book* (1922), and he sings in German—he is in one respect younger than his chronological age: He still frequently wets his bed. During the holidays, he is most affected by his mother's death; he has nightmares about it, and he insists on going out on Christmas Eve to sing at her grave. That terrorist act in Rome has robbed Jo of the remainder of his childhood; he is now a child struggling with an adult's awareness of the precarious nature of existence.

Too young to have understood the family tragedy (he apparently believes that his mother is away on an extended trip), Matthias is the unspoiled innocent of the novel, the child Corrie wants to protect, the little boy Jo has not been since their mother's death. Matthias eats with gusto, paints portraits of a "havverglumpus," eagerly opens doors on an Advent calendar (never having seen a harp, he mistakes one for a radiator), plays football, romps with the dog—all activities redolent of the joys of childhood. As yet, he is unaware that life has other, more painful experiences to offer.

The final character is Lilli, once an acclaimed illustrator of children's books in prewar Germany, then a refugee in London, and now a grandmother in a small English town. As the cozy, homely details of her paintings indicate, Lilli is as preoccupied as Corrie with preserving family traditions and the innocence of childhood as talismans against the evils of the world. In her careful attempt to provide a special Christmas for the motherless boys, Lilli makes it clear that hope, steadfastness, and faith—symbolized by the huge fir in her dining room—are values in which she believes, values that have helped her come to terms with a terrifying world that has taken away so many of her family and friends.

Themes and Meanings

All the novel's themes come together in a statement Lilli makes just after she asks Jo to sing a song about accepting the death of a child.

> I cannot agree that death is where a child belongs, that a child is best out of the world. . . . We *are* wandering, we *are* lost in darkness . . . but it is the children who will lead us out of this darkness. . . . With each child birth, they say, the world begins again. . . .

Incorporated into the novel's accounts of fantasylike family gatherings full of hope, love, and security are details about the suffering of innocents: several entire fairy tales by the Brothers Grimm, the television newscasts about the hostage children, excerpts from Anne Frank's *The Diary of a Young Girl* (1947), Bertolt Brecht's poem "Children's Crusade" (an alternative ending to "Hansel and Gretel" in which the children are devoured by the wicked witch in the dark forest), and the pleading letters from Germany. Clearly, the world is dangerous for children, and the very state of childhood is vulnerable in a society that thrives on destroying its magic; if the collage of references to endangered childhood is meant to represent the evil in the universe, however, then the good must be symbolized in the lovingly elucidated details of the everyday tasks and rituals within a family.

Kindergarten is the age-old story of the conflict between good and evil, and as happens in many of the fairy tales quoted in the narrative, good triumphs in the end. Thus, the novel ends in affirmation of the family, with Jo singing quietly to his grandmother as Corrie relives in his mind the last scene of Shakespeare's *The Winter's Tale* (c. 1610-1611), in which a long-dead wife is brought back to life by the love and tears of her family. Rushforth's benediction is the retelling of the finale of "Hansel and Gretel," this time the orthodox ending, in which the two children are saved from the witch and reunited with their father, to live happily ever after in the security of a family.

Critical Context

Kindergarten, first published in Great Britain in 1979 and later revised for the American edition in 1980, has elicited mixed reactions from critics, who agree that it is a compelling first novel. Winner of the Hawthornden Prize from Great Britain's Society of Authors in 1980, the novel has been hailed for the originality and intricacy of its montage structure, for its unusual filmic quality, for its intensely riveting story celebrating the strength of family ties, and for its reverberant and intriguing network of images and allusions. Commentators are unified in their praise for Rushforth's narrative skill and for his thoughtful treatment of the perils of childhood—a theme so easily over-sentimentalized by a less careful and perceptive writer. Most agree that the book requires, indeed demands, rereading for a thorough appreciation of its complexity and the richness of its imagery.

Oddly, it is *Kindergarten*'s very complexity that has been most strongly criticized, even by reviewers who find the novel extraordinarily well written. There is some truth to the accusations that Rushforth is almost heavy-handed with his use of related but extraneous material, thematically significant though that material might be. At times, the story of Corrie and his brothers is buried beneath a daunting multiplicity of allusions—to fairy tales, paintings, books, songs, poems, past experiences, and films—and then extricated, pages later, creating an otherworldly quality that occasionally turns the novel into one vast evocation of nostalgia at the expense of the story it is telling. Collagic structure notwithstanding, however, *Kindergarten* is a fine first novel. With its incredible profusion of detail and tableaux so fully realized in color that they call to mind exquisitely executed paintings or meticulously composed frames in a film, the book transcends the novel genre to become a modern fairy tale.

One of Rushforth's greatest achievements is the quality of fantasy he has incorporated into his all too painfully real tale. Imbued with the feeling of otherworldliness and remoteness, with the delicious possibility that perhaps Corrie, Jo, Matthias, and their grandmother live in a land far away and long ago, a land where family events are marked with celebrations and children are free to be children, *Kindergarten* nevertheless has a moral lesson for the real world. Childhood by its very nature will always be an endangered age, its precarious survival threatened by what Corrie instinctively senses as "the vague, powerful forces of the adult world . . . waiting, at the edges of childhood, unseen by the children." In the adult world, where the future inevitably brings loss and grief, where death is the only certainty, children have but one place of sanctuary where the forces of the outside world are temporarily held in abeyance, one refuge: the family circle secure at home.

Sources for Further Study

Cooke, Judy. Review in *New Statesman*. XCIX (June 20, 1980), p. 939.

Gunton, Sharon R., ed. *Contemporary Literary Criticism*. XIX (1981), pp. 405-407.

Judd, Inge. Review in *Library Journal*. CV (June 1, 1980), p. 1328.

Locher, Frances C., ed. *Contemporary Authors*. CI (1981), p. 425.

Yourgrau, Barry. Review in *The New York Times Book Review*. LXXXII (August 17, 1980), p. 10.

Edelma de Leon Huntley

KING JESUS

Author: Robert Graves (1895-1985)
Type of plot: Historical novel
Time of plot: The first century A.D.
Locale: Palestine
First published: 1946

> *Principal characters:*
> JESUS, the unacknowledged son of Prince Antipater,
>   anointed by John the Baptist as King of the Jews
> MARY, Jesus' mother, heiress of Michal, formerly a temple
>   virgin
> HEROD, King of the Jews, under the protection of the
>   Romans
> ANTIPATER, Herod's eldest son, the crown prince, secretly
>   married to Mary
> SIMON, the High Priest, who officiated at the secret marriage
> MARY THE HAIRDRESSER, the queen of the harlots (modeled
>   on Mary Magdalene)

The Novel

A first century Roman tells the story of the wonder-worker Jesus, born to Mary, a temple virgin and an "Heiress of Michal" (King David's wife). In ancient times, according to Simon, the High Priest, title to the land passed down from mother to youngest daughter by ultimogeniture. Thus David unified Israel by marrying the heiresses of the twelve tribes, and pharaohs of Egypt married their sisters. Therefore, Simon, in order to assure the claim to the throne of Prince Antipater, over his treacherous brothers, secretly marries Antipater to Mary. To protect the pregnant Mary from the dangerous intrigue of the unstable King Herod and his ambitious family, Simon announces her betrothal to Joseph, a kind and pious old man, instructing him to retain a small part of the bride price, without which the contract is not yet legal. Joseph assumes the role of protector, but after Herod murders his own son and seeks the child reportedly born in Bethlehem, Joseph pays the rest of the bride price to Simon and flees with Mary and the child Jesus into Egypt.

This novel creates a new legend of Jesus—his birth, ministry, and death—using much of Graves's knowledge, intuition, and speculation about Hebrew and pagan mythology, especially the cult of the Great Goddess. Here the goddess is Jesus' most important adversary. According to Clement of Alexandria, quoting from *The Gospel according to the Egyptians* (on the flyleaf), the Savior said, "I have come to destroy the works of the Female."

The novel has three sections, each containing unorthodox reinterpretations of the biblical story. The second section, for example, includes a ritual marriage to the second Mary, sister of Martha and Lazarus, though Jesus refuses to consummate the marriage. It also involves his strange relationship to Mary the Hairdresser, Queen of the Harlots. She is High Priestess of the love goddess, but Jesus exorcises her of the seven deadly sins.

The third section concerns the events leading to Jesus' death. Because he has refused his wife's right, under Jewish law, to a child, maintaining the celibacy he adopted among the Essenes, he feels obligated, in response to her plea, to bring her brother Lazarus back from the dead. This occult power demanded that a life be forfeited for the life regained. Unwilling to cause another's death, he accepts the forfeit of his own life. He decides to adopt the role of the Suffering Servant, prophesied by Isaiah, who takes upon himself the sins of the people. Such a person must be struck down by one close to him. Judas Iscariot is the unlucky disciple chosen for that role. Judas betrays him to the Romans, however, thinking that it will prevent Jesus from thus arranging his own death. Surely they would not execute him, since Jesus had no revolutionary political aspirations and spoke eloquently of a spiritual kingdom, not a secular one. Judas does not anticipate the terrible miscarriage of justice that occurs when Jesus refuses to defend himself before Pilate. In despair, Judas hangs himself in an attempt to ransom the life of Jesus.

Jesus is mourned at the cross by the three Marys, the implied representatives of the Triple Goddess who loved him: Mary the mother, Mary the bride, and Mary the Hairdresser, who is the layer-out (in death) of the sacred hero. Mary the Hairdresser says to Shelom the midwife, "His fault was this: that he tried to force the hour of doom by declaring war upon the Female. But the Female abides and cannot be hastened."

The Characters

Although Graves takes unusual liberties with biblical texts, he does not trivialize Jesus, or entirely demythologize his significance. While his birth is explained in more naturalistic terms and his temptation in the desert as ancient ritual with the aged Simon taking the part of the Devil's advocate, he is still the chosen sacred king, devoted to saving the world from sin and death. Some of his followers undoubtedly thought of this in political, revolutionary terms, casting the Romans as their adversaries, but Jesus is not interested in a secular kingdom.

The novel reveals both the high-minded dedication of Jesus as a man of innate vision trained by the austere Essenes and his essential humanity as a man of sorrows. The large gap in biblical records about his early life, for example, is partially explained as being the result of a psychic blow to his self-image. The elders of the synagogue discovered the discrepancy in time between his birth and Joseph's paying the bride price. They came to the obvious, logical conclusion that he was illegitimate. Bastards, no matter how precocious in wisdom, were denied access to the inner temple. The introspective, sensitive Jesus does not reveal his predicament to his mother, for fear of hurting her. Much later, Mary explains to him the unusual circumstances of his birth, not realizing that he has needlessly suffered the eclipse of his youthful dreams. This accounts plausibly for his relatively late emergence as a religious leader, especially since he is assumed to have spent several years among the Essenes.

Mary the Hairdresser is patterned after the biblical Mary Magdalene, but Graves has made her more than a simple harlot. She is representative of a more ancient religious orientation, in which worship focuses on the neolithic triple goddess of moon, earth, and underworld, controller of birth, love, and death. She and Jesus debate the significance of certain images in a religious shrine. Jesus interprets the pictures as scenes from the Hebrew Old Testament. Mary interprets them by the more ancient myth of Mother Eve bearing twin sons, who contend with each other for the love of the Second Eve, until sacrificed by the Third Eve.

Jesus cannot convert Mary the Hairdresser from her devotion to the pagan fertility goddess. At last turning to magic to exorcise her sins, however, he enlists at least her sympathy and devotion to his spiritual purposes. She is not misled, however, about Jesus' chances for replacing the law of nature with a spiritual kingdom defined by his masculine god Jahweh. "Nevertheless, Lord," she warns, "the end is not yet, and when the Mother summons me to my duty, I will not fail her." That duty is partly the traditional role of old women to prepare the dead body for burial, but it has mythological overtones of ritual acceptance of the sacrifice of the sacred king, which assures his immortality. Thus Jesus, in his high-minded devotion to a spiritual revolution that was to cancel out the material laws of nature, with their inexorable cycle of birth, copulation, and death, involuntarily reenacts the ancient drama of sacrificial death characteristic of pagan vegetation gods subservient to the goddess.

Themes and Meanings

In spite of the seeming defeat of Jesus, or at least his participation in rituals that predate both Judaism and Christianity, there is no satire or contempt implied in this treatment of the compassionate wonder-worker some called the Messiah. Neither is there any particular sentimentality. The narrator, who takes no part in the action but looks at it objectively as neither a Christian nor a Jew, maintains a respectful neutrality. He points out learnedly that there are five distinct meanings or assumptions about the Jewish Messiah, and the reader notes that no one of them is quite the same as the later Christian one. In any case, the Messiah was assumed to be human, though no doubt God's instrument, like Moses or David or Samson.

It does not offend such a narrator, accustomed to living in a world of many competing gods and cults, that the hero should be born, according to folklore, in the grotto of Tammuz outside Bethlehem. Absolute exclusiveness to particular mythic imagery is not yet necessary, nor is it especially desirable. Significance does not depend on absolutely unique action; on the contrary, it must resonate in a context of traditional meanings, enriched, not endangered, by the echoes of the past. To be sure, the Jews, with their single-minded devotion to the exclusively male deity, must struggle mightily with the forces of contamination around them, especially the goddess cults. One of the dangers of being ruled by mad King Herod was that he secretly sought to bring back the pagan desert god Set, which the Jews had known in Egypt— he who tore to pieces his brother Osiris and appeared to men in the guise of a wild ass.

Graves creates a mythopoeic world in which factual reality does not exclude the possibility of miracles. Some incidents, such as the resurrection of Lazarus from the tomb, have no rational explanation. Others, reported as miraculous, are apparently traditional symbolic rituals, such as the Temptation of Christ and the Scourging of Christ, the latter attributed in the Bible to Roman soldiers, but in the novel presented as a ceremonial scourging of the anointed king. Herod lived in political uncertainty partly because his power was dependent on Rome, but traditional kings of old had been chosen and anointed by the prophets, as Jesus was by John the Baptist.

Critical Context

This is probably the most daring and imaginative treatment of Christian myth that contemporary fiction has to offer. It is destined to fascinate and possibly shock readers for many years to come. D. H. Lawrence's defiant *The Man Who Died* (1931), which tried somewhat ineffectually to tie the crucified, but not dead, Jesus to a rejuvenation through sex with a priestess of Isis, pales in comparison with this complex novel so steeped in ancient lore of both pagan and Hebrew cults.

Even Graves's more fantastic imaginings have some correlation to rumor or legends of the period. Graves and Joshua Podro in *The Nazarene Gospel Restored* (1953) suggest that the idea of Jesus being spiritually begotten by God would have been greeted with horror in Palestine by Jews and ridicule by worldly Romans and Greeks, who would conclude that Jesus was a bastard. Some, however, took the epithet "King of the Jews" literally as indicating that he was Antipater's son.

One can hardly understand the dynamics of *King Jesus* without knowing something of Graves's obsessive fascination with what he called the White Goddess of ancient preclassical myth and cult. Though Graves insisted that this goddess is the poet's muse, the only appropriate object of the poet's devotion, this novel shows her more relentless aspect as the source of man's bondage to matter and the senses, and thus to sin and death. Jesus was in metaphysical revolt, on behalf of men and women too, against the bondage of the mind and spirit to material nature.

Graves and Podro wrote in *Jesus in Rome: A Historical Conjecture* (1957) that Jesus, like his fellow Apocalyptics, expected the world to end during his lifetime in a series of catastrophes, after which the Kingdom of Heaven would reign on earth for a thousand years. That was one reason Jesus insisted on celibacy and advised it for his disciples. Sexual intercourse made one ritually unclean for three days, and one needed to be constantly ready for God's imminent coming in glory. Both Jesus and all subsequent millenarians continue to be disappointed in this prophecy, for as Mary the Hairdresser so wisely pronounces, "the Female abides," in spite of all attempts to supplant the natural order with a supernatural one.

Graves read James Frazer and other anthropologists who have explored the similarities between Hebrew, Christian, and pagan traditions. He adds his own touch, however, to the obvious similarity of the Last Supper to certain well-known pagan rituals of symbolically eating the sacrificed god and drinking his blood. He makes a plausible case for Judas, as an educated and devout Hebrew, seeing this ceremony as deliberate blasphemy, a technique by which Jesus incriminates himself and therefore deserves the scapegoat death that he is determined to enact, a combination of Zechariah's "Worthless Shepherd" and Isaiah's "Suffering Servant." That subsequent Christians would accept this pagan rite, possibly originating in cannibalism, as a sacrament, probably pleased Graves's well-developed sense of irony. So, too, would the trick of making Judas, the Western world's quintessential traitor, the most misunderstood man in history.

Sources for Further Study
Cohen, J. M. *Robert Graves*, 1960.
Graves, Robert, and Joshua Podro. *Jesus in Rome: A Historical Conjecture*, 1957.
_____. *The Nazarene Gospel Restored*, 1953.
Seymour-Smith, Martin. *Robert Graves*, 1956.
Snipes, Katherine. *Robert Graves*, 1979.
Stade, George. *Robert Graves*, 1967.
Vickery, John B. *Robert Graves and the White Goddess*, 1972.
Ziolkowski, Theodore. *Fictional Transfigurations of Jesus*, 1972.

Katherine Snipes

THE KING MUST DIE
and
THE BULL FROM THE SEA

Author: Mary Renault (Mary Challans, 1905-1983)
Type of plot: Mythological romances
Time of plot: Sometime during the Mycenaean Age in Greece
Locale: Various sites on the Greek mainland as well as on Crete and other
  Aegean islands
First published: The King Must Die, 1958; *The Bull from the Sea,* 1962

Principal characters:
  THESEUS, a renowned Attican hero, who eventually succeeds
    his father, Aigeus, as king of Athens
  PITTHEUS, a king of Troizen, whose daughter, Aithra, is
    Theseus' mother
  ARIADNE, the eldest daughter of the king of Crete, Minos,
    and his queen, Pasiphae
  ASTERION (MINOTAUROS), Pasiphae's son from an adulterous
    union with an Assyrian bull-dancer
  ORPHEUS, the Thracian minstrel who assists Theseus in
    establishing a mystery religion at Eleusis
  POSEIDON, the Sea God and Earth-Shaker, who is Theseus'
    tutelary deity
  PIRITHOOS, the adventure-loving king of the Lapiths, with
    whom Theseus forms a fast friendship
  HIPPOLYTA, an Amazon queen, who becomes Theseus' lover
    and comrade-in-arms
  HIPPOLYTOS, the natural son of Theseus by Hippolyta
  OLD HANDY (CHIRON), a wise and gentle Kentaur
  OEDIPUS, the sightless Theban king now wandering about
    Greece in self-imposed exile
  PHAEDRA, the younger sister of Ariadne, whom Theseus
    formally weds after the death of Hippolyta
  MENESTHEUS, a demagogue who usurps the throne of Athens
    during Theseus' waning years

The Novels

The life of the legendary Attican hero Theseus spanned a period of
approximately fifty years. In *The King Must Die,* Mary Renault delineates
the course of his life up to the age of eighteen, when he assumes the kingship
of Athens; in *The Bull from the Sea,* she recounts the vicissitudes of Theseus'
subsequent career to his death on the Aegean isle of Skyros. The opening

section of Renault's earlier novel is set in the Peloponnesian city of Troizen, where Theseus' maternal grandfather, Pittheus, is king. It is here that King Aigeus of Athens once stopped over for the purpose of boarding a ship that would take him across the Saronic Gulf back to Attica. Aigeus was returning from a visit to the Delphic Oracle, whose advice he had sought on the matter of how best to put an end to his childless state. Unfortunately, the response of the priestess was too obscure to be of any help. While Aigeus is still in Troizen, Pittheus receives an oracle of his own from a local priestess directing him to sacrifice the maidenhead of his daughter, Aithra, to appease the wrath of the Earth Mother. He therefore arranges a sexual union between Aithra and his Athenian guest. Before Aigeus resumes his journey, he buries a sword and a pair of sandals under a huge rock and instructs Aithra to send any male offspring from their union to Athens when the child comes of age, provided that he is able to move the rock and retrieve the buried objects. A boy is born in due course and is named Theseus. Since enemies of Aigeus would surely attempt to kill any offspring of his who might have a claim to the kingship of Athens, the true identity of Theseus' father is kept secret from the people of Troizen as well as from the boy himself. Pittheus, moreover, adroitly encourages everyone to accept the rumor that Theseus is the son of Poseidon.

It is only when Theseus reaches the age of seventeen that his mother invites him to test his strength by lifting the rock under which Aigeus has buried the sword and the pair of sandals. After failing to dislodge the rock through sheer strength alone, Theseus decides to substitute wit for brawn by employing a lever to aid him in the task and thus succeeds in reclaiming the buried objects. He is, thereupon, informed for the very first time that he is the son of Aigeus and has now duly qualified himself to claim his birthright as the Athenian king's heir. Theseus chooses to go to Athens by the hazardous land route over the isthmus rather than by sea. At Eleusis, a city located fourteen miles northwest of Athens, Theseus finds himself forced to engage in mortal combat with a man named Kerkyon. After killing him, Theseus learns that Kerkyon's death was part of a matriarchal ritual in which the consort to the Queen is sacrificed annually and that he himself is the new Year-King. Acting on the basis of his own strong patriarchal instincts, Theseus quickly sets about organizing activities among the menfolk of Eleusis that are aimed at putting an end to the worship of the Earth Mother as well as to the social dominance of women. These efforts are strongly opposed by the Queen's brother. When the two fight a duel, the men of Eleusis side with Theseus and help him turn defeat into victory. Theseus then goes to Athens to be purified for having shed the blood of a kinsman and uses the occasion to reveal his identity to Aigeus. Even though Theseus is convinced that his destiny lies in Athens, he still returns to Eleusis briefly out of concern for the welfare of his comrades there. Once back in Eleusis, he is declared king and the queen commits suicide. Prior to departing for Athens again, Theseus replaces the matriarchal form of worship with a mystery religion espoused by an itinerant Thracian bard named Orpheus.

Many Greek cities at that time were obliged to pay tribute to the ruler of Crete because a member of his royal household had once been killed in a brawl on the mainland. It was mandated that a number of young men and women were to be dispatched on a periodical basis to serve as bull-dancers in the arena located within the labyrinthine palace at Knossus. In addition to providing amusement for the effete nobility of Crete, the highly lethal sport of bull-dancing constituted a religious ritual whose purpose was to appease the wrath of Earth-Shaker Poseidon. Following Theseus' return to Athens, seven youths and seven maidens were scheduled to be chosen by lot for the bullring at Knossus. Much to the dismay of Aigeus, who decided not to enter his son's name in the lottery, Theseus volunteers to replace one of the youths who was selected. Under his skillful coaching, the Athenian contingent not only manages to survive for a full year but also returns to Athens without the loss of a single member. Their escape from Crete occurs shortly after its ruler, Minos, requests Theseus to kill him as a means of thwarting the political machinations of his potential successor, Asterion, who is the illegitimate offspring of his deceased wife and an Assyrian bull-dancer. It turns out, however, that this power-hungry opportunist has already had sufficient time to coerce most of the island's nobility into supporting his claim to the kingship. When the coronation ceremony is disrupted by an earthquake, Theseus seizes the moment to slay Asterion. He then sets sail back to Greece along with the rest of his team. Accompanying them is Minos' eldest daughter, Ariadne, whose admiration for Theseus' daring performances in the bullring led her to become his lover. Theseus abandons her during a stopover at the island of Naxos, however, when he comes to view her with revulsion because of her zealous participation in the bestial orgies that take place during the annual slaying of the Year-King in the presence of Dionysos himself.

The concluding chapter of *The King Must Die* and the opening one of *The Bull from the Sea* overlap in content insofar as each of them recounts the incident of Theseus failing to replace the black sail with a white one as the vessel approaches the Greek mainland, so that Aigeus might receive advance notice of his son's safe return. Instead of keeping the promise that he made to his father, Theseus refers the matter to Poseidon and receives a sign instructing him to retain the black sail. Theseus is obviously impatient to become ruler of Attica. Grief-stricken at the sight of the black sail, Aigeus jumps over a cliff to his death, and Theseus sets foot in Athens as king. Among the more memorable incidents depicted in *The Bull from the Sea* is one in which Theseus encounters Oedipus outside Athens and is witness to the death of the former king of Thebes amid an earthquake. Another impressive episode deals with Theseus' participation in the legendary battle that erupts at the wedding of the Thessalian king named Pirithoos the Lapith, when a band of Kentaurs seeks to abduct the bride. The Kentaur king, Old Handy, is entirely different from his unruly subjects, and both Theseus and Pirithoos hold him in great esteem for his wisdom as well as his healing powers. A short time after the wedding, Pirithoos convinces Theseus that the two of them should join Jason in his quest for the Golden Fleece. While in the region of the Amazons at the eastern end of the Black Sea, Theseus is caught observing the secret rituals of the Moon-Maidens and is compelled to engage Queen Hippolyta in single combat. Victorious in the duel, Theseus takes her back to Athens as a concubine. She subsequently bears him a son, and he names the infant Hippolytos in her honor, although to do so is against custom in a patriarchal society. When the Amazons mount a rescue attempt on Hippolyta's behalf by forming the vanguard of a Scythian invasion of Greece, she sacrifices her life for Theseus while assisting him in repelling an enemy attack against the ramparts of the Acropolis.

Emotionally devastated by Hippolyta's death, Theseus takes to roving with Pirithoos and sacking cities throughout the Mediterranean. After having indulged himself in such nefarious activities for more than a dozen years, he directs his attention toward stabilizing political relations with the island of Crete. To this end, he decides to enter into matrimony with Phaedra, the younger sister of Ariadne. When she subsequently bears him a son, Theseus is convinced that the vassalage imposed on the island after he and his grandfather conquered it several decades earlier will now evolve into a permanent dynastic union with Athens. Before long, things go awry: Phaedra falls hopelessly in love with Hippolytos. Resentful because her advances are spurned, Phaedra falsely accuses Hippolytos of raping her in response to an omen bidding him to consecrate her as a priestess of the Earth Mother so as to restore the matriarchal form of worship. When Theseus confronts him, Hippolytos is unable to deny Phaedra's charges because of a priestly oath that he has sworn to remain silent. Theseus, thereupon, invokes the curse of Poseidon upon Hippolytos and sends him into exile. The truth comes to light only because Theseus' son by Phaedra informs him of Hippolytos' innocence. The boy makes this disclosure in the hope of appeasing the wrath of Poseidon after his father announces that an earthquake is imminent. The earthquake, nevertheless, occurs as Hippolytos is driving his chariot near the seashore, and both the driver and his team of horses are crushed by a tidal wave that engulfs them. Hippolytos is on the point of death when Theseus arrives on the scene, and there is barely time for a tearful reconciliation. Theseus' next encounter with Phaedra is a lethal one, for he strangles her forthwith. Once again, Theseus seeks distraction through piratical adventures, but he soon suffers a stroke that incapacitates him permanently. As a result, a new king is able to assume power in Athens and Theseus goes into exile on the island of Skyros. Broken in spirit as well as in body, Theseus is now convinced that his destiny has finally run its course, and he leaps into the sea from a cliff to his death.

The Characters

In accordance with mythological tradition, Mary Renault depicts Theseus as growing up with the conviction that Poseidon is his father. Her view of Theseus is, however, unique in two major ways. First, she endows Theseus with an "earthquake-aura" that enables him to sense in advance whenever an earthquake is imminent. This proof of Poseidon's partiality toward him manifested itself unequivocally in his final year of service at a temple dedicated to the sea god, where he was obliged to reside one out of every four months from age eight to age ten. Second, Renault rejects the view that Theseus was a man of gigantic size. In an author's note appended to *The King Must Die*, she argues to the contrary by stating that "a youth accepted for the bull-dance can only have had the slight, wiry build which its daring acrobatics demanded" and that Theseus' heroic feats may, in part, represent "the over-compensation of a small, assertive man." Within the novel itself, she describes how, while still a boy, Theseus found it difficult to reconcile his divine lineage with his smaller-than-average stature and how, on many occasions, he felt the need to reassure himself of his descent from Poseidon by performing deeds of great valor.

Theseus, at age six, is indoctrinated into the concept of kingship by his grandfather after witnessing the sacrifice of a noble white stallion in honor of Poseidon. Pittheus explains that the office of king is a sacred duty imposed by the gods themselves and that a true king must always be willing to sacrifice his life for the people whenever he receives a divine sign indicating that his *moira* (fate) is fulfilled. Both Aigeus and Pittheus exemplify all the qualities associated with a true king. Even Minos, for all of his faults, proves to be capable of sacrificing his life on behalf of his people when he finds it necessary to oppose Asterion. This villainous usurper, also called Minotauros (bull of Minos) because of his squat build, seeks the kingship of Crete without having received any indication of divine sanction, and Theseus welcomes the opportunity to punish him for this sacrilege. Although not immediately apparent, Asterion's half sisters—Ariadne and Phaedra—are in like manner morally corrupt and mirror the decadence of the semi-Hellenized nobility of Crete.

Hippolyta, notwithstanding her matriarchal proclivities, is Theseus' true love, for this warrior maiden fully shares his belief in the sacred nature of the kingship. Accordingly, Theseus views her selfless death on his behalf as the epitome of kingly virtue. His attitude toward Hippolytos, on the other hand, is fraught with ambiguity. Theseus is actually envious of his son's prepossessing appearance and tall stature. Theseus is also perplexed by the youth's androgynous character. In contrast to the uncompromising masculinity of his father, Hippolytos dedicates himself to the worship of the goddess Artemis and is still a virgin at age seventeen. He is, moreover, almost Christlike in his healing powers. Theseus never manages to advance to the moral level of Hippolytos, but owing to his steadfast willingness to consent to the dictates of destiny, he maintains an aura of genuine nobility throughout both novels.

Themes and Meanings

The sacred character of the kingship is one of the two major themes that link the ideological content of both novels. The other theme pertains to the conflict between matriarchal and patriarchal values. In the author's note accompanying *The Bull from the Sea*, Mary Renault summarizes the nature of this conflict for the benefit of those readers who are unfamiliar with the earlier novel. For the most part, she uses the occasion to reiterate the information related by Pittheus to Theseus in one of the opening chapters in *The King Must Die*. Here, Pittheus lectures his twelve-year-old grandson about the matriarchal societies that existed among the autochthonous inhabitants of Greece prior to their subjugation by Hellenic invaders. Throughout *The King Must Die*, Renault refers to these worshipers of the Earth Mother as "Minyans," a designation which is difficult to justify on historical grounds. "Pelasgians" would have been far more appropriate.) In *The Bull from the Sea*, however, she has a change of heart and switches to the term "Shorefolk." Theseus himself was to encounter two matriarchal societies at first hand, one at the city of Eleusis and the other on the island of Naxos. In each of these communities, a consort to the queen is put to death annually as part of an agricultural fertility rite similar to those delineated in the anthropological studies written by Sir James George Frazer and Jane Harrison.

It is clear that Renault finds both patriarchy and matriarchy to be one-sided and that she favors a fusion of the male and female principles. On an individual basis, such a fusion is best exemplified by the character traits of Hippolytos. The closest that Theseus ever comes to recognizing the merit of the feminine principle occurs when he joins Orpheus in establishing a mystery religion at Eleusis in honor of a goddess.

Critical Context

It is generally conceded that Mary Renault's first novel about Theseus is vastly superior to its sequel. While the plots of both novels are equally imaginative, *The Bull from the Sea* does not equal the aesthetic merit of *The King Must Die* either in terms of stylistic richness or in terms of character development. Especially fine is the section that depicts Theseus' adventures on the island of Crete. This section may very well be the finest achievement of Renault's entire literary oeuvre. There can, moreover, be no doubt that *The King Must Die* ranks, along with *The Last of the Wine* (1956) and *The Mask of Apollo* (1966), as one of Renault's most important novels. The literary establishment has, on the whole, chosen to regard novels written about mythological or historical subjects with condescension; few critics, with the exception of Peter Wolfe and Bernard F. Dick, have seen fit to undertake a serious analysis of Renault's career as a novelist. The reading public at large, however, has responded most positively to her writings, and there is every indication that *The King Must Die* and *The Bull from the Sea* will continue to enjoy popularity among those lovers of mythology who take delight in twice-told tales.

Sources for Further Study
Dick, Bernard F. *The Hellenism of Mary Renault*, 1972.
Ward, Anne G. *The Quest for Theseus*, 1970.
Wolfe, Peter. *Mary Renault*, 1969.

Victor Anthony Rudowski

LADY CHATTERLEY'S LOVER

Author: D. H. Lawrence (1885-1930)
Type of plot: Romantic tragedy
Time of plot: The early 1920's
Locale: Towns named Wragby and Tevershall, in the Midlands of England, and European cities, notably Venice
First published: 1928

Principal characters:

SIR CLIFFORD CHATTERLEY, the owner of an estate at Wragby
CONSTANCE CHATTERLEY, his wife
MICHAELIS, a playwright and family friend of the Chatterleys
ARNOLD HAMMOND, a friend of Sir Clifford, a writer
TOMMY DUKES, a brigadier general in the army
CHARLES MAY, another of Sir Clifford's friends, a writer on astronomy
OLIVER MELLORS, the gamekeeper at Wragby
CONNIE MELLORS, his young daughter
HILDA, Constance's sister
SIR MALCOLM REID, the father of Hilda and Constance
DUNCAN FORBES, a modern artist, who is unmarried

The Novel

The quest for fulfillment in a broken world is the central concern of this work, which became controversial for its frank and explicit depiction of sexual relations. The plot, which is relatively uncomplicated, deals with the travails of a loveless marriage and the attempt of the woman to find gratification elsewhere. At the outset, the events that join Sir Clifford and Constance Chatterley in marriage and their life together at his estate in Wragby are traced in a summary of the issues that later are to affect their separate destinies. When she was a girl, Constance studied music abroad and engaged in a brief liaison with a German lover in Dresden. Clifford, from an old aristocratic family, conducted research in the engineering of coal mining. His sexual fires evidently were stoked rather low all along; he had no experience of women before he married, and matters became much more difficult shortly thereafter. During World War I, he became a first lieutenant; his brother Herbert was killed in action in 1916, and early in 1918, not long after his wedding, he was wounded in Flanders. He was left partially paralyzed and impotent as well. He became permanently confined to a wheelchair. The family's hopes that his marriage with Constance might produce children, and thus ensure successors, seem doomed to frustration.

Vaguely chafing at her husband's incapacity, Constance initially falls prey to the charms of Michaelis, a waggish popular playwright who seduces her gently, leads her to climax, and then in a subsequent encounter complains that she has become too demanding. Under Clifford's watchful and occasionally suspicious eyes, other men come to Wragby Hall. Old acquaintances such as Arnold Hammond, Tommy Dukes, and Charles May, who had known Clifford during his university days or from the army, discuss the propriety of open discourse about sexual practices; they seem to believe that erotic urges impede the development of the mind. Constance, still perturbed by her affair with Michaelis, at times feels possessed by the need to conceive a child; in passing, she again considers taking a lover. She comes upon Oliver Mellors, the gamekeeper at Wragby, quite by chance, when he is scolding his younger daughter. Later, when he washes himself in the open air, she becomes fascinated with his firm, smooth, white skin and his air of unassuming naturalness. She is drawn to him even more when she encounters him at his hut; she asks him to have a separate key made for her. Sir Clifford now sends for his friends more rarely, and he seems more distant than ever from Constance. He maintains that they may have a child—there are intermittent hopes that medical treatment may restore some of the functions of his lower body—but only if she is certain that she wants one. On a fine clear day, Constance goes out on the grounds; she comes upon Mellors helping a pheasant hen bring a brood of baby chicks into the world. She is captivated by the raw natural beauty of their surroundings. Quite impulsively, she yields to his advances and they make love in his hut, in a tranquil, unhurried fashion that elicits from her the expressed desire for a later meeting.

Thereafter, Constance's continuing relations with Mellors become yet more vital, while her marriage with Clifford degenerates into open antagonism. Her intercourse with the gamekeeper reaches new levels of intensity: They reach simultaneous orgasm, and she feels enveloped in flame, as though she had become filled with molten lava. On another occasion, after his initial efforts prove unsatisfactory, he makes another spirited attempt and she feels as though she were caught up in surging waves of the sea. There is much graphic physical description: Constance's belly and buttocks and Mellors' loins and haunches are rendered in some detail in notable passages. On another front, bitter conflict erupts when the Chatterleys go for a drive in the country. Clifford's motorcar breaks down, and when Mellors tries to assist them the two men argue vehemently; Constance subsequently reproaches her husband for an attitude that, she maintains, is all too typical of the ruling classes. On a rainy day, when Constance meets Mellors again, they undress together and promenade about in the open air, with flowers nestled in their body hair. When Constance returns to Wragby Hall, the wary Clifford quarrels with her yet again. Her sister Hilda has arrived, and when they are alone Constance openly acknowledges that she has been having an affair and that she is carrying Mellors' child.

Suggestions of divorce come from various quarters; there is also some question about what Constance will do with her baby. The advice Constance receives from Hilda and from Sir Malcolm Reid, their father, is not particularly apt. They enlarge upon an earlier proposal of Sir Clifford, that Constance should travel abroad before reaching any lasting decisions. Although they get as far as Venice, nothing avails; Constance will have nothing of efforts, pending her separation from Sir Clifford, to arrange a union with Duncan Forbes. She finds this family acquaintance, a dissolute and self-important practitioner of modern art, actually somewhat repellent. Clifford, meanwhile, has finally grasped the full import of her relations with Mellors; he castigates her as perverted and sullied but will not hear of a divorce. He declares that he cares nothing about a prospective heir to the estate. Constance packs her most valued possessions and goes with Hilda to Scotland. The novel closes with a letter to Constance from Mellors, who has moved on to other work in the coal country; he expresses his yearning to be reunited with her when the next spring comes.

The Characters

This work has essentially to do with a love triangle that accentuates the diverse qualities and dispositions of those involved; other characters by their very shallowness heighten the contrasts that are developed in the novel's major encounters and confrontations. The romantic and sexual concerns of Constance Chatterley determine much of the action; it is a sense of self-discovery that impels her to pursue affairs that to many would be unthinkable for a woman of her social position. In the beginning, she is described as "full of unused energy" and not quite certain of what she wants. Nor does she realize immediately how stifling her marriage with Clifford will become. At the age of twenty-seven, she takes on extramarital lovers. After the affair with Michaelis, her sexual wants become identified with her longing for a child; with Mellors there are more openly sensual stirrings. Much of the narrative, albeit written in the third person, conveys Constance's point of view; her thoughts and impressions at many junctures are shared with the reader. Her reactions to sexual climax, as much as those of the men, are evoked in bright metaphorical language. More than the others, she is torn between the older ties of family, social class, and the life of the mind, on the one side, and on the other her own felt needs for affection and sexual gratification. The initial disharmony of the two spheres is great, and the realignment of her physical and moral selves is correspondingly painful.

In contrast to his wife, Clifford Chatterley seems to exist in a kind of unfeeling void, which is, in a sense, much broader than his disability: "[H]e was not in touch." His impotence and his restricted physical mobility in some ways seem to antedate his injury; while it is possible to ascribe some meanness to the author in rendering Clifford crippled as well as emotionally obtuse, from the novel's standpoint his condition seems to serve several purposes. The devastating effects of World War I are brought home most visibly in this way. Furthermore, Constance's infidelity is the more readily accepted in view of her husband's manifest inability to satisfy her or, indeed, to provide the heir his family seeks. Although by fits and starts he attempts some fiction writing, his consuming passion remains, as it was before the war, the effort to apply modern engineering processes to the production of coal. With his wife he is remote, pedantic, and given to oblique and rather ponderous locutions on the life of the mind. While in some places it is remarked that his scientific pursuits have "made a man of him," during his quarrels with Constance there are suggestions that he has regressed into a childlike state. He is not notably percipient, and though he is sporadically suspicious of his wife, he does not quite comprehend the nature or extent of her infidelity until rather late in the work.

Mellors is very much the opposite of Constance's husband. He is thirty-seven or thirty-eight years old; at one time he worked as a blacksmith. He was married for five or six years before his wife left him with their little girl, Connie, and went away. Like Clifford, he performed military service: For a time, he was in Egypt and India and was commissioned as a lieutenant in the cavalry. He is forthright and unassuming; his only affectation, if it is that, is a tendency to shift from the King's English into local dialect depending on whether he is speaking with his social betters or with those from similar walks of life. With Constance, he uses both forms of speech. Before he met Lady Chatterley, his experiences with women had brought him to regard them as cold and insensate. Yet he is capable of tenderness and a depth of feeling that are positively enthralling to her. His familiarity with natural surroundings and his gentleness in handling baby chicks and wild flowers belie the gruff, blunt manner he adopts when they meet for the first time. Although it is he who initiates their lovemaking, her gratification is a source of some satisfaction to him. In some passages, he pays tribute to the visible charms of her body in his quaint workman's language. Although ultimately he must go away, his concluding message to Constance makes clear his continuing affection for her.

Other characters make brief or intermittent appearances to espouse their own views of love and sex, and to consider other intellectual topics; some offer Constance advice. Some of Clifford's friends, such as Arnold Hammond and Tommy Dukes, consider sexuality beyond the pale of serious dignified discussion. Duncan Forbes, the aspiring artist whose modernistic renditions of nudes have the value of a religious cult for him, is alternately serious and sophomoric about Constance's chances for remarriage. Although they do not entirely comprehend her problems, Hilda and Sir Malcolm Reid provide some support, as well as a place of refuge, when Constance's marriage finally comes undone. That the fates of the leading and minor characters remain unresolved at the end suggests the significance of thematic concerns in the author's conception of his work.

Themes and Meanings

The outlook for English society at large, as depicted in this novel, is bleak and desolate. World War I, with its immense human sacrifices, has brought suffering and despair; neither gentry nor commoners have been spared. The German lovers of Hilda and Constance were both killed during the first year of hostilities; Clifford's brother fell later on, and Clifford himself came so close to death, and was so severely maimed, that he could never again seem lighthearted or flippant. Most of the men in the novel knew someone who was killed or wounded in action; some years after the armistice, ugly wounds remain in the nation's psyche from the "false inhuman war."

An older but equally insidious destructive force is the transformation of the countryside by industry, which has left sooty, blackened villages and towns to mark the passing of the old England. The pollution of the landscape imparts a darker tone to all that takes place in the nation's heartland: "The utter negation of natural beauty, the utter negation of the gladness of life" accompany the onward march of industrial growth. Human relations in some ways are still transfixed by the old bonds of class and property. The Reids and the Chatterleys continue to regard themselves as scions of the aristocracy; Sir Clifford's family ranks somewhat higher among the well-bred families of the kingdom, and he seeks further to advance his position by combining his inherited estate with the new wealth which industry and engineering have generated. Class prejudice appears to be as deeply rooted at the upper end of the scale as among the workmen. Clifford's contempt for those beneath him turns to vague, impotent hatred when he learns of Mellors' affair with his wife; what matters to him is the lowly common origins of his wife's lover rather than the actual fact of her infidelity.

In a world ravaged by industrial blight, class divisions, and dark brooding memories of the Great War, the author points to the life forces of love and sexuality as means of redemption. They are not inseparable: Desire may anticipate or exceed affection at times. Nor are such stirrings necessarily limited or confined by the ties of marriage. The author would seem to suggest that direct sexual gratification is an integral part of the love experience and must be taken independently of social conventions or traditional mores. This work neither advocates promiscuity as such nor promotes experimentation or novelty for their own sake. Nevertheless, to the same extent as romantic love, sexual intercourse legitimately may be portrayed, and the sensations aroused may be evoked, not merely in their indirect manifestations or as subjective drives but as essential events that must be taken as part of human experience. The insistence that explicit, unswerving depictions of sexual activities could be achieved in serious fiction brought this novel much notoriety upon its appearance in print and attached a scandalous reputation to it well after the bulk of D. H. Lawrence's work had been accepted as literature.

Critical Context

In his choice of a rural English setting for this, his last full-length novel, Lawrence returned to themes he had developed in his earlier work, but with some differences. While other efforts, notably *Kangaroo* (1923) and *The Plumed Serpent* (1926), were set in exotic locations such as Mexico and Australia, *Lady Chatterley's Lover* deals with issues and places that had also been featured in *Sons and Lovers* (1913) and *The Rainbow* (1915). The gloomy shadows cast by rampant industrial growth have been darkened in this last work by lingering memories of World War I; the characters are older and have become more deeply involved in marriage. The sexual relations that matter here are all extramarital. Initiation in romantic experience is not at issue as it was in Lawrence's first novels, but the quest for a union of the love experience with mature sexuality is a central concern. During his later years, Lawrence wrote extensively about pornography and obscenity and developed his own theories of the standards by which literature could be judged to be moral or improper. The checkered publishing history of *Lady Chatterley's Lover* was, in large part, a result of the comparatively graphic nature of the novel and the earthy language employed at certain points. In many ways, the work became a landmark: Its final acceptance marked the adoption of new conventions that expanded the boundaries of serious literary activity. At the same time, such controversies made it more difficult to assess the novel's position, on its own merits, within the overall body of Lawrence's work, or indeed within modern fiction.

In addition to unflinching descriptions of the physical act of sexual consummation, Lawrence allowed his characters, chiefly Mellors, to use a certain number of venerable four-letter, Anglo-Saxon words. In other writings, Lawrence suggested that such terms had become corrupted by generations of high-minded censors and low-minded pornographers. He contended that "the so-called obscene words" in and of themselves are inoffensive. Once society's moral guardians had driven sex underground and out of the serious novel, however, purveyors of lowly forms of entertainment and humor could "do dirt on sex" with impunity. On another level, and whatever the aesthetic issues, Lawrence's novel contains dialogue that has the ring of authenticity, however salty it may be in places. As was pointed out in later legal proceedings, the working classes, and many others as well, are often enough given to inelegant and repetitive expressions. Although it was originally published in Italy in 1928, the unexpurgated version of *Lady Chatterley's Lover* could not legally be distributed in the United States until 1959; in Great Britain it was successfully defended in a celebrated trial in 1960. The modern reader, once the question of obscenity has been set aside, may consider rather whether the novel succeeds in depicting the dynamics of mature sexual relations, even with its inconclusive plot; it may be considered as well whether Lawrence has accomplished his purpose in his experiments with language and with sexual imagery.

Sources for Further Study

Hewitt, Cecil Rolph, ed. *The Trial of Lady Chatterley: Regina v. Penguin Books Limited*, 1961.

Nehls, Edward, ed. *D. H. Lawrence: A Composite Biography*, 1959.

Squires, Michael. *The Creation of Lady Chatterley's Lover*, 1983.

Squires, Michael, and Dennis Jackson, eds. *D. H. Lawrence's "Lady": A New Look at Lady Chatterley's Lover*, 1985.

J. R. Broadus

LANARK
A Life in Four Books

Author: Alasdair Gray (1934-   )
Type of plot: Metafictional allegory
Time of plot: The unspecified present
Locale: Glasgow and imaginary under- and afterworlds
First published: 1981

> *Principal characters:*
> LANARK, the protagonist, a writer and the alter ego of
>   Duncan Thaw
> DUNCAN THAW, a Scottish painter and writer, the hero of the
>   interior narrative and Lanark's alter ego
> RIMA, Lanark's companion and the mother of his child
> PROFESSOR OZENFANT, a research scientist at the Institute
> MARJORY LAIDLAW, a Glasgow acquaintance of Duncan Thaw
> DUNCAN THAW, SR., the father of Duncan Thaw
> SLUDDEN, a politician and friend of Lanark

The Novel

Identification of the state with the human organism is, one of the narrators of *Lanark* tells the reader, a literary device at least as old as Plutarch. In this eccentric, compelling novel by a Scottish writer-painter whose sketches both illustrate and extend the text, the decay of the body politic is the controlling image. Swiftian in its intensity, *Lanark* is a metafictional allegory: Drawing on sources that range from Vergil to Johann Wolfgang von Goethe, from William Blake and Ralph Waldo Emerson to contemporary Scottish novelists, Alasdair Gray creates in the novel a series of worlds which function simultaneously as projections of a collective unconscious, contemporary versions of the classical underworld, and embodiments of a grim, anti-utopian social vision. Literary allusions, echoes, and conscious plagiarisms, both hidden and overt, enhance the text, lending power and often humor to the ultimate bleakness of the author's perspective.

The outline of the story is less complicated than the eccentric organization of the novel's component parts might suggest. Chapters 1 through 11, identified as book 3 in the table of contents, follow the adventures of the eponymous hero from the moment of his birth—or rebirth—in a railway car to the point at which, cured of a mysterious disease, he is told, in chapters 12 through 30 (books 1 and 2), the story of his alter ego, or previous self, Duncan Thaw. Lanark's story, a quest journey filled with archetypes and symbolic figures and scenes, is picked up again in the final third of the book, where it is at one point interrupted by an epilogue, also identified as a prologue, which provides among other things an index to the multiple plagiarisms embedded in the text. What seems at first to be merely a superficial manipulation of the reader's attention comes to make sense in the emotional rhythm of the fictive pattern and for the most part adds to the impact of the book.

Lanark first appears on the scene in an after-hours coffeehouse in a city that bears a strong resemblance to contemporary Glasgow. Drawn into a clique dominated by the charismatic politician Sludden, Lanark is attracted by one of Sludden's admirers, the girl Rima, who frustrates him by both inviting and repelling his advances.

It soon becomes apparent that the surface upon which the characters move is at once more and less substantial than it seems. People mysteriously disappear from the streets of the city, strange odors disturb Lanark's senses, authority figures representing some kind of military body try to recruit him. More disturbing is the evidence that strange diseases are spreading among the populace. Some people grow mouthlike sores on their limbs; Lanark finds his own skin turning crusty, glittering and cold. The progress of the rash, diagnosed by an unperturbed physician as "dragonhide," parallels the hero's growing inability to make human contact. Terrified, he tries to flee the city and, in a nightmarishly effective passage, plunges beneath the surface of the earth.

Lanark awakens in a mysterious Institute, a giant hospital filled with endless corridors and pulsing lights, where he is to undergo a course of treatment supervised by the sinister Professor Ozenfant, who plays the violin as he observes the death of human souls. By defying Ozenfant and breaking the rules of the Institute, Lanark manages to save the life of his fellow patient Rima and is rewarded by an oracle with his own story, the life of Duncan Thaw.

At this point in the book, conventional narrative supplants allegory. Thaw's story is a moving and straightforward history of that familiar figure in the literature of the West, the artist who is at odds with his environment and unable to find a place in the modern world. Thrashing about in postwar Glasgow, seething with ambition and frustration, Thaw is a doomed Lawrentian figure, condemned to destroy himself and others.

Gray notes in the epilogue that Thaw's story is in part autobiographical and that much of it was written before the "hull" of the novel—that is, Lanark's story—had been completely planned. Literally autobiographical or not, this part of the novel is raw and powerful, clearly fueled by memory and personal emotion. A talented and sensitive boy who suffers from asthma and disfiguring rashes, Thaw is imprisoned by poverty and by his own suffering. The various mentors he encounters—teachers, clergymen, parents, and friends—attempt to give him the intellectual and theological keys to a normal life but cannot help. Teased by girls who awaken his adolescent eroticism and tortured by unfocused guilt, he finds relief from his pain only in work.

By chance, Thaw is given the opportunity to decorate the interior of a decaying parish church. Into the giant mural he creates there, the painter pours his entire understanding of classical and biblical history, of the nature of society and the meaning of creation. Forbidden by the congregation to depict God, Thaw creates masses of natural and supernatural figures. When the congregation rebels and refuses to pay for the completion of the bizarre work, he continues anyway, finally sleeping on the floor of the church, forgetting to drink or eat and lecturing aloud to empty pews. When he is expelled from school, lampooned in the press, and rejected by a prostitute who recoils in horror from his eczema, Thaw explodes, consumed by his own energies.

In its final third, *Lanark* takes yet another turn. Thaw, whose experiences clearly formed the substructure of the opening chapters, disappears. The cured Lanark, discovering that the Institute runs on the energy released by human disintegration, escapes with Rima along a disorienting, *Godot*-like road back to the city, Unthank, where Sludden and his henchmen have now assumed control. Given the task of saving the city from the destruction planned for it by the governing Council, Lanark travels across an idealized landscape familiar from Thaw's childhood, to the prosperous town of Provan. Although he fails in his mission and cannot argue his case, he is rewarded by a role in the epilogue and by the foreknowledge of his death.

The Characters

Fully realized characters are seldom called for in allegory—in fact, they often impede its progress—so it is not surprising that many of the figures that appear in *Lanark*, often identified only by first names, are types rather than individuals. What reality they have is gained in part by a clever use of literary resonance, explained in the Index of Plagiarisms in the epilogue, and in part by Gray's structural gamesmanship, since characters who appear only in essence in the Lanark story take on the dimensions of the vivid personalities whose roles correspond to theirs in the Thaw section.

This kind of "structural characterization" is, for the most part, effective. It enables the author to underline his themes without seeming too obvious and to enliven what might otherwise be a rather dry excursion into didactic form by forcing the reader to make connections between conventional perspectives and their underlying role in psychophilosophical discourse. Several characters can be condensed into one and seen in terms of their function in Thaw's psychic life; their individuality is referential rather than specific, but they retain lingering traces of their original personalities. Rima, for example, is Marjory Laidlaw, Thaw's teasing nemesis, but she is also all the other women in Thaw's life, from his mother to the prostitute, who attract and then abandon him. Sludden, the archetypal taker and destroyer, is the underside of all the authority figures in Thaw's life, whose function in the interior narrative is more ambiguous and less self-serving.

In general, the most memorable figures in *Lanark* are those closest to the hero—not unusual in a narrative with some autobiographical roots. Thaw's father, a gentle and baffled rationalist who tries without success to take on the sufferings of his son, is moving and pathetic in his frustrated inability to provide Thaw with adequate weapons to ensure his survival. Thaw himself has far more complexity and energy than the cipherlike Lanark. An amalgam of Paul Morel (of D. H. Lawrence's *Sons and Lovers*, 1913), Stephen Daedalus (of James Joyces's *A Portrait of the Artist as a Young Man*, 1916), and Gulley Jimson (of Joyce Cary's *The Horse's Mouth*, 1944), Thaw is nevertheless firmly rooted in his time and his place. His combination of illness and talent may be both familiar and symbolic, but it is convincing and sufficiently particularized to make his final explosion almost unbearably painful.

Themes and Meanings

Lanark is primarily a philosophical novel, one in which the author calls on the combined resources of modern, medieval, and classical literary traditions in an attempt to express his convictions about the forces governing contemporary civilization. His particular subject is the destructive struggle for power that crushes the creative spirit of humankind, forcing human energy in upon itself and destroying the ability of the individual to save himself and others through the active exercise of love.

The figure who appears to Lanark in one of the final chapters of the novel and identifies himself to his hero as the author (who is also the king and creator of Unthank and Provan, a being once, but no longer, a part of God) describes the Institute as an embodiment of the Hobbesian state, a Leviathan into whose maw pour the resources of humanity, consuming the many to benefit the few until the food supply is exhausted and the creature has no choice but to consume itself. Thaw's miseries and his final outbreak of murderous violence are precisely analogous to the progressive repression of the individual by the state and to the Armageddon that comes as a relief to a civilization suffocating from its own stenches and poisoned, as Unthank is, by its own waste. Real human relationships of all kinds provide the only possible relief from the pain of existence, but these are unpredictable and difficult; social needs and economic pressures are all too likely to crush human beings into fodder for the self-perpetuating state.

Within this context, the artist-hero has a special role. Gray gives to the head of the governing Council the name James Burnett, Lord Monboddo, an eighteenth century Scottish anthropologist who anticipated Darwin by postulating the descent of man from the orangutan. The world presided over by Monboddo, essentially the world of Thaw's atheist father, is logical and not unkind, but cannot provide a place for the free spirit, for the creative intellect that demands eccentric nourishment and chafes under restraint. It is the artist, Gray suggests, who alone possesses the means to travel safely between the various worlds of human imagining and who may, like Lanark, be allowed a glimpse of eternity, but even the artist is unlikely to press his claims: Lanark, for example, misses his chance to argue for the fate of Unthank because he has been jailed as a public nuisance.

In the epilogue, the author figure—also called the "conjuror"—uses a discussion of the literature of the past two thousand years to illustrate to his hero the inevitability of human failure, but Lanark remains unconvinced: The works of art which the "author" cites are themselves testimony to the positive powers of the irrational. Lanark's death is not triumphant, but he is vouchsafed at the end some peace and some light.

Critical Context

When *Lanark* was published in Great Britain, several reviewers—among them novelist Anthony Burgess—hailed it as a masterpiece; critic G. Ross Roy described it as "a work which can be compared without disadvantage to Carlos Fuentes' *Terra Nostra.*" With its censorable illustrations (Gray is a painter and draftsman as well as a writer), its typographical play, its fantastic erudition, and its impudent wit, *Lanark* immediately established Gray as a metafictionist of the first rank.

Gray's subsequent works, while generally well received, have been less ambitious. A collection of short fiction, *Unlikely Stories, Mostly* (1983), plays with motifs from Franz Kafka and Jorge Luis Borges. The novel *1982, Janine* (1984) employs, on a smaller scale, some of the tricky devices of *Lanark* in its parodistic rendering of sadomasochistic pornography. *The Fall of Kelvin Walker: A Fable of the Sixties* (1985) is Gray's most conventional novel to date, a broadly satiric critique of the Calvinist values which he regards with loathing.

Sources for Further Study

The Atlantic. Review. CCLV (June, 1985), p. 104.

Fantasy Review. Review. VIII (June, 1985), p. 18.

The New York Times Book Review. Review. XC (May 5, 1985), p. 14.

Roy, G. Ross. Review in *World Literature Today.* LVI (Summer, 1982), p. 557.

The Village Voice Literary Supplement. Review. December, 1984, p. 15.

Jean Ashton

LAST AND FIRST MEN
A Story of the Near and Far Future

Author: Olaf Stapledon (1886-1950)
Type of plot: Science fiction
Time of plot: c. 1900 to c. two billion years A.D.
Locale: Earth, Mars, Venus, and Neptune
First published: 1930

> *Principal characters:*
> HUMAN NATURE, the character of humanity as revealed over
> billions of years
> THE NARRATOR, a member of the eighteenth species of man-
> kind, who speaks through the medium of the twentieth
> century writer of this narrative

The Novel

Last and First Men is an imitation history of mankind written from the point of view of a new species of humanity two billion years in the future. Though Olaf Stapledon presents some episodes in detail, most of the novel is very general, showing the broad sweep of a possible human history without attention to particular characters. The narrator's subject is human nature. The accounts of eighteen different human species add up to an exploration of potentials inherent in human nature and assertions about which of those potentials ought most to be valued. The eighteenth species exemplifies the fullest development that humanity achieves.

Contemporary humanity, the first species, is characterized by a childish individualism that repeatedly leads to self-destruction. During the centuries of this species' domination, humanity repeatedly rises toward common ideals of civilization only to decay into savagery. The first men deplete their resources and health through religious warfare. This pattern continues to characterize the early developments of subsequent species.

The second men are nearly destroyed by Martian invaders, who are incapable of understanding human consciousness. Because the nonanimal Martians cohere and reason by means of forms of radiation, they are unable to recognize humans as sentient beings. They assume that radio stations are intelligences and humans their servants. The second men destroy the Martians with a biological weapon that also destroys human civilization. When the third men achieve high culture, they use genetic engineering to produce the fourth men.

The fourth men are giant brains with immobile, partly mechanical, vestigial bodies. After the fourth men virtually destroy the apparently useless third species, they come to see that the life of the intellect is not satisfactory.

Without consciousness of physical existence, they are without passion or affection. They can neither know all that may be known nor sustain the desire to know when they encounter intellectually incomprehensible realities such as love and values. To escape despair, they create a fifth species that balances a maximum of intellect with the best of human passions.

As the fifth men approach a pinnacle of human culture, they are forced by cosmic disaster to move the race to Venus. The adjustments to a new planet involve creating the sixth men, who fare badly there until they develop the seventh men, a winged species which delights in the physical sensations of flight at the expense of intellectual pursuits. Without intellectual rigor, the flying race is happy and free but lacking in the tragic vision which derives from objectivity and a sweeping view of human history. When the more serious species that replaces the seventh men has achieved a high level of civilization, humanity is again forced by cosmic calamity to move, this time to Neptune.

Over millennia, the cycle of development, destruction, and decay is repeated until humanity again adjusts itself to an alien and hostile environment, balances conflicting potentials, and produces the eighteenth species, the highest level of human development presented in this "history."

Eighteenth men, of whom the narrator is one, learn that mankind will be destroyed by yet another cosmic disaster before the completion of the human destiny they imagine: to achieve a full racial consciousness, making the human race in all time and space conscious of itself as a whole. This goal was to be achieved by two means. The human past would be unified with the present by mental time travel of the kind exemplified in the narrator's use of a first-species writer. Eighteenth men plan to become acquainted with the minds of all people of the past and to commune with them. Full consciousness in the present would result from increasing telepathic union of the entire existing human race on Neptune. Having learned of the impending destruction of the solar system, the last men endeavor to continue the exploration of and union with the past while preparing a molecular dust which might carry the seeds of human potentiality into the cosmos. They hope that, before the end of the cosmos, humanity might again achieve high self-consciousness and reach the apparently ultimate human destiny of realizing a unified spiritual being, of making the universe conscious.

The Characters

The main character of *Last and First Men* is human nature. The narrator speaks as one of a species which has realized human nature to the fullest in his time. He speaks to the first men, who can hardly imagine what such humanity may be. Though many thematic issues are explored, the main subject is always the possibilities inherent in human consciousness, how they might be meaningfully and beautifully organized.

Stapledon sees human nature as divided between the individual passions that arise from the need for personal survival and group passions that arise from the need for species survival, between physical and emotional being on one hand and self-consciousness and the need to understand on the other, and between subjectivity and objectivity. The various species he presents illustrate the permutations of imbalances and balances among these main potentials. The eighteenth men represent an ideal manifestation of humanity because they have found a proper balance of these possibilities.

A proper balance includes a complete subordination of the individual to the race without the surrender of the individual. This seemingly impossible balance becomes possible only when telepathic communication allows a perfect understanding between individuals. It approaches the ideal on Neptune, where "families" of ninety-six members frequently experience complete mental union and where occasionally the whole race experiences such union. All these types of union depend upon the physical bonds of emotion and affection that these people cultivate. The regular experiences of "higher consciousness," or group mind, lead to a blending of objectivity and subjectivity that the narrator often characterizes as aesthetic and tragic.

Last men are able to look upon the entire history of humanity as a work of art, the expression of a cosmos that may be alive and purposefully attempting to achieve consciousness. The last men are able to accept humanity's failures and its ultimate defeat in time, for even if the cosmos achieves consciousness, it must end. To see and accept the beauty of this effort in the face of ultimate defeat the narrator characterizes as tragic nobility. This is the sort of "character" the narrator gives humanity. His narrative becomes the record of humanity's often blind and blundering reaching out in the direction of spiritual fulfillment.

Themes and Meanings

Stapledon, in his preface to *Last and First Men*, says that he wants to express "the highest admirations possible" within his culture. In each species, but especially in the fifth and eighteenth, Stapledon presents for both the reader's admiration and his criticism frequently praised human traits—for example, aesthetic appreciation, community, rationality, compassion, imagination, and dexterity. He not only makes clear that these traits must be balanced for humanity to realize itself most fully but also shows that the dark, destructive side of human nature often helps the species and, therefore, must be accepted and even affirmed.

John Huntington sees the thematic center of this novel in its dialectical approach: Stapledon's goal is "to teach a trust in the possibility of an understanding that must remain incomprehensible at the end." Each possible formulation of an ideal humanity points toward yet another possibility; therefore, there is no certain completion of human nature. Because the species must die before it can achieve a final formulation, its fate is tragic.

Huntington points out a second major theme that functions to reconcile narrator and reader to this tragic fate: musical form. Humanity is like a symphony with themes and variations, conflicts and resolutions. Though the themes are limited, the variations are innumerable. For a symphony to become beautiful and complete, it must end. The narrator dwells on this comparison, using it repeatedly as a means of reconciling himself and his readers to the paradoxes and injustices of a history filled with evil as well as good, suffering as well as fulfillment. Ultimately, the narrator uses the concept of humanity as a symphony to reconcile himself to the ends of mankind and of the cosmos.

Stapledon is sometimes seen as having written a theodicy like John Milton's *Paradise Lost* (1667), but from the point of view of an agnostic mystic. Instead of justifying the ways of God to man, Stapledon asks readers to contemplate the aesthetic beauty of the highest possibilities of human achievement against the background of the inevitable end of all things. Unable to affirm an intelligent will outside time and space that creates and sustains human meaning, Stapledon sees in human aspirations a will within history to create meaning and, ultimately, spirit. Unlike Milton's comic view of human destiny, Stapledon's view—sometimes called ecstatic fatalism—is tragic in this novel because, though humanity aspires to spiritual being, there is no clear evidence that the cosmos conspires with the species' struggle.

Critical Context

Though Stapledon is widely acknowledged as one of the founders of modern science fiction, his first novel, *Last and First Men*, has never been popular. Lacking characters and adventure, it does not recommend itself to casual readers. Nevertheless, it is widely admired by students and writers of science fiction. Eric S. Rabkin argues that Stapledon was one of the first to see the genre as useful for philosophic inquiry and fostering moral growth. Such well-known writers as C. S. Lewis, Arthur C. Clarke, Stanisław Lem, Doris Lessing, and H. G. Wells—who also influenced Stapledon—have acknowledged debts to him. For example, Lessing's "Canopus in Argos Archives" series (1979-1983) uses ideas of the group mind similar to those of Stapledon. While it is difficult to be sure of direct influence in every case, there are suggestive connections between Stapledon and several more recent writers. For example, the views of human nature and its relations to the future in Frank Herbert's "Dune" series (1965-1985) may owe a debt to Stapledon. When reading *Last and First Men*, one repeatedly recognizes devices and ideas that are encountered in other science fiction from Ray Bradbury to Kurt Vonnegut, Jr.

Even though the book was not very popular, it was successful enough to encourage Stapledon to continue writing science fiction as a part of his life's work of studying and teaching philosophy. His more important novels include *Odd John: A Story Between Jest and Earnest* (1935), *Star Maker* (1937), and *Sirius: A Fantasy of Love and Discord* (1944). In those books, he continued to explore and elaborate his ideas about human nature and the destiny of humanity.

Sources for Further Study

Goodheart, Eugene. "Olaf Stapledon's *Last and First Men*," in *No Place Else: Explorations in Utopian and Dystopian Fiction*. Edited by Eric S. Rabkin et al., 1983.

Huntington, John. "Olaf Stapledon and the Novel About the Future," in *Contemporary Literature*. XXII (1981), pp. 349-365.

――――――. "Remembrance of Things to Come: Narrative Technique in *Last and First Men*," in *Science-Fiction Studies*. IX (1982), pp. 257-264.

Kinnaird, Jack. *Olaf Stapledon: A Reader's Guide*, 1982, 1986.

Rabkin, Eric S. "The Composite Fiction of Olaf Stapledon," in *Science-Fiction Studies*. IX (1982), pp. 238-248.

Terry Heller

LEAVE IT TO PSMITH

Author: P. G. Wodehouse (1881-1975)
Type of plot: Comic melodrama
Time of plot: The late Edwardian era
Locale: Primarily Blandings Castle
First published: 1923

> *Principal characters:*
> PSMITH, the protagonist, an aristocrat with plenty of charm
> and little means
> EVE HALLIDAY, the heroine, who eventually marries Psmith
> LORD EMSWORTH, the owner of Blandings Castle, a large
> country estate
> THE HONORABLE FREDDIE THREEPWOOD, his son
> RUPERT BAXTER, Lord Emsworth's private secretary
> EDWARD COOTES, an American gangster
> LIZ (MISS PEAVEY), a poetess and partner of Cootes

The Novel

From the moment Lord Emsworth sticks his head out the window of his library in Blandings Castle in the opening scene, the plot of *Leave It to Psmith* proceeds as surely and inevitably as the rows of plantings in the manicured garden which is Emsworth's only preoccupation.

Broke and inept, Freddie Threepwood approaches his uncle, Mr. Keeble, hoping to wheedle from him a thousand pounds to offset his losses at the track and to invest in a bookmaking operation. A good-hearted soul, Keeble is distressed by his inability to help his stepdaughter and her husband buy a small house in the country: Keeble's wife, Lady Constance, is as tightfisted and inflexible as her husband is generous; she has never forgiven the young girl for marrying for love rather than money and has forbidden Keeble to send the young couple a check.

Always the opportunist when borrowing money is at stake, Freddie offers a simplemindedly melodramatic solution to the problem: Arrange to steal Lady Constance's famous necklace, replacing it with a new one and meanwhile selling the stolen one and sending the money to Keeble's stepdaughter. Freddie will keep a thousand pounds as a reward for his management of the affair. Keeble agrees and Freddie proceeds.

He answers a strange "position wanted" advertisement in a London newspaper. A person named Psmith—the "p" is silent—has offered his services for any job, in any capacity, "provided it has nothing to do with fish," and has urged his reader in all the self-assurance of bold type to "**Leave It to Psmith!**"

As instructed, Psmith meets Freddie in the lobby of a London hotel, and the deal to steal the necklace is struck. While in London, Psmith goes to his club, The Drones, where Lord Emsworth, also a member, wrongly takes him to be the fashionable poet Ralston McTodd, whom Lady Constance has invited to Blandings.

Far from disabusing Emsworth of his mistake, Psmith quietly listens to the old gentleman rhapsodize on his garden. While listening, he sees from the window pretty Eve Halliday running among the shops as she gets caught in a sudden downpour. Leaving Emsworth, who never notices, Psmith steals an umbrella, gives it to Eve, and strikes up an acquaintance with her. She has been hired by Emsworth to catalog the great library at Blandings. Psmith's attraction to Eve is even further inducement to his accepting Freddie's proposition.

At Blandings, Psmith assumes his role as poet with becoming ease, though he is immediately suspected by Rupert Baxter, Emsworth's efficient, officious private secretary, who awaits his chance to expose the impostor. Suspicious of him, too, is Miss Peavey, a female poet also invited as a houseguest.

Miss Peavey is really Liz, an American and a petty criminal who has made her way to Blandings solely to steal Lady Constance's famous necklace. Her accomplice is Edward Cootes, an inept crook who relies on his partner's female wit to redeem his incompetence. Liz's scheme is to snatch the necklace during a poetry reading scheduled by Lady Constance. When Psmith, alias Ralston McTodd, is called upon to read from his collected works, Cootes is to cut the electricity and run to the terrace where Liz, taking advantage of the confusion, plans to seize the jewels and throw them through the window into the waiting hands of Cootes.

Freddie, meanwhile, has fallen in love with Eve and doltishly proposes. Eve forcefully declines, preferring instead the immaculate self-possession of Psmith, who woos her with evening boat rides on the lake. In a last attempt to win her love, Freddie assures Eve of his impending wealth and blunderingly alludes to the scheme. Eve goes to Keeble, who reveals the details of the entire arrangement.

The climax occurs on the night of the poetry reading. Things go according to plan for Liz except for the incompetence of Cootes, who arrives too late to catch the jewels. Eve, who had been strolling on the terrace, sees the necklace fly through the window and fall to her feet. Picking it up, she quickly hides it in one of the flowerpots bordering the lawn.

In the confusion that evening, Rupert Baxter, burning with suspicion, runs into the garden in his pajamas, searching for the necklace which he is convinced has been hidden nearby. Finding himself locked out of the house, he attempts to wake someone by flinging a flowerpot through a window. The window belongs to Lord Emsworth, who is awakened, sees Baxter in his pajamas and dirty hands, and immediately concludes that his secretary is mad. The next day, he fires him.

The next day, too, Eve returns for the jewels but finds them missing. A search begins, and as in true musical comedy all the characters involved in the action come together in a final scene to a woodman's cottage on the estate, whither Psmith has retired. Psmith gives Eve the flowerpot which he had picked up on the terrace as a present for her. Liz and Cootes arrive and hold up the couple but are thwarted when Freddie, who has been searching upstairs, crashes through the rotten floorboards and allows Psmith to take advantage of the distraction to disarm the gangsters.

In the end, all is restored. Eve learns Psmith's true identity, and Psmith takes over as Emsworth's private secretary. He and Eve agree to be married, and Blandings subsides into a mindless tranquillity.

The Characters

The characters of *Leave It to Psmith* are deliberate stereotypes, but they are drawn with such precision and clarity, with such comic whimsy, that they are memorable in their own right. Psmith himself, for example, is the perfect embodiment of the Edwardian gentleman. He dresses impeccably, speaks with grammatical precision, and conducts himself with irreproachable panache. There is, in fact, something of the decadent in him, a distaste for the disagreeable in life that makes him at first glance merely superficial and brings him dangerously close to being irrelevant. Yet at the same time, he is resourceful. He survives by being always unperturbed: nothing irritates him, no turmoil ever ruffles his clothes or his grammar. Psmith's self-assurance is his hallmark. It is applied even to validate his most trivial accomplishments, making him truly incomparable. In proposing to Eve, for example, he recommends himself to her by listing among his fine points his ability to perform card tricks and, what he believes to be an irresistible asset, his skill at reciting Rudyard Kipling's "Gunga Din."

As for Eve Halliday, she is bright, clever, and as honest as Psmith is self-assured. She is one of those classic heroines who enjoy their independent minds, who can see things clearly yet feel deeply. She is attracted to the irritating charm of Psmith and is repelled by the dull, the commonplace, the unfeeling shallowness of Freddie Threepwood and his kind.

Too stupid and lazy to be malicious, and dependent on the Emsworth estate, Freddie has no social graces and no imagination; the bulk of his working knowledge, the sum of his vocabulary, and the essence of his behavior are all derived from the numerous movies he has seen, the plots of which he resorts to when in need of negotiating some of life's more troublesome turns.

His father, Lord Emsworth, negotiates nothing. Stolid and serene, he is locked in his own world, bounded by The Drones Club in London and his flower garden on the estate. He bovinely grazes among the safe opinions of his friends, and the only conflict in his life is the interminable argument he sustains with his gardener over the disposition of his hollyhocks.

Finally, the team of Liz and Cootes is more suitable for a vaudeville show than a life of crime. Cootes is sufficiently brainless as to be handled easily by Psmith, and though Liz Peavey is more cunning, she is not vicious, and her attraction to Cootes dooms any enterprise to failure.

Themes and Meanings

Leave It to Psmith makes no profound statement about life, art, or morality. It is a book that takes itself seriously only as entertainment, rather like Oscar Wilde's *The Importance of Being Earnest: A Trivial Comedy for Serious People* (1895), which exists as a well-designed play glorifying the absolutely trivial. To the extent that *Leave It to Psmith* pokes fun at the stolid upper class, it is something of a satire on a life-style quickly fading out of existence.

Yet the book's central purpose is not so much satirical, since the tone and direction of the plot avoid anger and righteous mockery, both indispensable to the satiric technique. Rather, the novel is a finely wrought comedy of style and rhetorical punctiliousness, a sort of literary cassation or divertimento, elegantly designed, without the slightest vulgarity and with no jarring unpleasantness. A tone of amiable, old-fashioned chattiness, not mockery, adds to the pastoral, good-natured quality of the humor, as if the events and the characters existed in a world immune to violence and void of peril and indecency.

Like the best of musical comedies, of which P. G. Wodehouse wrote several, *Leave It to Psmith* makes the romantic real. The result is a sort of mythical comedy of bumbling lords, debonair aristocrats, and pretty heroines in a never-never land of estates, gardens, and moonlit terraces.

Critical Context

Leave It to Psmith is the perfect introduction to classic Wodehouse. As a transition book, it looks back to the humorous magazine sketches of the author's earlier days, and it anticipates in style and character the famous novels featuring Jeeves, the butler, polished, clever, equably good-humored.

There is something of the butler in Psmith, in fact, a man's man who could serve with dignity and loyalty but with unmistakable independence. Additionally, the heroine is the typical Wodehouse female—young, bright, and fond of mayhem—though in this novel she is still the more traditional romantic figure.

Finally, *Leave It to Psmith* is characterized by the well-planned, complex plot and the curious blend of classical English and slang that are the hallmarks of the Wodehouse style.

Sources for Further Study
Orwell, George. *Critical Essays*, 1946.
Usborne, Richard. *Wodehouse at Work*, 1961.
Wodehouse, P. G. *Author, Author!*, 1962.

Edward Fiorelli

LESS THAN ANGELS

Author: Barbara Pym (1913-1980)
Type of plot: Comedy of manners
Time of plot: The 1950's
Locale: London, its suburbs, and the English countryside
First published: 1955

> *Principal characters:*
> CATHERINE OLIPHANT, the protagonist, a writer of romantic
>   fiction and journalism
> TOM MALLOW, her lover, an anthropologist
> DEIRDRE SWAN, a young student of anthropology
> ALARIC LYDGATE, a retired colonial administrator with
>   anthropological interests

The Novel

   Less than Angels, like Barbara Pym's other novels, is preeminently successful at creating a small world peopled with characters whose prosaic lives become interesting, even fascinating, because of the perspective from which they are presented. Here, the heart of the microcosm is the Learned Society, a fashionably situated London center for the social and intellectual pursuits of a group of established and aspiring anthropologists. Pym takes her readers from this center to Catherine Oliphant's flat on the "shabby side" of Regent's Park; to bourgeois Barnes, the suburb where Deirdre Swan lives with her mother, brother, and aunt; to Mallow Park, the manor from which Tom Mallow has escaped into academia; and to the Gothic country house where Professor Mainwaring, upper-class in his origins, as Tom is, takes refuge from the inelegant academics.

   Less than Angels is much concerned with the interplay of these various social subsets. At the Learned Society itself, there are American and French students to be contrasted with the English ones and a wide and memorable gallery of anthropologists to be contrasted with their students and with one another. In the suburbs, Mabel Swan, her sister Rhoda Wellcome, and their circle, the embodiments of middle-class comfort and conventionality, are counterbalanced by the academic people Deirdre meets at the Learned Society, with the imaginative bohemian Catherine Oliphant, who comes to stay with them, and with Alaric Lydgate, the eccentric retired colonial administrator who has settled next door. Catherine, a waifish and whimsical woman given to irony and gifted with a keen sense of the absurd, holds values and cherishes customs very different from those of her lover Tom Mallow, an anthropological researcher who shares her flat when he is home from the field. Tom, in turn, a rebel against upper-class rural standards he has not entirely left behind, seems an odd fish when he returns to the Shropshire village his family dominates, a tribal enclave as "exotic," if only one sees it that way, as is the African culture he studies. This ruling-class world which Tom has abandoned is one to which Professor Mainwaring, at the end of his eminent career, has returned, and according to whose values he wryly judges his colleagues and students, in much the same way that Tom's Sloane Ranger sister and his former girlfriend Elaine see Catherine and Deirdre when the four women meet for tea and mutual sympathy.

The story line making possible these cultural and personal contrasts is partly anthropological and partly romantic. Shaping the progress of life among the social scientists is the evolving future of the Learned Society, directed by the formidable Esther Clovis and underwritten by money which Professor Mainwaring has charmed out of a rich American widow, Minnie Foresight. After World War II, Barbara Pym began editorial and administrative work at University College London's International African Institute, and the details of life there provided her with richly comic materials for the Learned Society. The students, particularly the saturnine Mark, his blander sidekick Digby, the voluptuous Vanessa, and the strident activist Primrose, are competing to impress their professors and to obtain fellowship money provided by Mrs. Foresight, a grant that Father Gemini, an anthropologist in holy orders, cannily manages to snatch out from under Professor Mainwaring's patrician nose. This maneuver is but one example of how the professional anthropologists also compete with one another: Gemini, the linguist Miss Lydgate, and others are always debating obscure points and deprecating their colleagues who are absent in the field. Somewhere between students and teachers is Tom Mallow, home from his researches and writing his thesis; quite apart from them is Alaric Lydgate, brother to the linguist Gertrude and himself the frustrated possessor of boxes full of anthropological notes as yet not "written up," a man whose failure to achieve has turned him into an embittered debunker of others' achievements.

The chief romantic developments of the novel are framed by Tom Mallow's arrival in England and his return to Africa. Tom's liaison with Catherine, though informal, follows the typical pattern for marriage in Pym's world: The woman seeks love, the man comfort. To quote the cynical Mark, Tom and Catherine's relationship is "reciprocal": "the woman giving the food and shelter and doing some typing for him and the man giving the priceless gift of himself." Yet Tom, striving to write and disconcerted that Catherine's perpetual levity does not spare the anthropological efforts he holds sacred, needs more than comfort. He requires uncritical admiration, and this Deirdre can provide. A nineteen-year-old child of the suburbs just beginning her anthropological studies, Deirdre finds Tom irresistible: He is alien and superior in so many ways—ten years older, initiated into the profession by dint of his fieldwork, and, whether behaving like the academic or the country gentleman, very far removed from the middle-class proprieties of her home.

The fiction writer, like the anthropologist, must have a capacity for detachment, and at first Catherine sees Tom's semiconcealed assignations with Deirdre as "copy," a story to observe and file away. Eventually, though, the betrayed woman in love must surface. Catherine sends Tom, who is by no means ready to end their relationship, out of her flat to less agreeable bachelor quarters with Digby and Mark.

Shortly thereafter, Tom leaves for Africa, where he will resume his tribal studies and die absurdly rather than heroically in a political upheaval. The women who have unselfishly loved him are drawn together by this bereavement—and attracted to other men. Catherine goes out to stay with the Swans and, while at their house, renews her acquaintance with their next-door neighbor Lydgate, a lonely man who proves to be much in need of her companionship and her whimsical irony, which finally frees him from the burden of his unpublished research, a dead mass of notes the two of them excitedly burn in a Guy Fawkes Day bonfire. Deirdre, missing and mourning Tom, is comforted by Digby, the kindly student suited to her as the more worldly Mark is to the debutante he met at a dance given by Tom's aunt. Thus, the novel ends, if not with the romantic convention of marriage, with what in the real world is the next best thing, as Pym sees it: a "suitable attachment."

The Characters

One crucial affinity unites the otherwise diversified characters of *Less than Angels*: All, in their different ways, are observers of life. Much of the novel's humor comes from the recognized or unacknowledged ironies of this fact. Catherine Oliphant, writer of pulp pieces for feminine readers, is the most self-conscious and most self-deprecating of the observers. She is a woman without roots. No parents, home, husband, or children constrain or support her. Even her occupation is one she can hardly take seriously, for her taste and judgment exceed her talent and market. Thus, Catherine is detached in a way that the other characters are not. Like the authorial eye of Barbara Pym, Catherine's gaze sees the absurdity in her own behavior—in the queer customs of the anthropologists who, eager to study exotic customs abroad, are blind to the odd intricacies of their own professional rituals, hierarchies, taboos, and totems, and in the suburban niceties of the Swan household and the ruling-class code of Tom's female relations.

Catherine may be the chief of *Less than Angels'* informal social scientists, but many of the other characters are also keen observers of human behavior. Digby, Mark, and Deirdre, recently embarked on life and their studies, scrutinize the professional and personal actions of their elders. These senior people in their turn and in varied ways examine the young. Mabel and Rhoda show the middle-class gentlewoman's typical interest in the neighbors' doings and the children's social lives. Professor Mainwaring takes an Olympian view of his students and junior colleagues. Miss Clovis, though no anthropologist herself, watches over her social scientists with the proprietary benevolence of an informed outsider, much as a social scientist might study and protect "her" chimps in the wild. Even Tom, caught up as he is in thesis-writing, looks at the native culture to which he has returned, and especially at the ancestral manor and village, with the objective bemusement of an outsider.

The positive side of such detachment—or alienation, as one might as easily call it—is its way of permitting interest in and amusement at ordinary matters that are purely routine to the engaged and connected, the insiders. The negative side is loneliness. Catherine, self-sufficient though she tends to be, suffers moments when she envies other people their webs of relationships, however entangling, and their solid backgrounds, however oppressive. Yet the chief sufferer from alienation is Alaric Lydgate. Invalided out of the Colonial Service, blocked in his efforts to create order and meaning from his anthropological jottings, Lydgate has no successful professional identity, and that bulwark is more necessary for the male ego than for the female one in the Pym world. Lydgate's only connection is his unmarried sister, and her linguistic eminence is a reproach to a man whose only publications are reviews. A grim look hides Lydgate's morbid inability to deal with the society in which he must live—a graphic example of his state being the African mask he wears in moments of private leisure. His sensitive, insistently concealed spirit needs an ally—and he finds one in Catherine, under whose influence he learns to cast off the repression of professional expectations and with whom, masked or not, he learns to enjoy life and himself.

Themes and Meanings

Less than Angels, like Pym's other novels, is far more than its "theme." The brilliantly observed detail, the telling irony or quiet absurdity detected in the particulars of ordinary life, the well-noted nuance of character: These are the gems to be gained from Pym's novels, and these are the reasons readers cherish her works.

The rewards and responsibilities of such observation are as much as anything else Pym's theme in *Less than Angels*, a book that without being autobiographical borrows extensively and fruitfully from the specific events, people, remarks, and ideas that made up her life. In her journal for June, 1953, the period when she was writing *Less than Angels*, Pym quotes the following passage from *Notes and Queries in Anthropology* (1874), an extract that appears in revised form in the novel: "It is important that not even the slightest expression of amusement or disapproval should ever be displayed at the description of ridiculous, impossible or disgusting features in custom, cult or legend." The tolerance pompously prescribed in this passage is a real virtue, and it is the special genius of both Pym and her protagonist Catherine

Oliphant. Neither judging nor mocking, the clear-sighted and good-humored observer of human absurdity can find occupation, and even a measure of happiness, in the least promising personal situations.

Critical Context

Less than Angels, the fourth of Pym's novels to be published, is one of the most cheerfully comic of the early group, works that are in general lighter and happier than those Pym wrote later in her life. Like the other early novels, *Less than Angels* succeeded with Pym's select readership and with the critics when it first appeared. Like the others, it suffered eclipse during the 1960's and early 1970's, a period when Pym, discouraged, turned away from fiction writing.

Championed by Philip Larkin and Lord David Cecil in the 1977 list of underrated twentieth century writers published by *The Times Literary Supplement*, Pym was reborn as a literary figure worth reading and as a writer of novels who, after years of silence, produced three new works and saw her older ones reissued and widely rediscovered.

Sources for Further Study

Benet, Diana. *Something to Love: Barbara Pym's Novels*, 1986.

Long, Robert Emmet. *Barbara Pym*, 1986.

Nardin, Jane. *Barbara Pym*, 1985.

Pym, Barbara. *A Very Private Life: An Autobiography in Diaries and Letters*, 1984.

Peter W. Graham

LIFE & TIMES OF MICHAEL K

Author: J. M. Coetzee (1940-   )
Type of plot: Allegorical realism
Time of plot: The 1980's
Locale: Cape Town, South Africa, and the adjacent countryside
First published: 1983

> *Principal characters:*
> MICHAEL K, the protagonist, who is slow-witted and
>   harelipped but a survivor
> ANNA K, his dropsical mother, who dies
> A DOCTOR, the medical officer at a "retraining" camp where
>   Michael is interned

The Novel

Narrated mostly from the third-person point of view of Michael K, the novel begins with a summary of his bleak, uneventful life and family history. Michael is the third surviving child (all by different fathers, long gone) of Anna K, a Cape Town scrubwoman and domestic servant, herself the product of itinerant farm workers, including an alcoholic father. Michael is born with a harelip, which would be easily corrected by an operation, but no one ever bothers. Slow-witted, teased by other children, Michael grows up lonely and unschooled until his mother enters him in Huis Norenius, a state school for "variously afflicted and unfortunate children." At the age of fifteen, he becomes a gardener with the Cape Town Department of Parks and Gardens. There, he quietly passes the years, visiting his mother on weekends but otherwise not associating with women.

When Michael is thirty-one, this routine changes. His mother, grown dropsical and old before her time, longs to return to the farming country of her childhood to die. She persuades Michael to quit his work (just before he is laid off) and to accompany her. Their decision becomes more pressing when a riot almost destroys the neighborhood in which Anna works, leaving her unemployed and ill. The rioting, widespread unemployment, and homeless people roaming the streets are all symptoms of the social disintegration occurring as a result of the South African war—apparently a civil war that the government is slowly losing.

Because of the war, Michael and Anna's simple trip to the countryside becomes an odyssey—and another occasion for displaying the social disintegration. One institution that has not disintegrated but only grown and become worse is the state bureaucracy. Michael buys train tickets, but the insensitive bureaucracy keeps delaying their travel permits. Finally, they decide to leave on foot without permits, with Michael hauling his sick mother and her suitcase in a makeshift cart. During several days on the road, they meet other refugees, convoys of soldiers, and thieves, but the elements prove most baneful for Anna. She makes it only as far as Stellenbosch, where she dies in a hospital (another strangely insensitive institution). Michael proceeds alone to Prince Albert, being robbed of his mother's savings by a soldier and impressed into a temporary work gang along the way. Eventually, he reaches the now-deserted Visagies farm, where his mother once lived, and scatters her ashes.

With nowhere else to go, Michael stays on at the farm, planting corn and pumpkins and killing birds to eat. His quiet life there is interrupted, however, by the appearance of the Visagies' grandson, an army deserter. The grandson sends Michael into Prince Albert for supplies; instead, Michael flees into the mountains. There, he stays until he almost starves. When he comes down out of the mountains, Michael is picked up by soldiers and interned in Jakkalsdrif, a "resettlement" camp for homeless people—actually a guarded concentration camp and source of cheap labor for the railroad and nearby farmers. Only the children are fed; the adults have to work for their food. After a while, Michael escapes and returns to the Visagies farm. The grandson is either hiding or has disappeared, so Michael settles down in a nearby camouflaged den and grows a garden of melons and pumpkins. Once, a guerrilla group passes by without seeing him, but he is eventually discovered—just before he almost starves again—by soldiers, who return him to a Cape Town "retraining" camp, where he is hospitalized for malnutrition.

The guerrillas and soldiers, and Michael's return to Cape Town, are signs that the South African perimeter is shrinking. News filtering into the retraining camp—of railroad lines cut off and shipments of retrainees delayed—confirm this impression. The retraining camp scenes, forming a brief part 2 of the novel, are narrated from the first-person point of view of the camp doctor, who worries along with the camp director about soon facing war-crime charges. Fascinated by Michael's simple mentality and survival skills, the doctor sees him as an embodiment of the winning side. This impression is confirmed by an even briefer part 3, which shows Michael, having escaped from the retraining camp, joining a friendly band of hardy survivors, having his first sexual experience, and hiding out in the ruins of Cape Town until the war is over.

The Characters

The strangest (and ultimately most brilliant) feature of this novel is that J. M. Coetzee does not identify the race of his protagonist, Michael K, or of any of his characters—seemingly a highly pertinent fact in a novel about contemporary South Africa. The setting and circumstances of the novel encourage the reader to assume that Michael and Anna K are black, the soldiers and farmers white, the guerrillas black, the doctor white, and so on. At the same time, by pointedly omitting any mention of race, Coetzee presents the reader with an allegory of South Africa without the factor of race. He thereby encourages identification with his protagonist and understanding of his characters' basic humanity—and inhumanity. Stripped of its racist justifications, South Africa is revealed for what it basically is—a cruel police state, a vast bureaucracy of prison keepers and prisoners. Yet Coetzee shows that even in South Africa there are a few kind people left.

Michael K's Kafkaesque name and character are both consistent with the police-state atmosphere. As a realistic character, Michael is rather dull, an example of minimal man, without personality or social attachments, almost without a will to live. It is only as an allegorical figure, a victim and survivor of the police state, that Michael is interesting. Michael resembles Albert Camus' alienated stranger, but there is a basic difference: Slow-witted Michael still retains his loyalties, feelings, and primal instincts. He is loyal to his mother, visiting her faithfully and transporting her ashes to spread on the farm; he is capable of feeling hurt or responding to kindness; and his healthy primal instinct is to garden and grow seeds. It should not be held against Michael that he is a minimal man: That is what enables him to survive, the ability (as the novel's ending states) to live on spoonfuls of water dredged up from a destroyed well.

The doctor is rather blatantly the author's mouthpiece, acting as a kind of one-person chorus who interprets (unnecessarily) the action and Michael. As a realistic figure, he is even duller than Michael. He is, however, an interesting example of the ineffectual liberal who goes along with the regime but has a pained conscience, particularly late in the losing game. The doctor's maudlin efforts to identify with Michael make him perhaps a white shadow. He is reminiscent of Coetzee's earlier protagonist in *Waiting for the Barbarians* (1980).

Themes and Meanings

Life & Times of Michael K is organized around a double exemplum, an exposition of the two sides of the title. Despite the narrative form, plot is less important here than the display of conditions during the life and times of Michael K. The reader is encouraged to identify with Michael, but his life is no more important to the scheme of the novel than the times in which he lives. The novel consists, in essence, of the dissolution of the state of South Africa and the causes thereof, although these topics are not set forth in full. The times of Michael K give a partial picture of the dissolution, and his life suggests some of the causes.

The state is dissolving because it is under heavy attack; no fighting, however, is ever shown. This omission centers attention on the inner causes of dissolution—the soulless but also fatalistic nature of the state. The state is rotten at the core, as though established on the wrong basis to begin with and now incapable of change. Like a vast machine, the system grinds on even as it falls apart.

Stated simply, the wrong basis of the state is that it uses people rather than serves them, and two of its typical victims are Anna and Michael. Yet, like William Faulkner, Coetzee has his people who endure, and Michael K represents them. Michael cannot kill himself even when he tries. Although he tries to sleep himself to death, the semihibernation merely enables him to survive on little food. Even the system works to preserve him, waking him, interning him, and bringing him back to health each time he is on the verge of expiring. His insignificance keeps other people from seriously hurting him. All he has to do is wait, and he is an expert at waiting.

Critical Context

Coetzee has an apocalyptic imagination that prophetically projects the siege mentality of white South Africans under apartheid. His imagination first reached its true form in *Waiting for the Barbarians*, about an unnamed "civilization" under counterattack by indigenous "barbarians" whom it has quelled or pushed back. The protagonist is a frontier magistrate who questions his government's brutal treatment of the barbarians, gets a taste of the treatment himself, and ends in an ecstasy of guilt and identification waiting for the advancing barbarians. *Life & Times of Michael K* looks at a similar scenario from the other side, though the setting is much more explicit. Through these two works, Coetzee has established himself as an important part of the literary conscience of white South Africa.

Coetzee's technique, which suggests some combination of William Faulkner and Franz Kafka, has sometimes been called heavy-handed. As *Life & Times of Michael K* shows, however, Coetzee is capable of shrewdly using his technique to open up universal dimensions of his themes. Through his technique, Coetzee indicates that the imperial mentality and racism are not merely South Africa's problems.

Sources for Further Study

Blake, Patricia. Review in *Time*. CXXIII (January 2, 1984), p. 84.

Brink, André. "Writing Against Big Brother: Notes on Apocalyptic Fiction in South Africa," in *World Literature Today*. LVIII (Spring, 1984), pp. 189-194.

Daymond, M. J., et al., eds. *Momentum: On Recent South African Writing*, 1984.

Gordimer, Nadine. Review in *The New York Review of Books*. XXXI (February 2, 1984), p. 3.

Ozick, Cynthia. Review in *The New York Times Book Review*. LXXXIX (December 11, 1983), p. 1.

Prescott, Peter S. Review in *Newsweek*. CIII (January 2, 1984), p. 63.

Roberts, Sheila. "South African Post-Revolutionary Fiction," in *Standpunte*. XXXV (June, 1982), pp. 44-51.

Harold Branam

LIFE BEFORE MAN

Author: Margaret Atwood (1939-   )
Type of plot: Domestic realism
Time of plot: From October 29, 1976, to August 18, 1978, with flashbacks to
  earlier times
Locale: Toronto
First published: 1979

Principal characters:

ELIZABETH SCHOENHOF, the protagonist, age thirty-nine
NATE SCHOENHOF, her thirty-four-year-old husband
LESJE (pronounced "Lashia"), Nate's new lover
CHRIS, Elizabeth's former lover, who killed himself
MARTHA, Nate's former lover
WILLIAM, the man with whom Lesje is living at the opening of
  the novel
JANET and NACY, Nate and Elizabeth's young daughters
AUNTIE MURIEL, the woman who reared Elizabeth

The Novel

Life Before Man is a nineteenth century novel of manners translated into
twentieth century life, a detailed description of sexual manners and mores
among several modern couples. Where the earlier form would have been
essentially satiric, however, Margaret Atwood's novel is savage and sad.

The novel is divided into five parts; each part contains from eleven to fourteen short chapters of three to four pages, headed by a character and a date
and centering on one of the three main characters. The opening chapter in
part 1, for example, is titled "Elizabeth, Friday, October 29, 1976," and the
last chapter of part 5 is "Elizabeth, Friday, August 18, 1978." The novel thus
covers nearly two years (including two Nate chapters that are flashbacks to
1975 and 1976). Often, two or three chapters cover the same day, or the same
events are being described from the perspectives of Elizabeth, Nate, and/or
Lesje.

Given this busy and clever structure, the plot of *Life Before Man* is really
quite thin. Chris, Elizabeth's former lover, has killed himself a week before
the novel opens, and Elizabeth is trying to deal with his death: "I don't know
how I should live," reads the first line; "I live like a peeled snail." Chris
worked in the same museum of natural history where Elizabeth (in special
projects) and Lesje (an assistant paleontologist) still work, and Elizabeth
ended the relationship some weeks before (apparently because Chris wanted
more than a love affair), but her lover's shotgun blast has struck her as well,
at least figuratively, and she is in shock.

At the same time that Elizabeth has been letting Chris go, Nate has been concluding his affair with Martha, a secretary at the legal firm where he once worked, and is casting about for a new lover. He settles on Lesje and, over the course of the novel, courts and seduces her, gets her to leave William, moves in with her part-time, and, after still more indecision, moves in completely and accepts Elizabeth's plans for divorce. At the end, Nate is again working as a lawyer (he has been a woodworker) in order to make enough money to support two families, and Lesje has secretly stopped taking birth-control pills. The novel concludes almost as it began, however, with Elizabeth, "not lonely, but single, alone," wishing she were somewhere else.

The focus of the novel is not on this action but, rather, on the thoughts and feelings of the characters. Readers discover important information almost tangentially, as one character or another reveals facts about himself or about others. The fictional approach is rather oblique, but the novel takes the reader directly into the emotional lives of these three characters, into the various ways these people grapple with the messy machinations of their relationships. Elizabeth and Nate have what in the 1970's was called an "open marriage," and, while they no longer have a sexual relationship themselves, they still confide in each other about their affairs with others—or they did. Nate found out about Chris only indirectly, and when Elizabeth tells him that the affair with Chris is over, Nate starts to let Martha go to balance their life. Yet they still entertain together, parent together, and talk in the bathroom. It is all very civil, but it is also silly and sad.

If little actually happens in the course of the novel, three or four lives have been permanently changed by its end. Chris is dead, and Elizabeth has not been able to replace him; her one attempt at impersonal sex ends with adolescent fumbling in a parked car. Nate, however, is no longer there. The combined pressure of Elizabeth and Lesje has forced him to move out of Elizabeth's house and to return to the world of suits and legal aid, but he has yet to learn that he is about to become a father again. Lesje, by the end of the novel, is nostalgic for the simplicity of her life with William, and her pregnancy seems—like so many of the acts in *Life Before Man*—to be built on desperation.

If the various maneuverings of the several characters seem vaguely humorous, the more pervasive feeling in the novel is one of sadness. People run around, shift beds, manipulate one another. Yet no one finds happiness; no one, for more than a moment, finds anything but its opposite.

The Characters

Life Before Man is a novel of character over plot, and the central character in these tangled sexual skeins is Elizabeth Schoenhof. As readers learn from scattered bits of information, Elizabeth had a poor and painful childhood. Their mother an alcoholic, Elizabeth and her sister were reared by miserly Auntie Muriel, and both Elizabeth's mother and her sister died while

Elizabeth was still young. She is full of unrelieved grief and anger, much of it aimed at Auntie Muriel, but when her aunt is dying in the hospital, Elizabeth can only comfort and forgive her. Most important, her childhood has made Elizabeth strong, but with a strong need for security and control. (A friend tells Lesje that Elizabeth is "Haute Wasp," and that "Chris was the chauffeur" in her life.) For Chris, Elizabeth represented "what he wanted, power over a certain part of the world: she knew how to behave. . . ." She now knows that she treated Chris "the way men treat women," and she is having trouble dealing with Chris's death and her part in it. *"We are the numb,"* she thinks; "All she wants is oblivion. Temporary but complete. . . ." She knows that she will win in her legal and psychological battles with Nate—after all, that is probably why she married him—"and she hopes it will make her feel better." She has always controlled events around her, even the schedule of her husband's affairs. "You wanted to *supervise* us," Martha accuses her. "Like some kind of playground organizer." She lets Chris go, she sleeps with William, she lets Nate go. The only thing she cannot do is to learn to live her life with any happiness.

All the other characters in the novel appear in orbit around Elizabeth, and they all pale by comparison. Lesje has little self; she cannot endure other people's anger or desperation; she is "an appeaser and she knows it . . . cautious, afraid of saying the wrong thing; of being accused." At a dinner party that Elizabeth organizes (before Lesje is Nate's lover), Lesje spills coffee in her nervousness and flees to the bathroom to cry. She is afraid of Elizabeth, who wanders the museum "like some bereft queen out of a Shakespearean play"; she is afraid to ask Nate when he is going to move in; when he finally does, life is "painful" and she dreads the weekends with his children. In the end, she believes that Elizabeth has fired Nate as a husband for incompetence and that she has been hired "for a job she hasn't applied for. Apparently she is going to be tried out as a kind of governess." Her life is lived in reaction to Elizabeth's.

The men in the novel are weak. Chris has killed himself: *"At least he had the guts,"* Nate imagines Elizabeth thinking about himself. A man with little backbone and less moral sense, Nate "dropped out," in 1970's lingo, from the world of lawyering because he wanted his life to be "honest"; he has recently been a woodworker, making toys at home, but he seems the child for whom the toys are made, especially in his relationship with Elizabeth. His mother is a political activist, but Nate's "idealism and his disillusionment now bore him about equally." He has a vision—of when his two young daughters are grown up—of being tortured by three generations of women: "Motherless, childless, he sits at the kitchen table, the solitary wanderer, under the cold red stars." His metaphor is running, but it is never clear where he is going. He ends the novel mooning about Martha; the past begins to look more attractive than the present.

Themes and Meanings

The meaning of *Life Before Man* is not altogether clear, for, while there are a number of themes, the final message seems blurred. On one level, the novel is about the effect the past has on the present. All three major characters are who they are because of their childhoods: Nate and Lesje are still acting as children, and Elizabeth is living her life in reaction against her past. (It is interesting to note that few people in the novel know Elizabeth's background.)

Yet what kind of present is it? The best answer lies in the paleontological imagery that Atwood weaves into her story. Lesje sits each day sorting drawers of dinosaur teeth—yet she is barely able to keep the contents of her own life in order. When readers first meet her, "Lesje is wandering in prehistory." Later, living with Nate, she longs for "that prehistoric era during which she lived with William." The men in particular are like neanderthals, a dying breed, in their approach to women. The novel is about "life before man," about the prehistory to truly civilized sexual relations. "The dinosaurs didn't survive and it wasn't the end of the world," Lesje thinks at the beginning of the novel. "Dinosaurs are dead," Nate tells her one day. "But I'm still alive." "Are you sure?" she asks.

Little is lasting in the late 1970's—not lives, not marriages, not selves. Atwood's novel may be a fictional illustration of the kind of sociological analysis that one finds in a book such as Christopher Lasch's *The Culture of Narcissism: American Life in an Age of Diminishing Expectations* (1979), published in the same year as *Life Before Man*: Lasch suggests that people have become so concerned with themselves that they are incapable of merging with others or of finding any real happiness. Certainly, people in the novel—and especially those living together—seem to be incredibly isolated from one another.

Yet the situation in which the characters find themselves is also mildly humorous, a softly acidic portrait of modern marriage, of "prehistoric" sexual mores in the last quarter of the twentieth century. Nate takes Lesje to a cheap hotel—and spends their entire time explaining his complicated arrangement with Elizabeth; Chris invited Nate to a chess game in his apartment (in one of Nate's two flashbacks)—but only so Nate could see the jewelry that Elizabeth left there. When William finds out about Lesje's affair with Nate, he rapes her, and the humor turns to sadness. The men are ineffectual, the women weak—or, if strong, like Elizabeth, then unable to find anyone to tolerate. It is, readers hope, "the extinction of the dinosaurs." As Atwood says in one of the two epigraphs she uses:

> These fossils give us our only chance to see the extinct animals in action and to study their behavior, though definite identification is only possible where the animal has dropped dead in its tracks and become fossilized on the spot.

Atwood gives the reader few clues about what world will follow. In the present age, there are only pain and suicide and desperation.

Critical Context

Margaret Atwood's is one of the strongest North American literary voices in the last half of the twentieth century. Her novels, popular in her native Canada, are immensely popular in the United States as well. Primarily a novelist, she is also a short-story writer, poet, essayist, and literary critic of real merit. The range of her work, in fact, is broader than that of most of her contemporaries.

In *Surfacing* (1972), Atwood probes the psyche of one young woman, as she plunged into the depths of her own prehistory. While that short novel explores some of the sexual relationships around the central character, the focus is much more psychological. It is also mythological, and if the major metaphor in *Life Before Man* is paleontology, in *Surfacing* it is the ancient pictographs that the woman finds in the lake where she searches, symbolically as well as literally, for her father. In *The Handmaid's Tale* (1986), Atwood describes sexual and social relationships in some distant future when most women are slaves.

Atwood's interests parallel those of many other contemporary writers. Nate, for example, may remind readers of the characters in the novels of Saul Bellow or Bernard Malamud—like Tommy Wilhelm in Bellow's *Seize the Day* (1956), Nate is ineffectual and indecisive. Atwood's central focus on women's control of their own lives is certainly the concern of a number of women writers, from Marilyn French (*The Women's Room*, 1977) through Gail Godwin (*A Mother and Two Daughters*, 1982) and Ellen Gilchrist (*The Annunciation*, 1983) to any number of writers who continue to depict the changing world of sexual relationships.

Given its critical context and the changing roles and relationships in the modern world, *Life Before Man* itself seems something of a throwback. Its characters are mired in behavior and attitudes that are peculiarly those of the 1960's and the early 1970's, and from which many men and women have been trying to free themselves. The novel is alternately amusing and sad: amusing because the characters are so dated, and sad because they cannot find any happiness in their prehistoric world. Yet the novel does not point to any future; with its dinosaur imagery, it confirms that this is a life in danger of extinction. As for what lies ahead, Atwood does not attempt to predict.

Sources for Further Study

Davidson, Arnold E., and Cathy N. Davidson, eds. *The Art of Margaret Atwood: Essays in Criticism*, 1981.

Grace, Sherrill E., and Lorraine Weir, eds. *Margaret Atwood: Language, Text, and System*, 1983.

Gray, Paul. Review in *Time*. CXV (February 25, 1980), p. 89.
Harris, Lis. Review in *The New Yorker*. LVI (July 7, 1980), p. 98.
Prescott, P. S. Review in *Newsweek*. XCV (February 18, 1980), p. 108.

David Peck

LIGHT

Author: Eva Figes (1932-   )
Type of plot: Extended prose poem
Time of plot: A summer day in 1900
Locale: Giverny, France
First published: 1983

Principal characters:
    CLAUDE MONET, the Impressionist painter
    ALICE RAINGO HOSCHÉDÉ, Claude's second wife
    LILY BUTLER, Alice's granddaughter, the daughter of Alice's
        deceased daughter, Suzanne
    JIMMY BUTLER, Alice's grandson, Suzanne's son, and Lily's
        brother
    MARTHE HOSCHÉDÉ, Alice's elder daughter
    GERMAINE HOSCHÉDÉ, Alice's younger daughter
    JEAN-PIERRE HOSCHÉDÉ, Alice's son
    MICHEL MONET, Monet's son by Camille, his first wife
    OCTAVE MIRBEAU, a writer and close friend of the Monets
    ANATOLE TOUSSAINT, a parish priest
    THEODORE BUTLER, an American painter and father of Jimmy
        and Lily

The Novel

The action of *Light* takes place on a single day, from first light to nightfall, in the summer of 1900, and focuses on an artist in thrall to his craft and the people around him who live in a world dominated by him. In pursuit of his art, Claude Monet has built his own version of Eden at Giverny. He has painstakingly designed the gardens and even rerouted a stream to modify the lily pond which he carefully monitors.

The novel falls into three parts. The first period, chapters 1 through 6, from dawn to midday, presents the stream of consciousness of each character as he or she begins and progresses through the morning.

Monet arises in the predawn hour to go to the lily pond, while his wife lies awake in another room, suffering in the darkness from insomnia and claustrophobia. Obsessed with capturing the ephemeral truth, or light, of this world—waterlilies, people, flowers—Monet believes that he can penetrate, can see through to the essence of life only at dawn, when everything—sky, water, land—is in perfect balance, unified into one composite whole. On this particular day, at the instant in which Monet perceives that the one perfect moment of light has arrived, he believes that he is at the very center of the world.

While Monet's obsession isolates him from those around him, his wife, Alice Raingo Hoschédé, is, in her own way, just as isolated. Daily, she makes a pilgrimage to the grave of her daughter, Suzanne, and in her continuing grief, Alice feels outside time, as if "the wall separating night and day, the visible and invisible had crumbled. . . ." She can almost feel her own mother's hand stroking her hair. Such sensory apparitions make Alice feel more connected to the dead than to the living. She can breathe in the peace of the graveyard, lifesaving breath that is unavailable to her in her own home.

Lily Butler, her grandchild, awakes to a world newly created for her pleasure. In contrast to her grandmother's protest against this fleeting visible world, Lily glories in the sensory delights of the moment. She is entranced by light, sound, smell, weight, weightlessness, color (as manifested in rose petals), an astonishing cobweb, pebbles, prisms of light. For Lily, pansies have human faces so real that she has an urge to talk to them.

Jimmy Butler, unlike his younger sister, whom he naturally tries to control, lives in a fantasy world full of Indians, pretending that what he sees is really something else.

Germaine Hoschédé, Alice's younger daughter, awakes to her memory of the previous day. She will spend this day alternately elated and fearful, worrying whether Monet will permit her to accept Pierre Sisley's proposal of marriage. At lunch, she is aware that living in her stepfather's house is like being a powerless passenger on someone else's ship—unable to come or go without permission.

Having been trained by her mother to care for the younger children, Marthe Hoschédé, Alice's elder daughter, has full charge of Jimmy and Lily. Central to Marthe's character is her awareness that she has never been first with anyone. The two children she is rearing are not her own, and she fears that they will be taken away from her. Marthe's life has consisted of answering other people's needs, and she recognizes that should there be no needs to meet, she will not exist. To herself, Marthe must confess that she knows neither who she is nor what she might want. She cannot imagine doing anything by choice because she has never had the freedom to choose.

Michel Monet, Claude's son, cannot, will not, leave Giverny. His father holds him in thrall. To Michel, only his father's work is worth emulating, yet he cannot do it because he has neither Monet's vision nor his talent. Michel seems destined to a lifetime of feeling inadequate in comparison to his father.

The second period of *Light*, chapter 7, presents the family at lunch with their guest, writer Octave Mirbeau, and the late arrival of Anatole Toussaint, the local cleric. Lunch is the only time during the day when these characters indulge in conversation, and the most articulate of the group is the outsider, Mirbeau. Like Michel, he yearns for the artistic skill and vision of the artist, and he shares Monet's passion for botany, as does Toussaint.

The four chapters after lunch, which constitute the third period, cover the remainder of the afternoon, including dinner and the descent of darkness. Late in the afternoon, Theodore Butler, father of Jimmy and Lily, arrives and stuns Marthe by proposing marriage. Marthe accepts; the children will be hers. Theodore, however, proposes this marriage only because the union will enable him to remain in Monet's household and under the great artist's influence.

In the twilight, Monet and Alice walk together in the garden. Alice knows that despite all of her efforts to know her husband, a part of him remains un-attached either to her or to the home she has made for him. As they walk, Monet becomes aware that a point of starlight has just become visible, and once more, the mystery revealed to him in the dawn has eluded him. He must wait for a new day.

The Characters

Although the details of Monet's life are historically accurate, in *Light*, Eva Figes is dealing with the obsession of an artist, not with history or biography. The overriding desire of Monet is to show in his paintings "how light and those things it illumines are both transubstantial, both tenuous." His goal is to capture the shifting and disappearing substance of this world—both natu-ral and human substance—to see through the luminous cloud which envel-ops each person and part of nature. Only in the early morning hours can he seize, he believes, the actual tone and color of earthly life. Ultimately, Monet knows, he will die before he can complete his quest, but with each new day, he is reinvigorated with the challenge of trying.

Monet, in godlike fashion, has designed his estate at Giverny, with the lush gardens and the lily pond, as his own natural world. Yet the isolation of the characters in *Light* is inescapable. Alice talks to voices in her head at night; she and Monet have no mutually sustaining words or conversation. When there is something to see, Monet cannot hear. Marthe has felt closer to some of the servants than she has ever felt to members of her own family. Jean-Pierre can no longer get Michel to say anything.

The other members of the household recognize themselves in relation to the artist but not to one another. In their isolated inner struggles, Monet believes that the spiritual is omnipresent, while Alice yearns for knowledge of another realm where nothing is lost but where past and present, living and dead, somehow coexist.

Only the youngest person, the child Lily, perceives the difference between her grandparents: Her step-grandfather is all on the surface, to be seen, heard, smelled, touched. Her grandmother is just the opposite, someone whose essence is all on the inside, a secret indicated but not revealed by the expression on her face or by the odors coming from her clothes. While Lily's perceptions are credible and provide insight, her thoughts are presented in language far more sophisticated than one might expect of a six- or seven-year-old child. She functions neither as a child nor as an adult, yet within this novel, Lily is the one character most able to see things as they truly are.

Lily, like Monet, finds that she can perceive the essence of reality. In the first instance, she finally, after many failures, blows a perfect soap bubble: "The few seconds during which it held were enough for Lily. Memory holds the shining bubble, bright with the newborn glory of the world." With the revelation of what she has seen, Lily will always carry that moment in her memory, but whether she will be able to share her new awareness is another question.

In the second instance, Lily, concentrating on her new red balloon, sees the figure of her dead mother, her face lost in shadow behind the balloon. In Lily's vision, her mother looks like the angel Lily has been told she is. In each instance, the trigger for her epiphany is neither art nor nature.

Themes and Meanings

At least three themes inextricably manifest themselves in the course of this novel. Figes' focus is constantly on the artist and the question of the value of art itself: Can it achieve its goal? At what price in human terms? What worth can it claim for itself alone?

Monet's obsession with transforming life into paint on canvas is inevitably doomed to failure, for art is always once removed from life, however one defines either art or life. While Monet may look at Lily on the veranda and see Mimi, his daughter who died long ago, or look at Germaine and see his wife as a young woman, he has not really known these people. He has been too busy with his own work.

While Alice is depressed because she does not fully know her husband, however hard she has tried, Monet makes no comparable attempt to enter Alice's world. He recognizes that her life has been difficult: He has often been absent from home; they have had financial troubles; she has had to tend gravely ill children; she has been forced to manage on her own after her first husband left her; she has what Monet believes is an unfounded jealousy of other women. Nevertheless, he chooses to believe that her unhappiness is sadly misguided, that she is unhappy simply because she does not see things as they are. Yet the substance of Monet's carefully created world at Giverny—without the light and without the color—is perceived as incredibly limited and devoid of humanity. Monet serves his vision, magician that he is, while every human being around him is in servitude to his attempt to assume power over all that is constantly changing.

While the star that Monet sees in the predawn hour cannot possibly be the same star that he sees at the end of the day, the evening star reminds him of his quest. Hence, the final chapter, which is only one paragraph, is strikingly poignant. The moment is at night, and there are many stars shining on a deserted Giverny, after all the inhabitants of that summer day in 1900 have died or left. The moment serves as a reminder of both the timelessness and the elusiveness of each part of creation. Light—which is so apparent throughout the book that it becomes almost a character in itself—remains, even though the gardens are now overgrown and the pond is untended. The stars, which once signaled a perfect day to the artist, shine now without him and light other worlds.

As Toussaint implied in his rapture at seeing the actual flowers which he had previously seen only in books, no artist—no matter how skillful—can adequately represent the natural world through another medium. Whatever the efforts of man to control or to seize the natural world, nature forever eludes even the most gifted. The most painful irony, however, is that transcendent beauty, which the artist strives to capture and evoke, can be perceived without art. While Monet's desire is to make people see, they may well see without him, as Lily does, by means of a mere soap bubble or a red balloon. Figes suggests that while art may provide aesthetic pleasure and vision, and may transcend the temporal world, it is not the only means of transcendence or insight. When a person clings to the notion that art is somehow greater than life, he has lost an essential part of his own humanity.

Critical Context

Light, Figes' eighth novel, offers yet another departure from her earlier works, although the structure of her second novel is similar in that it is limited to a single day. Each of Figes' novels is an experiment, using a new mode to impose order on chaos, a mode different from any she has tried earlier. While Figes acknowledges the influence of T. S. Eliot, Franz Kafka, Samuel Beckett, and Virginia Woolf, her fiction is different and distinctly her own.

While one may think of Woolf's use of the stream-of-consciousness technique when reading *Light*, Figes uses the technique to quite different ends. The luncheon in *Light* differs radically from dinner with the Ramsays in *To the Lighthouse* (1927). There is no larger whole composed by the interrelated thoughts of different minds in *Light*. Mr. Ramsay needs reassurance from his wife and responses from everyone around him; Monet requires only submission. Lily's apprehension of the reality beyond appearance is hers alone. Not only does she fail to communicate her visions, but also it does not occur to anyone that her perceptions could be of interest.

When Figes became known for *Patriarchal Attitudes: Women in Society* in 1970, she had already won the Guardian Fiction Prize in 1967 for her second novel, *Winter Journey* (1967). Alienation, identity, lack of identity, the nature of reality versus the nature of art are Figes' themes. Her innovative power in creating new modes to express various facets of these subjects is beyond question. The aesthetic precision of *Light*, and the rich density of its imagery, provide a provocative view of art as it anatomizes the artist.

Sources for Further Study

Bannon, Barbara A. Review in *Publishers Weekly*. CCXXIV (August 26, 1983), p. 367.

De Feo, Ronald. Review in *The Nation*. CCXXXVII (January 7, 1984), p. 38.

Deveson, Richard. Review in *New Statesman*. CVI (September 2, 1983), p. 24.

Oates, Joyce Carol. Review in *The New York Times Book Review*. LXXXIX (October 7, 1984), p. 38.

Carol Bishop

THE LITTLE GIRLS

Author: Elizabeth Bowen (1899-1973)
Type of plot: Psychological realism
Time of plot: The late 1950's or early 1960's and 1914
Locale: Somerset and London
First published: 1964

> *Principal characters:*
> DINAH "DICEY" PIGGOTT DELACROIX, the protagonist, a well-to-do widow
> SHEILA "SHEIKIE" BEAKER ARTWORTH, a chic matron and schoolgirl friend of Dinah
> CLARE "MUMBO" BURKIN-JONES, a businesswoman and a schoolgirl friend of Dinah and Sheila

The Novel

It is appropriate that a novel whose theme involves the question of dealing with the past should take place in two time frames. The first and third sections of *The Little Girls* are set in the period after World War II, when Dinah "Dicey" Piggott Delacroix decides to recapture her childhood; the second section is set in the time just before World War I, when she and her friends were living that childhood.

Dinah's preoccupation with the past is evident in the first scene of the novel. Ostensibly from whim or boredom, actually from a deep need, Dinah has been collecting treasured objects from her friends with the intention of burying a sort of time capsule for the benefit of future scholars. Interestingly, she wishes to preserve the varied objects which seem essential to her friends. While she is discussing her project, Dinah suddenly recalls another cache of treasures, the coffer which she and two school friends buried when they were eleven, just before World War I. Despite the discouraging words of her suitor and neighbor, Major Frank Wilkins, who points out that one cannot go back in time, Dinah resolves to track down the school friends who shared the earlier burial and with them to find that long-forgotten box.

Like Frank, Sheila Beaker Artworth and Clare Burkin-Jones believe that a venture into the past may be dangerous. With typical zest, Dinah has advertised widely for her schoolmates, and it is primarily to stop the embarrassment caused by this publicity that Sheila and Clare agree to meet Dinah. As Clare points out, she and Sheila feel like the little pigs whose houses may be blown down at any moment. Clearly, their apprehensions are caused by more than a fear of publicity. For most adults, the present is a fragile construct whose stability depends partly on selective forgetting of the past. Fearlessly, however, Dinah persists, and the women dig up the buried coffer, which proves to be empty. Although they do reveal to one another what they had placed in the box, the schoolmates feel increasing tensions and even animosity toward one another. At the end of the novel, Dinah falls into a psychological collapse, perhaps the immediate result of a physical attack by Clare, perhaps the culmination of the schoolmates' exploration of their common past. The moment of danger passes, however, and it is clear that Dinah will recover to commit herself to the present.

The central section of the novel is the author's own account of the three girls' lives during the months before England's entry into World War I. It presents an interesting contrast to the fragmentary memories of the three adult women, as they are related in the other sections of the book, because it reveals the young girls as they were, not as they recall themselves and one another. Yet the story which Elizabeth Bowen tells is one which none of the three schoolmates will ever know, simply because it is an objective account.

Although Dinah, Sheila, and Clare will always have different perspectives on their common past, by the end of the novel Dinah has realized that reentering the past is more dangerous than she had supposed, and all the women have changed as a result of the experience.

The Characters

Describing herself, young Dicey says "I like looking for things . . . or hiding things, wondering who'll find them. Or doing anything I can do, like getting on people's nerves." Called "Circe" by Clare, young Dicey or older Dinah has the urge and the capability to draw her friends into her projects, even against their better judgment. It is not surprising that Dinah conceals a gun in the coffer which the girls bury; the symbol of action and danger, it would have appealed to Dinah, an emotional daredevil. Young or old, Dinah possesses great zest for life and captivating innocence. Therefore, it is to be expected that, though a grandmother, Dinah still has the energy to organize her suitor, her houseboy, and her friends, in what she never will admit are slightly mad projects. At the end of the novel, one assumes that the wiser Dinah, waking, will still have her appealing innocence.

The schoolmates, Sheila and Clare, are similarly symbolized by what they chose to bury in the coffer. Sheila, the talented dancer who has now become a beautifully dressed, perpetually dieting wife, buries her physical flaw, the sixth toe with which she was born. Always concerned with appearances, Sheila is nervous about the publicity which may arise from the newspaper advertisements, hesitant about seeing her friends again, frightened about opening the coffer. She has suppressed the guilt she feels for abandoning her dying lover. At the end of the novel, however, she throws herself into nursing Dinah, and there is the hope that by accepting both life and herself, flaws and all, Sheila has become capable of truly living. Clare, too, must learn to participate in life. Never able to commit herself to an adult relationship,

Clare, the efficient businesswoman, is still young "Mumbo," who could not permit herself to love Dinah. When Clare buries a copy of Percy Bysshe Shelley's poetry in the coffer, she is deliberately refusing passion, feeling, and life itself. When she refuses to stay with the adult Dinah, she is once again denying her own emotions. It is significant that at the end of the book Clare has returned to say a proper farewell to Dinah; though she will not let herself be enchanted by Circe, she will admit her feelings.

Themes and Meanings

Explaining Roman artifacts to young Dicey, an older woman says, "as time goes on things bury themselves." In this comment the two major themes of the novel are contained. Dinah, the adult Dicey, is just as fascinated with burying things as she had been as a child. Her elaborate project for burying the obsessions of her friends, described at the beginning of the novel, is a repetition of the coffer burial undertaken when she was eleven. Yet although Dinah buries things, she always looks toward the time when they will be dug up. "It's for someone or other to come upon in the *far future*" she explains, when the personalities of the buriers will long have been lost and forgotten. The impulse to dig up her own childhood coffer, rather than to leave it for future archaeologists, seems to break her own rules, but then, Dinah is not noticeably rational.

When Dinah and her friends come together to unbury the coffer, they then are violating the time scheme which kept them safe. After their deaths, after the end of their civilization, it would hardly have mattered what archaeologists thought about their find. The point of the story is that in her unreason, Dinah is correct. The lives of the friends can never be complete until they unbury their old obsessions, deal with them, and move on. Thus the unburial, painful though it may be, permits a kind of resurrection for all the women. The theme of time and the theme of burial-resurrection are united at the climax of the novel.

Critical Context

Although some critics of *The Little Girls* saw the work as a comedy which failed because it occasionally became serious, while other reviewers believed that in this work Elizabeth Bowen evidenced a loss of the capacity for serious or even tragic dimension which she demonstrated in *The Death of the Heart* (1938), later opinion has placed this novel with her others as a psychological masterpiece, as well as a book with something to say.

Like her other novels, *The Little Girls* is concerned with the issue of life as art. In many ways a religious writer, Bowen realized that man is limited by circumstances and by his own nature, yet he is able, within limits, to design his own life as a work of art. In order to do that, he must find his real identity, like the schoolmates in this novel, who must recover that which they buried, yet he cannot then live in the past but must decisively move into the future.

Bowen is also interested in the theme which is central to so much literature, the loss of innocence and the entrance into adulthood, a process which may seem a fortunate fall and yet which necessarily involves the discovery of evil. Finally, in *The Little Girls*, as in her other novels, Bowen emphasizes the quality without which life cannot truly be lived: the capacity for love. Looking at her friend, Clare understands that her life has been as empty as the box the girls dug up. "Never have I comforted you. Forgive me," she says, and at that point, Dinah awakes, and the spell of evil is broken. Above all, Bowen emphasizes the redeeming power of love.

Sources for Further Study

Adams, Phoebe. Review in *The Atlantic Monthly*. CCXIII (March, 1964), p. 187.

Austin, Allan E. *Elizabeth Bowen*, 1971.

Baro, Gene. Review in *The New York Times Book Review*. L (January 12, 1964), p. 4.

Blodgett, Harriet. *Patterns of Reality: Elizabeth Bowen's Novels*, 1975.

Hall, James. *The Lunatic Giant in the Drawing Room: The British and American Novel Since 1930*, 1968.

Kenney, Edwin J., Jr. *Elizabeth Bowen*, 1975.

Time. Review. LXXXIII (January 24, 1964), p. 70.

Rosemary M. Canfield-Reisman

THE LITTLE HOTEL

Author: Christina Stead (1902-1983)
Type of plot: Social criticism
Time of plot: The postwar 1940's
Locale: Switzerland
First published: 1973

> *Principal characters:*
> MADAME BONNARD, the narrator, the proprietor of the Hotel Swiss-Touring
> ROGER, her husband
> LILIA TROLLOPE, the protagonist, divorced and living with her "cousin"
> ROBERT WILKINS, her "cousin"/lover, a speculator in international currency
> MISS CHILLARD, a miserly Englishwoman, who is dying at the hotel
> THE MAYOR OF B., a Belgian politician undergoing psychiatric treatment in Switzerland
> MRS. POWELL, a "patriotic" American with racist views
> MRS. BLAISE, a wealthy drug addict whose money came from the Nazis
> DR. BLAISE, her selfish husband, who visits his wife and supplies her with drugs
> PRINCESS BILI, Lilia's friend, a wealthy woman in pursuit of her youth

The Novel

The Little Hotel is narrated by Madame Bonnard, who recounts the events that occur at her fourth-class hotel in a Swiss resort. While the eccentric activities of the Mayor of B. are her initial focus, the novel actually concerns the relationship between Lilia Trollope and Robert Wilkins, who maintain an unconvincing pose as "cousins." Although both are unattached, Robert refuses to marry Lilia not only because he promised his mother that he would never marry, so his inheritance is at risk, but also because he simply enjoys the existing situation. Lilia, whose funds Robert insists she bring out of England, begins to suspect that Robert is primarily after her money, and she regrets having put so much of it in his name, especially since he has apparently lost interest in her. (While they dine at the hotel, he reads his newspapers and simply ignores her.)

Faced with a static and futile relationship, Lilia turns to the other people at the hotel—people, she points out, with whom she would never have chosen to associate. Mrs. Powell, a rabidly racist American who believes Lilia to be "Asiatic"—Lilia's mother was in fact Dutch-Javanese—deliberately snubs her and determines to drive her from the hotel. Miss Chillard, a former hotel guest who has since returned to the hotel, has money but pleads poverty, thereby enabling her to exploit the generous Bonnards and to appeal to Lilia's compassion. Mrs. Blaise, who initially serves as Lilia's confidante and friend, turns against her and taunts her by discussing "gigolos," an indirect allusion to Robert that violates a confidence. Only Princess Bili seems willing to help her persuade Robert to "do the right thing."

The climax of the plot occurs at the dinner Robert and Lilia host to commemorate their first meeting twenty-seven years before. Their guests are the Blaises, the Pallintosts (they own the car that Robert wants Lilia to buy for his birthday), and Princess Bili, accompanied by her lapdog Angel, who "sings" "D'ye ken John Peel?" In the course of the party, the company becomes intoxicated, Dr. Blaise assumes command and attacks that institution of marriage, Princess Bili discusses her impending "face-lift" and marriage to a younger man, and Lilia concludes, justifiably, that it is "a very cruel age." As Lilia and Robert dance, they become the victims of that cruelty as the Blaises reward their hospitality by calling Robert a "little rubber salesman" and Lilia his "half-caste mistress."

After the dinner party, Lilia's plight becomes more desperate when Princess Bili unsuccessfully approaches Robert on her behalf. Convinced that Robert will never marry her—and worried that she would be "worse off" if he does—she resolves to leave him. After securing her funds from Robert, she tells him that she is leaving, but he does not believe her and further insults her by keeping her from meeting his sister Flo, who is visiting him. Mrs. Blaise subsequently insults Lilia, but the next day she inexplicably apologizes and asks her to visit in Basel, where, she says, she will be in danger from her husband. When Princess Bili abruptly departs, leaving Angel behind, Lilia is deserted. Giving her money to the miserly, opportunistic Miss Chillard, Lilia leaves Robert, and after visiting the Blaises, she returns to England—never, at least to Madame Bonnard's knowledge, to see Robert again. Mrs. Blaise dies of a suspicious heart attack and unaccountably leaves her estate to the housekeeper, Ermyntrude, if she marries Dr. Blaise. Madame Bonnard adds knowingly, "No doubt a wedding took place."

The Characters

The guests at the Hotel Swiss-Touring are individuals, refugees from domestic strife who nevertheless need relationships, regardless of how destructive those ties may be. Even though she has willingly left her family to follow Robert to Europe, Lilia misses them and feels their disapproval of her relationship; she salvages her "honor" and returns to England only after she leaves Robert. Initially, Robert seems less in need of the relationship, partly because of his ties to his mother and sisters, whose primacy is reaffirmed when he chooses his sister over Lilia. He cannot, however, accept her continued absence and declares, "I do not know what I am going to do without Mrs. Trollope." Lilia must choose between Robert and "some kind of freedom"; Robert discovers that his "freedom" from commitment has its cost in self-deception and aimless wandering.

Although they are married, the Blaises are not a "family," for they are bound only by their children and, more important, by Mrs. Blaise's money. Mrs. Blaise lives at the Hotel Swiss-Touring and vows never to return to her home in Basel, where her husband lives, but she depends on her husband for drugs and for the bitterness and cynicism she needs to augment her own hostility toward the outside world. So insulated is she that she is literally wrapped up in clothes to protect herself against infection from others and from advances from her husband. Yet she is addicted to their relationship, for her husband can help her transform her insecurity and jealousy of Lilia into self-righteous snobbery. Although he does help his wife in a perverse, destructive way (he also contributes to her addiction by giving her drugs), Dr. Blaise sees marriage as a curse which sanctions slavery, and he can free himself only by killing his wife. Mrs. Blaise is so cynical about family and marriage that she prefers homosexuality to marriage for her son and considers her daughter a "clown" for marrying a professor, a "capon." Her comments surely reflect on her own failed marriage and her family, which consists of isolated individuals.

The other guests at the hotel are equally isolated in the hotel, which serves as an inadequate "home" for the homeless. Although the characters live in spatial proximity, they do not nurture one another but instead feed off one another's insecurities. Mrs. Powell, an American insecure about her position in Europe, salves her ego by becoming exclusive, attempting to ostracize Lilia because she is "Asiatic." The "Admiral," an elderly woman despised by the servants, rages and bullies because she is alone and in poor health. Superficially, Miss Chillard's case is like the Admiral's, but Miss Chillard is in fact a manipulative invalid who preys on the compassion and wealth of those people who, like Lilia, truly want to be "home." Miss Chillard's isolation is not merely geographical but also emotional; when she first came to the hotel, she was with a "poor humble companion" who proved to be, to the surprise of other guests, her own mother. She is not even close to Lilia, her benefactor and "savior," whom she calls "Mrs. Collop" and "Mrs. Scallop." The Mayor of B., on the other hand, does reach out to the other people, particularly to the Bonnards: He gives unofficial title to his Zurich property to Olivier, their son, and seems determined to establish a hotel family to replace the Belgian family he left. Ironically, it is when he leaves his hotel home for another hotel that he is institutionalized, and his family acts in typical Stead fashion when they decide to take him to an asylum in Belgium.

Though most of the novel concerns the hotel guests, Stead devotes much attention to the Bonnards and the hotel staff, who do not escape the malaise that afflicts the guests. Madame Bonnard may be "Selda" (Lilia's eldest daughter's name) to the desperate Lilia, but Madame Bonnard states, "I am always looking for a friend," and adds that when you "grow up and marry, there is a shadow over everything; you can never really be happy again." Julie, her "best friend," undermines her confidence and her marriage, which is also threatened by her husband's drinking. Madame Bonnard must also deal with Charlie, the child molester/porter, who is separated from his wife, and with Clara, a malicious servant intent on destroying the marriage of Gennaro and Emma, two servants in the hotel. In the world of *The Little Hotel*, characters may reach out, but few connections are made.

Themes and Meanings

When Lilia reminds Robert that they "are one flesh," he quickly responds, "And one fortune," thereby suggesting the extent to which emotional and financial needs are confused in this novel. Money, not love, motivates the men who exploit the weaknesses and addictions of their women. Rather than converse with Lilia during their meals, Robert reads the financial pages of newspapers; when he realizes that Lilia will not return to him, he refers not to his emotional state, but to the "calculations" that she has upset. For him, the marriage is a merger that has not been consummated. Robert, who admits that he is selfish, has two ambitions, both of which involve the accumulation of money; he is so manipulative and greedy that he can quite accurately interpret Miss Chillard's behavior. The relationship between the Blaises is more complex because both, even to Lilia's somewhat naïve eye, are greedy. In fact, one of the sources of the novel is a short story named "A Household," which Stead has also titled "Greedy." The Leglands, a French couple in the short story, seem to have been the forerunners of the Blaises, but in the novel, it is the greedy husband, not the callous wife, who is the real villain. Dr. Blaise will be a "slave" for money only until he can use his wife's drug addiction to force her to return to Basel, where he will probably kill her and forge her will.

Money and materialism permeate this novel, which involves the lives of people who speculate in international currency, attempt to transfer funds out of England and America (the Nazi money is in the United States), and allow money to rule their lives. Robert charts his life according to the financial charts he devises daily, and he lets international currency rates determine where he and Lilia will live. Among the hotel staff the order that Madame Bonnard requires is threatened by theft, first of the one-hundred-franc note and then of the *forbici* (the scissors). Money also jeopardizes the Bonnards because Madame Bonnard apparently believes that her Zig-Zag Club debt may cost her Roger's love.

Despite her emphasis on the debilitating effect of money, Christina Stead does present her readers with a character who can accept the reality of her situation and choose freedom, such as it is. Lilia realizes that she "is on the shelf," that her alternatives involve being second to Robert's family or living alone with "some kind of freedom" at the age of fifty. In order to gain that freedom, Lilia must regain control of her business affairs and give the money Robert had to Miss Chillard. It is her "charity" that secures her individuality and independence, and at the end of the novel it is she, not Robert, who has found peace.

Critical Context

Although published in 1973, *The Little Hotel* is actually the result of Christina Stead's combining earlier material: "The Hotel-Keeper's Story" (1952), which concerns Madame Bonnard and the Mayor of B., and "The Woman in the Bed" (1968), which explains Lilia's break with Robert and her decision to give money to Miss Chillard. Because of the way the stories are yoked together, almost without alterations, the novel lacks unity and consistency in point of view. It is, however, very much of a piece with Stead's other works in terms of its view of families, its portraits of international wanderers, its treatment of money and the exploitation of women, and its concern for the isolated individual. Although in length it is little more than a novella, *The Little Hotel* closely resembles the much longer *House of All Nations* (1938) in its condemnation of a society motivated by greed. Stead indicates the exploitive capitalistic society with its decadent parasites who are priviliged guests in the hotel that serves as a microcosm of the world. It is this world setting and worldview that make her, unlike Patrick White, another great Australian novelist, almost "un-Australian"; although "feminist" in her portrait of Lilia, her opposition to exploitation extends beyond feminism to encompass all oppression.

Sources for Further Study

Bader, Rudolf. "Christina Stead and the *Bildungsroman*," in *World Literature Written in English*. XXIII, no. 1 (1984), pp. 31-39.

Geering, R. G. "What Is Normal? Two Recent Novels by Christina Stead," in *Southerly*. XXXVIII, no. 4 (1978), pp. 462-473.

Lidoff, Joan. *Christina Stead*, 1982.

Thomas L. Erskine

LIVES OF GIRLS AND WOMEN

Author: Alice Munro (1931-   )
Type of plot: Künstlerroman
Time of plot: The late 1950's and early 1960's
Locale: Jubilee, a small town in southwestern Ontario
First published: 1971

Principal characters:
DEL JORDAN, the protagonist and narrator, who comes of age
during the novel
ADA JORDAN, Del's mother
UNCLE BENNY, an eccentric neighbor
MARION SHERRIFF, an acquaintance of Del who commits
suicide
NAOMI, Del's high school friend and confidante

The Novel

Lives of Girls and Women, Alice Munro's only novel, is more a collection of connected short stories narrated by its protagonist, Del Jordan, than a fully conceived and unified narrative. Each of the novel's eight chapters is a basically self-contained tale that reveals one more significant set of facts about Del's evolving identity—specifically her coming of age in the small Ontario town of Jubilee.

The novel begins with "The Flats Road," an important retrospective of an episode in Del's childhood. In this chapter, she is first awakened to the romance of everydayness, when the world outside her parents' peaceable home clashes with the kingdom of the chaotic and eccentric exemplified by misfits such as Uncle Benny, whose world was "a troubling distorted reflection, the same but never at all the same." These early experiences train Del to focus on the details of life and not merely the broad shadows that individual lives sometimes cast.

Thus, what one critic calls "the symbolic geography of the book" is set, and Del emerges as a "chameleon" adventurer, surveying the land before her while she sharpens her senses for a future career as a writer. The subsequent episodes in *Lives of Girls and Women* survey the various models of womanhood that Del meets in Jubilee. There is, at one extreme, Naomi, Del's closest friend, who fulfills the "expected" role of ingenue, wife, and then mother, who "settles down," resigning herself to the familiar roles common to other Jubilee women. At the other extreme is Marion Sherriff, a wholly disenfranchised young woman, an unfortunate daughter in an unfortunate family, who takes her own life rather than live with the shame of motherhood out of wedlock.

Del, however, seeks a life of the mind, wanting men to love her, but not at the expense of her unique calling and gifts as a woman. Ada, Del's mother, thus surfaces as the most dominant and significant woman in her life. Though considered by Del's aunts and local townspeople as a "wildwoman" because of her erratic, sometimes unseemly behavior, she offers Del often profound advice and serves as the most credible example of womanhood to Del in the novel. "There is a change coming," she prophesies and warns Del, "in the lives of girls and women. . . . All women have had up till now has been their connection with men. . . . But I hope you will—use your brains."

At the end of "Baptizing," the next to last episode in the novel, the reader discovers that Del has listened well and is prepared for the journey toward maturity; in a tone of sober abandonment, she declares that "now at last without fantasies or self-deception, cut off from the mistakes and confusion of the past . . . like girls in movies leaving home, convents, lovers, I supposed I would get started on my real life."

In the final chapter, labeled "Epilogue," Del's "real life" becomes a story-within-a-story, the novel turning in on itself as Del steps out of her own narrative to describe how she went about crafting a novel about life in the small southwestern Ontario town in which she came to womanhood.

The Characters

Clearly, there is a double edge to Munro's stories. The novel not only is about Del but also is the record of her own growth as a writer. As narrator and protagonist in each of the eight stories in *Lives of Girls and Women*, the reader witnesses not only significant episodes in her own life but also those snapshots of the lives of women she has known who enrich and inform hers. It is important that the definite article, "the," is left off the title. These are "lives," not "The Lives," of girls and women. In this novel, Del's initiation takes on a more universal quality, becoming a lens through which every woman's movement toward selfhood and adulthood is elucidated.

Del's experience of the eccentric (literally, that which is "off-center"), becomes the open door through which she discovers the eccentricity of all women in a male-dominated world. This revelation increases her powers of observation, narration, and empathy for her sisters living under the constraints foisted upon their gender.

The only other fully developed character in the novel besides Del is her mother, Ada. Del is fond of quoting things that she remembers her mother telling her at various junctures in her life, and in these anecdotal portions, Ada becomes as real and as vibrant as Del herself. All the other characters in the stories are peripheral, but precisely because of their pronounced periphery, they stand out. Munro appropriately concludes the novel by having Del craft an epilogue that explores how the truth of the extraordinary nature of the peripheral in everyday life can be told in fiction, captured in the lives of the "dull, simple, amazing, and unfathomable—deep caves paved with kitchen linoleum."

Themes and Meanings

Under scrutiny by Alice Munro, the ordinary becomes extraordinary; the bits and pieces of lives—an errant look, a remembered epithet, a lingering impression—come together to form the composite meaning of an individual's life. Del's own conclusion, voiced in the epilogue to her narrative, equally befits the style and substance of her creator: Like Del, Munro strives to record "every last thing, every layer of speech and thought, stroke of light on bark or walls, every smell, pothole, pain, crack, delusion, held still and held together—radiant, everlasting."

Lives of Girls and Women momentarily moves its cast of characters beyond their ordinary trials into the realm of the heroic and tragic, the prose counterpart of an Edward Hopper painting. Though set in a southwest Ontario town, Jubilee is Everytown, while Del both is and is not Everywoman.

Alice Munro has few peers in her ability to explore and amplify the significance of the seemingly minor incidents of everyday life. There is a decidedly understated, supremely ironic grasp of the mundane that permeates all of Munro's stories and that climaxes in this novel. Consequently, *Lives of Girls and Women*, ostensibly a "novel," is best read as a series of discrete narratives woven together not by a plot, but by the overall thematic structure of a young woman moving into adulthood and sexual maturity by paying attention to the details of the landscape before her.

Critical Context

Alice Munro is one of the most celebrated Canadian writers of the twentieth century and, probably, one of the best living women prose writers in North America. Her short-story collections have won for her numerous literary awards, including the Governor General's Award for Canadian Fiction Writers in 1969 and 1978, and the Canada-Australia Literary Prize in 1977.

Munro has been criticized, however, for the limited range of her themes and characters: Most of her characters are young women passing through the stages of life or older women looking back on that experience. The initiation theme predominates in most of her stories, much as it does in Sherwood Anderson's tales of young men at the turn of the century.

Nevertheless, her work has been compared favorably with that of such regional writers as Eudora Welty and Flannery O'Connor, who wrote about the American South in much the way Munro has written of southwestern Ontario. This comparison is even more appropriate when one considers that Munro's forte is the short story, wherein her sharply focused characters and her eye for the details of ordinary life serve her narrative style forcefully.

Sources for Further Study

Bailey, Nancy I. "The Masculine Image in *Lives of Girls and Women*," in *Canadian Literature*. LXXX (Spring, 1979), pp. 113-118.

MacDonald, Rae McCarthy. "Structure and Detail in *Lives of Girls and Women*," in *Studies in Canadian Literature*. III (Summer, 1978), pp. 199-210.

MacKendrick, Louis, ed. *Probable Fictions: Alice Munro's Narrative Acts*, 1983.

Wallace, Brownen. "Women's Lives: Alice Munro," in *The Human Elements*, 1978. Edited by David Helwig.

Warwick, Susan. "Growing Up: The Novels of Alice Munro," in *Essays on Canadian Writing*. XXIX (Summer, 1984), pp. 204-225.

Bruce L. Edwards, Jr.

LIVING

Author: Henry Green (Henry Vincent Yorke, 1905-1973)
Type of plot: Neorealism
Time of plot: Early twentieth century
Locale: Birmingham and Liverpool, England
First published: 1929

>   *Principal characters:*
>   LILY GATES, a housekeeper and the daughter of a factory
>   worker
>   JOE GATES, her father
>   MR. CRAIGAN, her grandfather, also a factory worker
>   JIM DALE, a boarder in the Craigan household and Lily's
>   would-be lover
>   BERT JONES, a foundryman and Lily's lover
>   MR. DUPRET, the aged and sickly factory owner
>   RICHARD DUPRET, his son and heir to the factory
>   MR. BRIDGES, a foreman

The Novel

Like many of Henry Green's novels, *Living* portrays British domestic life in terms of a class struggle: The "upstairs/downstairs" conflicts of *Loving* (1945) are broadened in *Living* and in *Party Going* (1939) to encompass a clash between workers and the aristocratic owners of a Birmingham machine works and iron foundry. Yet class conflict in Green's novels is rarely presented in terms of actual battles, strikes, or violence; rather, he probes the psychological dimensions of this conflict through the subtle irony existing in a situation in which vast economic differences are countered by identical desires for love and survival. Green refuses either to romanticize the working class of *Living* or to condemn thoroughly Richard Dupret, the rich young man who takes on the management of the works after his father's death. Instead, Green attacks false romanticism itself in Lily Gates's failed elopement with the lackluster Bert Jones, in the dull Dupret's facile attachment to an equally dull socialite, and in the hubris of owners and workers alike who trample over the lives of others in order to enhance their own positions. Above all, *Living* scrutinizes forms of ritual and imitation which condemn all to hollow, mundane lives redeemed—sporadically, and never finally—by occasional visions of flight and escape into nature (represented in the novel's bird imagery). Like the island-bound inhabitants of James Joyce's *Dubliners* (1914), the workers and owners of *Living* are trapped within "life," which they struggle to endure and transcend.

In the conversations between bosses and workers which constitute much of the novel, the reader quickly learns that the world of the foundry is dichotomized between the very young and the very old, between those who have power over others and those who seek to gain such power. Mr. Bridges, the shop foreman, continually fears that, because of his age and slowness, he will be replaced; Joe Gates and Craigan are always on the defensive against younger men, such as Bert Jones, whose vague ambitions are undermined by a lack of effort. The workers not only squabble among themselves (to the extent of endangering one another's lives when, for example, a crane operator "accidentally" drops a spanner nearly onto the head of an enemy) but also engage in conflicts—many of them petty—with each level of management above them. Thus, the factory workers contest with the foremen, the foremen with the shop managers, and the shop managers with the architects and draftsmen. None of these conflicts is resolved in the novel: The old die, the young go on as before or move on to other factories, and in what seems to be a fatalistic vision, nothing changes. Yet Green's fatalism is matched by the irony and humor he perceives in situations such as when upper management has decreed that a guard be placed before the door of the factory lavatory so that workers will not loiter. The furor and gossip caused by this small event reflect Green's satiric commentary upon ritual and order within both the microcosm of the factory and a larger world which would fail to see that the insignificance of the lavatory episode parallels that of events usually assumed to have a more cosmic importance.

Without overt commentary or heavy plotting, Green creates in *Living* intricate parallels between the working world of the factory and the domestic lives of the workers and the owners. In the Craigan household, there is a power struggle over the future of Lily Gates, Craigan's granddaughter. Craigan rules the roost and acts as Lily's father, even though her real father lives in the same house: Joe Gates's sporadic attempts to assert authority over Lily rarely succeed. As the novel opens, Craigan seems pleased that Lily is attracted to his boarder, Jim Dale, since a marriage between them would ensure, in Craigan's mind, Lily's continued maintenance of the house and Dale's continued financial contribution to Craigan's imminent retirement. Yet Lily soon tires of Dale's passive advances and forms an intimate relationship with Bert Jones. The low-key rivalry between Dale and Jones, and the topic of "what to do with Lily," become the chief concerns of the Craigan household. Lily's aborted elopement with Jones to Canada precipitates a crisis which threatens to undermine thoroughly the domestic institution as Joe Gates is thrown in jail for swearing and Dale leaves in a fit of jealousy; Craigan, who has lain sick in bed for a long period, is forced to care for himself and for Lily, who returns emotionally distraught after Jones's cowardly departure from her in Liverpool. As men struggle for power and position in the factory in order to survive fluctuations in the economy and personal aggressions, so they struggle for possession of Lily, who becomes the sign or guarantee of continued order and existence. These attempts to acquire her strength and energy are parodied by Richard Dupret's halfhearted courtship of the shallow-minded Miss Glossop: In both cases, the biological fight for survival is disguised by a succession of social and domestic rituals whose disruption, like a threatened strike at the factory, could portend extinction.

The Characters

One of Green's primary achievements as a modern novelist is his success in creating characters almost solely through dialogue. When the characters of *Living* are not talking to one another about everyday woes and ambitions, they are engaging in habitual or minor actions which do little to distinguish them from the background of anonymity that is established at the beginning of the novel:

> Bridesley, Birmingham.
> Two o'clock. Thousands came back from dinner along the streets.
> "What we want is go, push," said the works manager to son of Mr. Dupret. "What I say to them is—let's get on with it, let's get the stuff out."
> Thousands came back to factories they worked in from their dinners.
> "I'm always at them but they know me. They know I'm a father and a mother to them. If they're in trouble they've but to come to me. And they turn out beautiful work, beautiful work. I'd do anything for 'em and they know it."
> Noise of lathes working began again in this factory. Hundreds went along road outside, men and girls. Some turned in to Dupret factory.

The manager's falsely paternalistic speech is composed almost entirely of hollow clichés which fail to mask the drudgery and ordinariness of the workers' lives. Against this gray backdrop "character" rarely emerges; the speech patterns and actions of the novel's principals, related through the deadpan, noncommittal voice of Green's narrator, become ritualistic and routine gestures only occasionally interrupted by a colorful flight of birds or an abrupt action such as Lily's departure for Liverpool with Jones. Even Richard Dupret, whose money and education should, according to the aristocratic philosophy, distinguish him from the crowd, can only speak in conventional phrases or not at all when convention fails him in a complex emotional situation. In a sense, *Living* is a novel without character, faithfully portraying the nature of the quotidian for both rich and poor. If "character" exists in a Green novel, it can be perceived in those unusual moments when a character such as Lily notices a slight alteration in or sudden movement of something that has been there all along—again, Green's birds serve this purpose. They are signs of an "otherness" which subtends the assumed and false naturalness of everyday life and of ritualized being.

Themes and Meanings

As the title suggests, *Living* is about survival, or more precisely, about the continuity of life in an entropic, leveled universe. In the novel, old Dupret dies, Craigan is forced into early retirement, workers move listlessly from factory to factory, and the old men at the foundry labor with increasing slowness, while the young men talk of escape to Australia and Canada. The picture is one of a dying world in which worsening economic conditions are abetted by inefficient management and a labyrinthine, gossipy bureaucracy. Death itself seems to become part of a tiresome cycle or ritual, as if life were a long period of waiting for yet another ordinary event. Yet within the quotidian, arising out of it, Green depicts surprising instances of light, irony, humor, song, and motion, which might be seen as the resistances to death. For example, in speaking of the dying old Dupret, two factory managers quite unconsciously manage to redeem from cliché and dullness an unacknowledged humorous moment: "'He was a grand fine man,' Mr. Walters said, 'a grand man,' in his dull voice. 'Is 'e as sick as that?' said Mr. Bridges." Yet there is birth as well as death in *Living*: One birth in particular serves as the occasion for a rare intrusion of song into the mundane world of the workers. At the foundry, a Welshman's celebration of his son's birth is portrayed in lyrical detail, his "silver voice" disrupting the routine of the "black grimed men," just as the birth of a child remains an extraordinary event in the most ordinary of worlds.

At the end of the novel, a child is born to Lily Gates's neighbor, a symbolic event that represents all the irony and ambiguity inherent in a work in which life and survival are not always necessarily equal. To Lily, the child may be seen as a sign of what she may never have; yet, amid a flutter of pigeons and raucous sounds, the infant, simply because it demands a special kind of attention—another intrusion into the ordinary—becomes a sign of continuance and life. In this scene, as in the novel as a whole, loss (Lily's loss of Jones, her failure to escape) is countered by a momentary presence, a point of interest represented by the child's grasping hand as it reaches for a pigeon and the pigeon's "fierce red eye" as it appears ready to peck at the baby. In Green's attenuated universe, such moments are charismatic, transforming, and, if only momentarily, redemptive.

Critical Context

Among the giants of literary modernism, Henry Green is still (and will probably continue to be) considered a minor novelist. While his novels are exemplars of a lucid realistic style that is, finally, far more interesting than Ernest Hemingway's attempts at minimalization, and while Green's experiments with syntax successfully represent and counter the repetitiveness and communicative breakdowns of modern life, for many his work is too mannered or schematic. On the large scale, one can observe repeatedly in most of his novels the same class dichotomies and ironic parallels that characterize his early effort in *Living*. Yet in looking for the more grandiose experiments and epic vision of a James Joyce in Henry Green (though Green's combined lyricism and transparency derive from *Dubliners* and *A Portrait of the Artist as a Young Man*, 1916), readers may miss Green's subtlety, his construction of a world in which a turn of phrase or a sudden gesture can mean much, though it may change little. There are strong political overtones in Green's work, yet he is not a polemicist. Rather, he sees the world divided along arbitrary class lines, and he is interested in portraying the similarities of human nature which cross these lines. One of these similarities is desire, which is repressed or made routine in Green's novels but which manifests itself at odd moments of projection or longing. *Living* is parablelike at such moments, for Green perceives behind the façade of everyday life, or between class lines, a largely unattainable transcendence. If the characters of his novels are only able to "see" these instances obliquely, for his readers, Green provides sudden and subtle insights into another nature disguised by "modern life."

Sources for Further Study

Bassoff, Bruce. *Toward Loving: The Poetics of the Novel and the Practice of Henry Green*, 1975.
Mengham, Rod. *The Idiom of the Time: The Writings of Henry Green*, 1982.
North, Michael. *Henry Green and the Writing of his Generation*, 1984.
Odom, Keith. *Henry Green*, 1978.
Weatherhead, A. Kingsley. *A Reading of Henry Green*, 1961.

Patrick O'Donnell